This book is a companion volume to

The Architecture of Southern England
by John Julius Norwich
also published by Macmillan London

The Architecture of
NORTHERN ENGLAND

JOHN MARTIN ROBINSON

with a Foreword by John Julius Norwich

PHOTOGRAPHY BY JORGE LEWINSKI AND MAYOTTE MAGNUS

MACMILLAN LONDON

First published 1986 by
MACMILLAN LONDON LIMITED
4 Little Essex Street London WC2R 3LF
and Basingstoke

Associated companies in Auckland, Delhi, Dublin, Gaborone,
Hamburg, Harare, Hong Kong, Johannesburg, Kuala Lumpur,
Lagos, Manzini, Melbourne, Mexico City, Nairobi, New York,
Singapore and Tokyo

Designed by Robert Updegraff

Maps by Hilary Evans

Filmset in Apollo by Filmtype Services Limited, Scarborough,
North Yorkshire

Printed in Hong Kong

British Library Cataloguing in Publication Data

Robinson, John Martin
    The architecture of Northern England.
    1. Architecture—England, Northern
    I. Title
    720'.9427   NA995.N6

ISBN 0-333-37396-0

Contents

How to Use the Book

For every county there is a main selection of the best buildings – some of which are additionally distinguished by a star. Liverpool and Manchester, including the towns and properties falling within those metropolitan counties, have separate sections at the end of Lancashire.

Entries are normally listed under place name, with specific buildings picked out in small capitals. The exceptions are when a single house stands alone, or when it is considerably better known than its nearest town or village.

In the line printed in italics immediately below each heading, the first figure is that by which the entry is marked on the relevant map, the entries in each county being numbered separately. There follows a brief indication of the whereabouts of the place or building in question – not precise in every case, but sufficiently so to enable the reader to locate it on any good road map. If a building is illustrated by a colour photograph, the plate number is given in brackets at the end of the line.

The letters *NT* at the beginning of the italic line signify that the building concerned is the property of the National Trust. Further details of these buildings, including the days and times of opening to the public, are given in publications available at any National Trust shop, or can be obtained from the National Trust, 36 Queen Anne's Gate, London SW1 (Telephone 01-222 9251). For buildings not belonging to the Trust, information can usually be found in the annually issued *Historic Houses, Castles and Gardens in Great Britain and Ireland*, published by British Leisure Publications, East Grinstead, and obtainable from most bookshops and bookstalls.

A bold number at the end of the italic line indicates a colour photograph in one of the three plate sections.

There are four area maps (pp. 350–7) on which every entry in the book is marked. Entries are numbered from *1* within their county and a key to the buildings of each county is provided.

Foreword

This foreword is, essentially, an expression of gratitude. Ten years or more ago, I was asked by Messrs Macmillan to produce for them what amounted to an architectural anthology: a guide to what I considered the best buildings in England, with a short description of each. Delighted with the prospect of a virtually unlimited future of free sightseeing, I buckled down with a will — only to discover that England was far, far richer in superb architecture than I could ever have thought possible, and that in consequence the job I had taken on, while every bit as enjoyable as I had expected, was infinitely more demanding. I slogged away as long as I could, but at last in despair returned to the publishers with my confession: the whole country was too much for me — I had bitten off more than I could hope to chew. Would they, I wondered, allow me to sign off when I had finished the 24 counties comprising the South of England and leave the North to someone younger and rather more — dared I say it — spry?

They agreed, bless them, and this book is the result. It contains a few contributions of my own, merely because I used a good deal of Staffordshire as an early *ballon d'essai* and also because, in the years when I still hoped to cover the whole country, I took advantage of any occasional visit to the North to write up any buildings that I happened to visit while I was there. But the overwhelming majority of these essays are the work of my friend and colleague John Martin Robinson, and I am immeasurably grateful to him for having taken on the job where I left off. The book that you now hold in your hands is his and his alone. Follow him with confidence, and mark his words well.

John Julius Norwich
London
November 1985

Introduction

This volume covers that part of England that lies between the Cotswolds and the Scottish Borders, between the Welsh Marches and the North Sea. Though called 'the North', it includes much of the Midlands too. I suppose we all have different definitions of 'the North'. Mine is the northern province of the Church of England, York not Canterbury, and the boundary runs through Renishaw Park in Derbyshire and along the River Trent. To me, Leicestershire, Lincolnshire, Warwickshire, Staffordshire and Shropshire, let alone Worcestershire and Herefordshire, are the Midlands. Not everybody may agree. I was somewhat surprised the other day to see Geoffrey Grigson referring to Grantham (on the edge of the Vale of Belvoir) as being in the 'north-east'!

The area covered here, however, is unified by the fact that it was nearly all involved in the eighteenth- and nineteenth-century Industrial Revolution, from Shropshire to Northumberland. For 200 years this was the most prosperous manufacturing area in the world. The majority of this old industry has now gone, or is in rapid decline, but it was responsible for much of the architecture described in these pages. One of the differences between this volume and its companion on the South lies in the type of building described. Here are to be found the great towns and cities of the Industrial Revolution: Liverpool, Manchester, Leeds, Halifax, Newcastle, Sheffield, Preston, Bolton, Birmingham and Leicester; but there are also magnificent churches, houses and model villages in the countryside erected by those lucky enough to have been enriched by coal, cotton, iron and shipping. This adds an extra dimension to the castles, medieval churches, abbey ruins, old market towns, Elizabethan country houses and pretty villages that can be found throughout England, and one to which I have tried to do justice in my selection.

It may be noticed too that more Catholic churches appear in this volume than in that on the South. This is owing to the strong recusant element in Lancashire, Staffordshire, parts of Yorkshire and the north-east — and this again is a distinctive historical characteristic of the conservative and independent North.

Another important feature of the area under discussion is the landscape, which contains some of the most beautiful and dramatic English scenery: the Welsh Marches and the Malverns, the Peak District, the Yorkshire Dales, the Lake District, the North York Moors, the hills of Northumberland. No fewer than five of England's National Parks are covered by this volume. Most of the buildings (even towns like Sheffield and Halifax) in these pages are therefore to be found against wonderful natural backdrops. There is a scale and nobility about much of the landscape and architecture which is thrilling. For those who prefer grandeur to mere prettiness, the North is for them.

This book was written at a period of transition as the old-established industries that had formed the economic backbone of the area for centuries were shrinking at an alarming rate. Cotton, coal, iron, wool, shipbuilding and docks have almost ceased to exist. Many of the nineteenth-century cities are for the moment like fat men who have suddenly lost weight and find that they no longer fill their good old clothes. At the same time, however, the destructive planning policies that did so much damage in the 1960s and early 1970s have lost their impetus and in many places there are heartwarming signs of improvement, shown in the change to tourism and a service economy allied to more imaginative policies of preservation and a better standard of new buildings. So it is possible now to feel more optimistic than would have been the case travelling around in pursuit of good buildings ten or fifteen years ago. In the remoter rural areas, of course, things carry on much as they have done for centuries, through good times and bad. Shropshire, Derbyshire, North Yorkshire, Cumbria and Northumberland convey an almost pre-war impression of rural England, with well-kept country houses and estates, old-fashioned market towns, and their churches still open during the day.

A word or two on access may be in place. Many, but by no means all, of the houses mentioned are open to the public, at least occasionally for charity if not on a regular basis. But it would be best to check in *Historic Houses, Castles and Gardens in Great Britain and Ireland* (published annually by British Leisure Publications, Windsor Court, East Grinstead House, East Grinstead, West Sussex RH19 1XA) before arranging a visit to a particular place. In towns, if you are seriously interested, it is usually possible to have a quick look at the town hall murals or whatever by asking the doorman politely. Churches are the real problem nowadays. While in some rural areas they are still open, this is hardly ever the case in towns or suburbs, and in certain dioceses like Southwell there seems to be a policy of keeping all the churches locked all the time. As most of the vicarages and rectories have been sold off and one incumbent may look after three or four churches and live in a remote bungalow, it can be almost impossible to find the key. Where a church is kept locked, it should be made compulsory to post a note in the porch stating the whereabouts of the key.

I am grateful to a considerable number of people for help in preparing this book. In the first place John Julius Norwich and Mollie Philipps generously gave me their notes and information on buildings that they had visited but had not written up themselves. Jorge Lewinski and Mayotte Magnus, as well as specially taking all the photographs, very kindly reported back with bits of extra information or corrections that they thought ought to be included. Many people in strategically placed counties generously offered hospitality or drove me to interesting houses, churches and towns, including my sister Anne, Mrs Andrew Baird, Mr and Mrs Jeffrey Haworth, Mr James Miller, The Rev. Henry Thorold and Mr David Wakefield. And of course I am indebted above all to the owners of the houses described in these pages, whose kindness and patience in granting me access to their homes and in providing me with much invaluable information has been immense.

A word should be said about the division of labour on this volume between myself and John Julius Norwich. Cheshire, Derbyshire and Staffordshire are joint efforts; in Warwickshire and Shropshire there are odd entries by John Julius, but Lancashire, Cumbria, Yorkshire, Northumberland, Durham and Lincolnshire are mine. We had thought of identifying our individual entries, but on reflection decided not to, as the reader might have more fun in guessing.

John Martin Robinson
London
November 1985

Photographers' Note

At one time architectural photographers considered only one kind of camera – the large, cumbersome view camera initially used for plates and later for cut film. Superb images of cathedrals and sumptuous interiors could be created with this camera, but it demanded great patience and a leisurely approach as the photographer had to spend an interminable amount of time with his head under the black cloth, viewing, arranging and focusing. Although we took some of the photographs for this book – especially the interiors of cathedrals – in a similar way, with a 5 × 4 inch Linhof Technica, if we had used such a camera for all the shots it would have taken us perhaps five years to complete the project instead of one. Modern cameras, lenses and photographic materials, however, have improved so much that nowadays a smaller-sized negative provides an image of more than adequate quality. Consequently we chose two basic cameras for our task – the Pentax 6 × 7cm and the Nikon FA, the latter often used with one of the excellent PC (Perspective Corrective) lenses.

The great advantage of a view camera such as our Linhof Technica is its flexibility. The lens is mounted on a panel that can be shifted in all directions (as can the back of the camera), which means that the photographer can virtually shoot around the corner of a building, so to speak. But its main advantage is that, from relatively close to the building, it allows the correction of optically distorted verticals so that they appear perfectly parallel in the photograph. Most ordinary modern cameras have to be tilted to include the higher parts of a building, and the resulting photographs show the verticals – towers or spires, say – converging towards the top. The effect can be dramatic – and in fact this is how the eye sees the building most of the time – but it is often preferable to avoid it. The view camera with its 'rising front' does just that, but it is a convenience that was denied owners of small cameras until the invention of the PC lens. Our Nikon PC lens is fitted with a movable front element: it can be shifted up or to the side without tilting the camera, and we have taken advantage of that feature in many of these photographs.

Yet in spite of the first-class sharpness and resolution that Nikon lenses always provide, there are a number of reasons why an architectural photographer may still prefer a larger format. For one thing, the 35mm format often calls for a fine grain, making it necessary to use slower negative and positive materials, and in a dark interior this may mean excessively long exposures. In addition, all the colour reproductions in a book or a magazine invariably come from colour transparencies and not from prints and so it is much more satisfactory to view relatively large 6 × 7cm rather than small 36mm colour slides. Similarly, the quality of a black-and-white negative is much easier to maintain on a large format than on a small one. Some photographers also prefer to use a short film (10–12 exposures) and then switch to a new roll for the next building, rather than rely on a long 35mm film, believing that with shorter rolls and fewer frames one tends to concentrate and shoot with more care – though this is arguable.

More recently, too late as far as this book was concerned, Pentax have put on the market an excellent PC lens to fit their 6 × 7cm Pentax camera, and this new addition is great news for us. Now we can have both the quality of a large negative and the ability to correct perspective in architectural photography.

Finally a note about light. Because we had to cover so many buildings in such a relatively short time, unfortunately we could not always wait for the ideal moment or ideal light. But morning, with its low rays of soft, diffused light, is perhaps the most interesting and beautiful time for photography, especially for exterior shots. Hard, mid-day sun is certainly least suitable with its uncompromising contrast of deep shadows and burnt-out highlights. For general purposes, reasonably bright, overcast conditions are often best, allowing a building to be photographed successfully from many angles, and bringing out the texture of the fabric of the building.

We would like to express our deepest thanks to all the house owners who so kindly allowed us to photograph their properties.

Jorge Lewinski and Mayotte Magnus
London
November 1985

Cheshire

Most people have no very clear idea of Cheshire. If pressed, they might say it is flat, and of course would know about the picturesque 'black-and-white' and the unique 'Rows' of Chester. But it would surprise many outsiders to be told that Cheshire is one of the most unspoilt, prosperous and attractive counties in the whole of England. In the first place, it is not at all flat. The centre of the county, the Cheshire Plain, is rolling, hilly, wooded and dotted with meres or small lakes, while towards the Welsh border rises the dramatic outcrop of the Beeston and Peckforton Hills, like baby brothers of the Malverns in Worcestershire. To the east, beyond Macclesfield, dramatic moors and crags form the foothills of the Peak – mountain country by English standards.

Cheshire has been extremely lucky in the past century, for though close to nineteenth- and twentieth-century industry, it has also been protected from it in such a way as to reap all the peripheral benefits of prosperity without too many of the hideous visual side-effects. Thus the urban development of Manchester and Liverpool has been held at bay, but waves of moneyed Lancastrians have set themselves up in the county and used their riches to beautify it. Cheshire's farming has also long been geared almost entirely to dairy production, to supply the cities and towns north of its borders, and so it was not affected by the late nineteenth-century agricultural depression that blighted some of the more arable parts of England. By accident, therefore, the balance in Cheshire is almost exactly right: most of the towns are small, the farmers are prosperous dairymen who do not need to tear out their hedges and trees, while modern industry, like ICI, is concentrated and does not scar whole tracts of the landscape. The only real horrors are sudden outcrops of vulgar villas for commuters, which tend to sprout in the cracks between the great landed estates.

The chief cause of the preservation of Cheshire's rural landscape is that most of the land belongs to old-established estates, the owners of which have been able to resist 'development'. More ancient landed families survive in their houses in Cheshire than in almost any other county. Some of them have passed through the female line but retain their old names, the antiquity of which is attested by their clipped pronunciation: Leghs, Cholmondeleys, Leches, Egertons, Grosvenors, Wilbrahams, Bromley-Davenports, Lancelyn-Greens, and many others. A number of these families have been here since the twelfth century, thus perpetuating the original pattern of sub-infeudation after the Norman Conquest. Their houses are one of the major attractions of Cheshire, whether still privately owned or preserved by the National Trust. The oldest of these houses – like Adlington, Bramall, Gawsworth and Little Moreton – are romantically timber-framed, but there are also grand Jacobean houses of brick or stone, including Crewe Hall, Dorfold, Peover, Lyme Park and Brereton. Others were developed out of monasteries after the Dissolution, with bits added on at different dates – such as Vale Royal and Combermere, the latter in a most spectacular setting overlooking a large mere surrounded by wooded slopes. There is a series of palatial eighteenth-century houses, of which both Lyme Park and Dunham Massey now belong to the National Trust and are open to the public. The grandest of the Victorian houses, the Duke of Westminster's Eaton Hall, has been demolished and replaced by a large new house in the Modern style, although its Victorian chapel and elaborate formal gardens remain, kept in spanking condition, and are occasionally opened for charity. Of the surviving Victorian houses, by far the most striking is Peckforton, a convincing castle by Salvin on top of a wooded hill.

Cheshire is also a county of attractive small market towns: Knutsford, Nantwich, Sandbach and Malpas, all with more or less well-kept buildings of different dates and styles. The city of Chester itself, with its Roman remains, complete city walls, medieval cathedral and cross-plan of four picturesque main streets is, of course, one of the great historic cities of England. Much has been done in the last fifteen years to preserve Chester's fabric, but it is a pity that the insensitive inner ring-road was built before the concern for conservation began – it should never have been allowed to breach the walls.

Macclesfield is less picturesque and less venerable, so has fared less well than the county town. It used to be a remarkably interesting eighteenth-century silk-weaving town, with Georgian brick houses and mills. Post-war planning has done its best to wreck this, but even here much has been done in recent years to preserve what remains. To compensate for losses elsewhere, one of the most intact eighteenth-century industrial villages in England is to be found at Styal, where the mill and cottages now all belong to the National Trust, which preserves them perfectly.

This is a good county for all-of-a-piece Perpendicular churches. For some reason that has never been properly explained, Cheshire was very prosperous in the later Middle Ages; perhaps it was just the profits of agriculture and those of salt-extraction at the three salt towns (or 'wiches') that paid for this outburst of church-building. Anyway, as a result, there is a series of ambitious Perpendicular churches, of which those at Astbury, Great Budworth, Gawsworth, Malpas and Northwich are especially memorable. The curious thing is that, outside Chester, there is little architecture in the county dating from before the fourteenth century.

Apart from the late medieval churches, the little country towns, and the Elizabethan and Georgian country houses, what else is there to see in Cheshire? The answer is a great deal of Victorian work by both national and local architects. One of the best locals was John Douglas of Chester. He was responsible for many of the picturesque restorations and reconstructions in his native town, which deceive the casual visitor into thinking they are the real thing. His too are the wonderful estate buildings around Eaton Hall — lodges, kennels, farms and whole villages. Even the old buildings in Cheshire owe a great deal to Victorian restoration. Much of the impact of Chester Cathedral, for instance, is due to G.G. Scott's restoration, while the whole interior of Crewe Hall, destroyed by a fire in 1866, is the work of E.M. Barry — and remarkably sumptuous it is.

Coming into the twentieth century, Lord Leverhulme's model village for his soap-workers at Port Sunlight is a pioneering example of English garden-city development and is still beautifully maintained by the original firm, now Unilever. Lord Leverhulme's more rural model village and his large country house at Thornton Hough are equally interesting and perfectly represent the international taste of rich Edwardian industrialists on both sides of the Atlantic — Chester County, New York, as much as Cheshire, England.

Adlington Hall
1; 4 miles N of Macclesfield on A523
This interesting quadrangular house, exhibiting Tudor, Caroline and Georgian features, is reputedly built on the site of a Saxon hunting lodge. It has been the home of the Legh family since 1315, but the oldest part of the building to survive is the Hall built by Thomas Legh in 1505. The next stage in the development of the house was undertaken by another Thomas Legh, who in 1581 refaced the Hall and made substantial additions on either side. A further small addition was made to the north of the Hall in c.1660. In the early eighteenth century John Legh altered the interior of the Hall, but it was his son Charles who was responsible for extensive alterations to the house and its surroundings. He completed the west side of the quadrangle by building a new brick wing containing Dining Room, Drawing Room, Library and staircase; he also built the stables with a pedimented centre in 1749 and in 1757 he rebuilt the south side of the quadrangle with a tall Ionic portico. There is no record of Charles Legh having employed an architect for his alterations and it is possible that he designed them himself, for he had 'tastes for music, poetry, painting and architecture', and was, incidentally, a friend of Handel, who set to music a hunting song written by Legh.

Charles Legh's son predeceased him and the property descended to his niece, Elizabeth Rowlls, who took the name of Legh — the first of several excursions into the female line, and in fact each subsequent owner has taken the name of Legh. The house was reduced in size in 1929, when outlying portions of the Georgian work were demolished and the interior modernised to the design of Sir Hubert Worthington.

The Hall retains its original speres at the screen end, a canopy over the dais, and its roof — which, carved with angels bearing coats of arms, is very similar to that of Rufford Old Hall in Lancashire (*q.v.*) — but it was altered in 1670, when the then Thomas Legh inserted the splendid Baroque organ and the wall paintings depicting the history of Troy. These were later covered up and only rediscovered in 1859 when an energetic game of shuttlecock disturbed a piece of plaster. The eighteenth-century rooms have simple plaster ceilings and good panelling by Sefton. The Drawing Room has Corinthian pilasters and an overmantel carved with fruit and flowers, with the overdoors depicting Neptune, Bacchus, Juno and Ceres. The Chapel in the north wing dates from 1936 and incorporates the fittings of the eighteenth-century chapel from the demolished part of the house.

In the grounds are a lime avenue, yew walk, an eighteenth-century rotunda and a little summerhouse lined with shells. Adlington is open to the public in the summer.

Arley Hall
2; 8 miles SE of Warrington off B5356
Arley is the ancestral seat of the Warburtons, who acquired the manor in c.1190 and built their first house on the site in 1469. The estate is still occupied by their descendants and forms an oasis of unspoilt countryside before one enters the heavily populated area across the county boundary to the north.

The present house was built between 1832 and 1845 by Rowland Egerton-Warburton to the designs of the Nantwich architect George Latham. An important example of the Victorian Jacobethan style, it has fine plaster ceilings and oak panelling. Adjoining the house is a large Gothic Chapel designed by Anthony Salvin and completed in 1845. The north aisle, added in 1856–7, is the work of G.E. Street. The house was originally much larger and the Chapel formed part of the main block, but in 1968 the rear of the building, including the kitchens and servants' quarters, was demolished. Surviving from

The church of St Mary, Astbury.

the original Tudor buildings is a splendid cruck barn, which was surmounted in the nineteenth century by a picturesque Bavarian clock tower.

Arley is particularly notable for its GARDENS, which overlook beautiful parkland and provide a great variety of style and design. Originally laid out in the mid-nineteenth century, their outstanding feature is the double herbaceous border established in 1846 – one of the earliest in England. Other features from that period include the fine yew hedges, the Furlong Walk (220 yards long), an avenue of pleached lime trees, and the Ilex Avenue, which consists of fourteen large ilex trees clipped to the shape of giant cylinders. The house and gardens are regularly open to the public in summer.

Astbury

3; 2 miles S of Congleton on A34

The approach to the CHURCH OF ST MARY from the main Congleton–Newcastle road is highly effective – a short, wide village street with red brick and black-and-white timbered cottages, the Egerton Arms pub, and mown grass and trees on either side neatly framing the impressive west end of the church. This is an unusual composition, with an older spire to one side of the Perpendicular bulk of the main body of the church and a projecting three-storeyed porch in the centre. The exterior of weathered sandstone is sturdy and grand. The interior is even grander, with the nave and chancel all in one, wide aisles to either side, and remarkably tall clerestory windows. It is a plan of textbook perfection, the grandeur of space matched by the high quality of detail and the range of good fittings. The low-pitched oak ceiling has moulded and cambered beams and is richly em-

bellished with carved bosses and heraldry. The stone aisle piers are of a finely moulded uniform design; the nave is divided from the chancel by a rich Perpendicular rood-screen and, hanging from the roof, a large open-work pendant boss like a lantern, which presumably once contained a statue or crucifix. The pulpit, font cover and box pews all date from the mid-seventeenth century and are in a sturdy Jacobean style. The font cover looks a bit like a grandfather clock with a pedimented top. The pulpit was moved and altered in the nineteenth century. Originally it was a three-decker; the base and sounding board have been made into a table which stands in the vestry. The chancel is surrounded by the original Perpendicular parclose screens of carved oak, incorporating choir stalls with linenfold panelled fronts. The vast east window has colourful stained glass by Warrington dated 1858, and the communion rails, decorated with an unusual pattern of acorns, are mid-seventeenth century. Over the altar is a huge ceiling boss carved with the five wounds of Christ. The aisle walls are dotted with marble tablets commemorating local families, including the Shakerleys of Somerford Park, the Ackers of Moreton Hall and the Swetenhams of Somerford Booths. Over the west door hang the Royal Arms of Charles II.

Astbury is altogether one of the most impressive of the large Perpendicular parish churches of Cheshire, and the Jacobean fittings are a unique survival. If it is locked, the key can be obtained from THE RECTORY, the impressive red brick Georgian house standing in its own grounds just to the north of the graveyard. It is a great relief to find that this has not yet been sold off by the Church Commissioners.

Birkenhead

4; 15 miles NW of Chester on A41

This town on the south side of the Mersey, facing Liverpool, was one of the great success stories of the nineteenth century – a fact probably not easy to grasp now as one surveys the aftermath. In the course of the last century, however, its population increased from 100 souls to over 100,000. Birkenhead grew with shipbuilding, and has declined with it. The shipbuilding yard was founded by William Laird, a Scotsman, in 1824, and he employed the Edinburgh architect James Gillespie Graham to lay out a new town on a grid-plan. This was one of the most ambitious pieces of town planning in the nineteenth century and, if completed, would have produced results comparable to the New Town of Edinburgh. In the event, only the public buildings and Hamilton Square were executed as envisaged; the remainder of the town filled up later with inferior buildings. Post-war 'planning' has wrought the usual devastation: roadworks, 'slum' clearance, and mediocre shopping developments have done much to ruin what remained of the early nineteenth-century layout.

HAMILTON SQUARE, however, survives in remarkably good condition and does indeed look just like a chunk of Edinburgh New Town strayed south of the border. It is very large and dignified, though its appearance is somewhat marred by the weedy municipal planting of the central area. It needs grass and full-scale forest trees, not little formal flower beds. How is it that the nation that produced Capability Brown and Humphry Repton seems to have lost all sense of large-scale planting and landscape layout? The focal point of the square's east side is now the TOWN HALL, built in 1883–7 to the design of C.O. Ellison, with a tall clock tower, which was partly reconstructed in 1901, after a fire, by Henry Hartley. It is

Bramall Hall.

a handsome classical piece with a rusticated granite plinth and grand Corinthian portico. The terraces surrounding the square were built in the 1830s and 1840s and are basically uniform, with three main storeys and an attic all faced in Storeton stone. The classical detail, however, varies from terrace to terrace, with Roman Doric columns and pilasters articulating the symmetrical layout.

Apart from Hamilton Square, the only other part of the town really worth looking at is BIRKENHEAD PARK. This was laid out in 1843–7 by no less than Sir Joseph Paxton and is among the best of all Victorian town parks, with an elegant carriage drive, a lake, boathouse, excellent tree planting and a series of delightful stone entrance lodges in different styles. Even here, however, the original concept has been marred by the misplaced efforts of more recent municipal gardeners. The park was intended to be surrounded by a Picturesque development of prosperous villas. Some of these were built in the 1840s and 1850s, but the original plan for the area was never completed and it has been somewhat spoilt during this century by insensitive piecemeal redevelopment.

Bramall Hall

5; 3 miles S of Stockport on A5102

Bramall is one of the major surviving black-and-white timber-framed houses in Cheshire, although it was much restored in c.1883 and its fenestration and ornamental brick chimneys are Victorian. The house dates from the fifteenth century but was greatly enlarged in the 1590s, and again in 1609 to form a quadrangle like that at Speke in Lancashire (*q.v.*), though one side of this was removed in the late eighteenth century. The house is eminently picturesque, with gables and multifarious bay windows, its timber-framing making dazzling lozenge- and cross-shaped patterns and its park still hilly and wild-seeming, despite the close proximity of Stockport.

Inside, the Hall was originally full height, but a ceiling was put in c.1590 to form the Drawing Room above. The latter has a stucco ceiling with pendants in quatrefoils and a plaster Mannerist chimneypiece with bulging caryatids. The south wing, which was the medieval solar, has a splendid roof with arched braces and two and a half tiers of wind-braces, and interesting wall paintings. The Chapel has early sixteenth-century stained glass and some brought-in carved woodwork, including a pew from the Davenport Chapel at Stockport. The Great Hall has some modest late sixteenth-century plasterwork and there is a late sixteenth-century Long Gallery along the top of the house. The terraced gardens were laid out in the nineteenth century.

Bramall belonged to the Davenports from the early sixteenth century till the death of William Davenport in 1829. He had no legitimate issue but adopted two daughters, one of whom married Admiral Sir Salisbury Price, who took the name Davenport. The estate was sold in 1877 and, after a period of uncertainty, the house was acquired by C.H. Nevill, who carried out the late Victorian restoration. It now belongs to the local council and is maintained as a museum.

Brereton Hall
6; 8 miles W of Congleton on A50

Brereton Hall has what is in many ways the best Elizabethan façade in the county. The house, which is now a school, was built by Sir William Brereton in 1586 on a site that had been occupied by his family since the twelfth century. Many of the medieval heads of the family (all of whom were called William) had been involved in the French wars of Edward III and Henry V; one was bailiff of Caen and another was killed at Harfleur. (The Sir William Brereton of Henry VIII's reign, who was unfortunate enough to know Anne Boleyn and in 1536 was executed for adultery with her, was a cousin – but of Malpas (*q.v.*), not of Brereton.)

Brereton is of brick of delightful colour and texture. Its symmetrical nine-bay façade has gabled ends and a central gatehouse, which is embellished with strapwork and heraldry and flanked by octagonal turrets; originally these had onion cupolas like those at Melford in Suffolk, but they were truncated and castellated in c.1830, though they had in fact already lost their original tops in the eighteenth century. The windows are mullioned and the canted bays in the projecting ends have little pediments showing the influence of old Somerset House in London. There are further canted bays at the sides.

The interior, with its Jacobethan plasterwork, is largely the result of nineteenth-century alterations, but several genuine sixteenth- and seventeenth-century carved chimneypieces, now *ex situ*, remain.

Capesthorne
7; 6 miles N of Congleton on A34

A large Jacobean house of brick, Capesthorne is a thoroughgoing Victorian reconstruction of a seven-bay early eighteenth-century house. It was designed in 1732–3 by Francis Smith for John Ward and incorporates flanking wings of 1720 by William Smith. Some interior reconstruction and decoration was done in the late eighteenth century but nothing of this survives. The Victorian remodelling was carried out in 1839–42 by Edward Davies Davenport to the design of Edward Blore, with shaped gables, Hatfield-inspired turrets, and a colonnade across the entrance front. The centre was gutted by fire in 1861 and rebuilt to the design of Anthony Salvin; further work was done by Salvin in 1879. The present interior is largely Salvin's, with restrained Jacobean plaster ceilings and heraldic stained glass by Willement. The unusual drawing-room chimneypieces of 1789 are of Coade stone and were brought from the family house in Belgrave Square, but their origin is unknown. The staircase has an iron balustrade incorporating the Bromley and Davenport crests; the latter (a felon with a rope round his neck) is a portrait of Gladstone, the political enemy of the arch-Tory William Bromley-Davenport.

Some traces of the early Georgian house can still be seen at the back, but the only substantial Georgian work at Capesthorne today is the adjoining but detached Chapel built in 1722. It has round-arched windows and a balustraded parapet. In 1959 the timber cupola was restored to the original design. The interior was beautified in 1887 by Mrs William Bromley-Davenport as a memorial to her husband, with wood-carving, terracotta panels by George Tinworth (of Doulton), and mosaic by Salviati. The conservatory designed by Paxton, which used to connect the Chapel to the house, was demolished in c.1920.

Cheadle
8; 3 miles W of Stockport on A560

The TOWN HALL (formerly Abney Hall), a sombre brick, Tudor-Gothic house, is the result of three phases of Victorian building work by prosperous Manchester businessmen. The original house is of 1847 and incorporates a fanciful Neo-Norman entrance doorway. It was enlarged in 1849 to the design of Travis & Mangnall and again in 1893 to the design of G.F. Armitage. The work in 1849 was done for Sir James Watts, a rich wholesale draper and Mayor of Manchester. The interior was decorated for him in the Puginian manner by J.G. Crace in 1852–7 and survives largely in the original state, with Hardman chandeliers, Minton tiles and heraldic stained glass. Its present function as Cheadle Town Hall is an imaginative re-use, and it is good to be able to record that a building in public ownership is well cared for.

Chester★
9; 15 miles S of Liverpool on A56 [1]

Chester's history is long and distinguished. From the Romans it took both its name (*castra*, a camp – though they themselves called it *Deva*) and its street-plan; to the Normans it owes the beginnings of its cathedral and that marvellous, if truncated, church of St John the Baptist. Norman, too, though on Roman foundations, is a large part of the CITY WALLS. Nearly 2 miles in circumference, between 15 and 25 feet high, they have been preserved *in toto*, making Chester, with York (*q.v.*), the most completely walled city in England. Where civilian architecture is concerned, however, Chester is famous above all for its black-and-white timber-framed houses, many of them built with covered galleries at first-floor level which connect with each other, providing pedestrians with a second, superimposed, thoroughfare along the principal streets. It is these 'ROWS' that make Chester unique; so agreeable are they, and so practical, that one wonders why no modern town has adopted the idea.

The Rows are genuinely medieval; they were there already in the thirteenth century. The black-and-white houses, it must now be admitted, are almost all Victorian or later. There were three local architects who made themselves specialists in the *genre* – T.M. Penson, T.M. Lockwood and John Douglas; and their work bears roughly the same relationship to the genuine sixteenth- and seventeenth-century stuff as the work of, say, William Butterfield bears to genuine Early English. Purists may complain (and often do); and it is perfectly true that, after an hour's perambulation through the world's largest permanent exhibition of Op Art, the eye lingers with relief on the occasional stone or stucco front. Nonetheless, it is the black-and-white more than anything else that has given Chester its highly individual personality, and I for one would not have it different.

THE CASTLE

There has been a castle above the Dee at this point since Norman times, but the present buildings, the work of that local genius Thomas Harrison between 1785 and 1822, are castle in nothing but name: what they are, to quote Pevsner, is 'one of the most powerful monuments of the Greek Revival in the whole of England.' The whole complex surrounds a gigantic Parade Ground – full marks to the city council for not turning it into a car park – of which the long central block has a Doric portico (containing a beautiful semi-circular SHIRE HALL) and the two shorter projecting ranges have Ionic half-columns. Apart from these basic classical features and the quite sparing use of rustication – that on the sides of the main building makes a nice contrast with the ashlared centre – the whole concept impresses by its quite exceptional lack of decoration; its argument relies entirely on form and proportion, and a very strong argument it is.

The fourth side of the Parade Ground is closed by tripartite Doric propylaea, which since 1865 have neatly framed an equestrian statue of Lord Combermere. But, 20 yards behind that, there rises one of the most insensitive buildings I have seen anywhere in Europe: an eight-storey block, faced by what appears to be concrete Ryvita and topped by a forest of aerials. Enquiry revealed it to be the County Police Headquarters. It would look terrible anywhere; but here, precisely centred as it is on the axis of Harrison's *tour de force*, it is nothing short of sacrilege. How the council can have allowed it defies explanation.

THE CATHEDRAL AND IMMEDIATE ENVIRONS

The first thing to be said about Chester Cathedral is that almost all the visible exterior, with a few exceptions like the base of the crossing-tower, the clerestory windows of the nave and the west door, is nineteenth-century restoration, carried out by R.C. Hussey in the 1840s, George Gilbert Scott in the 1860s and 1870s, and Sir Arthur Blomfield in the 1880s. This is not to say that the cathedral is not worth looking at: Scott at least could be a very fine architect indeed, and much of his work (and that of the other two) may well have closely followed what was already there. The trouble was that Chester, like its neighbouring cathedrals at Worcester, Lichfield and Carlisle (*qq.v.*), was built of a notoriously friable red sandstone: Scott described it as being 'so horribly and lamentably decayed as to reduce it to a mere wreck, like a mouldering sandstone cliff.' If the Victorians had not moved in when they did, there would be little of it left today.

Once inside, the situation becomes a good deal more cheerful. There is majestic Norman work to be found in the north transept and the north-west corner of the nave, and a lovely late thirteenth-century Lady Chapel with an east window of five stepped lancets and side-windows of three. Here, though the actual stonework has nearly all been replaced, remarkably little of the beauty has been lost. Some of us will find more to complain about in the way every line of moulding in the vault, supporting piers and (especially) sedilia has been picked out in red, blue and gold. These features may not be genuinely medieval; nonetheless, it cannot have been right to trick them out like a merry-go-round. Best of all is the choir, with its tall, closely set, late fourteenth-century canopies rising up in a veritable forest of crocketed spirelets – Gothic wood-carving at its flamboyant best. The misericords, too, are as good as any in the country: well worth careful inspection, at whatever cost to the vertebrae.

Until 1540, Chester Cathedral was a Benedictine abbey, and it has preserved many of its monastic buildings. Best of all is the CHAPTER HOUSE; it begins with a fascinating vestibule which, Pevsner tells us, is one of the earliest examples of piers running into vaults without intervening capitals – the effect is vaguely vegetable and not unpleasing. The Chapter House itself is rectangular – not, alas, polygonal as so often at this date – but beautifully proportioned, richly vaulted and generously fenestrated with tall lancets. Then there is the REFECTORY, the best part of which is the delicate stairway, cut into the thickness of the wall, that leads up to the reading pulpit. Finally comes ST ANSELM'S CHAPEL, best approached from Abbey Square (see below). Built up against the north wall of the cathedral at gallery level, it provides an unexpected and enjoyable view down on to the Norman north-west tower. Indeed, it is very palpably Norman itself, if you can ignore the nasty nineteenth-century plaster vault. Here, surely, George Gilbert Scott should have known better, particularly when he had a so much more satisfactory model to hand: the seventeenth-century stucco ceiling over the chancel bay.

A *bonne-bouche* as a postscript: outside, on the south wall of the south transept and barely above eye level, there are two delightful corbels, pure Tenniel. In the first, Gladstone, quill pen clutched firmly in his mouth, undermines the claims of the Church of Rome, toppling a huge tiara as he does so; in the second, Disraeli as the British Lion takes up arms against Republicanism.

THE CITY

Northgate runs up from THE CROSS to the north. It begins quietly enough with Thomas Harrison's CITY CLUB, then immediately explodes into a riot of black-and-white called SHOEMAKER'S ROW, blatantly bogus and cheerfully admitting the fact with a little statue of Edward VII in a niche. Soon comes the splendidly Victorian TOWN HALL (built in 1867 by W.H. Lynn of Belfast) and, opposite it, the fourteenth-century ABBEY GATEWAY, leading into ABBEY SQUARE. This is really a sort of cathedral close, Georgian and elegant. From it you get the only easily available good view of the north side of the cathedral – though, if the truth be told, it's not up to much. Far more rewarding is the short detour into St Anselm's Chapel (see above). The next stop in Northgate is Harrison's NORTHGATE itself, proudly signed and dated, and then, just beyond it, a pretty little BLUECOAT SCHOOL with ALMSHOUSES behind.

Back to the Cross again – possibly ignoring the Roman hypocaust in the basement of Miss Selfridge – and turn left into EASTGATE, the Roman *via principalis*. Now it is almost all Victorian, but as there is no other Victorian

Eastgate, Chester.

street remotely like it anywhere, it is well worth looking at – as is Douglas's extraordinary development in ST WERBURGH STREET, which leads off to the left. (This time the statue is of Queen Victoria herself, in full regalia.) Beyond the Diamond Jubilee clock – Douglas again – Eastgate becomes Foregate Street, towards the bottom of which, to the right, runs BATH STREET, where Douglas has erected a little row of brick houses with tiny cone-capped turrets, straight out of a French fairy tale, which, for sheer curiosity value, take a lot of beating.

Off Foregate Street, to the south, stands ST JOHN THE BAPTIST. Little on the outside of this church prepares you for what lies within – Victorian Gothic it seems, at its most unimaginative. Go in regardless – but brace yourself for a shock. Suddenly it's the early twelfth century, and you are standing in a Norman abbey – a small cathedral, even. (St John's actually had cathedral status in the eleventh century, and kept the title until the sixteenth.) There before you looms a great pink Norman nave, with transitional triforium and Early English clerestory, marching up four bays to a magnificent crossing. Unfortunately, the church has been amputated at each end and each side; the transepts are gone, the nave was two bays longer, and even the chancel now extends only a single bay before we reach the distinctly peculiar east window – the Victorian idea of how the Normans would have done a five-light lancet. The extraordinary

thing is how little any of this seems to matter. It is the genuine Norman that comes across, the massive strength and confidence of it all. What a masterpiece this might have been!

A detour to the north brings you to the GENERAL STATION. This ranks with York, Newcastle, Monkwearmouth (*qq.v.*) and the best of the London termini in the very top league of early railway stations. It is Italianate, by Francis Thompson in 1847–8.

South from the Cross runs Bridge Street. Here, and in its continuation Lower Bridge Street, some excellent older buildings have survived – notably the BEAR AND BILLET (1664); GAMUL HOUSE (1700) with its strange elliptical windows, which was beautifully restored for Architectural Heritage Year in 1975; the seventeenth-century OLD KING'S HEAD; and THE FALCON (1626), whose continuous band of windows at first-floor level with quatrefoils below is a special delight.

The last main artery is Watergate Street. Now, at last, come the most distinguished sixteenth- and seventeenth-century buildings in Chester, led by the LECHE HOUSE (1560 or thereabouts) and BISHOP LLOYD'S HOUSE, which, despite Lockwood's restoration at the turn of the century, remains the best of the lot. The two other buildings most often pointed out, GOD'S PROVIDENCE HOUSE and the STANLEY PALACE, are largely reconstructions.

Cholmondeley Castle

10; 6 miles N of Whitchurch off A49

This seat of the Cholmondeleys has passed down in the direct male line since the twelfth century. The present house is a rebuilding between 1801 and 1805 by the 1st Marquess, who, though having inherited Houghton in Norfolk, decided to go on living here because of the remarkable continuity of the family connection, and that is also why he chose the Gothic style.

The founder of the family, Robert de Chelmundeleigh, was a younger son of a Norman marcher baron. His grandson Robert built the private Chapel, of which the chancel survives (with a flat hammerbeam roof dated 1300), though the nave was rebuilt to the design of William Smith in 1716 and the transepts were added in 1829. The Chapel contains splendidly preserved Jacobean fittings.

The ancient house was timber-framed and moated. Hugh Cholmondeley, an able and ambitious soldier who supported William III, was created Earl in 1706 and reconstructed the house from 1704–13 as a classical, brick, U-shaped pile to the design of William Smith of Warwick. He employed first-rate craftsmen: Tijou and Robert Bakewell for ironwork, Van Nost and Samuel Watson as carvers. Bakewell's gate-screen and staircase balustrade still survive, re-incorporated into the present park and house. The 4th Earl was created 1st Marquess and, when he inherited, the 1st Earl's house was so dilapidated that it was in danger of collapsing, so it was demolished and a new site chosen on a hill overlooking the whole park and the two lakes (landscaped by John Webb). The new house was begun in 1801 to the Marquess's own design, with William Turner of Whitchurch as executant architect. Additions in the same style were made by the 2nd Marquess in 1817–19; more were carried out in 1829–30 to the design of Smirke. The result is a charming, irregular Gothick castle, with octagonal and circular turrets and pointed windows with Gothick glazing bars (many of them restored *c.*1970). Of the principal interiors, the two-storeyed Hall is Gothick, but the Dining Room is plain classical and the Drawing Room has a simple Gothick frieze and marble chimneypiece.

Many improvements to both house and grounds have been carried out by the present Marquess. The interior has been redecorated to the design of John Fowler and the gardens redesigned by James Russell. A Gothick Pavilion overlooking the swimming pool was built *c.*1972 to the design of Roderick Gradidge. The gardens are sometimes open to the public.

Combermere Abbey

11; 6 miles SW of Nantwich on A530

With the Dissolution of the Monasteries, this great Cistercian house became the property of Sir George Cotton (Comptroller of the Household to Henry VIII's bastard son the Duke of Richmond) and remained with his descendants, later Baronets and Viscounts Combermere, until after the First World War. The abbey stands in a spectacular setting, encircled by wooded slopes on the bank of a mere that was enlarged out of two smaller pieces of water in the late eighteenth century.

Richard Cotton (son of Sir George) built the house in 1563; in his time it was a gabled black-and-white, half-timbered affair, some of the structure of which still survives inside, but of which nothing is visible from without. The exterior of the house was encased in brick and stuccoed in 'imitation of pointed Gothic style' by Sir Robert Cotton in 1795, possibly to his own design. The pinnacles on the roof are of carved wood.

The 1st Viscount intended to demolish the house and replace it with a new one designed by the Irish Morrisons; fortunately, this drastic proposal was not carried out and the only Morrison contribution is the Tudor-bethan Stone Lodge at the main entrance to the park. The 1st Viscount employed Blore to design the handsome brick 'Elizabethan' stable block with twin towers to the north of the house in 1837; he also added an armoury wing (since demolished) to the entrance front. Some restoration, to the design of John Tarring, was done *c.*1860.

The best interior, now called the Library, is the old Great Hall on the first floor, originally approached by an external flight of steps. It has a sixteenth-century frieze showing the arms of the Cottons and their connections, and a geometrical ribbed plaster ceiling. Some of the other rooms have old panelling, but they are chiefly simple Gothick work of 1795 – especially the Porter's Hall with its pretty clustered columns.

In the seventeenth century a formal garden and avenue were laid out in front of the house on the tongue of land that was later cut away to form the present superb, three-quarter-mile-long lake. The Gothick cottage, called DRAKELOWE FOLLY, on the opposite side of the mere was built in 1797, its interior decorated by Sir Robert's daughters with patchwork made out of old gowns. There they had a little model dairy, wrote many of their letters and in summer rowed across the lake after dinner to have tea in the cottage while they watched the sunset. The obelisk in the park was erected in 1890 to commemorate Stapleton Cotton, 1st Viscount Combermere.

Plans were considered in 1971 for refacing the house to the design of Raymond Erith and Quinlan Terry, but they were shelved; instead, part of the house was restored *c.*1975 to the design of A.N. Brown of A.H. Brotherton & Partners.

Crewe Hall

12; 2 miles SE of Crewe on A5020 [2]

In the nineteenth century this was one of the most admired houses in England – the Jacobean mansion *par excellence*, despite the fact that it was gutted by fire in 1866 and reinstated to the design of E.M. Barry, who heightened all the architectural effects to some tune. Crewe, which gave its name to the adjoining railway junction, was the seat of the Crewes from the Middle Ages until the Second World War. The present house was built by Sir Randolph Crewe in 1615–36. The 1st Lord Crewe added a service wing, redecorated much of the interior and landscaped the park to the design of Humphry Repton and John Webb in the 1790s:

Thus it happens at Crewe, where, tho' Taste overflows,
One Repton's called in to display what he knows.

The 3rd Lord Crewe restored the house in 1837–42 to the design of Edward Blore, replacing the late eighteenth-century neo-classical work with more sympathetic Jacobethan decoration at a cost of £30,000. All this was destroyed in 1866.

At the time of Barry's restoration (also for the 3rd Lord Crewe), the gardens were redesigned by W.A. Nesfield, and Eden Nesfield designed some delightful lesser estate buildings – lodges, cottages and farmhouses. Barry's work was intended to be an accurate recreation of the original house and therefore throws interesting light on Victorian attitudes to restoration. Barry stated that 'the greatest care has been taken to recover the design of Sir Randolph for such of the work as it has been possible to restore ... although with less roughness of execution and uncouthness of detail, particularly in respect of the human figure.' Further work was done at the end of the nineteenth century by the 1st Earl Crewe, when the service wing was extended to the design of Thomas Bower in 1896.

Despite all these alterations and additions, the exterior of the main block is still in essentials as it was built in the seventeenth century and most of the diapered brickwork was original. The main front is of seven bays and two storeys, with a columned centrepiece, canted bay windows and shaped gables. In the centre of the east side is a large bow window lighting the Chapel. On the west side are the later additions, dominated by Barry's distinctive tower with ogee spirelet on top, which can be seen for miles around and is easily visible from Crewe railway station. The interior is richly appointed in the High Victorian manner, with marble, alabaster, stucco and carved woodwork, and Barry's hand is more clearly discernible here than in the exterior. Some of the plasterwork and chimneypieces are replicas of the original but most of the decoration is frankly Victorian. The main suite of state apartments – Library, Drawing Rooms and two State Rooms – were decorated by J.G. Crace with exuberant plasterwork and stone chimneypieces. Stained glass was provided by Clayton & Bell, and decorative sculpture by J. Birnie Philip and J. Mabey.

Sir Randolph Crewe was Lord Chief Justice in the last year of James I's reign and is remembered for his noble summing up in the Oxford Peerage case: 'Where is Bohun? Where is Mortimer? Nay what is more, and most of all, where is Plantagenet? They are entombed in the urns and sepulchres of mortality.' The male line of the Crewes died out in the eighteenth century and the Chief Justice's great-granddaughter Anne married John Offley of Madeley in Shropshire. Their son changed his name to Crewe and after a long political career was created 1st Lord Crewe of Crewe. The line again died out in the late nineteenth century and after the death of the 3rd Lord Crewe in 1893 Crewe was inherited by the 2nd Lord Houghton, son of Richard Monckton Milnes, politician and man of letters, who had married Arabella Hungerford Crewe. The Crewe title was revived in 1895 as an earldom in favour of Lord Houghton, and in the Coronation Honours of 1911 he was advanced to a marquessate, a recognition of his own public career as a Liberal politician and of the fact that he represented three families all of whom had been distinguished in the legal, political and cultural life of England during the centuries of British ascendancy. On his death his titles became extinct, but the estate has been preserved by the Duchy of Lancaster, which now owns it.

Crewe Hall.

Doddington Hall
13; 4 miles SE of Nantwich on A51

Doddington Hall is Samuel Wyatt's masterpiece and, until recently, was the seat of the Delves Broughtons. The estate belonged to the Delves family from the Middle Ages until 1727, when it passed by marriage to the Broughtons. It was sold by Sir Evelyn Delves Broughton, the 12th Baronet, in 1979, but the house was retained.

The original house comprised a fortified pele tower, licence to crenellate which was granted to Sir John Delves in 1365, and a seventeenth-century block with a fanciful porch, topped by a balustrade and statues of the Black Prince, Lord Audley and four squires (one of whom was a Delves). Sir Thomas Delves Broughton demolished the Jacobean house but left the porch and the pele tower as an eye-catcher in the park. A completely new house, to the design of Samuel Wyatt in 1776–98, was built on a different site, 200 yards further south on axis with the tower. The long-drawn-out construction programme was the result of Sir Thomas's decision to fund the building in annual instalments from his income. His epitaph in Broughton church (*q.v.*), Staffordshire, states 'Let it not be forgotten that . . . he began to build Doddington Hall in the year 1777 and finished it in 1798 without encumbering his family estates with a shilling'.

The new house is faced in perfect ashlar and the austerity of the façades is relieved by tripartite windows inset under blank arches, a domed bow in the centre of the garden front, and crisp Coade-stone plaques showing the signs of the zodiac. The interior is symmetrically arranged with duplicated staircases, and the principal rooms on the *piano nobile* are embellished with elegant plasterwork by Joseph Rose, scagliola columns and elegant white marble chimneypieces. The finest room is the circular Saloon behind the bow, with its looking-glass panels, and pilaster strips painted by McLacklan, an artist otherwise known only as a decorator of china at the Derby porcelain factory. An interesting piece of geometrical planning is the neat arrangement of two hexagonal bedrooms in the space over the Saloon.

Wyatt also designed the stables, joined to the house by a segmental office wing, the cubic lodges and the geometrically planned home farm. The park was landscaped by Capability Brown, but has largely reverted to agriculture.

Dorfold Hall
14; 2 miles W of Nantwich on A534

Ralph Wilbraham built the present house in 1616 and it is one of the finest examples of Jacobean architecture in Cheshire. Constructed of red brick with stone mullions, it has gables and octangular shafted chimneys. The entrance front is symmetrical, with a recessed centre and projecting wings, and is flanked by subsidiary L-shaped pavilions with Flemish-style gables. The Victorian forecourt is enclosed by a stone balustrade and in the centre stands a sculptural group, depicting a mastiff and her whelps, from the Paris Exhibition of 1855. The front gates are from the same source. The whole approach to the house – lodges, avenue and forecourt – was designed by William Nesfield in 1862.

Dorfold Hall.

The plan of the house is unusual: a double pile with rooms behind the Hall and Great Chamber. The latter, the best room in the house, is on the first floor and has a coved stucco ceiling with geometrical patterns and hanging pendants; the original panelling of Mannerist design also survives. Other rooms contain lesser examples of Jacobean plasterwork and panelling: the King James Room has an armorial chimneypiece of 1621 and the Oak Room has attractive woodwork. Some of the rooms on the ground floor were redecorated in the eighteenth century. The Dining Room (formerly the Hall), has a mid-eighteenth-century ceiling, and the Library in the south-west corner was redesigned by Samuel Wyatt in 1772 with an Adamesque plaster ceiling executed for James Tomkinson, a successful lawyer from Nantwich who bought the Dorfold estate from the Wilbrahams in 1754. The Rev. James Tomkinson carried out some restoration work in 1837 and 1843 to the design of Edward Blore, including installing new 'Jacobean' chimneypieces; does that include the large stone one in the Great Chamber? In the nineteenth century the house descended through the female line to the Tollemaches and then to the Roundells by the marriage of Julia Tollemache to Charles Roundell. The present owner is Mr R.C. Roundell.

In the garden, the gateway from Robert Wilbraham's almshouses in Nantwich has been re-erected as an eye-catcher. It is a jolly mid-seventeenth-century Mannerist design, with busts in niches and a raised pedimented centre.

Dunham Massey
NT; 15; 3 miles SW of Altrincham off A56

Dunham Massey was once the seat of the Booths, later Earls of Warrington, and of the Greys, Earls of Stamford. The presence of a mound suggests that there was possibly a Norman castle on the site, although this may simply be an eighteenth-century garden feature. The existence of a chapel was recorded in 1307. Sir George Booth built a gabled quadrangular house in *c.*1600, some of the walls of which survive in the present house, reconstructed in 1732–40 by George Booth, 2nd Earl of Warrington, to the design of John Norris. This was a plain quadrangle of red brick, which has been heightened and elaborated at a later date. The east side was altered in 1822 by the 6th Earl of Stamford to the design of John Shaw and in 1905–7 the main front was given its sumptuous stone Jacobethan frontispiece, based on that at Lyme Park (*q.v.*), with tiers of columns to the design of J.C. Hall. Hall also 'improved' the internal elevations, especially that of the Great Hall; indeed, part of the character of the house as it is today derives from the Edwardian remodelling.

Much of the interior decoration was carried out at that period under the supervision of Percy Macquoid, the furniture historian. Both the Entrance Hall and the Dining Room are wholly Edwardian. The Great Hall has panelling and a chimneypiece of *c.*1740, but the Caroline-style stucco of the ceiling and upper parts of the walls is by Percy Macquoid. The Chapel retains old panelling and pews; the Library has original bookshelves and the overmantel frames Grinling Gibbons' masterpiece, a version in carved wood of Tintoretto's *Crucifixion*. The Green Saloon of 1822 is by John Shaw and has a large segmental bow, screened from the body of the room by four Ionic columns of *verde antico* scagliola.

The great deer park has held back the spread of Manchester for over a century. It contains several subsidiary buildings, including two handsome and dissimilar stable blocks of *c.*1720, two obelisks, a deer barn of 1744 and an Orangery.

The estate passed from the Booths to the Greys in 1736 by the marriage of Lady Mary Booth to Harry, 4th Earl of Stamford. There was a dispute *c.*1900 following the death of the Rev. Harry Grey, 8th Earl of Stamford, who had spent much of his life as a missionary, and considerable doubt existed as to whether his black son in South Africa was legitimate. The matter was resolved in a famous lawsuit, the court finding in favour of the Rev. Earl's nephew, William Grey. He inherited a house stripped of many of its contents, but was able to buy back a good deal, and it was he who restored and embellished the building between 1905 and 1907. On his death in 1910 he was succeeded by his son Roger, the 10th Earl, who lived in splendid seclusion at Dunham Massey until his death in 1976 and added further to the family collections, securing some of the magnificent early eighteenth-century Booth silver, which is now displayed in a room especially adapted for it. Dunham Massey was bequeathed to the National Trust in 1976.

23

Eaton Hall

16; 3 miles S of Chester off A483

Alfred Waterhouse's magnificent Gothic palace built for the 1st Duke of Westminster in 1870–83 was largely demolished in 1961–5 and has subsequently been replaced by a new house in the Modern style. Built on the same site in 1970–2 by the 5th Duke of Westminster to the design of John Dennys and Ove Arup, it is on a scale unequalled by any other recent English country house.

Eaton came into the possession of the Grosvenor family in the fifteenth century, but it was the acquisition by marriage in the late seventeenth century of extensive London estates (including what were to become Mayfair and Belgravia) that brought fabulous riches to subsequent generations. The first house on the present site, parts of which survived till 1961, was built in 1675–83 by Sir Thomas Grosvenor, 3rd Baronet, to the design of William Samwell, a gentleman-architect. It was of brick, a sophisticated version of the favourite type of Caroline house: a double-pile plan with a hipped roof, central cupola and pedimented three-bay centrepieces on both fronts. In 1803–12 it was enlarged and remodelled by the 1st Marquess of Westminster to the design of William Porden, forming an extravagant Gothic fantasy with an endless pinnacled skyline and cast-iron window tracery, once referred to by a relation as the 'Eternal Gothic of Eaton'. The house was later enlarged by Benjamin Gummow, who added the wings in 1823–5. The 2nd Marquess had the more frivolous elements shaved off and the house made more serious to the design of William Burn in 1845–54 and then, in 1870–83, it was totally transformed for the 1st Duke by Waterhouse at a cost of £600,000. The main part of the house was given up by the 2nd Duke at the outbreak of the Second World War and it was subsequently leased to the War Office to serve as an Officer Cadet School; when National Service came to an end in 1962, however, the lease was surrendered and, though the Army paid substantial compensation, it was unfortunately decided that the house was too large and in too poor a condition to restore.

The new house is a rectangle of concrete and glass, faced externally in white mosaic. An attempt to give the building a height and scale appropriate to its setting was made by raising the main rooms over a sub-storey containing a games room and heated swimming pool; this makes the house three storeys high. Ingenious use was made of the fall in ground levels to contrive a split-level entrance from the *porte-cochère*, with a wide flight of steps leading up to the entrance lobby on the *piano nobile*. The centre of the house is filled by the large Hall, which serves as a general sitting area, on the Edwardian model. It forms the main internal feature and is spatially interesting, as it rises through two storeys, has views through glazed doors and windows to the gardens, and is spanned at second-floor level by a bridge linking the principal bedroom suites in the north and south corners of the house.

The most important rooms are the Dining Room, Library and Drawing Room, which face the garden and have large windows with marvellous views eastwards across the terraces to the Cheshire Plain and Peckforton Hills. There is also plenty of wall space for paintings – a specific requirement of the client. The main rooms have wood-block floors, the Drawing Room is hung with silk and the Library has fitted bookcases. These, like all the internal joinery, are of teak and cedar supplied by Venables of Stafford. The standard of workmanship throughout is impressively high, closer to the norm in American architecture than in English. The remainder of the *piano nobile* is occupied by a Study, lavatories and, at the north end adjoining the Dining Room, the kitchen. The rest of the service accommodation is beneath the kitchen, on the lower floor, and the service entrance is by sunken access, concealed from the forecourt by a parapet wall. The floors at that level are tiled or of reconstituted marble, and the swimming pool at the south end is surrounded by Cosmati-work columns and marble statues salvaged from the Victorian house.

The top floor contains twelve bedrooms, two dressing rooms, two private sitting rooms, seven bathrooms, a laundry, servery, linen rooms and valet's room. The family bedrooms face the garden; the guest bedrooms overlook the forecourt, Belgrave Avenue and the distant Welsh hills.

Waterhouse's magnificent apsidal Chapel, with mosaics and stained glass designed by Frederick Shields and a tall *campanile* with carillon of bells, has been retained, as has the huge stable quadrangle, part of which has been converted into a gallery to display the overflow of works of art from the Duke of Westminster's collection.

The house is approached from Belgrave (a hamlet of three cottages which gave its name to a whole district of London) along a 2-mile avenue established in the seventeenth century, and is heralded by an obelisk of 1890 and the dazzling early eighteenth-century gilded wrought-iron gates, extended in the same style by Skidmore in 1871. The centrepiece of the forecourt is G.F. Watts's bronze equestrian statue of Hugh Lupus, and in the stable yard is the bronze statue of a rearing horse by Boehm. On the far side of the house are vast formal GARDENS with terraces, statuary, canals, temples and a camellia house 120 feet long. These gardens are among the grandest in England; they were originally designed by W.A. Nesfield in the mid-nineteenth century but were further embellished later by a succession of first-rate designers, including Lutyens, C.E. Mallows and Detmar Blow. They have been partly restored and replanted since the mid-1970s.

Eaton is set in the middle of a large park, landscaped by John Webb in 1805, with its own golf course, cricket field and stud farm, and long drives lead to it from all the surrounding immaculately maintained estate villages. There is an almost infinite number of subsidiary Victorian estate buildings, all of extremely high architectural quality – gates, bridges, cottages, temples, schools, farmhouses – many of them by the Chester architect John Douglas.

Eaton is not generally accessible, but the gardens are open once or twice a year for charity.

Eccleston

17; 2 miles S of Chester off A483

Eccleston is the prettiest of the Eaton estate villages. It has one or two early nineteenth-century cottages, but the most interesting buildings are those designed in varied toy Gothic for the 1st Duke of Westminster in the 1870s and 1880s by Douglas and Fordham; some are brick, some stone and some half timber. They include the SCHOOL, PUMP HOUSE and many cottages.

In the centre of the village is the CHURCH OF ST MARY. Standing in an ample churchyard with sprucely mown grass, it is approached through an eighteenth-century gateway (brought in the 1950s from Emral Hall, Flintshire, as a memorial to the 2nd Duke) and along a wide, straight path flanked by pleached limes. The church was built in 1899 to the design of G.F. Bodley, and was paid for by the 1st Duke. It is as noble and perfect as it is possible to be. There is a west tower, aisles and clerestory with flying buttresses, all executed in immaculate red sandstone ashlar. The interior is stone-vaulted throughout, the floor paved with black and white marble, the benches richly carved, the windows filled with stained glass by Burlison & Grylls; all the chancel fittings were designed by Bodley – as was the 1st Duke's own tomb, which has an effigy carved by Chavalliaud. Nothing detracts from the harmony. All is redolent of 'scholarly and patrician Anglicanism'.

Gawsworth

18; 3 miles S of Macclesfield off A536

The village of Gawsworth is especially attractive as a result of being arranged around three little meres or pools, with several grand houses in its centre, as well as the Perpendicular parish church. ST JAMES'S was built *c*.1500 by Randle Fitton and has an unusual plan with a wide nave but no aisles, and an embattled west tower. The interior contains Fitton monuments and a manorial pew recently embellished with Pugin woodwork brought from Scarisbrick Hall in Lancashire (*q.v.*) by the late Mr Raymond Richards. Near to the church is the OLD RECTORY, a large fifteenth-century black-and-white timber-framed house of the type in which Cheshire abounds. It owes something of its picturesque character to Victorian restoration, the porch, canted bay window and north wing all dating from the nineteenth century.

GAWSWORTH HALL is an L-shaped timber-framed house of medieval origins; it once formed a quadrangle, but the west wing and part of the south wing were demolished in the seventeenth century. It was formerly a seat of the Fitton family and is associated with Mary Fitton, Maid of Honour to Queen Elizabeth and mistress of the Earl of Pembroke. Shakespeare dedicated the First Folio of his works to her and she has sometimes been identified with the 'Dark Lady' of the Sonnets. The most notable architectural feature of the house is the jettied three-storey bay, the leaded lights of which have their original glass. In a recent restoration, sculpture was brought from Lowther Castle in Cumbria (*q.v.*) and library bookcases by Pugin from Scarisbrick Hall. The house overlooks one of the pools, in which its picturesque elevations are reflected.

GAWSWORTH NEW HALL is a large, plain brick Georgian house of fifteen bays, built by the Earl of Harrington in 1707–12 and altered earlier this century to the design of Sir Hubert Worthington, who added the Neo-Georgian front door. It is now an Old People's Home.

Gawsworth Hall.

Great Budworth

19; 4 miles N of Northwich off A559

ST MARY'S is a grand church, superbly sited on rising ground above this charming village. Although the red sandstone of Cheshire can often be deeply depressing to the spirit, in a Perpendicular church of this kind, with the light flooding through tall windows and a high clerestory, it is warm and welcoming. There is something comforting and protective about those broad aisles; this church, one feels, will stand for ever. The fine fourteenth-century Lady Chapel on the north side is sadly marred by hideous modern glass.

Jodrell Bank

20; 9 miles W of Macclesfield on A535

As one drives around the gentle, undulating country of the Cheshire Plain, one constantly gets glimpses of what seems to be the moon in broad daylight. This is the Jodrell Bank telescope – a thrilling piece of post-war British technology, very much more impressive than a great deal of the architecture and sculpture of the same decades, which strives after a similar effect but without any sense of purpose.

Conventional telescopes receive light-waves by means of a lens; Jodrell Bank was designed to receive radio-waves and the lenses were here replaced by huge shallow bowls or dishes. The station has five receiving bowls of various sizes. The largest is the oldest: Mark I. It was initiated in 1949 and built in 1952–7 under the direction of Bernard Lovell (later Sir Bernard) for the Radio Astronomy Laboratory of Manchester University. It has a circular steel bowl 250 feet in diameter supported by steel lattice triangles 180 feet high. When it was built it was the largest fully steerable radio telescope in the world. Mark II was added in 1960–4; it is an elliptic paraboloid 125 feet across its larger axis and is made of pre-stressed concrete. Mark III, built in 1963–6, has a bowl of open meshwork 50 feet in diameter and is supported on a massive concrete frame. The complex also includes other smaller telescopes with similar bowls used for tracking space probes.

The slight disappointment about Jodrell Bank is that, close up, the pristine sculptural splendour of the more distant views is somewhat compromised by the flat-roofed laboratory buildings and a mess of aerials. In the general landscape, however, the telescopes look like a twentieth-century reinterpretation of eighteenth-century garden design, with these huge, white geometrical shapes taking the place of classical temples and Gothick follies.

Knutsford

21; 12 miles SW of Manchester on A50

The Dorking of the north, immortalised by Mrs Gaskell as Cranford, Knutsford is a small and dainty place full of tea shops and genteel Manchester commuters. The spine of the town is KING STREET, at the top end of which is a noble pedimented triumphal arch designed in 1810 by Lewis Wyatt as the main entrance to Tatton Park (*q.v.*). The presence of the park and the Egerton estate immediately to the north acted as a natural green belt for the town, protecting it from large-scale development in the nineteenth and twentieth centuries. King Street is largely neat Georgian brick, with two-storeyed houses, boutique-style shops, restaurants, one or two Victorian banks, and the handsome Royal George Hotel. These act as a foil to the crazy interpolations built by Richard Harding Watt in the years around 1900. At the north end are the RUSKIN ROOMS of 1899–1902, with their domed turret and minaret; further down the street are the GASKELL MEMORIAL TOWER and KING'S COFFEE HOUSE of 1907–8, built of stone with crazy round-arched windows, battlements, a cupola and Arts and Crafts ironwork. There is nothing else like this in England – Gaudi in Barcelona is the nearest thing that comes to mind. At the south end of the street, Church Hill is reached. Here is the parish CHURCH OF ST JOHN THE BAPTIST. Plain and solid red brick Georgian with a west tower crowned with urns, it was designed by J. Garlive in 1741–4. The interior has giant Tuscan columns and side-galleries, but is nothing very special. The east end is Victorian.

Church Hill, steeply sloping and still cobbled, contains one or two good Georgian houses. It leads up to Princess Street and Toft Road, where the TOWN HALL (Gothic by Waterhouse), is situated, together with the former SESSIONS HOUSE. This, the best building in Knutsford, was designed by Thomas Harrison of Chester in 1815–18 and is a characteristic exercise in severe Grecian neo-classicism. The windowless façade is faced in smooth ashlar stone with a portico of unfluted Ionic columns in the centre, and the projecting wings to either side each have a large rusticated archway. It is a powerful and sombre piece of architecture.

To the west of the town centre is THE HEATH, an open area of grass with straight lines of lime trees, overlooked by Georgian and Victorian houses, forming an informal but pleasant piece of town planning. To the south of the centre are attractive nineteenth- and early twentieth-century suburbs with prosperous villas surrounded by trees and rhododendrons. In LEGH ROAD is another crop of buildings by Watt and his architects – dotty villas in a variety of styles, with towers, weird chimneystacks and domed turrets. All quite mad!

Little Moreton Hall★

NT; 22; 6 miles SW of Congleton on A34

The first sight of Little Moreton Hall cannot possibly disappoint. After all the travel posters, jigsaw puzzles and National Trust calendars, one cannot but fear some slight anti-climax; but no. There it stands, or rather lurches, as drunkenly, impossibly, endearingly as ever – not in any sense beautiful, but everybody's favourite black-and-white house.

Much of the charm, it must be said, is due to the south range, which is essentially a gatehouse, overhanging on three sides and topped by the dottiest Long Gallery in England. The Moretons always tended to give themselves airs; the trouble was that, whenever they tried to follow the fashions set by their richer, more sophisticated contemporaries, they invariably came a cropper. As can be seen clearly above the entrance, it was no good giving the local carpenter a Renaissance pattern-book

Lyme Park.

and hoping that he would produce decorations that would pass muster at Hampton Court; he wouldn't, and he didn't. The same applied to that Gallery. Although it may well have been built at the same time as the rest of the range – probably about 1570 – there can be little doubt that, so far as the designs were concerned, it was an afterthought. It played havoc with the alignment of the roof and, indeed, the stability of the entire structure, and even in their own day must have made the Moretons look more than a little foolish. How lucky, nonetheless, that they persisted; without the Long Gallery, the Hall would be a lesser place today.

The north range across the courtyard betrays the same determination to keep up with the fashion, and the same disastrous results. It was originally built in the late fifteenth century. In 1559, however – as the proud inscription makes clear – William Moreton determined to impress his neighbours by lighting his Hall with bay windows: a man felt such a fool without bay windows. Unfortunately, there was no room for them; the only possibility was to squash them together at right angles so that each cut out the light from the other. Consequently, that particular corner of the courtyard looks distinctly cross-eyed.

The Hall is still sadly under-furnished. What the National Trust needs is some benefactor who will present a few pieces of good Elizabethan furniture, particularly for the smaller rooms.

Lyme Park★
NT; 23; 6 miles SE of Stockport off A6
The largest house in Cheshire and one of the grandest, set superbly in a magnificent park, Lyme is part Elizabethan, part early eighteenth- and part early

nineteenth-century. It is the Elizabethan aspect that hits you first – and slightly below the belt – with a huge and pompous frontispiece, rising the whole height of the north front, almost as inept as if it had been dreamt up at Little Moreton Hall (*q.v.*). It is not often that one sees an Ionic column balanced on the apex of a triangular pediment! The south front, on the other hand, rising serenely above the lake, radiates sophisticated elegance. It is by Giacomo Leoni, translator and – with Colen Campbell – introducer of Palladianism to eighteenth-century England. At Lyme, however, he has tempered the style with distinctly Baroque giant pilasters separating the bays, even those partly concealed by his detached portico. (The square and graceless block above the roofline, for all the world like the fly-tower of a theatre, is not Leoni's fault, but that of Lewis Wyatt, commissioned in 1816 to provide more servants' bedrooms.)

Within the house, and once through Leoni's Palladian courtyard, Elizabethan preponderates, with the noble panelled Drawing Room, the Stag Parlour, and the Long Gallery above; all three have overmantels with the Royal Arms. To Leoni belong only the Entrance Hall, the expansive staircase and the Saloon, where the brilliantly assured limewood carvings are almost certainly the work of Grinling Gibbons. In addition, at the east end of the house, there is a Dining Room by Wyatt, but in late seventeenth-century style – 'a rare example', writes Pevsner, 'of so early a use of the Wrenaissance.'

A mile or so from the house, on a windy hill in the park, stands LYME CAGE. Originally built in about 1520 as a hunting lodge, it also seems to have been used as a temporary prison for local criminals on their way to Chester Assizes. It was Giacomo Leoni who added the four capped turrets in 1726.

Macclesfield

24; 15 miles SE of Manchester on A523

Macclesfield is of ancient origin. A charter was granted in 1261 by Edward I, when Earl of Chester, but it was not till the eighteenth century that the place expanded significantly. This was a result of the silk industry, and today it is as an eighteenth-century industrial town that Macclesfield is worth visiting, though the street pattern and some bits of the parish church are ancient. The creator of eighteenth-century Macclesfield, Charles Roe, founded his business as a silk-twist manufacturer in 1744 and introduced water-powered silk-throwing into the town in 1756, thus ensuring his own and Macclesfield's prosperity. He also opened a copper works in the town. The silk industry continued to flourish intermittently in the nineteenth century, but has declined since; the last handloom business closed in 1981. But Macclesfield retains much of its eighteenth-century character, and several of the Georgian mill buildings survive as impressive architectural features.

It is best to arrive by train. On emerging from the station, one encounters an empty space in front. This is Waters Green, and the River Bollin, which supplied the water power for the eighteenth-century mills, flows underneath in a culvert. Next to the station is the cast-iron Victorian façade of Arighi Bianchi, and opposite is a dramatically steep hill with the parish church on top. This can be approached either by the 108 STEPS or up CHURCH LANE. The latter is a curving, sett-paved street which immediately sets the Macclesfield scene. It has pleasant red brick Georgian houses, some with local stone-flagged roofs, and painted-timber Victorian shop-fronts. Note the good cast-iron street signs here and throughout the town. At the top is the medieval MARKET PLACE – small, irregular and also sett-paved. Coming from this direction, you see first the Blot – the lumpish new National Westminster Bank – on the west side. The only way to deal with such bad manners is to turn your back.

On the east side the parish church and the Town Hall form an excellent group. The churchyard has eighteenth-century railings and mown grass. The CHURCH OF ST MICHAEL was mainly rebuilt in 1898–1901 by Sir Arthur Blomfield in a respectable Perpendicular style. The west tower is part ancient but much enriched by Blomfield. On the south side the Savage Chapel, with a three-storeyed porch almost like another small tower, is genuine Perpendicular, having been built between 1501 and 1507 by Thomas Savage, Archbishop of York. There is handsome Edwardian stained glass by various well-known firms and the chancel fittings are by Sir Charles Nicholson. The chief interest of the church lies in the large array of fifteenth- and sixteenth-century alabaster monuments to the Savage family, the largest accumulation of such monuments in any Cheshire church.

The TOWN HALL, in contrast, is purest Grecian. It is the earliest work of Francis Goodwin, built in 1823–4. Goodwin's façade, with its fine Ionic portico, faces the churchyard. At right-angles to it, an almost identical façade – with another Ionic portico – is an example of Victorian keeping-in-keeping, having been added in 1869–71 by James Stevens, a versatile local architect. Inside, the Staircase Hall is embellished with Victorian white marble sculpture by Thornycroft and others. (A surprising number of well-known Victorian sculptors were born in the Macclesfield area.)

North of the Market Place stretches Jordangate. This is rather gappy, but contains two of the best Georgian houses in the town. The first is the MACCLESFIELD ARMS HOTEL, of five bays and four storeys, with lower pedimental side-wings containing Venetian windows. 'Um . . . 1770s,' you might say to yourself. In fact it dates from 1811; everything in Macclesfield is later than you think. On the opposite side of the street is JORDANGATE HOUSE, dated 1728. It is of three storeys and five bays, and has a Corinthian doorcase and florid lead rainwater heads. It was formerly the home of the Brocklehursts, a leading Macclesfield family.

Returning down the Market Place to the Town Hall, the next foray is along CHESTERGATE to the west. This is a narrow Georgian street and nicely frames the Victorian front of the Town Hall when you look back. The red brick houses have Victorian, or more recent, shop-fronts. A short way along, the street is bisected by Churchill Way. Any new road called 'Way' immediately suggests the worst, and this is indeed one of those ridiculous new road 'improvements' planned about thirty years ago, though only now being completed. It is to be regretted that it was not abandoned. On the corner of Churchill Way is CHARLES ROE HOUSE, the finest early eighteenth-century house in the town, its cornice decorated with carved acanthus leaves and its doorway with a curly open pediment. This building has recently been restored and an asymmetrical shop-front that disfigured the façade removed. Beyond, the street slopes gently downhill and is more cottagey in scale. Almost a quarter of a mile along, it forks into Prestbury Road and Chester Road, both of which contain some nice late Georgian houses.

In Chester Road is the Roman Catholic CHURCH OF ST ALBAN, part paid for by the Earl of Shrewsbury for Fr John Hall, and designed by A.W.N. Pugin. It is one of Pugin's major churches, begun in 1838 and opened in 1841. The style is East Anglian Perpendicular and the local sandstone is dressed with a 'rock-faced' finish which is deceiving and makes it difficult to date. The large west tower is incomplete. The impressive nave is remarkably spacious, with tall elegant arcades carrying a clerestory. The recent liturgical rearrangement has been tactfully done, with a simple new altar placed in front of the rood-screen, leaving the chancel intact with Pugin's stencilled decoration, east window with stained glass by Warrington and high altar with six brass candlesticks. Over the screen is a magnificent carved hanging rood, the focus of the church. Only the new, shiny metal light-fittings obtrude on the harmony of the original design.

Back to the Town Hall, this time turning to the south, down Mill Street. This is the main shopping area and not very special, but at the bottom is Park Green with several good features. The LIBRARY, dated 1874–6, is by James

Stevens in wild Ruskinian Gothic and shows him letting off steam after his tactful Town Hall extension. On the opposite side is the amazing Doric portico front of BARCLAYS BANK (originally the Macclesfield Savings Bank, built in 1841–2), then the tight fit of the Gothic CONGREGATIONAL CHURCH, with next to it an even worse National Westminster Bank than that in the Market Place. What does the NatWest have against poor Macclesfield? You will not be surprised to learn that it replaces a delightful Edwardian Baroque building. Shame! Forming an excellent view-stopper at the south end of Park Green is the brick-built Georgian MILL, dated 1785 and built by Daintry and Ryle. It is of thirteen bays and four storeys, with a stone-flagged roof, cupola, pediment and (working) clock. On the corner of Sunderland Street is a Georgian house of unusual design with a swept-up gable over an arrangement of lunette, Venetian window and doorway all under a blank arch. Behind the Library, in Park Lane, is PARADISE MILL, of twenty-two bays and four storeys, with a large pediment. It dates from the early nineteenth century and is now a museum open to the public, with working demonstrations of handloom weaving.

Returning up Mill Street, an opening on the west leads to Roe Street, in which is situated the SUNDAY SCHOOL, currently being restored as a museum of the silk industry. It is a large, brick block of four storeys with a pair of Tuscan doorcases. The parapet displays a deeply incised inscription 'SUNDAY SCHOOL' in gold letters, and 'ERECTED BY VOLUNTARY CONTRIBUTIONS A.D. 1813'. In front is a marble urn commemorating John Whitaker, the founder, carved in 1846 by Alfred Gatley (a local sculptor who later migrated to Italy). Next door to the Sunday School, the Salvation Army occupies a pretty classical chapel with a stuccoed front, built in 1829. Further west along Roe Street, and opening off it, are terraces of desirable, smaller Georgian houses, their date hinted at by their names – Waterloo Street, for example. It is a pity that these are currently being spoilt by the sporadic replacement of their original panelled front doors and double-hung sash windows with incorrect, off-the-peg substitutes.

In the middle of this pleasant area is CHRIST CHURCH, the best Georgian building in the town. It dates from 1775–6 and was paid for by Charles Roe himself. Despite the fact that it is situated in the middle of a residential area, it has been unnecessarily declared 'redundant' and its window panes are being smashed by local vandals. It is due to be vested in the Historic Churches Preservation Trust and preserved by that admirable body. Nevertheless, it is a disgrace that it should have been closed as a parish church – but typical of the Church of England's treatment of its 'redundant plant'. Christ Church is a case that strongly reinforces the view that there is no such thing as a redundant church. The architect of Christ Church is not known, but it is a handsome, somewhat unlettered design comprising a large, brick rectangular box with a tall, thin west tower. The east end is the most satisfying part of the composition, with a Venetian window flanked by a pair of *œils-de-bœuf*. The stolid character of the exterior is enlivened by the odd

Gothic touch, such as the Y-shaped glazing bars in the windows, and the battlements round the tower. The interior is plain but undisturbed, with a horseshoe-shaped gallery, box pews, eighteenth-century communion rails and tall pulpit, and a monument by John Bacon to Charles Roe with a relief of his silk mill and smoking copper works on the plinth. So much for the old chestnut that the English are not proud of mercantile achievement.

Malpas
25; 6 miles NW of Whitchurch on B5395

Malpas stands on a slight rise and in distant views is dominated by the parish church with its tall nave clerestory, lower chancel, short west tower and gold weathervane glinting in the sun. There are two main streets – Church Street and High Street – forming a Y, with nice cobbled verges and, at the junction, a pinnacled Gothic CROSS on an old stepped base, erected in 1877 to the memory of the Rev. Charles Augustus Thurlow, Chancellor of the Diocese of Chester. Adjoining is the MARKET HOUSE, early eighteenth-century, of brick with a stone colonnade of Tuscan columns along the ground floor; it is now a good restaurant. Opposite is Eyre's chemist's shop, its two-storeyed Victorian shop-front painted maroon and its cast-iron gutters embellished with frilly curlicues.

Church Street contains one or two seemly Georgian houses and the single-storeyed range of the CHOLMON-DELEY ALMSHOUSES, founded in 1721 by the Earl of Cholmondeley. They were substantially reconstructed in 1955, but have a nice carving of the Cholmondeley arms in the central pediment, and decent, green-painted front doors. The High Street has several attractive shops, all with carefully controlled signs, as well as the OLD SCHOOL HOUSE, which is dated 1745 but looks seventeenth-century. Behind the church is a mound, thought to be the motte of a Norman border castle built as a defence against the Welsh, the name 'Malpas' being a corruption of the Norman French for 'difficult passage'.

The parish CHURCH OF ST OSWALD is the principal monument of Malpas – a beautiful church, beautifully maintained. The graveyard has pleached lime trees and two sets of eighteenth-century gateways with urn-capped stone piers and iron gates. It is built of pink sandstone and, at first glance, looks all-of-a-piece Perpendicular, though in fact it was begun in the fourteenth century and its building history straddles the transition from Decorated to Perpendicular. There are good eighteenth-century lead downpipes and a dignified eighteenth-century brick vestry tucked against the north wall of the chancel. The nave is of six bays, with moulded piers supporting the clerestory of large, four-light windows. The eye is immediately caught by the magnificent timber roof, low-pitched, with carved, painted and gilded bosses and angels. The chancel is lower, with fourteenth-century sedilia and piscina. Over the chancel arch is a large oil painting of *St Peter's Denial* by Francis Hayman, given to the church in 1778 by Assheton Curzon of Hagley, Staffordshire. The east

Mow Cop.

Mow Cop
NT; 26; 3 miles NE of Kidsgrove off A34
Perched high on a steep escarpment over 1000 feet above
sea level, Mow Cop looks from a distance more like a
Syrian crusader castle than a Gothick folly. It was in fact
built as an eye-catcher by the squire of nearby Rode Hall
(*q.v.*), Randle Wilbraham, in 1750 – making it one of the
earliest sham ruins in the country. It possesses another
distinction, too: on 31 May 1807 it was the scene of a
twelve-hour prayer meeting, which ultimately gave
birth to Primitive Methodism. In 1907 the centenary was
marked by another meeting attended by no less than
70,000 people. Mr Wilbraham must have spun in his
grave.

Nantwich
27; 4 miles SW of Crewe on A534
This old town still contains much of interest, despite
having been treated unintelligently for the last twenty
years. It is proud to be a 'historic' town but has spent
money on all the wrong things, while good buildings
have been left to rot or have been demolished. The view
from the High Street has been ruined by an unnecessary
large-scale shopping development in Out Market of
sadly mediocre design for such a prominent site; the
parish church is full of touristy trappings and brash
modern needlework; huge sums of public cash have
been spent on indifferent brick paving and pedestrianisation of the High Street – sums which could
have been better used in the form of grants to some of the
decaying listed buildings that line the street.

Despite this, Nantwich is still worth a visit. The centre
of the town is the fourteenth-century CHURCH OF ST
MARY (the parish church), one of the most ambitious
churches in the county. It is large and cruciform in plan,
with an octagonal tower over the central crossing. The
exterior stonework (soft pink sandstone) had to be drastically restored in the nineteenth century and the west
front, with anachronistic details, is largely by G.G. Scott.
It faces a churchyard that has something of the character
of a formal town square, with grass, trees and a war
memorial in the middle, and Victorian banks and commercial buildings round it. You enter through the two-
storeyed south porch, where you have to fight your way
through modern plate-glass doors and past a large
souvenir shop (money-changers in the temple). The
lavishness of the church is presumably explained by
Nantwich having been the centre of England's salt
industry in the Middle Ages (it declined from the seventeenth century and so, as there was no need to redevelop
for new functions, much of historic interest survived
into the twentieth century), although when it was built
this mini-cathedral was merely a chapel-of-ease, not
even a parish church. Once in the nave, you are immediately struck by the impressive scale, and the richness of the architecture, which is a transitional blend of
Decorated and Perpendicular. The nave is tall and the
stonework a pleasant light pink, while the aisles have
fine strainer arches to support the clerestory. It is best to
turn your back on the modern appliqué hangings at the
west end (commemorating the Queen's Silver Jubilee in

ends of the aisles are formed into separate chapels by
carved Perpendicular screens of oak. One (north) is the
Cholmondeley Chapel, commemorating Sir Hugh Cholmondeley and his wife, and the other (south) the Brereton
Chapel, in memory of Randle Brereton and his wife. The
centrepiece of each is a magnificent alabaster tomb-chest
with carved effigies, both of them in perfect condition,
lovingly čared for; one imagines the housekeeper from
Cholmondeley Castle (*q.v.*) coming over to give them a
dust and polish every now and then. There are white
marble tablets to later Cholmondeleys in their chapel, as
well as excellent panels of sixteenth-century Flemish
stained glass in the windows. At the west end of the nave
is a rare medieval chest decorated with beautiful ironwork scrolls, and near the south door is the church-
warden's box pew. Bishop Heber of Calcutta was born
in 1783 at the Rectory in Malpas, where his father was
rector. The author of such hymns as 'From Greenland's
Icy Mountains' and 'Holy, Holy, Holy' would be pleased
to know that on a table at the back of Malpas parish
church, adjoining the guide-books, can be found a leaflet
– 'In Defence of Our Spiritual Heritage' – denouncing the
'dreary committee language' of modern alternative litur-
gies and defending the *Book of Common Prayer*.

1977); they look like religious bedspreads. Much more interesting is the faded Victorian stencilled decoration by Scott over the crossing-arch; it ought to be restored. The chancel is the *pièce de résistance*, stone-vaulted throughout in an intricate pattern with carved bosses, and richly furnished. There is a Victorian mosaic floor and a splendid series of late fourteenth-century choir stalls with rich tabernacled canopies and entertaining carved misericords showing foxes, nuns, wrestlers, dragons and a wife hitting her husband with a large kitchen spoon. The altar is an Elizabethan table with bulbous legs and behind, beneath the huge Perpendicular east window, is a carved reredos with wooden figures. The low, dark crossing forms an effective spatial contrast to the tall nave and elegant chancel. In it stands the original fifteenth-century pulpit, like a carved stone egg-cup. The transepts contain interesting furnishings, including screens with sixteenth-century painted heraldic panels brought from elsewhere, a seventeenth-century wall tomb to Sir Thomas Smith of Hough, and some medieval alabasters.

To the north-east of the churchyard is DYSART BUILDINGS, a tall brick Georgian terrace of the type you would expect to see in Liverpool. To the west is the HIGH STREET. On the curve opposite the church is a modern National Westminster Bank of restless concrete sections, trying too hard to be 'of our time yet in keeping', and then follows an excellent group of sixteenth-century black-and-white half-timbered buildings with one Georgian brick façade. Of these, the Crown Hotel, built *c.*1584, is the best. This group is in surprisingly poor condition, and gravely disfigured by unsympathetic shop-fronts. Further down on the other side is the new shopping development surrounded by silver birches

and raised brick flower-beds: the less said the better. Continuing beyond this, you reach WELSH ROW, with several more good black-and-white buildings. Retracing your steps and continuing along the High Street in the other direction (to the south), you discover more (neglected) timber-framed buildings and YE OLD VAULTS, a Georgian pub, the ground floor of which has an excellent frontage of fluted Doric columns, wood-grained, and a *verre églomisé* fascia sign. The continuation of the High Street is PILLORY STREET, with simple Georgian brick buildings on a cottagey scale, one or two bright tomato-red Victorian interpolations, and the stocks — the eponymous pillory. Off this to the east opens Hospital Street, which contains the black-and-white SWEETBRIAR HALL, several good Georgian brick houses with pretty porches, and, at the end, CHURCH'S MANSION, built in 1577 by Thomas Cleese for a rich merchant. It is the finest timber-framed building in Nantwich, now a restaurant and done up to the nines.

The old town centre of Nantwich is joined by twentieth-century ribbon development to Crewe and is embedded in suburbs of Barratt-type housing. Some of the new bungalows could win a prize for vulgarity.

Northwich
28; 16 miles NE of Chester on A556
ST HELEN'S, Witton, reminds one at first of St Mary's, Great Budworth (*q.v.*). It too is of the local red stone, all embattled, and proudly set on a hill above the surrounding houses. Inside, its glories are the polygonal apse of *c.*1525 and, of the same date, the roof of the nave and chancel, adorned with painted bosses large and small. Heavily restored in the 1860s, it has managed to keep its early sixteenth-century atmosphere remarkably well.

High Street, Nantwich.

Peckforton Castle.

Over Peover

29; 4 miles S of Knutsford off A50

The property of the Mainwarings from 1086 to 1919, PEOVER HALL, a timber-framed building, was refaced in brick by Sir Ralph Mainwaring *c.*1585. A large eighteenth-century wing was demolished in 1960 and a new front contrived on that side to match the style of the Elizabethan house. There is a fine Great Hall with an unusual magpie ceiling, and the house has been refurbished by the present owner, who has brought in panelling and furniture from elsewhere. The STABLES – dated 1654 and perhaps more important architecturally than the house – have Tuscan columns and arches, and a strapwork plaster ceiling. The adjoining Coach House is dated 1764 and has a central pediment and cupola. The house is set in a pretty garden with topiary and lily pond.

Peckforton Castle★

30; 12 miles SE of Chester off A49

In splendid Victorian self-confidence, Peckforton Castle rivals the genuine medieval ruins of Beeston Castle on an adjoining hilltop. And that self-confidence is not misplaced, for it *is* bigger and better than the real thing. 'The largest and most carefully and learnedly executed Gothic mansion of the present day is not only a castle in name . . . but it is a real and carefully constructed medieval fortress, capable of standing a siege from an Edwardian army. . . .' Thus wrote Sir George Gilbert Scott in disapproving tones. The character of the house owes a great deal to its builder, John, 1st Lord Tollemache, who inherited the 26,000-acre Cheshire estate from his mother, sister of the last Earl of Dysart. The original family house had been pulled down in the eighteenth-century and so he built Peckforton to replace it. He had a patriarchal picture of his position, fathered twenty-five children, spent £280,000 rebuilding the farms and cottages on his estates and a further £69,000 on his modern feudal castle, the seat of his 'benevolent autocracy'.

Lord Tollemache's medieval ideal was executed in solid stone by Anthony Salvin from 1844–50 – 'good, simple and free from extravagance'. It forms an irregularly shaped courtyard, as if dictated by defensive requirements, with a circular, keep-like tower dominating the rest. The individual parts are solid and sober with little ornament, just large expanses of well-executed masonry. The main rooms are ingeniously planned and vaulted in stone; they enjoy splendid views on all sides. They are now empty of family contents, as the house has not been continuously inhabited since the Second World War, though let from time to time. The present Lord Tollemache lives at his other seat, the moated brick Helmingham in Suffolk. The Peckforton estate, however, is splendidly maintained and, like Eaton (*q.v.*), possesses one of the best groups of Victorian model farms and cottage buildings in England. I may have had too much to drink at lunch, but I seem to remember one of the latter having a model elephant in its front garden.

Peover Hall

See Over Peover.

Port Sunlight★
31; 4 miles S of Birkenhead on A41

In 1888, William Hesketh Lever, later 1st Viscount Leverhulme, moved his soap factory from Warrington to a new site of 56 acres on the opposite bank of the Mersey, 3 miles from Birkenhead. The factory occupied 24 acres and the remaining 32 acres were used to house his workers in a 'garden village'. More land was bought later and the scale increased to include over 1000 houses. The original layout-plan for this exemplary model village, with its gardens, avenues, vistas and well-built houses, was Lever's own, though the first buildings and various refinements to the plan were the work of a Warrington architect, William Owen. It combines the Picturesque tradition of landscaped urban layout, inherited from Nash, with the paternalistic workers' housing of the more enlightened Victorian industrial employers. William Owen's design for the first twenty-eight cottages and the entrance lodge were awarded the Grand Prix at the 1910 Brussels Exhibition.

Port Sunlight survives as a complete museum-piece of *fin de siècle* architecture, showing the influence of the Pre-Raphaelites. The main plan is formal with a cruciform pattern of boulevards as the centrepiece. These − THE DIAMOND and THE CAUSEWAY − were developed in 1910. At the main crossing is a magnificent war memorial of bronze and granite by Sir William Goscombe John. The Diamond is a long formal garden with avenues on each side and symmetrical groups of cottages. The end of the vista is marked at one extreme by a stone triumphal arch with Tuscan pilasters and pediment, designed by J. Lomax-Simpson, and at the other by the LADY LEVER ART GALLERY, designed in 1914 by William Owen's son Segar in a refined *Beaux Arts*

classical style, with shallow dome and Ionic portico. The Gallery contains Lord Leverhulme's amazing collection of Pre-Raphaelite paintings and eighteenth-century English furniture, including the state bed from Stowe. In scale, quality and strong period character, these are the English equivalent of the eighteenth-century French art in the Wallace Collection in London. At right-angles to the Diamond is the Causeway, equally formal but slightly narrower; its focus is CHRIST CHURCH, again by William and Segar Owen, and a *chef-d'œuvre* of expensive Edwardian Perpendicular architecture executed in pink sandstone.

The cottages themselves range from semi-detached pairs to short terraces; all have their own gardens (originally allotments) and were well designed by a series of distinguished local architects, including Grayson and Ould, Douglas and Fordham, J. Lomax-Simpson and Sir Charles Reilly, as well as more famous names from London, such as Sir Edwin Lutyens and Ernest George. Many of the cottages are in the Cheshire half-timbered style and recall the similar model cottages around the Duke of Westminster's estate at Eaton (*q.v.*). The social centre of the village is the Bowling Green, with the LYCEUM (by Douglas and Fordham), a men's club, and the HULME HALL (by William and Segar Owen) used for functions. There is also a pub in the village, the BRIDGE INN, designed by Grayson and Ould as a romantic evocation of an old English coaching inn. It was originally a non-alcoholic establishment, but after an 85 per cent vote in favour of a licence it was turned into a proper pub. It is a good place for a pint after a morning's sight-seeing!

Portal
See Tarporley.

Port Sunlight.

Rode Hall

32; 6 miles S of Congleton off A34

Rode Hall is a substantial Georgian house of red brick with a somewhat complex building history. The original portion of the house was built by the first Randle Wilbraham, who purchased the estate from his cousin, Randle Rode Wilbraham; the house was described as newly completed in 1708. It has a hipped roof, a five-bay recessed centre and wings with Venetian windows and *œils-de-bœuf*. The onion cupola, which is similar to that to be seen on the nearby stable block of c.1750, is a later addition.

A completely new house was added to the north-west by the second Randle Wilbraham in 1752, at which time the old wing became the kitchen offices. The new block is much taller, two and a half storeys, and is five bays by four. Originally the windows had stone architraves but these were removed in the next stage of alterations, carried out between 1799 and 1800 on behalf of her youngest son by Mrs Richard Wilbraham-Bootle, who in her own words had a 'great turn for building'. At that time the house was re-oriented, the polygonal bays on the ends of the 1752 block made segmental, and a new, almost symmetrical, entrance front created to the south-west. All this was done to the design of John Hope of Liverpool. Finally, in 1810, a similar extension was made on the opposite side of the house to contain a new Dining Room designed by Lewis Wyatt. The exterior was also stuccoed at that time, but fortunately the stucco was removed in 1927 and the red brick restored under the supervision of Darcy Braddell, who also added a handsome Ionic portico to the entrance.

The Drawing Room and Library, divided by an octagonal anteroom, are plain Regency rooms by John Hope; the Entrance Hall is also largely his, with two screens of Tuscan columns. The Staircase Hall, lit by a big Venetian window and with Rococo plasterwork, is the only mid-eighteenth-century work surviving inside. But the best room is Lewis Wyatt's Dining Room, with its shallow segmental vault, an apse at one end with a screen of *verde antico* scagliola Ionic columns, and a severe black marble chimneypiece. Humphry Repton produced a Red Book for the park (preserved at the house) in 1790 but was told that it 'would not be requisite'.

Sandbach

33; 6 miles NE of Crewe on A534

A nice little market town, despite its modern suburbs, Sandbach is best approached from the east, where the main road is flanked on one side by the OLD HALL HOTEL, a famous black-and-white timber-framed building dated 1656, and on the other by a group of Victorian brick ALMSHOUSES and estate cottages, followed by the parish CHURCH OF ST MARY. This was designed by George Gilbert Scott and built in 1847–9, though it incorporates some bits from a previous church on the site. It is Perpendicular in style and has a well-proportioned, square west tower carried on open arches and said to be a reproduction of the original. Clustered round its base are the broken shafts of some Saxon crosses moved here from the Market Place in 1956 (where they had been grouped round the two big Crosses like little children at their parents' feet).

The HIGH STREET is lined with brick buildings of a pleasantly cottagey scale, mainly Georgian, but some, alas, disfigured by unsightly modern shop-fronts. The OLD MARKET PLACE opens up on the right almost immediately after the church. It is an attractive space, quite small and roughly square, still with cobbled paving and surrounded by old red brick or black-and-white timber-framed buildings, of which the OLD BLACK BEAR, dated 1634, is the best. It is a pity about the new post office for, though it tries hard to be inoffensive, the brick is the wrong colour and this sort of bland 'conservation-area style' is just not good enough. Why cannot a rich public organisation like the Post Office commission decent architecture?

In the centre of the Market Place are the two famous SANDBACH CROSSES. They are Saxon and are thought to date from the ninth century. They have stood in this position since at least the sixteenth-century, and have possibly always been here, though their present arrangement on a high-stepped plinth of worn stone dates from 1817. They are very tall and covered with interlacing carvings of scenes from the life of Christ. They lean slightly and look a bit like a pair of venerable old totem poles, just as they do in richly *chiaroscuro* nineteenth-century lithographs. There is something extraordinarily thrilling about the way these ancient, weathered relics stand nonchalantly amidst the trappings of everyday life, at Christmas with decorative coloured light bulbs looped around them. No careful museum display can ever match the shock of immediacy conveyed by works of art that have been left in their original setting.

Continuing up the High Street, a coarse but jolly red brick Victorian pub forms a good view-stopper at the end, and on the right is the TOWN HALL, built in 1889 to the design of Thomas Bower of Nantwich and paid for by Lord Crewe. It is Gothic, of red brick decorated with stone statues in niches and with the Crewe arms; it has an open arcaded ground floor to serve as a market house for the New Market Place at the back.

Turning left into High Town Square, and Crewe Road, there is a remarkably complete ensemble of Victorian Gothic buildings, including a good pub, the LITERARY INSTITUTE of 1857 by G.G. Scott, and the SAVINGS BANK, dated 1854. These are of diapered red brick with stone trimmings and make a picturesque group. In front is a stone fountain by Thomas Bower, dated 1897, and forming a little Jacobean-type rotunda with Tuscan columns. Finally, there is SANDBACH SCHOOL, gloomily Gothic in red brick with blue diapers and also by Scott, c.1850. Just looking at it conveys a *frisson* of waiting outside the headmaster's door.

As is so often the case in Cheshire, Sandbach owes the preservation of its Crosses, and its good Victorian buildings, to the beneficence of rich, enlightened and public-spirited nineteenth-century landowners. If only modern local authorities were able to do their jobs as well!

Styal

NT; 34; 1¼ miles N of Wilmslow off B5166
Includes Quarry Bank Mill (NT)

This remarkably well-preserved patriarchal industrial village in the wooded valley of the River Bollin, near Manchester Airport, now belongs to the National Trust and is imaginatively preserved and shown to the public. Its nucleus is QUARRY BANK MILL (NT), built as a silk mill in 1784 by Samuel Greg (who came from Belfast). It looks just like a Georgian stable block, of red brick, with small-paned windows, central pediment framing a clock, and little domed cupola on the roof. To the north is QUARRY BANK HOUSE (the Gregs' house) and to the south is the mill manager's house. Cottages for the workers, and the apprentices' house, are situated up the hill. It is all complete and was given to the Trust in 1939 by the Greg family.

Tabley House

35; 3 miles W of Knutsford off A556

This red brick mansion on the Palladian model was built on a new site, to the design of John Carr of York, in 1760–7 by Sir Peter Leicester, Bt, to replace Tabley Old Hall. The main block is of nine and seven bays with a rusticated basement, and has the main rooms on the *piano nobile*. The garden front was the original entrance front and has a giant portico of unfluted Doric columns, while the *piano nobile* windows are pedimented. The side elevations have canted bays; the present entrance front has a pediment, and a porch added in 1914. Attached to the main block by convex quadrants are four-bay pavilions and opposite the entrance forecourt is the long, simple stable block.

The principal rooms have good stucco and fireplaces. According to Howard Colvin, the whole west side of the house, formerly consisting of three rooms, was made into a Picture Gallery in *c.*1810 by the 1st Lord de Tabley to the design of Harrison of Chester; the three parts were separated by segmental arches. The Gallery contained his famous collection of paintings, including works by the best late eighteenth- and early nineteenth-century English artists, such as Romney, Constable and Turner. The de Tabley title died out in the late nineteenth century; the estate then passed to the Leicester-Warrens and later, through her mother, to Mrs Davenport of Davenport in Shropshire, who took the name Leicester-Warren. Her son, the late Colonel John Leicester-Warren, ran a boys' school in the house, but on his death it and the park were given to Manchester University.

The Old Hall fell victim to subsidence caused by the subterranean extraction of brine in the area in the 1920s and has since collapsed. The house had a medieval Great

Quarry Bank Mill, Styal.

Hall with a good timbered ceiling and a symmetrical brick front added in the seventeenth century, and stood on an island in the lake. It formed an extremely picturesque composition, with the adjoining seventeenth-century Chapel (which was rescued and rebuilt on the mainland in 1927–9), and was painted by Turner and other artists.

Tarporley
36; 12 miles SE of Chester on A51

Tarporley is a main-road village that looks like a film-set for some roistering costume-piece with stagecoaches and bucolic squires. It comprises one handsome wide street, the High Street, lined with eighteenth-century brick houses and coaching inns. The two petrol-filling stations are an intrusion, but could be worse. At the south end, forming a view-stopper, is the gabled MANOR HOUSE, dated 1586. It was originally brick but has been plastered. The lower end of the street has terraces of two-storeyed late eighteenth-century houses and the SWAN HOTEL of three storeys with canted bay windows.

The CHURCH OF ST HELEN is tucked away to the west of the High Street and looks a completely Victorian rebuilding. In fact, the Victorian exterior is only a 'restoration' of an older church, carried out by J.S. Crowther of Manchester for the Haddingtons of Arderne Hall, *the* prominent local landowners whose Victorian Gothic house, also by Crowther, has been demolished. The interior of the church is genuine Perpendicular, but mainly worth visiting for its rich nineteenth-century fittings, including stained glass by Kempe and an unusual iron chancel screen. There are seventeenth- and eighteenth-century memorials to the Crewe and Done families. In the churchyard is the former school, now the DONE RECREATION ROOM — a delightful little Jacobean building of diapered brick built in 1636 under the terms of the will of Sir John Done and embellished with his arms surrounded by carved strapwork.

To the north of Tarporley is PORTAL, a 'modern' timber-framed house, bigger and better than the real thing. It is built around a courtyard and was designed by W.E. Tower, a pupil of Bodley c.1900–5. Both the main fronts are symmetrical, with elaborately bargeboarded gables and canted bow windows. A lot of the beams are in fact old ones re-used, and include some fifteenth-century timberwork in one of the rooms. The interior has old brought-in panelling and some sixteenth-century Swiss stained glass. Throughout the building there is a real feel for the quality and character of timber-framing; there is a marvellous sense of craftsmanship, which makes it one of the best of the timber-frame revival buildings in Cheshire. Portal is a private house and is not open to the public.

Tatton Park
NT; 37; 6 miles SW of Altrincham off A556

Tatton was for centuries the seat of the Egertons, the descendants of Sir Thomas Egerton, Viscount Brackley, Lord Chancellor of England, who acquired the estate in c.1598. The origin of the present house was a three-storeyed early eighteenth-century brick building (the

date 1718 is in a cellar), to which a new Dining Room and Drawing Rooms with rich Rococo plasterwork designed by T.F. Pritchard were added in the middle of the century. Samuel Egerton, who had been a merchant in Venice, planned to remodel the house to the design of Samuel Wyatt in the 1770s, but it was his nephew William Egerton who started to rebuild to Wyatt's design in 1785. The available money ran out while work was in progress and it was finished only in 1807–22, by Wilbraham Egerton, to a much reduced design by Lewis Wyatt.

Most of the interiors are by Lewis Wyatt, notably the neo-classical Entrance Hall (with porphyry scagliola columns inspired by Henry Holland's hall at Carlton House), the extension to Samuel Wyatt's Staircase Hall and the richly decorated and much-gilded Drawing Room and Music Room. The Library, also by Lewis Wyatt, was given a new Neo-Georgian ceiling late in the nineteenth century. Of the earlier building, only Pritchard's Dining Room was retained (with a new chimneypiece by Westmacott). Much of the furniture was provided by Gillow in c.1820, and there is an interesting collection of continental paintings. The servants' quarters are shown as they were when the Egertons lived at Tatton.

The large flat PARK with two meres (one natural and one caused by subsidence), avenues and impressively long drives was landscaped by Humphry Repton and John Webb in the 1790s. The gardens round the house were much elaborated by Joseph Paxton in the mid-nineteenth and early twentieth centuries. Various small additions were also made to the house in the mid-nineteenth century, including an extra storey to the subsidiary wing, designed by G.H. Stokes in 1861–2, and a pair of ugly yellow terracotta archways flanking the forecourt, designed by Lord Egerton himself in 1884.

Of the various subsidiary buildings, the stable block was designed by Samuel Wyatt, and the Orangery and the Knutsford Lodge by Lewis Wyatt. The Rostherne Lodge was designed by James Hakewill in 1833, and a version of the Choragic Monument of Lysicrates, terminating a vista in the grounds, was the work of William Cole of Chester c.1820. The Shinto temple was imported from Japan in c.1910.

The 4th and last Lord Egerton of Tatton was a bachelor who spent much of his time big-game hunting and on exploratory expeditions abroad. In 1935 he added a 'Tenant's Hall' with a museum for his trophies, and an organ; the family state coach and the Victorian Tatton fire engine are also on view there. On his death in 1958, the 4th Lord Egerton bequeathed the house to the National Trust.

Thornton Hough
38; 6 miles SW of Birkenhead on B5136

Thornton Hough in the form we see it today was created by William Hesketh Lever, 1st Viscount Leverhulme, the self-made soap millionaire and founder of Port Sunlight (*q.v.*). He rented the estate from 1888 and then bought it in 1891. He built the model village with neat stone cottages, laid out 5 miles of avenues, made vast and elaborate gardens to the design of Thomas Mawson, and, not least, extended and remodelled the house to form the large, rambling Elizabethan-style manor house that exists today and is still the seat of Viscount Leverhulme.

The first alterations to the house were designed by William and Segar Owen, but they were followed by more substantial work c.1896 by Douglas and Fordham, of which two shaped gables and semi-circular bay windows on the south-east front still remain. But it is the later, grander additions that give the house its special character, including the gigantic Music Room or Picture Gallery by J.J. Talbot, with its segmental stuccoed ceiling and a two-storeyed marble inglenook fireplace incorporating an organ! Next came the kitchen and service wings, designed by Grayson and Ould; finally, the garden front was totally rebuilt (involving the demolition of some of Douglas and Fordham's work) by J. Lomax-Simpson as a long E-shaped composition. It incorporates the main rooms, which are all in different styles and incorporate eighteenth-century marble chimneypieces and other brought-in antique fittings of high quality. There is something of a transatlantic atmosphere about it all: Thornton could be on Long Island or in Connecticut.

Tirley Garth
See Willington.

Vale Royal
39; 3 miles SW of Nantwich off A556
Despite its romantic name and long history, Vale Royal looks, and virtually is, a large nineteenth-century L-shaped house. It occupies part of the site of the cloisters of a Cistercian abbey – the largest Cistercian foundation in England – which at the Dissolution was acquired by Sir Thomas Holcroft. It was sold to Lady Cholmondeley in 1616 and belonged to her descendants, the Lords Delamere, until the mid-twentieth century, when they emigrated to Kenya.

Thomas Holcroft built an H-plan mansion, part of the structure of which is incorporated in the present house; it was of stone and timber-framing. The Great Hall on the first floor was approached from outside by a straight flight of steps. This sixteenth-century house was remodelled by the 1st Lord Delamere c.1812; he truncated the wings and part-faced the house in ashlar, as well as redecorating the state rooms. The architect for all this is unknown; could it have been Lewis Wyatt? The exterior was altered again and Elizabethanised by Blore in the 1830s. Finally, much was done in the 1860s and 1870s, including the remodelling of the south-east wing; the clock turret and a new porch were designed by John Douglas.

The principal rooms are large and Victorianised, with brought-in 'Wardour Street' woodwork, though the timber roof of the Great Hall is old. There are various other bits and pieces re-set about the house, including a handsome classical doorcase of c.1750 in the Dining Room, which also has a late Georgian coved ceiling. The main staircase dates from the late seventeenth century and has attractive twisted balusters. Vale Royal is now converted into flats.

Warrington
40; 18 miles SW of Manchester on A57
Warrington, of course, is really Lancashire, and it is to be regretted that a slip of a bureaucrat's pen in 1974 should have transferred it to another county. Since 1872 a splendid mid-eighteenth-century country house has been its TOWN HALL and has been proudly maintained by the Corporation. It was originally called Bank Hall and was built by Thomas Patten to the design of James Gibbs in 1750 (the date is on the rainwater heads); it is the best house of its date in the area. The main block, of red brick, is three storeys and nine bays wide, with a rusticated ground floor and attached octostyle portico with giant Composite columns and the Patten arms in the pediment. The entrance is on the *piano nobile* and is approached by an elegant wrought-iron balustrade. One-storeyed links lead to a pair of large projecting office wings, each two storeys and thirteen bays, with rusticated three-bay pedimented centres. The whole forms a most satisfying composition. The interior has an unusual, somewhat Venetian plan: the transverse Hall runs back through the centre of the house flanked by a pair of staircases in the middle of the sides and, beyond them, three rooms along the garden front; of these, the Saloon and Music Rooms are now joined together but retain their excellent Rococo stucco ceilings and friezes. The best staircase also has stucco decorations, a mahogany dado and an elegant wrought-iron balustrade of lyre pattern. The smaller rooms have simple coved ceilings. The foundations of the house are said to be formed of moulded blocks of copper slag from the smelting works at Bank Quay, which made the Patten family fortunes in the late seventeenth century.

Willington
41; 10 miles W of Northwich off A54
TIRLEY GARTH is an Arts and Crafts Neo-Elizabethan house begun c.1906 by Mr Bryan Leesmith, a director of Brunner Mond (now ICI) and completed c.1912 by Mr R.A. Prestwich, a director of Burberrys. It was designed by C.E. Mallows and is quadrangular, the pretty internal courtyard being surrounded by cloister walks. The exterior is pebble-dashed and the main façade, facing south towards the dramatic line of hills crowned by Beeston and Peckforton (*q.v.*) Castles, is symmetrical with varied gables and bow windows with mullions and transoms. The interior has a full-height Living Hall with an open timber roof and a gallery on three sides, while the former Billiards Room has a domed plaster ceiling. The beautiful gardens were laid out in 1912 by Thomas Mawson, who wrote: 'At Tirley Garth we are impressed with the variety and completeness of the several parts of the site, beginning with terrace and pool gardens, merging into the freer landscape treatment, where undulating lawns sweep in pleasing curves under the shrubberies and specimen trees.' The entrance lodges were also designed by Mallows. Tirley Garth is self-consciously simple and 'socialist' – the absolute contrast to the rich cosmopolitan style of Lord Leverhulme's contemporary house at Thornton Hough (*q.v.*).

The Town Hall, Warrington.

Winnington Hall

42; ½ mile NW of Northwich on A533

It is strange to think that one of the greatest of our industrial Leviathans, ICI, was born in this medium-sized hybrid of a house – seventeenth-century timber-framed on one side and eighteenth-century ashlared neo-classical on the other. But so it was: Ludwig Mond and John Brunner, the firm's co-founders, shared the house with their respective families – the Monds, in the eighteenth-century part, getting very much the best of the deal – and their first factory sprang up all around.

The factory is still there and detracts not a little, it must be admitted, from Winnington's desirability. On the other hand, the house itself, now used as a guest house and club for senior ICI staff, is tended with loving care. The timber-framed part was too much restored in 1894 to be worthy of much attention now; judging from old photographs, it looked a great deal better with the Regency castellated stucco façade it had in the middle of the last century. The later addition, by contrast, is very fine indeed and provides the major architectural interest of the house.

Winnington Hall was built *c.*1778 by Richard Pennant, 1st Lord Penrhyn, after the estate, which had belonged to the Warburtons (a junior branch of the Arley family), was carried to the Pennants by the marriage of Anne Susanna Warburton to Richard Pennant.

The Wyatt wing is curiously asymmetrical, as if it is only a fragment of a larger scheme, but if this is the case, it is difficult to imagine what the overall plan could have been. There is also the problem of which Wyatt was responsible for the design. Stylistically it is much more likely to have been James than Samuel, the interior decoration being very close to that at Heaton. The Gallery, with a plaster tunnel vault, columns, niches and roundels along the walls, the oval staircase, the Dining Room, with an apse for the sideboard, and the Octagon Room, with stucco ceiling, marble chimneypiece (and originally with Chinese wallpaper), are all neo-classical rooms of the highest quality. This Wyatt decoration should, however, be viewed with a certain amount of caution, because more was added as part of Darcy Braddell's excellent restoration of 1920–2. A lost Wyatt feature at Winnington is the semi-circular poultry house 140 feet wide, which was almost certainly by Samuel Wyatt and was considered to be the finest in England.

After the 1st Lord Penrhyn's death, Winnington was purchased by the Stanleys of Alderley and then, in the mid-nineteenth century, became a girls' school (and regularly welcomed, as an assiduous visitor, John Ruskin); it was bought by John Brunner and Ludwig Mond in 1872. With rare imagination and care, ICI has not only retained the house but maintains it perfectly. A wonderful place to come back to after a hard day at the lab.

Cumbria

The best place to see all of Cumbria is from Hartside on the moorland road from Alston. Suddenly, as one rounds a bend, there is the most staggering prospect: at one's feet, far below, is the fertile Vale of Eden with its prosperous farms, country houses and old stone villages; in the middle, and sweeping far away to the south and west, the hills, fells and mountains of the Lake District recede chain upon chain into the distance; to the north there is a flatter agricultural landscape, stretching beyond Carlisle, with the waters of the Solway Firth and the Irish Sea glittering far behind. I know of no other view in England to compare with this. On an autumn afternoon, if there is a spectacular sunset and the whole of the vast, sublime landscape is filled with coloured light, it reminds me of nothing so much as the background to Altdorfer's *Battle of the Isthmus*.

The modern administrative unit of Cumbria combines the counties of Cumberland, Westmorland and the Furness division of Lancashire. It is partly very well known and partly not known at all. The Lake District, with its incomparably beautiful landscape of mountains and lakes, has been a place of pilgrimage for tourists in search of the picturesque since the middle of the eighteenth century, and in high summer the roads and hotels can be choked with visitors. The fringes of the area, however, are hardly known to outsiders: the flat farming country between Keswick and the Solway; the stark moors and lovely river valleys of the Eden and Lune to the east; the remote, forlorn eighteenth-century industrial towns and ports down the west coast; the attractive, almost Umbrian, landscape south of Kendal and Windermere. It is these fringe areas that contain the county's chief architectural sights; nor is their landscape to be despised. If it were anywhere but in the shadow of the mountains and lakes, this beautiful country would be justly famous; but those who cherish secret worlds will be glad that it is not.

Cumbria is Border country. For centuries it was disputed with the Scots and vulnerable to enemy raids. Perhaps the most distinctive feature of the architecture in the area is the series of pele towers or fortified houses. Hundreds of them survive, some in ruins but many as the nucleus of later country houses. They often have great halls attached, as well as sixteenth- or eighteenth-century wings and Victorian excrescences. Yanwath is an example of such a fortified house still in pristine medieval condition, while Levens and Sizergh show how the pele tower was transformed by the Elizabethans into a comfortable country house with larger mullion windows and panelled rooms. More often, however, the pele has been submerged in a mass of later buildings – Georgian or Victorian – as at Dalemain, Greystoke, Rose Castle and Hutton-in-the-Forest.

Because of its remote and wild state, the area was attractive to monastic foundations in the Middle Ages – Cistercian, Benedictine and Augustinian. Carlisle Cathedral began life as a Benedictine abbey and several of its buildings remain, as well as the cathedral church, which makes up for its truncated condition by the beauty of its fittings and the faultless taste with which it is maintained. In several other places much is still to be seen. At Lanercost half the church and many of the buildings are still roofed and used. At St Bees the church largely survives, and at Cartmel the whole of the priory church still stands, its bulk riding high over the low-roofed houses of the little town just as it did in the Middle Ages. But the greatest of all, the Cistercian house at Furness (which in the medieval period was the second largest in England), is now entirely a ruin – and poignantly beautiful it is, with its broken walls and arches of pink stone framed by wooded slopes in a secret valley close to, but out of sight of, the nineteenth-century town of Barrow-in-Furness.

The sixteenth century was a traumatic period in these remote northern counties. The Dissolution of the Monasteries destroyed much that for centuries had formed the economic focus of the area, and political troubles culminating in the ignominious failure of the rising of the northern Earls against Elizabeth I completed the ruin. There is something of an architectural hiatus, therefore, until the late seventeenth and early eighteenth centuries, when there was a renewal of economic enterprise in Cumberland with the development of coastal ports engaged in trade with the American colonies. Whitehaven is the best of these and was the first planned town to be built in England after the Middle Ages; something still survives from its Georgian heyday and is *at last* being preserved. The 'discovery' of the Lake District from the 1750s onwards by poets, painters and *nouveaux riches* immigrants was a crucial factor in its architectural development. Many delightful villas and country houses were built amidst carefully landscaped grounds. Belle Isle, a miniature Pantheon constructed in the 1770s on an island in the middle of Lake Windermere, is the plum of these. Much development followed the coming of the railways in the mid-nineteenth century and many of the old houses were restored and rebuilt. Anthony Salvin, in particular, cornered the market in this type of work and his competent hand can be found everywhere in Cumbria. The end of the century saw a great burst of Arts and Crafts activity, with the influence of the Keswick School of Industrial Arts in the north and a whole range of important houses by architects like Voysey and Dan Gibson in the south.

The main architectural pleasures of Cumbria, however, are quiet and unassuming. There are good-looking villages with large greens and simple stone cottages; prosperous little market towns like Penrith, Brampton, Kendal and Appleby; old country houses that continue to function as the centres of agricultural estates. On the whole, the churches are open during the day – something all too rare now, and for which we can be profoundly grateful. Altogether, this is one of the least spoilt parts of England.

Abbot Hall
See Kendal.

Acorn Bank
See Temple Sowerby.

Appleby
1; 12 miles SE of Penrith on A66

Appleby, though scarcely bigger than a village, is the ancient county town of Westmorland and is possessed of remarkable dignity and urban presence. It is built on the hillside sloping down from the castle to the River Eden. The main street, Boroughgate, is unusually wide, with the castle at the top and the parish church at the bottom. The lowest part has the old MOOT HALL of 1596 in the middle, raised over an arcaded ground floor. The surrounding premises are banks, shops and pubs but, as the street climbs the hill, these give way to solid Georgian houses of the type to be expected in a county town, and the roadway is flanked by lime trees and strips of mown grass protected by white posts and chains. The monumental air of this handsome street is accentuated at the top and bottom by the stone Tuscan columns carrying sundials – LOW CROSS and HIGH CROSS. Of individual buildings to look for on the way up, three are especially interesting. The RED HOUSE is dated 1717 and has a handsome doorway with a segmental pediment. The WHITE HOUSE opposite was built in 1756 by Jack Robinson ('Before you can say Jack Robinson!'), who was political agent to 'Wicked Jimmy', Earl of Lonsdale. Appleby was one of nine parliamentary boroughs – the Ninepins – controlled by the Lowthers in the Tory interest in the eighteenth century. The White House is Gothick, with ogee-arched windows and doorcase copied from Batty Langley. It was almost certainly designed by Henry Bellhouse, a talented local carpenter who was also responsible for a similar Gothick house near Brough, Hellbeck Hall. Further up the hill, near the castle, is ST ANNE'S HOSPITAL, founded by Lady Anne Clifford in 1651. It is a plain seventeenth-century quadrangle of two-storeyed almshouses, entered through a segmental arch under a carved panel with the Clifford arms, and it has an inner court with cobbled paving and a Victorian fountain.

The best building in Appleby is the CASTLE, founded by the Vetriponts in the twelfth century and the property of the Cliffords from the thirteenth century until the death in the late seventeenth of Lady Anne Clifford, the last survivor of a family that had been among the most powerful in the north for centuries. Lady Anne, 'hereditary sheriffess of Westmorland' (according to her epitaph in the parish church), restored the castle after the Civil War. From her earliest youth she had been imbued with the traditions of her family and as a result 'had a passion for the pomp of her family heraldry' and an abiding love for Westmorland, which coloured all her architectural ventures with a self-conscious historicism. After two not very happy marriages, she took up residence in the north in 1649 and lived there continuously in one or other of her castles until her death in 1676 – a memorable figure, the centre of a little, almost medieval, court of family and dependants. Her distinctive country clothes were described by Bishop Rainbow of Carlisle: 'her dress, not disliked by any, was yet imitated by none.' She restored various churches and castles on her lands in a deliberately archaistic Gothic manner. (Her second husband, the Earl of Pembroke, had of course employed Inigo Jones, Isaac de Caux and John Webb at Wilton.) At Appleby, which had been derelict for nearly 100 years, she began the repairs in 1651, re-flooring and re-roofing the twelfth-century keep, which she called 'Caesar's Tower', and mending the twelfth-century curtain wall. She also built the stable quadrangle, which survives, as does her Bee House with its stone pyramid roof.

After Lady Anne's death, the Westmorland estates with Appleby, Brough and Brougham Castles passed to her son-in-law Thomas Tufton, 6th Earl of Thanet, who concentrated on Appleby and in 1686–8 rebuilt the east range as a stately new house to the design of the Rev. Thomas Machell, using stone from Brougham and Brough Castles for the purpose. It is an L-shaped building of seven by six bays, with pedimented dormers in the roof and an elegant swan-neck pediment over the door. Further work was done *c*.1784, when the pretty little lanterns were added to the four corners of the keep, the Gothic south tower of the east range was built, and

The church of St Lawrence, Appleby.

probably the present simple Gothic ceiling of the two-storeyed Hall was installed. The Hall otherwise retains good seventeenth-century panelling, and the main staircase with twisted balusters is also seventeenth century.

The castle remained in the Tufton family (latterly Lords Hothfield) until 1963, when the estate was sold. After a further short period as a private house, the castle was converted tactfully into offices by Ferguson Industrial Holdings Ltd.

At the opposite end of Boroughgate from the castle is the CHURCH OF ST LAWRENCE, the parish church, approached from the street through a Regency Gothick arcade, designed by Sir Robert Smirke, with seven pointed arches and flanking square towers. The church itself dates mainly from the fourteenth century and is part Decorated and part Perpendicular, its west tower and clerestory ornamented with gargoyles and battlements. The church, like the castle, was restored by Lady Anne after the Civil War; she built the chancel and adjoining Clifford family chapel, re-using some fifteenth-century screens between the dividing arches. In the Clifford Chapel are monuments to Lady Anne and her mother, Margaret, Countess of Cumberland. The latter has a beautiful alabaster effigy, with a gilded coronet, on a carved tomb-chest. Lady Anne's monument was erected in her own lifetime and is embellished with a lavish display of Clifford heraldry, including the twenty-four principal quarterings brought into the family by heiresses over the centuries. Apart from the Clifford Chapel, the chief object of interest in St Lawrence's is the organ. The oldest in England, it was brought here from Carlisle

Cathedral (*q.v.*) and dates from the seventeenth century, although it incorporates part of an early sixteenth-century case with Renaissance decoration. It was carefully repaired and put back in its correct position at the west end of the nave in the early 1980s. Otherwise, the church has a comfortable, unrestored feel, mainly due to the early nineteenth-century Gothick plaster ceiling over the nave which the Victorians suffered to remain. The churchyard is pleasantly situated on the bank of the river and is well worth walking round.

Askham Hall
See Lowther.

Barrow-in-Furness
2; 8 miles SE of Ulverston on A590

The ruins of FURNESS ABBEY, the second most important Cistercian abbey in England, lie in a picturesque wooded valley just beyond the edge of the modern town of Barrow. The suppression of the abbey in 1537 removed the cultural and economic focus of the south Lakeland and Furness, and neither the later country houses nor the Victorian industrial town have supplied an equivalent substitute.

The abbey was founded in 1123 at Tulketh, near Preston, by Stephen, Count of Boulogne and Mortain, and later King of England. Four years later it moved to its present, more remote site, which, surrounded on all sides by the sea or mountains, was considered at the time to be an island. The monks owned and developed the

Furness Abbey, Barrow-in-Furness.

whole Furness peninsula and much else besides. They began the exploitation of the rich iron deposits of the district; created large sheep farms and fisheries; made the first harbour at Walney Island, protected by PEEL CASTLE, the crumbling fourteenth-century ruins of which remain dramatically silhouetted against the sea. The abbey also administered the King's law in the area, having the right to appoint its own coroner and the abbot being perpetual sheriff. (The ABBEY COURT HOUSE survives in the centre of the little town of Dalton to the east and now belongs to the National Trust.) The abbey ruins of weathered red sandstone form a perfect composition, framed by steep and luxuriantly wooded banks. Only the hideous brick 'interpretation centre', built in the late 1970s by the Department of the Environment, detracts from the idyllic setting.

Because of the narrowness of the valley there is no conventional approach from the west, and the main entrance is through a doorway straight into the north transept of the church. The abbey church is cruciform in plan, 276 feet long. The east end and transepts, and the west tower survive almost to full height, though the nave has largely gone. The church was built in the second half of the twelfth century, and is a characteristic example of the early Cistercian Gothic style, but the east end was partly rebuilt in the fifteenth century, with square chapels replacing the original apsidal arrange-

ment and large Perpendicular windows the smaller lancets. The west tower was added *c.*1500 after an attempt to heighten the central belfry had to be abandoned because of structural problems; it fills the west bay of the nave and is supported on an exceedingly tall arch reminiscent of a painting by Caspar David Friedrich. The stone base of the high altar and foundations of the choir stalls survive, but the most important feature of the church is the combined piscina and sedilia, with exquisite canopied heads and tall pinnacles of carved stone.

The outline of the conventual buildings can be followed clearly. The foundations of the rectangular cloisters to the south of the church are surrounded on all sides by remains of the original accommodation: the lay brothers' quarters to the west, the Refectory and large Infirmary to the south, and the Chapter House and Dormitory to the east. The latter is the best preserved range, parts of the walls still standing above first-floor level. The magnificent series of five round-headed arches facing the Cloister Walk is one of the architectural glories of the abbey. The first and third of these are book alcoves and flank the entrance to the Chapter House. Built in the thirteenth century, this is a fine square room with aisles of four bays, twin lancet windows and, originally, a vaulted roof (which collapsed in the eighteenth century). It must have been a very handsome room when intact, and makes a poignantly beautiful ruin now. To the east of these buildings a little-damaged section of the abbey's carefully planned drainage system can be explored. On the far side are the ruins of the Abbot's House, and all round the valley can be traced sections of the long stone wall that enclosed the 73 acres of the monastic precinct.

After the abbey, the Victorian town of Barrow may seem a bit of a Pugin contrast. But it is worth a visit as a good example of a planned industrial town, with wide, tree-lined streets, mediocre but solid brick houses and public buildings, bronze statues of local worthies on the key traffic roundabouts, and a very grand Victorian Gothic TOWN HALL, with a tall tower and octagonal lantern on top. It is a great pity that the area in front of this is ruined by a 1960s' Civic Centre of grey concrete – just the perfect choice of material for a town otherwise built entirely of red brick and red stone!

The late nineteenth-century DOCKS behind the Town Hall are constructed in the natural channel between the mainland and Barrow Island, and are rather splendid. Unlike almost anywhere else in England, the docks are still busy with shipbuilding, as it is here that nuclear submarines are built for the Royal Navy. Despite this, there is a spooky air of transience and unreality about Barrow: one feels that in another 400 years the abbey ruins may still be very much as now, but that the town will have reverted to the insignificant hamlet it was before the arrival of the railway in 1846. The steel works, the largest in the world in the late nineteenth century, have already gone.

Belle Isle
See Windermere.

Birket Houses
See Cartmel Fell.

Blencow Hall
See Greystoke.

Brackenburgh Tower
See Plumpton Wall.

Brampton
3; 10 miles NE of Carlisle on A69
A small market town, which happily preserves the character that Cockermouth (*q.v.*) has lost, Brampton comprises two principal streets running parallel to each other. MAIN STREET has Georgian houses but, as its name implies, is an A-road and carries heavy through-traffic. FRONT STREET, by contrast, is quiet and pleasantly traffic-free, but without the deadness of 'pedestrianisation'. It has wide cobbled verges and is lined with buildings of pink sandstone or colour-washed plaster. There are decent painted-timber shop-fronts and several dignified banks, an unspoilt pub and a hotel, the Howard Arms. Front Street widens to the east to form a market place, with the octagonal Gothick MOOT HALL of 1817 (now a tourist office) in the centre; it has pointed windows and a clock cupola.

At the west end of Front Street, the tower of ST MARTIN'S CHURCH forms an equally good view-stopper. This is Brampton's major building. It was designed in 1874–8 by Philip Webb for the 9th Earl of Carlisle, whose unusually discriminating patronage is responsible for so much of high artistic quality in the area (including Naworth and Lanercost (*qq.v.*)). It is Webb's only church, and an inventive and original exercise in Gothic Revival style. The interior has a timber roof – not quite a fan vault – painted a pale Arts and Crafts green, and the windows have first-rate stained glass made by Morris & Co., and designed by William Morris and Sir Edward Burne-Jones.

Webb designed one or two other buildings for the Earl of Carlisle, including the CHURCH HALL and FOUR GABLES, a house for the Earl's estate agent, just outside the town towards Naworth. Like the church, this latter is a highly individual design, combining Queen Anne sash windows with Jacobethan gables, mullions and corner bartizans – the latter an appropriate tribute to the Borders' vernacular.

Broadleys
See Cartmel Fell.

Broughton in Furness
4; 12 miles N of Barrow-in-Furness on A595
Before meddling with the county boundaries in 1974 transferred Furness to Cumbria, Broughton was the most northerly town in Lancashire. It has the atmosphere of a toy town, with everything on a miniature scale, and all is remote and undisturbed. There is an old stone parish church, a formal Market Place, and even a little 'castle' to complete the picture.

The CHURCH OF ST MARY MAGDALENE is on the edge of the town, surrounded by open fields. It is late Perpendicular (early sixteenth-century) with a Norman doorway, but was largely reconstructed by Paley and Austin in the late nineteenth century; the squat tower is theirs, as is much of the interior. The castle is called BROUGHTON TOWER. It is approached from the north corner of the Market Place up a straight drive lined with clipped laurels, and is set in a pretty park with good views over the beautiful Duddon Valley, a landscape immortalised by Wordsworth. It is basically an eighteenth-century house (dated 1744), Gothicked by the Sawrey Gilpins in 1777, almost certainly to the design of John Hird of Cartmel, the pioneer of Gothick in the area; it is one of the earliest examples of Gothic Revival in the Lake District. All the windows are ogee-headed and the porch has columns with feather capitals. The flanking wings in the same style were added in 1882–4 and are remarkably harmonious and sympathetic for their date.

The Market Place was planned in a regular manner in the eighteenth century. It is surrounded on three sides by plain three-storeyed houses, and on the south side is the TOWN HALL, with an arcade, now filled, along the ground floor and a clock cupola on top. In the centre of the square is an obelisk erected in 1810 to celebrate the fiftieth year of the reign of George III. It is flanked by four sycamore trees, and some stone bench-like constructions which are used as market stalls on Saturdays.

The Market Place, Broughton in Furness.

Carlisle

5; 18 miles NW of Penrith on A6

A Roman fort, a medieval city with castle and cathedral, an eighteenth-century market town and a nineteenth-century industrial centre, Carlisle stands near the west end of Hadrian's Wall. For 250 years it was an administrative and military outpost on the northern frontier of the Roman Empire, before it succumbed to the barbarian invasions. The revival of the town in the Middle Ages was due to William Rufus, who began the city walls, castle and priory (later cathedral) in 1092. But for seven centuries after that, Carlisle developed little because of its uneasy situation on the Scottish border. Its unusually turbulent (by English standards) history is largely the reason for the lack of many ambitious old buildings. The old city received a near-mortal blow in the 1960s when a dual-track motorway was driven bang through the middle, between the castle and cathedral, bisecting the ancient core and destroying the historic meaning of the place.

The now isolated CASTLE stands on the banks of the River Eden and has a well-preserved rectangular stone keep and curtain wall built by Henry II *c.*1157. The square outer bailey is occupied by a quadrangle of simple late Georgian barracks built in 1819. The fourteenth-century Captain's Tower, or inner gatehouse, gives access to the triangular inner bailey dominated by the Norman keep. It is worth going inside this to see the fourteenth- and fifteenth-century prisoners' carvings in the window embrasure on the second floor.

Returning towards the cathedral (and somehow crossing that beastly new road), Carlisle's three best streets are reached – Abbey Street, Castle Street and Fisher Street – all running more or less parallel to each other and with several decent late seventeenth- and eighteenth-century houses. TULLIE HOUSE in Abbey Street is the most ambitious; it was built in 1689 and is a distinguished classical design, with alternating pediments over the windows. It is now a museum, full of Roman altars and other remains. A stone gatehouse leads into the cathedral precincts; they are still known as 'THE ABBEY', recalling the priory founded by Rufus, which Henry II made into the see of the bishop. Various bits of the medieval buildings survive, including part of the Cloisters and the Perpendicular Refectory, which form a picturesque contrast to the Georgian Canonries with which they are interspersed.

The CATHEDRAL itself is the least of English medieval cathedrals, but not without its points all the same. The exterior is its worst aspect, with a mean little central tower and rudely truncated west end. The Scots, under General Leslie, tore down two-thirds of the Norman nave after the siege in 1645 in order to provide stone for reinforcing the city walls. The interior is better, and has benefited from the taste and wisdom of Stephen Dykes Bower, who has been consultant architect to the cathedral for over thirty years. On entering through the south transept, one is immediately faced with a splendid fifteenth-century carved Flemish altarpiece in the north transept. This was brought to England *c.*1820 by Lord Brougham for the church at Brougham. It has recently been re-assembled by the Victoria and Albert Museum and placed here, with the polychrome and gilding of its carvings restored to their original freshness. The stump of the Norman nave is now the chapel of the Border Regiment and is enclosed by iron screens (designed in 1949 by Stephen Dykes Bower) and hung with old military banners, recalling some of the smaller cathedrals of central Spain. The choir and chancel, part Early English and part Decorated, are the best features of the building. The large east window – 51 feet high – is a gorgeous piece of flowing tracery, with rich Victorian glass by Hardman. The timber roof has painted decoration in royal blue with gold stars, originally designed by Owen Jones in the 1850s but renewed in 1970, and there is a magnificent, carved, painted and gilded *baldacchino* by Sir Charles Nicholson (recently recoloured by Dykes Bower) over the high altar. The choir stalls date from the early fifteenth century and have rich carved canopies and amusing misericords (one of them shows a Scotsman in a kilt being swallowed by a dragon); an unusual feature is the series of contemporary paintings on their backs of stories from the life of St Anthony, St Augustine and St Cuthbert. Another rarity is the carved wooden screen in the north choir aisle, given to the cathedral by Dean Salkeld *c.*1541 – a fine example of sophisticated English Renaissance decoration before the advancing Reformation caused an artistic relapse into rude provincialism.

To the south-east of the cathedral is the MARKET PLACE – an attractive funnel-shaped space decently paved and pedestrianised. In the centre is the Market Cross of 1682, an Ionic column supporting a sundial and rampant lion holding the city arms aloft. The west side is occupied by the TOWN HALL, a lovable Georgian building begun in 1717 and altered later. It has only two low storeys, and for that reason looks as if it is sinking into the ground. On top is a lead clock cupola dated 1800, and at one end a Victorian glass-and-iron lean-to shelter has been informally tacked on. Peering out of a corner behind the Town Hall is the recently restored fifteenth-century GUILDHALL of brick and half-timber, with jettied storeys and carved and painted corbels. Along the north side of the Market Place, and running into Scotch Street, is a large area of redevelopment with an amazing new façade comprising Georgian replicas interspersed with Post-Modern jollities in brick and stone designed by the Building Design Partnership, an architectural firm which until recently was distinguished for its impeccable Modern credentials. Pevsner, 'thou shouldst be living at this hour'. It is a pity that the windows are plate-glass in pivoting metal frames and not double-hung timber sashes.

South-east of the Market Place, English Street leads towards the CITADEL and RAILWAY STATION. This area was rebuilt at different dates in the nineteenth century and is more regular in layout and larger in scale than the streets nearer the cathedral. There are several good banks, of which the classical TRUSTEE SAVINGS BANK, formerly the Athenaeum, forms a striking *point de vue* at the end of Devonshire Street. The Citadel was originally built by Henry VIII, but in 1810 was rebuilt to the design of Sir Robert Smirke as Assize Courts and gaol, with two fat, castellated, round towers flanking the entrance to English Street and making a monumental formal entrance to the town centre from the south. The buildings facing the Citadel complete a remarkably grand urban composition and include the Tudorbethan station of 1847 by Sir William Tite, the County Hotel by Salvin, and the Red Lion Hotel and Midland Bank with Frenchy mansard roofs. To the north-east is a planned early nineteenth-century development – Lowther Street, Lonsdale Street and Victoria Place – brick and stone houses with Ionic doorcases. South-west of the centre, across the railway tracks and not to be missed, is the great block of DIXON'S COTTON MILLS of 1836 – a monumental neo-classical pile with a chimney 300 feet high. It was designed by Robert Tattersall of Manchester and is one of the most impressive industrial buildings in all England.

Cartmel
6; 2 miles NW of Grange-over-Sands off B5277
Includes Cartmel Priory Gatehouse (NT)

The grey mass of CARTMEL PRIORY rising above the roofs and chimneys of the little town conveys a truly medieval image of the dominance of the Church in the life of the country. It is a picture that has altered only in detail over a period of 800 years. In 1185 King John gave 'the land of Cartmel' to William Marshal who, following his marriage, founded there a priory of Augustinian canons in 1188. The present building is the result of three major phases of construction: the choir and transepts were begun in the 1190s and are impressive examples of transitional Gothic; the GATEHOUSE (NT) in the Town Square and the Harrington Chapel were built in the 1340s; the nave and belfry tower date from the early fifteenth century. The cloisters and conventual buildings, originally on the south side of the church, were rebuilt to the north in the fifteenth century, but no trace of them now survives. The church itself was saved at the Dissolution of the Monasteries because the local people claimed it all as their parish church and so it was allowed to survive. Most of the priory estates were subsequently acquired by the Preston family of Holker (*q.v.*) and have passed down by descent through the Lowthers to the Cavendishes, who still own them today. This partly explains the remarkable feeling of continuity at Cartmel.

The church rises out of a graveyard grazed happily by sheep. The old tombstones include one to Wordsworth's schoolmaster, who, on his return to England after the French Revolution, was the subject of a memorable sonnet by the poet. The most idiosyncratic feature of the church's exterior, and the cause of its unique silhouette, is the diagonal belfry tower over the crossing. This was designed for practical rather than aesthetic reasons, helping to reduce the strain on the stone corner piers, which rest not on rock but on a bed of soft peat. The south doorway, with its carved round arch, is the oldest part of the building. (The new light-oak panelled doors, replacing an ancient studded one, are an unfortunate alteration: why was this allowed?) The nave seems somewhat homespun compared to the francophile dig-

Carlisle Cathedral.

nity of the east end: it has rubble stone walls, rather than ashlar, and run-of-the-mill octagonal stone piers like those of any other Perpendicular parish church in the north-west. The eye is immediately caught by a cluster of Lowther and Cavendish hatchments in the opposite corner. Beneath them is the noble monument to Lord Frederick Cavendish (murdered in Phoenix Park by an Irish Nationalist). His white marble effigy by Thomas Woolner rests on a tomb-chest of Derbyshire alabaster and Cornish marbles. Looking at this, it is interesting to recall that, as a token of Christian forgiveness, Lord Frederick's bereaved widow sent one of his cufflinks to the murderer, who was awaiting execution in a Dublin gaol. On a wooden shelf on the south-west crossing-pier a loaf of bread is still laid out for the benefit of the poor of the district in accordance with some old charity; I always wonder, as I pass, whether I am entitled to a nibble. The transepts have splendid late nineteenth-century stained glass by Shrigley & Hunt of Lancaster, the leading local firm; and both here and in the choir aisle there are several genteel marble tablets to local families, such as the Robinsons of Fell Foot. The choir is the most beautiful and interesting part of the building. The stalls retain twenty-five original carved misericords, but the choir screens date from the restoration of the church in the 1620s by George Preston of Holker; they are an important example of early Gothic Revival and are carved with

Cartmel Priory.

symbols of the Passion. At the same time Preston also gave an organ, but this was destroyed during the Civil War by an outlying posse of Parliamentary troops who had nothing better to do. The huge east window was originally fitted with stained glass similar to that of York Minster (*q.v.*). Some of this has disappeared, but enough remains and was restored in 1970. It is one of the pleasures of the early-morning Communion service at Cartmel to watch the light through this window. The present altarpiece, with curtains and gilt riddel-posts, is a tasteful sub-Comper affair but replaces a High Victorian Gothic alabaster reredos given to the church by Lady Louisa Egerton.

Between the choir and the Harrington Chapel is the tomb to John, Lord Harrington, and his wife Joan. This dates from the 1340s and was originally free-standing in the centre of the chapel, with an altar at the west end (like Henry VII's tomb in his eponymous chapel at Westminster Abbey); it is thought that it was moved to its present position in the sixteenth century to protect it from the attentions of the Reformers and iconoclasts. It is a fine piece of fourteenth-century sculpture, with little *pleureurs* round the base. Traces of the original painted decoration can be seen on the wooden boards of the canopy. The east window of the chapel was a Jesse window, and some of the original rich stained glass survives in the upper lights. In the Middle Ages this chapel alone served as the local parish church. We can be grateful for the

pride and loyalty that made the local population claim the whole building for their own in the 1530s; grateful also to George Preston for restoring the church. Without them there would be only ruins today.

The parish of Cartmel, stretching from the west shores of Windermere to the Winster Valley, encompasses some of the most beautiful landscape in England, with narrow, hedged lanes winding through hilly pasture and well-maintained woods. The fellside CHURCH OF ST ANTHONY is difficult to find, but worth the effort. It is a humble late Perpendicular chapel with a low west tower. Inside, the floor slopes down towards the altar, following the contour of the hillside. It is memorable for its old fittings, which include sixteenth- and seventeenth-century pews and screens, and a rare three-decker pulpit. The east window has medieval stained glass from Cartmel Priory, and in the vestry is an exceptional treasure – a thirteenth-century wooden crucifix, which somehow survived the iconoclasm of the Reformation.

In the area are several turn-of-the-century Arts and Crafts country houses of the first importance to architectural historians, and of European significance.

BIRKET HOUSES is an Edwardian whitewashed and gabled house in a sensitive revived brand of the Lakeland vernacular, with round chimneys and mullioned windows. It is the principal work of Dan Gibson, an architect (for a time in partnership with Thomas Mawson) who specialised in houses of this type in the area. The new building replaced a simple eighteenth-century house, for long the home of the Birkets, and was devised to contain an unusual collection of local furniture. The interior comprises a Hall (entered through a screen passage like a great hall), Dining Room, Drawing Room and Library. The Hall and Dining Room have 'Jacobean' oak panelling, while the Drawing Room is 'Georgian'. Throughout the house there is sound and beautiful craftsmanship, especially the simple, decorative plasterwork and oak joinery. The gardens were designed by Mawson and the hillside setting adds enormously to the building's appeal.

BROADLEYS was designed by C.F.A. Voysey for Henry Currer Briggs, a Yorkshire colliery owner. Voysey's commission extended to the design of most of the furniture, including a clock and a toast-rack. (Briggs also employed Voysey to design some buildings for him at the Whitwood Colliery in Yorkshire's West Riding.) The grounds of Broadleys, overlooking Lake Windermere, were beautifully landscaped by Thomas Mawson and form a perfect setting for the house. The building is L-shaped and the wing towards the lake, with three segmental bow windows, contains the main rooms, which are arranged around a two-storeyed Living Hall, with an inglenook fireplace, and the main staircase. The other wing, running back towards the road, contains the service quarters. A characteristic feature of Voysey's houses is the care devoted to the rooms provided for the servants; these are unusually spacious and often enjoy views from their windows nearly as attractive as those from the principal rooms.

Broadleys is now the Windermere Yacht Club and is well cared for. Architecturally, it is one of the finest of its date in Europe and is generally considered to be Voysey's masterpiece. One cannot but agree with Pevsner that: 'There is nothing on the continent to come up to [its] standard. The future and the past blend effortlessly indeed ... twentieth-century pioneer work and yet free Tudor.'

MOOR CRAG was also designed by Voysey, this time in 1898 for J.W. Buckley, a Manchester businessman. Again, the grounds were landscaped by Mawson. Until recent years the house contained most of the furniture and fittings designed for it by Voysey, but these have now been dispersed. The double bed from the principal bedroom is now in Brighton Museum; it was considered so extraordinary by the family that it was long confined to the attic.

Cockermouth

7; 10 miles E of Workington on A66
Includes Wordsworth House (NT)

This old market town with its CASTLE, standing at the confluence of the Rivers Cocker and Derwent, occupies a naturally defensive site, first taken advantage of by the Romans. Stone from their fort at Papcastle was used in 1134 by Waltheof of Dunbar to begin the present castle, the substantial ruins of which are the most impressive sight in Cockermouth. It is now the property of Lord Egremont and is still the administrative centre of large Cumberland estates derived from the medieval holdings of the Percys. These came to the Wyndhams, like Petworth in Sussex, through the marriage of Catherine Seymour, daughter of Lady Elizabeth Percy, to Sir William Wyndham in the early eighteenth century. In its present form, the castle was largely rebuilt in c.1360–70 and comprises two spacious baileys, the inner one with the Great Hall, kitchen and medieval living quarters, all of which are now in ruins. The outer bailey was patched up c.1800 by the 3rd Earl of Egremont as an occasional residence, while the Victorian estate office along the south side next to the mid-twelfth-century gatehouse was built c.1860.

The town itself is largely plain Georgian and comprises a Y of two broad streets – Main Street, lined with pollarded lime trees, continued in narrower form as Castlegate, and, branching off it, Market Place. Most of the houses have plastered and painted fronts, though there is some ashlar stone. WORDSWORTH HOUSE (NT) (where the poet was born) in Main Street is a mid-eighteenth-century house of nine bays, with impressive stone gatepiers punctuating the garden wall in front. Nearby, in the middle of the street, is a marble statue of Lord Mayo, MP for Cockermouth in the nineteenth century. He was blown off his tall pedestal in a storm, but escaped without so much as a chip and was put back again with block and tackle.

The general effect of Cockermouth has been eroded in recent years by a rash of unsophisticated 'tarting up'. The old shop-fronts and panelled house-doors, for instance, have given way to cheap, off-the-peg joinery with bubble-glass panes, plastic Dutch blinds and inappropriate colours of paint. All this bespeaks a lamentable failure on the part of the local authority to implement a positive planning policy. There has also

been some misguided and unnecessary 'slum' clearing of backland, which has had a deleterious effect on the once picturesque area between the PARISH CHURCH and the river. The parish church itself, with its spindly central spire, is a boring Victorian rebuilding of 1852–4 by a dim London architect, Joseph Clarke. The churchyard, however, is pleasant, with eighteenth-century red sandstone headstones and a good view of the castle.

Apart from Wordsworth, Cockermouth's most famous son is Fletcher Christian, leader of the Mutiny on the *Bounty*.

Conishead Priory

See Ulverston.

Corby Castle

8; 5 miles E of Carlisle off A69

Corby Castle is the seat of a branch of the Howards, who are descended from Lord William Howard of Naworth (*q.v.*), a younger son of the 4th Duke of Norfolk. The origin of the present house is a thirteenth-century pele tower, to which, in the late seventeenth century, the Howards added a three-storeyed wing in a rustic classical style, with pedimented windows alternately triangular and semi-circular. But as it now is, Corby is essentially a severe but handsome Greek Revival house built in 1812–17 by Henry Howard, author of the *Memorials of the Howard Family*. It was designed by the Cumberland County Surveyor, Peter Nicholson, whose masterpiece it is. It forms a three-storeyed rectangle of five bays by seven, both the main fronts being faced in pinkish sandstone ashlar, each with fluted Greek Doric porches and with the Howard lion crest standing proudly in the centre of the parapet. Inside are a number of early eighteenth-century features, including the staircase and the stucco ceilings of the rooms at the rear. Nicholson's front rooms have restrained classical decoration. Over the chimneypiece in the Entrance Hall is a monument to Thomas Mowbray, Duke of Norfolk, who was banished by Richard II for quarrelling with Bolingbroke and who died in Venice. It was brought from St Mark's, Venice, and was saved because a workman who was ordered to destroy it instead used it upside down as a paving stone. It was rescued and brought to Corby by Henry Howard at the time when he was gathering material for his *Memorials*. The Howards of Corby are Roman Catholic, and there is a private Chapel in the house with a black-and-gold seventeenth-century reredos made in Rome; it is said to have been the property of Viscount Stafford, who was unjustly executed at the time of the Titus Oates' plot in 1680.

The most attractive feature of Corby, however, is its dramatic landscaped GARDEN, which won the praises of a succession of Georgian tourists and which exploits the spectacular sloping site overlooking the River Eden. The garden was laid out by Thomas Howard in the early eighteenth century and is the most interesting of its date in the north, embellished with statues, a cascade and two temples, one of which has attractive murals by Nutter of Carlisle. The garden is sometimes open to the public, but the castle is not.

Crosthwaite
9; 1 mile NW of Keswick on A66

Canon Rawnsley, disciple of Ruskin, founder of the Keswick School of Industrial Arts and one of the co-founders of the National Trust, was vicar of Crosthwaite from 1883–1917, and his character is still strongly felt in the large CHURCH OF ST KENTIGERN. It was rebuilt in the early sixteenth century as a typical example of simple, northern late Perpendicular architecture, and was sweepingly restored by Sir George Gilbert Scott in 1844 (an early job of his). The interior has no chancel arch and the nave flows imperceptibly into the sanctuary — a typical northern feature. The church is unique in retaining its original consecration crosses, nine inside and twelve on the outside, while the churchyard is notable for a series of exquisitely carved slate headstones, thought to be the work of a local sculptor, William Bromley. The interior is embellished with many works of the Keswick School of Industrial Arts, including beaten-copper electroliers and several mildly *art nouveau* metal memorial tablets. The carved reredos behind the altar was designed by C.J. Ferguson, the Carlisle diocesan architect, and the mosaic floor of the chancel shows legends from the life of St Kentigern. Robert Southey, Poet Laureate from 1813–43, is buried in the graveyard and his striking memorial inside the church, with a white marble effigy by Lough showing him reclining in academic robes on a Gothic tomb-chest, was designed by Gilbert Scott. The Baptistery at the back of the church is a memorial to Canon Rawnsley and was designed by Paley and Austin of Lancaster, though the font itself, with its elaborate carving, dates from 1395.

Dacre Castle
See Dalemain.

Dalemain
10; 2 miles N of Ullswater on A5920 [3]

Dalemain is an archetypal squire's house of different dates, enclosing a small inner courtyard. The oldest part is the west range, a former pele tower, probably dating from the fifteenth century but extended *c*.1600. The rough, palimpsest quality of the rear elevation with its mullion windows gives away the early date, but the main nine-bay façade to the east, built by Edward Hasell *c*.1750, is a serene classical design of smooth pinkish sandstone ashlar, the windows with moulded architraves and the central door with fluted Ionic pilasters and pediment. Unfortunately, the architect is unknown. The principal rooms form a continuous enfilade behind this front, mainly with sober eighteenth-century raised and fielded oak panelling by a London carpenter, though one room is decorated with good Chinese wallpaper and has a fantastic Chippendale Rococo wood chimneypiece. The Drawing Room has especially handsome joinery, with good doorcases and a carved chimneypiece. The large Dining Room was made in 1785, with a plaster frieze and two niches in the side-wall. The setting of Dalemain has been landscaped and beautifully planted over the centuries so that it is now as placid and serene as the house itself.

Situated on the Dalemain estate, to which it has belonged since 1715, is DACRE CASTLE, a large pele tower with a moated *enceinte* standing above a beck in an idyllic pastoral valley that belies a warlike past. The castle's origins are almost legendary. The Venerable Bede mentions a monastery on the site in the eighth century; in 1131 William of Malmesbury mentions Dacre as the place where Constantine, King of the Scots, and Eugenius, King of Cumberland, put themselves under the English King Athelstan after the battle of Brunanburh in 937. The present building, however, dates only from the fourteenth century, when William Dacre received a licence to crenellate from Edward II. The exterior was altered *c*.1700 by Thomas, Lord Dacre, later created Earl of Sussex; he inserted the mullion-and-transom windows and the present main entrance, approached by a flight of steps on the first floor and embellished with his arms. This gives access to the Hall, with vaulted rooms underneath and the solar and King's Chamber above.

Dallam Tower
11; 1 mile W of Milnthorpe off A6

Seen from the bridge over the River Bela coming from Milnthorpe, Dallam presents the perfect picture of an English country house: sheep and deer grazing in the well-maintained park, the even grey façade urbane and reserved, with the Wilson standard bearing three wolves' heads fluttering lazily overhead. There could be no more ideal backdrop to shooting-party photographs.

Dallam is a Georgian mansion, albeit of moderate size, and the seat of a Whig dynasty — a great rarity in Westmorland. The main block of 1720–2 was built by Daniel Wilson, MP for Westmorland, and is of seven bays with a hipped roof and little pedimented dormers; the centrepiece is delineated by channelled pilaster strips. The house was considerably altered and extended in 1826 by George (Smyth) Wilson to the design of George Webster; they stuccoed the exterior, added the dignified Tuscan porch on the entrance front, the symmetrical side-wings and the pair of balanced outer-office pavilions, each with an elegant white-painted cupola. The detailing of the pavilions is slightly asymmetrical and the incorporation of one or two seventeenth-century mullion windows from older buildings on the site is curiously wilful. Inside the house, the Dining Room, with elaborate Edwardian plasterwork, is Webster's, but the Hall and Drawing Room in the main block have enriched early Georgian panelling of high quality, as have the bedrooms. The Library has fitted oak bookcases by Gillow. The main staircase is of chestnut, walnut and yew, with parquetry landings and slender turned balusters. The secondary staircase is hardly less handsome. Both give access to a cross-corridor on the first floor. There is some re-used Jacobean panelling, either brought in or from the previous house on the site, and a carved oak chimneypiece, dated 1602, in one of the bedrooms is reported to come from Nether Levens but has been added to.

The gateway into the kitchen garden, dated 1683, is probably the original front door of the previous house. The grounds and park are beautifully landscaped, with a herd of fallow deer and some interesting subsidiary buildings designed by Webster, including the quadrangular home farm, the Tuscan deer house and an extremely rare early nineteenth-century iron-and-glass conservatory.

The estate has passed three times through the female line – to the Smyths, Bromleys and Tryons – but each time the inheritor has taken the name and arms of Wilson. The present owner is Brigadier C.E. Tryon-Wilson, and he has recently restored the house after fire damage. There are interesting family portraits and a wide range of furniture, from sixteenth-century oak to Gillow mahogany.

Dalton Hall
12; 2 miles S of Burton off A6070
Designed in 1968–70 and completed in his ninetieth year, this was the last work of Clough Williams-Ellis. As he commented himself: 'It is very warming to have ended my long building career with so satisfactory a last fling.' It replaces a large and rather ugly Victorian house by E.G. Paley, which looked a bit like one of the hotels at Windermere. There was a Georgian wing, and the original plan was to extract and restore this, but it proved too badly infected with dry rot; so instead Clough used the columns from the porch to make a circular temple in the garden, with a copper dome and characteristic golden ball finial on top.

The new house is symmetrical on all four elevations, like a doll's house, with classical centrepieces of applied Tuscan pilasters and pediments front and back. Much of the impact of the design is due to the well-proportioned sash windows and the hipped roof of Westmorland slate with a pair of tall chimneystacks. The exterior is stuccoed and painted pink, looking cheerful and welcoming at any time of year and in any light. The new house occupies only part of the site of the old one; Clough ingeniously used the remaining foundations and lower parts of the walls to make a formal forecourt with cobbled paving, pleached limes, central circular grass plot and wrought-iron gates. He also designed the garden layout on the other side of the house, enclosing the garden in a large semi-circular sweep of yew hedge with a pair of tall gateposts carrying stone eagles on the central axis. One of the great attractions of Clough's architecture, however flimsy and stagey some of his buildings may seem, is the way he fitted his houses into the landscape, and the care with which he contrived their immediate setting. Dalton shows that, even at the end, this ability was unimpaired.

Dent
13; 6 miles S of Sedbergh off A684
This little town, the only one in Dentdale, is eminently picturesque with a narrow, curving cobbled main street lined with cottages of grey limestone or with whitewashed fronts. They have sashed windows and front doors reached up one or two steps from the street. Against one cottage is a large monolith of unpolished Shap granite – more boulder than obelisk. This is the memorial to Adam Sedgwick, the son of a nineteenth-century vicar of Dent and a pioneer geologist. ST ANDREW'S, the parish church, is an uneventful north-country job with a Norman door and humble tower of uncertifiable date, but the nave and chancel are largely Perpendicular, albeit much restored by energetic Victorians.

Dent is still remarkably unspoilt, despite the fact that it is now mainly dependent on tourism for its living. It may be because it attracts the more outdoor type of visitor that it has not become too 'twee'. It makes a good centre for walkers in the Dales, being close to the steep slopes of Whernside (the highest point in the Pennines), Great Coum, Middleton Fell and Rise Hill, and the cobbles of its streets resound to hobnailed hiking boots.

Furness Abbey
See Barrow-in-Furness.

Dallam Tower.

Grange-over-Sands
14; 12 miles SW of Kendal on B5277

The name Grange-over-Sands was invented by a Victorian vicar, and the place is entirely a nineteenth-century creation. It is a remarkably complete little Victorian resort, with buildings of grey limestone, elaborate municipal bedding-out, monkey puzzles, bandstands and gabled boarding houses. There is no great architecture in Grange, but the overall impression is very pleasant, and its setting on the north side of Morecambe Bay is sublime, affording views across the sands towards Silverdale and the distant Pennines, and behind to the mountains of the Lake District.

The oldest part of the town is the group of somewhat Italianate villas built in the 1830s by the Websters of Kendal. These were cut off from the sea by the Furness Railway when it was built along the front in 1847. In compensation the railway company laid out the little park with a small lake, rockery and evergreen planting next to the railway station. The arrival of the railway was the main cause of Grange's development; in the late nineteenth century three or four enormous hotels were built on the hill behind the town with names like the 'Cumbria Grand Hotel', and looking for all the world like health hydros in Switzerland. The best of the hotels, however, the NETHERWOOD, was originally a private house called Blawith, first designed by Webster and then in the 1890s rebuilt to the design of Willink and Thicknesse in full-blown Tudor style. The garden in front consists entirely of topiary crenellation of clipped laurels.

Grange has two towerless Victorian Gothic churches of little interest, one Catholic and one Anglican. The lack of a church tower, however, is made good by the CLOCK TOWER at the top of the High Street, a distinctive exercise in an Arts and Crafts style, with battered corner buttresses and a slated cap on top, culminating in a twisted finial of wrought-iron. It dates from 1912, but nobody seems to know the name of the architect.

The RAILWAY STATION is a remarkable period piece, as it preserves its cast-iron and glass canopies and all its original gabled buildings. The side facing the sea has glazed windows so that waiting passengers can enjoy the view. It is a very exciting experience to approach Grange by train, as the railway crosses the estuary on a long, low iron viaduct so that when the tide is in you feel as if you are in a boat.

HOLME ISLAND, which projects into the Kent estuary, was connected to the mainland by Alexander Brogden, engineer of the Furness Railway, who built the charming castellated cottage there for his own use.

Greystoke
15: 6 miles W of Penrith on B5288

GREYSTOKE CASTLE is the capital seat of the medieval barony of Greystoke, one of the territorial subdivisions of Cumberland. After the Norman Conquest, it was granted to Ranulph de Meschines, Earl of Northumberland, and then passed down through the de Greystokes and Dacres of Gilsland to the Howards, with whom it remains. The castle, faced in pink-grey stone, is largely Victorian but incorporates a large original pele tower of 1353 with a vaulted ground floor. The present handsome Tudorbethan front, with large mullion windows, replaces a classical one added in the early eighteenth century by Charles Howard, possibly to the design of James Gibbs.

In the late eighteenth century the 11th Duke of Norfolk Gothicised part of the house, probably to his own design, adding a long wing with a Banqueting Hall, extra bedrooms and three octagonal towers (now mainly demolished). In 1778 he also built several dotty Gothic farms named after American victories in the War of Independence – FORT PUTNAM and BUNKERS HILL, for instance – to annoy Tory neighbours such as the Earl of Lonsdale. They can be seen from the approach to Greystoke from the east and are charming follies. SPIRE HOUSE, with a spire on top, is supposed to have been a practical joke played on a tenant who belonged to a religious sect that claimed that churches were not necessary and that worship should take place in the open air.

Salvin designed the main part of the house in the Elizabethan manner in 1836–47. The interior was part gutted by fire in 1867 and subsequently restored, again by Salvin. The present appearance of the Great Hall dates from after the fire; it has a Gallery and grand oak staircase made in London, and the windows contain heraldic glass. The Drawing Room, Library and Dining Room are all attractive, well-proportioned rooms with good oak joinery, largely made by estate craftsmen at the time of Salvin's restoration. The main rooms contain family portraits and other features of interest. In the front Hall is a rare marble bust by Dieussart of Thomas Howard, the 'collector' Earl of Arundel; he was the first of the great English collectors and was responsible for assembling the Arundel Marbles in the Ashmolean Museum at Oxford.

GREYSTOKE PARK, an area of 5000 acres, was formed in the late eighteenth century by the 11th Duke of Norfolk, who bought several neighbouring properties for the purpose. As they were thereafter used as farmhouses, these buildings have survived in remarkably unaltered condition. They include BLENCOW HALL, bought in 1802 – a picturesque and interesting specimen of traditional architectural taste in the area. It comprises a hall range between two low towers. The centre of the house was built by Henry Blencow and is dated 1590, but the north tower is probably mid-fifteenth century. The south tower is a shell. In front is a walled courtyard with the remains of a chapel on the side opposite the house.

JOHNBY HALL is on the eastern boundary of the park, and is another dependent manor of the barony of Greystoke. It is an L-shaped house standing within a courtyard and surrounded by an extensive clutter of seventeenth-century farm buildings. It comprises a hall range of three storeys with a hipped roof and a small, projecting tower. Above the doorway is an inscription dated 1582 set in a curious egg-timer-shaped moulded stone framework. The whole of the ground floor is vaulted and there is a spiral staircase of 1582, the stone newel of which continues as a little column supporting a ribbed groin vault. The hall on the first floor is 36 by 30 feet and has a large stone fireplace.

Holker Hall.

HUTTON JOHN further down the valley is not part of the Greystoke estate, but is the seat of the Hudlestons. It too was one of the manor houses held from the barony of Greystoke in the Middle Ages. The core of the house, on which have been clustered the subsequent additions, is a square castellated pele, possible dating from the thirteenth century. To this tower a hall range was later added to the south, and then a larger wing to the north by Andrew Hudleston in 1662. The latter is still in the Jacobean tradition, with mullions in the windows; it now contains the principal living rooms. An interesting feature is the Catholic symbolism of the heart-shaped windows (recalling Sir Thomas Tresham's buildings in Northamptonshire). Various minor works occurred in the eighteenth century, including the sashing of the windows in the pele and the new pedimented doorway dated 1739. Some of the windows in the hall block were restored in 1830, but the major nineteenth-century restoration was carried out in 1866 under the supervision of George Ledwell Taylor, who was related to the Hudlestons by marriage. The Entrance Hall and Library are wholly of this date, and smaller alterations by Taylor, such as chimneypieces, can be found throughout the house.

Holker Hall
16; 3 miles W of Grange-over-Sands on B5278
Holker is one of the largest houses in the north still lived in as a private house. The present L-shaped building occupies the site of an early seventeenth-century house, but is essentially a Victorian rebuilding in two phases:

one wing of 1840 by George Webster, and the other, after a fire, of 1873 by Paley and Austin. Both were built for the 7th Duke of Devonshire and the different character of each admirably demonstrates the development of Victorian architecture within one generation, from the reticent stuccoed Jacobean of Webster's old wing to the demonstrative, even flamboyant, work of Paley and Austin carried out in pink sandstone with a square tower, ogee cupola of green copper, projecting bay windows and gabled dormers.

The interior of the new wing, which is the part open to visitors, is well planned, with the Library, Drawing Room, Billiards Room and Dining Room all opening off a long Entrance Hall. Some of the interior decoration was designed by Crace, and the craftsmanship throughout is of excellent quality. The main rooms are furnished with a mixture of eighteenth- and nineteenth-century furniture, much of it brought from Chatsworth (*q.v.*) after the fire at Holker. The Library contains books that belonged to Henry Cavendish, the eccentric eighteenth-century scientist.

Holker is set in a beautiful park. The gardens round the house were laid out in 1835–6, redesigned by Thomas Mawson in 1910, and remodelled again in 1983. Joseph Paxton himself carried out various works at Holker: his large conservatory at the end of the old wing has disappeared, but a monkey puzzle planted by him, one of the first four in England, still thrives. Outside the lodge gate is a MODEL VILLAGE of early nineteenth-century cottages designed by Webster with fancy cast-iron casements.

Hutton-in-the-Forest
17; 6 miles NW of Penrith off A6

Hutton-in-the-Forest is an intensely romantic place, approached down long avenues through the park, which was laid out by Beaumont in the late seventeenth century and naturalised by William Gilpin in c.1800. The house is an amalgam of contributions of different dates, though the dominant impression is of the seventeenth and nineteenth centuries. The basis of the house is a fourteenth-century pele tower with a vaulted ground floor; a hall range, of which some of the masonry may still remain, was added later and, in 1826, a further tower, largely reconstructed by Francis Vane to the design of George Webster, was built to create the present Dining Room and Drawing Room, one over the other. The estate was bought from Lancelot Hutton by Richard Fletcher of Cockermouth, a rich merchant, in 1606. His son Sir Henry Fletcher, 1st Baronet, added the Long Gallery to the east in 1641–5, almost certainly to the design of Alexander Pogmire, the 'excellent skilful mason and carver' employed by Sir John Lowther at Lowther (*q.v.*). It has a central canted bay and the ground floor was originally an open arcade, but the arches were later enclosed and glazed. They are notable as an early piece of Gothic Revival with 'medieval' capitals. It is not known whether it was ever intended to balance this wing by another on the south side of the forecourt, so making the entrance front symmetrical; the nineteenth-century alterations to the south tower have in any case further reduced any attempt at symmetry. Today much of the special character of the house derives from the clear-cut difference between the various additions. The most striking feature of the façade is the swagger Baroque five-bay centrepiece erected in 1680 by Sir George Fletcher to the design of the mason Edward Addison; it is busy with rustication, Corinthian capitals, garlands, alternating pediments, rich stone-carving and urns on top. Some external alterations to the south front were made to the design of Charles Nixon in the late eighteenth century, and much of the remainder of the exterior was remodelled by Webster in the Gothic manner. The present front door was formed and new offices added by Salvin from 1860 onwards. The interior contains a magnificent carved wooden staircase of 1680, with acanthus scrolls and cherubs, no longer in its original position. Some rooms upstairs retain eighteenth-century decorations, including a good plaster ceiling and original Morris wallpapers. Other rooms also have Victorian wallpaper and Arts and Crafts fittings, as in the late nineteenth century Lady Vane was a patron of the Keswick School of Industrial Arts.

Hutton John
See Greystoke.

Isel Hall
18: 6 miles N of Cockermouth off A595

The large and ancient house of Isel stands dramatically above the north bank of the Derwent, about 3 miles from Cockermouth, in the middle of beautiful wooded and undulating country. The fourteenth-century pele tower at one end is of the usual plan, with a vaulted ground floor, and to one side of it is the sixteenth-century domestic range. This latter is the most imposing domestic building of its date in the county, three storeys high and 126 feet long. The original mullion windows and entrance door survive, and along the top is an Elizabethan parapet sparsely embellished with little conical pinnacles. The interior contains an impressive series of rooms, many of which are lined with very good sixteenth-century panelling, some of it linenfold pattern and some painted in imitation of intarsia. A carved chimneypiece in one of the rooms is dated 1631, but there is little to show later in date than this, because during the eighteenth and nineteenth centuries the Lawsons lived at their other Cumberland house, Brayton Hall (which was destroyed by fire c.1940). Isel is still owned by the Lawson-Austin-Leigh family. It is not open to the public.

The parish CHURCH OF ST MICHAEL on the opposite side of the river is an endearing little building, mainly Norman, set in an attractive grassy graveyard with yew trees. The interior was restored in 1901 in Arts and Crafts taste, and has splendid hanging oil-lamps of wrought-iron designed by Bainbridge Reynolds, clear glass in the windows, dark oak pews and an organ case with carved and gilded decoration. The biblical texts on painted boards hanging round the walls are probably eighteenth-century.

Johnby Hall
See Greystoke.

Kendal
19; 7 miles SE of Windermere on A6

Kendal is a prosperous country town of grey limestone surrounded on all sides by fells, which can be seen at the ends of most of the streets, and this adds greatly to the attractions of the general townscape. The spine of the town is one long street which changes its name three times – Kirkland, Highgate, Stricklandgate – and lies parallel to the River Kent. A unique feature of the town plan was the series of 'yards' – narrow enclosed ways through to the river surrounded by houses and small warehouses on the site of the old back gardens. Most of these were demolished in the 1950s and 1960s by the town council under a misguided scheme of 'slum' clearance. This has greatly weakened the impact of the town, for anybody turning off the main street through one of the surviving archways, instead of finding himself in a picturesque, almost Italian, backwater, will find only empty wastelands and dreary council housing.

The main street, however, still has many attractions. In STRICKLANDGATE several former townhouses survive, including the local council offices with a pedimented doorcase, and the YWCA, formerly the house of the Stricklands of Sizergh (*q.v.*) and displaying their crest on the lead rainwater pipes. Briggs's shop (established in 1865) has a shop-front with four fluted columns painted black and gold, and a former brush shop retains its old sign – a hog made out of bristles. HIGHGATE has more good early nineteenth-century shop-fronts, including

The church of the Holy Trinity, Kendal.

the black-and-gold Highgate pharmacy, with a Grecian fascia and gold mortar and pestle on top; Titus Wilson, the printer, with no less than three small-paned bows; and Farrer's, the tea merchant's, of *c*.1823. The MARKET PLACE, opening off to one side, was given a Civic Trust scheme in the 1960s and all the stuccoed fronts are picked out in pastel colours. The NEW SHAMBLES is a remarkably well-preserved Victorian development of single-storeyed shops, painted two shades of dark green, flanking a cobbled footpath and with original gas-lamp brackets. Back in Highgate, the handsome early nineteenth-century Grecian MIDLAND BANK, with pilasters and a stone lion on the parapet, was designed by the Websters, the highly successful local firm of architects. Older buildings include the sixteenth-century FLEECE INN, with jettied upper storeys, and the SANDES ALMSHOUSES, founded in 1659 by a local wool merchant. These, and the name of the Fleece Inn, are a reminder that the fifteenth- and sixteenth-century prosperity of Kendal was based on the production of woollen cloth. Further down, the HIGHGATE HOTEL, dated 1769, has a pair of milestones on either side of the front door which give the distance to London (258 miles) and Edinburgh (135 miles). Lowther Street, which branches off next to the florid Victorian TOWN HALL, contains the premises of the KENDAL BROWN SNUFF MANUFACTURERS and has a colourful painted sign in the form of a Turk in turban and baggy trousers.

From Kirkland, fine eighteenth-century wrought-iron gates, hung from rusticated piers topped with urns, lead to the CHURCH OF THE HOLY TRINITY, a prosperous wool church of the fifteenth and early sixteenth centuries. In plan it is a large rectangle with no fewer than five aisles, two on either side of the nave, and a west tower. The interior is, as a result, spatially impressive, but has little else to offer, thanks to a particularly drastic restoration in 1850 when lots of nice old junk was ruthlessly thrown out, and thanks also to some horrid modern fittings. The trendy central altar, with a frontal of tango-orange sackcloth, is made even worse by a hanging corona in the vague form of a crown of thorns. The most impressive thing about the parish church is the exterior view of the east front, with its five wide gables and five large Victorian Gothic windows.

Viewed from the river, which is nicely landscaped through the length of the town, the church makes a handsome picture together with ABBOT HALL, the best building in Kendal. Really a country house in a town setting, it stands in a little park facing the river and has its own stable block behind. It was reputedly designed in 1759 by John Carr of York for Colonel George Wilson, and cost £8000; the building material is dressed local limestone. The central portion of the house has three bays and there are slightly lower attached wings. The entrance front presents an austere angular U-shape, while the riverside façade is more elegant, with canted bays and Palladian windows. The main rooms on the ground floor contain original cornices, carved doorcases and chimneypieces. The Entrance Hall runs through the house from front to back and is partially divided in two by fluted Doric columns at either side. The wooden staircase has turned balusters. The first-floor rooms, while retaining their fine original proportions, have been decorated in an unobtrusive modern style to house changing exhibitions, as the building is now an excellent small art gallery and museum. The newly built addition to the museum has as its elevation the reconstructed façade of the old Kendal Gas Works, dated 1825, with a pediment, Tuscan columns and the amusing inscription: 'EX FUMO LUCEM'.

Kirkby Stephen
20; 6 miles S of Brough on A685

The centre of the town is a tiny MARKET PLACE next to the churchyard, entrance to the latter being through a Tuscan colonnade built in 1810 by George Gibson. The columns are painted toffee-colour and white, and there is a little cupola with a gold ball on top. The Market Place opens off the long main street and is lined with eighteenth- and nineteenth-century two- and three-storeyed buildings – harmonious enough, but none of them very special. To the east is the TEMPERANCE HALL of 1856, with a jolly stucco façade and what looks like a statue of Our Lady in blue robes in a niche over the door, but which must actually be meant to be of the goddess of health. The most important building is the parish church, dedicated to ST STEPHEN. It is built of red sandstone and has a Perpendicular west tower built *c*.1506, which is much taller and more imposing than the usual north-country medieval stump. The architectural interest of the interior is largely thirteenth-century. The nave arcades, with circular piers and double-chamfered arches, date from then, as do the fine sedilia and piscina in the chancel, with carved leaves on their capitals and trefoil arches; these were re-incorporated when the chancel was rebuilt as part of a general restoration in 1847.

Kirkoswald
21; 8 miles NE of Penrith on B6412

An odd feature of this village, as it is approached, is the way the bell-tower looks as if it has become detached from the main body of the church and has climbed a nearby hill. It is a stumpy stone belfry dating only from 1897, but it replaces an earlier timber structure. The CHURCH OF ST OSWALD looks slightly truncated without it. The nave dates from the twelfth and thirteenth centuries, but it is the chancel that gives the building its air of nobility. It was built in 1523 by Lord Dacre of Gilsland as a collegiate chapel, served by six priests, and it is a remarkably consistent and uniform piece of late Perpendicular architecture, with a five-light east window and three-light side-windows with round-arched heads, just like those at Naworth Castle (*q.v.*); both were partly rebuilt by Lord Dacre in the early sixteenth century.

The COLLEGE itself is now a country house and belongs to the Fetherstonhaughs, whose ancestor Henry Fetherstonhaugh bought the building in 1590 for £140. Some fabric of the old college survives in the present mansion, including an old pele tower of the Dacres, and there are also traces of early seventeenth-century work, including panelling dated 1619 in the Oak Room on the first floor and a carved wooden chimneypiece dated 1641. The special distinction of the house derives, however, from the beautiful pink sandstone entrance front built in 1696 by Timothy Fetherstonhaugh. It is the best of its kind in the north-west, and more a Home Counties' type, with a hipped flagged roof, projecting ends, five-bay recessed centre and front door with a curly swan-necked pediment. Inside, the centre of the house is filled with the large transverse Hall, which has a beamed ceiling and carved stone fireplace incorporating a sixteenth-

century panel with the arms of Lord Dacre of Gilsland, brought from Kirkoswald Castle when it was demolished. The spacious open-well staircase that opens off the Hall dates from the late seventeenth century and has a barley-sugar-twist balustrade. The large square Drawing Room was added *c*.1839–42 and the incongruously 'Jacobean' office wing dates from the same time.

In the garden is an unusual cruciform sundial. The College contains Fetherstonhaugh family portraits from the seventeenth to the twentieth centuries, as well as interesting furniture and china, including much Chinese Export showing the family arms.

Lanercost Priory
22; 2 miles NE of Brampton off A69

Lanercost's peaceful rustic setting disguises a violent history. The priory was founded *c*.1166 for Augustinian canons, but was severely damaged by Scottish raiders on three separate occasions in subsequent centuries. After the Dissolution in 1536 the buildings passed to the Dacre family of Naworth Castle (*q.v.*), which stands just across the River Irthing to the south. Part was converted by Sir Thomas Dacre into a house, while the nave continued to be used as the local parish church. This explains the unusually well-preserved state of Lanercost. Only the east range of the cloisters, with the chapter house, has disappeared. Otherwise, all remains standing to a substantial height and over half is still roofed. Some of the buildings are a working farm and this also helps to prevent the dead, antiseptic feel found in some too neatly maintained monastic ruins. The field in front of the church, where you park your car, is full of placidly grazing cows, and the west door sports a notice: 'This church is open. Our cows eat aerials and mirrors. We suggest you retract them.' The walled graveyard to the east of the church is most attractive, with old pink or grey headstones, unmown grass and wild flowers. Most of the church dates from the thirteenth century and is good Early English work, with tall elegant lancets. The chancel, now roofless, is particularly beautiful. The nave is simpler and, to make room for the cloisters, has an aisle on one side only. The western limb was repaired *c*.1740 when the present dividing wall, with a large three-light window, was inserted at the crossing. The church was again restored in the late nineteenth century by Rosalind, Countess of Carlisle (wife of the artist 9th Earl), and the timber barrel ceiling, carved oak pews and rich organ case date from that time. So do the stained-glass side-windows, made by Morris & Co. The eighteenth-century east window has clear lights, but with three small sixteenth-century heraldic glass panels. There are several late nineteenth-century monuments to different members of the Howard family, including three bronze tablets of high artistic quality designed by Burne-Jones and made by Sir Edgar Boehm. Boehm was also responsible for the touching effigy in terracotta of the infant Lady Elizabeth Howard in the north transept. At the west door is a tent-like arrangement of heraldic curtains made by parishioners out of blankets in 1954 'for the adornment, comfort and dignity' of the church.

On going out of the church, it is worth studying the statue of St Mary Magdalene, the priory's patron saint, in the niche high up in the west gable. It is a well-preserved piece of thirteenth-century sculpture, similar in style to the statues at Lincoln Cathedral (*q.v.*), and is the finest medieval work of art in Cumberland.

Levens Hall★

23; 4 miles S of Kendal on A6

Levens Hall itself is a remarkable example of Elizabethan architecture, with rich, carved wooden fireplaces, plasterwork and panelling, while the famous topiary garden of *c.*1700 is the finest surviving example of its kind in England and without equal in Europe. Although most of the architectural features one sees now are Elizabethan, the core of the house is much older and was built on the typical Westmorland plan of pele tower and hall. It was remodelled in 1595 by James Bellingham to create the present mansion. Soon after Sir James Graham acquired the house in the late seventeenth century (according to tradition, he won it at a game of cards), he added the south wing to contain new offices. He laid out the gardens and bought the magnificent late seventeenth-century furniture, which is one of the glories of the house. Thereafter, Levens passed by descent to the Bagots, the present owners (but often through the female line, entailing innumerable changes of name), and was used as a dower-house for most of the eighteenth century, which partly accounts for its remarkably unaltered state.

The exterior is attractively informal, with gables, mullion-and-transom windows, a castellated tower and fat round chimneys. The walls are harled and in the eighteenth century were whitewashed like those of central European castles. The interior is grand but comfortable. The Hall, in the medieval position, has an elegant plaster ceiling and a coloured heraldic frieze, while the two Drawing Rooms have fantastic carved oak chimneypieces of 1595, continuing and elaborating on the style of those at Sizergh Castle (*q.v.*), also near Kendal. The overmantel in the small Drawing Room has figures of Samson, Hercules and the Senses, as well as allegorical panels of the Four Seasons and Four Elements. The Dining Room walls are hung with seventeenth-century Cordova leather − a rare survival. Originally there was a Long Gallery above the Hall, but this has been subdivided. Some interesting alterations were made to the house in 1810−20 to the design of Francis Webster of Kendal; these were carefully detailed to match the original work, including the panelling in the Library and some of the bedrooms. The tall Bathroom Tower was added then, fitted with a marble bath and water closets designed and made by Gillow. The estate agent at the time remarked of them: 'I, of course, have no Experience of such Conveniences.'

The most famous feature of Levens is the formal GARDEN laid out *c.*1700 for Sir James Graham by William Beaumont, a French designer who was formerly gardener to James II, and who also worked at Stonyhurst, Hutton-in-the-Forest (*qq.v.*) and Edenhall. As well as the clipped yews, there are vast, amorphous beech hedges. The PARK, which is separated from the house and gardens by the eighteenth-century turnpike road (now the A6), was laid out at the same time as the garden, and includes an impressive oak avenue over a mile long focusing on a pretty view of the River Kent − an early example of landscape appreciation. The park contains a rare herd of black fallow deer (actually dark brown). There is a local superstition that, whenever an albino fawn is born, some change will take place in the house.

Lanercost Priory.

Lowther Castle.

Lowther

24; 4 miles S of Penrith off A6

The princely seat of the Lowthers, Earls of Lonsdale, embodies in itself a potted history of architecture. What is now visible on the ground, namely the beautiful pink-grey ashlar shell of Dance and Smirke's CASTLE of 1802—11, is merely the tip of a submerged iceberg of lost or unexecuted designs by many of the greatest names in English architecture. The first Lowther Hall (the change of name to Castle was made in the early nineteenth century) was a symmetrical castellated house of five bays and three storeys flanked by square fourteenth- or fifteenth-century towers with stepped-up corner battlements on the model of Bolton Castle in Yorkshire (*q.v.*). It was remodelled in 1631 when the centre was rebuilt with large mullion-and-transom windows, a centrepiece with an elaborate frilly parapet and an ogee-capped cupola on the roof. A classical porch was added in 1642 by the 'excellent skilful mayson and carver' Alexander Pogmire, who in 1655 also added the gallery on the east side of the front, similar to that at Hutton-in-the-Forest (*q.v.*). The main house was demolished *c.*1690 by John, 1st Viscount Lonsdale, to make room for the new house built in 1692—5. Several architects were consulted over the design of this, including Sir Robert Hooke and William Talman, but in the event none of them got the commission, though Lord Lonsdale may have used Talman's design for the elevation; together with the master mason, Edward Addison, he himself may have evolved the design as built. The new house was of fifteen bays with projecting wings (one of them Pogmire's gallery of 1655), enclosing an inner court and, beyond that, a further pair of symmetrical office wings flanking an outer court. The interior was embellished with a series of painted ceilings by Antonio Verrio depicting Olympian scenes of gods and goddesses sprawling amidst clouds and rainbows. The new house was barely completed before it was badly damaged by fire in 1718. Although Lord Lonsdale consulted both Colen Campbell and James Gibbs about rebuilding, nothing was done and the house remained a ruin for nearly 100 years.

With the accession in 1750 of James Lowther ('Wicked Jimmy'), later 1st Earl of Lonsdale of the first creation, schemes for rebuilding the house began to fall as thick as confetti. Lord Lonsdale, the son-in-law of Lord Bute, wielded enormous political power in the Tory interest, and had also accumulated a considerable fortune, partly out of money-lending, partly out of the development of Whitehaven and the coal-mines there. Nevertheless, he never managed to get any of his architects' designs for a new house beyond the drawing board. The roll-call of architects consulted by him exceeded even the 1st Viscount's, and included Mathew Brettingham, Capability Brown, James and Robert Adam, Thomas Harrison and the Websters. Of all these, the Adams' various plans of 1765 were the most spectacular: they envisaged a vast, symmetrical, castellated house with geometric courtyards, about as big as Diocletian's palace at Spalatro. Not surprisingly, this came to nothing, but the Adams did design a neat neo-

classical MODEL VILLAGE (which still survives) on the edge of the park, with a crescent, little square and miniature terraces.

At the end of his life, Lord Lonsdale had more or less determined on the conversion and enlargement of the surviving west wing of the old house, despite its poor relationship with the great avenue in the park, the principal survivor of the 1st Viscount's layout. Both Harrison of Chester and the Websters produced designs and work was started from 1800–2, with Bernasconi being paid for plastering; however, Lord Lonsdale died in 1802 before things had progressed very far. He was succeeded by a cousin, who became 1st Earl of Lonsdale of the second creation, and it was he who immediately set about building the present castle. The foundation stone was laid in 1802 and the general form of the design, with its attractively composed masses and varied heights, was determined by the second George Dance, whose designs are dated 1803. Dance, however, was unable to continue with the work and so recommended that his pupil, the young Robert Smirke, should take over in 1806; construction was completed by 1814. The result was the spectacular house of which the ruin still survives.

The mansion is 420 feet long, the entrance front being of more severely castellated character than the park front, which is more ecclesiastical. As Wordsworth put it:

> *Lowther! in thy majestic pile are seen*
> *Cathedral pomp and grace, in apt accord*
> *With the baronial castle's sterner mien.*

The principal rooms were arranged around a large, imperial-plan staircase in a central Hall 60 feet square under a keep-like tower 90 feet high, which was latterly embellished with stained glass given by Kaiser Wilhelm II. The Library, Saloon, Dining Room and Drawing Rooms were adorned with Perpendicular plasterwork by Bernasconi and contained an important collection of paintings, antique and modern sculpture, furniture, books and silver; the collection is now largely dispersed.

Lowther is set in a large and beautiful PARK, landscaped by John Webb in 1807 and made even larger early in this century by the 5th Earl, the celebrated 'Yellow Earl', in order to impress the Kaiser; the lodge gates date from then. The Yellow Earl was famous for his tall stories and exaggeration; he drove the Kaiser for miles and miles over the neighbouring county *en route* from Penrith station, claiming that everything they passed was his land. He is remembered for capping a dinner-table story about Arctic exploration with the remark, 'I myself have been to the North Pole – indeed, I have been a good deal further.' Towards the end of his life, in the mid-1930s, he was forced as an economy measure to give up living in the castle and, apart from wartime occupation by the Army, it was never again lived in. The roof was removed by the present Earl of Lonsdale in 1957, but the shell of the building was kept as a landscape feature at the heart of the park and great estate.

From the centre of the castle, an oak avenue of early eighteenth-century origin sweeps into the distance. To one side, in splendid isolation, is ST MICHAEL'S, the parish church, beautifully situated on a natural terrace overlooking the River Lowther. It is cruciform in plan and was remodelled externally in 1686 by Sir John Lowther. At that time a dome was added to the centre, but unfortunately this was converted into a more conventional Gothic tower in 1856. The large, plain interior has arcades dating from the twelfth century, but is chiefly remarkable for the Lowther family memorials and hatchments, dating from the seventeenth to the twentieth centuries. That by William Stanton to the 1st Viscount is especially good: a marble effigy of the deceased reclining with his elbow on a cushion and nonchalantly holding his coronet in his hand. In the churchyard is a little Gothic MAUSOLEUM of 1857, containing a seated white marble statue of the 2nd Earl, all alone with a few dead leaves drifting round his pedestal.

From here there is a good view across the river to ASKHAM HALL, the house of the present Earl. It is an irregular quadrangle dating from the fourteenth to the seventeenth centuries, with one grander front of 1685–90. The latter has cross-mullion windows and a segmental pediment over the door, which faces a garden of formal terraces and clipped yews. The best feature of the interior, the staircase, is of the same date. The rooms are furnished with the remains of the family collection from Lowther Castle, including many interesting eighteenth-century paintings and portraits. The landscape for miles around is a model of good farming and forestry.

Moor Crag

See Cartmel Fell.

The church of St Lawrence, Morland.

Morland

25; 6 miles SE of Penrith off A66

The CHURCH OF ST LAWRENCE has the only Saxon church tower in the north-west of England, a sturdy pink stone affair with narrow, round-headed doors, double-arched windows and a pretty sixteenth-century lead spirelet on top. The body of the church was rebuilt in the twelfth century with a wide nave and sturdily buttressed transepts. The arcades, with well-proportioned round columns, are very beautiful. The chancel was re-modelled in the sixteenth century and the north aisle rebuilt with classical round-headed windows in the eighteenth; they let in more light than the twelfth-century lancets in the south aisle and transepts. Much of the cheerful impact of the interior of the church is due to late nineteenth-century restoration. The nave was done by C.J. Ferguson of Carlisle in 1896, and the chancel was by W.D. Caröe. The walls of the nave are plastered and pink-washed, and there are decent Arts and Crafts benches of pale oak. The windows have clear glazing, so the church is always full of light. Only the east window has stained glass, by Powell of Blackfriars; it is a memorial to Joseph Torbock of Cross Rigg Hall. The carved oak reredos below was designed by Caröe, but the altar rails are seventeenth-century and the pulpit with sounding board eighteenth-century. The elegant little font with a carved conical cover is dated 1662. Behind it, the oak pew with round knobs was originally that of the Stanwix Nevinson family of Newby Hall; it was moved here during the restoration in 1896. The boards, showing the Our Father and Creed, were painted for the church by William Dobson in the mid-eighteenth century, and the Royal Arms are those of George III. Note also the seventeenth-century poor-box, hollowed out of a single log.

Muncaster Castle

26; 1 mile E of Ravenglass on A595

This pink granite castle of the Penningtons enjoys one of the finest sites in England, above the Roman harbour at Ravenglass and guarding the entrance to Eskdale described by Ruskin as the 'gateway to paradise'. The castle is the result of extensive reconstructions at the end of the eighteenth century by the 1st Lord Muncaster, to his own design, and again between 1860 and 1864 by the 4th Lord Muncaster to designs by Anthony Salvin.

The pele tower, the oldest part of the present castle, was erected in 1325. The Hall and kitchens were added in the fifteenth century. The late eighteenth-century alterations comprised the addition of an octagonal Library, a new north wing, and general internal and external remodelling – the former in the classical taste and the latter in castellated Gothic. Salvin swept most of this away, replacing it with more solid and serious work. The Library was recased, but retains its octagonal shape, and some eighteenth-century traces are still visible in the present Dining Room; otherwise, all is now by Salvin's hand. He also added a second tower at the north-west angle to balance the original pele.

Lord Muncaster died while work was in progress and the reconstruction was finished off as rapidly and economically as possible by the trustees, which explains why the rooms are relatively plain – though the Drawing Room has a handsome segmental plaster barrel ceiling and has recently been adorned with a superb white marble chimneypiece designed by Robert Adam and brought from Byram Park in Yorkshire. A feature of the rooms is the quantity of English and continental woodwork, panelling, carved chimneypieces and furniture brought from elsewhere. There is also a good series of family portraits.

Henry VI is traditionally said to have hidden at Muncaster after the battle of Towton in 1461, and the famous glass bowl, the 'Luck of Muncaster' (a copy is displayed in the Dining Room), is supposed to have been given by him to Sir John Pennington. An eighteenth-century folly tower on a nearby hillside marks the spot where a shepherd is supposed to have discovered the King. The surrounding landscape owes a great deal to the 1st Lord Muncaster, who was a pioneer agricultural improver. The most magnificent feature of the gardens is the half-mile long terrace, which follows the contours of the hillside overlooking Eskdale and leads the eye up to Sca Fell and the mountains at the head of the valley. At the back of the terrace are two summerhouses built of twigs, dated 1891. The famous rhododendrons were planted by Sir John Ramsden, 5th Baronet, from 1917 onwards. The stables and main entrance survive from *c.*1781 and are pretty Gothic work, bearing comparison with the 'Drunken Duke' of Norfolk's Gothic farms at Greystoke (*q.v.*).

Naworth Castle

27; 1½ miles NE of Brampton off A69

From the drive, as one descends gently towards the castle, a vast view can be had over the Border country and far into Scotland. Lady Georgiana Fullerton's anagram for Naworth Castle was 'War to the Clans', neatly summarising its historic role as a fortress against the Scots. A licence to crenellate the naturally defensive site was granted by Edward III to Ralph Dacre in 1335 and the castle was enlarged by Thomas, Lord Dacre of Gilsland, *c.*1520; the large Perpendicular windows date from that time. Naworth passed to the Howards as a result of the marriage of Elizabeth Dacre to Lord William Howard, third son of the 4th Duke of Norfolk and ancestor of the Earls of Carlisle, whose seat it remains. The Dacre inheritance included Henderskelfe (later Castle Howard (*q.v.*)) in Yorkshire, but the estates were split in the early twentieth century, the Yorkshire estates and Castle Howard going to a younger son and Naworth remaining with the earldom.

Lord William Howard, 'Belted Will', was a remarkable figure – a soldier but also a scholar with antiquarian and historical tastes, who carried out investigations of the Roman remains on his estates and formed an interesting library, part of which still survives at Naworth. He found the castle 'in very great decay' and set about repairing it and converting it into a mansion. He restored the Carlisle Tower in 1619, and in 1622 moved the (happily still existing) Gothic timber roof of *c.*1350 from Kirkoswald Castle (*q.v.*) to the third floor of the tower, together with other fittings; these, which included a ceiling with paintings of kings in the Great Hall, have since been destroyed.

Some work was carried out in the early eighteenth century by the 3rd Earl of Carlisle, who employed Hawksmoor and Vanbrugh at Castle Howard, and it was stated by the architect C.W. Ferguson in 1879 that Vanbrugh designed a music gallery and screen for the Hall at Naworth. The 5th Earl employed Charles Tatham to design further alterations in the late eighteenth century, but no trace of this work, either Baroque or neo-classical,

survived the disastrous fire of 1844, which gutted most of the interior, leaving only the outer walls.

The castle was reinstated between 1846 and 1848 by Anthony Salvin, whose work was remarkably faithful to the medieval original. The Great Hall, the largest in the north-west, is his; it has an open timber roof and carved heraldic beasts down the sides of the room (which escaped the fire). The magnificent tapestries were brought by the 5th Earl from the Orléans collection. (The collection of Philippe Egalité, Duc d'Orléans, was the best in eighteenth-century Europe; at the outbreak of the French Revolution it was sold in London.) The 9th Earl of Carlisle was a friend of the Pre-Raphaelites and was himself an artist of considerable merit. He employed Philip Webb to design his town house in London and also consulted him about work at Naworth, commissioning him to design the agent's house on the estate, now called FOUR GABLES. The old Library is the best of the castle's late nineteenth-century rooms and has a gesso overmantel depicting the battle of Flodden, designed and painted by Burne-Jones and modelled by Boehm. The present Earl of Carlisle and his wife bravely moved back into the castle after inheriting it; they have adapted it for continued family life, re-roofing the Hall, and opened it to the public for the first time in 1984.

Penrith

28; 18 miles S of Carlisle on A6

Penrith is the model of the small, prosperous market town and is the best of its kind in the north-west, being far less damaged by modern redevelopment than Kendal (*q.v.*). It is full of solid, old-fashioned, red stone buildings (reflecting the red faces of the farmers), nice timber shop-fronts, butchers selling properly cured bacon, and greengrocers with a sideline in seed potatoes and bedding plants. It also has an agreeably complex street-plan with, as its nucleus, various irregular and informal spaces loosely linked to each other in the Market Place, the Cornmarket and the churchyard of St Andrew's. It is these rather homely attractions, rather than any especially spectacular sights, that make Penrith a draw. Although there is a CASTLE, built in the fourteenth century by Archbishop Strickland, it is not a very impressive ruin and received its *coup de grâce* in the nineteenth century when the London Midland and Scottish Railway Company demolished half of it to make way for the station – an unfortunate piece of Victorian vandalism.

The parish CHURCH OF ST ANDREW was largely rebuilt in 1720, with the result that it now has a Georgian body and a medieval west tower. It stands in a handsome graveyard with good iron railings, mown grass and trees, and is surrounded by decent-looking houses. In the graveyard are several pieces of Saxon sculpture, including the bases of two tenth-century crosses and some hogback coffins; they are known locally as the Giant's Thumb and the Giant's Grave. The interior of the church is a plain Georgian box with two tiers of Tuscan columns, galleries and a solid, carved oak pulpit. The present colour scheme is somewhat startling but not unpleasant. Even more startling are the large wall paintings in the apse, signed by Jacob Thompson and dated 1845: they

St John the Evangelist, Plumpton Wall.

show the angels appearing to the shepherds and the Agony in the Garden in a full-blown, sentimental, early nineteenth-century style.

The MARKET PLACE is a good space surrounded by appropriate buildings: Arnison's, the old-established draper's, which has an especially well-preserved Victorian shop-front; the George Hotel, a dignified, red sandstone Georgian hostelry, most of which, rather amazingly, was built in 1924; and three good banks in various styles, notably Barclays, a red stone Tudor job. In the centre is a Gothic CLOCK TOWER, built in 1861 to commemorate the son of a local squire, Philip Musgrave of Edenhall, who died in Madrid at the age of twenty-six. The adjoining CORNMARKET has a new, oval timber shelter in the centre, which is remarkably good-looking – a positive asset. Behind it is the GLOUCESTER ARMS, a sixteenth-century pub with a projecting porch carved with the Royal Arms and a dark, cosy interior with panelling and beams.

Now incorporated in the town and serving as public buildings are two former country houses of interest. HUTTON HALL was the original manor house of Penrith and comprises a fifteenth-century pele tower with additions. The seven-bay classical red stone front is mid-eighteenth-century, and there are good interiors of the same date. It is now the Penrith Masonic Lodge. The MANSION HOUSE was built c.1750 by Thomas Whelpdale, attorney and steward to the Duke of Portland. It has a five-bay centre and end pavilions with Venetian windows. It now serves as District Council offices.

The most prominent feature of Penrith in any distant view (from the M6, for instance) is the fell behind the town, planted with conifers and topped off with the BEACON TOWER, dating from 1719 – a red stone pyramid on a square base. It has the slightly haunted quality of a painting by Caspar David Friedrich – just the place for witches on a moonlit night.

Plumpton Wall
29; 6 miles N of Penrith on A6

BRACKENBURGH TOWER, the house of the Harris family, colliery owners, was designed for them in 1902–3 by the best Scottish architect of his day, Sir Robert Lorimer. It is a good example of his work and bears comparison with that of his English contemporary, Sir Edwin Lutyens. Like much of the latter's work, Brackenburgh is an exercise in free Tudor, well-handled to create an impressive asymmetrical composition with large mullion-and-transom windows and low-pitched roofs and gables. The exterior is more impressive than the interior. The Great Hall is the principal room, with finely carved oak joinery, though the overall effect is perhaps more ecclesiastical than domestic. At the back, Lorimer's house incorporated part of a previous house on the site, including an old pele tower and a wing designed by William Atkinson in 1852. In recent years the kitchen wing has been demolished and the interior slightly rearranged in order to provide separate accommodation for two generations of the family.

The church at Plumpton Wall, dedicated to ST JOHN THE EVANGELIST, was also designed for the Harris family by Lorimer in 1907. It is an excellent piece of Edwardian Gothic Revival – one of the best churches in Cumbria.

Rose Castle
30; 7 miles SW of Carlisle off B5299

Rose Castle has been the residential seat of the Bishops of Carlisle since the thirteenth century. It is set in beautiful, rolling, fertile country to the south of the city. The medieval castle formed an irregular quadrangle but was damaged by fire in the Civil War in 1646, and after the Restoration two ranges were demolished by Bishop Rainbow, leaving the present L-shape which he remodelled to the design of the Rev. Thomas Machell. No trace of Machell's work is now apparent. The oldest part is a pele tower of c.1300 called the Strickland Tower, which is almost detached at the north end. The main block incorporates Bishop Bell's Tower of c.1488 and at right-angles the Chapel, also built originally by Bishop Bell in 1487–9 but rebuilt by Bishop Rainbow c.1665–70.

When Bishop Lyttelton was at Rose Castle in the mid-eighteenth century, Horace Walpole wrote to him and suggested that he should 'change it for Farnham or Hartlebury Castles – so that Pitt and I can come with our Gothic trowels', implying that Carlisle was impossibly remote. However, Pitt may have advised his uncle when he ceiled the interior of the chapel and roofed the Strickland Tower in 1763. The Chapel and the whole castle were again refaced and somewhat drastically remodelled in 1828–31 by Bishop Percy to the design of Thomas Rickman, and further work was done by Salvin in 1853; it is this nineteenth-century Gothic work that now determines the character of the house. The landscaping of the grounds was done for Bishop Percy by Paxton. The interior contains a number of large, rather severe, early nineteenth-century Gothic rooms, including the Dining and Drawing Rooms one above the other, with impressive Gothic stone fireplaces, and the main staircase. The Chapel has old panelling from Lambeth Palace.

St Bees

31; 4 miles S of Whitehaven on B5345

St Bees is a remote spot near the sea, but lying in a sheltered hollow, and now strongly redolent of 'muscular Christianity'. St Bega, or Bees, was an Irish virgin and saint who, according to the early eighteenth-century antiquarian Nathaniel Buck, 'is said to have lived here some time in great abstinence and piety'. A nunnery was founded *c.*650, but destroyed by the Vikings. It was refounded as a Benedictine priory in the reign of Henry I by William de Meschines, Lord of Egremont, and was a cell of St Mary's Abbey, York (*q.v.*).

At the Reformation all of the CHURCH OF ST MARY AND ST BEGA except the east end was preserved as the parish church, but nothing remains above ground of the other priory buildings. Despite the dedication to female saints, the architecture of St Bees is sternly masculine. The church is cruciform, of pink sandstone, with a plain, square tower over the crossing. The best surviving Norman feature is the west door – heavyweight Romanesque work with three recessed round arches decorated with weathered zigzag ornament. Three lancets above and simple flanking buttresses complete an austere but satisfying façade. Inset in the wall opposite is a carved lintel with interlaced ornament and the figure of St Michael or St George killing a dragon; it is said to be Norman but looks earlier. The doors have elaborate scrolling ironwork hinges. They were designed by William Butterfield, who carried out a sweeping restoration in 1855–68, and it is his unmistakable hand that is largely responsible for the architectural impact. The nave is Early English, with pointed arches carried on alternately round and octagonal piers. The clerestory has simple late Perpendicular windows, which may date from 1611, when considerable repairs are known to have been carried out following post-Reformation neglect. The aisles are largely Butterfield's, as is the chunky timber ceiling of the nave. The south aisle has, near its west end, a cluster of elegant Georgian marble memorials, and a heavy, plain font of Devon marble by Butterfield. At the time of writing, the pews in the nave have been rearranged into an irritatingly askew pattern and the floor covered with cheap lino tiles – most unworthy. This, however, is completely overshadowed by the simple grandeur of Butterfield's east end. The whole of the crossing-arch is filled with a great iron screen designed in 1886 by Butterfield in memory of William Fox. It is painted in authentic shades of brick red, biscuit and blue. Beyond it is the crossing, under the tower, flanked by short transepts, and then the one-bay chancel. The crossing has a simple timber ceiling with bold stencilled patterns, and the whole of the east wall, originally erected in 1539, was treated as a reredos by Butterfield, with bold, simple, geometrical decoration – just three great arches and two circles, sparsely inlaid with coloured tiles, marble and sgraffito decoration. Against the north wall of the chancel is the monument to Maria Claudine Lumb, in whose memory the chancel was restored in 1867. She is represented as a sleeping marble babe clutching a sprig of lily of the valley. The whole of the south transept is filled with a splendid large organ in a richly carved oak case. This is of considerable interest as it was made by Father Henry Willis in 1899; it is the last major instrument to have been supervised by him personally and is one of the finest pieces of his work.

The remainder of the chancel, which is beautiful Early English work with tall thin lancets, fell into ruin at the Reformation but was re-roofed, with a flat plaster ceiling, in 1817 to serve as the lecture hall for the theological college founded at St Bees by Bishop Law of Chester to train clergy for the expanding industrial towns of the north. This was the first modern theological college in the country and survived till 1894. It is now used by ST BEES SCHOOL, the main buildings of which lie on the other side of the road. The old grammar school at St Bees was founded by Archbishop Grindal of York in 1583. In the nineteenth century, like so many old foundations, it became a public school and expanded, though it is still quite small. The buildings form an open quadrangle facing the old east end of the chancel. The north wing, with mullion windows, is the original schoolhouse of 1587. The two other wings are elegant, papery Tudor work of pink ashlar stone erected in 1842–4. Behind are later buildings, including the Chapel and Library, both by Paley and Austin. The school forms an attractive group, though it would benefit from a few more trees, and it is disgraceful that the local planning authority has permitted a rash of bungalows on the skyline above.

Scaleby Castle

32; 6 miles NE of Carlisle off A6071

The approach to the castle from Scaleby village is by means of an impressive oak avenue over half a mile long. A circular moat encloses an exceptionally large piece of ground (about 5 acres) with the part-ruined castle in the centre. This was the family home of William Gilpin, high priest of the Picturesque, and 'in his later imaginary landscapes it appeared as the prototype of the romantic ruin. So it seems appropriate that the earliest drawings of William Gilpin to have survived should be of Scaleby Castle.'

The property was originally granted by Edward I to Richard Tilliol, and licence to crenellate was granted to Robert Tilliol in 1307; the lower courses of masonry right round the building, including the Gatehouse, date from that time and the fifteenth-century east range retains original tunnel vaulting throughout its whole length – a rare survival. The Great Hall was over the southern end. The Tilliols died out in 1435, after which Scaleby passed to the Musgraves. They altered the Gatehouse and added the multi-angular tower in the early sixteenth century. The north part is now a ruin and today the habitable bit of the castle is the southern half, which was rebuilt by Sir Edward Musgrave in 1596 and altered later. Some early seventeenth-century windows survive, particularly on the courtyard elevation, and there are massive buttresses of indeterminate date, but the south-west corner, which contains the Drawing Room, was remodelled, possibly to Thomas Rickman's design, in 1838. The Gilpins inherited from the Musgraves in the seventeenth century and Scaleby is now the seat of the 8th Lord Henley, whose father bought the castle in 1952 and restored it.

Sizergh Castle.

Sizergh Castle
NT; 33; 2 miles S of Kendal on A6

This ancient seat of the Stricklands consists of a pele tower dating from c.1340, a fifteenth-century Great Hall, remodelled in the eighteenth century, an Elizabethan central block adjoining the Great Hall, and two long Elizabethan wings flanking the forecourt (one containing the private apartments and the other a Catholic chapel). The rubble stonework is harled and was once whitewashed, as at nearby Levens Hall (q.v.). The central block was partly remodelled c.1770 to the design of John Hird of Cartmel. George Webster made some minor alterations in the early nineteenth century, and various restoration works were carried out earlier this century, including the castellated front porch by John Curwen and the unfortunate terrace on the garden front.

The interior is of interest largely for its sixteenth-century Renaissance woodwork, which is of a quality unequalled anywhere in England. It includes a carved screen, dated 1555, in the Entrance Hall and no fewer than five carved oak chimneypieces, dating from between 1563 and 1575. There is also much panelling of different designs and dates, including some early linenfold, though the especially fine inlaid panelling from the Inlaid Chamber is now in the Victoria and Albert Museum in London. The ceilings are mainly of the sixteenth-century type with thin timber ribs, except in the Inlaid Chamber, where there is an elaborate stucco ceiling with pendants, ribs and floral motifs of c.1575.

The Strickland family history is well documented. They were frequently knighted in the Middle Ages,

played their part in sporadic northern warfare against the Scots, and every generation from 1258 until the late seventeenth century (when they were excluded on religious grounds) sat in Parliament as Member for Westmorland. The family remained Catholic after the Reformation and, as recusants, Royalists and Jacobites, suffered grievously from compositions and sequestrations. The castle contains an interesting collection of Jacobite portraits and relics, as well as family portraits and furniture of many dates. It now belongs to the National Trust and is regularly open to the public.

Swarthmoor Hall
See Ulverston.

Temple Sowerby
NT; 34; 6 miles E of Penrith on A66

ACORN BANK (NT) dates from c.1600 and is a three-storeyed block of reddish sandstone. It was extended by John Dalson in 1656 and altered in the eighteenth century, when the nine-bay south front was totally refaced and given a central doorway with segmental pediment and lower projecting wings with Venetian windows. Inside the house there are some fireplaces, ceilings and two panelled rooms of c.1600, but the best features date from the mid-eighteenth century, including decorative plasterwork and handsome chimneypieces.

The property now belongs to the National Trust; the house, however, is not open to the public, as it is let as a Cheshire Home, though the nicely planted gardens are accessible.

Ulverston

35; 8 miles NE of Barrow-in-Furness on A59

The most eccentric feature to strike the visitor approaching Ulverston for the first time is a full-scale copy of Eddystone Lighthouse on the hill above the town. This is a Victorian monument to Sir John Barrow, a local lad who became Admiralty cartographer in the early nineteenth century. Ulverston is otherwise an unassuming little market town with a friendly character. The main street is cobbled and widens at one end to form the MARKET PLACE with the Market Cross in the centre and a handsome Grecian bank by the Websters of Kendal as the backdrop. The equally handsome SAVINGS BANK, with a clock cupola whose bell loudly chimes the hours, marks the other end of the street. ST MARY'S, the parish church, is away from the centre and quite difficult to find; it dates from the 1540s (apart from the Norman south doorway) and is the characteristic north-country Perpendicular, with a tower, clerestory and timber hammerbeam roof. It was extensively restored and reconstructed by E.G. Paley in 1864–6 – the chancel is almost entirely his. The church contains a number of unusual odds and ends, including stained glass after Reynolds's at New College, Oxford; it was made for the east window but in the nineteenth century was moved to the back of the church. This and the former altarpiece, a deposition by Ghizardi, were given to the church by Colonel Braddyll of Conishead Priory, who also restored the sixteenth-century monument to William Sandys. The effigies are now almost entirely early nineteenth-century and of Coade stone, which explains the good quality of the carving noted by Pevsner. For those interested in sculpture, the little marble nymphet by Pasquale Romanelli should not be missed; she is kneeling on a revolving (of course) pedestal and has an unbearably soapy expression. Ulverston's other Anglican church, HOLY TRINITY by Salvin, has been converted into a sports club and contains squash courts and a Jacuzzi bath.

In the locality are two interesting country houses: Conishead Priory and Swarthmoor Hall. CONISHEAD PRIORY occupies the site of an Augustinian priory (suppressed in 1535) and is now owned by the Manjushri Institute, a college of Tibetan Buddhist studies. It was built between 1821 and 1836 by Colonel Thomas Richmond-Gale-Braddyll to the design of Philip Wyatt, the brilliant but feckless youngest son of James Wyatt. Wyatt's design is an ambitious exercise in Perpendicular Gothic, with turrets, battlements, spires, oriels and lofty plaster vaults. Wyatt was dismissed while work was in progress and Colonel Braddyll turned instead to George Webster, who designed a bridge in the park and a lodge, *c.*1834–40. There is much old woodwork from Samlesbury Hall in Lancashire (*q.v.*), brought here in 1834. This is chiefly arranged in the Oak Room, a typical creation of its time.

SWARTHMOOR HALL is a late seventeenth-century house, rough-cast and with mullion windows. It was once the home of George Fox and the northern headquarters of the Quaker Movement, the Quaker connection having developed from the marriage of Judge Thomas Fell, Chancellor of the Duchy of Lancaster, to Margaret Askew, who was a leading follower of the Movement and after Fell's death married George Fox, its founder.

This is the type of house that provided the inspiration for the late nineteenth-century Lake District Tudor-bethan style. Inside, there is some fine panelling, part original and part replacement, dating from the period between the First and Second World Wars when the house was rescued from near ruin. The staircase is especially worth noting.

The Market Place, Ulverston.

Warwick Bridge

36; 8 miles E of Carlisle off A69

In the eighteenth century Warwick Bridge was a nest of Popish recusancy of a type more usually encountered in Lancashire than in Cumberland. WARWICK HALL and HOLME EDEN HALL stand in little parks on either side of the River Eden. The latter is a splendid Tudorbethan mansion of pink sandstone with an ornamental skyline bristling with chimneys and finials. It was designed in 1837 for Peter Dixon by John Dobson of Newcastle. It has been occupied for most of this century by Benedictine nuns. Warwick Hall belonged to the recusant and Jacobite Warwicks, and Jane Warwick entertained Bonnie Prince Charlie there in 1745. The present house was built in 1930 by Colonel R.G.G.J. Elwes (a privy chamberlain to Pope Pius XII) to the design of his brother Guy Elwes, and is a distinguished twentieth-century Neo-Georgian design of pink sandstone ashlar, with a copper domed cupola in the centre of the roof. Inside, the staircase is the finest feature, circular in plan with ritzy decoration. The neo-classical stables and entrance lodge date from 1828 and survive from the previous house, which was burnt down in 1930.

The little Catholic chapel of OUR LADY AND ST WILFRED in the centre of the village was designed in 1841 by A.W.N. Pugin for Henry Howard of Corby (*q.v.*). Although small, with a bellcote rather than a tower and without aisles, it is one of the finest surviving examples of Pugin's English parish churches. It is an exercise in archaeologically correct Gothic – stone with a slated roof, alternating lancets and two-light windows with Decorated tracery. The stepped buttresses at the sides and corners help to establish a feeling of solidity. The interior remains almost exactly as designed by Pugin, its original dark decoration miraculously intact. The nave has an open timber roof painted with *fleurons* and inscriptions. The rood-screen is still *in situ*, with a large cross, part-coloured and -gilded statues of Our Lady and St Wilfred, and six brass candlesticks on top. The chancel retains its original stencilled decoration, obviously by the same artist as that at Cheadle in Staffordshire (*q.v.*). The panelled ceiling is covered with crosses and IHS monograms, while the walls have fleurs-de-lis and M monograms. Twin circular brass coronas, each carrying six candles, hang from the roof. The altar has a gilded reredos and six candlesticks, all designed by Pugin, as was much of the church plate, including a holy-water bucket and sprinkler. In the north wall of the chancel, in an arched recess based on a medieval Easter sepulchre, is the tomb of the founder; he died the year after the church was built.

Wetheral

37; 4 miles SE of Carlisle on B6263

This village, near Carlisle, is full of prosperous Victorian villas and has a small triangular green. The main reason for visiting Wetheral is HOLY TRINITY, the parish church. It is well sited above the River Eden, opposite Corby Castle (*q.v.*), and is early sixteenth-century, of pink stone, but drastically restored in the 1870s and 1880s. The great thrill of the place is the HOWARD MAUSOLEUM,

private and solemn, added to one side of the chancel in 1791 in the most fragile and spidery Gothick, with funny little pinnacles on top and thin cast-iron tracery in the windows. The interior has a plaster vault painted to look like stone. The architect is not known, but may have been Henry Howard himself, who had antiquarian and historical tastes. He built the chapel to house the memorial to his wife, the Hon. Maria Howard, who died in childbirth in 1789 at the age of twenty-three. It is of white marble by Joseph Nollekens, whose monumental masterpiece it is, and it is one of the most important pieces of neo-classical sculpture in England. (Nolleken's contract, still preserved in the Howard of Corby archives, is dated 23 March 1790.) At the other end of the chapel is a life-size plaster cast of a kneeling woman. Who or what is it?

Wharton Hall

38; 1 mile S of Kirkby Stephen on A685

Wharton Hall was the seat of the Wharton family from the Middle Ages down to the early eighteenth century. The main block, consisting of a Hall with two cross-wings, was built in the late fourteenth or early fifteenth century. A larger Great Hall, 68 by 27 feet with a kitchen beyond, was added c.1540 to the south-east of an earlier house on the spot by Thomas, 1st Lord Wharton. The Gatehouse opposite and the north-west range were added c.1559. The original block fell into ruin in the course of the eighteenth century but the oldest part was restored in 1785 by the 1st Earl of Lonsdale for use as a shooting lodge and this part alone still remains roofed. The stone buildings surround an irregular courtyard and form an impressive ensemble, with gables and sixteenth-century mullion-and-transom windows. The sixteenth-century Great Hall is unfortunately a complete ruin, but the shell of the great kitchen alongside survives; it is a very lofty and impressive apartment with a vaulted undercroft and two huge fireplaces. The Gatehouse has a segmental archway and is embellished with a panel bearing the quartered arms of Wharton and the motto 'PLEASUR IN ACTS DARMYS'. As these ruins suggest, the Whartons came to a spectacularly bad end. Philip, 5th Lord Wharton, was created a Marquess for strenuously supporting William of Orange; his son, who was William's godson, was advanced to a dukedom in 1718, but died in Spain in 1731 at the age of thirty-two – a ruined spendthrift, rebel and outlaw, having adopted the Jacobite cause and the Catholic religion. Alexander Pope portrayed his character in the lines:

> *Wharton the scorn and wonder of our days,*
> *Whose ruling passion was the lust of praise,*
> *Born with whate'er could win it from the wise,*
> *Women or fools must like him, or he dies.*

His confiscated estates were bought by Robert Lowther of Maulds Meaburn and descended to the Earls of Lonsdale, like much else in Westmorland. The family portraits by Van Dyck were acquired by Sir Robert Walpole and passed, with the rest of his collection, to Catherine the Great of Russia. It is poignant in these sad ruins to imagine them amid the gilding of St Petersburg.

1 *Chester Cathedral, Cheshire.*

2 *Crewe Hall, Cheshire.*

3 *Dalemain, Cumbria.*

4 *The church of St Mary, Wreay, Cumbria.*

8 *St Mary and All Saints, Chesterfield, Derbyshire.*

9 *Kedlestone Hall, Derbyshire.*

10 *The birdcage, Melbourne Hall, Derbyshire.*

11 *Renishaw Hall, Derbyshire.*

12 *Sudbury Hall, Derbyshire.*

13 *Wirksworth, Derbyshire.*

14 *Durham Cathedral.*

15 *The church of St John the Evangelist, Escomb, Durham.*

16 *Gibside Chapel, Durham.*

17 *Berrington Hall, Hereford and Worcester.*

18 *Croft Castle, Hereford and Worcester.*

19 *Eastnor Castle, Hereford and Worcester.*

20 *Hanbury Hall, Hereford and Worcester.*

Whitehaven

39; 8 miles S of Workington on A595

In Whitehaven you feel as if you are in the most remote town in England, stranded between the mountains of the Lake District and the Irish Sea. The hills of south-west Scotland are visible from the harbour on a clear day. The forlorn atmosphere is due to the decline of the town's economic base. Once a thriving port – an entrepôt for the Virginian tobacco trade – and a centre of coal-mining, it is now largely derelict, dependent on one remaining coal-mine (the workings of which stretch far under the sea) and the British Atomic Energy Authority.

Whitehaven is a planned town, the first in England after the Middle Ages; it was founded by Sir John Lowther in 1690 and finished by James Lowther, 1st Earl of Lonsdale, in the mid-eighteenth century. (The latter was the most notorious member of his family – 'Wicked Jimmy' or 'the imperious and morose tyrant of Cumberland and Westmorland'.) The estate was bought in the early seventeenth century by Sir Christopher Lowther, who died in 1644. Sir John, as well as laying out the town, also built a house for himself in 1694, called Flatt Hall. Wicked Jimmy remodelled and regularised this in 1766–9 and renamed it WHITEHAVEN CASTLE. His architect was no less than Robert Adam, and Whitehaven Castle, with its neat stone battlements, ashlar façades, central canted bay windows and square corner towers, is one of the earliest of Adam's castle houses. It survives, but has been somewhat spoilt by its present use as a hospital. The exterior is festooned with fire escapes and nothing much is left of the interior decoration with the apses and ovals and delicately coloured plasterwork shown on Adam's drawings (preserved in Sir John Soane's Museum in London). Although only a shadow of its original glory remains, it is still historically important and antedates Adam's Scottish houses in this style.

Most of the interesting street architecture in Whitehaven is early to mid-Georgian. Much restoration work has been carried out recently under a Town Scheme organised by the Historic Buildings Council, though the grain of the town has been disturbed by the large new Co-op, which spoils several of the best streets, and the burning of the central parish CHURCH OF ST NICHOLAS. Looking at the pathetic ruins of the latter in a half-demolished square, it is hard to believe that this is the centrepiece and culmination of Sir John Lowther's grid-plan. It could be redeemed by demolishing all the church ruins except the tower, planting proper trees in the square and rebuilding the demolished houses along the sides. Part of the pleasure for the visitor to Whitehaven consists of improving the place in the mind's eye, as with some care it could still be a very handsome town.

The main axis is Lowther Street, which runs from the castle to the harbour. It is long and narrow, lined for the main part with decent, understated buildings interspersed with the odd stronger accent, notably three classical banks. The TRUSTEE SAVINGS BANK of 1833 is especially handsome, with a Doric portico and a stucco façade painted cream and coffee with the Royal Arms picked out in colours. To the north-east, up a steep hill on axis with the central square, is ST JAMES'S CHURCH. Its immediate surroundings have been ruined by council housing of the dreariest description, but the church itself is a fine building and the only survivor of the three classical churches that graced eighteenth-century Whitehaven. It was built in 1752–3, is faced in red sandstone ashlar and has a square west tower with obelisk pinnacles. It boasted the finest Georgian church interior in the county, but recently this has been grievously spoilt by a series of ill-considered suburban 'improvements' aimed at introducing the comforts of a bungalow front room to the House of God. The floor is covered with wall-to-wall green carpet. The pulpit has been mutilated and taken off its tall columnar pedestal, the eighteenth-century altar rails removed and a corny central altar on a circular dais installed in the chancel. The walls have been painted avocado green and the chandeliers have crinkly yellow-glass shades. The pulpit pedestal is now used for 'flower arrangements' and the other discarded eighteenth-century fittings can be seen in the south gallery. Despite all this misguided effort, the beauties of the original architecture can just be discerned: the ceiling, with its lively stucco roundels of New Testament subjects; the two tiers of well-proportioned Tuscan and Ionic columns supporting galleries on three sides; and the apse, which was embellished in 1871 when the important altarpiece painted by Procaccini was given to the church by the Lowthers.

Parallel to Lowther Street runs Duke Street, with the TOWN HALL at the south-east end on the site of the late seventeenth-century Mansion House and still incorporating part of its masonry, though it was largely reconstructed in 1851 by William Barnes. Nearby is SOMERSET HOUSE, recently restored by the Council and a nice piece of Batty Langley Gothick. The best-preserved Georgian streets lie to the west, and much careful repair and rehabilitation work has been carried out in them in the last few years. Scotch Street, Irish Street and Queen Street all have good early eighteenth-century houses with original doorcases. The long, narrow Market Place along the south-west side of the town centre is best when full of market stalls and Salvation Army bands; on other days it seems rather forlorn and melancholy.

The most exciting part of Whitehaven is the HARBOUR, with its impressive stone quays. The oldest part dates from 1687 but there were extensions and alterations in 1741 and again from 1824–39, the latter work being by John Rennie. There are two LIGHTHOUSES, one of them also early nineteenth-century by Rennie, but the small circular one is of 1730. On the steep hill to the south-west are the buildings of the WELLINGTON PIT, with an elaborate chimney of 1840 said to be copied on a larger scale from one of Lord Lonsdale's dining-room candlesticks. These days there are only one or two small fishing boats in the harbour, but with its salty mud smells, the clutter of nautical junk lying around on the quays, and the cries of seagulls, it still has a convincing seafaring atmosphere: it is easy to imagine the day when Paul Jones, a Whitehaven boy, came back during the American War of Independence and fired the ships in the harbour, earning a reputation as a pirate – or as the glorious founder of the United States Navy, according to your point of view.

The last – and best – view of Whitehaven is to be enjoyed from the main road to Workington, which climbs up and sweeps round the steep hill to the north-east of the town, giving an astonishing aerial view of the grid-planned centre and quays.

Wigton
40; 14 miles SW of Carlisle on A596
Set on a wide plain with views south to Skiddaw and north to the hills of Dumfriesshire, Wigton could be a very attractive small market town if only the heavy traffic could be got out of the main street and if its buildings were more intelligently cared for. Still, it is a rare pleasure in England to find a small country town of character, free from all signs of modernisation or gentrification.

In plan Wigton is T-shaped, and at the main cross-roads there is something worth travelling a long way to see. This is the FOUNTAIN erected in 1872 as a memorial to his wife by George Moore of Whitehall, a millionaire lace manufacturer and High Sheriff of Cumberland. It was designed by J.T. Knowles (architect of the Grosvenor Hotel at London's Victoria Station) and is of pink granite with a spire 20 feet high. On top is a gilded cross and the granite is carved with naturalistic leaf decoration, also gilded. Round the plinth are four beautiful bronze reliefs by Thomas Woolner, showing various acts of charity: Clothing the Naked, Teaching the Ignorant, Consoling the Afflicted and Feeding the Hungry. It is a princely job, worthy of St Petersburg, the gilding still kept brightly burnished by an endowment provided by the founder. Until recent years the granite was also given a weekly wash by the town's fire engine.

The general architecture of the streets is decently Georgian with nice doorcases and fanlights. ST MARY'S, the parish church, is also Georgian, having been rebuilt in 1788 by Nixons and Parkin, the masons, and Pattinson and Holmes, the joiners. It is of red sandstone with a square-cut west tower and round-arched windows. The graveyard has unfortunately been ruined and the excellent eighteenth-century headstones used as paving – a disgrace. The interior of the church has two tiers of Tuscan columns supporting galleries on three sides. For some reason the central arch of the Venetian window over the altar has been partly filled with hardboard, which rather spoils the effect – as does the peculiar 1950s' colour scheme. There is an eighteenth-century pulpit of carved oak and a very fierce wooden-eagle lectern of indeterminate date. The supposedly sixteenth-century Flemish retable over a side-altar looks like the front of an old chest.

The Catholic CHURCH OF ST CUTHBERT at the other end of the town was designed by Ignatius Bonomi and paid for by Miss Elizabeth Aglionby of Wigton Hall. It is red sandstone Gothic and quite ambitious for an early nineteenth-century Catholic chapel in a small country town outside Lancashire. It forms a nice group with the PRESBYTERY and SCHOOL. The most prominent landmark of Wigton is to the south of the town. This is the wild clock tower added to his house HIGHMOOR in 1887 by William Banks, a prosperous draper who made his fortune in the export trade. It is 136 feet high, and the florid clock on top is curiously lop-sided – as if a housemaid dusting has not put it back in the right place. It originally contained one large bell, weighing 8 tons 16 cwt, which could be heard 12 miles away, as well as a carillon of ten bells cast by Severn van Aerscholt of Louvain. This tower is best admired from a distance, as its immediate setting has been spoilt by a development of council houses. Again and again in English towns it seems to be the public authorities, who ought to know better, who do the most visual damage.

WIGTON HALL, at the far end of West Street, appears to be an early nineteenth-century Gothic design of symmetrical character. In fact it is an older house of different dates, with a heterogeneous collection of rooms that bear no relationship to the symmetrical stone front stuck on by the Rev. Richard Matthews *c.*1830.

Windermere
41; 8 miles NW of Kendal on A591
'The first house that was built in the Lake District for the sake of the beauty of the country was the work of a Mr English, who had travelled in Italy,' wrote Wordsworth of BELLE ISLE, the late eighteenth-century house set on an island in the middle of Lake Windermere. It was sold unfinished in 1781 to Isabella Curwen of Workington Hall (*q.v.*), who had married her cousin John Christian. The Christian-Curwens completed Belle Isle as a villa for summer use, thereby setting an important new trend that was to transform the banks of Windermere, hitherto sparsely inhabited by a few farmers, into a desirable place of residence for men of means and taste. As a result, the surroundings of the lake are today an almost continuous piece of late eighteenth- and nineteenth-century Picturesque design and planting, with villas and *cottages ornés* in beautifully landscaped grounds.

As the starting point of this whole movement in the history of English architecture and landscape design, Belle Isle is therefore of great importance. It is no exaggeration to say that, despite its small size, it is one of the key monuments of Picturesque neo-classicism in Europe; it is a reduced version of the Pantheon, fifty-four feet in diameter and unique as the first cylindrical mansion in England. It was designed in 1774 by John Plaw, an accomplished but not a prolific architect, who designed a number of interesting and unusual buildings, including the church of St Mary in Paddington Green.

The romantic landscaping of the grounds of Belle Isle, which so perfectly complements the architecture of the house and makes the whole island one of the most attractive features of Lake Windermere, was carried out in 1786 by the Christian-Curwens to the design of Thomas White of Retford, a follower of Capability Brown; his signed plan still hangs in the house. As well as landscaping the island itself, they also acquired and planted the HAWKSHEAD COMMONS on the far side of the lake, using over 3 million trees, including a good number of larches, which were then a recent introduction to England and much disliked by Wordsworth, who had an irrational prejudice against them. Since that time many exotic trees have been added to the original planting on the island.

The principal exterior feature of the house is an Ionic portico, ingeniously incorporating the steps to the front door so that a visitor could climb them under cover – an important consideration in an area deemed the second wettest part of England. In niches flanking the door are white marble statues of Autumn and Spring by the early nineteenth-century Italian sculptor Rinaldo Rinaldi. The ceiling of the portico is embellished with the Curwen arms in coloured plaster, and the Ionic capitals of the columns which look like stone are in fact of carved wood – one of those eighteenth-century architectural 'frauds' that were to evoke strong disapproval in the breasts of moralising Victorian critics such as Ruskin. This device was made necessary by the somewhat coarse quality of the local stone, which did not lend itself readily to fine carving.

Inside, the rooms are small but charming. In the centre is the staircase, which rises the full height of the house and is lit by the cupola on top of the dome (which also conceals the chimneystacks by a clever arrangement of the flues). Both the Drawing and Dining Rooms have neo-classical chimneypieces and plasterwork, the former decorated with musical instruments and urns, the latter with foxes' masks. The elegant cast-iron grates were made by Wilkinson. The paintings include a pair of De Loutherburg views of Windermere, with Belle Isle, in calm and stormy weather, and some of the furniture is by Gillow.

Witherslack

42; 6 miles NE of Grange-over-Sands off A590

The surrounding landscape with its delicate, grey stony hills and dense woods of hazel, yew and little oak trees can, in certain lights and seasons, recall the beauties of Umbria. The view from the graveyard across the Winster Valley in early spring, when the grass is white with snowdrops, is my favourite. ST PAUL'S CHURCH was built in 1669 under the will of John Barwick, Dean of St Paul's, and his brother, physician to Charles II – a gift to their native village from two local lads who had had successful careers. There is a short west tower and the nave has stone-mullioned windows with round-arched heads. The outside walls are covered with roughcast and were originally sprucely whitewashed, although now they are grey and weathered. The interior is light and tranquil. The plain coved plaster ceiling and the Ionic columns framing the chancel were inserted in 1768 by John Hird of Cartmel, a local architect who also worked at Sizergh Castle (*q.v.*). The windows are largely clear-glazed, apart from some good seventeenth-century heraldic roundels attributed to Henry Gyles. There are also hatchments with the arms of John Barwick impaling those of St Paul's Cathedral. The pulpit is original, with carved panels, but was cut down in 1880; it gives the cue for the benches of the same date. On a windowsill near the chancel end is a monument to Geoffrey Stanley, who died young in 1871; it shows a white marble baby clutching a poppy. Not signed, it can be attributed to Sir Edgar Boehm and is very similar to that to Lady Elizabeth Howard at Lanercost (*q.v.*).

Workington

43; 8 miles W of Cockermouth on A66

Workington is a depressingly run-down industrial town, almost a byword for unemployment. It was one of the west-coast ports that thrived on American and West Indian trade in the eighteenth century, and was a centre of coal-mining and iron-founding. But it has now been in decline for over a century and the last coal-mine closed in 1973. It is worth visiting, however, for two important buildings: Workington Hall – a ruin, but one of Cumberland's most important and historic houses – and the remarkably impressive neo-classical St John's Church.

The ruined shell of WORKINGTON HALL, the large, castellated house of the Curwens, remains on the outskirts of the town. The east range, poised at the edge of a precipice above the River Derwent, represents the fourteenth-century house, with vaulted basements surviving at its northern end and a pele tower at its southern. The Elizabethan north and south ranges joined the medieval range to the medieval Gatehouse and so completed the quadrangle. The house was entirely remodelled from 1782 onwards by John Carr of York for John and Isabella Christian-Curwen, new furniture being supplied by Gillow. But, alas, nothing much survives of their interior decoration. The suite of Dining Room, Saloon and high Library along the east front formed the finest sequence of neo-classical rooms in Cumberland, with excellent plasterwork, marble chimneypieces and painted *grisaille* decoration. They were allowed to fall into a desperate state of decay by the local authority, to whom the Curwen family were unwise enough to give their house when they retreated to Belle Isle (*q.v.*). Although £30,000 was spent on making the Hall a 'safe ruin' in 1970 (with the advice of the Royal Commission on Historical Monuments, which considered the ancient masonry more important than the Carr interior) the result is depressing in the extreme.

Belle Isle, Windermere.

The Curwens were the oldest family in Cumberland, producing many Knights and Sheriffs in the Middle Ages. Sir Henry Curwen gave refuge to Mary Queen of Scots in 1568 after she fled across the Solway. John Christian-Curwen, Whig MP for Carlisle, who married the heiress Isabella Curwen in 1782, was one of the leading improvers of the Agricultural Revolution. He held his own annual agricultural show in Workington, built a castellated model farm at the Schoose – fragments of which still survive in a caravan site – and did much to stimulate local industry and prosperity, now all dissipated.

The first impression of ST JOHN'S CHURCH is of a bigger and better version of Inigo Jones's St Paul's, Covent Garden. This is not misleading, for Thomas Hardwick, the architect of St John's, had restored St Paul's after a fire in 1795 and then applied what he had learnt when he came to design this church in 1823. It is larger than the London church, built of stone with a short clock tower added on top of the portico in 1846. The large Tuscan portico is especially impressive. The interior comes as a surprise, for much of it is by Sir Ninian Comper. It is formed of one generous rectangular space with the original galleries decorated with triglyphs along the sides and, at the west end, supported on slim, reeded iron columns. The needlework panel depicting the Royal Arms on the west gallery dates from 1846 and was made by one of the sisters of the rector of the day, but nearly everything else is twentieth century. In 1904 the interior had been turned back to front, and the altar placed at the west end, spoiling the church's character. Sir Ninian Comper was employed in 1930–1 by the Rev. J.R. Croft to restore and embellish the interior as a deliberate gesture in the depths of the inter-war depression – with the splendid results we see today. The altar was put back in its proper place and provided with an impressive classical *baldacchino* with Corinthian columns, painted dark blue with masses of gold and, hanging within, a medallion of St John the Baptist surrounded by golden rays. Most of the other furnishings are also by Comper, including the octagonal font cover with a spire, painted dark blue and gold, the oak lectern and altar rails, the base and steps of the pulpit, the light-fittings and the organ case. Comper also designed the attractive ceiling plasterwork in an Arts and Crafts classical manner, with a rib pattern and pretty leaf motifs painted pale blue and white. It is altogether an amazing effort. In many ways, the interior of St John's is more successful than Comper's remodelling of the interior of the Grosvenor Chapel in Mayfair, and it deserves to be far better known than it is.

Wreay
44; 8 miles SE of Carlisle off A6 [4]
The CHURCH OF ST MARY, consecrated in 1842, is an extraordinary apparition – a small Roman basilica stranded on a village green and full of mind-blowing church furnishings, partly inspired by fossils from the coal-measures. It was built and designed by Miss Sara Losh, the daughter of a rich local landowner and industrialist, as a memorial to her sister Katherine, who died young in 1835. The Losh graves in the churchyard are strikingly

odd and personal, too: they comprise naturalistic boulder-like slabs carved with shells, branches and palm trees. In one corner a stone pine-cone commemorates some pine-seeds sent to Sara Losh by a friend serving in the Army in India. The interior of the cyclopean mausoleum to Katherine is effectively lit from two small side windows through which light shines directly on to her 'pallid image' in white marble. This seated statue by Dunbar was based on a sketch made by Sara while on holiday near Naples. In front of the mausoleum is a full-scale variation on the Bewcastle Cross commemorating the Losh parents. The architecture of the church shows a remarkable range of sources, illustrating the breadth of Sara's learning and intended to recall her and her sister's travels together. Much of the decoration is symbolic, especially the weird sculpture by a local boy, William Hindson. The building is quite small, and solidly constructed of fine ashlar stone, with an apse. The west gable is decorated with stepped blank arches, and the west door and west windows have plain moulded surrounds carved with stylised butterflies, poppies, wheatears and monkey-puzzle twigs – like specimens in a Victorian album. Even odder, but equally enjoyable, are the gargoyles representing tortoises, snakes and an alligator. The inside of the church comprises a small rectangular nave, which is relatively plain, and the semi-circular apse surrounded by Romanesque columns, with a continuous clerestory of narrow round arches above. The windows are glazed with a mosaic of fragments of medieval glass. The altar is of green marble supported on brass eagles; the pulpit and lecterns are of black bog-oak; the Byzantine font of alabaster was carved by Sara herself.

One is often tempted to call a building unique – in this instance no other word will do. What on earth did the villagers, let alone the ecclesiastical authorities, think of it when it was opened? They are very proud of it now, and speak of 'Miss Sara' as if she were still alive.

Yanwath Hall
45; 2 miles S of Penrith off A6
This house, which is one of the best surviving medieval fortified houses in the country, forms three sides of a courtyard and comprises a pele tower built by John de Sutton in 1322, a hall range and east wing built by the Threlkeld family in the fifteenth century, and an early seventeenth-century north wing built by the Dudleys, who inherited the property from the Threlkelds in the reign of Henry VIII. The pele tower has battlements and Elizabethan mullion-and-transom windows. The Hall was sub-divided internally in the sixteenth century, but retains its original roof, still visible upstairs, with king-posts and curved and moulded braces, as well as a projecting bay window at the dais end. Other parts of the house have interesting sixteenth-century features, including several fireplaces and some modest plasterwork. Yanwath was bought by Sir John Lowther in 1654 from Christopher Dudley and still forms part of the Lowther estate. Its excellent state of preservation and the absence of eighteenth- or nineteenth-century alterations is due to its having been a farmhouse for so long.

Derbyshire

A Victorian lady traveller writing home to a friend described Switzerland as 'the Derbyshire of Europe'. With English prejudice, it is possible to prefer the austerely elegant landscape of peak and dale in Derbyshire to the overstated scenery of Switzerland. The architecture is certainly better, thanks to centuries of prosperity derived from the abundant mineral wealth of the county – lead, copper, coal, fluorspar and lime. The Crescent in Buxton, for instance, is reputed to have been paid for by the 5th Duke of Devonshire out of a single year's revenue from copper. Lead was mined in the county by the Romans and for centuries Wirksworth was the centre of the English lead-mining industry. Today, the most important quarrying and mining activity in the county is the limestone-working near Buxton (which produces one of the main ingredients for cement and concrete), and the coal-mining all down the Erewash Valley on the eastern fringe of the county next to Nottinghamshire – from Eckington in the north to Swadlincote in the south. Industry in Derbyshire is not restricted to mining, however. The county was one of the birthplaces of the Industrial Revolution in the seventeenth and eighteenth centuries, with pioneer iron works at Renishaw, cotton mills at Glossop, Cromford and Belper; silk mills at Derby and Long Eaton; porcelain manufacture at Pinxton and Derby. From the 1830s and 1840s, the railways spread throughout the county, the Midland Railway establishing its headquarters and locomotive works at Derby, and heavier industry followed. Many of the magnificently engineered lines were closed, alas, in the 1960s, but Derby continues to be the centre of British Rail's locomotive design and manufacture. Today, the county town and its sprawling suburbs make up the county's chief centre of modern industry, for, though cotton is still spun at Cromford and Belper, those towns have something of the character of living museums of industrial archaeology, while places like Glossop are now entirely commuter towns. Derbyshire is dotted with magnificent industrial relics: breathtaking railway viaducts, pretty railway stations like that at South Wingfield, eighteenth-century mills like Arkwright's at Cromford, handsome old limekilns, grand classical warehouses – for many visitors these are among the most interesting and memorable sights of the county. Only the colliery villages of mean brick houses east of the A61 are actively ugly.

While not being in the absolute first league for important church architecture, Derbyshire nevertheless possesses many fine old churches of all periods. There are important and well-preserved Saxon sculptural fragments at Eyam and Wirksworth – a cross and a coffin cover respectively – and an atmospheric little crypt at Repton. At Melbourne there is an ambitious Norman church, the interior of which substantially survives, and there is more fragmentary Norman work elsewhere. There are major medieval town churches at Ashbourne, Chesterfield, Tideswell and Wirksworth, all with transepts and dominant towers or spires. Many a village church has good fittings and an array of family monuments and hatchments. At Foremark there is a rare seventeenth-century Gothic Survival church, complete with all its fittings; and Gibbs's All Saints, Derby (now the cathedral), is a first-rate eighteenth-century town church. There are many nineteenth-century churches in Derbyshire, but none of them is of the quality of the best in the neighbouring counties of Cheshire, Staffordshire and Nottinghamshire – although the Duke of Devonshire's estate church at Edensor, a *chef-d'œuvre* by Sir George Gilbert Scott, is impressive with its high stone spire.

There are several good towns in Derbyshire, but these do not include Derby itself, the centre of which has been ruined by 'planning' since the early 1960s. Ashbourne, however, is an excellent old market town with a perfect main street and cobbled market place. Wirksworth, too, is a good-looking town with a lot of atmosphere. There are no fewer than three spa towns in the county: Bakewell, Buxton and Matlock. All three have much to offer, but Buxton is the best, with impressive stone buildings and parks set amidst dramatic moorland scenery. Chesterfield, though surrounded by dingy industrial suburbs, still has a visually satisfying centre with a large cobbled market place recently saved from unnecessary redevelopment. Cromford, Belper and Glossop, all children of the Industrial Revolution, are good examples of planned eighteenth- and early nineteenth-century manufacturing towns that would benefit from much more care and attention than they have received in recent years. The villages of Derbyshire are also worth looking at, whether haphazard assemblages of old vernacular buildings like Eyam, or immaculate unified estate establishments like Edensor or the Fitzherberts' at Tissington, which has the unique quality of being set in the middle of a park and approached by a gatelodge and lime avenue. Many of these places are the settings for ancient rituals and customs, just like the old hill towns and villages of central Italy. But how many English people who have seen the Palio in Siena or the race of the Ceri at Gubbio have also witnessed the Shrove Tuesday football match at Ashbourne, or the Ascension Day well-dressing at Tissington?

The supreme architectural glory of Derbyshire, however, is its country houses. Perhaps only Northamptonshire, or possibly Wiltshire, can compare with it in concentration of first-rank houses. Chatsworth, Haddon, Hardwick, Kedleston are *the* exemplars of their age and style, and would have to appear in any general history of English architecture – but they are only the tip of the iceberg, and houses like Bolsover, Calke Abbey, Locko, Longford, Melbourne, Radburne, Renishaw or Sudbury are hardly less distinguished.

The finest of all, and indeed the greatest of all English country houses, is Chatsworth. It is not just the architecture of the house that inspires awe, but the incomparable collections, gardens, park, estate, and the way it is all maintained and managed today. No matter from which direction you approach, as you draw near to Chatsworth you feel you are entering 'Alternative Civilization plc'. In their different ways, the others are equally moving. Haddon is the dream medieval castle or manor house, clinging to the side of a wooded hill as if glimpsed in the background of a tapestry. It is a house *en grisaille*, with its grey stone walls, silvery sheen of old timber beams and panelling, and faded medieval wall paintings in the Chapel. It owes much to the miraculous restoration carried out in the first half of this century by the 9th Duke of Rutland, who brought it all gently back to life after the house had lain empty for 200 years.

Both Chatsworth and Haddon can show the work of different centuries and different hands; Hardwick and Kedleston, on the other hand, are each the supreme unified masterpieces of their age, complete with their original furnishings and pictures. Hardwick is unrivalled for its Elizabethan architecture, and its tapestries, needlework, marquetry, coloured plasterwork and carvings of local 'marbles' all convey the serene yet vigorous poetry of the Renaissance in its belated northern flowering. Kedleston, meanwhile, is the most assured and sophisticated of neo-classical palaces, with Adam plasterwork, superb alabaster columns, Grand Tour paintings, casts after famous antique statues, and furniture by leading cabinetmakers; it makes the products of almost any other period or place seem barbaric by comparison.

So much for the architecture – and that would be worth a pilgrimage even if it were embedded in the suburbs of London. But what makes Derbyshire more worth visiting than almost anywhere else in England is the landscape setting. The county is three times as long as it is wide, and divided into five geological strips by three rivers flowing in L-formations from north to south – the Dove, Derwent and Erewash. This last runs through the coal measures and is the part of the county which in conventional terms is the most 'spoilt' – covered with collieries, the M1 and dreary 'urban' development. Even here, however, there are fascinating things to see and magnificent contrasts – not least Renishaw, Bolsover and Hardwick glittering in the sunlight or lowering in the rain on their respective hilltops. It is a landscape immortalised by the Sitwells. The Derwent and Dove valleys, by contrast, have been tourist territory since the late seventeenth century, the former running through sandstone country and the latter through limestone. To the north is the Peak itself – great bare sweeps of moor and rocky outcrops, rising to over 2000 feet at Kinder Scout. The south of the county below Ashbourne is unassuming Midlands country with good farmland, comely red brick houses and villages, and many good old trees. It is difficult to say which is the most beautiful part of Derbyshire: perhaps it is the sweeping uplands, with limestone walls and dramatic valleys, towards Dovedale – especially in winter when there is snow on the ground and everything is silver, grey, white or black, with no colour to detract from the beautiful bones of the landscape.

Perhaps it is dangerous to end on a note of optimism, but it has to be admitted that Derbyshire is probably better-looking today than it was 100 years ago. While the wild landscape has been successfully preserved in a relatively unchanging state, the farming landscape too has kept its trees and hedges and has benefited from a lot of new planting. Even the industrial landscape of the Erewash Valley has been improved by the landscaping of slag heaps and extensive new planting. All the major country houses have undergone substantial restoration or stylish rejuvenation in this century, and now even some of the towns, notably Ashbourne and Wirksworth, are being looked after with renewed care and sensitivity. 'There are things in Derbyshire as noble as Greece,' wrote Lord Byron. And after even a short visit here, one can only agree.

Ashbourne

1; 12 miles W of Belper on A517

Ashbourne stands on the frontier between the mild Midlands landscape of south Derbyshire and the hills and dales of the Peak District. It is a remarkably well-preserved old market town of brick and stone and has an air of 'by appointment to the gentry of south Derbyshire' about it. Approaching from the west, after a small stretch of undistinguished suburb, you come straight to the parish CHURCH OF ST OSWALD, surrounded on two sides by open fields and dominating the scene with its beautiful fourteenth-century spire, which soars aloft to 212 feet and looks as if it has strayed from Lichfield Cathedral (*q.v.*). The churchyard is entered through impressive wrought-iron gates, the stone piers of which carry obelisks supported on little carved skulls. The long chancel is Early English with lancets, but the transepts have huge Decorated windows. On entering, the warm, light pink of the stonework is immediately attractive. An odd feature of the nave is that it has an aisle on one side only and is not centred on the chancel arch, creating the feeling that the south arcade has taken one or two steps forward from where it should be. The great glory of the church is the north transept, within which the Boothby Chapel is particularly splendid. This is so full of monuments to the Cockayne and Boothby families that it looks more like a shop selling funerary sculpture or a section of the Cast Court at the Victoria and Albert Museum than a chapel. There are no fewer than six large medieval table-tombs with alabaster effigies, as well as an array of unusual Georgian monuments of marble and alabaster. That to Sir Brooke Boothby (an extraordinary portrait by Wright of Derby showing him reclining and communing with Nature hangs in the Tate Gallery in London) is a Greek coffer on a base covered with naturalistic trails of carved ivy by Jos Evans. In a corner is a large Baroque marble urn commemorating Ann Boothby. But what takes everybody's eye is the beautiful little white marble monument to Penelope Boothby by Thomas Banks — a masterpiece of English neo-classical sculpture. It shows the dead girl in a long Regency frock, lying as if asleep on a naturalistic mattress on top of a Grecian sarcophagus. Queen Charlotte is reputed to have burst into tears when she saw it exhibited at the Royal Academy. The inscriptions include lines from Dante and the famous epitaph: 'THE UNFORTUNATE PARENTS VENTURED THEIR ALL ON THIS FRAIL BARK. AND THE WRECK WAS TOTAL'. The chancel is richly furnished with Gothic stalls by George Gilbert Scott and remarkably good Victorian encaustic tiles patterned with birds, butterflies and fleur-de-lis. The low-pitched ceiling has painted decoration done under the direction of Stephen Dykes Bower in 1963.

The main artery of Ashbourne is Church Street. Beginning by the church at the west end, first comes the FREE GRAMMAR SCHOOL founded by Sir Thomas Cockayne in 1585. It is a symmetrical Elizabethan building with gables and mullion windows. The lower courses of the façade stonework are deeply incised with the names or initials of generations of schoolboys. Facing each other, just beyond, are two remarkably handsome Georgian townhouses, both of which betray the hand of Joseph Pickford of Derby. THE GREY HOUSE next to the school is faced in stone and has a Venetian window and Doric porch. Opposite is the MANSION HOUSE, actually seventeenth-century, but refaced in red brick *c.*1750 for the Rev. John Taylor, who was a friend of Dr Johnson. Behind is a large garden, and in the centre of the rear side of the building is a domed octagonal Music Room with good Rococo plasterwork inside. Beyond the Mansion House are the OWLFIELD ALMSHOUSES, founded in 1640 and repaired in 1848. Other, less ambitious, Georgian houses line the rest of the street, where there are also several antique shops and an imposing stone Italianate Trustee Savings Bank of 1843. The eye is caught, however, by the remarkable sign of the GREEN MAN WITH BLACK'S HEAD; hanging right across the street, it is formed of a blackamoor's head perched in the middle of a wooden beam.

Opening off Church Street near here is the hillside MARKET PLACE — steep and cobbled with an island of houses in the middle. The first little bit, once the Shambles and now called VICTORIA SQUARE, has a good Victorian iron lamp standard erected in 1864 by the Ashbourne Gas Company under the direction of S. Evans, 'Gas Engineer'; it was restored in 1977. The main Market Place is triangular and surrounded by cheerful buildings, including the GEORGE AND DRAGON pub with its brightly coloured plaster relief of St George; Kennedy's Bicycle Shop with a sign 'Raleigh Cycles' and a nice pre-war atmosphere; and the stone-faced TOWN HALL of 1861 by Benjamin Wilson, topped by a florid clock such as you would expect to find in the middle of a Victorian mantelpiece. It is in the Market Place that the 'kick-off' takes place for the Shrove Tuesday football match — a free-for-all with goals three miles apart! Ashbourne has been considerably smartened up since the mid-1970s, and it is now a very good-looking place indeed.

The church of St Oswald, Ashbourne.

Bakewell

2; 10 miles NW of Matlock on A6

The quiet distinction of Bakewell is due, more than anything else, to the attempt made by the Duke of Rutland around 1800 to transform it into a fashionable – and profitable – watering-place, just as his neighbour and rival the Duke of Devonshire had done at Buxton (*q.v.*) a few miles away. He was not entirely successful, but he gave Bakewell a number of fine stone houses – notably the RUTLAND ARMS in Rutland Square and those in CASTLE STREET nearby. In Bath Street – off the Buxton Road – the BATH HOUSE is also well worth a visit; built for the 1st Duke in 1697, the original bath is still there under a low vault in the basement, fed by that chalybeate spring which never quite fulfilled its early promise. For me, however, the best thing in the town is the marvellous BRIDGE, whose five low, pointed arches, supported on broad breakwaters, have been spanning the swift waters of the Wye for close on seven centuries. (There is a delightful riverside walk to the south of it from which it can be seen to perfection.)

ALL SAINTS' CHURCH is finely sited on its hill; its octagonal tower, spire and splendid battlements cannot fail to impress – at least from a distance. Alas, closer inspection reveals that despite a largely Norman west front, all too much of the rest is rather heavy-handed Victorian restoration.

Barlborough Hall

3; 7½ miles NE of Chesterfield on A619

Latterly the seat of the Locker-Lampsons, Barlborough is 'The House Next Door' of Sir Osbert Sitwell's autobiography. He tells the story of his father, Sir George, standing on the terrace at Renishaw (*q.v.*) and saying to Evelyn Waugh, 'You see, there is *no one* between us and the Locker-Lampsons', as they gazed over the valley with its railway, colliery, iron works and the 'densely teeming streets of men who worked there' towards the opposite hilltop.

Barlborough, approached from the village by a long lime avenue, is now a Catholic prep school run by the Jesuits. It is one of the smaller Elizabethan prodigy houses and has been attributed on stylistic grounds to Robert Smythson. It was built by Sir Francis Rhodes, a judge in the Court of Common Pleas who worked for the Earl of Shrewsbury (husband of Bess of Hardwick). It is dated 1583 on the porch and 1584 on the chimneypiece in the Great Chamber. In form and plan it is very similar to the exactly contemporary Heath Old Hall in Yorkshire, which was demolished a few years ago; both of them had compact square plans with two principal storeys over a basement. The main façade is extremely beautiful – symmetrical with large mullion-and-transom windows, a central projecting porch, the entrance approached by a straight flight of steps, and flanking canted bay windows, which are carried up above the castellated parapet of the main block in the form of octagonal turrets or gazebos, very similar to the arrangement at the Earl of Shrewsbury's Worksop Manor (*q.v.*), which was destroyed by fire in the mid-eighteenth century. In the middle of the flat roof is another circular

cupola with large mullion windows lighting the original spiral staircase. The result is sturdily and romantically English, but a hint of the Italian Renaissance is introduced by the old stucco covering the outside walls and the little classical busts in roundels below the first-floor windows of the projecting bays. It is romantic and beautiful, and would be an exceedingly desirable house were it not for the proximity of so much industry and the M1.

Inside, the kitchen and offices are at basement level with the Great Hall over, and the Great Chamber (now the Chapel) at right angles to it. The latter has an original carved stone chimneypiece with classical columns and figures of Wisdom and Justice. The interior was otherwise greatly altered in 1825. The panelling in the Great Hall dates from then, as does the main staircase inserted in the small inner courtyard and lit from above through a glazed roof.

Belper

4; 8 miles N of Derby on A6

Here is the archetypal gritty northern industrial town, its small streets of terraced houses adjoining a large red cotton mill. There is much to be said for visiting Belper on a winter's evening when the frost glints from the stone paving of the streets and the buildings are bathed in the barley-bright glow of orange sodium lighting. Its setting in the Derwent Valley, by the river and surrounded by wooded cliffs, is dramatic: it was this combination of industry and landscape that gave eighteenth-century tourists to Derbyshire such a thrill and proved a major source of inspiration to the local artist, Joseph Wright of Derby. The industrial development of Belper is thanks to the Strutt family. Jedediah Strutt (in partnership with Richard Arkwright) built the town's first mill in 1776. Subsequently, Arkwright concentrated on Cromford (*q.v.*) and the Strutts developed Belper as a model patriarchal industrial settlement with no fewer than five cotton mills and a rough grid-plan of terraced cottages for their employees. Round the edge, a number of farms were built by the Strutts to supply dairy produce. None of the original eighteenth-century mills survives; they were all replaced in the early nineteenth century by Jedediah's engineer son William, who developed his own form of fire-proof iron construction. Four of these were disgracefully demolished in the 1960s, but the NORTH MILL of 1804 survives by the river. It is a substantial T-shaped building, five storeys high, faced in brick but with an advanced form of iron-framed construction. From the main road it is overshadowed by the huge EAST MILL of 1912, a seven-storeyed pile of harsh red Accrington brick which dominates Belper like a fortress and still functions as a cotton mill. The North Mill overlooks an impressive semi-circular stone weir in the river, constructed in 1796–8 by Thomas Sykes, the County Surveyor, and there are attractive gardens along the river bank. The streets of late eighteenth-century workers' houses line the slopes to the south of the mill. The best is LONG ROW – an impressive layout which lives up to its name, especially when seen from the top looking down. The terraces of brick and stone are mainly three

Bolsover Castle.

storeys high, surprisingly substantial for early workers' housing. The original stone street-paving survives, but it is a great pity that the old sash windows and front doors are being removed and replaced with off-the-peg 'builders' allsorts'. The planning authority should take steps to stop this erosion. At the top of the hill is ST PETER'S CHURCH, designed by Matthew Habershon in 1824 – a well-preserved 'Commissioners' Gothic' church with a pleasant, light interior.

Bolsover★

5; 7 miles E of Chesterfield on A632

BOLSOVER CASTLE is a proud and romantic spectacle, standing high on its hilltop above the smoking collieries and drab terraced houses of the town. It has a long history, going back to William the Conqueror, although it was largely rebuilt in the early seventeenth century by Sir Charles Cavendish, the favourite son of Bess of Hardwick, to the design of the mason-architects Robert and John Smythson. The keep, begun in 1612, is one of the best-preserved expressions of late Elizabethan and Jacobean romantic neo-medieval taste. The exterior is square and compact with 'posthumous-Gothic' turrets and cupola.

The interiors are even more theatrical, with ribbed vaults, fantastic carved chimneypieces and painted decorations after Primaticcio and Marten de Vos. Sir

Charles's son William Cavendish, later 1st Duke of Newcastle, added a large domestic range with a Long Gallery and Great Hall as well as a riding school, all to John Smythson's design and, though the state apartments are now in ruins, their splendid Mannerist façades vie with the keep in dramatic effect. The rooms of the keep, which have been over-restored recently, have no contents. Nevertheless, the Pillar Parlour, the Star Chamber, the Marble Closet, the Elysium and the Heaven Room can still show some of the finest surviving Jacobean Mannerist decoration in England.

The whole house has an incomparable atmosphere, grandiose and theatrical, which Sacheverell Sitwell has captured well: 'Bolsover Castle, dead, dead, as the Mayan ruins of Uxmal or Chichen Itza, and as remote from us, but with a ghostly poetry that fires the imagination, that can never be forgotten, and that never cools.'

Buxton

6; 10 miles E of Macclesfield on A6

Situated 1000 feet up in the Peak, Buxton is the highest town in England. It consists of two parts – the old market town, with its funnel-shaped Market Place, humble old CHURCH OF ST ANNE and relatively small-scale seventeenth- and eighteenth-century stone buildings; and the spa, which lies in a more sheltered hollow below. The mineral springs were known to the Romans but the development of Buxton into a spa proper was the work of the eighteenth- and nineteenth-century Dukes of Devonshire, who were (and are) lords of the manor. The 1st Duke built a bathhouse on the site of the Roman baths in 1710, but it was the 5th Duke who initiated development on a scale intended to rival Bath; his work was continued by the 6th and 7th Dukes, reaching a climax in the late nineteenth century.

Buxton is among the most attractive of English spa towns, not least because of its wonderful site, surrounded on all sides by wooded hills and moors. Being built entirely of solid local sandstone, it also has a uniform dignity denied towns like Cheltenham with their rather tawdry peeling stucco. Another advantage is that Buxton is not at all large, so the splendid Italianate and francophile buildings have the feeling of being gathered together on the side of a mountain to make a Rex Whistler capriccio, rather than forming part of a real town. The classic English spa contains several ingredients – a crescent, glass-and-iron winter gardens, parks, mineral wells and baths, a theatre or opera house and solid Regency or Victorian villas. Buxton comprises all these ingredients to perfection.

The centrepiece is THE CRESCENT, designed for the 5th Duke by John Carr of York in 1781. It is semi-circular, with a rusticated arcade supporting fluted Tuscan pilasters, a triglyph frieze and top balustrade. In the centre of the latter is a weathered carving of the Devonshire arms. One wing of the Crescent contains St Anne's Hotel, its interior a real horror to me. The other wing, once also a hotel, was converted into a library by the county council in 1970. Upstairs survives the original ASSEMBLY ROOM, one of the most beautiful eighteenth-century interiors in the north of England, with an Adamesque coved ceiling, Corinthian pilasters, a pair of marble chimneypieces and original glass chandeliers. It was an imaginative and praiseworthy project to make this a library, but it is a huge pity that it has been done with so little taste. Here was a chance to create a library comparable to those at Oxford or Cambridge; instead we have the usual local-government blend of expensive mediocrity.

Facing the Crescent is ST ANNE'S WELL (now a 'micrarium' – a word not in my dictionary) and THE SLOPES – an area of pleasure grounds laid out by Sir Jeffrey Wyatville in 1818 but using genuine eighteenth-century carved stone urns from Londesborough (Lord Burlington's house in Yorkshire). The equally appropriate obelisk turns out on close inspection to be the war memorial. At the end of the Crescent is THE SQUARE, in a plainer version of Carr's style and incomplete. It looks out at the PAVILION GARDENS – a beautifully landscaped park of 25 acres with the River Wye running through, two little lakes and several Victorian cast-iron bridges. Along the south side is BROADWALK, with Italianate stone terraces and villas, while to the north is THE PAVILION itself, and the OPERA HOUSE. This is the Covent Garden of Buxton in more ways than one. The Pavilion was erected in the 1870s and restored in 1982 by the town council to form a winter garden, several cafés, a restaurant and a concert hall. The interior is an Experience, especially on a cold winter's day when the warmth, palm trees and scented plants in the winter garden come as a great surprise. The coffee shop and bar in the central pavilion have been kitted out in a 1980s' 'hi-tech' style, which blends remarkably well with the original cast-iron and glass; it is a credit to Buxton. So too is the Opera House behind, designed in 1904 by Frank Matcham, the doyen of Edwardian theatre designers. The interior, recently restored, is a *tour de force* of Rococo and gilt, with elaborate ceiling paintings. It is all remarkably well preserved, even down to such details as the original stained-glass canopy over the entrance. To the north is THE PARK, laid out by Paxton with a circular boundary road intended to be lined with villas in the manner of Nash's Regent's Park; it was not completed at the time, however, and the intended effect has been somewhat spoilt by newer development of inappropriate scale and design.

The CHURCH OF ST JOHN THE BAPTIST is a handsome neo-classical church, a variation on the Tuscan mode inspired by St Paul's, Covent Garden. Long attributed to Wyatt, it is now known to have been designed by John White. The interior is dull but the outside is very handsome. When first built it had a portico at the east end (like St Paul's) but this was later filled in to make a new chancel. At the west end is an attractive domed tower, which makes one of the best features in the Buxton skyline when admired from the Town Hall at the top of the Slopes. Next to St John's is the huge pile of the DEVONSHIRE HOSPITAL; this was originally a stable and riding school designed for the 5th Duke by Carr of York at the same time as the Crescent. It is a typical piece of neo-classical geometry, the overall shape being an irregular octagon with a circular courtyard in the centre. In 1880 the courtyard was covered with an enormous dome, larger than that of Santa Sofia at Constantinople; when built, it was the largest in the world. The florid clock tower was added at the same time by Benjamin Currey, the 7th Duke of Devonshire's architect at Buxton. Currey was also responsible for the PALACE HOTEL, a Frenchy mansard-roofed pile, the whacking bulk of which dominates the centre of Buxton like a section of the Tuileries gone into northern exile. From here THE QUADRANT, a planned Victorian shopping street with attractive iron-and-glass canopies, leads back to the Crescent where we started.

Calke Abbey
NT; 7; 10 miles S of Derby off A514

After centuries of complete obscurity Calke was dragged reluctantly into the limelight in 1983 when it looked as if it was threatened with extinction as a result of capital transfer tax on the death of the penultimate in the line of its eccentric reclusive owners. As *The Times* explained: 'The later Harpur-Crewes were slow to embrace the amenities of modernity. The motor car came to Calke in 1949, the electric light in 1960, the arts of tax avoidance never.' In the event, the house – but not the estate – was saved by the government and given to the National Trust.

It is a large and handsome square stone block of three storeys, built in 1703 by Sir John Harpur. The name of the architect is not known but the house displays several unusual features, such as the florid Ionic capitals of the pilasters, which are derived from Philibert Delorme's treatise and are unique in English architecture. There are also particularly splendid lead downpipes decorated with the family crest. The house is based on the Ragley prototype with four corner blocks, each one originally containing an apartment. Like Ragley in Warwickshire (*q.v.*), it is embellished with a later Ionic portico; in the case of Calke, designed by William Wilkins, Senior, in 1804. Like many houses on medieval sites, Calke is hidden romantically in a low-lying hollow, embosomed in the middle of a huge and beautiful park that contains several lakes and a herd of deer. Houses on abbatial sites always have a particular mystery and charm; they tug at the heart in a special way.

Inside Calke, the main rooms are on the first floor, approached by an early eighteenth-century timber staircase. In the centre, behind the portico, is the large Saloon, with early eighteenth-century panelling and an early Victorian ceiling. On one side are the Library and Drawing Room, and on the other the Breakfast Room and Dining Room. The latter is a pretty neo-classical design with porphyry scagliola columns, elegant plasterwork and little inset paintings of cherubs against a pink ground.

The great appeal of Calke's interior, however, lies not in the architecture but in the amazingly undisturbed Victorian atmosphere that pervades the rooms. 'As if the outcome of a successful experiment with time', the furnishings and hangings, furniture, specimen cabinets and bric-à-brac of the Victorian age are preserved fresh and in full. The Saloon, for instance, is crammed full of glass cases of stuffed birds, shells, minerals, an alligator's skull, Russian buttons from Inkerman and, labelled in a faded hand, a 'Collection of Egyptian curiosities brought by me from Egypt'. The Drawing Room has its Victorian wallpaper still fresh, and all the furniture, paintings and ornaments in the exact positions shown in photographs taken in the 1880s. The accumulation and fossilisation continue in room after room, on floor after floor. As areas silted up, the family simply shut them and moved on. It still has to be seen whether the National Trust can cope successfully with the difficult problem of preserving and displaying all this without affecting the unique atmosphere of the place.

On a hump in front of the house is the parish CHURCH OF ST GILES, a little early nineteenth-century Gothick design with cast-iron window tracery and tower; the whole thing looks like a toy model. Behind the house is an attractive early eighteenth-century brick stable quadrangle with original timber cross-mullion windows.

Calke Abbey.

Chatsworth★

8; 8 miles W of Chesterfield off A619 [5]

None of the great houses of England – not even Longleat – possesses a more spectacular approach than Chatsworth. The best is from the south, where the A623 from Rowsley and Matlock (*q.v.*) crosses a narrow one-arch bridge, takes a sharp turn to the right and enters the park. Almost at once the house comes into view, looking deceptively small at first but already unquestionably a palace, in its setting of gardens, meadows and gently rolling hills, of copse and woodland, of lake, fountain and cascade – a green and glorious vision of a dream England which, on a sunny summer day or (as I first saw it) through the gentle misty rain of an autumn evening, has no rival anywhere. Chatsworth is indeed the grandest house in England; everything about it is superb: the landscape, the traditionally maintained estate, the great park, the formal gardens, the architecture – an amalgam of Baroque and neo-classical at its most glorious – and the rich and varied collections.

The first house on the site of which any record survives was begun by Sir William Cavendish and his wife Bess of Hardwick in 1551, three years after they had bought the estate; its quadrangular plan dictates the form of the present main block. It was reconstructed in stages by the 1st Duke of Devonshire from 1686 onwards, partly to his own design, partly to that of William Talman and Thomas Archer, creating the magnificent façades of golden stone carved with the neatness of 'wrought plate', as Horace Walpole noted.

The landscaping of the park by Capability Brown and the construction of the stable block and bridge over the River Derwent by James Paine were put in hand by the 4th Duke in the mid-eighteenth century, but it was the 6th Duke in the early nineteenth century who made Chatsworth the finest house in England. He built the model village at Edensor (*q.v.*), remodelled the gardens with the aid of Joseph Paxton and doubled the size of the house by adding the brilliantly Picturesque north wing, to the design of Sir Jeffrey Wyatville but expressing his own ideas as much as his architect's. The interior of Chatsworth is equally interesting as an expression of the 1st Duke's late seventeenth-century and the 6th Duke's early nineteenth-century taste; it is, moreover, enriched with the superb early eighteenth-century collections from Chiswick House and Devonshire House in London, formed by Lord Burlington and by the 2nd and 3rd Dukes of Devonshire respectively.

The entrance to Chatsworth is through a succession of halls and corridors that result from a series of accidents but are cleverly turned to advantage to create a number of spatial surprises – through James Paine's Doric Entrance Hall, up a flight of stairs, along the 6th Duke's marble-floored corridor, into the 1st Duke's Painted Hall (with murals by Laguerre) and so to the Great Stairs, which lead to the 1st Duke's State Apartment on the second floor (like its Elizabethan predecessor). The five state rooms have painted ceilings *à la* Versailles by Verrio and Laguerre; the walls are wainscotted and embellished with excellent wood-carving by Samuel Watson, Lobb, Young and Davis, and are hung with stamped and gilded leather or tapestry. They contain some of their original seventeenth-century furnishings, of which the silver chandelier in the Dressing Room is exceptional. The many other treasures include the state bed in which George II died, a collection of malachite given to the 6th Duke by Tsar Nicholas I and gilt furniture by William Kent. After descending by the West Stairs, with a ceiling by Thornhill, the visitor sees the Chapel which, now that Charles II's work at Windsor has been largely destroyed, is the finest seventeenth-century ensemble of its type in England.

Even grander than the 1st Duke's apartments are the 6th Duke's, which stretch in an enormous enfilade on the first floor along the whole of the east side of the house. They begin with three princely Libraries, of which the principal one is formed out of the original Long Gallery and has a unique seventeenth-century ceiling with gilded plasterwork and circular paintings by Verrio (restored in 1983). The library at Chatsworth is the finest in private hands and, as well as 45,000 printed books (including over 500 *incunabula*, an assemblage only exceeded among historic collections by that of the King of Spain), has a world-famous collection of Old Master drawings. The white-and-gold Dining Room is entirely Wyatville's creation and is hung with oyster-coloured watered silk and a group of excellent full-length portraits by Van Dyck and his contemporaries. Beyond is the 6th Duke's Sculpture Gallery – the best place to see the output of those artists who worked in Rome in the early nineteenth century; to some extent it was conceived as a memorial to the great Canova (a number of whose works adorn it). It is to be regretted that the original arrangement was disturbed earlier this century and it is to be hoped that one day it will be put right. More

Chatsworth.

sculpture is displayed in the Orangery, which now serves mainly as a gift shop. From the Orangery, the visitor enters the garden, which occupies over 100 acres and, like the house itself, is a superb and rich amalgam of different styles and features from four centuries.

Chesterfield

9; 10 miles S of Sheffield on A61 [8]

Nowadays Chesterfield is above all famous for the crooked spire of its parish church, ST MARY AND ALL SAINTS, which has done for the town, on a more modest scale, much the same as the Leaning Tower has done for Pisa. Why the timber-and-lead construction should have warped in so unique a way is a mystery; but the result is irresistibly funny, like a bishop with hiccups. There can have been few more fortunate architectural accidents, since it has resulted in the church – and, by extension, the whole town – being loved in a way it would never otherwise have been.

Inside, the church strikes one as imposing, cavernous and faintly pompous – it is very much the creation of the rich, self-made fourteenth-century Derbyshire merchants who built it; the very last church, in fact, that would have wished such a spire upon itself. Its most interesting features are the two Lady Chapels off the south transept – one (the Lesser) with a polygonal apse, which is something of a rarity in England, and the other boasting the astonishing collection of tombs of the Foljambe family. They include a kneeling figure in full armour with his visor *down*, and another, also anonymous and even more bizarre, of a body all bundled up in a shroud as if about to be thrown into the Bosporus, surmounted by standing figures of Death, Childhood and Old Age. The lack of any identifying inscription somehow makes it more sinister still.

In Elder Way, the Unitarian ELDER YARD CHAPEL of 1697 is not easy to find; but it is well worth seeking out for those who have the time. The MARKET PLACE is also worth a glance, as it nearly disappeared to make way for a hideous new shopping centre. In the event, such was the strength of public feeling that it was preserved and many of the surrounding old buildings repaired – a heart-warming success story.

Cromford

10; 2 miles S of Matlock on A6

The ghost of Richard Arkwright, inventor of the first water-powered COTTON MILL in 1771, broods heavily over Cromford. His original buildings still stand, dark and undeniably satanic, on the banks of the Derwent; so too does the not particularly memorable CHURCH OF ST MARY, which he built near the fifteenth-century bridge and, on the hill above, the turreted and battlemented WILLERSLEY CASTLE, which he ordered for himself towards the end of his life and never lived to inhabit. (Faintly ridiculous but commanding a sensational view across the valley, it is now a Methodist Rest Home.) At the other end of the bridge stands an early eighteenth-century fishing pavilion inscribed 'PISCATORIBUS SACRUM' – an agreeable conceit, but not quite pretty enough. Back in the village proper – across the A6 – NORTH STREET consists almost entirely of houses built by Arkwright for his workers.

Arkwright's Mill, Cromford.

A mile or two outside the town on the Derby road you will see on the left a tall chimney with a cast-iron top, looking more like a Doric column than anything else. It belongs to a delightful old PUMPING HOUSE, the purpose of which was to deliver water up to the canal which flows at this point on a high AQUEDUCT over the Derwent. A few yards beyond the chimney, a little track turns back to the left in a descending hairpin to the building itself, where the original engine is said to have been recently restored to working order. From here, after two minutes' walk southwards along the canal bank, you find yourself standing on the aqueduct high above the river. (To obtain a view of the bridge from below is possible but, owing to the dense woodland, much harder.)

Dale Abbey★
11; 6 miles NE of Derby off A6096
Virtually nothing remains of the original twelfth-century abbey of Premonstratensian canons, except the great arch of the east window and parts of the Chapter House standing lonely in a field; alone, they would not have found a place in this book. The joy of the village, however, is ALL SAINTS, its parish church, surely one of the dottiest in England. At first glance it is barely recognisable as a church at all, since it now shares a roof with a rather seedy farmhouse café (where, incidentally, the key can be found); only a second closer look reveals Norman walls and a rough Norman doorway – humble, minute, but unmistakably genuine.

Inside, all is higgledy-piggledy. The whole church is less than 9 yards square, yet it manages to contain an incredible quantity of box pews, an upstairs gallery (the stairs being outside, at the back), a 1634 pulpit *behind* the altar, lurching drunkenly a good 20° from the vertical, a surprisingly well-preserved series of thirteenth-century wall paintings (including a wonderful Visitation), a battered harmonium, countless coathooks too high to hang anything on, and the most dangerous-looking system of electric wiring I have ever seen. Go there soon, before somebody tidies it up or the whole thing goes up in smoke.

Derby
12; 11 miles NE of Burton upon Trent on A52
Today Derby is a drab and dingy Midlands red brick industrial town, its centre greatly spoiled since the 1960s, in my view, by new roads and the mediocre redevelopment of the Market Place. It is still worth visiting, however, for the parish CHURCH OF ALL SAINTS, since 1927 the CATHEDRAL: it is one of the best eighteenth-century town churches in the country. The old church had become so decrepit by the early eighteenth century that the parishioners used to rush out of services 'at every crack of Wind'. The vicar of the day, Dr Michael Hutchinson, determined to rebuild all except the handsome early sixteenth-century Perpendicular west tower. Designs for rebuilding were obtained in 1718 from the Smiths of Warwick. The Yorkshire architect Ralph

Tunnicliffe was also consulted, but in the event a new design from no less than James Gibbs himself was adopted, with the Smiths relegated to the role of contractors. The vicar raised the necessary money by subscription and then secretly ordered the old church to be demolished in order to forestall the mayor and corporation, who had been dragging their feet – thus leaving no option 'but for everyone to lend his helping hand' towards building the new church.

The exterior of the new nave is deliberately plain to render it 'more suitable to the old steeple'. Its interior is dignified with giant Roman Doric columns supporting a semi-circular plaster vault similar in form to that of St Martin-in-the-Fields, but without the decorative stucco. There were never any side-galleries because, as Gibbs wrote, they 'clog up and spoil the Inside of Churches, and take away from that right Proportion which they otherwise would have'. These noble arcades lead the eye to the magnificent wrought-iron screen with the Royal Arms on top; this is the *chef-d'œuvre* of the virtuoso Derbyshire smith Robert Bakewell. The original east end was replaced by a new, larger chancel between 1954 and 1972, following the elevation of the church to cathedral status. It was designed by Sebastian Comper in strict conformity with Gibbs's style and is a worthy addition to the church. He designed the *baldacchino* over the altar with a canopy on Corinthian columns. The modern stained glass in the east windows of the aisles by Ceri Richards and Patrick Reyntiens is somewhat strident; clear glass always seems a more appropriate accompaniment to classical architecture. The south choir aisle is the Cavendish family chapel, with their burial vault below. It contains several monuments, of which the chief one is that to Bess of Hardwick (which she ordered in her lifetime), with an alabaster effigy, black marble columns, obelisks and fanfare of heraldry.

Edensor

13; 2 miles NE of Bakewell on B6012

Pronounced 'Ensor', this is the 6th Duke of Devonshire's model village, which he moved to its present site in 1838–42, considering its earlier location too close to Chatsworth (*q.v.*). The planning he entrusted to his head gardener, Joseph Paxton – later to build the Crystal Palace – who was joined in the design of the individual houses by one John Robertson of Derby. Architecturally, it must be admitted that Edensor is a pretty odd mix; the deliberately quirkish and fanciful houses reflect a welter of styles like a contemporary pattern book – Norman, Tudor, Swiss chalet, even Italian Renaissance. No matter: there is a charmingly carefree quality about its general layout, while the setting among the rolling green hills of Chatsworth park make it a delightful village that is little short of idyllic on a sunny summer morning.

Sir George Gilbert Scott's CHURCH of 1867 is perhaps too big for its surroundings but impressive nevertheless with its tall spire. It is worth entering for the stunning alabaster tomb, at the east end of the south aisle, of the 1st Earl of Devonshire and his brother, the two elder sons of Bess of Hardwick.

Eyam

14; 4 miles NW of Baslow on B6521

Eyam stands in limestone country, surrounded by crags, gorges and wooded hills, but the village itself is built mainly of gritstone. It is one of the show villages of Derbyshire (as the over-elaborate street lighting makes clear) and is famous as the 'Plague village'. In 1666, when the Plague was brought to the village in a parcel of clothing from London, the inhabitants went into voluntary quarantine; many of them died but by their action the Plague was prevented from spreading to the rest of Derbyshire. Several of the cottages have painted boards recording the names of the Plague victims.

The village street is lined with substantial eighteenth-century stone cottages with stone-flagged roofs and grandish architectural details, including the odd Venetian window. The parish CHURCH OF ST LAWRENCE stands in a handsome graveyard, with undulating grass, lime trees and open views over the surrounding hills to the north. In front of the church is a notable Saxon CROSS thought to date from the eighth century and carved with interlacing patterns and Christian symbols. It is one of the very few such crosses to preserve its head and arms as well as its shaft. The church itself is the usual village mixture, with an Early English chancel and Perpendicular tower. It was sweepingly restored in the nineteenth century, when the aisles were rebuilt. An unusual feature of the interior are the late Elizabethan paintings round the nave at clerestory level showing the signs of the twelve tribes of Israel and, at the west end, a lifelike skeleton – if that is not a contradiction.

Overlooking the village street, a little to the west of the church, is EYAM HALL – a perfect example of Derbyshire Jacobean vernacular, albeit a late one. It is dated 1676 and has an H-plan and a symmetrical façade with tiny gables and mullion windows, the myriad panes of which glint in the afternoon sun.

Edensor.

Foremark Hall
15; 2 miles E of Repton off B5008

Now a prep school and with the rather kicked-about look of houses inhabited by lots of small boys, Foremark Hall was built in 1759–61 for Sir Francis Burdett. It is a late Palladian design, showing a Rococo softening – typical of the second-generation Palladians – in the pair of canted bay windows with domes on top. The architect was David Hiorn of Warwick, and the contractor Joseph Pickford of Derby. The main block has an Ionic portico on the entrance front, approached by sweeping stone staircases. On either side there are curved screen walls with niches and pedimented doorways connecting with small flanking pavilions on the Palladian model. Bad-tempered Lord Torrington described these as 'Venetian Vanities' and dismissed the whole place as 'vile architecture'. The main rooms are on the first floor and have well-preserved marble chimneypieces, plasterwork and good joinery of the period. The principal rooms are the Entrance Hall and large Saloon on the main axis. The other rooms are smaller.

At the edge of the Hall grounds is ST SAVIOUR'S CHURCH, built by Sir Francis Burdett in 1762 and an interesting example of Gothic Survival. It has a castellated west tower and Perpendicular windows. The interior is special because it retains all its original furnishings: box pews, three-decker pulpit with canopy, carved altar and a wonderful Jacobean rood-screen with enriched arches, fretwork panels, little obelisks on top and a steep central pediment framing a painted glass panel depicting the Holy Ghost and angels. The pretty eighteenth-century wrought-iron altar rails are almost certainly by Robert Bakewell. The ensemble is completed by fine Burdett family memorials and hatchments.

Glossop
16; 7 miles E of Manchester on A57

Surrounded by high, desolate moors and approached by the famous Snake Pass, Glossop is really two places in one – the old village around the parish church, with dark stone cottages dating from the seventeenth century and an ancient stone cross forming a picturesque group; and the nineteenth-century town. The latter is called HOWARD TOWN and was developed for the Howards, Dukes of Norfolk, by their northern estate agent Matthew Ellison. They built the reservoirs up the valley between the hills to the north-east in order to provide water power for the new cotton mills, and laid out the town centre on a dignified grid-plan. It developed round NORFOLK SQUARE, an impressive space for a small industrial town, with the classical TOWN HALL of 1838, built for the 12th Duke of Norfolk by M.E. Hadfield; behind is the MARKET HALL, added by the 13th Duke in 1844; and to one side is a chemist's shop with a Victorian shop-front painted maroon and distinguished by a nineteenth-century warrant: 'By appointment to His Grace The Duke of Norfolk'. Does His Grace still drop in for the odd tube of toothpaste, one wonders? The square itself is surrounded by decent stone buildings of various dates, banks, shops and offices, and has a twentieth-

century war memorial in the centre. To one side is the Norfolk Arms and behind that the RAILWAY STATION, built by the 13th Duke of Norfolk in 1847 with the Howard lion crest proudly silhouetted on the roof over the entrance.

Glossop Hall itself, once a Howard seat, has been demolished, but the PARK is partly preserved as an attractive public open space, and opposite the lodge is the Catholic ALL SAINTS' CHURCH, designed by M.E. Hadfield for the 12th Duke. It is an austere Tuscan composition, with pilasters, pediments and wide eaves, inspired by St Paul's in Covent Garden. The interior has an apse for the altar and a coved ceiling, but the nineteenth-century painted decoration which formed an important part of the ensemble has been covered over. Glossop is now a dormitory town for Manchester and none of the cotton mills still serves its original purpose, though the buildings survive. These, and the cyclopean stone-revetted reservoirs, and the impressive railway tunnels and cuttings through the surrounding hills, all add up to a dour but impressive monument to early nineteenth-century industrial enterprise.

Haddon Hall⋆
17; 3 miles SE of Bakewell on A6 [7]

Haddon Hall lies only 3 miles or so from Chatsworth (*q.v.*); yet no two houses could be more different in spirit. This difference is already apparent on the approach. You reach Chatsworth at the end of a carefully contrived crescendo of park and river; Haddon reveals itself suddenly, yet seeming so natural a part of the hills above the Wye that it seems to have grown organically out of them. It is that rarest of things – a welcoming castle. There is nothing forbidding, still less aggressive, about those battlemented towers; all is gentle, quiet, mellow with age and wisdom. As one gazes up at it, across the murmuring river and the seventeenth-century bridge, that dreadful word 'romantic' springs all unbidden to the mind; one seems to have wandered out of the workaday world straight into the pages of Sir Walter Scott. But Haddon is real to the last stone. Abandoned at the beginning of the eighteenth century when the Duke of Rutland transferred his household to his other great castle of Belvoir, it lay empty until the beginning of the twentieth, thus escaping the attentions of *dilettanti* Gothicisers and Victorian restorers alike. Time, however, continued to take its toll. Only in 1912 did the 9th Duke return to the lonely old house, determined to save it before it crumbled away. For thirty years – the rest of his life – he worked with dedication, devotion and profound scholarship; and the preservation of one of the loveliest buildings of England – perhaps its very survival – is in large measure due to him.

The history of Haddon goes back to the eleventh century, when William the Conqueror granted the fief to his bastard William Peveril. The Peverils lasted less than 100 years, but it was they who built Peveril's Tower at the north-east corner; parts of the flanking walls and the bastions along the south and west also go back to the early twelfth century at least, as does the south aisle of the Chapel, once the parish church of the long-vanished village of Nether Haddon. Then, around 1170, the castle passed to another great local family, the Vernons. They possessed considerably more staying power – they flourish in Derbyshire to this day – and most of the Haddon that we see today is Vernon work, including the remainder of the Chapel (with its memorable fifteenth-century wall paintings), the Great Hall of 1370 (or perhaps a little earlier) with its superb panelled and traceried screen and, around it, the usual offices of kitchen, pantry and buttery in their traditional positions. Just south of the Hall is the Parlour – now known as the Dining Room – with the Great Chamber immediately above it. Originally the two probably formed a single room, a solar, of the same height as the Hall itself; but they were separated by Sir Henry Vernon around 1500 – a decision that led to the glorious painted ceiling of the Parlour, which still survives, miraculously, as in Sir Henry's day.

In 1558 Dorothy, younger daughter of Sir George Vernon of Haddon, married John Manners, second son of the Earl of Rutland. Tradition has it that they eloped and, Haddon being Haddon, has clothed the elopement with all the trappings of a Scott novel – the father's opposition, the daughter's confinement, the lover's disguise and the final flight during the wedding ball of the elder sister, with the beautiful Dorothy slipping away from the dancing and the music, then flying along the terrace and away down the long flight of steps to the narrow packhorse bridge where John Manners was waiting to bear her away to Belvoir. One longs for it all to be true; the legend does not, however, explain why Sir George should have objected to such an eminently suitable match, nor why he subsequently bequeathed his estate to the errant couple in preference to his elder daughter and his own younger brother. But bequeath it he did, fortunately for the Mannerses, sadly for the Vernons; and Haddon has remained Rutland property ever since.

That same John Manners was responsible, in his old age, for the building of one of the greatest glories of this glorious house – the Long Gallery. It is 110 feet long and 17 feet across, and lit on three sides with huge leaded windows, mullioned and transomed, that seem to flood it with perpetual sunshine; the pale Renaissance panelling makes it lighter and lovelier still. It possesses too, in abundance, another wonderful quality of long galleries – that of looking just as beautiful from the outside. When, on a summer evening, one stands in the terraced garden to the south, watching the declining sun flickering and flashing over its windows – whose leaded lights are set on purpose at irregular angles to give precisely this effect – then one knows, beyond all doubt, that Haddon is one of the magic places of the earth, and feels for the hundredth time a surge of gratitude to the man who nursed it so tenderly back to life.

The Chapel, Haddon Hall.

Hardwick Hall.

Hardwick Hall★

NT; 18; 7 miles SE of Chesterfield off A617 [6]

There is not one of the great houses of England that possesses more of a sense of unity than does Hardwick Hall. It was built in just seven years, between 1590 and 1597, by one of the most remarkable women of her age, and has scarcely been touched since her death, eleven years after its completion, at the age of nearly ninety.

> *Four times the nuptial bed she warm'd,*
> *And every time so well perform'd,*
> *That when death spoil'd each husband's billing*
> *He left the widow every shilling.*
> *Fond was the dame, but not dejected;*
> *Five stately mansions she erected. . . .*

So wrote Horace Walpole of Bess of Hardwick; and, with the possible exception of the word 'fond', he wrote no more than the truth. She was born and brought up in the old Hall whose ruins still stand within sight of the house. Despite its size, her father John Hardwick was not rich, and Bess was still a child when she was married off to a well-to-do cousin who died shortly afterwards, leaving her a widow before she was sixteen. For her second marriage she set her sights considerably higher – on no less a personage than Sir William Cavendish, Treasurer of the Chamber to the King. This was the period immediately following Henry VIII's Dissolution of the Monasteries; as Commissioner for Monastic Estates in Derbyshire, Sir William was in an unrivalled position to turn the iniquitous decree to his own advantage, and his already considerable wealth was increasing hour by hour. Now at last Bess could indulge in her passion for building. In

1549 she bought the Chatsworth estate (*q.v.*). The fine old house was demolished, and in its place she built, at a cost of £80,000, a splendid new palace more in keeping with her new station in life.

Less than ten years later Sir William died in his turn, leaving his widow with six children and vast estates all over the Midlands. Still only in her late thirties, Bess now married Sir William St Loe, Captain of the Queen's Guard and Grand Butler of England. He had children by a former marriage, but she was careful to arrange that he too should leave all his money and properties to her, so that on his death in 1565 she must have been one of the richest women in the Kingdom. Her fourth and last husband, however, was still richer, and considerably more influential than any of his predecessors: George Talbot, Earl of Shrewsbury. It was typical of her that, to make quite sure of his wealth, she simultaneously arranged for the wedding of two of her children to two of his. This fourth marriage was quite simply one of convenience – her own. She seldom saw her husband, who within a year was unfortunate enough to be appointed custodian of Mary Queen of Scots. Bess grew furiously jealous – more through wounded pride than anything else – and in 1583 there was a formal separation; poor Shrewsbury was to spend the rest of his life defending himself from her attacks and bringing endless unsuccessful actions against her in his efforts to regain at least some of the properties of which she had managed to dispossess him. But she did not care. By now she had little time for anything but building – additions to Chatsworth and her family mansion at Hardwick, her husband's old castle at Bolsover and his new palace at Worksop (*qq.v.*), besides any number of smaller houses and manors up and down the country.

It was not, however, until after Shrewsbury's death in 1590 that Bess embarked on the grandest venture of them all, and the one that was to prove her permanent memorial. Her new great house at Hardwick is, by any standards, one of the most sublime *tours de force* of English secular architecture. We have no documentary proof for the architect, but all the circumstantial and stylistic evidence points in the same direction – to Robert Smythson, who had recently designed Wollaton (*q.v.*), only 15 miles away, and had previously worked for Sir John Thynne at Longleat. There can be no doubt, on the other hand, that most of the details – and indeed even some of the structural features – are the work of Bess herself; and when she crowned the corner towers with her own tremendous initials, E.S. – for Elizabeth Shrewsbury – fourteen times repeated, it was with well-justified pride in the knowledge that, despite her seventy-nine years, this magnificent edifice was her own creation.

Like Haddon (*q.v.*), Hardwick has gained immeasurably for having been, for all its splendour, only a secondary home for the family to which it belonged. The original decoration survives to a remarkable degree and since *c*.1700 the house has been maintained much in its old state, the Cavendish family devoting most of their energies to the embellishment and improvement of Chatsworth, though the 6th Duke of Devonshire was responsible for some sympathetic alterations in the early nineteenth century.

The forecourt is surrounded by the original screen wall with an array of little obelisks on top. The colonnade was probably intended to stretch all round the house, but in the event was confined to the centre only. The Entrance Hall is two storeys high and shows a decisive break from medieval precedent in its symmetrical position and transverse plan. On screens are displayed panels of sixteenth-century needlework, immediately introducing the visitor to one of the chief glories of the house.

The plan of Hardwick is arranged with two complete sets of apartments – the state apartment, including the Long Gallery, High Great Chamber and State Bedroom on the top floor, and a set of less elaborate rooms, for Bess of Hardwick's own use, on the first floor. The latter are typical examples of Elizabethan decoration, with ash panelling and plaster heraldic overmantels. The state rooms on the top floor, however, are of outstanding interest. They are reached by a long staircase, which drifts romantically upwards in flights of shallow stone steps across the middle of the house. The Long Gallery is the finest to survive and has two handsome chimneypieces of alabaster and marble, a geometrical stucco ceiling and walls covered with tapestry, on top of which hangs a series of sixteenth-century portraits, including one of Queen Elizabeth I given by that monarch herself to Bess of Hardwick. The High Great Chamber is also partly hung with tapestry, but the wonder of the room is the deep plaster frieze by Abraham Smith, copied from engravings after designs by Marten de Vos and still retaining its original colouring. Nothing could be more evocative than this large Renaissance room with its faded colours, needlework and marquetry furniture glowing in the subdued light filtering through the curtained windows.

Horsley
19; 6 miles N of Derby on A61
The first sight of ST CLEMENT'S CHURCH as you come in through the churchyard gate raises high expectations indeed. Since it is set on a hill, you see it obliquely from below in an unusual, almost exciting, perspective, with its low spire broached and lucarned, its ubiquitous crenellations and splendid gargoyles. The churchyard is beautiful too, ablaze with roses, looking out benevolently over the surrounding country. Within, the building reveals itself as earlier than one had thought – well before 1350, and quietly distinguished throughout. But that first thrill is never quite repeated.

Kedleston Hall★
20; 3 miles NW of Derby off A52 [9]
At first sight Kedleston appears to be all of one piece – the unified late eighteenth-century creation of Nathaniel Curzon, 1st Lord Scarsdale. As such it tends to conceal rather than disclose the complicated story of its design, as well as the 850-year-long history of the Curzon occupation of the site. Only the medieval church survives from before the second half of the eighteenth-century; everything else – the old house, rectory and village – was swept away to create the magnificent house and landscaped park that exist today.

The design of Kedleston is the brainchild of its owner but the work of several architects. Mathew Brettingham the Younger, whose father had built Holkham in Norfolk, provided the basic Palladian plan, with a central block and flanking wings. But soon after the north-east wing (the family residence) was begun in 1759 Brettingham was superseded by James Paine, who revised all the plans. Paine himself, however, was soon passed over for the interior decoration when Lord Scarsdale consulted James 'Athenian' Stuart, who made designs for the Dining Room and various furnishings. Lord Scarsdale was obviously determined to break away from the old-fashioned Palladian architecture of Brettingham and Paine and to have the interior of his house done out in the newest neo-classical taste. At this stage Robert Adam, recently returned from Italy, was able to convince Lord Scarsdale of his more brilliant abilities and to push Stuart aside and take over the decoration of the interior. The result is one of Adam's most magnificent ensembles, though incorporating many of the ideas of his predecessors, such as Paine's columned Hall and Stuart's scheme of lining the Dining Room with fitted paintings. Adam promoted the very young Samuel Wyatt to be clerk of works to supervise building on site and Kedleston thus became Wyatt's first important independent employment. The palatial results well justified the effort that went into the design.

The principal rooms are grouped round the Marble Hall on the *piano nobile*. This Hall is one of the grandest

The Hall, Kedleston Hall.

eighteenth-century rooms in the whole country. It is surrounded by superb Corinthian columns of Derbyshire alabaster supporting a coved stucco ceiling, designed by George Richardson. In niches round the walls are plaster casts of famous antique statues provided by Brettingham. On axis with the Hall on the garden front is the circular Saloon – an English Pantheon rising the full height of the house. The present appearance of the room, with inset classical paintings and scagliola Ionic doorcases, is Adam's second scheme for the room; his earlier decoration, with niches for statues, still exists underneath.

On the east side of the house are the Music Room, Library and State Drawing Room, all with stucco ceilings by Joseph Rose and hung with Lord Scarsdale's important collection of Flemish and Italian sixteenth- and seventeenth-century paintings. The Library has fitted bookcases made by Samuel Wyatt. The Drawing Room has alabaster doorcases and gilded sofas (made by John Linnell) decorated with dolphins and palm branches. To the west is the state apartment, comprising a Boudoir or Dressing Room and the State Bedroom, both hung with blue brocade and family portraits, and containing spectacular pier glasses and a bed decorated with gilded palm trees. The principal rooms are completed by the State Dining Room, where the side-tables are arranged in an apse (according to an idea by Adam) for the display of the family silver and a jasper wine cooler. The ormolu incense-burning tripod on the table was designed by 'Athenian' Stuart and is of considerable historical importance as one of the earliest examples of the English neo-classical style.

Locko Park

21; 4 miles NE of Derby on A6096

The sprawling subtopia between Derby and Nottingham seems an unlikely place to find a house still inhabited and beautifully maintained, but only 2 miles north of Spondon is the secluded park of Locko, one of Derbyshire's most retiring and least-known country houses. The main block was built in about 1730 in the style of Smith of Warwick and is stone faced, with rusticated Tuscan pilasters and a top balustrade. It is flanked on either side by the earlier Chapel (dated 1669) and a balancing eighteenth-century Drawing Room. The large, undulating park, with woods, deer and a wide lake, was landscaped by William Eames in the 1790s. But the dominant character of Locko is Victorian, the result of the work carried out by William Drury-Lowe in the 1850s. He employed Henry Stevens of Derby to remodel much of the interior as a setting for his notable collection of Italian paintings, and to add the Osborne-like tower, the Picture Gallery and the Dining Room. The latter is an impressive room, its walls still painted the original porphyry red as a background to the seventeenth-century Italian pictures that hang here; the coved ceiling is decorated with coloured arabesque patterns by an Italian artist called Romoli. The Picture Gallery also has a coved ceiling with arabesques by Romoli. Here the early Italian pictures, bought by William Drury-Lowe in Florence in the 1840s, are hung against brocade in serried rows three deep, and very impressive they look with their gold grounds. These formal rooms, with their *palazzo* air and grand contents, alternate with cosier lower-ceilinged rooms in the old main block, like the

Book Room and the Old Hall. The seventeenth-century Chapel has an original carved wooden ceiling with panels and hanging pendants, a chamber organ by Snetzler and the original pulpit with sounding board, brought back recently from the parish church at Denby to which it had migrated in the nineteenth century. The Drawing Room was remodelled in 1780 with an elegant plaster frieze of that date. It has recently been redecorated with yellow walls and eighteenth-century family portraits to enhance its late Georgian character.

Longford

22; 9 miles W of Derby off A52

Hall and church form a good group, standing side by side away from the village amidst cedars, clipped yews and well-maintained lawns. LONGFORD HALL is of warm red brick with stone dressings and is the result of an eighteenth-century modernisation of a Tudor house. Thus it has tall sash windows with white-painted glazing bars, and Tudor chimneys on top. The interior was burnt in 1942 but has since been reconstructed.

The large and handsome CHURCH OF ST CHAD, with a prominent Perpendicular west tower, is partly Norman, as can be seen clearly inside. The north arcade of the nave comprises fat round columns with scalloped capitals and semi-circular arches; the south arcade also has Norman piers, but the capitals and arches were altered *c.*1300 when the aisles and chancel were rebuilt. At the east end of the south aisle is an array of alabaster effigies of the Longford family, who owned the manor, beginning in 1357 and ending in 1610. On the death of the last Longford the property passed to Clement Coke, younger son of Chief Justice Sir Edward Coke, founder of the Holkham family. When the 1st Earl of Leicester of the first creation died in 1759, Holkham was inherited by the Longford branch of the Coke family. 'Coke of Norfolk', 1st Earl of Leicester of the second creation, was born at Longford and was buried here on his death in 1842. His monument takes the form of a large marble wall tablet in a Gothic surround, with a bust by John Francis; it is a place of pilgrimage for English agriculturalists. In the nineteenth-century, Longford was occupied by younger sons of the Holkham family.

Matlock

23; 16 miles N of Derby on A6

Nearly all spa towns are architecturally enjoyable, and some are even distinguished; Matlock falls within the first category. It is really a group of five separate villages, of which the earliest, OLD MATLOCK, is of the least interest – for the obvious reason that much of it predates the town's development as a watering-place. Most rewarding is MATLOCK BATH, a mile or so to the south on the Derby road. It had its origins around the old wooden bath of 1698 (now vanished), and boasts a fascinating collection of eighteenth- and nineteenth-century houses and hotels for the Quality, of which latter the Temple, the New Bath (Ruskin's favourite) and Hodgkinson's all have much to recommend them. Here the Derwent Valley has narrowed into a veritable gorge, above which to the west climb the so-called HEIGHTS OF ABRAHAM –

early nineteenth-century pleasure gardens, with steep leafy walks leading to two great caverns where lead has been mined since Roman times and, at the top, the VICTORIA PROSPECT TOWER of 1844. Lower down are two other still more enjoyable towers in castellated Gothick and, in Cliff Road, another unexpected bonus in the shape of the Arts-and-Craftsy chapel-of-ease of ST JOHN THE BAPTIST, designed by Guy Dawber in 1897.

To the north is MATLOCK BANK, where the hosiery manufacturer John Smedley built in 1853 the great HYDRO that was to bring wealth and popularity to the town for the best part of a century: a terrifying pile, now the headquarters of the county council – I for one should have preferred the vaguely orientalising ROCKSIDE HYDRO of 1903–6, today part of the College of Education. But it was Smedley, nonetheless, who dominated Matlock, and symbolised the fact in the 1860s by building himself his fairy-tale RIBER CASTLE, like a child's toy fort, on the high hill to the east – the perfect eye-catcher for the more romantically inclined of his patients in the town below. Today's visitors will find the castle only an empty shell, and will do better to turn their attention to the seventeenth-century HALL and MANOR HOUSE nearby.

Another equally lovely manor house, Elizabethan this time, can be found at SNITTERTON, a mile or so to the west of Matlock.

The Dining Room, Locko Park.

Melbourne

24; 6 miles S of Derby on B587 [10]

An unspoilt little town in the centre of a fascinating stretch of country on the Leicestershire–Derbyshire border – an area stuffed with architectural goodies, including Staunton Harold, Ashby-de-la-Zouch and Calke Abbey (*qq.v.*). Melbourne has a French air and is a rather pleasanter version of Petworth, with the Big House in the town and the parish church nearby. The town is a nice mixture of brick and stone, with the odd cruck cottage. It comprises three streets, which meet at a triangular 'square', where stand a drinking fountain and a shelter that looks like a witch's hat. POTTER STREET is the most agreeable and leads down to the Market Place, which has a cast-iron lamp of 1830 in the middle.

The CHURCH OF ST MICHAEL AND ST MARY is an unusually ambitious Norman building, with transepts, apsidal chancel, central tower and two west towers. The towers and the apse, unfortunately, have been truncated and mutilated, which detracts from the appearance of the exterior. The interior, however, is surprisingly impressive, with fat round columns and cushion capitals, the round arches of the nave carved with zigzag moulding, and a clerestory above. The crossing is spectacular, as it is open into the tower and has blank arcading round the sides, like the Romanesque churches of France. On one side of the arch facing the nave is a medieval painting of a devil with curly horns. Several hatchments hang on the walls, including that of Lord Melbourne, Queen Victoria's mentor and favourite Prime Minister; near it is the flag of Melbourne, Australia, which is called after him.

MELBOURNE HALL's chief fame lies in the formal gardens laid out *c.*1700 by the royal gardeners George London and Henry Wise; it is one of only a few examples of their work to survive. The lead statuary by John van Nost and the wrought-iron birdcage, or arbour, by Robert Bakewell are of exceptional quality.

The house itself dates from the early seventeenth century and forms a U-shape, its principal façade overlooking the garden. This front was added *c.*1720 and may have been designed by Smith of Warwick. The best rooms also owe their appearance to early eighteenth-century improvements, including their painted panelling and marble chimneypieces. The rooms are furnished with good Georgian furniture and family portraits, among them those of Lord Melbourne, Lady Caroline Lamb and Lady Palmerston, all of whom lived here. The Hall is now a seat of the Marquess of Lothian.

Radburne Hall

25; 3 miles W of Derby off B5020

Described by eighteenth-century topographers as 'a plain house of brick', Radburne is one of the lesser known of Derbyshire's many great houses. It is the seat of the Chandos-Pole family and was built for their ancestor, German Pole, in 1735, probably by William Smith of Warwick. It stands well on the highest part of the estate, surveying the prosperous and undisturbed Midlands landscape of south Derbyshire. Much of the impact of the house today comes from the exemplary restoration carried out for the present owner in 1958–60 by Frank

Scarlett and John Fowler. They restored glazing bars to the windows and redecorated the interior with faultless taste. The main rooms are on the *piano nobile* and the front door is approached by an impressive flight of wide stone steps. The Entrance Hall has a screen of Ionic columns at the back, pedimented doorcases, and a two-tiered chimneypiece that is balanced opposite by a niche under a pediment. On the opposite side of the house to the Hall is the Saloon, which is the finest room at Radburne; it contains a series of paintings by Joseph Wright of Derby, commissioned for the room in the 1770s and framed into the walls with plaster Palladian architraves. The other rooms are smaller and more homely. The Dining Room has eighteenth-century panelling and family portraits; the Library is lined with bookcases and offers lovely views of the grounds. In the rooms on the ground floor much of the seventeenth-century panelling is re-used from an earlier house on the site. Tradition has it that Bonnie Prince Charlie lunched here with the Poles in 1745 when he reached Derby.

Renishaw Hall

26; 1 mile S of Eckington on A616 [11]

The legendary seat of the Sitwells stands high on a hill amidst the industrial landscape of north-east Derbyshire but out of sight of the steel works and nineteenth-century village at its feet. These are the successors to the iron works established by the Sitwell family in the seventeenth century, thereby restoring their fortune after the depredations of the Civil War. The Sitwells came to Renishaw in 1625 and the core of the house dates from that time; it is sandwiched between large additions designed by Joseph Badger of Sheffield in the years 1793–1808 for Sir Sitwell Sitwell. It is this later work that is responsible for the romantic castellated exterior. The two sides of the house have strikingly different characters. The north front, which is the entrance front, is dark, austere and overlooks somewhat sombre parkland; it gives one a slight *frisson* on arriving. The south front, on the other hand, is charming and light, with an air of fantasy; it overlooks the famous terrace gardens made in the 1890s by Sir George Sitwell, with topiary, statues, fountains and formal pools. Their planting has recently been rejuvenated with flair and imagination by Reresby Sitwell, the present owner. Below is the lake, formed by Sir George, and beyond are plantations artfully placed to blot out the industry in the valley below. On a sunny day in summer one could be in Italy, rather than 6 miles from Sheffield.

The interior of Renishaw has a strong and delightful character all its own. Part of its charm derives from the contrast between the large, grand Georgian rooms at either end and the smaller, cosier, low-ceilinged rooms in the old part of the house. The contents are also remarkable for an English country house, embracing a strong representation of twentieth-century English art and Italian Baroque alongside the standard family portraits and Georgian mahogany. Both Sir Osbert and now Reresby Sitwell have added considerably to the collections. Much renovation and redecoration has also been undertaken in recent years. The tone is immediately set

Renishaw Hall.

by the Entrance Hall, which is lined with paintings by John Piper and enlivened by Venetian statues of blackamoors. In the east wing, the Drawing Room, Anteroom and Ballroom are all on a grand scale, enhanced by elegant plaster friezes and excellent marble chimneypieces designed by Sir William Chambers. They were removed from Albany when it was converted into bachelor apartments by Henry Holland in the 1790s and rescued then for Renishaw. The Anteroom was remodelled in an appropriately monumental style, with Tuscan columns and a coved ceiling, by Sir Edwin Lutyens in 1909. He also designed a bathroom upstairs, but this has since been dismantled. At the other end of the house, the Georgian Dining Room of 1797 is by Joseph Badger and has an apsidal recess for the sideboard. In the old house, the Library is the best-preserved room, its original plaster ceiling decorated with squirrels, dolphins and mermaids. Upstairs, as his own sitting room, Reresby Sitwell has recently made a Print Room on the eighteenth-century model, with Italian prints (found loose in the attic) pasted on to a yellow ground.

Repton

27; 7 miles SW of Derby on B5008

This is a pleasant little town, once the capital of the kingdom of Mercia. It retains its character despite the proximity of power stations and coalfields. It is dominated by the school founded by Sir John Port in 1557, which occupies the site and remaining buildings of an Augustinian priory; like all English public schools, it expanded enormously in the nineteenth century.

The most important building in the town is the CHURCH OF ST WYSTAN, which is famous for its well-preserved Saxon crypt. There has been much scholarly debate as to the exact date of this structure; though founded in the seventh century, it was damaged by the Danes in 874 and presumably rebuilt afterwards. The Saxon church was cruciform with a central tower. Of this building, the crypt, chancel, north transept and part of the crossing survive. The nave and aisles were rebuilt in the thirteenth and fourteenth centuries and the west tower and spire, rising to 212 feet, were completed in 1340. The two-storeyed porch and the nave clerestory, with Perpendicular windows and timber roof, are fifteenth-century. Most visitors will make straight for the crypt, which is small and dark and awe-inspiring. It is approximately 16 feet square, divided into nine bays by spiral-patterned columns carrying a tunnel vault. At the sides are recesses that are thought to have contained the tombs of Kings Aethelbald and Wiglaf. The general effect is reminiscent of the Romanesque crypts under the choirs of ancient monastic churches in central Italy.

REPTON SCHOOL is entered through the old gateway in the original precinct wall of the priory. The War Memorial Garth occupies the site of the cloisters, surrounded by Jacobean-looking buildings that contain some of the fabric of the medieval structures. Beneath the west range is an impressive undercroft with circular columns. Of the priory church, some low stretches of ruined wall and stumps of columns remain. The fifteenth-century prior's lodging, called Prior Overton's Tower, is incorporated in the late seventeenth-century REPTON HALL (now the headmaster's house). The prior's study on the first floor, with its carved timber ceiling, is a remarkably interesting medieval interior. The Victorian school buildings are run-of-the-mill public-school Gothic, and include a Chapel by Stevens of Derby and a large Hall by Sir Arthur Blomfield. The attractive Neo-Georgian theatre was designed in 1957 by Marshall Sisson. The town forms an agreeable foil to all this, with some timber-framed buildings and Georgian houses.

Sandiacre

28; 8 miles E of Derby on A52

I arrived at ST GILES'S CHURCH to find the vicar busy clearing away the debris of two tremendous trees that had just been felled in the churchyard. They were dead, he told me, and their removal meant that for the first time the church would be seen and admired from the roadway, as it deserved to be. He was right. It is a wonderful church, with a terrific Norman chancel arch surmounted by a small Saxon-looking opening, its aisleless nave pierced by two Norman windows that have been extended downwards at some later date. Beyond the arch is a fourteenth-century Decorated chancel, almost as long as the nave, with a glorious six-light east window (in which the Victorian glass is not at all bad), and sedilia and piscina most majestic under their canopies. Flanking the south door there are two beautiful crowned heads – Edward III and Queen Philippa? – she with a lovely filleted hairnet.

South Wingfield

29; 7 miles SE of Matlock on B5035

A dramatic ruin if ever there was one; and an object lesson of what could so easily have happened to Haddon Hall (*q.v.*) – which, on its completion in the 1450s, WINGFIELD MANOR must closely have resembled. Built by Ralph, Lord Cromwell (who had recently finished Tattershall in Lincolnshire (*q.v.*)), it was soon afterwards sold to the Shrewsburys and four times sheltered Mary Queen of Scots during her 'guardianship' by the 6th Earl, Bess of Hardwick's husband. Wingfield is now a roofless skeleton of a house; but one can still identify, grouped around its two courtyards, the Gatehouse, Hall, state rooms and Great Chamber. Despite its condition – it is now the property of a local farmer, who has used much of the floor space for his kitchen garden – it still keeps a lot of its atmosphere and, as so often in this part of Derbyshire, commands a wonderful view over the surrounding country.

Connoisseurs of early railway history should not miss the STATION, just beyond the bridge to the east. Built in 1839–40 and now derelict, it is the only complete surviving station built by Francis Thompson for Stephenson's Midland Railway.

Sudbury Hall

NT; 30; 4½ miles E of Uttoxeter on A50 [12]

The Vernons had held the manor of Sudbury since the beginning of the sixteenth century; but it was not until 1665 or thereabouts – 100 years after their old seat at Haddon (*q.v.*) had passed to the Mannerses – that George Vernon began work on the Hall. He seems to have been his own architect, a phenomenon not at all rare in the seventeenth century and one that would do a lot to explain the house's style, which must at the time have looked distinctly old-fashioned. The E-shaped plan, the diapered pattern of the brickwork, the tracery in some of the windows, the suggestion of strapwork in the lower cornice and (despite its Baroque tendencies) the two-storey porch – all these speak much more of Jacobean times than those of the Restoration; and the Long Gallery

of about 1676 must surely be the last ever built without deliberate archaising intent. Only the hipped roof and cupola were thoroughly up to date; but by the time Vernon had got to these he was probably growing more sophisticated.

Once the structure was completed, he could start on the decoration; and it is the decoration that makes Sudbury the sensational house it is. No building of its period is more richly, exuberantly ornate. Edward Pierce provided a carved staircase, with baskets of fruit on the newel-posts that could be replaced at night with candelabra; Louis Laguerre, fresh from Chatsworth (*q.v.*), embellished it further with a ceiling painting on the underside of the upper landing and another beneath the slope of the stairs themselves. The two also worked together in the Saloon, where Pierce's carvings are in every way comparable with those in the Drawing Room next door by Grinling Gibbons himself – and that is praise indeed. Yet what one remembers above all else at Sudbury is the plasterwork, the best of it by the two London plasterers Robert Bradbury and James Pettifer. Surprisingly little is known about these two consummate craftsmen, but their work at Sudbury is enough to ensure them a place in history. Pettifer apparently left after he had finished the Staircase Hall and Saloon, but Bradbury seems to have stayed on to tackle the greatest task of his career: the ceiling of the Long Gallery – a formidable undertaking which he completed with breathtaking virtuosity, covering its 138-foot length and 20-foot breadth with dragons, wild boars, horses emerging from cornucopiae, emperors' heads, shells and a series of particularly irresistible grasshoppers, at a total cost of £101.2s.0d.

In 1965 the Hall became the property of the National Trust, which almost immediately embarked on a flamboyant programme of restoration and redecoration under the direction of the late John Fowler. Sudbury falls into the second league of English country houses, yet no visitor coming to it from Kedleston, Hardwick or Chatsworth (*qq.v*) need fear disappointment or any sense of anticlimax. In its own way it has just as much to offer; and it is certainly a good deal less awe-inspiring. To live in one of those prodigious piles could not, one feels, be other than a challenge; to live at Sudbury – if only one could afford it – would be pure delight.

The discreetly sited Victorian wing (by George Devey, 1876–83) copies the style of the main house. In it, Sudbury's curator John Hodgson has created a MUSEUM OF CHILDHOOD, enchanting to adults and children alike.

Sutton Scarsdale

31; 5 miles SE of Chesterfield off A617

The shell remains of this splendid Baroque house designed by Francis Smith of Warwick in 1724, which, according to local legend, was the house of the Rake in Hogarth's *Rake's Progress*. It was saved from demolition after the Second World War by Sir Osbert Sitwell, who bought it; and the intention is that it should be preserved as a grandly beautiful ruin. The interior had magnificent Italianate plasterwork by Artari and Vassali but this has all gone, though one or two rooms from the house have

Sudbury Hall.

been re-erected in the Museum of Fine Art in Philadelphia. Both façades are beautiful, with a perfectly controlled balance between the horizontal channelling of the rusticated stonework and the perpendicular fluting of the Corinthian columns and pilasters. The capitals are finely carved; so is the pediment on the east front, showing the arms of the Leeke family who owned the place down to their extinction in the early nineteenth century. It was then bought by the Arkwrights, but abandoned by them after the First World War in the face of the spreading blight from the coal-mines around Bolsover (*q.v.*). There is a vivid description of the house by Sir Sacheverell Sitwell in *British Architects and Craftsmen*: 'When we saw it, the ceiling of the lower room had fallen in, so that there was the extraordinary spectacle of four Venetian mantelpieces, all of the richest work imaginable, richer, by far, than anything in a Venetian palace, hanging in the air, with the remains of the coloured stucco in panels and niches upon the walls .... Such was the fate of what was, certainly, the finest work of Artari or any of the Italians in England. ... The violent force of this revelation of the Venetian eighteenth century may be imagined.'

Tideswell

32; 6 miles NE of Buxton on B6049

This little town lies in a slight hollow in the Peak and the first view is of the four serrated pinnacles of the church tower sticking up above the roofs of the surrounding houses like the snouts of four swordfish. The town itself is built of grey limestone, with unassuming shops and houses; the unmistakable aroma of fish and chips permeates the air. Indeed, Tideswell has a surprisingly unspoilt and workaday character – very much the Flookburgh of Derbyshire. The great sight, of course, is the CHURCH OF ST JOHN THE BAPTIST, a massive and uniform fourteenth-century structure. It was begun in 1340 and completed fifty years later, the hiatus in construction having been caused by the Black Death. The style changes almost imperceptibly from Decorated to Perpendicular. The tower (completed last) is at the west end and the overall plan is cruciform, with transepts and chancel all sharing an even roofline. A visually most effective touch is the little fretted bellcote crowning the roof-ridge at the junction between the crossing and chancel. When seen broadside on from the village street, you are immediately struck by the beautiful Decorated tracery in the large transept window and the almost Puginian perfection of the chancel, its tall square-headed three-light windows separated from each other by narrow buttresses. The interior makes an immediate impression of noble simplicity with its ample proportions, symmetry and uniform architectural character. The enormous west window has stained glass of 1907 by Hardman (described in the guide-books as 'good modern glass'!). The chunky timber roof of the nave is the original, and the early nineteenth-century Gothick box pews are most attractive. The south transept contains a medieval table-tomb with battered knightly effigies, while the north transept is almost entirely filled by a huge Victorian organ with an array of stencilled pipes in a carved oak case. This, and the richly appointed choir stalls and other late Victorian furnishings were partly the work of 'Suffolk craftsmen' and partly the work of

St Mary's church, Tissington.

Advent Hunstone, a local wood-carver. The tall chancel has an attractive timber roof decorated with a sparse flutter of carved angels. In the centre of the chancel is an alabaster table-tomb; scattered round the walls are one or two hatchments and memorial tablets, creating a comfortably furnished look. The low stone reredos screen behind the altar is an unusual but not unique feature (a similar arrangement can be found in the Fitzalan Chapel at Arundel in Sussex). The two limewood statues filling the niches were carved in 1950 by Jethro Harris of Oxford. The beautiful Victorian glass in the large east window, depicting the tree of Jesse, was made in 1875 by Heaton, Butler and Bayne. The side-windows have clear glass, which lets in the light and forms an effective contrast to the rich glow of colours above the altar. If you look back, you can still see the jagged outline of the previous smaller chancel visible in the stonework around the west arch. I wonder why it was never smoothed over?

Tissington
33; 6 miles N of Ashbourne on A515
From the Buxton–Ashbourne road, the village of Tissington is approached through a lodge gate and down an ancient lime avenue. (A new outer line of trees, which will take the place of the older trees in due course, has recently been planted.) Tissington is a patriarchal estate village of stone, neatly kept, and without any jarring note. There is a small triangular green with a little stream down one side fed by the village's five wells. On Ascension Day each year these are dressed with flowers, mosses and berries in mosaic patterns – an ancient custom for which the place is well known.

ST MARY'S CHURCH and the HALL face each other across the village. The church is 'Norman' with a low west tower. Much of the detail, including the aisle arcade, is due to nineteenth-century reconstruction, but the interior retains an attractive atmosphere, with its whitewashed walls, dark beamed roof, old pews, Jacobean two-decker pulpit, hatchments and the serried monuments of the Fitzherbert family, who have been lords of the manor of Tissington since the fifteenth century. Their Hall is set back behind low stone walls and a sloping lawn, approached through an arch with a fine wrought-iron gate. The centre is the original Jacobean house, forming a compact square block enlivened by a projecting two-storeyed porch in the centre and mullion windows glittering with small panes of glass. The austere effect is considerably softened by the massed array of columnar chimneys bristling on the skyline, and extensions to either side. To the left are attractive eighteenth-century stables, and to the right is a wing nearly as big again as the old house, added in 1910 to the design of Arnold Mitchell in a sensitive evocation of the original style. It is these additions that are partly responsible for the attraction of the Hall, transforming it into the *beau idéal* of the rambling old English manor house. The back of the house, facing the terraced garden, was Georgianised in the eighteenth century. The Strawberry Hill Gothick chimneypiece and plaster cornice in the Hall also date from that time, but the handsome panelling there and in the upstairs Drawing Room is good original Jacobean work.

Wingfield Manor
See South Wingfield.

Wirksworth

34; 6 miles S of Matlock on B5035 [13]

Formerly the centre of the English lead-mining industry, and until recently rather a forlorn place, Wirksworth has a dramatic setting in a craggy valley. It is a little town of brick and stone huddling round an ambitious medieval church. It has benefited considerably over the last ten years from a Historic Buildings Council Town Scheme and the activities of the Derbyshire Historic Buildings Trust. As a result, many fine buildings that were on the verge of dereliction have been carefully repaired. This restoration programme has been remarkably successful in rejuvenating the architectural fabric without making the town look too tarted-up and today Wirksworth is a pleasant place to spend an hour or two.

There are two curving main streets, with several good three-storeyed Georgian houses, meeting at a triangular MARKET PLACE with old-established shops and pubs. Among the shops, Payne's Chemist's Shop, established in 1756, has an original Georgian shop-front with two little bows; Marsden's Ironmonger's was established in 1764 and is still going strong; Braziers and General Ironmongers have gone but the shop-front, with its red-and-gold *verre églomisé* fascia sign, survives. The Red Lion pub, with a central feature of an archway, Venetian window and pediment, makes a good view-stopper out of one corner of the Market Place.

The CHURCH OF ST MARY is concealed from the main street by buildings and has a surprise approach through an eighteenth-century wrought-iron gate, which has urn-capped stone piers dated 1721. These lead into a grassy graveyard surrounded by nice houses – rather like a miniature cathedral close. Round it are simple iron railings with little acorns on top. In one corner is the former GRAMMAR SCHOOL – a delightful Gothick structure bristling with pinnacles, dating from 1828. (Next to it in bathetic contrast is the new office of the Derbyshire Rural Community Council in purest Bungaloid style.) The church is a magnificent cruciform structure, with a thirteenth-century central tower, showing examples of most phases of English medieval architecture but heavily restored in the nineteenth century by Sir George Gilbert Scott. The interior is spatially exciting; it contains interesting monuments to the Gell family of Hopton Hall, as well as a Highly Important Saxon coffin lid which sends archaeologists into raptures and has been the subject of many long and learned articles relating its iconography to Byzantine art.

One of the most attractive features of Wirksworth is the series of narrow little lanes lined higgledy-piggledy with old houses, opening off the main streets; these are well worth exploring on foot. The best sequence is DALE END and GREENHILL, which winds uphill out of a corner of the Market Place and is lined with sixteenth-, seventeenth- and eighteenth-century houses and cottages, now being repaired after years of neglect. The gem is BABINGTON HOUSE – a Jacobean building with gables and mullion windows. There is perhaps something of the feel of an old Italian hill town about Wirksworth; it is certainly a place with an unusual atmosphere. It also has a very good fish-and-chip shop.

Youlgreave

35; 4 miles S of Bakewell off B5056

ALL SAINTS' CHURCH is a rare treasure. Outside it appears grandly Perpendicular, all pinnacled and battlemented and with a mighty west tower second only to that of Derby (*q.v.*) itself. The first surprise comes immediately on entering, when one discovers that the building is a good deal earlier than it pretends to be. The south arcade is late Norman at its best – simple and strong, its piers circular, their capitals scalloped; the northern is just a little later, its arches being ever so slightly, almost tentatively, pointed and the capitals curiously adorned with scrolls and heads, both human and animal. Just to the west is a delightful little carving of a pilgrim, traditionally carved by a wandering friar in return for hospitality. The north aisle contains an endearing Jacobean monument and a wondrously beautiful alabaster panel of the late fifteenth century to Robert Gylbert, his wife and seventeen children.

Up the steps to the chancel; and there, most dramatically in the centre, lies the tiny alabaster figure of Thomas Cokayne. He wears full armour; his head rests on his helm, which is surmounted by a crowing cock. His diminutive size is generally explained by the fact that he died young (in a brawl as it happened, on his way to the church); but his droopy moustache suggests that he was already fully grown, or nearly so. All around him, the rest of the chancel is essentially Victorian in feeling, the result of a conscientious restoration by Norman Shaw in 1869–70. Shaw's are the choir stalls and reredos, Burne-Jones's the excellent east window – and, *pace* Pevsner, the south window nearby, though it doesn't look like it to me.

On leaving, don't miss the font: dating from about 1200, it is the only one in the country with, projecting from its side, a separate stoup, supported by a salamander and designed, presumably, for holy oil.

Wirksworth.

Durham

The old county of Durham is unlike anything else in England, for it was an episcopal palatinate, the Bishop having been responsible for law, government administration and defence against the Scots from the Norman Conquest onwards. This wonderful anomaly survived down to the 1830s, when the structure of the Church of England, the most medieval institution in Europe to survive the French Revolution, was dismantled by the Whigs in a series of philistine 'reforms' not equalled until the Heath–Walker destruction of the ancient counties of England in the early 1970s. County Durham suffered from the latter too, losing its northern fringe to a bureaucratic unit with the imaginative name of 'Tyne and Wear', and its southern fringe to Cleveland (which at least is better than Teesside). But we ignore that here. Durham is essentially that area between the Tyne and the Tees, between the North Sea and the bleak moors on the borders of Cumberland and Westmorland. The county is bisected by the Great North Road (the A1), now a motorway. To the east is a landscape once heavily industrialised and built up with mines, colliery villages, and former shipbuilding towns and coal ports. To the west is wild, open country – desolate moorland in the north, and attractive pastoral and farming country in the south. The valley of the River Wear is austerely splendid, while the valley of the Tees is softer but equally beautiful, with unspoilt country and good-looking villages built round large greens. The ancient market town of Barnard Castle, with its handsome wide streets; the Raby estate, with its magnificent medieval castle, well-managed farms and woodland, and whitewashed houses and cottages; and the arable plain round Darlington form the southern frontier of the county.

Although now mainly rural, the landscape of Durham was everywhere shaped by industry. Lead-mining and coal-mining are thought to have been begun here by the Romans. Coal was the dominant force for centuries, and the source of the bishopric's great wealth (the mineral rights belonged to the palatinate). Now King Coal is in retreat. Since the Second World War many inland mines have been closed, slag heaps grassed over, and even the colliery villages – those graded D in the 1954 County Development Plan – demolished. Today most of the coal mined in the county comes from the pits along the coast, whose rich seams stretch far out under the sea. Second only to coal in the nineteenth century were steel and shipbuilding, but they have gone entirely; the great steel works at Consett closed in 1980 and have now been pulled down. Their place has been taken to an extent by the chemical industry, developed since the 1920s at Billingham near the mouth of the River Tees, and 'light industry' in the new towns of Peterlee, Newton Aycliffe, Washington and elsewhere. Since the war, all the centres of the old industrial towns have been destroyed by 'comprehensive redevelopment', so none of them finds a place in this guide. It is one of the peculiarities of modern Britain that the economic collapse of the old industrial areas has involved the destruction of much of their architecture, whereas in the past, economic decline was the surest way of preserving the fabric of towns, as is demonstrated by Flanders and Italy, or East Anglia and the Cotswolds.

The great architectural thrills of County Durham are its churches, beginning with the three important Saxon churches at Monkwearmouth, Jarrow and Escomb. The latter is one of only three complete Saxon churches in the country. Norman work is represented at a supreme level by Durham Cathedral. Gothic also appears at the highest standard of excellence in the Chapel of the Nine Altars added to Durham Cathedral in the thirteenth century and showing the Early English style at its most maturely beautiful; Gothic is found on a lesser scale, too, in several parish churches, such as that at Chester-le-Street. After the Reformation, the tradition is continued in Bishop Cosin's Gothic-Baroque woodwork of the late seventeenth century, and the perfect Georgian church at Gibside designed by James Paine as if it were a particularly grand garden temple with a dome and portico facing down an avenue of oaks. Victorian Gothic, redolent of Pugin, and indeed with many fittings by him, is to be found in the chapel of the Catholic seminary at Ushaw. And, finally, there is the amazing early twentieth-century Arts and Crafts Gothic of St Andrew's, Roker – a masterpiece by E.S. Prior.

Country houses are thinner on the ground than in some other counties. The most magnificent is the Londonderry seat at Wynyard – an early nineteenth-century neo-classical palace by Philip Wyatt. But Durham is a good county for castles – both ruins, like Barnard Castle, and continuously inhabited ones, like Raby, Lumley, and Durham Castle itself, all of which are accessible to the public.

County Durham is, as you might expect from its idiosyncratic and independent history, a good place in which to find eccentric buildings, whether the extra-ordinary apparition of the Penshaw Monument – that blackened northern Parthenon – or the francophile Bowes Museum at Barnard Castle – a dislocated piece of Napoleon III's Paris. But all roads lead back to the county town itself – one of the great architectural experiences of the world which, with its magnificent complex of an-cient buildings and streets on a rock, was compared by Pevsner to Prague or Avignon. It is rare in England for money, power, piety and art to meet in one place – but, to coin a phrase, 'the effect is shattering'.

Barnard Castle
1; 15 miles W of Darlington on A67

This attractive old market town in Teesdale takes its name from the castle founded in 1112 by Bernard, son of Guy de Baliol. The ruins of the castle survive, guarding the sixteenth-century bridge over the Tees, and even today give an impression of military might, with their four wards, earthworks, stone walls and fourteenth-century round tower. The views to the moors are im-pressive, recalling Sir Walter Scott's lines:

> *What prospects from his watchtower high,*
> *gleam gradual on the warder's eye.*

The town itself is wrapped round two sides of the castle and has a continuous sequence of impressive main streets lined with three-storeyed stone-built houses with stone-flagged roofs and many old painted-timber shop-fronts.

The centre of the town, and the place to begin a walk, is the MARKET CROSS at the bottom of the Market Place. It is a handsome two-storeyed octagon with a Tuscan colonnade round the ground floor and a cupola on top. The main room, on the first floor, where the town council used to meet, is lit by Venetian windows. The Cross was built in 1747 at the expense of Thomas Breaks and was referred to 100 years later by Robert Surtees, creator of Jorrocks and a famous son of Durham, as 'a heavy modern town hall in the centre of the street'. In the weathervane are two bullet holes made in 1804 by two locals who fired at it from a distance of 100 yards to settle a bet. Across the road, and set back slightly, is ST MARY'S, the parish church, of largely Perpendicular appearance but drastically restored in 1873 when the tower was rebuilt by Hodgson Fowler.

Following the main street steeply downhill towards the river, this stretch is called the Bank and has one or two special buildings, including BLAGRAVE HOUSE, which dates from the sixteenth century and is an ex-ample of the local vernacular, with mullion windows and a gabled bay. The three little figures on brackets are relatively modern; they look like Toby jugs. At the bottom of the hill, Thorngate has a few sycamore trees and THORNGATE HOUSE gives a touch of grandeur. By the river are a row of weavers' cottages and THORN-GATE MILL, a memento of Barnard Castle's eighteenth-century woollen industry. An iron footbridge made in

Barnard Castle.

Darlington in 1892 leads across the river and gives good views of the rapids in their stony channel below the castle crag – a subject painted by several of the early nineteenth-century Romantics.

Returning up the hill to the Market Cross and beyond to the MARKET PLACE and its continuation the HORSE-MARKET, the visitor is rewarded by a remarkably good stretch of townscape with curving stretches of stone houses, banks and shops. The street itself is 40 yards wide. The Golden Lion pub is Georgian but endearingly painted black and white to look like half-timber; the Italianate façade of the King's Head Hotel conceals an older building, where Dickens stayed in February 1838 while collecting material for *Nicholas Nickleby*; and there is a collection of seemly banks. At the end of the Horsemarket is a townscape surprise, for the street suddenly turns at right-angles into GALGATE, a further stretch of wide tree-lined street with good-looking buildings on both sides. The most famous sight in Barnard Castle, however, is the BOWES MUSEUM situated in Newgate on the other side of the town, past the parish church. This spectacular display of Second Empire splendour was founded in 1869 by John Bowes of Streatlam Castle, the illegitimate son of the 10th Earl of Strathmore. It was designed by Jules Pellechet and is of four towering storeys with a mansard roof, and looks for all the world like a stretch of the Louvre that has descended on County Durham. It stands amidst well-maintained Victorian gardens with specimen trees and formal bedding-out, and gazes across the river to open country. The contents are as rich and cosmopolitan as the architecture – silver, china, textiles and an interesting collection of paintings, of which those by Spanish masters form the only assemblage of the type in England. The museum is now well run by Durham County Council, but one wishes that the tall, gaunt galleries at the top of the building could be restored to their Victorian colour schemes and the paintings hung several tiers deep on the walls; this need not disturb the run of masterpieces at eye-level, as there are plenty of 'second-eleven' paintings that could go above them, and it would improve the appearance of these three huge rooms.

Biddick Hall
See Penshaw Monument.

Chester-le-Street
2; 6 miles N of Durham on A167
The site of the CHURCH OF ST MARY AND ST CUTHBERT is a venerable one: there was a Saxon church here in the eighth century and in the ninth it was briefly the seat of the bishopric, until this removed to Durham in 995. The present collegiate church was built in 1286. The nave survives from that time, with circular piers and pointed arches. The octagonal spire, however, which is the dominant feature, was added to the earlier tower in the fourteenth century. The west front is very picturesque – not least because built into the end of the north aisle is an anchorage where a hermit lived in the fourteenth century. It has little rooms inside and a squint opening into the church so that he could follow the services.

The interior of the church is impressively dark, thanks to the Victorian stained glass that fills all the windows. The major interest resides in the Lumley monuments, which line the north aisle and are one of the country's most striking demonstrations of Elizabethan antiquarian taste. John, 7th Lord Lumley of Lumley Castle (*q.v.*), was among the founder-members of the Elizabethan Society of Antiquaries – a collector, bibliophile, Catholic recusant, and patron of William Byrd. He was passionately interested in his family's history – so much so that King James I, on a visit to Lumley Castle, interrupted a recitation of his host's ancestors with the words, 'I didna' ken Adam's name was Lumley.' At Chester-le-Street, Lumley erected monuments to his forebears: no fewer than fourteen knightly effigies on tomb-chests. Some are genuine, brought here under licence from Durham Cathedral or from suppressed monasteries, but the majority were specially made in neo-medieval style in the late sixteenth century. There was not quite enough room to cram them all in, so some have their feet missing. Above them are inscriptions written by Lord Lumley, which explain who is meant to be who and begin with a long description of the family descent from Liulph in the reign of Edward the Confessor. (In fact, the Lumley pedigree cannot be traced before the twelfth century but, as Edward Gibbon remarked, 'The proudest families are content to lose in the darkness of the Middle Ages, the tree of their pedigree.')

Durham ★
3; 17 miles N of Darlington on A167 [14]
More than most places in England, Durham is a city of cultural contrasts. The Low Town round the bus station is squalid, with graffiti on the walls, new buildings, filthy footpaths and nasty shops. The High Town, on the other hand, is ancient, dignified, a seat of learning and a national shrine. Such a contrast in this setting strikes the visitor as convincingly medieval. Castle, cathedral and old town stand on a rock that is almost encircled by a loop of the River Wear. The site was chosen for defensive reasons, to protect the tomb of St Cuthbert from marauders from across the seas or from Scotland to the north. St Cuthbert was moved here from Lindisfarne in 995, but it was the Normans in the eleventh and twelfth centuries who were responsible for the unforgettable silhouette, 'half church of God, half castle 'gainst the Scot'. The view from the railway – as the train north suddenly emerges from a rocky cutting on to a 100-foot-high viaduct – of castle, cathedral and old city looming majestically across the river is the single most dramatic architectural apparition in the whole of England.

THE CASTLE
Until 1836 this impressive stone pile was the seat of the Prince-Bishops of Durham and the administrative centre of their palatinate. In that year it was turned over to the newly founded University (the third oldest in England) and it has been occupied by one of its colleges ever since.

The castle was founded in 1072 and retains its original layout, with a large shell keep, reconstructed in the nineteenth century, and bailey. The Great Hall, one of the largest medieval halls in Europe, was built in 1284, and the kitchens date from the fifteenth century. There are two chapels – one Norman (1072) and one sixteenth-century. Bishop Cosin carried out an extensive programme of repairs in the 1660s following damage in the Civil War; the tapestry-hung state rooms and the staircase with its carved balustrade of black oak are his. Further restoration was done in the late eighteenth century by Bishop Shute Barrington under the direction of James Wyatt, and the pretty Gothick GATEHOUSE leading from Castle Green is almost certainly Wyatt's. Finally, the University undertook some rebuilding under the direction of Anthony Salvin in the 1840s, and much of the present appearance of the keep is due to him. Most of the building provides student accommodation, but the Great Hall serves as the Dining Hall and the Bishop's state rooms have been maintained in their old condition and appropriately furnished. They are open to the public.

THE CATHEDRAL AND IMMEDIATE ENVIRONS

Durham Cathedral is the grandest Romanesque church in Christendom. Only the east transept, the three towers and the Cloisters date from later than the twelfth century. Externally, this great cathedral makes an overwhelming impact because of its vast size. It forms a spectacular, picturesque composition from wherever it is viewed, but nothing can compare with the cathedral and the strongly buttressed masses of its outbuildings as seen from Prebends Bridge to the south-west, rising above the steep wooded banks of the river, with a little red-roofed mill in the foreground to give scale. The close-up view of the north side from Palace Green is hardly less impressive.

The first thing the visitor to the cathedral encounters is the famous bronze sanctuary knocker on the main door. The moment of entering the nave, to quote Alec Clifton-Taylor, 'provides an architectural experience never to be forgotten; one of the greatest which England has to offer'. The original Norman building is unusually well preserved and the design is of an incomparable nobility and grandeur. The proportions are satisfying, the nave columns are round and tall, and, if they were hollow, would be fat enough to lie down in. The double-arched tribune provides deep, dark shadows, and overhead is the noble vaulted roof – the earliest high-level rib vault in Europe. As you stand at the back of the church and your eye passes down the immensely solemn vista, it seems incredible that all the Norman work was completed within forty years of the starting date in 1093. The nave and choir piers alternate between composite shafted columns and cylindrical columns. The latter are decorated with incised geometrical patterns – a flourish of unforgettable audacity. There are four different patterns: diaper, chevron, spiral and vertical flute. The vault ribs are also carved with chevron or zigzag ornament, which makes a further appearance in the interlacing arcades round the lower parts of the walls. This rich but simple decoration helps to mitigate the domineering character of the masses of stone masonry.

Before progressing up the nave, it is best to look at the Galilee Chapel at the west end. Durham has no west front, as this Chapel occupies the narrow ledge between the body of the cathedral and the precipice overlooking the River Wear. (Wyatt was stopped from pulling it down to make a carriage drive – a proposal that led to him being blackballed from the Society of Antiquaries!) There are dizzy views down from the west windows. The Galilee is late twelfth-century, having been finished *c.*1189. It shows Norman work at its most light and fanciful, with slender columns supporting arches lavishly carved with chevron ornament; the effect is almost Moorish in its extravagance. The Perpendicular windows admit more light than the original Norman windows in the nave aisles, and this, too, contributes to the elegant effect. In the recess behind the altar survive important traces of late twelfth-century wall paintings and there are patchwork assemblages of medieval stained glass in the windows. But the most moving object in the Galilee is the tomb of Bede – a plain stone chest with a black marble slab on top inscribed in Latin: 'IN THIS TOMB ARE THE BONES OF THE VENERABLE BEDE'. He was brought to Durham in 1020.

The principal furnishing in the nave is the lofty font cover, 40 feet tall. It was erected by Bishop Cosin in 1663. The cathedral had been damaged by the Scots during the Civil War. (They had, for instance, burnt all the medi-

The sanctuary knocker, Durham Cathedral.

eval woodwork, including the choir stalls, to keep themselves warm.) At the Restoration, Bishop Cosin went to great lengths to restore his churches, and episcopal powers. At Durham he was responsible for many elaborate furnishings, deliberately combining classical and Gothic elements to create a unique Baroque effect. The font cover is the most gorgeous of these effusions, with Gothic tracery and crocketed gables. In the south aisle is the post-Restoration organ case – a massive piece of Baroque woodwork, originally on top of the rood-screen but removed by the Victorian 'restorers' and only reassembled here in 1903. The grey marble line across the nave floor marks the point beyond which, until the beginning of the Reformation, women were not allowed to go. As you walk up the nave, your eye is caught by Sir George Gilbert Scott's rood-screen and behind, at the east end, James Wyatt's cobweb-like rose window. The screen is of open Gothic design with shafts of Frosterly marble; it provides just the right note of punctuation in the massive vista. The transepts and choir are almost identical in design to the nave, though built first; Durham, like most cathedrals, was begun at the east end. In the south transept is an amazingly theatrical clock, part Gothic, part Jacobean, and looking like a motif from a medieval illuminated manuscript writ large. It was erected in the late fifteenth century by Prior Castell and remodelled in 1630. Removed in 1845, it was restored in 1938 by Stephen Dykes Bower. The painted doors in the base lead to the Cloisters; you almost expect them to open at the hours and some equestrian automaton to ride out. The large clock face, gilded and painted, is supported on marbled shafts and crowned by an open dome and lofty finial.

The choir is a scene of magnificence. Here the Catholic mass was said for the last time in an English cathedral during the rebellion of the northern Earls in 1572. Bishop Cosin's elaborate Baroque-Gothic choir stalls and fretted canopies stand out against the pale stone of the Norman arcades. The floor is paved with marble. The Bishop's throne is elevated above the gilded tomb of Bishop Hatfield – a unique arrangement. The high altar is backed by the Neville Screen, given by John, Lord Neville, in c.1380 and one of the most beautiful Gothic artefacts in England, with its openwork turrets and pinnacles of pale Caen stone, like an eighteenth-century dream of spiky Gothic. Behind, on a raised platform, is the tomb of St Cuthbert. The medieval shrine was destroyed at the Reformation and the tomb is marked now by a simple slab inscribed with the name 'CUTHBERTUS' – more impressive amidst all the grandeur than gold and jewels, for this is the *raison d'être* for the whole vast edifice. Hanging high above is a gilded tester by Sir Ninian Comper, and round the platform is a restored sixteenth-century timber screen. The final surprise at Durham is the east end: the original Norman apsidal arrangement was replaced between 1242 and 1280 by a transeptal CHAPEL OF THE NINE ALTARS – like Fountains Abbey, but an arrangement unique in cathedral architecture. Here is Gothic work that harmonises perfectly with the Norman architecture because it shares the same robust magnificence. The piers form massed shafts of grey Frosterly marble shooting up to the vault. The whole of the north wall is occupied by one huge window with double geometrical tracery – an effect of surprising richness.

The CLOISTERS lie to the south side of the church and were restored in the mid-eighteenth century, when the rather striking Gothick tracery was inserted in the windows. Durham, like several other English cathedrals, was served by Benedictine monks, not secular canons – an anomaly going back to Saxon times and unique to this Kingdom. Many of their buildings survive, opening off the Cloisters. The MONKS' DORMITORY is a museum containing many precious objects; the REFECTORY is the cathedral Library, with seventeenth-century bookcases. The vaulted undercroft is now the TREASURY and visitors' restaurant. Here used to be the Durham whale – a vast, dusty skeleton beloved of children. She was washed up on the shore of Sunderland in the 1660s and brought to Durham at the command of Bishop Cosin, who was intent on restoring *all* his palatine powers. Where is she now?

Beyond the Cloisters is COLLEGE GREEN – a perfect English scene with lawn and trees surrounded by cobbled paths and buildings of all ages, including the fifteenth-century DEANERY, several solid eighteenth-century canons' houses, the Tudor-Gothick CHOIR SCHOOL, and the delicious Gothick CONDUIT HOUSE of 1751 – all approached from the outer world through a late fifteenth-century GATEHOUSE. The old monastic KITCHEN is now used to store the archives. A mysterious, cobbled, tunnel-like passage called the DARK ENTRY leads from College Green to a romantic walkway along the river bank at the west end of the cathedral.

THE CITY

The old town forms a perfect foil to the cathedral and castle. Coming from the station, the peninsula is entered across Framwellgate Bridge and up Silver Street, a curving thoroughfare that is now pedestrianised and lined with shops. At the top is the MARKET PLACE, given character by the Victorian Gothic of ST NICHOLAS'S CHURCH (built by J.P. Pritchett in 1857) and the TOWN HALL (by P.C. Hardwick in 1851). In the centre is a large green-bronze equestrian statue of the 3rd Marquess of Londonderry by Rafael Monti (the sculptor responsible for the proscenium arch at Covent Garden). This is known to the locals as 'The Horse', recalling Queen Victoria's rebuke to a guest at Windsor who had inadvertently referred to 'the Copper Horse' – 'Do you mean the equestrian statue of Our Grandfather?' From here, the approach to PALACE GREEN and the cathedral via Saddler Street and Owengate is a classic demonstration of 'kynetic townscape'; as you walk up the curving cobbled lane, the bulk of the cathedral, culminating in the west towers, is gradually revealed. It is like watching a film being slowly unwound. On Palace Green, the terrific broadside impact of the cathedral is the visual knock-out, but there are also several Georgian houses, all restored and occupied by the University, as well as the toy-fort Gothick of the eighteenth-century gateway to the castle.

Along the east side of the peninsula, the most attractive street in the old city runs along the line of the medieval fortifications – NORTH BAILEY and SOUTH BAILEY. Quiet and well kept, it forms a gentle curve round the outside of the cathedral precincts and leads down to PREBENDS BRIDGE (built by George Nicholson in 1772–8), with fine balustraded parapets and *the* wonderful view. The street itself is lined with a variety of attractive houses – some brick, some stone and some stuccoed – once the town residences of the Durham gentry. They have Georgian façades but are older inside. Many of them are occupied by the University and have been well converted and restored. The former Eden townhouse is now ST JOHN'S COLLEGE. It is a stately stone-fronted building of 1730. The college CHAPEL is the old parish church of St Mary-the-Less – a Norman church rebuilt in 1846 but incorporating several old features. ST CHAD'S COLLEGE occupies several more old houses and also has sympathetic new buildings designed by Francis Johnson. Next to it is the little church of ST MARY-LE-BOW, seventeenth-century with an eighteenth-century tower and an interior stuffed with old woodwork in the Cosin tradition. No longer used as a church, it is now a 'heritage centre'. The former Red Lion Hotel has become HATFIELD COLLEGE, the second oldest in the university. The additions in Tudor style were Salvin's in 1848.

Returning to the neck of the peninsula, the medieval Elvet Bridge crosses the river to Old Elvet, a spacious street with many grand eighteenth-century houses, the fiery red brick former SHIRE HALL (now used by the University) and the CATHOLIC CHURCH of 1827 by Bonomi, with its unspoilt Gothick interior and its sanctuary decorated with the arms of local recusant families. The ASSIZE COURTS and GAOL behind are sombre early nineteenth-century neo-classical with a Tuscan portico. If one could choose one's prison on architectural grounds, this might be the place to go.

Egglestone Abbey

4; 3 miles SE of Barnard Castle off A66
The ruins of the Premonstratensian abbey lie in a beautiful position by the River Tees a few miles from Barnard Castle (*q.v.*) and make a perfect picturesque composition. Cows graze the surrounding fields, the ruins are framed by old trees, and a farmhouse and one or two stone cottages complete the ensemble. The abbey was founded at the end of the twelfth century by Ralph de Malton. The first church was built then but extensively reconstructed in the late thirteenth century, when the chancel was rebuilt and the windows altered. It is this later work that adds so much to the beauty of the ruins, especially the broken tracery of the large windows. The church is the best-preserved part, most of the walls standing to a good height. The monastic buildings are more fragmentary, and in 1548, after the Dissolution, the north range was converted into a house. It, too, is now in ruins, but it still sports Elizabethan mullion windows. One of the most impressive surviving features of the monastic buildings is the drainage system with deep stone-lined culverts leading to the rushing waters of the river below.

Gibside Chapel.

Escomb★

5; 1 mile W of Bishop Auckland off B6282 [15]
The CHURCH OF ST JOHN THE EVANGELIST is the most intact of the Durham churches surviving from the time of Bede, and one of only three complete Saxon churches in England. As is so often the case, the survival of this building is due to neglect, a Victorian church (now demolished) on another site having superseded the old one. Escomb was brought back into use, sympathetically restored and furnished, under the supervision of Sir Albert Richardson in 1965. The church is tiny, comprising a tall, narrow nave and smaller chancel. The exterior of darkened rubble stone is awesomely venerable: only the larger windows are a later alteration; everything else is untouched. The interior is whitewashed with a simple, open timber roof and an impressive chancel arch thought to be built of Roman stonework from the fort at Binchester. Sir Albert's new pews and altar are becomingly simple. The whole has a convincing atmosphere of ancient piety, which transcends the rather dreary industrialised valley in which the church is set.

Gibside★

6; 6 miles SW of Gateshead off A692 [16]
Includes Gibside Chapel and Avenue (both NT)
The Jacobean mansion is a ruined shell, but the bones of the eighteenth-century park survive, as do one or two of the ornamental buildings. Of these, the finest is the CHAPEL (NT), which, because it is looked after by the National Trust, is in pristine condition. It could easily be

in the park of one of the Russian imperial palaces around St Petersburg – Pavlovsk, say, or Tsarsko Selo – with its dome, projecting portico and richly carved detail. It was obviously inspired by Palladio but much elaborated, as befitted the deeper purse of an eighteenth-century English aristocrat. The architect was James Paine and building began in 1760 under the terms of the will of George Bowes; it was completed in 1810 by his grandson, the 10th Earl of Strathmore. The hiatus in building was caused by George Bowes's daughter and heiress, 'the unhappy Countess', marrying as her second husband a 'penniless Irish adventurer' who tried to grab her fortune.

The chapel has a cruciform plan, the Ionic portico facing down the avenue being approached by balustraded steps. The handling of the internal space, with apses in the transepts, little domes over the corner spaces and attached Corinthian columns supporting the central dome, survives as devised by Paine, but much of the detail is early nineteenth-century. The most prominent of the elegant cherry-wood furnishings is the triple-decker pulpit with pretty umbrella-shaped sounding-board supported on an Ionic column. The side apses contain box pews for servants and visitors; the pews for the owner, his agent and chaplain, and an enclosure for the font occupy the four corners. An unusual aspect of the design is the central position, under the dome, of the communion table. The chapel has been well restored by the National Trust, which has executed an authentic scheme of decoration in shades of stone colour – a welcome change from the ubiquitous, unhistorical Wedgwood blue-and-white to be found in eighteenth-century churches.

The chapel stands at one end of an impressive AVENUE (NT) of Turkey oaks running along the top of a ridge. A mile away at the other end is the COLUMN OF BRITISH LIBERTY. It is 140 feet high, taller than Nelson's Column, and the statue on top was originally gilded.

Apart from the chapel, the other substantial building at Gibside is the BANQUETING HOUSE designed by Daniel Garrett in 1751. This is a fantastic Gothick folly, its central bow crowned with three gables looking like bishops' mitres – very appropriate in an episcopal palatinate. After standing roofless and ruined for many years this entertaining whim was rescued and restored by the admirable Landmark Trust in 1980. It is now a little holiday cottage where it is possible to stay. The Banqueting Room itself fills the full width of the building and has reinstated Gothick plasterwork and a coved ceiling. It is to be hoped that in due course the rest of the park, including the derelict Tuscan Orangery, will be as well restored.

Jarrow

7; 5 miles E of Newcastle upon Tyne on A185

The CHURCH OF ST PAUL at Jarrow is one of the Holy Places of the English race. Here Bede lived and wrote his *Ecclesiastical History*, and here he died on the Eve of Ascension in 735. The Benedictine MONASTERY was founded by Benedict Biscop in 681 on land given by King Ecgfrith, like Monkwearmouth (*q.v.*), and it was run jointly with that establishment. The monastic buildings were begun in 682 and the church in 685. The dedicatory inscription miraculously survives, with Roman-looking lettering on a stone slab: 'DEDICATIO BASILICAE SCI. PAULI VIII KL MAI ANNO XV ECFRIDI REG. CEOLFRIDI ABB. EIUSDEM Q. Q. ECCLES. DO. AUCTORE CONDITORIS ANNO III'. It is the oldest surviving church dedication in the country. Excavations have shown that the Saxon church was 170 feet long and 45 feet wide, with a west porch, nave, chancel link and east church. Of this, the lower stages of the link survive as the base of the Norman tower, while the present chancel is the body of the Saxon east church. Most of the nave was demolished in 1782 and has been replaced by a Victorian structure designed by George Gilbert Scott. The exterior of the chancel is the most interesting part, with roughly coursed stonework and little round-arched windows.

South of the church, ruined walls survive from the monastery buildings, part Norman but including some Saxon work. The immediate surroundings have been tidied up to make a grassy park, but on every hand are prospects of utter desolation: post-industrial squalor, motorways and tower blocks as far as the eye can see. There is something immensely impressive, however, about the survival of this ancient church amidst surroundings that are almost a caricature of all that is worst in the aftermath of the Industrial Revolution. A beacon in the wilderness.

Monkwearmouth
See Sunderland.

Lambton Castle
See Penshaw Monument.

The church of St Paul, Jarrow.

Lumley Castle.

Lumley Castle

8; 6 miles N of Durham on B1284

Robert Surtees, the nineteenth-century historian of County Durham (not to be confused with the creator of Jorrocks), described Lumley Castle as standing 'glittering with a bright open aspect on a fine gradual elevation above the Wear'. This is a view now vouchsafed to the motorist on the A1 as he speeds north. Licence to crenellate was granted by Bishop Skirlaw of Durham in 1389 to Ralph, 1st Lord Lumley, and was confirmed by King Richard II in 1392. The building operations that ensued left the exterior of Lumley much as it is today, with four ranges enclosing a courtyard and four massive corner towers like Bolton Castle in Yorkshire (*q.v.*). Unlike that building, however, Lumley has continued to be occupied, and much of the interior is now Elizabethan and early Georgian. The later work is as interesting as the original medieval architecture. The Elizabethan alterations were done for John, 7th Lord Lumley, the leading art collector of his age and a passionate antiquarian who was exceedingly proud of his family history; the early eighteenth-century work was designed by Vanbrugh for the 2nd Earl of Scarbrough in the 1720s. The castle still belongs to the Lumleys, though now let to a hotel.

Although close to industry, the castle stands well in a wooded park, looking very impressive in distant views with its mighty four-square silhouette, towers, turrets and battlements. The original Gatehouse, with a double arch and heraldic decoration, leads to the inner courtyard. This is part paved, part lawn, and is planted with old laburnum trees, which help to soften the powerful architecture. Many of the inner windows have mullions and transoms installed by John, Lord Lumley,

who was also responsible for the display of heraldry – no fewer than eighteen shields – that adorns the main entrance opposite the Gatehouse. The ground floor is all stone-vaulted, as at Bolton Castle, and the main rooms are on the first floor. The Great Hall was remodelled by John, Lord Lumley, whose grand stone fireplace survives, the overmantel with Mannerist Renaissance decoration and the Lumley arms. The series of full-length portraits of ancestors commissioned by John, and the marble fountain with a pelican which adorned the room until recently, have been removed for the time being to Sandbeck Park, Yorkshire (*q.v.*), Lord Scarbrough's other seat. The eighteenth-century state rooms, made by Vanbrugh but decorated over a long period, fill an enfilade along the south front. The first and grandest is the Garter Room, with superb stucco decoration by Italian craftsmen on the walls and high coved ceiling. The design of the latter incorporates the Garter Star, which has given its name to the room. The former Dining Room next door has early eighteenth-century panelling with original grained decoration – a rare survival. (The name of the painter-stainer responsible is written into the pattern.) The Saloon and Boudoir have especially pretty Rococo plaster ceilings. Downstairs, the room now used as the hotel dining room was formed by Vanbrugh as a library, and its shallow-vaulted ceiling is supported on deeply cut rusticated columns.

Lumley is a most impressive house, but its long-term future must give cause for worry. The hotel that occupies it looks rather shaky, and the stonework of the walls, corroded by two centuries of atmospheric pollution, is in need of substantial restoration work.

Penshaw Monument.

Penshaw Monument

NT; 9; 6 miles NE of Barnard Castle on A688

This improbable blackened Parthenon, with chunky Doric columns and pediment, stares out under northern skies at a landscape of collieries and new towns. It is a monument to John George Lambton, 1st Earl of Durham – 'King Jog' ('A man can jog along on £40,000 a year.') It was erected in 1842 by public subscription and was designed by John and Benjamin Green of Newcastle. The design is a half-size copy of the Theseum in Athens. Lord Durham was the architect of the Great Reform Bill, British Ambassador to St Petersburg, first Governor-General of Canada, and a popular Liberal statesman. As he drove round the county, crowds of children would tag along behind his carriage shouting 'Lord Durham for ever!' The monument now belongs to the National Trust, so it is possible to see it close to, although it is better glimpsed from afar as a punctuation of the distant horizon. The best view is to be had from LAMBTON PARK, from where it is seen framed by trees.

The park of LAMBTON CASTLE is an amazing oasis of 2000 acres, comprising the best example in the county of early nineteenth-century Picturesque layout. It takes full advantage of the natural beauties of the steep banks of the River Wear. Lambton Castle, a Gothic remodelling by Bonomi of an earlier house, was drastically curtailed in the 1930s, but still forms an effective ornament in the landscape. The Lambtons now live at BIDDICK HALL on the edge of the park, approached by an ancient avenue. It is an early eighteenth-century brick Baroque house and was extended in the 1950s by Trenwith Wills. Another new addition is a group of *chinoiserie* beehives in the garden, designed by the present Lord Lambton.

Raby Castle★

10; 6 miles NE of Chester-le-Street off A183

The once bleak northern landscape has been humanised by generations of improving landowners and landscaping so that the country for miles around Raby now exudes an air of eighteenth-century well-being. The exterior of the castle itself is largely as built by the Nevilles in the fourteenth and fifteenth centuries, though much of the fenestration is unobtrusive Victorian restoration. The interior, on the other hand, is largely eighteenth- and nineteenth-century, apart from the Chapel and the wonderfully undisturbed Great Kitchen and Servants' Hall, which were constructed in the fourteenth century. It is this Georgian and Victorian dimension that adds enormously to the interest of the castle. The whole building has been magnificently restored over the last twenty years with the help of grants from the Historic Buildings Council.

The eighteenth-century work was designed by James Paine, Daniel Garrett and John Carr of York, while the nineteenth-century work was by William Burn, except for the Library, which is the work of one Joseph Browne. The rooms have a pleasant, faded character and the contents are of high quality. The pictures include a very good group of sporting paintings by Ben Marshall, J.F. Herring, Francis Sartorius and H. Chalon. They are hung in the Small Drawing Room. There are many family portraits, the best concentrated in the Dining Room and the Baron's Hall, including fine works by Lely and Reynolds. The continental paintings, attributed to Murillo, Ricci, Claude, Teniers and various others, are of less interest.

All the original contents of the castle were sold in 1714 and the present furniture has been acquired since then. It comprises one of the largest groups of Gillow furniture in the country, but there is also much by other manufacturers. The set of Gothick furniture is particularly notable. In purely architectural terms, the best rooms are Carr's Entrance Hall – with its octagonal columns and vaulted ceiling worthy of the Castle of Otranto, and its splendid Louis XIV Mazarin marquetry desk – and Burn's Octagon Drawing Room. This has rich white-and-gold Jacobethan plasterwork, yellow damask wall hangings and gilt chairs, and a *tête-à-tête* provided by Morant – the perfect setting for one of Disraeli's novels. The other gilt furniture is possibly by Gillow but so far has not been satisfactorily identified as such. The Octagon Drawing Room also boasts a fine Louis XV desk, typical of the early nineteenth-century taste for luxury French furniture.

The park is magnificent and there are many mid-eighteenth-century Gothick estate buildings, including PARK FARM by James Paine and an entertaining GARDENER'S COTTAGE in the walled garden. The farmhouses on the surrounding hillsides are all whitewashed – it is said because a nineteenth-century owner of the castle wished to be able to identify his own property when out in the country. The distant view of the castle in autumn, crouching amidst bracken and old oak trees, is the nearest thing to a Turner watercolour that you are ever likely to see.

Rokeby Hall

11; 10 miles W of Scotch Corner off A66

Perhaps best known for having given its name to the *Rokeby Venus* by Velasquez (once here but now in the National Gallery in London), this is in itself a fascinating Palladian-style villa. It is the only one of the English eighteenth-century villas to be painted a strong Italian terracotta colour. The recipe for this is an old one and the paint is specially mixed on the premises. Even on a wet, grey day it gives the house a warm southern look. The composition too is remarkably lively, the pyramidal-roofed centre block flanked by lower recessed cubic wings marshalled in a stepped-back formation. Rokeby goes a long way to dispel the illusion that Anglo-Palladian architecture is dull and pedantic. Perhaps one of the reasons for this is that it was designed not by a professional architect but by its owner, 'Long Sir Tom' — Sir Thomas Robinson, son-in-law of the Earl of Carlisle and a notable amateur designer. He inherited the estate (bought by his father, a merchant of London) in 1720 and described the house as being complete in 1731. He was himself an eccentric and lively character. One French visitor who came across his tall, gawky figure — he resembled a pair of scissors — in London mistook him for Robinson Crusoe. He was, among other things, a Member of Parliament, Governor of Barbados, and director of Ranelagh Gardens. Unfortunately, his financial extravagances forced him to sell his estate in 1760 to John Sawrey Moritt, whose descendants still own the property. Moritt's son was a friend of Sir Walter Scott, who often stayed here and wrote a long poem about the medieval Rokebys.

The house is entered through a single-storeyed Tuscan colonnade into a low, pillared Hall. On either side are comfortable, low-ceilinged rooms for everyday living, including a Library and Breakfast Room. The latter is a charming example of the eighteenth-century taste for print decoration, with engravings glued to the wall to form patterns. The *piano nobile*, by contrast, was intended for state and parade. Most of the main block is filled with a two-storeyed Saloon, where the *Rokeby Venus* once hung. This excellently proportioned room has a richly decorated coved ceiling and grandly detailed doorcase with pediment and Corinthian columns. It was perhaps with reference to this that Sir Thomas wrote to Lord Carlisle: 'My chief expense has been in Palladian doors.'

The park at Rokeby and the landscape setting by the River Tees is exceedingly beautiful — a source of inspiration to Romantic painters and poets alike in the early nineteenth century. GRETA BRIDGE at the south end of the park was designed by Carr of York in 1773, and immortalised in Girtin's famous watercolour. It is a great pity, though, that the new road has cut off one of the entrance lodges and slices through the edge of the park. God save us from road engineers.

Raby Castle.

St Andrew's church, Roker.

Roker

12; 1½ miles N of Sunderland on A183

'The cathedral of the Arts and Crafts Movement', proclaims the noticeboard outside – with justifiable pride, for ST ANDREW'S CHURCH is one of the most extraordinary parish churches of its date in the whole of England. It was built in 1906–7 at the expense of John Priestman, a self-made millionaire who had started life as a shipyard labourer; it was to serve a new suburb of red brick houses, and was designed by E.S. Prior. The style is Gothic, but simplified and with wonderfully original details, like the triangular arches to the windows and their angular tracery. The outside is low and broad and massive, faced in rough-hewn local Marsden stone and with a domineering crossing-tower sitting astride the east end. The bold masonry gives it a strong, primitive quality. Inside, the nave is exceedingly wide, spanned by stone-faced concrete arches and a concrete-and-timber roof, no doubt intended to look like the hull of a ship. Tiny aisles tunnel through the bases of these arches and the lower part of the nave walls has austere planked oak panelling. The chancel is much narrower than the nave and, as a result, the transept arches linking the two are askew – a curious effect. The chancel is the most richly decorated part, and its painted decorations (designed by Prior) are a deliberate contrast to the bare stonework of the body of the church. Under the tower is a shallow dome, treated as the heavens with a large gold sun in the middle (containing a light fitting) and round it a painted

sky with the moon, gold stars and, over the altar, the hand of God emerging from a cloud. This was executed in 1927 by Macdonald Gill and restored in 1967 – it had suffered from the effects of damp. As is only to be expected in an Arts and Crafts creation, all the fittings are subtly designed and superbly made. The reredos is a tapestry by Burne-Jones, woven by Morris & Co.; the chancel carpet is a Morris design. The cross and candlesticks on the altar were designed by Ernest Gimson, who was also responsible for the lectern (with leaf- and chevron-patterned inlay of silver, ebony and mother-of-pearl), the choir stalls and the pulpit. There is lettering by Eric Gill, stained glass by H.A. Payne (especially in the south transept window, with angels sweeping across regardless of the stone tracery) and a font by Randall Wells. The simple oak cover was made by Thompson of Kilburn – note his carved-mouse signature.

Roker is a perfect and unified museum-piece of Arts and Crafts taste, quite unlike anything else in the north of England. It cleverly unites boldness of structure and form with a richness and warmth in its details and fittings rare in twentieth-century British architecture.

Sunderland

13; 7 miles SE of Newcastle upon Tyne on A184

The venerable CHURCH OF ST PETER WITH ST CUTHBERT, Monkwearmouth, is now surrounded by subtopian sprawl, though the immediate environs have been cleared and grassed over by the local council. The church was founded in 675 by St Benedict Biscop, a Northumbrian monk of noble birth, on land granted by King Ecgfrith on the north bank of the Wear estuary. The church was monastic until 1536; after the Dissolution it became the parish church. Of the Saxon building, the tower and nave survive; the chancel is fourteenth-century and the north aisle is Victorian. The nave, as at Escomb (*q.v.*), is exceedingly tall and narrow, with a steeply pitched roof. The tower is of different dates, the lowest parts c.675, the second storey c.700, and the top storeys built up in the tenth century – including the two-light windows under round arches. All the Saxon stonework is rough rubble, but traces of sculptural decoration can still be seen on the tower walls. Benedict Biscop's church was much more elaborate than the present one, with a western narthex and side-chapels. Nothing remains of the monastic buildings that lay to the south of the church, though excavations have revealed something of their layout. A number of interesting Saxon inscriptions, carved capitals and so forth, are displayed in the new octagonal PARISH HALL at the east end of the church.

Ushaw

14; 3 miles W of Durham on B6302

ST CUTHBERT'S COLLEGE is a successor to the English College at Douai in Flanders, which was founded by Cardinal Allen in the late sixteenth century and suppressed by the French Revolutionaries in 1793, its staff and pupils returning to England and establishing themselves here and at Ware. The Ushaw estate was bought in 1799 and the college building, a huge barracks-like classical block, built between 1804 and 1819. This quadrangle survives at the centre of a spreading complex of Victorian Gothic buildings. The CHAPEL, as rich as the other buildings are plain, is by Dunn and Hansom and was built in 1882–4. It is partly a reproduction, double the size, of a previous chapel by Pugin on the site (which had proved too small) and contains several of his fittings, including stained glass by Hardman. It is T-shaped, with an ante-chapel, as at Magdalen, Merton or New College, Oxford, divided from the Chapel-proper by a large screen. The chancel is apsidal, with lavishly carved late Victorian fittings and painted decorations. The Lady Chapel was redecorated in 1894 by J.F. Bentley, the architect of Westminster Cathedral, who kept to the Puginian manner and re-used the tiles, stained glass and Lady altar from Pugin's Lady Chapel. The Sacred Heart Chapel also re-uses Pugin's original high altar and reredos. The Perpendicular screen enclosing this chapel, however, was designed by Basil Champneys as a memorial to the son of Coventry Patmore, the Victorian Catholic poet.

North of the Chapel is a long cloister corridor lined with a series of little chapels, begun by Pugin in the 1850s and completed by his son, E.W. Pugin. All are splendidly decorated and contain Victorian carvings, paintings and stained glass by artists who worked almost exclusively for Catholic patrons and so are not especially well known, but interesting nonetheless.

The fine Library at Ushaw contains an important group of books from the English College in Lisbon.

Wynyard Park

15; 3 miles S of Sedgefield on A689

Wynyard is a feudal oasis situated between the bleak moors south-east of Durham, dotted with even bleaker mining villages, and the hinterland of Billingham, where belching cooling-towers, chimneys and all the apparatus of the chemical industry form a landscape of almost surrealist horror. It is an unlikely setting for one of the finest estates and most splendid houses in the north of England, but, like the city of Durham itself, Wynyard Park is grand enough in scale to hold its own and to maintain a proud independence amidst alien surroundings. Indeed, the house and its landscape draw an additional romantic attraction from the proximity of the trappings of 'heroic materialism'.

Wynyard is the creation of the 3rd Marquess of Londonderry and his formidable wife Frances Anne, who was described by Princess Lieven as being like 'one of those effigies you see in Greek churches with no colour or shading but loaded with jewels'. It was designed in the 1820s by Philip Wyatt, the feckless younger son of James Wyatt. He had to be paid off before the work was finished 'because', according to Lord Londonderry, 'his extreme incompetence made him impossible to deal with', and then in 1841 the interior was gutted by fire, but restored to its original appearance under the supervision of Ignatius Bonomi, using Wyatt's original drawings. Faced in grey stone with a huge Corinthian portico on the entrance front, the house is in fact very close to the unexecuted scheme for a Waterloo Palace for the Duke of Wellington.

The interior is on a princely scale. The centre is taken up by a large Sculpture Gallery, 120 feet long and 60 feet high, with pilasters of jasper on plinths of Egyptian green marble, the doorcases of Siena marble and the floor paved with white marble. The dome in the middle has rich stained glass by Wailes. The state rooms along the south front – Boudoir, Library, Vestibule, Drawing Room and Ballroom – are all fitted up in a rich cosmopolitan style with classical ceiling paintings, gilt plasterwork, enormous sheets of looking-glass, Boulle panels and marble pilasters and doorcases. Throughout this enfilade, the floors are of mahogany inlaid with rosewood and satinwood. Even today, when the rooms have lost most of their original furniture, the effect is still magnificent.

The present Lord Londonderry has formed a self-contained house at the east end of the old mansion; the famous portraits by Sir Thomas Lawrence and the grand Regency furniture from Londonderry House in London now enrich these rooms. The Chapel at the west end is embellished with marble and mosaic in Edwardian Byzantine style. It is approached through the Monument Room, created in 1855–7 as a memorial to the 3rd Marquess of Londonderry.

The park at Wynyard was landscaped by a Mr Gilpin in 1822 and is very handsome, with a lake, eighteenth-century ornamental bridge, tall obelisk commemorating the Duke of Wellington, classical temples and a Victorian dogs' graveyard. Much tree planting has been carried out recently to restore the original landscape effect.

Hereford and Worcester

The new county combines old Worcestershire and old Herefordshire, but despite this enforced marriage each retains much of its former individuality, with its own cathedral city (and former county town). It is an unforgettable experience to enter this part of England from Wales in the west. Kingswood Common, on a little ridge beyond Kington, for instance, commands a view as beautiful as any in Europe. Below is the valley of the Wye, and beyond the central plain of England stretches forever into the distance, interrupted here and there by sudden abrupt hills such as the Malverns. After the wildness of Wales it all looks incredibly prosperous and civilised – neatly hedged farms and orchards, old oak trees, woods and parks, houses and villages. Coming from the east, the landscape of Worcestershire and more particularly that of Herefordshire seems wonderfully hilly after the flatter landscape of the central Midlands, and always in the far distance, forming a splendid backdrop to the general views, are the hills and mountains of Wales. It is a landscape of strong and varied colours: the ploughed fields have reddish soil, and there is a remarkably wide array of building materials – red brick, black-and-white half-timber, and three or four different colours of stone. Hence Housman's 'coloured counties'.

Of the two, Worcestershire has been the more spoilt since the introduction of town and country planning in 1947. Birmingham has burst through the natural barrier of the Clent Hills, engulfing Hagley in suburbia and spreading its malign influence far into the heart of the county in the form of new town development round Redditch. The ancient cathedral city of Worcester wrecked itself in the 1960s in the interests of unnecessary new roads, hotels and shops; anybody looking at it today would find it difficult to believe that it was not bombed during the war. The rural parts of the county have also come in for their share of ugliness. The Vale of Evesham, with its prosperous market gardens, sounds idyllic. In fact, this type of farming is more hideous than modern coal-mining because it involves huge glass-houses the size of major factories, and every plot of a few acres is able to pay for a peasant-millionaire's bungalow to the detriment of the landscape harmonies. The best bits of Worcestershire are the south and west fringes: the

outlying portion of the Cotswolds round Overbury and Broadway, those immaculately maintained villages, and the rolling country along the Herefordshire border, where red brick or black-and-white farmhouses still stand in the midst of old-fashioned dairy farms with meadows, trees and hedges. And of course the Malverns introduce a dash of miniature mountain scenery. Herefordshire, on the other hand, is still a county of exceptional overall beauty, almost totally free from industrialisation, and with a remote and secret feel to it.

The architecture of the two counties is similar. There is the same vernacular of black-and-white half-timber in the farms and villages. Little towns like Pembridge and Weobley in Herefordshire are almost entirely 'black-and-white', as are such Worcestershire villages as Abbots Morton and Rous Lench; and there are elaborate Elizabethan country houses in this style – Besford Court, for example. The greatest architectural interest of the two counties, however, lies in their Norman parish churches, which survive on a scale encountered nowhere else in England. They are distinguished for rich Romanesque sculptured decoration in doorways, fonts and chancel arches; Kilpeck in Herefordshire is perhaps the most perfect of these. Both counties have interesting cathedrals, which, while not in the absolute first rank of English medieval cathedrals, and heavily restored in the nineteenth century, contain bits of most periods – some, notably the north transept at Hereford and the Lady Chapel at Worcester, of exquisite beauty. Hardly less grand are the abbey churches that have survived in parish use: Pershore, Malvern and Evesham in Worcestershire, and Abbey Dore in Herefordshire, which is perhaps the most romantic monastic church in England.

Herefordshire and Worcestershire continued prosperous in the seventeenth and eighteenth centuries thanks to dairy farms, cider orchards and, in Worcestershire, pioneer industrial enterprise, like the Worcester China Factory. This provided the means to build well, and there are many Caroline and Georgian houses and churches. Holme Lacy in Herefordshire is a huge Charles II house with the finest plasterwork in England, while the eighteenth-century church at Great Witley has an equally exceptional interior, with Italian Baroque decoration from Canons. There are many decent mid- to late eighteenth-century houses in both counties, as well as a handful of houses of national importance – notably Berrington Hall, Downton Castle and Croome Court (the latter unfortunately despoiled). Worcestershire, in particular, benefited in the nineteenth century from the industrial profits of nearby Birmingham and the Black Country. Witley Court is now a ruined shell, but Hewell Grange and Madresfield are both spectacular Victorian country houses. From the later nineteenth and early twentieth century there is much attractive Arts and Crafts vernacular revival with good use of the varied local materials, notably in Randall Wells's additions to Besford Court, and the sensitive new buildings and restorations in places like Broadway. If only this standard had been maintained into the later twentieth century!

Abbey Dore★

1; 11 miles SW of Hereford on B4357

The CHURCH OF ST MARY, formerly a Cistercian abbey, lies remote in a beautiful valley. It is approached through a farmyard. One's first impression is of the terrific broadside of the transepts and the blocked central arch where the nave once was. The church fell into decay after the Dissolution and now comprises the transepts and choir only. It was repaired and re-roofed in 1632 by John, 1st Viscount Scudamore, 'the Good Lord Scudamore', under the influence of Archbishop Laud. A further restoration, remarkable for its sensitivity, was carried out in 1902 under the supervision of R.W. Paul, an SPAB (Society for the Protection of Ancient Buildings) man. The interior of the church is a dream of ancient, time-ravaged beauty. The architecture is Early English, simple and pure, with pointed arches, clustered columns and lancet windows. The transepts and crossing create an effect of height. The texture of the walls is romantic in the extreme, with old limewashed plaster and faded mural paintings of scriptural texts in decorative borders – King David with his harp, Father Time with a scythe, and the Royal Arms of Queen Anne. The ceilings of silvery-grey timber with beams on carved brackets are those erected for Lord Scudamore in 1632 by John Abel. He was also responsible for most of the furnishings, including the dramatic screen at the entrance to the choir, embellished with turned balusters and topped by an elaborate cresting of heraldic cartouches and obelisks. The chancel is an almost untouched example of a Laudian layout, with rails round the stone medieval altar, stalls, pulpit and other furnishings all by Abel. On either side are some medieval floor tiles showing the arms of various benefactors; these were found and re-set by R.W. Paul. The choir aisles are stone-vaulted, and behind the altar there is a beautiful vaulted ambulatory with excellent thirteenth-century bosses and many architectural fragments from the demolished parts of the church. Before you leave, note the seventeenth-century poor-box with the inscription: 'He that from ye poor his eyes turn away. The Lord will turn His eyes from him in ye later day.'

The church of St Mary, Abbey Dore.

Abbots Morton.

Abbots Morton
2; 11 miles E of Worcester off A422

A pretty timber-framed village that retains its medieval plan, Abbots Morton is all extraordinarily picturesque, with houses set higgledy-piggledy along the sloping village street. They are all of different shapes and sizes, and remarkably cosy looking, some of them with thatched roofs. The smaller cottages are built at right-angles to the village street so that you see their gables in enfilade. They have narrow strip gardens behind. The grander houses are at the upper end of the street near the CHURCH OF ST PETER, which has a stone tower and an un-restored·interior with Jacobean woodwork and a plaster cartouche over the chancel arch.

Berrington Hall★
NT; 3; 3 miles N of Leominster on A49 [17]

Thomas Harley, younger son of the 3rd Earl of Oxford, made a fortune as a banker and as a government contrac-tor for the British Army in North America during the Seven Years' War. He bought Berrington in 1775 and immediately started to lay out the park to designs by Capability Brown. In 1778 he demolished the old house and built a new one on a better site, employing as his architect Brown's son-in-law, Henry Holland. The work was finished by 1784, when the diarist John Byng described it as 'furnished in all modern elegance, com-manding beautiful views, a fine piece of water and . . . throughout a scene of elegance and refinement'. It sur-vives almost untouched as a remarkable late eighteenth-century ensemble. The house forms a crisp rectangle of rose-coloured stone, with an Ionic portico on the main front and a compact courtyard of offices to the rear linked to the main house by quadrant walls. In one of the rear blocks is an exquisite eighteenth-century dairy lined with white and green Wedgwood tiles, and with a marble floor.

The interior is a perfect example of Holland's French brand of neo-classicism. The Hall employs the Doric order and has a marble floor, reflecting the design on the ceiling, and plaster trophies in roundels over the doors. It is flanked by the Drawing Room and Library. The for-mer has a carved chimneypiece of purest Carrara marble and the finest of the decorated ceilings in the house, its delicate plasterwork inset with painted roundels. The grate in the fireplace is inlaid with Wedgwood medal-lions – a most unusual feature. The Library has pedimen-ted bookcases designed as part of the architecture of the room. The pier glasses between the windows are origi-nal, and the beautiful Axminster carpet was woven for the room in the early nineteenth century. Inset in the ceiling and round the top of the walls are *grisaille* paint-ings of great authors, including Shakespeare and Milton. The Dining Room has a sumptuous marble chimneypiece and carved doorcases with rams' heads and anthemion. It contains three great sea pieces by (or after) Thomas Luny, depicting Admiral Rodney's sea battles; also in the room are satinwood side-tables original to this house. The most distinguished feature is the Staircase Hall, which rises the full height of the house and is a brilliant exercise in spatial design, with screens of Siena scagliola Corinthian columns at first-floor level, and light stream-ing down from the glazed dome in the ceiling. The prin-cipal rooms are completed by the exquisite little Boudoir with its barrel ceiling, and apse and semi-dome screened by scagliola columns simulating lapis lazuli. All these rooms retain their Edwardian colour schemes of bistre, blue, pink, white and gold.

Berrington was bought by the first Lord Cawley in 1900, together with some of the original contents. Other pieces were brought by him from elsewhere, including the books in the Library, some of which came from Heaton Hall, Manchester (*q.v.*). The house is set in a large park with fine views over the surrounding country.

Besford

4; 2 miles E of Pershore off A4104

The CHURCH OF ST PETER was built in the fourteenth century entirely of timber-framing, like the old cottages to be found in many Worcestershire villages. It was restored in the 1880s when the thin tower with spire was added. The interior is a handsome display of joinery, with a queenpost roof and medieval screen, and Jacobean woodwork, including panelling and communion rails.

BESFORD COURT is a beautiful black-and-white timber-framed house of *c*.1500 with extensions of 1912 by Randall Wells in a sensitive Arts and Crafts evocation of Tudor domestic architecture reminiscent of Lutyens.

Bredon

5; 3½ miles NE of Tewkesbury on B4079
Includes Bredon Barn (NT)

Housman country, and a beautiful village with a splendid group of old buildings clustering round the parish church, including the Elizabethan RECTORY, the Jacobean OLD MANSION, the Georgian MANOR HOUSE and a terrific thirteenth-century TITHE BARN (NT) with an aisled interior. The CHURCH OF ST GILES has a Norman nave, a crossing-tower with a spire, and an Early English chancel. The latter has traces of original red trellis-patterned wall paintings and heraldic floor tiles depicting the arms of local families.

Bredwardine

6; 12 miles W of Hereford on B4352

ST ANDREW'S is a little Norman church in a beautiful stretch of the Wye Valley, approached by a short avenue of beech trees. Francis Kilvert was parson here from 1877 until his death at the age of thirty-eight in 1879; his diaries, edited by William Plomer, give a vivid and sympathetic picture of the life of a Victorian country parson. The church has changed little since his time. There is an attractive grassy graveyard with eighteenth-century headstones, and daffodils in spring. The interior is a bare, barn-like space with rubble stone walls and rough beamed roof. The plan is noticeably crooked as you look east towards the chancel. There are several endearing touches, including a woolly mat in the chancel depicting symbols of the Four Evangelists, and the hymn numbers chalked up on a slate on the chancel wall.

Brinsop

7; 5 miles NW of Hereford off A480

Up a track in the middle of a field, with no more in the way of a village than a couple of cottages, stands the CHURCH OF ST GEORGE. It is a fourteenth-century rebuilding but incorporates an important carved Norman tympanum of St George (built into the inside wall of the nave) from a previous Norman church. The exterior is simple, with a little wooden bell-turret. The interior is of great beauty. There is no break between nave and chancel, and an arcade (with circular piers) to one side only. The walls are limewashed – always a more cheerful effect than bare rubble – and there are exquisite furnishings by Sir Ninian Comper. He restored the Perpendicular rood-screen, adding the gilt figures of angels holding candles and the crucifix on top. The altarpiece is also by Comper, carved from translucent alabaster, tinted with azure and touched with gold. Above hangs a gilded tester, and on either side are stunning brass statues of St George and St Martin. The east window contains fourteenth-century stained-glass panels, but the other windows are all by Comper. One is a memorial to Wordsworth – 'a frequent sojourner in this parish'.

The church of St George, Brinsop.

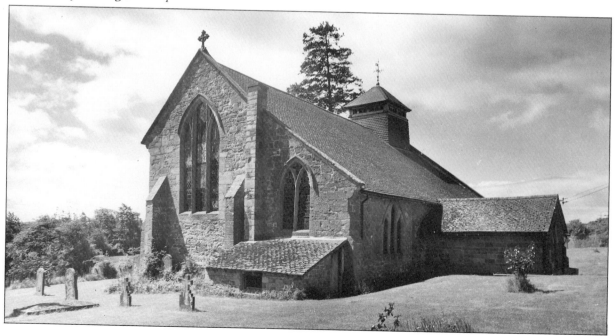

Broadway

8; 6 miles SE of Evesham on A44

Anybody who is a fan of E.F. Benson's Lucia novels will find it difficult to keep a straight face in Broadway, his model for Riseholme. Which of these desirable Tudor residences could be Lucia's? And is that Georgie we can see, stepping daintily over the crazy-paving paths of a herb garden? Broadway is a beautiful village, beautifully kept. Some may find it *too* genteel, and it is certainly too full of tourists in summer, but I prefer this sort of intelligent, well-heeled upkeep to the un-intelligent non-upkeep so often encountered in English villages which were once handsome but, not being famous showplaces, are now ruined beyond redemption.

Broadway, as its name implies, comprises one long, wide street – the HIGH STREET – lined with splendid houses and cottages dating from the sixteenth to the twentieth century, but all built of Cotswold stone and forming a cumulative harmony. There are grass verges all along the street, and well-maintained front gardens. Not to be underestimated is the late nineteenth- and early twentieth-century Arts and Crafts contribution, such as the Post Office of 1899 by Guy Dawber, or the extensions of 1910 to the Lygon Arms by C.E. Bateman, or Lloyds Bank of 1915 by G.H. Hunt. It is this sensitive later work that makes places like Broadway so special – Tudor and Georgian houses can be found anywhere – and it is an architectural pleasure unique to England. It is one of the tragedies of our century that the art of sensitive vernacular-style building in old villages has been lost. Think of the recent ruination of the oolite villages of Rutland and Leicestershire and compare the quality of building being done for the same type of clients (Midlands businessmen) in Broadway and the other Cotswold villages a mere fifty or sixty years earlier.

At the top of Broadway Hill is the FISH INN, built as a seventeenth-century rustic classical gazebo. Further along the top of the hill is BROADWAY TOWER, designed by James Wyatt for the Earl of Coventry in 1800 in Neo-Norman style. It enjoys spectacular views.

Burton Court

9; 5 miles W of Leominster off A44

This early nineteenth-century house on a hilltop was remodelled to the design of the Hereford architect F.R. Kempson in the 1860s. Further work was done in 1912 to the design of Sir Clough Williams-Ellis, who gave the east front its free Tudor treatment and simplified the south front by substituting a clean parapet for gables. The Great Hall, however, is a remarkable survival dating from the fourteenth century. It has its original roof with curved wind-braces and collar-beams of chestnut, but the carved oak fireplace is a wonderful 'Wardour Street' production with 'Flemish' carved angels and 'Elizabethan' panels.

Chaddesley Corbett

10; 4 miles SE of Kidderminster on A448

The village street contains a good mixture of Georgian brick and old black-and-white cottages and houses.

TUDOR HOUSE is a charming eighteenth-century hybrid job, with ogee gables and arches hinting at Gothic, Venetian windows in the bays, and the doorcase staying resolutely classical. A country builder hedging his bets or perhaps losing his place in Batty Langley while at the drawing board? The street leads down to the churchyard and the CHURCH OF ST CASSIAN. The dominating tower and spire is an eighteenth-century rebuilding, but the glory of the church is the spectacular Decorated chancel, the east window a splendid piece of curvilinear tracery. The nave is part Norman and the font is a spectacular piece of late Norman sculpture, the writhing dragons and interlacing Viking ornament with which it is covered making it look like a petrified basket.

Croft Castle

NT; 11; 6 miles NW of Leominster on B4362 [18]

The Crofts are among the oldest families in England. Bernard de Croft was recorded as holding Croft in the Domesday Book in 1086 and the present Baron is descended from his heirs in the male line. The castle itself, however, was mortgaged to the Knight family in the eighteenth century and was only bought back in 1923. It became the property of the National Trust in 1957 but is still occupied by different members of the Croft family.

The castle stands in a beautiful park beneath the Iron Age fort of CROFT AMBREY and is approached by noble avenues of chestnut, lime, oak and beech. It is square in plan and the outer walls and cylindrical corner towers date from the fourteenth century. The mullion windows were inserted in the sixteenth century, and considerable alterations were carried out by the Knights in the eighteenth to the design of T.F. Pritchard. The pretty Gothick bay windows of the east front are his, though his oriel and porch have been replaced. The outer stone walls are a nice patchwork of pink, yellow and grey, like pot-pourri, while the inner court, somewhat surprisingly, is homely Georgian red brick. The principal interiors are by Pritchard. The staircase is a good example of Gothick work, its plasterwork recently restored. The Anteroom, Library and Blue Room are all Rococo Gothick. The latter has old panelling painted in the eighteenth century with a gold boss in the centre of each panel. The Drawing Room, however, is conventionally early Georgian with Elizabethan panelling painted in the eighteenth century but since stripped, while the Dining Room was re-done in 1913 in Neo-Georgian style with green-and-white panelling. All these rooms are nice, low-ceilinged and beautifully furnished.

The small CHAPEL sitting in the garden next to the house dates from the fourteenth century but has a seventeenth-century bell-tower with a Chinese hat on top and a blue-and-gold clock face. The interior has eighteenth-century box pews, medieval floor tiles, whitewashed walls and an oak roof. The tomb of Sir Richard Croft, who died in 1509, is a good piece of late medieval sculpture; it has recently been cleaned and restored. It comprises a tomb-chest surmounted by carved angels and impressive effigies. On a lighter note are the four pretty carved and painted eighteenth-century angels' heads arranged around the bottom of the roof.

Croft Castle.

Croome Court

12; 6 miles S of Worcester off A38

The glory is departed, but Croome is still an important unified eighteenth-century work of art. House, PARK and CHURCH were all built by the 6th Earl of Coventry in the mid-eighteenth century to the design of Capability Brown. The church is Gothick and the house classical, with a grand Ionic portico. The park is one of Brown's finest, with a lake and a plethora of garden buildings, now all rather neglected as the estate has been broken up. It is a great pity that the park was not acquired by the National Trust.

The great importance of Croome lies in the contribution of Robert Adam, who was called in to finish off Brown's work. The interior of the church is by Adam, with dainty Gothick stucco work and exquisite furnishings, including the little carved classical font. Adam was also largely responsible for the interior of the house, though this has been much despoiled by the religious institution that occupied Croome till recently and quietly sold many of the fixtures and fittings without listed building consent. The Tapestry Room (including the plaster ceiling and marble chimneypiece) is now in the Metropolitan Museum, New York. The Library bookcases are in the Victoria and Albert Museum, while the antique plaster casts from the Gallery are at Kenwood and elsewhere. None of these should have left the house. The Hall and Saloon, with pre-Adam Palladian decora-

tion, survive (presumably there was less of a market for their decorations) and Adam's Long Gallery retains its plaster ceiling and fine marble chimneypiece with caryatids.

The garden buildings are now a better monument to Adam's genius than the rooms inside the house. Greenhouse, summerhouse, rotunda, various sets of lodge gates and a panorama tower are all in the chastest neoclassical taste, their crisp stonework embellished with garlands and plaques.

Dinmore Manor

13; 8 miles N of Hereford off A49

In the Middle Ages Dinmore belonged to the Knights of St John and a few fragments from this time survive, including the fourteenth-century Chapel and some parts of the east wing of the house; the latter date from c.1600 and the range next to it from the seventeenth century. Most of the house (including the large west wing), however, dates from 1923–36 and was designed by Ford and Beddington for Richard Hollis Murray of Hereford in a full-blooded, Gothic style with a large Great Hall – now the Music Room – and Cloisters. The setting in a secluded, wooded valley is very romantic. Only the garden, Chapel, Cloisters and Music Room are open to the public. There is some stained glass of a vulgarity hardly to be imagined, showing a sunset and palm trees, in a grotto off the Cloisters.

Downton Castle

14; 2 miles SE of Leintwardine off A4113

This Picturesque castle in a romantic setting overlooking the deep wooded valley of the River Teme consciously evokes a painting by Gaspar Poussin, and was designed for himself in 1774–8 by Richard Payne Knight, the grandson of a rich iron-founder. With his neighbour Uvedale Price, Payne Knight was joint prophet of the Picturesque as an aesthetic philosophy, and in this building he put his thesis into practice. He described Downton as a house 'ornamented with what are called Gothic towers and battlements without, with Grecian columns and entablatures within' and spoke of the advantages of the design, which combined an exterior that looked picturesque with 'an elegant and convenient dwelling ... capable of receiving alterations and additions in almost any direction without injury to its genuine and original character'. This latter has proved to be true; various Victorian Gothic additions of the 1860s and 1870s (by Haycock of Shrewsbury), have merely increased the drama of the design. The overall composition is effectively asymmetrical, with strong simple shapes and good stonemasonry. A large square central tower dominates the main south front, with flanking octagonal and square towers at either end. The composition looks best, however, when seen from the north-west with the twin cylindrical towers of the gatehouse-type main entrance projecting forward at the end of the west wing and the rest of the building, including the Victorian parts, irregularly disposed behind.

Payne Knight's interior, by contrast, is wholly classical, with elegant Adamesque plasterwork, mahogany doors, marble chimneypieces and porphyry columns. The main rooms form an impressive enfilade along the south front, and enjoy beautiful views over the valley. The large square tower contains the Dining Room – a full-height rotunda on the model of the Pantheon. The coffered domed ceiling is painted blue, red and gold, and the little apses in the walls have porphyry Corinthian columns, but the marbled decoration in green, yellow and red on the walls has most regrettably been painted over. The original Entrance Hall (later the Morning Room) has a bold Doric frieze and a rich chimneypiece of porphyry and ormolu, while the adjoining Drawing Room has a screen of porphyry columns at the west end and a doorcase framed in porphyry columns bought in Italy. The Library in the west wing has large mahogany bookcases especially designed for Payne Knight.

Downton, though still a private house, no longer belongs to Payne Knight's descendants, and during this century his great art collection, which included several Rembrandts, Poussins, Ruisdaels, Salvator Rosas and works by English artists, has all been dispersed.

Eastnor Castle

15; 2 miles E of Ledbury on A438 [19]

Situated in a beautiful part of the Welsh marcher country, Eastnor is a splendid expression of the aspirations of an early nineteenth-century Tory peer, an evocation in stone of the political views put into effect by Lord Liverpool's government at the time of Waterloo.

Eastnor was built in 1810 by John, 2nd Lord Somers, to the design of the young Robert Smirke, who here perfected his design for a symmetrical Neo-Gothic castle-house first developed at Lowther in Westmorland (*q.v.*) for Lord Lonsdale, another Tory peer. The 3rd Earl Somers redecorated three of the principal rooms to the designs of A.W. Pugin and George Fox (who also worked at Longleat and Warwick (*q.v.*)) and they survive as a remarkable example of early Victorian interior decoration.

The Great Hall is in the Norman style with marble columns and carving by James Forsyth. The upper parts of the wall are painted in a stencilled pattern derived from an old altar cloth in Toulouse Cathedral, while round the lower part is displayed the important collection of fifteenth- and sixteenth-century armour assembled by the 3rd Earl Somers and now the only collection of its sort to remain in an English country house. The Dining Room is chiefly notable for a good series of family portraits by Lely, Kneller, Romney and Reynolds. The Drawing Room was redecorated in 1849 by A.W. Pugin in the style of the House of Lords and its rich Gothic stencilling provides an unusual but effective setting for a splendid set of seventeenth-century Brussels tapestries. The Long Library recalls Fox's work at Longleat, with inlaid walnut bookcases inspired by the sacristy of Santa Maria delle Grazie in Milan. Above them hang French tapestries devoted to mythological themes. The Staircase Hall is dominated by the four Watts' frescoes of the Elements.

Evesham

16; 14 miles SE of Worcester on A44

Evesham is quite a handsome town with some fine open spaces and streets lined with agreeable buildings. The usual spread of bland new shops does not quite succeed in wrecking the townscape. Everything is well kept, neat and prosperous. There is something very appealing about this type of small English town, with its public library; smartly painted telephone boxes; prosperous banks; variety of churches; dozens of pubs; self-conscious trees; innumerable public lavatories; the odd antique dealer, secondhand bookshop, art dealer or gunsmith amidst the standard stores; the little local museum; the public park with municipal bedding-out and green benches; the almshouses and the odd meteorological eccentricity. The latter at Evesham takes the form of a wind-dial and barometer fixed on to the outside wall of the Town Hall – the bequest to his native town of a local worthy.

Evesham grew up around the ABBEY founded in 714 by Bishop Egwin of Worcester. Little now remains of the monastic buildings apart from some low stretches of wall, but the splendid early sixteenth-century BELL-TOWER built by Abbot Lichfield survives. It is a free-standing Perpendicular piece over 100 feet high with all-over decoration of blank panels, corner buttresses, openwork battlements and elegant narrow pinnacles. Two GATEHOUSES also remain, the Norman Gate with a later timber-framed upper storey and the Great Gate now built into an eighteenth-century house.

A unique feature of the Evesham precinct is the presence of two parish churches, and this explains why the abbey church was allowed to disappear at the Reformation. Otherwise the townspeople might have claimed it as their own, as happened elsewhere, and so saved it from destruction. The predominant architectural interest of both churches is Perpendicular, though they have older bits. ALL SAINTS' CHURCH is Norman with a well-preserved west door of *c*.1200. The tower with a spire and the porch are both rich Perpendicular work, the latter with openwork battlements and pinnacles like the bell-tower. The great thrill inside is the Lichfield Chapel built by Abbot Lichfield as his own burial chapel. It has a fan vault and rich carved detail. The CHURCH OF ST LAWRENCE also has a Perpendicular west tower with spire, but in this case the spire was added in 1836 by H. Eginton, who was responsible at that time for a sweeping restoration of the whole building which increased the perfection of the Perpendicular effect. He added the roof, for instance, to St Clement's Chantry – another of the early sixteenth-century works of Abbot Clement. The south chapel has a stone fan vault with central pendant boss. The large east window contains stained glass by Willement.

Leaving the abbey precincts through the Norman Gate, the Market Place is reached. This is given dignity by a group of handsome public buildings, including the Neo-Georgian LIBRARY of 1908 by G.H. Hunt and the

TOWN HALL, remodelled in 1884 also by Hunt. The best building is the fifteenth-century BATH HALL, originally an inn. It is an ambitious three-storeyed timber-framed building with jettied upper storeys and two gables, and was carefully restored in the 1960s. From here the three main streets open off – Bridge Street, Vine Street and High Street. All retain some nice Georgian houses of middling quality.

Goodrich Castle
17; 6 miles SW of Ross-on-Wye on B4228

This is a splendid red sandstone ruin, perched high on a spur above the Wye. The name means Godric's Castle. It was the last stronghold in Herefordshire to hold out for Charles I, and finally fell to an assault by a locally made cannon called 'Roaring Meg', the walls being breached on the south side. Most of the present building was erected in the late thirteenth century, but incorporating parts of the Norman castle that had stood on the site.

The castle is approached by a powerful semi-circular Barbican and is surrounded by a deep moat cut into the rock. The Gatehouse, too, has a mighty semi-circular tower, housing the Chapel. Inside, there is a square courtyard with ranges of buildings and towers in the corners. The oldest is the small square Norman keep. The Great Hall, in the west range, is 65 feet long and has traceried windows. The principal living quarters opened off it at the high-table end.

Goodrich Castle.

The church of St Michael, Great Witley.

Great Malvern

18; 8 miles NE of Ledbury on A449

The dramatic outcrop of the Malvern Hills is the principal landscape feature of Worcestershire. This town, which is scattered over the steep slopes, developed as a spa in the mid-nineteenth century and is essentially Victorian – rather like an English hill station in India. In the Middle Ages the Benedictine MALVERN PRIORY was here, with a little village outside its gates. The church survives because, as so often happened, it became the parish church at the Dissolution.

This majestic church contains important Norman work, and Perpendicular work. It is the latter that is most in evidence from the outside. The aisles, clerestory, porch, east and west ends are uniformly Perpendicular, with huge traceried windows – the east and west windows are vast – and openwork traceried parapets. The whole is dominated by the square central tower with its sumptuous all-over decoration of blank tracery and thin buttresses, culminating in an openwork battlemented crown and four square corner turrets with concave tops. It is obviously related to the crossing-tower of Gloucester Cathedral – a younger brother, I should think, though possibly a first cousin.

The interior is a breathtaking experience. The Norman arcades survive in the nave, with low round columns and plain capitals and arches. These arcades are remarkably austere, and they make a powerful contrast to the filigree elaboration of the Perpendicular work all around. Above soars the fifteenth-century clerestory, remarkably tall in juxtaposition to the Norman arches. The flat timber roof was restored by the ubiquitous George Gilbert Scott. The crossing under the tower has an elaborate stone lierne vault and this makes an effec-

tive transition to the chancel, which is pure Perpendicular with all-over tracery, blank between the arcades and the large triforium windows. The east wall is formed entirely of one giant window over a low reredos, also of blank traceried pattern; again the model is Gloucester. This chancel was intended to have a stone vault, but it was never built and there is a flat timber roof like the nave. As so much of the building consists of large Perpendicular windows it is a wonderful chance that more fifteenth-century glass survives at Malvern than anywhere else in England; the interior glows with the characteristic yellows and blues of late medieval glass. Hardly less remarkable a survival are the tiles in the screen walls round the chancel – the only medieval wall tiles in England. They are beautifully coloured in pink, brown and lavender and have ninety different patterns of heraldry, religious symbols and inscriptions. They were a rich source of inspiration to Victorian architects in the nineteenth-century revival of encaustic tile-making, though this never quite reached the beauty of the real thing, as seen here.

Great Witley★

19; 15 miles NW of Worcester on A443

The ruins of the palatial Victorian house and the dignified eighteenth-century parish church next to it, like a private chapel, overlook the shattered terraces and fountains of W.H. Nesfield's formal gardens. *Sic transit* . . . The house was spectacularly remodelled in the mid-nineteenth century by Samuel Dawkes for the fabulously rich (coal and iron) 1st Earl of Dudley. It was burnt in 1937, leaving just the stone shell with huge Ionic porticos and balustrades. The classical restraint of Dawkes's façade forms an appropriate backdrop to the Baroque PERSEUS FOUNTAIN by James Forsyth, with its carved rock-work and more than life-size figures on a plinth 26 feet high.

The parish CHURCH OF ST MICHAEL is attached to the ruins of the house. The architect is not definitely known, but James Gibbs has been suggested. The exterior is a plain rectangle, faced in stone by Dawkes but originally of red brick, with an open cupola over the west end. The interior has some of the finest eighteenth-century Baroque decoration in England, derived from the chapel of the Duke of Chandos at Canons in Middlesex (where Handel had been the *Kapellmeister*). When Canons was sold up in 1747, Lord Foley, the builder of Great Witley, bought the stained glass, organ and ceiling paintings, and took moulds of the plasterwork. These bits were all fitted together again by Gibbs. All the decoration (papier mâché, not stucco) is white and gold, including the elaborate wall panels and the coving of the ceiling. The latter re-incorporates the circular panels from Canons painted by the Venetian artist Antonio Bellucci, who came to England in the 1720s. The Canons' stained glass was designed by another Italian artist, Francesco Sleter, and made by Joshua Price, the leading English glass painter of the day. The Baroque effect was enhanced in the mid-nineteenth century by Dawkes, who designed many of the fittings, including the pulpit, pews and lectern, and was generally responsible for the aura of velvet-upholstered luxury. On either side of the altar are little transepts, that to the north containing the huge eighteenth-century monument to the 1st Lord Foley by Rysbrack, of grey-and-white marble, with a fanfare of marble urns and drapery around the semi-reclining effigy of the deceased. It is the sort of thing you can imagine a starving eighteenth-century sculptor doodling without ever expecting to have the chance of actually carrying it out.

Hagley Hall

20; 5 miles SW of Halesowen on A456

A late example of the English Palladian house with corner towers on the model of Wilton, Hagley Hall was designed by Sanderson Miller for the 1st Lord Lyttelton in 1754–60 and is notable for its landscape PARK with a 'ruined castle' by Sanderson Miller, an obelisk, and the Temple of Theseus by James 'Athenian' Stuart, which is the earliest example of Greek Revival architecture in Europe.

The interior of the house contains very good Rococo decoration, skilfully restored after a serious fire in 1925. The main rooms are on the *piano nobile*. The Entrance Hall has pretty stucco decoration by Vassali, including a relief of a satyr and Cupid above the fireplace, and antique statues in niches round the walls. The Saloon, on axis, has splendid Rococo plasterwork with lush trophies, which frame paintings and represent Music, Painting, Acting, Hunting and War. The whole of the south side of the house is occupied by the Gallery, which has a Rococo ceiling and screens of Corinthian columns at either end; the appearance of this room has been greatly improved by its redecoration in 1981. The Dining Room,

Library and Tapestry Room, though smaller, also have nice plasterwork, carved marble chimneypieces and their original eighteenth-century furniture.

Hanbury Hall

NT; 21; 2 miles E of Droitwich off B4090 [20]

'A sweet place and a noble estate,' Bishop Hough called it in 1733. The house was completed in 1701 and is a good example of the time, though somewhat old-fashioned with its red brick elevations, hipped roof, central white-painted cupola crowned with a large gold ball, and well-carved stone details. It was built by Thomas Vernon, a successful Chancery barrister, who, according to his own estimation, amassed in forty years' practice a fortune of £112,000 in fees. The name of his architect is not known.

The present forecourt and fussy Chinese pavilions are Victorian, but otherwise the house is largely unaltered externally. The principal interior feature is the Hall and staircase with mural decorations by Sir James Thornhill carried out in 1710. In a niche over the Hall fireplace is a good marble bust of Thomas Vernon. The adjoining Parlour has an original bolection-moulded chimneypiece, similar to that in the Entrance Hall, and is hung with Vernon family portraits. The Long Room was formed out of two rooms, as revealed by the disposition of Thornhill's ceiling paintings. Here is displayed the late R.S. Watney's gift of eighteenth-century English porcelain and Dutch flower pictures. The Drawing Room was remodelled in the late eighteenth century and has a neoclassical stucco cornice and chimneypiece; the wooden floor has a rare painted border. The house has been prettily decorated and furnished by the National Trust.

Hanbury Hall.

Harvington Hall.

Hartlebury Castle
22; 2 miles E of Stourport-on-Severn on B4193

Hartlebury is the residential seat of the Bishops of Worcester, and one of the most attractive of English episcopal palaces. The old castle was largely destroyed in the Civil War and rebuilt later in the seventeenth century as a comfortable country house. In the mid-eighteenth century some Gothick alterations were made, including the addition of battlements and a delicious conical-roofed cupola to the Hall roof in the centre, and the conversion of the ground-floor windows to pointed arches with elegant Y glazing bars. The Chapel, with pretty plaster fan vaulting, is known to have been done by Henry Keene (the Surveyor to Westminster Abbey), so perhaps he was responsible for all the Gothick alterations. The interior has a seventeenth-century staircase, Saloon with a Rococo plaster ceiling, and a late eighteenth-century Library with screens of columns and fitted bookcases.

Harvington Hall
23; 3 miles SE of Kidderminster off A448

Harvington is famous for its series of ingenious priests' hiding holes, which number no less than seven – a reflection of the recusancy of its owners, the Pakingtons. It is the perfect setting for a nineteenth-century Gothic novel or historical melodrama. The house itself is a somewhat amorphous red brick Elizabethan building, modernised by John Pakington in the 1570s, with gables and mullion windows. The interior contains much original panelling as well as some very interesting Elizabethan wall paintings showing nude figures, arabesques, animals, and a series depicting the Nine Worthies. Further alterations were made by the Throckmorton family in *c.*1700, including the removal of the drawbridge and the transfer of the original staircase to Coughton Court in Warwickshire (*q.v.*); a replica was left in its place. In this century the Roman Catholic Diocesan owners have done a certain amount of restoration on the house.

Hellen's
24; 5 miles SW of Ledbury on B4024

A fragment of a much larger Jacobean mansion of red brick with mullion windows and incorporating some older sections, Hellen's is remotely situated and unspoilt. It is said to have been visited by both the Black Prince and Bloody Mary. The interior contains several notable items of Jacobean decoration, including a Jacobean staircase with oak balusters, a fine plaster frieze in one of the ground-floor rooms and a couple of rooms on the first floor with ribbed plaster ceilings and elaborate carved chimneypieces. The Cordova Room is lined with seventeenth-century embossed leather hangings.

Hereford

25; 18 miles N of Monmouth on A49

Hereford itself is not one of England's foremost historic towns, nor is its cathedral of the first rank. The centre is a good example of 1970s' civic improvement, complete with pedestrianisation, raised flower-beds, pastel-coloured façades and unobtrusive street lighting. It is not bad in its own way, but how one wishes that old towns in England could be more than shopping centres. At times it seems as if all our historic towns are merely brightly maintained façades to one huge, dead super-market-chainstore – despite good intentions and a certain amount of careful restoration work. A new ring-road has recently been built around the outside of the medieval city walls, isolating the centre from the suburbs.

HEREFORD CATHEDRAL, unlike most English cathedrals, is not secluded in its own close; instead the west front faces directly into Broad Street across a strip of lawn. The exterior is almost entirely Victorian restoration, the usual trouble with soft red sandstone being exacerbated here by the collapse of the Norman west tower in 1786. The west front, for instance, is a completely new design by Oldrid Scott, replacing one by James Wyatt. The most impressive external feature is the majestic fourteenth-century crossing-tower, encrusted with ball-flower decoration. The interior also owes much to eighteenth- and nineteenth-century restorers. The nave has lost two of its bays; the building nevertheless does not feel out of proportion. In the nave the arcades of fat circular Norman columns and round arches with zigzag carving survive, but the upper parts were damaged by the fall of the west tower and reconstructed by Wyatt. His is the triforium with Y-tracery and the vault, which is of wood – though you cannot tell that, as it is attractively painted with Victorian stencilled patterns of dull brown and blue on a stone-coloured ground. The crossing was partly reconstructed in the 1840s by Cottingham but, like Wyatt's work in the nave, this is relatively unobtrusive. The south transept is Norman. Over the altar is a south German triptych dating from *c.*1530. The north transept is a *tour de force* of mid-thirteenth-century Gothic, erected by Bishop Aquablanca, with enormously tall traceried windows and triangular arches. The piers have Purbeck marble shafts inspired by Westminster Abbey. Bishop Aquablanca's own monument is in the same style as his transept, with a tall gabled canopy, thin pinnacles and geometrical tracery carried on elegant Purbeck shafts; it is among the most important medieval tombs in England. The choir is part Norman, but again the dominant impression comes from the Victorian restoration. It is a pity the vault is so low. The east end, with a curious double arch behind the altar giving an enticing vista through to the Lady Chapel, is Cottingham's while the fourteenth-century choir stalls were restored by George Gilbert Scott, who also designed the tiled pavement. Unfortunately, the latter's magnificent metalwork screen, studded with semi-precious stones and comparable to that at Lichfield (*q.v.*), was removed in the 1960s (bits were made into table-lamps!) by the then Dean, who did not like Victorian art, but there is now a chance that it may be reinstated.

Behind the altar is the thirteenth-century Lady Chapel – a self-contained rectangular room of exquisite beauty, with a rib vault, and lancet windows containing rich, dark medieval and Victorian stained glass. There is a seemly modern altarpiece of gold and colours. Several medieval tombs have had their colouring restored, including the early sixteenth-century chantry of Bishop Audley. Baron Peter Grandison, who died in 1358, rests his feet on a large pet dog with its tongue hanging out licking its master's knee. The outside of the Lady Chapel was restored by Gilbert Scott so that it looks like a medieval relic casket with a tall roof culminating in a decorative cresting along the ridge.

To the south of the cathedral are fragments of the Cloisters and the BISHOP'S PALACE, which stands in a pretty position, its lawns and trees stretching down to the river. The Palace has a Georgian façade and Norman Hall.

Broad Street still has character despite some 1950s' rebuilding. There are Georgian houses and Victorian banks; the Catholic CHURCH OF ST FRANCIS XAVIER has a Doric portico front; the GREEN DRAGON HOTEL has a jolly green-painted dragon in the pediment; and at the north end, the thirteenth-century steeple of ALL SAINTS'

Hereford Cathedral.

CHURCH makes a good view-stopper. Turning east, High Town – the continuation of the High Street – is reached, with the OLD HOUSE of 1621, wildly timber-framed, and the nineteenth-century MARKET HALL with a clock turret on top. In St Peter Street is ST PETER'S CHURCH, neatly filling the end of the vista. It is Victorianised medieval with a spire. Tacked on to one side is a Victorian glass-and-iron shelter, like something from the seaside. In the middle of the street is a war memorial cross. To the east is the SHIRE HALL of 1817–19 by Sir Robert Smirke, coolly Grecian with a majestic Parthenon portico. St Owen Street contains Georgian brick houses as a foil to the jolly brown terracotta fantasy of the TOWN HALL, designed by H.A. Cheers in 1902–4. More decent eighteenth-century houses can be found in the network of streets leading south towards the cathedral. North of the junction of High Street and High Town is Widemarsh Street, at the end of which is the CONINGSBY HOSPITAL, founded in 1614. Just behind it is the only surviving FRIARS' PREACHING CROSS in England.

Hewell Grange
26; 3 miles SE of Bromsgrove off A441

This splendid former seat of the Earls of Plymouth in a Repton park was sold after the Second World War and is now a borstal. This has one advantage, in that the boys provide plentiful labour for the upkeep of the grounds, though the elaborate Neo-Jacobean topiary garden has been swept away. Why can't it be restored?

Hewell Grange.

The present house was built in 1884–91 by Bodley and Garner for the 1st Earl of Plymouth, a notable patron of the arts. It is in a super-Jacobean style, three storeys high, faced in red sandstone with elaborate gables and large mullion-and-transom windows. The entrance front is somewhat severe and has a two-storeyed porch flanked by stepped-back wings; but the garden front is jollier, with two little pyramidal-roofed towers, bay windows and an arched *loggia*. The interior impresses with its scale and lavishness. The front door leads straight into an incredibly vast Hall, which occupies about half the total space of the house. At either end are two tiers of marble-columned arcades, which owe more to Italian *quattrocento* precedent than to Jacobean England. The Chapel is even more sumptuous, fitted out with a carved wooden ceiling designed by Detmar Blow and a palatial floor of marble and lapis lazuli.

Perhaps the most amazing feature of Hewell is that the shell of the previous house, a large square Baroque pile of eleven bays by eleven, attributed to Thomas Archer, still stands in the park. The four entrance lodges by Cundy were, of course, designed for this rather than for the present house.

Holme Lacy
27; 3 miles SE of Hereford on B4399

Holme Lacy is a very large house, though, being of undemonstrative architecture, it does not immediately convey its true scale. It was built by the 2nd Viscount Scudamore in the 1670s, almost certainly to the design of Hugh May, who had remodelled Windsor Castle for Charles II. The exterior is a good example of Anglo-Dutch architecture, serene and well-proportioned, with hipped roofs, balustraded parapets and large pediments containing florid cartouches. The interior contains a rich sequence of eight state rooms on the ground floor, which have the best plaster ceilings of their date in England – amazingly elaborate after the plain dignity of the façades. How much better is Caroline stucco work of this type than the flaccid mythological ceiling painting of Verrio and Laguerre! Hardly less grand is the Edwardian decoration carried out in 1910 in a ritzy manner, including the palatial Grand Staircase. Having for many years been occupied by a mental hospital, Holme Lacy is currently empty. With luck a sympathetic user will be found.

Holt
28; 5 miles N of Worcester off A443

The little CHURCH OF ST MARTIN stands next to the remains of Holt Castle (now a private house). It is one of the finest Norman churches in a county rich in Norman architecture, and is lavishly decorated inside and out. The doorway and round-arched windows all have profuse carving. Inside, the arcade has round columns with scallop capitals, and the Norman chancel arch has zigzag carving. Over it is a Victorian mosaic copied from Ravenna. The pulpit and lectern are Victorian Neo-Norman. Pevsner quotes an amusing passage from an 1858 issue of *Building News*: 'We refuse to criticize, as they are the work of a lady and it is pleasing to find them taking an interest in these matters.'

The church of St Mary and St David, Kilpeck.

Kilpeck★
29; 8 miles SW of Hereford off A465

The CHURCH OF ST MARY AND ST DAVID is situated in a particularly beautiful part of Herefordshire. A new avenue of chestnut trees leads towards the apsidal east end of the church, which was completed *c*.1150 and has hardly been altered since. It contains some of the best work of the Herefordshire school of Norman sculpture. The church is quite small, and consists of a rectangular nave without aisles, and an apsidal sanctuary. Over the west end is a little bellcote. The exterior is richly embellished with carving of Scandinavian character. There is a corbel table round the top encrusted with over seventy grotesque carvings: falcons, deer, wild boar, rams' heads, a dog, a rabbit, wrestlers, lovers, musicians. The south door is the great treasure of the church, with carved tympanum, columns and arches. It depicts the Garden of Eden and the Fall of Man; on the right-hand jamb Adam is being tempted to eat the forbidden fruit; the arches, ornamented with all manner of birds, beasts and fish, and the tympanum, which shows the Tree of Life, represent the Garden of Eden.

The interior has whitewashed walls – an excellent foil to the carved pink stonework of the chancel arch. This is a unique arrangement, with little saints standing on top of each other. The little apsidal sanctuary has a rib-vaulted ceiling. The huge plain font is Norman. At the back of the church is a seventeenth-century wooden gallery. By the crossing-arch, note also the ancient holy-water stoup, carved to represent a pair of hands.

Kingsland
30; 3 miles NW of Leominster off A44

Kingsland is heralded by cedar trees, always a sign of civilisation, in the garden of the late seventeenth-century Big House. It is a pretty village of brick Georgian houses and older black-and-white cottages grouped loosely along the main street. The CHURCH OF ST MICHAEL AND ALL ANGELS stands in a grassy churchyard with a large yew tree, and has a big square west tower and a little bellcote over the crossing-gable. It is a grand all-of-a-piece job, dating from *c*.1300, and has some unusual touches, such as the circular windows in the clerestory. Entering through the north door, you are immediately confronted by the most extraordinary feature of the church – a little chantry chapel opening directly off the porch; it is unique in England. The nave is tall and regular with symmetrical arcades. The walls are washed a light pink colour and there is an open timber roof. The chancel has a barrel ceiling of timber with painted stencilled patterns designed by G.F. Bodley, who restored the church in 1866–8. He also designed the pulpit, lectern and choir stalls, but his screen has since been removed. The encaustic tiles in the sanctuary are by Godwin and the east window retains some medieval stained glass. Over the Lady altar is a cartoon of the Crucifixion by Frank Brangwyn. The overall atmosphere is of good-taste Anglo-Catholicism.

Ledbury
31; 8 miles SW of Great Malvern on A449

The CHURCH OF ST MICHAEL stands in an attractive churchyard, reached from the picturesque High Street of this little hill town by a narrow cobbled lane flanked with black-and-white houses. It is the grandest parish church in Herefordshire, with parts of different dates from Norman onwards, though it is mainly fourteenth-century. It has an unusually wide nave and aisles. The west door with zigzag carving is Norman, as is the chancel arcade with its sturdy round pillars. The early thirteenth-century bell-tower is detached from the church and stands on its own to the north. The stone spire was built in 1727–34 by Nathaniel Wilkinson of Worcester to replace a timber one. The general aspect of the exterior is Decorated with large geometrical traceried windows. The north chapel windows, studded with ball-flower carving, are very similar to those at Leominster (*q.v.*) and are obviously by the same masons. The nave is grand and spacious. The arcades have octagonal piers and the aisles have good timber roofs. There is a great deal of Victorian stained glass by Kempe.

The church is unusually rich in monuments, including a whole series to the Skynner and Biddulph families, which features works by such leading sculptors as Westmacott, Flaxman and Thornycroft. In the north aisle is a monument by Lough to Edward Moulton Barrett, the stern father of Elizabeth Barrett Browning. The Jacobean Skynner monument is the most impressive: on it, five slightly bearded sons and five daughters kneel beneath the beruffed effigies of their parents.

Leominster

32; 11 miles W of Bromyard on A44

Leominster is basically a superb place, but today, sadly, its condition strikes one as that mixture of neglect and insensitive new work that is always so profoundly depressing in old English country towns – neither the graceful mellow decay of Italy, nor the self-conscious spruceness of New England. It was a wool town in the Middle Ages and the sixteenth century, but prosperity departed long ago. The general townscape is a mixture of Georgian red brick and medieval or sixteenth-century black-and-white timber-framing. The main street, the High Street, has some unspoilt Victorian and late Georgian shop-fronts of painted timber; it is continued on a grander scale by Broad Street. To the east is Corn Square, a little market place with the Victorian Gothic CORN EXCHANGE and a black-and-white house dating from *c.*1400. DRAPERS LANE, a paved pedestrian alley which runs parallel, is a picturesque backwater with timber-framed buildings. Church Street has several good eighteenth-century houses, such as THE FORBURY, which has a pediment on top and a fluted Doric doorcase. The street approaches the church at an angle – a good townscape effect.

The CHURCH OF ST PETER AND ST PAUL was a Benedictine priory, which explains its grandeur. When approaching from the town centre, the first impression is of the splendid array of five Decorated windows, with geometrical tracery and ball-flower carving, in the south aisle; the huge Perpendicular window in the centre of the west end; and the Norman doorway in the base of the tower. From the outside, though asymmetrical, the church forms a balanced composition that suggests a nave flanked by two spacious aisles. The interior therefore comes as a surprise, because it comprises two churches side by side – or, at least, two large and splendid naves, one Early English with a Decorated aisle, and one Norman. The explanation for this curious state of affairs is that the Norman nave was monastic, whereas the other nave was added in the thirteenth century

to serve as the parish church. The Norman nave has cylindrical columns with cushion capitals and a flat beamed ceiling with stencilled patterns. It contains some interesting bric-à-brac, including a seventeenth-century ducking stool. The other nave still serves as the parish church. It was restored in the nineteenth century by Sir George Gilbert Scott, and the piers in the south arcade are his. The best object is the organ case dating from 1739.

South of the church is GRANGE COURT, an ultra-picturesque black-and-white structure with an interesting history. It is the old Town Hall of Leominster, and once stood at the junction of the High Street and Broad Street. It was built by John Abel in 1633 and is two storeys high; originally the ground floor was open with Ionic columns on plinths. The upper part is elaborately decorated with fancy patterns of beams and shallow canted bay windows.

Little Malvern Court

33; 3 miles S of Great Malvern on A449

This house is of interest because it incorporates the early fourteenth-century refectory, or Prior's Hall, of a former Benedictine priory. Part of the priory CHURCH survives too and is now the parish church. Bits of the present building owe their appearance to a restoration and remodelling carried out to the design of Charles Hansom in 1860. The interior of the Prior's Hall, however, is perfectly preserved and has recently been carefully restored. The whole of the open medieval roof survives, with double purlins and cusped wind-braces. Only the Hall itself is open to the public.

Lower Brockhampton

NT; 34; 2 miles E of Bromyard on A44

A small and delightful medieval timber-framed manor house, which still forms the centre of a proper working farm. The house is moated and approached by a tiny fifteenth-century timber gatehouse. Of the main building, only the central Great Hall and one wing survive; both date from the fourteenth century and the Hall has an interesting timber roof. The house belongs to the National Trust and the Hall is open to the public during the summer.

Madley

35; 7 miles W of Hereford on B4352

The square Early English tower of the CHURCH OF THE NATIVITY OF THE VIRGIN, with lancet windows and embattled top, is a prominent feature in the landscape. The gilt clock face was erected in 1901 in memory of Queen Victoria. A large porch, almost on the scale of a transept, gives access to the light, spacious Early English nave, which is among the most beautiful in Herefordshire. The arcades are symmetrical, with round piers supporting a clerestory of lancet windows. The aisles have plain stone walls and are on the same generous scale as the nave, which adds to the feeling of spaciousness. The chancel is Decorated and, most unusually for an English church, takes the form of a polygonal apse. In the east window there survives some beautiful medieval stained glass, albeit arranged rather like a patchwork quilt. The sedilia is carved with ball-flower decoration, there are plain old oak choir stalls, and the floor is paved with Victorian encaustic tiles. Other furnishings include, in the north aisle, an old family pew like a four-poster bed, and, in the south aisle, an altarpiece made up out of Flemish or Spanish Baroque woodwork. An unusual feature of Madley, by parish church standards, is the existence of a little crypt beneath the chancel, formed by the slope in the lie of the land. This has a stone rib vault supported on a central octagonal pier.

Madresfield Court
36; 2 miles E of Great Malvern off A449
The seat of the Earls Beauchamp, of diapered brick and half-timber, moated, gabled and asymmetrically composed, Madresfield Court is a romantic Victorian evocation of a medieval château. It was designed largely by P.C. Hardwick in the 1860s. Further work was done earlier this century, including the Staircase Hall with crystal balusters, and the Chapel – a *chef-d'œuvre* of Arts and Crafts decoration, which formed the inspiration for Evelyn Waugh's description of the chapel at Brideshead. It was a wedding present from the 7th Earl to his wife. The correct response to this fantasy of painted decoration and ornamental glass and hand-beaten metalwork and pale oak woodwork is – 'Gosh!'

Malvern Priory
See Great Malvern.

Moccas Court
37; 10 miles W of Hereford off A438
The perfection of one type of late eighteenth-century landscape composition: a crisp red brick box of a house in a ravishing park, planted under the direction of both Capability Brown and Humphry Repton, overlooking the River Wye. The house itself was built for Sir George Cornewell in the years 1775–81 by Anthony Keck, a local man, who, however, worked loosely from drawings and plans prepared by no less a figure than Robert Adam.

The house is notable for its fine series of rooms. The staircase is oval with cantilevered stone steps and a delicate iron balustrade; beyond is the circular Drawing Room behind the central bow on the river front. This is one of the finest ensembles of its type in the country, its walls hung with a superb French Etruscan-style wallpaper. Other rooms contain reticent but exquisite plasterwork and handsome carved marble chimneypieces. Both house and park have been restored by the present owner.

Ombersley
38; 9 miles N of Worcester on A449
This is an estate village and therefore not ruined by inept suburban in-fill. The MAIN STREET is one of the best village streets in Worcestershire, with old timber-framed cottages (some of them medieval) and several stately Georgian brick buildings, including the Vicarage and post office.

OMBERSLEY COURT was built in 1723–6 for the 1st Lord Sandys by Francis Smith of Warwick. It was altered in 1812–14 by John Webb, who was responsible for the plain Regency exterior. Rather more of Smith's work survives inside, including an enfilade of state rooms with classical panelling, and the staircase with turned wooden balusters. Upstairs is a rare Regency Chinese Room with silk wall panels and Regency furniture.

The CHURCH OF ST ANDREW stands in the grounds of the house and is a typical nineteenth-century landowner's job – large, elaborate and solid. It was designed by Thomas Rickman in Decorated style and built from 1825–9. It has a grand west tower with a spire. The interior still has a Georgian feel, with a plaster rib vault, box pews and a Gothic cast-iron stove. Part of the chancel of the medieval church survives as the Sandys Mausoleum and contains many monuments to the family.

Overbury
39; 5 miles E of Tewkesbury off B4079
A trim, bankers' village, Overbury has a great deal of Arts and Crafts work to show. There are stone and timber-framed cottages, all of different dates. Some of them were improved in the late nineteenth century by R. Norman Shaw, who in 1895 also designed the VILLAGE HALL in Neo-Tudor style for the Holland-Martins. Their house, OVERBURY COURT, in the middle of the village, was restored to its eighteenth-century state in 1959 by Victor Heal. It stands amidst formal gardens and has a dignified stone façade with a central pediment and segment-headed windows. The adjoining CHURCH OF ST FAITH is Norman but with a Perpendicular central tower. Its immaculately kept churchyard, which feels like an extension of the house grounds, is entered through a stocky timber lich-gate designed by Sir Herbert Baker.

Pembridge
40; 8 miles W of Leominster on A44
Pembridge is a pretty little town with black-and-white timber-framed cottages and a small Market Place. In many ways it is even more attractive than Weobley (*q.v.*), because it is less self-conscious. The CHURCH OF ST MARY, set back behind other buildings, is reached by a flight of steps. It is basically Norman but, as so often in Herefordshire, it was partly rebuilt in the fourteenth century. The most remarkable feature is the BELL-HOUSE, a detached structure, like a pagoda, in the graveyard. It has a low stone base carrying a steep pyramidal roof and weatherboarded bell stage. The interior is a mighty piece of timber-framing thought to date from the late fourteenth century.

Pershore
41; 13 miles SE of Worcester on A44
Pershore is an unspoilt little town, mainly of Georgian red brick, with a market square – Broad Street – and one principal street lined with seemly eighteenth- and nineteenth-century buildings.

The ABBEY was founded by King Oswald in the seventh century but destroyed by the Vikings; it was

Pershore Abbey.

rebuilt by the Normans in the twelfth century. The church survives to a large extent, but the west end of the nave is missing, which unbalances the exterior views. The transept and what remains of the nave is Norman. The beautiful crossing-tower has ball-flower decoration; the chancel – a piece of Early English perfection – has moulded arches, clustered columns and tall triple lancets in the clerestory. It has an elaborate Decorated stone vault, which harmonises well but – my only criticism – seems too low for the space. The bosses, elaborately carved with naturalistic foliage, are of high quality.

Rock

42; 12 miles E of Tenbury Wells off A456
The CHURCH OF ST PETER is a large and lavish Norman church, thought to date from around 1170. The north door is a rich design, with flanking colonnettes and zigzag carving. The windows are also flanked by little columns. Inside, the eye is taken by the chancel arch, which has rich carving on the capitals of the flanking columns and zigzag on the arches. The Norman font is an attractive rounded shape with sparse decoration.

Ross-on-Wye

43; 16 miles NW of Gloucester on A40
Ross-on-Wye is a good little town situated on a ridge above the River Wye, silhouetted against a backdrop of hills as you approach from the east. The town centre has a complex plan with steep sloping streets and buildings of different dates. The CHURCH OF ST MARY stands well at the top of the town, its tower and spire the dominant motif in the general scene. The nave has excessively tall arcades with round piers (heightened in 1743) and very wide aisles, so the effect is more like three naves. Unfortunately, the walls were stripped in the nineteenth century to reveal the ugly rubble stonework. Your eye is immediately caught by a cluster of church monuments in the south-east corner looking as if they are holding a conversation. They are of different dates and include two Tudor table-tombs to the Rudhall family with alabaster effigies, and an almost life-size mid-seventeenth-century statue of Colonel William Rudhall in classical armour. In front of him is a monument to Thomas Westfaling, which has a good marble bust by Theed and a pedestal relief of Charity. Skirting the unpleasant new central altar, it is possible to penetrate the chancel to see the memorial to Ross's most famous son, John Kyrle, 'the Man of Ross', whose extensive benefactions still distinguish his native town. Note his heraldic crest: a porcupine.

John Kyrle was responsible for the public garden known as THE PROSPECT to the south of the church. The north part was redeveloped in 1836; a new road was cut below the red sandstone cliff and on the top was built the picturesque ROYAL HOTEL, as well as a neo-medieval PROSPECT TOWER that looks like the part-survival of a Gothic castle. To the east of the church are the RUDHALL ALMSHOUSES – pink sandstone Elizabethan, dated 1575 and restored in 1960. The main streets form a Y with the MARKET HOUSE at the junction. It is of red sandstone with an open arcaded ground floor and was built in 1660–74. A medallion of the newly restored King Charles II adorns one side and there is a pretty clock turret on the roof. The upper room is now the town library. The central group is completed by some picturesque black-and-white houses, including the one where the Man of Ross lived (and died in 1724 at the age of eighty-eight), and a series of comparatively carefully rebuilt red brick Georgian houses with a curving frontage. Notice throughout the town the attractive blue-enamel street-name signs. BROAD STREET stretches downhill with many old houses, timber-framed underneath but stuccoed on top. It is a great pity to see how decayed some of these are, and how they are being tampered with by jobbing builders. Sadly, one gets the impression that the town is not as well cared for as it deserves to be.

Rous Lench

44; 12 miles E of Worcester off A422
An ultra-picturesque village with brick and timber-framed buildings round a green. Many of these are genuine sixteenth- and seventeenth-century but they owe much to the prettifying efforts of Victorian landowners. Note the letterbox to ROUS LENCH COURT: it looks

like a dovecote. The Court is an equally picturesque black-and-white mansion, now L-shaped but once upon a time two complete quadrangles. It has been much embellished in this century with architectural fragments brought-in from elsewhere.

The CHURCH OF ST PETER is Norman but was enlarged in the thirteenth century and restored in the 1880s in a Neo-Norman style grander than the original. The best original feature is the south doorway, which is embellished with spiral fluted columns, a zigzag carved arch and a noble relief of Christ in Glory set into a little carved niche above.

Shobdon★

45; 8 miles NW of Leominster on B4362

The hillside park at Shobdon has recently been replanted with mixed trees and a new beech avenue. One pavilion of the old MANOR HOUSE survives and has been converted to a new house; together with the large brick stable, octagonal dovecote and the church it forms an attractive manorial group. The great thrill of Shobdon is, of course, the CHURCH OF ST JOHN THE EVANGELIST – more like a proprietary chapel than a parish church. It was rebuilt between 1752 and 1756 by Richard Bateman, the local squire, who was a friend of Horace Walpole, and, like Walpole, had embraced the Gothick style. The exterior is surprisingly solid, of ashlar stone, cruciform, with battlements and the retained medieval west tower.

Only the ogee arches of the windows are demonstrably eighteenth-century. The interior, by contrast, is as filigree and fantastic as could be hoped for; it is among the most attractive examples of mid-eighteenth-century Batty Langley Gothick anywhere in England – all painted blue and white with Gothick stucco decoration on the walls and coved ceiling. The arches to the transepts and chancel consist of tripartite ogee arrangements with hanging pendants; the north transept was for the household staff and the south transept, with a fireplace (copied straight out of Batty Langley) was the family pew. The Gothick furnishings are as inventive and delightful as the architecture, especially the three-decker pulpit, the very fine armchairs in the chancel and the pretty pews, which look as if made out of Gothick sledges. The side-windows retain their brightly coloured eighteenth-century glass, but that in the east window has been replaced with more serious stained glass of 1907 and only fragments of the original remain, mounted in a screen in the north transept.

Stoke Edith

46; 7 miles E of Hereford on A438

You come suddenly to Stoke Edith, feudal and forlorn on the side of a hill. Stop awhile to see what it has to offer: the FOLEY ARMS, a pretty plum brick RECTORY, a couple of classic lodges, dark plantations and, in particular, ST MARY'S CHURCH, its medieval tower and truncated

The church of St John the Evangelist, Shobdon.

needle spire looking like an obelisk when first glimpsed over the treetops, its churchyard full of snowdrops in spring. The body of the church is simple, robust eighteenth-century classical, stuccoed, with round-arched windows; it contains all the romance and sad elegiac poetry of England. The musty, cream-painted interior has box pews, old hymn books, faded marbling round the chancel, a Victorian harmonium and moth-eaten red-baize linings to the family pew. The marble wall plaques and memorials, mainly to the Foleys, include one to Tom Onslow, who was killed in action in 1917 aged nineteen – a year after winning a scholarship to Magdalene College, Cambridge.

The same forlorn, haunted character pervades the PARK (landscaped by Repton) with its broken-branched cedars, and the abandoned site of the great seventeenth-century house – one of the most beautiful in England but burnt down in 1927, its shell finally abandoned and demolished in the 1950s. Its glorious painted decorations by Thornhill, rare needlework hangings and gilt plaster-work are now no more than a memory.

Weobley
47; 9 miles SW of Leominster on B4230

Weobley is a famously black-and-white little town situated in the middle of a broad valley with wooded hills behind and the prominent spire of the parish CHURCH OF ST PETER AND ST PAUL sailing over all. Weobley is set off the main road, so it is now a pleasantly quiet backwater. So often in the Midlands black-and-white houses are mixed with red brick Georgian façades to create a uniquely English townscape that it comes as a bit of a shock to see a whole town composed of early black-and-white houses – like a film set for Chaucer's *Canterbury Tales*. BROAD STREET is the main street and sets the tone, the upper storeys of the houses being exaggeratedly 'wobbly', jettied and timbered. The Red Lion Inn has a good sign portraying a jolly red lion. Many of the houses here and in CHAMBER WALK date from the fourteenth century, albeit much restored and prettified.

Worcester
48; 24 miles SW of Birmingham on A38
Includes The Greyfriars (NT)

Worcester is a typical example of the damage so often inflicted on a historic city by 1960s' redevelopment. The scars still show, especially the appalling dual-track road, hotel and multi-storey car park opposite the east end of the cathedral. There is, nevertheless, much of interest still, and if only the city council would adopt a vigorous conservation policy like that of York, or Chester, or even Nottingham (*qq.v.*), it would not be impossible to stitch the bits of the town centre back together.

The place to begin is the CATHEDRAL, magnificently situated on the banks of the Severn. The original church on this site was built by St Oswald in the tenth century and rebuilt by St Wulfstan after the Norman Conquest. The Norman crypt survives, but the body of the church was rebuilt from 1224 onwards in Early English style, the choir being by the same mason as the nave of Lincoln Cathedral (*q.v.*). The rebuilding proceeded unabated in

the same style for over 100 years and the architecture, as a result, blends harmoniously. The proportions are also very beautiful and this adds enormously to the aesthetic appeal of the building. On the debit side, at least externally, is the drastic nineteenth-century restoration begun by Perkins in 1857 and continued by Sir George Gilbert Scott from 1864; all the red sandstone of the exterior is renewed, just like a 'medieval' building in Germany. Inside, however, the Victorian work – where it has not been tampered with in recent years – has a splendour of its own. There is rich dark stained glass by Hardman and Lavers and Barraud. The choir vaults display the faded magnificence of Hardman's stencilled decoration, though the aisle vaults have for some inexplicable reason been whitewashed. Most of Gilbert Scott's fittings in the choir and sanctuary survive, including the iron screen, organ case, Bishop's throne, rich paving, and magnificent carved and gilded alabaster reredos. In the nave, however, many of the beautiful carved oak benches (presented to the cathedral by the Earl of Dudley) have been removed and replaced with ignoble grey plastic chairs. The most beautiful part of the Early English work at Worcester is the exquisitely proportioned eastern Lady Chapel, lavishly embellished with Purbeck marble and carving. The cathedral is full of interesting fittings and furnishings of all dates, including thirty-seven medieval misericords incorporated in Scott's choir stalls, and a rich crop of monuments and memorials, including two royal ones. King John is buried in front of the high altar under a beautiful Purbeck marble effigy, and to the right is the late Perpendicular chantry chapel of Prince Arthur, elder brother of Henry VIII. Note how Catharine of Aragon's Arms have been tampered with in order to curry favour with the authorities.

South of the cathedral are well-preserved precincts, including handsome fourteenth-century CLOISTERS, the original circular Norman CHAPTER HOUSE, and COLLEGE GREEN, guarded by a thirteenth-century gate and surrounded by attractive Georgian houses. The DEANERY, the best of these eighteenth-century houses, is characteristically no longer lived in by the Dean. Further south, beyond the precincts, is the ROYAL WORCESTER PORCELAIN FACTORY, founded by Dr Wall in 1751 and the only one of the eighteenth-century English porcelain factories still in production. It contains a good museum of Worcester china.

As for the area immediately to the north of the cathedral, it is probably best to draw a veil. Deansway replaces much of historic interest. As a modern road it could be mitigated by some decent landscaping, though ideally the stretch past the cathedral should, of course, be deleted altogether. The former BISHOP'S PALACE has a handsome early eighteenth-century front of pink stone with a segmental pediment, and lots of medieval interest inside. The eighteenth-century spire of ST ANDREW'S CHURCH, 155 feet high and nicknamed the 'Glover's Needle', is a dominant landmark; unfortunately, the body of the church was demolished after the Second World War and replaced by a garden. Opposite is the Countess of Huntingdon's CHAPEL, a precious eighteenth-century Nonconformist survival now being

Weobley.

repaired after years of neglect. ALL SAINTS' CHURCH, built in 1739–42 and attributed to Richard Squire, was gone over by Aston Webb in 1889; note how the public lavatory at the west end tactfully keeps to the same Georgian style as the church. The noble red sandstone BRIDGE over the Severn was built by John Gwynn between 1771 and 1780 and from it can be enjoyed the world-famous view of the façade and central fourteenth-century tower of the cathedral rising from riverside gardens.

Returning uphill, it is worth finding FRIAR STREET, Worcester's best medieval street, lined with picturesque overhanging timber-framed houses. These were preserved, let it not be forgotten, by private effort, not by the city council. Mr and Miss Matley Moore bought and restored THE GREYFRIARS (NT) and the houses round it after the Second World War and gave them to the National Trust. The Greyfriars was built in 1480 as a prosperous merchant's house. As restored in 1949 to the design of Maurice Jones, with rugs and needlework and polished oak, and things painted the colours of barges, it has a strong period flavour. At the back, against the city wall, is a well-planted little garden.

The main axis of Worcester extends in a long line to the north of the cathedral, beginning with the High Street. This is 'pedestrianised', with globe lights and similar municipal clutter, but above the 'snowline' the remains of many eighteenth-century brick house fronts can be seen. And on the west side the early eighteenth-century GUILDHALL, restored in the 1870s by – of all unlikely people – Gilbert Scott and expensively refurbished recently, presents a cheerful Baroque spectacle,

its carved decoration all gilded and painted in bright colours.

The continuation of the High Street is called The Cross; it is the junction of the main thoroughfares in the town. Bond Street to the west has several nice Georgian houses and the former Crown Hotel (now a shopping arcade) retains some splendid George IV lanterns. In The Cross an air of grandeur is introduced by LLOYDS BANK – a stone Italianate *palazzo* by Elmslie, dated 1861 – and ST NICHOLAS'S CHURCH, built in 1730–5 by Humphrey Hollins in a style derived from Gibbs. On the pavement here are two jolly cast-iron tram (now bus) shelters painted maroon and looking as if they have escaped from a pier at the seaside. Foregate Street is cut across by the RAILWAY BRIDGE, a strong and florid cast-iron interpolation not to be sniffed at. Even more florid is the CORNMARKET – a terracotta fantasy recently restored. It faces the BERKELEY HOSPITAL rebuilt in 1703 with brick houses and chapel surrounding a courtyard. The CROWN COURT of 1834 is a handsome Grecian design with an Ionic portico; the former JUDGE'S LODGING at the back is an even more extreme manifestation of the same style. The continuation of Foregate Street is called The Tything and is lined with many Georgian houses, of which BRITANNIA HOUSE is the best. KAY'S SHOE FACTORY of 1907 is by Maxwell Ayrton – a handsome piece of Arts and Crafts architecture. To the west is a substantial stretch of Regency town development – Albany Terrace, York Place, Britannia Square and St George's Square – with brick and painted stuccoed houses adjacent to the racecourse; it provides a welcome oasis of civilisation.

Lancashire

No county in England can show such contrasts as Lancashire, from the undisturbed beauty of the north to the post-industrial squalor of the south. It is tempting to see the former as the survival of a pre-industrial Golden Age and the latter as the aftermath of the Industrial Revolution. In fact this would be quite wrong; the picturesque appearance of the rural part of the county is just as much a product of the prosperity of the eighteenth, nineteenth and early twentieth centuries as are the industrial towns of the south. The tree planting, country houses and Victorian churches of the Lune Valley, fells and the Fylde were paid for by the fortunes made in coal, ships, cotton, iron and banking, just as much as were the public buildings, civic monuments and Victorian churches of the nineteenth-century towns. Indeed, thanks to the economic collapse of the English manufacturing industry and destructive post-war 'planning', the countryside in north Lancashire is now a better-preserved monument than are the towns to the creative prosperity that made this county the greatest industrial area in the world.

Lancashire is in many ways exceptional, not least because of its unique religious history. The Elizabethan church settlement found little favour in the county. The south-east, based on the cloth-manufacturing towns of Manchester and Bolton, was a centre of Puritan Nonconformity, and supported Parliament in the Civil War. The north and west of the county, cut off from main routes by meres, marshes and mountains, remained Catholic, and were later Royalist and Jacobite. The gentry sent their sons abroad to be educated and maintained Catholic chapels and priests in their houses. This made them backward-looking and sympathetic to the Middle Ages. A feature of Lancashire are the huge, dark stone antiquarian houses of the recusant families — Stonyhurst, Townley and Hoghton Tower. Anybody looking at them would assume that they were medieval castles brought up to date later; in fact, nearly everything that makes them so venerable was done by their owners in the sixteenth, seventeenth and eighteenth centuries.

Considering the degree of urbanisation and industrialisation that the county has undergone, it is amazing that so many old houses have survived. As well as the large stone houses already mentioned, there are also several picturesque half-timbered black-and-white houses, of which Rufford and Samlesbury are the best known.

The great age in Lancashire was from the late eighteenth century onwards. Although there have been terrible demolitions of country houses as increasing industrialisation has driven their owners away, many still survive. Lytham Hall in the Fylde, designed by Carr of York, is a good example of a prosperous eighteenth-century Lancashire squire's house — solid and red brick without, but embellished with beautiful plasterwork inside. Elaborate plasterwork by Italian *stuccatores* is a special feature of Lancashire. The best surviving examples are in the Hall at Townley, the Music Room at Lancaster and the interiors of Burrow Hall. Perhaps the *émigré* Italian craftsmen found Catholic Lancashire especially sympathetic to work in.

The Gothic Revival also took root in the county. The façade of Leighton Hall, in a beautiful park with views towards the Lake District mountains, is a particularly pretty piece of stage scenery. The Lune Valley is an almost continuous sequence of late eighteenth- and early nineteenth-century castellated or Tudorbethan houses in beautiful parks; driving along it is almost like turning the pages in a Regency book of 'seats' and admiring the aquatint illustrations. The Gothic Revival has its apotheosis in Pugin's Scarisbrick Hall, near Southport — a *tour de force* of passionate Gothic with much of the original carved, painted and gilded decoration still intact, though the house is now a school.

Lancashire would not be the first county on most people's lists for beautiful towns, but it has much of interest nevertheless. Lancaster, the county town, is a handsome place of stone-built Georgian houses, with a castle, medieval parish church, grand Edwardian Baroque Town Hall and the most amazing folly in England — the Ashton Memorial, surmounted by a prominent green copper dome, paid for out of the profits of linoleum. Clitheroe is a more conventional little market town with a ruined castle on a hill and a steep main street lined with agreeable shops, houses and pubs. Fleetwood can show the abortive remains of a grand neo-classical layout, including two of the prettiest lighthouses in the country. But even the larger industrial towns have much to offer, though their architectural glories tend to be isolated and bitty rather than adding up to a grand urban ensemble. Bolton, for instance, has a magnificent group of public buildings in the centre, several good country houses preserved in the suburbs, and a number of impressive cotton mills. Preston too has much to show, including a whole Georgian quarter of red brick houses and the best group of Catholic churches in any town in the country; St Wilfred's need not fear comparison with Brompton Oratory.

The cities of Liverpool and Manchester are really now both independent counties and so have been treated as separate sections at the end of Lancashire itself. The houses and small towns that lie within their metropolitan areas are accordingly described there.

Abbeystead
1; 6 miles SE of Lancaster off A6

Abbeystead is a large shooting lodge built by the Earl of Sefton in 1886 to the design of Douglas and Fordham of Chester; it now belongs to the Duke of Westminster. It is a sensitive Elizabethan design soundly executed in local sandstone, with mullion-and-transom windows, gables and three canted bays along the symmetrical main front which rises from balustraded terraces and flights of steps. The setting is highly romantic, in a valley leading through the fells to the Trough of Bowland; streams, a reservoir and old plantations of Scots pine heighten the landscape effect. Many of the estate buildings, farms and cottages are small-scale echoes of the architecture of the house and were also designed by Douglas and Fordham.

Astley Hall
See Chorley.

Bolton
See Manchester section.

Borwick
2; 8 miles NE of Lancaster off A6

BORWICK HALL is a good example of the north-country house that comprises a pele tower and a lower Elizabethan range. At Borwick the tower is fourteenth-century and the rest was built in 1595 by Robert Bindloss, a Kendal clothier; his mason was Alexander Brinsmead. The asymmetrical yet balanced façade has small gables, mullion-and-transom windows and the porch in the middle. The chimneys are diagonally set and there is a picturesque open timber gallery to the courtyard at the rear. The Gatehouse is dated 1650 but is identical in style to the main house. The adjoining stables are dated 1590. Inside, the Great Hall is single-storeyed and the main staircase, which ascends between solid walls, has an unusual arrangement of stone Tuscan columns on top of the central newel.

The house was carefully restored in 1910–12 by Mr J.A. Fuller-Maitland, music critic of *The Times*, to the design of R.H.P. Huddart. It now belongs to the county council and is used as a hostel, but is open to the public from time to time.

Borwick Hall.

Browsholme Hall

3; 6 miles N of Clitheroe on B6478

This is one of those amazing houses crammed with objects of all dates and looking as if nobody has ever thrown anything away. It owes some of its effect, however, to the early nineteenth-century antiquarianism of Thomas Lister Parker, who employed Jeffrey Wyatville to remodel one wing of the house in 1806.

The first stone-built house on the site dated from 1507. It was refronted in 1604 by Thomas Parker to the design of Thomas Holt of York, with a columned frontispiece and projecting end wings. This largely survives, although its top storey was removed in the eighteenth century. There are seven different types of panelling in the house and a fine collection of oak chests and cupboards, many of them with Parker initials and dated. One chimneypiece is made from an Elizabethan bedstead. The large square Drawing Room is the finest room; it was designed by Wyatville, with handsome mahogany doors provided by Gillow and plasterwork vaguely Jacobethan in style. The Entrance Hall contains a wonderful mixture of objects, including Stone Age weapons, eighteenth-century hats, the buckskin coat of a member of the family killed at the battle of Newbury in 1643, an aluminium girder from the first Zeppelin shot down in the First World War, a martyr's skull, and a dresser made out of the fronts of three seventeenth-century chests and a thirteenth-century reredos.

Browsholme has belonged to the Parkers, hereditary Park-keepers of the Royal Forest of Bowland, since the fourteenth century and it is still their home. Restoration work has recently been undertaken in both the house and grounds, where the lake has been dredged and refilled.

Burrow

4; 10 miles NE of Lancaster on A683

The site of BURROW HALL is that of a Roman fort but the origins of the present building go back only to the early seventeenth century, when a new house was erected by Edward Briggs. This was sold in 1690 to John Fenwick, a lawyer and member of the large Northumberland clan who owned the property right down to 1945. In about 1740 Robert Fenwick (also a successful lawyer, Attorney General and King's Serjeant of the Palatinate of Lancaster, MP for Lancaster from 1734–46 and an amateur archaeologist) reconstructed the house, giving it its present dignified front designed by Westby Gill and built by John Platt. It forms a handsome overture to the interior, with its series of exceedingly rich Baroque plaster ceilings by Vassali and Quadri, with medallions of Roman Emperors, mythological scenes, baskets of flowers and elaborate scrollwork.

Chorley

5; 10 miles S of Preston on A6

ASTLEY HALL belonged successively to the Charnock, Brooke and Townley-Parker families and all have left their mark. The Charnocks, who acquired the property from the Knights of St John of Jerusalem, built the original timber-framed house round a small courtyard in the sixteenth century. On the death in 1653 of Robert 'One Eyed' Charnock, his daughter and her husband, Richard Brooke of Mere in Cheshire, built the grand front range of brick, with a pair of vast mullion-and-transom bay windows which are the principal architectural feature of the building. The Brookes also failed in the male line and the house descended to the Townley-Parkers of Cuerden, who added the south wing in 1825 and stuccoed the exterior, probably to the design of Lewis Wyatt. In 1922 the house and its contents, including family portraits and furniture, were given by Reginald Tatton, who had inherited from the Townley-Parkers, to Chorley Corporation as a memorial to the local men killed in the First World War.

The interior is notable for the staggering mid-seventeenth-century plasterwork, adorned with heavy wreaths and disporting cherubs, that decorates the ceilings of the Great Hall and Drawing Room. The lower parts of the Hall are panelled with inset paintings of a curious selection of famous figures, including Philip II of Spain, Elizabeth I, Mohammed II and Tamerlane. The staircase is of the same period; it has a coarse but vigorously carved acanthus-scroll balustrade and square newels topped by vases of flowers. The whole width of the house on the top floor is occupied by a Long Gallery, which contains what must be the finest shovel-board table in existence – 23½ feet long, with twenty legs. The Dining Room in the early nineteenth-century wing has inlaid sixteenth-century panelling brought in from elsewhere.

The grounds of Astley Hall, which include a small lake, were landscaped by John Webb, and the plain classical brick stable block with pedimented centre is of *c*.1800.

Clitheroe

6; 16 miles NE of Preston on A59

Clitheroe has been a borough since the twelfth century, protected by a CASTLE perched on a solid rock. It was founded by Robert de Lacy in 1100 and he built the small square keep, said to be the smallest in the country. Some of the curtain wall survives as well, and was incorporated in the late eighteenth century into a Gothick house, south of the keep, with tall chimneystacks and pointed windows. This is now council offices, and the castle grounds are a small municipal park, embellished with a turret from the Houses of Parliament. The town itself is built of grey limestone and comprises one long, sloping street, running from west to east. This principal street, and the best in Clitheroe, is CASTLE STREET and is lined mainly with two- or three-storeyed Georgian buildings, some with Victorian shop-fronts and interspersed with 1830s' Jacobean revival inns, such as the Swan and Royal, perhaps by the Websters of Kendal. Just after the castle, the street splits into two, with the CARNEGIE LIBRARY on the corner making a great townscape effect. It was designed by Briggs and Wolstenholme in 1900 in *art nouveau* Gothic and has a splendid rounded corner bow like the poop of a galleon. Behind is the TOWN HALL by Rickman, dated 1820 – staid late Georgian Gothic.

Clitheroe Castle.

The parish CHURCH OF ST MARY MAGDALENE still contains odd medieval fragments but it was mainly rebuilt in 1828–9 by Rickman and is a competent example of his brand of Gothic Revival. The octagonal top stage to the tower and the thin spire were added in 1844 and compete with the castle keep for townscape effect, though in distant views both are dwarfed by the two chimneys of the Ribble cement factory to the east.

Just outside the confines of the town is an interesting country house, STANDEN HALL – a solid, dignified Palladian design of seven bays and two and a half storeys with an applied portico of Tuscan columns. It was largely built in the mid-eighteenth century by John Aspinall to replace an older building; the dates 1748 and 1757 are recorded. The house has good original interiors with nice joinery and chimneypieces, and a pretty staircase. The large Drawing Room at the back is Victorian. From the wooded park there is a good view of the top of Pendle Hill, a majestic outcrop of the Pennines famous as the haunt of the Lancashire witches.

Croxteth Hall
See Liverpool section.

Downham
7; 3 miles NE of Clitheroe off A59
Everything at Downham is perfect and perfectly maintained: the stone-built village, the beautifully planted park on the north slopes of Pendle, with its clumps and avenues of beech trees (dating from 1721, 1805 and later), and the cool neo-classical architecture of DOWNHAM HALL, remodelled in 1834–5 by the second William Assheton to the design of George Webster. In fact, the Hall is partly ancient and Webster's task consisted as much of tidying up and refronting as of entirely new work. It is H-shaped, faced in rough Pendle stone but with ashlar dressings and an ashlar centrepiece of Longridge stone on the north front, with pediment and Doric porch. The old carved shields let into the wall above the porch carry the arms of Henry Lacy, Earl of Lincoln, and John of Gaunt, Duke of Lancaster, and are reputed to have come from the ruins of Sawley Abbey. The south front is plainer and traces of old mullion windows are still visible in the stonework, as well as an appropriately classical new porch designed by Tom Mellor. The schoolroom wing was added in 1880 and the whole house was thoroughly restored and improved *c.*1910, at which time the Adam-style Drawing Room was formed and decorated. The finest of the Webster interiors is the Library – Grecian, like the exterior, with bookcases of alternating height and projection painted dark green and gold. The staircase is of plain oak and mahogany, while the Dining Room has a continuous sequence of Assheton portraits back to the sixteenth century.

Downham has been the property of the Assheton family since 1558, when it was bought by Sir Richard Assheton, Receiver-General of monastic lands in Lancashire. His descendant was created Lord Clitheroe in 1955 and the house now belongs to his son.

Close to the Hall, the CHURCH OF ST LEONARD benefits from the same benevolent paternalism as the rest of Downham and is beautifully cared for. It was rebuilt, apart from its Perpendicular tower, in 1910 by the Asshetons to the design of Mervyn Macartney. The interior is light and cheerful, with stone walls and mainly clear glass in the windows. The east window, however, has stained glass designed and made in 1859 for the previous church by the brothers Ralph and Richard Assheton. There are several Assheton monuments; that of William Assheton, who died in 1858, was made, says *Murray's Guide*, to a design 'drawn by Mr Carter of Preston from a sketch of one made by Richard Orme Assheton in the Campo Santo at Pisa'. There are also a number of good furnishings, including brass Georgian chandeliers and an organ by Schmidt.

Droylsden
See Manchester section.

Farnworth
See Liverpool section.

Fleetwood
8; 8 miles N of Blackpool on A587
'The abomination of desolation; a modern Greek town is insupportable. I am sitting in a Grecian coffee room in the Grecian hotel with a Grecian mahogany table close to a Grecian marble chimneypiece, surmounted by a Grecian pier glass and to increase my horror the waiter has brought in my breakfast on a Grecian sort of tray with a pat of butter stamped with the infernal Greek scroll.' So wrote A.W. Pugin on 26 July 1842 to his greatest Gothic patron, the Earl of Shrewsbury. Fleetwood was the brainchild of Sir Peter Hesketh Fleetwood, a Lancashire baronet who wished to build on his estate a kind of northern St Leonards combined with a commercial port. It was begun in 1836 and rapidly developed but, for reasons that have never been explained satisfactorily, the scheme floundered before it was completed and Sir Peter was forced to sell most of his estates to pay his debts – though Fleetwood itself later flourished as a fishing port, its trawlers once filling the seas from Portugal to Archangel. Only the bones of Sir Peter's grand plan of radiating streets and one or two classical buildings by his chosen architect, Decimus Burton, survive as an indication of the intended appearance of this great neo-classical enterprise.

The earliest important building at Fleetwood is the CUSTOMS HOUSE, built in 1839. It is faced in ashlar stone and has a projecting Doric portico. On either side are flanking brick houses called the LOWER QUEEN'S TERRACE; these were followed by the UPPER QUEEN'S TERRACE of 1840–4, much larger and faced in stone with three pediments and iron balconies. It faces the railway station, until 1847 the terminus of the main line north from Euston (passengers completed the journey to Scotland by steamer). Originally there was also a layout of commercial buildings to serve the harbour, but these have gone, apart from the two stone lighthouses, which are among the most handsome in England. The taller of the two, the LARGE PHAROS, resembles a Tuscan column on a raked rusticated base. The SMALL PHAROS at the other end of the same street is a beautifully proportioned square tower with a colonnaded shelter round the base and an octagonal cupola on top. Both were designed by Decimus Burton but the lights were organised by Commander H.M. Denham, and originally they were fuelled by the Fleetwood Gas Company. Decimus Burton's largest building in Fleetwood is the NORTH EUSTON HOTEL, built in 1841; it was this that so horrified Pugin. It is like a London club with a Doric portico and a grand central staircase, and, though now rather faded, in its early days it was the acme of modern luxury, with gas lighting, steam heating, a complicated system of bells, and iron cooking ranges in the kitchen.

Gawthorpe Hall
NT; 9; 1 mile NE of Padiham on A671
The present house was built by the Rev. Lawrence Shuttleworth between 1599 and 1603. Anthony Whitehead was the master mason, though the influence of Robert Smythson is apparent in the compact square plan. The interior was richly decorated and the Drawing Room and Long Gallery, which both survive, have the best Jacobean plasterwork in Lancashire, while the former also retains particularly good carved and inlaid oak panelling.

Lawrence Shuttleworth was succeeded by his nephew, Richard 'the Roundhead', and after his death in 1699 the house was abandoned for over a century. It was not until the reign of Queen Victoria that Gawthorpe was restored – and then to something rather more than its former glory – by the heiress Janet Shuttleworth and her husband Sir James Kay-Shuttleworth, the prophet of popular education and first Secretary of the Committee of Council on Education. They employed Sir Charles Barry between 1849 and 1850 to raise the silhouette and to sprinkle the house with improving mottoes – 'KYND KYNN KNAWEN KEPE' and 'WASTE NOT WANT NOT'. Barry's Entrance Hall, Dining Room and Library blend well with the genuine Jacobean decoration in the other rooms.

The Kay-Shuttleworth's son, Ughtred, became Under-Secretary of State for India, was created Lord Shuttleworth and lived at Gawthorpe until his death in 1939 at the age of ninety-five. His grandson, with the help of an indomitable aunt, Rachel Kay-Shuttleworth, secured the future of the house by transferring it to the National Trust, with a lease to Lancashire County Council.

Hall i' th' Wood
See Bolton (Manchester section).

Heaton Hall
See Manchester section.

Hoghton Tower
10; 6 miles SE of Preston off A675
'Hoghton Tower', wrote Whitaker, 'is the only true baronial residence in Lancashire with upper and base

courts which from its summit of its lofty ridge and from its extent appears at a distance almost like a fortified town.' Dark, aloof, romantic, it looks older than it is. Hoghton is one of the few houses in Lancashire that has descended directly in the male line from remote times and has never passed through the female side. The Hoghtons have owned land here since the beginning of the thirteenth century; they were made baronets by James I in 1611 and provided MPs for Preston all through the eighteenth century. The present castellated house was built in 1562–5 by Thomas Hoghton, a Catholic recusant and friend of Edmund Campion and Cardinal Allen; he eventually went into exile for 'conscience sake' and is buried at Douai. Later generations, swinging to the other extreme, were noted for Presbyterian Nonconformity, but the family eventually reverted to Catholicism. Hoghton's moment of glory came in April 1617 when James I was received here with great state, to the detriment of the family fortune. As the King advanced up the drive to the sound of trumpets he beheld a boulder bearing the words 'TORNE ME O'RE AND I'LL TELL THEE PLAIN'. After much labour the stone was turned over and the oracle's reply read 'HOT POORITCH SOFTENS HARD BUTTER-CAKES, SO TORNE ME O'ER AGAIN'. In the eighteenth century the family moved to Walton Hall and Hoghton gradually fell into decay, but restoration was begun in the 1860s by Sir Henry de Hoghton (the 'de' he added to his name was a sign of the antiquarian enthusiasm that made him move back to Hoghton). He employed Paley and Austin as his architects. The work was finished in 1901 by Sir James de Hoghton to the design of R.D. Oliver, much of the joinery, particularly the new panelling in the ballroom, being by Gillow. It

was an excellent restoration and makes one thankful that George Webster's less sensitive scheme of *c*.1830 was never executed.

It is an impressive experience to climb the long straight drive up the hill and to pass through the towered stone gateway and outer court to the inner court, so enclosed and seemingly remote from the world. The principal rooms are grouped round this. The state apartment is on the first floor, approached by a staircase with barley-sugar-twist columns. The succession of rooms has late seventeenth-century panelling, moulded box cornices and large mullioned windows. The largest room is the Banqueting Hall, which is two storeys high and fills the north range. It has an unusual screen decorated with turned balusters and at the dais end is the Jacobean table where James I dined and is reputed to have knighted the sirloin of beef. The bill of fare for that occasion is still displayed alongside.

Hornby
11; 8 miles NE of Lancaster on A683

HORNBY CASTLE is the *beau idéal* of the romantic nineteenth-century castle, especially when seen from the bridge over the River Lune. It is, however, of ancient origin; Whitaker thought the site was occupied in Roman times and Camden ascribed the foundation of the castle to Roger de Montbegon in the early twelfth century. In the Middle Ages the estate was held successively by the Nevilles and Harringtons, and in the early sixteenth century was acquired by Sir Edward Stanley, younger son of the 1st Earl of Derby, created Lord Monteagle for his part in the English victory at Flodden. Lord Monteagle added the upper storeys of the pele tower, the

The gateway, Hoghton Tower.

Hornby Castle.

lower part of which dates from the early thirteenth century. The castle remained the property of the Monteagles until 1713 when it was sold to Colonel Francis Charteris, 'the Wicked Lord', who created a modern sash-windowed mansion in front of the tower and built a gazebo on top of the octagonal turret. This Georgian house was successfully refaced in the Gothic style in 1849–52 to the design of Sharpe and Paley of Lancaster for Pudsey Dawson, a Yorkshire financier. They disguised the original symmetry by adding bay windows and a castellated porch with a pointed entrance arch; they also added new battlements to the pele tower and stair turret.

By the gate to the castle is the parish CHURCH OF ST MARGARET. It was mainly rebuilt in the nineteenth century but retains an unusual octagonal west tower of the early sixteenth, built by Lord Monteagle. Opposite is the Catholic CHAPEL OF ST MARY. This was built in 1820 by Dr John Lingard, the historian. Its façade is decorated with busts of ancient Roman worthies.

Ince Blundell Hall
See Liverpool section.

Knowsley Hall
See Liverpool section.

Lancaster
12; 18 miles N of Preston on A6

Lancaster is a small, stone-built city of considerable character. As the name implies, it began as a Roman camp but only a few feet of unimpressive wall survive, near the quay, from that period. The castle, priory church and street-plan bear witness to its medieval past, but essentially the town in its present form is Georgian and Edwardian. In the eighteenth century Lancaster was one of the main ports on the west coast, but at the end of the century the Lune estuary silted up and the American and West Indian trade moved to Liverpool. In the closing

years of the nineteenth century and in the early twentieth there was, however, a second burst of prosperity based on the manufacture of linoleum, which paid for several important public buildings, including the TOWN HALL in Dalton Square.

The Town Hall was the gift of Lord Ashton, linoleum magnate, and was designed by E.W. Mountford in 1906. It is the epitome of Edwardian pomp and circumstance, with a huge Ionic portico and domed clock tower. The VICTORIA MEMORIAL in the centre of Dalton Square was also the gift of Lord Ashton and was designed by Herbert Hampton in 1907; its plinth has bronze reliefs of high quality showing the great and the good, and the Queen herself slightly averting her gaze from Edward VII, who is to be seen in the pediment of the Town Hall. Dalton Square itself was laid out with plain stone houses in the 1790s by the Daltons of Thurnham Hall (*q.v.*). Over the canal bridge to the east is the CATHOLIC CATHEDRAL. It has a prominent spire, and inside is a carved and painted triptych by Sir Giles Gilbert Scott, originally the reredos but now stacked away ignominiously at the back of the nave. A short walk to the north of the Square leads to ST JOHN'S CHURCH, a handsome anonymous Georgian design of 1754–5. The circular lantern and obelisk spire were added by Thomas Harrison in 1784. The interior, restored by Sir Albert Richardson in 1955 and now vested in the Redundant Churches Fund, retains original fittings.

Church Street, with the seventeenth-century JUDGE'S LODGING forming a view-stopper at one end, is the best of Lancaster's Georgian streets, containing several good stone early eighteenth-century houses. In a backyard off this street is the MUSIC ROOM – a Baroque pavilion with an elaborately carved façade and an interior with rich Baroque plasterwork of the Muses by Italian *stuccatores*. Having fallen into deplorable condition, the Music Room has been rescued and excellently restored by the Landmark Trust. There is a little flat at the top which it is possible to rent as a base for a holiday in the area.

Parallel to Church Street, the Market Square is dominated by the OLD TOWN HALL, now the museum. Designed in a sturdy Tuscan style by Major Jarratt in 1781–3, the cupola on top was added by Thomas Harrison to the great benefit of the overall design. The interior contains a fascinating jumble of local memorabilia and relics, from Roman tombstones to Queen Adelaide's tea cup, and a moving array of mementoes of Lancashire regiments' far-distant campaigns.

The best part of Lancaster is the area round the CASTLE, where steep cobbled streets lined with good Georgian houses lead up to the picturesque mass of the castle itself. This is of Norman foundation and has an old keep, grand Gatehouse built by Henry IV, and one or two medieval towers, but was otherwise rebuilt in the early nineteenth century as a model gaol in castellated style by Thomas Harrison and Joseph Gandy. It still serves as gaol and law courts – a highly appropriate use for an historic castle. Only parts of it are open to the public, including the CROWN COURT and SHIRE HALL, both beautiful Gothick rooms with decorative plasterwork and the original Gothick furniture provided by Gillow. The latter is particularly impressive, with a semi-circular plan and vaulted ceiling carried on thin columns. Round the walls is an array of shields depicting the arms of all the High Sheriffs of Lancashire from the reign of Richard II down to the present.

Next to the castle, the PRIORY CHURCH OF ST MARY has a medieval nave and chancel, but much of its presence comes from the eighteenth-century Gothick tower designed by Henry Sephton in 1784. The spatial effect of the interior is much enhanced by the beautiful Boer War memorial aisle added by Austin and Paley in 1903, with its fine carved woodwork and regimental banners. In the choir are important Decorated choir stalls, with carved misericords brought here from Cockersands Abbey at the Dissolution of the Monasteries. From the graveyard and ST MARY'S STEPS there are fine views over the roofs of the town towards the ASHTON MEMORIAL on the far horizon. This amazing Edwardian copper-domed folly was by John Belcher in 1906–9 for Lord Ashton and is reminiscent of Lord Curzon's Victoria Hall in Calcutta.

A short walk downhill leads to ST GEORGE'S QUAY, constructed in 1749, where a group of tall warehouses and the pedimented CUSTOMS HOUSE by Richard Gillow recall Lancaster's brief heyday as a prosperous port. Upriver from here are two splendid pieces of late Georgian engineering – SKERTON BRIDGE, the main road bridge over the Lune, by Thomas Harrison, and, perhaps even nobler, the LUNE AQUEDUCT by John Rennie and D.A. Alexander, which carries the Lancaster–Kendal Canal over the river at Halton in a blaze of Doric splendour worthy of Rome.

Leighton Hall
13; 8 miles N of Lancaster off A6 [23]

Leighton was bought in 1822 by Richard Gillow of the famous Lancaster furniture-making firm and has descended to the present owner, Mr R.J.R. Reynolds, through his mother. An older house was plainly Georgianised by George Townley in 1765 to the design of the carpenter John Hird and then refronted in a delightful Gothick style *c.*1822 to the design, perhaps, of Robert Roper, who was responsible for a similar façade at Thurnham Hall (*q.v.*) near Lancaster. The left-hand wing, which makes the overall composition one of controlled asymmetry, was added by the local architects Paley and Austin in 1870. The interior is more mildly Gothick than the exterior; it has attractive rooms and, as is only to be expected, much interesting Gillow furniture. The Dining Room, formerly the Billiards Room, has decorative eighteenth-century landscape paintings inset into the panelling and it still retains its central skylight. The landscaped setting could not be bettered, the saucer-shaped park framing views to the Lake District mountains in the background with the white limestone of the house looking like stage scenery in certain lights.

Leighton strikingly reflects the Catholic tradition of the county. Though the house has three times changed hands through the Middletons, Worswicks and Gillows, every owner since the Reformation has subscribed to the old faith. The Gillows in particular are synonymous with Catholicism in Lancashire, Joseph Gillow being the author of the standard *Biographical Dictionary of English Catholics*.

Lancaster Castle.

The church of St Mary and St John the Baptist, Pleasington.

Lytham St Anne's

14; 6 miles S of Blackpool on A584

The Cliftons were an old Lancashire family seated originally at Clifton-with-Salwick; they bought LYTHAM HALL in 1606 and it remained their property down to 1963. Before the Dissolution of the Monasteries the estate belonged to the monks of Durham, who had a cell or a manor house on the coast, the site of which is buried under sand-dunes. The first house on the present site, a mile inland, was built in the mid-seventeenth century but was demolished in 1759, two years after the present house was begun by Thomas Clifton to the design of John Carr of York. The stables were built in 1758 and the interior fitting up continued into the 1760s. Carr produced a competent, dignified mansion of red brick with an attached Ionic portico and rusticated architraves to the ground-floor windows. The main rooms are on the ground floor, an early example of the break from the *piano nobile* of Palladian tradition. The rooms are chiefly decorated in the robust Rococo of the mid-eighteenth century 'York School', with excellent joinery and chimneypieces, and plasterwork by Giuseppe Cortese, though the Dining Room, which was the last to be finished, shows the influence of Adam in its more delicate plasterwork in the apsidal sideboard alcove. The finest feature is the central Staircase Hall based on James Paine's design for the Doncaster Mansion House (*q.v.*). The staircase of mahogany rises beyond a screen of Ionic columns in one flight and returns in two, under a richly coffered and stuccoed ceiling with a central medallion of Jupiter by Cortese. The columns of the upper landing are echoed by those in the Venetian window opposite.

Middleton

See Manchester section.

Ordsall Hall

See Rusholm (Manchester section).

Platt Hall

See Salford (Manchester section).

Pleasington

15; 3 miles W of Blackburn off A674 [25]

Rural Lancashire is dotted with pre-Emancipation Catholic chapels, but most of them are simple classical boxes. It therefore comes as a surprise to find what looks like a full-blown variation on King's College Chapel rearing above the fields by the River Darwen, not far from Blackburn. The CHURCH OF ST MARY AND ST JOHN THE BAPTIST was built in 1816–19 by John Francis Butler of Pleasington Hall, a local Catholic landowner and the descendant of the Butlers of Rawcliffe who had been attainted as Jacobites after the 1715 Rebellion. The architect was John Palmer of Manchester, who was himself a Catholic and a local pioneer of Gothic Revival. His intention at Pleasington, as he explained, was that 'the different styles of architecture that prevailed in this kingdom from the days of King Ethelbert down to Henry VIII will be introduced into the building'. The stone came from Butler's own quarry at Butler's Delph. The overall impression is, in fact, free Perpendicular, despite some earlier features. The church is tall with aisles and clerestory, and a polygonal apse. The west front has a prominent entrance with an enriched archway, a rose window above, and two flanking octagonal turrets on either side. The names of the architect and the sculptor are carved on the blank niches at the ends of the aisles: on the right 'JOHANNES PALMER, ARCHITECTUS' and on the left 'THOMAS OWEN, SCULPTOR'. Owen was responsible for the statues of Counter-Reformation saints on the pinnacles at the ends of the aisles and for the almost Baroque figures of Our Lady and St John the Baptist over the west doorway. The latter stands on a corbel carved with a bust which Pevsner thought was Butler but which is no less than King George III himself – making the point that, while the English Catholics accepted the Pope as head of the Church, they recognised as the civil power no other than the English Crown. On the gable is inscribed the dedication in Latin: 'DEO OMNIPOTENTI IN HONOREM BEATAE MARIAE SEMPER VIRGINE' – 'To all powerful God in honour of the Blessed Virgin Mary'.

Suitably impressed, we pass inside. The nave is lofty and light, of five bays, with moulded piers, arches with dogtooth decoration and plaster vaults. The nave bosses, by Owen, are very entertaining. The altar is set in an apse, with stained-glass windows above and reliefs by Owen on either side, showing the beheading of St John the Baptist, and St Mary Magdalene. It is altogether the most extraordinary performance, and almost unremarked in the literature of art history. Many happy hours could be spent tracing the sources of the church's different features. The west door, for instance, is inspired by that to the Chapter House at Whalley Abbey (*q.v.*).

Preston

16; 18 miles S of Lancaster on A6

An old market town and borough, Preston developed into an important centre of the cotton industry in the eighteenth and nineteenth centuries. The old layout of the streets in the centre survives, but all the old buildings have gone and the architectural interest now dates almost entirely from the nineteenth century. There are fine public buildings, an amazing group of Catholic churches, and an intact late Georgian residential area with a large square and attractively landscaped park on the bank above the River Ribble.

The most impressive of the Victorian public buildings is the HARRIS ART GALLERY AND LIBRARY in the Market Place. It was built in 1882–93 to the design of the local architect James Hibbert and is a remarkably fine, and remarkably late, example of the Greek Revival. It has a large Ionic portico with richly carved pediment, rusticated stone basement of Whittle stone and a square lantern over the centre. The friezes are carved with inscriptions explaining the dedication of the building to art and learning. Inside there are three storeys arranged round a central rotunda, and galleries. On the ground floor is the public library, on the first floor the museum and on the top floor the art gallery. This last contains one of the best middle-sized collections of English eighteenth- and nineteenth-century art, including a whole room devoted to the work of Arthur Devis, who was born in Preston, and many works by nineteenth- and early twentieth-century Royal Academicians of a type now becoming fashionable again.

A unique feature of Preston is the concentration of impressive Catholic churches in the centre, some of them classical and some Gothic; they are a striking testimony to Lancastrian religious recusancy. The oldest is ST MARY'S CHURCH, approached through an archway off Friargate. It was founded in 1605, rebuilt on the present site in 1761, then wrecked in an election riot and finally reconstructed in 1856. It is a simple classical building of brick, the west front forming a nice composition with its stucco door surround, an inscription 'SALVE VIRGO MATER DEI' – 'Hail the Virgin, Mother of God', and a painted statue of Our Lady in a niche above. The interior has marbled walls with Ionic pilasters, and a rich Italian-style altar of marble and mosaic, with alabaster altar rails and brass gates in front.

The CHURCH OF ST AUGUSTINE OF CANTERBURY in St Austin's Place is also classical; it is a distinguished design reminiscent of nineteenth-century French church architecture. It was built in 1838–40 to the design of the Preston architect A. Tuach, but was enlarged in 1878–9 when the apsidal sanctuary was added to the design of James O'Byrne of Liverpool. In 1890 the church was further enlarged at the west end: the nave was extended by 20 feet, the two west towers with cupolas added and the original Ionic portico reset; these alterations were designed by Sinnott, Sinnott and Powell. The adjoining Clergy House was built in 1856 to the design of J.A. Hansom. Despite this complicated building history and the involvement of many different architects, a great effort has been made to keep to the original style, and the result appears very much all of a piece. The interior is

The Harris Art Institute, Preston.

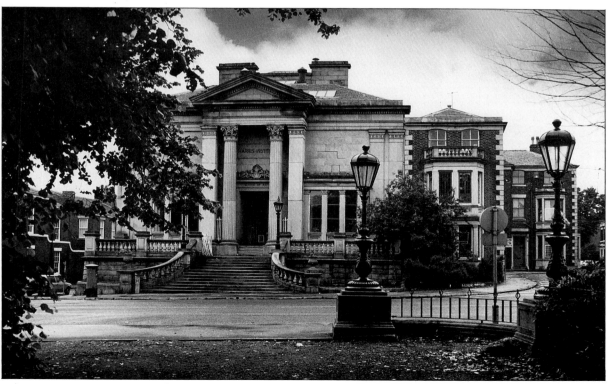

St Wilfred's church, Preston.

impressive, with a coffered tunnel ceiling by Sinnott, Sinnott and Powell, and O'Byrne's marble altar in the apse.

ST WILFRED'S, off Winckley Square, is the finest of Preston's classical churches. It was built in 1793, but was rebuilt and enlarged between 1839 and 1843 then progressively enriched throughout the nineteenth century to create a remarkably monumental and richly decorated interior. The exterior is of red brick with yellow terracotta decoration in early Renaissance style, and is a recasing of the old walls carried out in 1892 by S.J. Nicholl. The west front, which is hemmed in by other buildings, has three doors with fine moulded tympana and a circular window above. The appearance of the main body of the interior dates from a remodelling of 1879–80 to the design of S.J. Nicholl. It forms a noble basilica, with ten proud Corinthian columns of pink Shap granite. The penetrated barrel-vaulted ceiling has sumptuous moulded plasterwork, while the aisle walls are lined with yellow marble and have pink marble pilasters. The apsidal sanctuary has two semi-circular niches with marble screens flanking the altar. The ceiling has gilded octagonal coffering, while the high altar itself is of marble and was designed by Fr Scoles, a Jesuit priest and son of the architect S.J. Scoles. The floor is paved with marble and the altar rails have gates of gilt metal. Over the altar is a white marble crucifix against a gold mosaic background designed by W.C. Mangan in 1961 to replace an oil painting. The other fittings in the church, and the side-chapels, are equally rich. St Joseph's Chapel was designed by J.J. Scoles in 1844 from a model in Rome and decorated by Taylor Bulmer. The Chapel of Our Lady was designed by Fr Scoles and over the altar has a marble relief of the Coronation of the Virgin designed by Pugin and Pugin and carved by R.L. Boulton. The chapels of the Holy Ghost and the Sacred Heart have marble altars designed by J.J. Nicholl. The Baptistery, by Edmund Kirby of Liverpool, is as late as 1902, with a domed ceiling, stucco emblems of the Four Evangelists in the pendentives, and a marble relief of the Baptism of Christ against the rear wall. The west gallery has the pre-1879 altar rails re-used as its balustrade.

Preston's Gothic churches are as impressive as its classical ones. The CHURCH OF ST IGNATIUS in Meadow Street was designed by J.J. Scoles in 1836. It is cruciform and Perpendicular, with a west tower and spire – the first on any church in Preston. In 1859 the chancel was added by J.A. Hanson and this was further enriched in 1883–6 when the high altar and reredos in excellent Puginian Gothic were installed to the design of Charles Hadfield. The flanking chapels of Our Lady and St Joseph have vaulted ceilings, and carved alabaster altars and statues, all designed by Hadfield. The Sacred Heart Chapel was also Hadfield's, but the marble, mosaic and granite altar and the statue were added by Edmund Kirby in 1907.

The CHURCH OF ST THOMAS OF CANTERBURY AND THE ENGLISH MARTYRS in Garstang Road was designed by E.W. Pugin in 1865–7 and the exterior, with its dramatic west front, is a typical example of his Flamboyant/Decorated Gothic. The interior is less exciting; the east end was enlarged in 1887–8 to the design of Peter Paul Pugin. There are elaborate Gothic altars of Caen stone and alabaster, and good Victorian stained glass by

Hardman in the sanctuary, by Mayer of Munich in St Joseph's chapel and by Barraud and Westlake in the Lady Chapel.

ST WALBURGE'S in Weston Street is the most important of the town's Gothic churches. It was erected in 1850–4 under the auspices of the Rector of Stonyhurst (*q.v.*) on the site of the Hospital of St Mary Magdalene (founded in 1293). It was designed by J.A. Hansom and is his most original design. The apse was added in 1872 to the design of S.J. Nicholl. The most striking feature of the exterior is the spire of white limestone rising 303 feet above the railway sidings and back streets of little red brick terraced houses – one of the most dramatic architectural contrasts in any English town. The interior is no less striking. It is one space without aisles, 165 feet long and 55 feet wide, making the proportions three squares. The roof, remarkably steep and tall, is as high as the sidewalls and is of timber hammerbeam design, decorated with twenty-six carved statues. Many of the fittings are by S.J. Nicholl, including the altars, organ case and squat font; they are as 'rogue Gothic' as Hansom's extraordinary roof. There is stained glass by both Hardman and Mayer of Munich.

Apart from the churches, the best architectural feature of Preston is the Georgian quarter between Fishergate, the main street, and the River Ribble. The centrepiece of this is WINCKLEY SQUARE – large and hilly with good tree planting. Although begun in the late eighteenth century, much of the area was not built up until the 1850s, so it is later than it seems. The effect is remarkably unified: red brick houses with stone doorcases and sash windows. The slopes above the River Ribble were landscaped in 1873 to form MILLER PARK, an especially good piece of Victorian municipal park layout, the terraces on its fringes giving way to individual villas, including one or two in the Jacobean and Italianate styles, and BUSHELL PLACE, a formal promenade with stone balustrade and cast-iron Victorian lamps, overlooked by the HARRIS INSTITUTE, a stone classical building designed in 1846–7 by John Welsh.

Rainhill

See Liverpool section.

Rivington

17; 5 miles NW of Bolton off A673
This moorland estate in the centre of the county belonged anciently to the Pilkingtons but was sold in the seventeenth century to the Levers. Jane Lever married a Mr Andrews in the mid-eighteenth century and they built the neat Georgian RIVINGTON HALL in 1774. It is of red brick, with a pedimented one-bay centre and tripartite entrance. At the rear are the remains of an older stone-built house showing the dates 1694 and 1700. But what makes Rivington a spectacularly exciting place to visit is the contribution of the 1st Lord Leverhulme, the self-made soap millionaire, around the beginning of this century. (He bought the property presumably because of its Lever connection.) He built himself an ill-fated country house, Roynton Cottage, higher up the hill behind the Hall. It was first burnt by suffragettes, then

rebuilt, and finally demolished by Liverpool Corporation after the Second World War as part of a comprehensive policy of destruction throughout the catchment area surrounding their reservoirs on the edge of the moors. The Hall is now used for catering and entertainment in association with the old cruck barn alongside, which was well restored by Lord Leverhulme.

The dramatic landscape GARDENS laid out by Thomas Mawson in 1905 still survive, however, in a state of romantic decay, with stone summerhouses and bridges recalling the work of H.H. Richardson in the USA; the avenues that Lord Leverhulme laid out to criss-cross the park below have not yet reached maturity, but are extremely impressive nonetheless. On the edge of a lake-like reservoir in the park is a full-scale replica of Liverpool Castle built by Lord Leverhulme, while other towers and follies dot the moors above. The whole adds up to an outlandish combination of landscape and architecture, which seems a million miles away from the surrounding industrial towns and deserves to be much better known and much better cared for.

Rufford Old Hall

NT; 18; 10 miles SW of Preston on A59
This is an important fragment of a black-and-white half-timbered house built between 1480 and 1523 by Thomas Hesketh to a typical medieval plan, with east and west wings joined by a Great Hall. The west wing, containing private rooms, was destroyed long ago; the east wing was reconstructed in brick in 1662 and further works, aimed at making the house habitable and heightening the romantic effect, were carried out in 1821. The

The Great Hall, Rufford Old Hall.

result is a composite L-shaped building, half brick and half black-and-white, the two parts of which do not harmonise.

The Great Hall is the finest feature and the best preserved of all the Lancashire and Cheshire halls of its type. The timbers are richly carved – especially the elaborate roof, which is embellished with armorial bosses and angels holding shields of arms. At the west end is a coved sixteenth-century canopy over the site of the high table and at the east end there is an arch supported by a spere truss, whose octagonal supports descend to the floor. Between them stands the unique movable screen. This massive piece of furniture is embellished with three elaborate pinnacles, more like primitive totems from the South Seas than the work of a Lancashire craftsman.

The 1821 wing, comprising a Dining Room set below a Drawing Room, has a canted bay window to the garden intended to blend with the black-and-white architecture of the Hall. The interior is relatively plain, apart from the Dining Room ceiling, which has moulded timbers. The house contains oak furniture and some armour collected by the 1st Lord Hesketh, who gave Rufford to the National Trust.

Rusholme
See Manchester section.

Scarisbrick Hall.

Salford
See Manchester section.

Samlesbury Old Hall
19; 5 miles E of Preston on A59
Gilbert Southworth acquired Samlesbury by marriage and built the first house on the present site c.1325. The Southworths were a distinguished family in the medieval period – frequently knighted, fighting at Harfleur, Agincourt and Flodden – but were ruined in the late sixteenth and early seventeenth centuries because of their adherence to Catholicism. One member of the family was martyred at Tyburn in 1654 and has been canonised: St John Southworth, whose remains, after several adventures, are now enshrined in Westminster Cathedral. In 1678, as a result of fines and mortgages, Edward Southworth was forced to sell and the estate was bought by Thomas Braddyll, a lucky speculator whose son married the heiress of Conishead. The Braddyll family owned Samlesbury until 1846 but never lived there, the house being converted into tenements and later becoming a public house. Originally it took the shape of a moated quadrangle but only two wings survive, forming a truncated L-shape.

The house, which was greatly altered in 1835 – further 'restoration' took place in 1862 – is partly of brick, partly timber-framed, while the brick portions of the south wing, dated 1545, demonstrate the earliest use of brick in Lancashire. The Hall, in particular, has suffered, and the movable screen, dated 1532 and similar to that at Rufford (*q.v.*), although in need of restoration, has been dismantled and re-erected incongruously at the dais end. The main room in the south wing is the two-storeyed Chapel, which has, however, lost most of its carved fittings to Conishead. The Entrance Hall and Parlour are largely of 1835.

Scarisbrick Hall★
20; 5 miles SE of Southport off A57 [**24**]
This is by far the best Victorian house in Lancashire, and A.W.N. Pugin's 'old English Catholic mansion' *par excellence*: 'To those who have prayed and hoped and loved, the realization of all their longing desires appears truly ravishing. . . . Oh then what delight! What joy unspeakable! When one of the solemn piles is presented to them.' Charles Scarisbrick, Pugin's patron, was the scion of an ancient Catholic family seated at Scarisbrick since the thirteenth century, but whose fortune had been considerably amplified by the draining of Martin Mere and its reclamation for agriculture, and by the development of the modern seaside resort of Southport over Scarisbrick land. Charles Scarisbrick does not seem to have shared Pugin's romantic Catholic outlook, but he did want an impressive medieval-looking house. The idea of building a new Gothic house at Scarisbrick had been first aired in Humphry Repton's Red Book of 1803; he had recommended Gothic because at 'Scarrisbrick [*sic*] a Mansion of this character is more consonant to the antiquity of the Family and the extent of the property annexed'. In 1812–16 Thomas Scarisbrick (who re-adopted the ancient patronymic in place of Eccleston,

which the family had briefly adopted in the eighteenth century in connection with another inheritance) built a new west wing in a very dull Gothic to the design of Thomas Rickman and John Slater. Following Thomas's death, his son Charles turned to Pugin, then aged only twenty-four, and, from 1837–45, between them they thoroughly reconstructed Scarisbrick, creating a fantastic and romantic evocation of the Middle Ages. It comprises a central block with a full-height Great Hall, embellished with brought-in continental wood-carving. The west wing was remodelled to contain a Dining Room and two richly decorated Drawing Rooms, glowing with red-and-gold wallpapers, dark carved woodwork, and painted and stencilled ceilings – foreshadowing Pugin's decoration of the Houses of Parliament. The carved oak west staircase incorporates in the balustrade pictures of Pugin's design for the house. These rooms were the setting for Charles Scarisbrick's jackjaw collections, including several Rembrandts and twenty John Martins, all of which were sold after his death. Charles, educated at Stonyhurst (*q.v.*), was a miserly eccentric recluse who never married but lived at Scarisbrick with a mistress and a string of illegitimate children. On his death in 1860 he was succeeded by his sister Anne, Lady Hunloke, who called herself Lady Scarisbrick and, at the age of seventy-two, entered into her inheritance with a zest heightened by dislike of her brother. She employed Pugin's son, Edward Welby (who, like his father, ended his days in a lunatic asylum) to remodel the east wing in an 'ornate and caparisoned' style intended to outdo the rest of the house. In particular, she added the soaring tower, culminating in a slated spire with gilded iron finials (now lost), which alters the balance of the composition and dominates the landscape for miles in every direction. Inside the new east wing another Drawing Room was created, as well as a Chapel and another staircase – all decorated by Crace with stained glass by Hardman (that on the staircase with portraits of Lady Scarisbrick and E.W. Pugin) and 'A.S.' monograms lavishly sprinkled around. The stables were also added at this time and form a charmingly frivolous fortified appendage. The house now belongs to an evangelical interdenominational boarding school, which acquired it in 1963, but it can be visited by appointment.

Sefton
See Liverpool section.

Smithills Hall
See Bolton (Manchester section).

Speke Hall
See Liverpool section.

Standen Hall
See Clitheroe.

Stonyhurst★
21; 10 miles NE of Preston on B6243
Oliver Cromwell, who was an unwelcome guest of the Royalist and Catholic Sherburnes (or Shireburnes), in

1648 pronounced Stonyhurst to be the finest half-house he had ever seen – alluding to the fact that the north side of the quadrangle had not been built; it was, in fact, completed only in the nineteenth century. The Sherburnes, who had changed their name from Bayley on marrying an heiress in 1377, had owned Stonyhurst since the thirteenth century and had occupied a house on the site from at least 1372. In 1592 Sir Richard Sherburne began the great quadrangle that makes Stonyhurst the most important Elizabethan house in Lancashire. The fantastic Gatehouse, with its four tiers of the classical orders, recalls the work of the Yorkshire mason John Ackroyd in the Old Schools quadrangle at Oxford and is paralleled in a number of northern houses.

After the death of Sir Richard, work ceased, leaving the house incomplete until the time of Sir Nicholas Sherburne, who was created Baronet by James II. He celebrated the dawn of what seemed easier times for Catholics by making great improvements to the house and gardens, using artists and craftsmen of the first rank. Henry Wise designed the formal gardens, including the canals flanking the avenues; Jean Tijou provided ironwork; John Nost was responsible for the lead statues; and Edward and William Stanton were the masons. Sir Nicholas added the twin Baroque cupolas with stone eagles (carved in Antwerp) to the top of the Gatehouse; these give Stonyhurst its special silhouette, in distant views reminiscent of Drayton.

Sir Nicholas's only son died young and Stonyhurst was inherited by his daughter, Maria Winifreda Francesca, Duchess of Norfolk. She retired to this, her northern seat, after the death of her husband, the 8th Duke, and there practised her faith and nursed her Tory-Jacobite sympathies in peace, in company with Peregrine Widdrington. (It is not certain whether she married this gentleman; some authorities say she did, and some say she ought to have done.) She made various alterations aimed at heightening the antique effect – such as installing the Gothic window from Bayley Hall (the former family seat, demolished in the eighteenth century) in the end of the south wing.

The Duchess died in September 1754 and the house passed to the Welds of Lulworth, who never occupied it. When his old school, the English Academy at Liège, was expelled in 1794 by the advancing armies of Revolutionary France, Charles Weld offered his Lancashire estate as a substitute and so Stonyhurst began its second career as a Catholic public school and principal home of the English Jesuits. They added the Neo-Perpendicular chapel – a variation on the theme of King's College Chapel – designed by J.J. Scoles in 1832–5. In 1888 the large new school range was built to the south, facing the gardens, to the design of Dunn and Hansom in a highly successful and pleasing Victorian version of Elizabethan architecture.

In the nearby village of Hurst Green are the splendid SHIREBURNE ALMSHOUSES, dating from the seventeenth century. Originally they stood remote on Longridge Fell, but they were brought down and reconstructed here after the Second World War. It is well worth making a detour to see them.

Townley Hall.

Thurnham Hall

22; 4 miles SW of Lancaster on A588

The antiquity of Thurnham is partly concealed by the 'elegant modern Gothic' façade added in 1823 to the design of Robert Roper, but it is only a skin, varying in thickness from 2 to 18 inches, attached by metal ties to the irregular mid-sixteenth-century house built around a thirteenth-century pele tower.

In early times Thurnham belonged to various families, including the Flemings and the Grays; but in 1556 it was bought by Robert Dalton and remained in the Dalton family, though with sidesteps through the female line, until 1973 when it was sold to Mr S.H. Crabtree. He has carried out a radical restoration, revealing the earlier fabric at the expense of nineteenth-century features.

The Hall has a sixteenth-century ribbed plaster ceiling, moulded frieze with vines and grotesque heads, and restored panelling. The main staircase, with sturdy turned balusters, is seventeenth-century. One priest's hole, and the elaborate Gothic private chapel added by Miss Elizabeth Dalton in 1854, attest to Thurnham's Catholic past.

Townley Hall

23; 1 mile SE of Burnley on A646

Originally a quadrangle and now a hollow U of dramatic, sombre castellated architecture, Townley was the seat of the Townleys from the thirteenth century until 1902, when Lady O'Hagan (Alice Mary Townley) sold the house to Burnley Corporation for a nominal sum. The present house was begun *c.*1400, but its architectural history is almost unbelievably complicated and, though there are traces of fifteenth-century work in the south wing, most of the features that give the house its medieval appearance are deceptive and are the product of three centuries of conscious antiquarianism on the part of the Townleys.

The Long Gallery was formed in the seventeenth century. The corner buttresses are part of the original structure; they were enlarged by Wyatville. One extension to the north was added by William Townley *c.*1776. The Chapel was originally a detached sixteenth-century building but it was taken down in 1700 by Charles Townley and reconstructed out of the old materials as another extension to the north wing. Richard Townley's major work, the new Hall in the centre, however, is frankly Baroque; it presents a severe 'Gibbsian' elevation to the back of the house and is richly embellished with plasterwork by Francesco Vassali and Martino Quadri.

Charles Townley, the famous connoisseur whose collection of antique marbles was sold to the British Museum after his death, remodelled the interior of the south wing in 1767 to the design of Carr of York, providing an enfilade of neo-classical rooms to display some of his collection. These, however, were swept away by his successor, Peregrine Townley, who employed Wyatville to alter the rooms and to give the whole exterior a tidier baronial flavour. The turrets, battlements, front porch and much of the fenestration are all Wyatville's work. The final alteration was the bathroom tower added to the north wing by Charles Townley in 1851. He re-used an eighteenth-century doorway and two Georgian windows, as if deliberately trying to confuse later historians. The house has been well maintained this century as a museum and art gallery.

Whalley

24; 5 miles NE of Blackburn on A59

This little town lies on the south side of the Ribble Valley, just to the north-east of Blackburn, and is well known for the ruins of the Cistercian abbey founded here in 1296. It has a bit of the feeling, though, of a suburb rather than of an old country town. It is protected from industrial Lancashire by the wooded eminences of Whalley Nab and Clark Hill, and in distant views across the valley is dominated by the long brick arcade of a mid-Victorian railway viaduct. On the Blackburn side, below Whalley Nab, are two rows of pretty estate cottages in the Gothick taste. The main street, KING STREET, has eighteenth-century brick and stone houses and two good eighteenth-century inns; but also a terrible 1960s' gap, with a tastefully landscaped car park, which badly needs filling with appropriate buildings.

The parish church and abbey ruins lie to the north of King Street. ST MARY'S CHURCH faces a little square with some done-up cottages, a Jacobean house with mullion windows, and a once pretty Victorian Gothic school severely damaged by insensitive additions in the 1960s' Official-County-Council style. The church is a palimpsest of different dates – Norman, Early English and Perpendicular. It was restored *c.*1900, at which date the curious gabled dormer windows were inserted in the stone-flagged aisle roofs and the porches added. It is a pity, however, that the plaster has been stripped from the inside walls.

The chief beauty of the church lies in its fine fittings. These include fifteenth-century choir stalls from the abbey church, with carved canopies and misericords. In the chancel and flanking chapels are restored Perpendicular parclose screens. There are several good seventeenth- and eighteenth-century pews: 'St Anton's Cage' is a welter of elaborate seventeenth-century woodwork; the Churchwardens' Pew is dated 1690; and the Constable's Pew is dated 1714. The beautiful eighteenth-century organ case at the west end was made for Lancaster parish church and brought here in the nineteenth century; the brass chandelier in the chancel is another excellent eighteenth-century piece. The east window contains good modern heraldic glass, showing the arms of many old Lancashire families. The monuments to be seen inside the church include one to Dr Whitaker, the local historian.

Round the corner from the church (and ignoring the new bungalow on the right), the gatehouse to WHALLEY ABBEY is reached down a short cobbled way flanked by lime trees. This inner gatehouse, with corner buttresses and battlements, dates from the fifteenth century. The larger, older and more impressive outer gatehouse straddles the road to the north-east. Through the inner gatehouse, you find yourself in a cobbled courtyard with ranges of stone sixteenth-century outbuildings along two sides and an Elizabethan-looking country house opposite, with shaped gables and mullion or sashed windows. This is said to incorporate part of the Abbot's Lodging and was converted into a country house by the Asshetons after the Dissolution; much of its external appearance, however, is due to early nineteenth-century remodelling. It is now a retreat house of the Anglican diocese of Blackburn. Of the abbey church, only the foundations, outlined in the lawn, survive; but parts of the buildings round the cloister still stand to a reasonable height. The best feature is the entrance to the Chapter House – an impressive Decorated composition with an enriched archway flanked by a pair of ogee windows. It is a pity that the whole place is kept up like an elaborate rock garden, with over-neat edges, crazy paving and inappropriate planting of heather and alpines. Simple grass and some creeper would be preferable. Indeed, it might show a better sense of priorities to spend any available money on the upkeep of the ruins themselves (which need attention) rather than on unnecessary and, in my view at least, undesirable gardening.

Widnes

See Liverpool section.

Winstanley Hall

See Manchester section.

Worsley

See Manchester section.

Wythenshawe Hall

See Manchester section.

The inner gatehouse, Whalley Abbey.

LIVERPOOL★

25; 15 miles N of Chester on M62 [26]

Liverpool, like Antwerp or Venice, was once a great seaport; and, like those cities, it has lost its commercial base. No sea-going boats fill the river now, and the great merchant and shipping families have all departed elsewhere. But some of the architecture survives, despite the ravages of German bombing in the Second World War and those wreaked by its own council in the decades since then. The decline of Liverpool is tragic, for it is the greatest of English provincial cities and it hurts to see this magnificent town, with its superb Water Front, its Georgian 'West End', and its many architectural masterpieces, all slowly dying. It is a sad but splendid place and it is impossible to forget that for two centuries it was the greatest European port of world-wide trade. The ocean-going liners transferred to Southampton in the 1920s and since the Second World War most of the overseas trade has been driven to Rotterdam (whence it is transported in little boats to the small ports and private docks of East Anglia, the staff of which do not form part of the National Dock Labour Scheme). The office of Lord Mayor of Liverpool was abolished in 1983 – a symbolic gesture which neatly gives a *terminus ad quem* to the history of the city.

Liverpool was made a 'city' by Royal Charter at the height of her glory on 11 May 1880, but in her heyday she was inordinately proud of her bogus medieval ancestry. King John gave the place a Charter in 1207, hoping that she might become an alternative to Chester (*q.v.*) as a port for Ireland. In fact she remained a tiny fishing village of less than 500 souls down to the sixteenth century. It was only then that she began to develop as an independent port, slowly gathering momentum over the following 100 years. The first cargo from America is recorded in 1648 and in 1658 she was officially recognised as a customs port in her own right. The decisive step for Liverpool was taken in 1700 when, with great courage and foresight, a group of local merchants initiated the pioneering dock scheme which made such an outstanding contribution to the maritime history of Britain. Despite its setting on a very wide river, Liverpool had great natural disadvantages as a port: a tidal range of over 30 feet, strong winds, swift currents, and over 20,000 acres of shifting sandbanks in the Mersey. The solution to this, masterminded by the engineer Thomas Steers, was to develop the wet-dock, an enclosed piece of water, the wooden gates of which held the water inside and the ships afloat regardless of the state of the tide. This was built in 1710 and completed by 1715 – the first wet-dock in the world. Success was immediate, and in the eighteenth century Liverpool was able to secure the lion's share of the American and West Indian trade – including the slave trade, which was made a British monopoly by the Treaty of Utrecht in 1715 (and was abolished by Parliament in 1807). By the end of the eighteenth century 45,000 tons of shipping were passing annually through the port, and by the late nineteenth century this had risen to 12,400,000 tons of merchant shipping – about 40 per cent of the world's trade. This prosperity was the basis of a great burst of civic pride, expressed in a series of magnificent architectural projects that made Liverpool one of the great neo-classical cities of northern Europe.

The 'Down Town' Area

The centre of Liverpool between the Water Front and municipal buildings, between Exchange Station and Canning Square is the site of the original seventeenth- and eighteenth-century town and is still an important provincial centre of banking, insurance and finance. Its well-kept streets are lined with largely homogenous classical buildings of stone and marble dating from the late eighteenth to the early twentieth century. The last sunset rays of a vanished prosperity still linger here.

The centrepiece of this part of the city is the TOWN HALL, one of the best Georgian public buildings in England. It was originally designed in 1749–54 by John Wood (the Elder) of Bath, but following a fire in 1795 the interior was remodelled and the dome added by James Wyatt, who designed it, and John Foster, who was executant architect. The Wyatt–Foster work continued intermittently until 1812. The ground floor was originally an open arcade for use as an exchange and there was a courtyard in the middle. Wyatt and Foster's rooms on the first floor are splendidly maintained and were redecorated in their original colours by John Fowler in 1970. Much of the furniture was acquired in the 1820s and there are many full-length portraits of good quality. The staircase is of imperial plan, rising under the dome. Both are dated 1802. The statue of Canning on the half-landing was executed by Sir Francis Chantrey in 1832; the paintings in the pendentives are by Charles Furse, *c.*1900. On the first floor three spacious Drawing Rooms fill the south front, facing Castle Street. They have excellent Wyatt plasterwork and magnificent pivoted mahogany doors. The centre room has a shallow-domed ceiling with fan-patterned pendentives, while the two side rooms have segmental plaster vaults. The Small Ballroom has shallow apses at either end and a segmental ceiling with Wyatt plasterwork. Beyond it is the Large Ballroom, added along the back of the whole building by Wyatt in 1789 and redecorated after the fire. It is lined with Siena scagliola Corinthian pilasters and there is a coffered exedra for musicians in the centre of the rear wall. The three great glass chandeliers are among the most magnificent in England. (Wall panels added by Romaine-Walker in 1905 have been removed.) The Dining Room was decorated in 1811. It has Corinthian scagliola pilasters simulating Carinola marble, beautiful porphyry urns in niches and extravagant gilt stoves and lamps. The painted roundels of cherubs are by Matthew Cotes Wyatt. It was intended that he should also paint the ceiling panels, but these were never executed.

EXCHANGE FLAGS, the square behind the Town Hall, was laid out by James Wyatt and John Foster in 1807. The surrounding buildings, unfortunately, have been replaced by not very good examples of inter-war commercial architecture, but the centrepiece survives: it is the NELSON MONUMENT designed by M.C. Wyatt in 1807 and cast in bronze by Richard Westmacott in 1808–13. The first time I saw it, on a Sunday morning, six work-

The Town Hall, Liverpool.

men with ladders and mops were giving it a good clean and polish. As part of an overall scheme for improving this area, CASTLE STREET, on the south side of the Town Hall, was widened in 1786 and James Wyatt designed new symmetrical façades for the west side. These have all gone and the street is now mainly Victorian classical. C.R. Cockerell's BANK OF ENGLAND is of 1845–8 and is a building of international importance, its majestic façade composed of Roman Doric columns with an Ionic aedicule on top. Next to it, the Huddersfield Building Society has Corinthian columns and a richly carved pediment. Opposite, Norman Shaw's National Westminster Bank has a lively façade striped with red marble. Similarly impressive Victorian and Edwardian classical banks and insurance buildings are still to be found in Water Street and Dale Street to the east and west of the Town Hall. At the south end of Castle Street is Derby Square, the site of the medieval Liverpool Castle (a replica of which can be found at Rivington (*q.v.*)). It now contains the QUEEN VICTORIA MONUMENT – a characteristic piece of Edwardian pomp and circumstance, with the statue of the Queen placed under an Ionic domed *baldacchino* and surrounded by sculptural bronze groups representing Industry, Commerce, Education and Agriculture. Beyond, at the end of the axis, is CANNING SQUARE, the

site of the original wet-dock of 1710. Here once stood the neo-classical Customs House, with a dome and massive Greek Ionic portico, designed by John Foster in 1828 and completed in 1839. It was gutted by incendiary bombs in the Second World War; the immensely strong shell survived and could easily have been restored (as it would have been in Leningrad) but instead it was torn down by the city council 'in order to provide work for the unemployed'. North of Derby Place is Lord Street (ignobly rebuilt after bomb damage) and at the end, off Church Street, is the BLUECOAT SCHOOL. This is the earliest surviving piece of Georgian architecture in Liverpool – an exceptionally large early eighteenth-century school building. It was built in 1714–18 with three wings of red brick and painted stone dressings, and was almost certainly designed by Henry Sephton, the leading Liverpool mason-architect of the time, whose best work is Ince Blundell Hall (*q.v.*). The Bluecoat School was rescued and repaired by the 1st Viscount Leverhulme (with money received as libel damages from the *Daily Mail*). It too was gutted in the Second World War but was carefully reinstated afterwards – an exceptional act of piety for post-war Liverpool. The cobbled courtyard is very attractive and is often used for outdoor art exhibitions.

The Plateau

On the high central area of the city, overlooking the old town and the docks, a new civic centre was developed in the nineteenth century, creating one of the most impressive pieces of Picturesque town planning in Europe. Although the majority of the buildings are grandly classical, they are sited informally, following the contours of the hill. For the visitor approaching by train, this is his first impression of Liverpool, for LIME STREET STATION is among the nineteenth-century public buildings overlooking the Plateau. The present station is the third to have been erected on the site within forty years – striking evidence of the dynamism of Liverpool in the mid-nineteenth century. The original terminus of the Liverpool–Manchester Railway – the first passenger railway in the world – was at Crown Street, further out; the station was moved closer in, to Lime Street, in 1836. There the first train-shed had a timber roof and a classical frontage by John Foster. The second train-shed was completed in 1851; its curved roof of iron and glass was the largest single-span roof in the world at the time it was built. It was replaced by the present station in 1874, with an even more impressive roof of glass and iron – again the largest span in the world when built. It survives as a confident monument to nineteenth-century prosperity. The turreted stone front building, originally a hotel and now offices, was designed by Alfred Waterhouse, who was born in Liverpool.

Opposite the station, the Plateau is adorned with recently restored geometrical paving, well-designed cast-iron Victorian lamp-posts with entwined dolphins, and dignified civic monuments and statues. Rising from this is the finest piece of monumental classical architecture in England, described by Sir Charles Reilly, one-time professor of architecture at Liverpool University, as 'a building for all times, one of the great edifices of the world'. This is ST GEORGE'S HALL, combining a concert hall and former assize courts in one majestic public building. Reilly called it 'not only the best Graeco–Roman building in Europe but representing the climax of a long movement'. It was conceived in 1836 and building work began in 1838 to the design of Harvey Londsdale Elmes (chosen by competition). Elmes died in 1847 and C.R. Cockerell completed the building, including the superb interior decoration. The overall concept owes much to the influence of the German neo-classicists Schinkel and von Klenze, whose work Elmes had studied.

The entrance doors are of bronze, intricately cast, to Cockerell's design. The Great Hall is 151 feet long and is flanked by red granite columns carrying a tunnel-vaulted ceiling inspired by Blouet's reconstruction of the Baths of Caracalla. The colourful floor of Minton tiles is said to have been designed by Professor Ludwig Grüner from Dresden and the white marble statues of worthies are by various neo-classical sculptors, including Chantrey, Noble and Liverpool's own John Gibson. The other major interior is the circular Concert Room on the first floor, which has a balcony carried on caryatids and a rich frieze inspired by Desgodetz.

St George's Hall, Liverpool.

William Brown Street, Liverpool.

The Victorian colour schemes, rich and sombre, which add so much to the splendour of this incomparable interior, have been excellently restored. But it is a pity that the exterior stone cleaning has been done so badly and the sculpture removed from the pediment. Even worse, the Law Courts, which occupied much of the building, have recently been decanted to a new building on the Water Front (covered with white tiles and looking like a large public lavatory), leaving St George's Hall without a use, and the city council is refusing to accept the additional responsibility for the upkeep of this major monument.

Opposite St George's Hall, in William Brown Street, a group of nineteenth-century civic buildings, all classical in style, form a splendid foil. They comprise the SESSIONS HOUSE, built in 1882–4 by F. and G. Holme, with a portico; the WALKER ART GALLERY of 1874–7 by Sherlock and Vale, in pure Roman style; the PICTON READING ROOM, executed in 1875–9 by Cornelius Sherlock, with a dramatic semi-circular façade; the WILLIAM BROWN LIBRARY AND MUSEUM of 1857–60 by Thomas Allom, taking its cue from St George's Hall with a Corinthian portico; the COLLEGE OF TECHNOLOGY, built in 1896–1902 by E.W. Mountford in a blaze of Edwardian Imperial Baroque. At the top of the hill is the WELLINGTON MONUMENT, a Tuscan column with a statue on top, acting as an effective full stop or exclamation mark. The Walker Art Gallery has the finest of all English provincial art collections, with rich holdings of nineteenth- and early twentieth-century painting and sculpture – the fruits of

Victorian and Edwardian prosperity and generosity – and also a good range of continental Old Masters, including a precious group of Italian Primitives originally belonging to the Royal Liverpool Institution and bought with the advice of William Roscoe, the Liverpool banker and author of *The Life of Lorenzo de' Medici*, who in 1817 became the Institution's first president.

The Water Front

The most impressive part of Liverpool is the river, which here is three-quarters of a mile wide. A series of late eighteenth- and nineteenth-century docks, with gigantic warehouses, hydraulic towers and other ancillary buildings, stretches along it for 7 miles. Although all now disused, and partly demolished, much more survives in Liverpool than in London, which had the only comparable group of large-scale dock buildings in England. The climax is the PIER HEAD, with its three majestic Edwardian piles, flanked on one side by the parish CHURCH OF OUR LADY AND ST NICHOLAS – which has a fanciful early nineteenth-century Gothic spire designed by Thomas Harrison of Chester (the body of the church was destroyed in the Second World War) – and on the other by the ALBERT DOCK – the peak of Liverpool's dock architecture. It is possible to see the river frontage from one of the small pleasure boats that still ply the river from the Pier Head, and this is strongly recommended.

The tallest of the three Pier Head blocks is the ROYAL LIVER BUILDING of 1908–10, designed by W. Aubrey Thomas. It is his *chef-d'œuvre* and has no counterpart in

Pier Head, Liverpool.

England, though similar early twentieth-century buildings can be found in the USA. It is a massive pile of reinforced concrete faced in grey stone, with two *art nouveau* clock turrets on top supporting gilded versions of the mythical Liver Birds. The offices of the MERSEY DOCK AND HARBOUR BOARD balance the Liver Building on the other side of Pier Head. They were designed by Arnold Thornley in collaboration with Briggs and Wolstenholme, and built in 1907 in full-blown English Baroque style. The huge central copper dome is copied almost 'word for word' from Sir Charles Reilly's competition design for the Anglican cathedral of 1902. In the centre, the CUNARD BUILDING again has a strong American accent – this time *Beaux Arts* classical in the manner of Carrère and Hastings, or McKim, Mead and White in New York. It was designed in 1913 by the local firm of Willink and Thicknesse, with Arthur Davis (of Mewes and Davis) as consultant. It is a giant Italianate *palazzo* of reinforced concrete, faced in gleaming Portland stone. The majestic carved frieze and boldly projecting cornice are not easily matched in English architecture; this is classical architecture on the grandest scale and with an incomparable river setting.

The Albert Dock

After forty years of neglect by the city council, the Albert Dock has recently been rescued by outside intervention and enterprise. It is the most important group of dock buildings in Europe and, in its different way, a neoclassical masterpiece as impressive as St George's Hall (*q.v.*). To have pulled it down would have been an almost inconceivable disgrace, but this has consistently been planned. All credit then to the current programme of restoration as art gallery, museum and a mixture of residential and commercial accommodation. It is a pity,

though, that the brick has been cleaned; it looked more impressive when it was dark. There is always a degree of excessive gentrification in schemes of this type – but better gentrified than demolished!

The Albert Dock was designed in 1839 and opened in 1845 by Prince Albert, whose name it bears. It comprises an enclosed dock of 7 acres, surrounded by symmetrical ranges of five-storey fireproof warehouses with arcades of squat Doric columns along the ground floor. These, and all the internal structure, are of cast-iron, as are the roofs and the window frames. The quays and retaining walls are of massive granite blocks; the nineteenth-century local historian J.A. Picton thought they looked like a 'gigantic crazy paving of Cyclopean masonry put together with the precision of a jig-saw puzzle'. They were designed by Jesse Hartley, who was appointed Liverpool Dock Engineer in 1824 and was responsible for the incomparable architectural grandeur of the city's docks. 'He had grand ideas and carried them into execution with a strength, solidity and skill which have never been exceeded,' approved Picton. The DOCK TRAFFIC OFFICE, a version in cast-iron of St Paul's, Covent Garden, was designed by Philip Hardwick. As well as the buildings and granite retaining walls, the architectural impact of the docks derives from the cast-iron bollards, swing bridges and similar details that enliven the quays.

The Georgian West End

Georgian Liverpool stretches along the hillside southeast of the city centre from Abercromby Square to Upper Parliament Street; long streets of three-storeyed red brick or stucco houses with sash windows, columned porches and elegant fanlights survive on a scale not otherwise seen outside London. Physically, the area has deteriorated badly; many houses have been demolished piecemeal and others long ago degenerated into slums. Some sporadic efforts at rehabilitation have been made in recent years, but much more could be done. Why, for instance, has the city council not made more effort to use the historic buildings' laws to protect and enhance the area?

The way up to the West End from the city centre is along BOLD STREET – a major shopping street, although now much declined from its pre-war status. It is redeemed, at either end, by Thomas Harrison's stately LYCEUM CLUB and the handsome shell of John Foster's ST LUKE'S CHURCH. The former was reprieved by Michael Heseltine (when Secretary of State for the Environment) after the city council had given consent for its demolition, and it is now to be restored as a post office. It is a well-proportioned neo-classical building of stone, with an Ionic portico. St Luke's was gutted in the war, but the shell was retained as a landmark; the 'cardboard Gothic' west tower makes a very handsome street ornament.

RODNEY STREET is the best-preserved of the Georgian streets. It was built between 1780 and 1840 and is famous as Gladstone's birthplace (NO. 62) in 1809. Many of the houses are now offices, but well maintained. At the end, ST ANDREW'S PRESBYTERIAN CHURCH was the best remaining building by Foster in Liverpool, but it has been allowed to deteriorate sadly. At least the façade should be preserved. The sight of buildings of this quality falling into irredeemable ruin makes one despair. To the north of Rodney Street is Mount Pleasant, with the pretty classical PICTON ROOMS of 1845, and ABERCROMBY SQUARE. The latter is among the latest in date of Liverpool's London-type squares and was developed after 1820 to a design by John Foster. Its original focus was the Ionic portico of St Catherine's Church, but this has been demolished by LIVERPOOL UNIVERSITY, which, sorry to say, has also pulled down the Regency stucco houses in Bedford Street and in their place erected a group of hybrid Modern buildings. East of Rodney Street is a large area stretching from Gambier Terrace to Faulkener Square, all of which is still more or less intact. These streets were laid out to a gridiron pattern in 1800 by John Foster, the Corporation Surveyor, but many of the houses were not built until the 1830s or later. The best street is PERCY STREET, entirely stone-faced, with good carved detail and cast-iron balconies; but CANNING STREET and HUSKISSON STREET also contain good houses. It is hereabouts that, with the help of the Historic Buildings Council, a belated programme of rehabilitation has been initiated – but better late than never.

Dominating the Georgian area are the two Liverpool cathedrals, situated at either end of Hope Street. The ANGLICAN CATHEDRAL has a magnificent site overlooking ST JAMES'S CEMETERY, a former stone quarry turned into a dramatic necropolis by Foster in 1827 and, despite excessive and crude tidying, still endowed with a powerful Piranesian atmosphere. The cemetery CHAPEL survives at the west end of the cathedral – a baby classical neighbour beside that vast Gothic pile; it has recently been restored by the Walker Art Gallery as a museum of neo-classical sculpture. Three cheers! The cathedral is fully worthy of its site. Like much else in Liverpool, the closest parallel is not English but American; only in New York and Washington are there modern Gothic cathedrals on this scale. It is appropriate, therefore, that when the nave of Liverpool Cathedral was finally completed in 1978, the stonemasons moved on to Washington to finish the cathedral there.

Liverpool Cathedral was begun in 1903 and was designed by Sir Giles Gilbert Scott who worked on it for fifty-nine years. The exterior makes a magnificent composition, with the choir and nave of equal size balancing each other on either side of the transepts and the massive central tower, 331 feet high. The tower is beautifully proportioned and of a most original design, the octagonal turrets at the corners terminating below the final octagonal corona with its miniscule pinnacles. It is sometimes nicknamed the 'Corned Beef Tower', as it was paid for by the Vesteys. The cathedral is built of warm red sandstone from the Wirral, and much of the Gothic detail is derived from Spanish rather than English precedent. The main impact, however, comes from the huge scale, the perfect proportions, the considered contrasts between blank stonework and richly carved decoration, and the faultless handling of the masses. It looks magnificent in all distant views, and succeeds in dominating the city. Here is the grand finale of the English Gothic Revival. It has the romantic grandeur to be found in Edwardian dream architectural drawings, but all solidly expressed in stone.

The Anglican Cathedral, Liverpool.

The interior makes an immediate and overwhelming impact by reason of its vastness and splendour. There is an effective contrast between, on the one hand, the low side-aisles tunnelling through the walls and, on the other, the tall wide spaces of the choir and nave and the immensely high space under the tower. An equally dramatic feature is the stone bridge arching across the nave, sometimes illuminated by sudden shafts of light from the stained-glass windows. It is a pity that, on the whole, the fittings are so weak, with their light oak and sentimental sculpture, but the vast Spanish-style gilded reredos towering over the high altar is very effective. The most beautiful part of the interior is the Lady Chapel, an almost detached structure reached by the south choir aisle. This was built in 1906, and Scott was helped by Bodley in its design. It has a stone vault with curved ribs, a richly carved triforium and a black-and-white marble floor. The impressive altarpiece was also designed by Bodley and Scott. In the cathedral, it is in here only that you feel the urge to pray.

The CATHOLIC CATHEDRAL was commissioned from Sir Edwin Lutyens in 1930 and work began in 1933 but stopped in 1940, at which point only the crypt had been built. The detailed drawings and a large wooden model survive, demonstrating that this was to be the resounding climax of English classical architecture, with its carefully calculated build-up of geometrical masses and its enormous central dome. (Rumour had it that there was to have been an illuminated cross on top which would have been visible in Ireland.) The crypt alone is an amazing experience, with its complicated plan, seemingly infinite vistas and unplastered brick vaults that make you feel as if you are inside the substructure of some gigantic Roman ruin. This is quite simply the most impressive spatial experience in English architecture. By an immense stroke of luck, the concrete funnel-shaped structure built in the 1960s to the design of Sir Frederick Gibberd to serve as a cathedral was not placed on top of the crypt but to one side of it. This means that the rest of Lutyens' cathedral could still be built (in the meantime using Frederick Gibberd's concrete church as a temporary cathedral). This project should be started as soon as possible. It would make a very good 'job-creation' scheme, and would not be excessively expensive by the standards of such public-funded ventures. It would endow Liverpool with the greatest English building of the twentieth century and make doubly sure that, when the commercial tide finally runs out, this city – like Venice – could continue to live off its visitors and outside admirers.

Croxteth Hall

26; 5 miles NE of Liverpool centre off A580

Croxteth Hall was the seat of the Molyneux family, who became Earls of Sefton in 1771, and was given to the city of Liverpool on the death of the 7th and last Earl in 1972. The first Croxteth Hall was built sometime in the second half of the sixteenth century, but the only parts from this period still visible are two gables with mullion windows to the left of the gatehouse. The house has grown over the centuries into a large, irregular quadrangle sur-

rounding a courtyard. The spectacular south front was added in 1702–14 by William, 4th Viscount Molyneux, at the time when Sefton Hall (*q.v.*) was demolished and Croxteth became the main family seat. The north-east ranges, including the Gatehouse, nursery wing and kitchens, were built in 1874–8 in a gabled Tudor style to the design of Thomas Henry Wyatt, whose cousin was agent to the Croxteth estate at that time; a separate dining-room wing was added at the same time in the style of the Queen Anne front. Finally, the west range was rebuilt between 1902 and 1904 to replace a wing of 1790. It is the work of J. MacVicar Anderson in the same modified version of the style of the south front as the dining-room wing. The south wing was badly damaged by fire in 1952 and its enfilade of panelled rooms largely destroyed, so the architectural interest of the interior is now more or less confined to MacVicar Anderson's contribution – in particular the excellent Grand Staircase with florid wrought-iron balustrades, and Wyatt's Dining Room with its Caroline-style stucco ceiling.

Croxteth, though almost surrounded by suburban Liverpool, is set in a large park and has some very good Victorian estate buildings, including a laundry block by Nesfield, kennels by John Douglas of Chester, and a home farm, which has a Gothic house by Nesfield and a charming Gothic dairy of 1861–70, also by Nesfield,

Ince Blundell Hall.

lined with blue and white tiles, the ceiling painted with daffodils and *cross-moulines* (emblem of the Sefton arms) by Albert Moore.

Farnworth
27; 9 miles SE of Liverpool centre on A568

The CHURCH OF ST LUKE is an ancient one, but, alas, much restored and reconstructed in the nineteenth century. The whole of the north side, and the pitch-pine nave roof, date from a partial rebuilding in 1855; further 'restoration' was done in 1892–5 when many Georgian fittings, including the galleries and pews, were thrown out. It is a sad story. There are bits of possibly Norman stonework, but the general effect is Perpendicular, with a fourteenth-century tower and fifteenth-century chancel which has a handsome carved timber roof.

The special feature of the church is the Bold Chapel at the end of the north side; it contains the monuments and tombs of the extinct family of Bold of Bold Hall, and an impressive series of their hatchments hangs aloft in the nave. The best of the monuments is the beautiful neo-classical tablet to Mary Bold, Princess Sapieha, who married Prince Eustace Sapieha of Dereczyn in Lithuania. It was made in Rome in 1824 and is by Pietro Tenerani, a leading sculptor of the early nineteenth century who

trained under Thorwaldsen. The Princess lies on a Grecian couch and limply holds the outstretched arm of an angel, who is showing her an hour-glass with the sand run out. Her surviving husband leans, weeping, on the end of the sofa. The plaster model for this monument is in the Tenerani Museum in Rome. There is something cheeringly improbable about the quirk of dynastic history that deposited this work of art of international interest in a dim little town on the outskirts of Liverpool.

Ince Blundell Hall
28; 10 miles N of Liverpool centre on A565

The woods of the park of Ince Blundell Hall form an island in the once-remote flat arable landscape between Southport and Liverpool. The main lodge on the Southport road, a triumphal arch with stone lions, is based on a painting by Sebastiano Ricci which once hung at the house. For centuries this was the seat of one of Lancashire's leading recusant families, the Blundells, later Weld-Blundells, who maintained here into the mid-twentieth century a 'stately and devout life' beyond anything imagined by Evelyn Waugh – the family sitting together after dinner talking away in their distinctive loud voices and embroidering vestments. In the eighteenth century Ince Blundell was a headquarters of the Jesuits, who were guests of the family, with Fr Babworth a superior to thirty priests employed on the Lancashire mission. It now belongs to the Augustinian nuns, who maintain it well as a convalescent home.

The first mention of a house on the site is in the thirteenth century, but the present grand Georgian house was built by Robert Blundell *c*.1720. For long the architect was a mystery, but it is now known to have been Henry Sephton, the leading Liverpool mason-architect of the second quarter of the eighteenth century. (Sephton's signed design is preserved among the Everingham papers deposited by the Duke of Norfolk in Hull University Library.) The principal façade faces the garden and is a handsome brick and stone Baroque composition derived, with variations, from the original Buckingham House, London. The house was altered in 1802, and again in 1847–50, by Henry Blundell. His major addition was the Pantheon, built to hold the celebrated sculpture collection he began as a young man on his Grand Tour. (One of Piranesi's plates in *Vasi, Candelabri* is dedicated to him.) The Pantheon was originally an independent building but was later joined to the house to serve as an entrance hall. The design was Blundell's own, with advice from his friend Charles Townley of Townley (*q.v.*), but the executant architect was John Hope. This important neo-classical ensemble was unnecessarily disrupted when the sculpture was given to the Liverpool Museum *c*.1960 at the time when the house became a convent. There is no practical reason, however, why it should not be returned to the Pantheon as an out-station of the museum and every effort should be made to achieve this. The mid-Victorian work, apart from a large new Dining Room, consisted chiefly of redecoration by Crace of the main rooms with pretty Raphaelesque *Grotteschi*. The Drawing Room has an excellent mid-eighteenth-century Rococo plaster ceiling, a great rarity in Lancashire. Several of the chimneypieces have unfortunately been removed.

The house has a beautiful park, with lake, temple and extensive outbuildings – including a Chapel of 1858 by J.J. Scoles, which serves as the parish church. A unique feature is the circular PRIEST'S HOUSE at the edge of the park.

Knowsley Hall
29; 7 miles NE of Liverpool centre off B5194
Knowsley Hall is still the seat of the Stanleys, Earls of Derby, though the main house is part-let to the Lancashire County Constabulary and the present Lord Derby, who was Lord Lieutenant of Lancashire from 1951 to 1968, resides in a large, new Neo-Georgian house in the park designed by Claud Phillimore *c*.1960. The Knowsley estate is almost encircled by motorways and the modern expansion of Liverpool, yet the great PARK, with its high stone wall, woods and surrounding farms, makes up an oasis that is both big enough and beautiful enough to ignore the world outside and to preserve its own values. Red deer and fallow deer roam the park, which also contains an African wildlife reserve, successor to the nineteenth-century zoo of which Edward Lear's father was keeper.

Knowsley is essentially a very large L-shaped twentieth-century Neo-Georgian house, the result of two phases of remodelling an inchoate assemblage of older buildings of different dates. These included substantial early eighteenth-century bits (dated 1731–7), which provided the key for the reconstruction. The first phase was carried out by the 17th Earl of Derby, 'King of Lancashire', to the design of Romaine-Walker in 1912. In Lord Derby's own words, 'It is more of a restoration to what never existed, to use an Irishism, than an old house.' The second phase was carried out by the present (18th) Lord Derby to the design of Claud Phillimore in 1954.

A twentieth-century house on this scale is exceptional in England and perhaps reflects the equally exceptional survival into the twentieth century of the Stanleys' political and territorial influence. The long garden front of the main block has a three-storeyed, nine-bay centre by Romaine-Walker, replacing a monstrous Victorian saddleback-roofed tower. The entrance front of brick with painted stone dressings is partly by Romaine-Walker, who added the top storey to the centre and sashed the windows, and partly by Claud Phillimore, who removed a *porte-cochère*, the terrace hiding the basement, and added the present entrance porch; he also made the forecourt and *claire-voie*. The west wing contains the oldest fabric, but it has been extensively remodelled. The north front of the west wing is late seventeenth-century, with castellations by John Foster, but the west end is by Claud Phillimore, designed to replace demolished sections. The isolated Dynamo Tower is by William Burn. The rear of the west wing is a jumble of castellated bits of different dates, which were built partly by John Foster in 1820 and partly by William Burn in 1836–9.

Knowsley became the principal Stanley seat only after the destruction of Lathom in the Civil War, and it was the 10th Earl who, *c*.1732, was responsible for the early Georgian aggrandisement of the house – probably to the design of Henry Sephton. The main external survivor from his time is the two-tier timber colonnade, Doric and Ionic, at the south end of the east wing, based on Leoni's edition of Palladio. A tablet written by the 10th Earl records the ingratitude of Charles II to the Stanley family: 'James, Earl of Derby, Lord of Man and the Isles, Grandson of James Earl of Derby and of Charlotte, Daughter of Claude Duke of Tremouille whose husband James was beheaded at Bolton XV October, 1652, for strenuously adhering to King Charles II, who refused a bill unanimously passed by both Houses of Parliament for restoring to the family the estates which he lost by his loyalty to him 1732.' The other major survivor of the 10th Earl's time, though *ex situ*, is the Baroque stucco doorcase, dated 1733, in the Long Gallery. The adjoining Stucco Room, resplendent with plasterwork of the same type, is probably Edwardian in its present form, though there was an eighteenth-century Stucco Room at Knowsley with 'beautiful medallion heads of the twelve Caesars in *Basso Relievo*'. The other major rooms, in a variety of 'period' styles, are also by Romaine-Walker; they include the tripartite Entrance Hall, the spectacular

'Caroline' staircase and the 'Luis XV' Walnut Drawing Room – where, however, the French *boiseries* are said to be genuine. The Queen's Rooms are Edwardian neo-Adam, recalling the lost glories of the Adam townhouse in Grosvenor Square and Adam's unexecuted scheme for a huge castellated mansion at Knowsley. The brobdingnagian State Dining Room is by Foster and dates from 1820, although it was remodelled in 1890 and is like a Great Hall. It is entered through doors 30 feet high. As Creevey asked: 'Pray, are those vast doors to be opened for every pat of butter that comes into the room?'

Rainhill

30; 12 miles E of Liverpool on A57

'This Sacred temple is a very handsome building; the finest in all probability of any of the kind to be met with in any part of the rural districts of the county,' proclaimed a local newspaper at the time of the opening of the CHURCH OF ST BARTHOLOMEW. Like all the best Lancashire Catholic churches, it was the gift of a rich local landowner: it was erected in 1840 by Bartholomew Bretherton, who had made a fortune out of the stage-coach between St Helens and Liverpool, and is built of pink sandstone from Bretherton's own quarry nearby. The architect was Joshua Dawson of Preston, whom Bretherton sent to Rome to study the architecture there before designing this miniature basilica in Lancashire. Dawson took as his model S. Bartolomeo on the Isola Tiberina, which is a genuine Roman temple converted into a Christian church. Hence at Rainhill the exterior combines a handsome Roman Ionic portico at the front with a short Lombardic *campanile* at the side. The interior is splendid, with a tunnel-vaulted and coffered ceiling carried on ten giant Corinthian columns, originally painted to resemble grey granite. The east end forms an apse and has good paintings of St Peter, St Paul and St Bartholomew, with the Resurrection in the half-dome, all by a Preston artist named Carter. The altar was of Siena marble, but unfortunately has been moved from its original position. It is sad to record that the impact of this wonderful interior has been seriously affected by unnecessary alterations carried out in 1984 – yet another example of the anomaly whereby ecclesiastical buildings in use are exempt from all the listed-building controls that apply to secular monuments.

Sefton

31; 10 miles N of Liverpool centre on B5422

Amidst the flat fields just to the north of Liverpool's suburbs, the fourteenth-century spire of the CHURCH OF ST HELEN is a conspicuous landmark. The body of the church was largely rebuilt between 1535 and 1540, when a member of the Molyneux family was rector. Indeed, the church owes its interest to generations of this family, who were lords of the manor of Sefton from 1100, when it was granted to them by Roger de Poitou, down to the death of the last Earl of Sefton in 1972.

The style of the church is latest Gothic, with large traceried windows and long horizontal castellated parapets concealing the low-pitched roof. The impressive interior has a continuous oak roof, with

The church of St Helen, Sefton.

moulded beams and carved bosses, running from end to end without a break or chancel arch. The remarkable carved-wood fittings include elaborate screens, stalls and pews, all of the early sixteenth century, and a pulpit dated 1735. The noble rood-screen is the finest in the north-west, its intricate small-scale decoration just beginning to show the impact of the Renaissance, and the traceried screens along the sides of the chancel and round the Sefton Pew are scarcely less ornate. The classical reredos with Ionic pilasters in the chancel was given by Anne Molyneux in 1765. Hanging in the nave are two splendid eighteenth-century brass chandeliers with doves on top. There is an extensive group of medieval and Tudor monuments and brasses to members of the Molyneux family, beginning with a stone effigy in chain-mail of *c.*1296 and leading up to a table-tomb with brasses of 1568; the absence of later monuments is due to the fact that the family remained Catholic until 1750. Of their ancient manor house nothing remains except the moated site and a small section of brick park wall; it was given up in 1702 when the Molyneux moved to Croxteth (*q.v.*).

Speke Hall

32; 8 miles S of Liverpool centre off A581

Speke is one of the most richly half-timbered houses in England, its setting unfortunately ruined beyond redemption by the runway of Speke Airport on one side and large modern factories on the other. The history of the manor goes back to the Domesday Book, but by 1170 it had passed into the hands of the Master Foresters of Lancashire and later came to the Molyneux. The Norreys (later Norris) family acquired the estate in the fourteenth century. The present house was begun in *c*.1490 by Sir William Norreys, who built a Hall that formed the nucleus around which the house has grown.

Speke is extremely picturesque from all angles because of its stone-flagged roofs, many gables and the varying patterns of the timbering. It is, moreover, almost entirely free, externally, from the nineteenth-century embellishments that so compromised the authenticity of other 'mansions of olden time'.

The inner courtyard has cobbled paving and is filled by two large yew trees, one male and one female, called Adam and Eve. It is surrounded by galleries, or passages, giving access to the main rooms, many of which have Elizabethan panelling and fireplaces. The finest rooms are the Great Chamber and Great Hall. The former has an elaborate stucco ceiling with vines, filberts and rosetrails, comparable with that in the Drawing Room at Gawthorpe (*q.v.*). The overmantel has endearingly naïve carvings representing three generations of the Norris family. The Hall is embellished with a patchwork of panelling of different designs, presumably brought in from elsewhere – though the legend that it was looted from Holyrood House in 1544 is ludicrous. One suspects that here, as elsewhere in the house, the antique effect was judiciously supplemented with introductions from 'Wardour Street' by the second Richard Watt as part of his early nineteenth-century restoration.

The first Richard Watt, a Liverpool merchant who made a fortune in Jamaica, bought the estate in 1797 for £73,500 after the Norris family, staunchly recusant and Royalist, had failed in the male line and when Topham Beauclerk (the son of a female Norris) sold Speke to pay his gambling debts. The series of fascinating hiding holes and escape passages is a memento of the house's recusant past.

Widnes

33; 12 miles SE of Liverpool on A562

The industrial landscape along the Mersey at this point is reminiscent of the Ruhr, with smoking chemical factories, power stations and the wide expanse of the river. This grim grandeur forms the background to the ROAD AND RAILWAY BRIDGES that cross the Mersey, side by side. The latter carries the main line from London to Liverpool and is approached by long, arched viaducts of stone. It was built in 1864–8, of iron with castellated archways of blackened stone at either end. The road bridge is even more spectacular; it was erected in 1956–61 by Mott, Hay and Anderson, and comprises a huge steel-lattice arch from which the road deck is suspended on wires. With a total length of 1628 feet, it was the largest steel arch in Europe at the time at which it was built. The two bridges look especially impressive when seen from upstream on the south bank of the Mersey, silhouetted against a smoky sunset on an autumn or winter afternoon. Heroic materialism indeed.

Speke Hall.

MANCHESTER★

34; 30 miles SE of Preston on A6

Manchester is the best Victorian city in England, and until well into this century was the commercial centre of the greatest manufacturing district in the world. The industrial base has shrunk since the Second World War, but Manchester remains a provincial centre of banking, insurance, government administration, newspaper printing and television, and still retains the air of a northern capital. The city has a medieval past, the textile industry having been started here by Flemish weavers introduced by Edward III in the fourteenth century, but little survives from then apart from the collegiate parish church, now the cathedral, and its domestic buildings, now Chetham's Hospital. Most of the site of the old town – Market Street and High Street – was redeveloped in the 1960s and 1970s to make one of the largest – and surely one of the ugliest – new shopping precincts in the whole country, so the architectural interest of the city centre is almost entirely and resoundingly Victorian.

Nearly everything worthwhile in Manchester was paid for by cotton, which was introduced alongside wool in the sixteenth century and, aided by the damp Lancashire climate, superseded it in the eighteenth. The huge expansion of the cotton trade was encouraged by the improvements in communications – the Mersey and Irwell Navigation opened in 1721, the Bridgewater Canal in 1756 – and the use of steam power for spinning from 1781 onwards. Between 1750 and 1800 the population rose from 17,000 to over 70,000. The greatest age of development, however, was the nineteenth century, when the population grew to nearly a million and the whole city centre was rebuilt with magnificent buildings in massive gritstone, or hard-pressed red brick with terracotta and faience decoration, or shiny granite, forming extraordinary fretted fantasies. These were the entrepôt for the Lancashire cotton industry which clothed the world. Comparatively little damage was done in the Second World War; but since then several good buildings have been unnecessarily demolished and replaced with new ones, which are, alas, universally inferior to their predecessors. The heart of Manchester forms a triangle between the three main railway stations – Victoria, Piccadilly and Central (now closed). Within, much of the Victorian fabric still survives and is now being preserved. Outside this triangle, however, swathes of 'slum' clearance and road building have created urban deserts. In the late 1970s and 1980s there has been something of a revival of the city centre, manifested in such things as the re-opening of the Opera House (after a decade devoted to bingo), new theatres, the spectacular improvement of the City Art Gallery and the ambitious restoration of Central Station as a conference centre.

The City Centre

Like all Victorian cities, Manchester is best approached by train. PICCADILLY STATION has four impressive glass-and-iron train-sheds of 1862, but the front building, in the form of a piece of serpentine 1960s' curtain walling, is a characteristic work by Colonel Seifort. Piccadilly

itself retains an array of Victorian buildings, not yet refurbished – but no doubt they will be? PICCADILLY PLAZA, with a gaudy municipal garden on the site of the eighteenth-century Manchester Infirmary and an 'ultra-modern' office and hotel complex, is an entertaining piece of 1960s' vulgarity that already has a certain period charm.

In Portland Street, just off the Plaza, there is one especially splendid Victorian building – the former COOK AND WATTS' WAREHOUSE, designed in 1851 by Travis and Mangnall as a Venetian *palazzo* 300 feet wide and 100 feet high. It has recently been converted into a hotel – rather crudely, but at least the magnificent stone shell has been preserved. Portland Street is crossed by PRINCESS STREET which leads to WHITWORTH STREET and this in turn to OXFORD STREET. This grid of wide streets lined with vast commercial premises is the best-preserved area of Victorian Manchester and in scale and self-confident grandeur should be counted among the wonders of the world. Princess Street is an almost undisturbed Victorian commercial street, with red brick buildings decorated with terracotta and faience; many of them are in the Venetian Gothic style, which caught on in Manchester thanks to the influence of Ruskin. The note of imperial glory is struck not just by the architecture but by the names – Asia House, Rhodesia House, and so forth. The smaller Italianate block was the birthplace of the TUC, and has recently been restored. Whitworth Street is similar, but its character is later than Princess Street – more Edwardian than Victorian. The width of the street and the architectural splendour of the office blocks recall Chicago. BRIDGEWATER HOUSE is a spectacular confection of stone and faience, dripping with elaborate detail. LANCASTER HOUSE, with a tall turret on the corner, is Baroque by Harry Fairhurst. The INSTITUTE OF SCIENCE AND TECHNOLOGY is also Baroque, in red and yellow terracotta, designed by Bradshaw, Gass and Hope in 1927 and completed as late as 1957. This Bolton firm was among the most accomplished purveyors of twentieth-century classical architecture in the north and could be well worth a special study. But the *clou* is the headquarters of REFUGE ASSURANCE – a vast red-and-yellow *palazzo* in a Baroque-cum-Flemish style, with a tall tower and cupola. It was designed by Paul Waterhouse (son of Alfred) and built between 1891 and 1912. Rumour has it that 'the Refuge' is due to move out because of the high rates – a pity, as they maintain their building beautifully. It stands on the corner of OXFORD STREET, the triumphal way into the city centre from the south. Beyond the railway bridge stretches the post-war wasteland of concrete redevelopment, but this merely heightens the effect of being inside the city gates. Much of the grandeur of Oxford Street derives from ST JAMES'S BUILDINGS, a huge Baroque pile of 1912 designed by Charles Clegg and Son and faced entirely in Portland stone – an alien material as exotic in Manchester as marble.

Oxford Street leads straight to the centrepiece of the city: ST PETER'S SQUARE, with the Central Library, the Town Hall Extension and the back of the TOWN HALL itself. From this side they form an original and thrilling

The Town Hall, Manchester.

geometrical architectural composition. The landscaping of the central area lacks the nobility demanded by the situation, but it is partly redeemed by Lutyens' CENOTAPH. The square, an irregular space formed in this century, stands on St Peter's Fields, notorious as the site of Peterloo, the violent dispersal of an unarmed working-class meeting in 1819. At the south-west end of the square is the MIDLAND HOTEL – a gleaming and elaborate brown faience concoction. And out of the north-east corner stretches Mosley Street. The first building of note in this direction is the CITY ART GALLERY, which comprises two buildings, both by Sir Charles Barry. The main building at the front was raised for the Royal Manchester Institution in 1824–35 and is Grecian with an Ionic portico. Behind is the former Athenaeum of 1837 in Barry's better-known Pall Mall Italianate style, recalling the Palazzo Farnese in Rome. The ground floor of the Athenaeum is one room with scagliola granite columns and is used for changing exhibitions. The best interior, however, is not open to the public – the former Lecture Theatre at the top, with its elaborate coved stucco ceiling. The interior of the main Art Gallery building has recently been redecorated in an exemplary manner, recreating the colour schemes and elaborate stencilled patterns of the 1840s. The major space is the Entrance Hall, rising the full height of the building, with an impressive stone staircase, white marble neo-classical statues, new light fittings with Greek-key borders and

brass snakes holding the ends of their supporting chains and, inset into the walls, plaster casts of the Elgin Marbles given by George IV. The walls and ceiling are richly painted and stencilled in different shades of stone colour, terracotta and Pompeian red. The galleries themselves continue the same theme, with new Victorian-pattern stencilled friezes and ceilings and the walls painted dark red or green. The collection of paintings includes an incomparable group of Pre-Raphaelite works and some superb continental paintings. The holdings of the latter have been greatly improved recently, and Manchester looks set to overtake Liverpool as possessor of England's best provincial art collection.

The rest of Mosley Street fails to sustain the standard set by the Art Gallery. There is an impressive WILLIAMS AND GLYN'S BANK, originally the Manchester and Salford Bank. This twin *palazzo* was designed by Edward Walters in two parts, one in the 1860s and the other, replicating it, in the 1880s. Randolph Caldecott, the artist, was a bank clerk here. On the other side of the street is the PORTICO LIBRARY, a noble Ionic building designed by Thomas Harrison in 1802–6. Milne Buildings, however, a large warehouse with Egyptian columns, has been demolished. A disgrace!

Now back to the Town Hall, which must be entered through the main entrance from ALBERT SQUARE. The square itself was laid out a little before the Town Hall, which is of 1868, and the Gothic ALBERT MEMORIAL by

Thomas Worthington in the centre was designed in 1862 – what Manchester does today, London does tomorrow. The short sides of the square have smaller-scale Victorian buildings, mainly Venetian Gothic, while the side opposite the Town Hall is in the recent conservation-area style. The Town Hall is, of course, the major architectural monument of Manchester and among the half dozen most important Victorian buildings in England. It is the *chef-d'œuvre* of Alfred Waterhouse and *the* High Victorian Gothic masterpiece. The site is triangular, a fact which Waterhouse turned to great advantage in his plan, placing the subsidiary staircases at the three points, and devoting the main side, facing Albert Square, to ceremony while placing the Great Hall in the middle, with internal courtyards on either side surrounded by offices. The façade is symmetrical and dominated by the magnificent clock tower, 286 feet high with an octagonal spire on top and containing a notable carillon of bells.

The main entrance leads into a sequence of low-vaulted halls and corridors, and the symmetrically duplicated main staircase to the *piano nobile*. Vistas stretch on all sides, with stone vaults, columns of polished granite, and glistening statues and busts of white marble. The latter comprise the finest collection of Victorian civic sculpture in the country. The main stairs mount in semi-circles under high vaults painted dark blue with gold stars; they meet at a landing with a coloured glass ceiling recording the names of all the Lord Mayors of Manchester and a mosaic floor decorated with bees – the emblem of Manchester's Victorian work ethic – and intertwining cotton threads. The Great Hall, 100 feet long, has a hammerbeam roof with painted heraldry, showing the city's chief trading partners – foreign countries and British cities – in the nineteenth century. There are wrought-iron gasoliers (well converted to electricity), statues and busts of Victorian worthies, a huge organ by Cavaillé-Coll of Paris in a case designed by Waterhouse, and, last but not least, round the lower part of the walls is the famous cycle of Pre-Raphaelite wall paintings by Ford Madox Brown depicting the history of Manchester. The clear glass in the windows, where one might have expected stained glass, was a deliberate choice in order to admit as much light as possible on to the murals. The state rooms – Banqueting Room, Anteroom, Reception Room and old Council Chamber – stretch in sequence along the Albert Square front and are miraculously well preserved, with carved alabaster chimneypieces and stencilled ceilings, their walls with oak panelling round the bottom and peacock-blue paint round the top as a background to full-length portraits. The original wrought-iron gasoliers and Waterhouse-designed furniture survive throughout. Indeed, one of the amazing features of Manchester is the prodigious quantity of Victorian furniture that is still *in situ* in the settings for which it was made.

Vincent Harris's TOWN HALL EXTENSION and circular CENTRAL LIBRARY were designed in 1925 and are perfect examples of architectural good manners. The Extension, with its high pitched roof, has a Gothic air which acts as the transition between Waterhouse and the undiluted Roman classicism of the Library. This latter is a rotunda of Portland stone encircled by Tuscan columns and entered through a Corinthian portico. The interior has a spare elegance that recalls twentieth-century American classicism. The Hall is two storeyed, the walls lined with Hoptonwood stone, the ceiling carved and painted. It is a pity about the tawdry clutter and rubber floormats that disfigure the lower stages of the room. The main Reading Room, upstairs, is a large circular space with a plain segmental dome, Siena-marble doorcases and all its original furniture: chairs, tables and an amusing gilt wrought-iron clock on bright green marble columns in the centre of the booking counter.

The Town Hall Extension and Central Library, Manchester.

North of the Town Hall is an area of smaller-scale streets, containing a rich mixture of Victorian architecture. KENNEDY STREET, though one side is half rebuilt, still retains on the south side an entertaining procession of narrow Victorian façades, each in a different style: Jacobean, Venetian Gothic, Flemish, Perpendicular. The LAW SOCIETY of 1885 by Thomas Hontas has stained glass with portraits of judges in the windows lighting the library. FOUNTAIN STREET, stretching north, is partly rebuilt, but No. 46 by Worthington, the former Poor Law Commissioners, is a good Italianate block with *palazzi di Genova* details. York Street leads to SPRING GARDENS, parallel to Fountain Street. On the corner is a red sandstone Edwardian Baroque bank of 1902 by Charles Heathcote. Between Spring Gardens and King Street is the MANCHESTER CLUB, the most accomplished of Manchester's many Venetian Gothic buildings. It was built in 1870–1 to the design of Edward Salomans. King Street used to be the best street in Manchester but has suffered from 1960s' rebuilding. It still retains one or two excellent classical banks, notably Lutyens' MIDLAND BANK of 1929 – a characteristic example of his late stepped-up geometrical classicism, with Corinthian flourishes above the snowline. No less impressive is C.R. Cockerell's BANK OF ENGLAND, dated 1845–6, which has giant Tuscan columns and pediment. Cutting across King Street is Cross Street, which leads to the horrors of the new Arndale Shopping Centre; but it is not necessary to proceed that far, because first there is the grandiloquent interpolation of the COTTON EXCHANGE – a veritable temple of Mammon. The original Exchange was built in

Bridges between the Town Hall and Town Hall Extension, Manchester.

1729, rebuilt by Thomas Harrison in 1806, enlarged and reconstructed by Mills and Murgatroyd in 1869 and redone by Bradshaw, Gass and Hope in 1914–21 as a halcyon monument to the cotton trade, which for 150 years had made Manchester the world's most important textile city. Trading ceased on 31 December 1968. The Exchange is a stone classical pile with giant Corinthian columns and pilasters rolling round the outside, and a clock tower 180 feet high. The interior is even more impressive – a vast Hall with three glass domes and giant columns of red marble. Free-standing in the centre is the Exchange Theatre for theatre in the round – an exciting piece of 1970s' hi-tech design and a brilliant way of using this gigantic redundant space. A board high up at the end of the room still displays the closing prices for cotton in places like Alexandria on the last day of trading. What a way to go! It is like a Metro-Goldwyn-Mayer set for *The Decline and Fall of the Roman Empire* – you expect Attila the Hun and his hordes to come riding in at any moment dressed in animal pelts and shining steel helmets, their horses laden with the fruits of rape, pillage and loot. (The City Art Gallery is rich in paintings of this type.)

Leaving by the opposite entrance, steps lead down to ST ANNE'S SQUARE. This has just been well repaved and is embellished with new cast-iron lamp-posts, bollards and litter boxes decorated with embossed bees. In the middle is a bronze statue of Cobden by Marshall Wood on a granite base. The square was laid out in 1709 by Lady Bland, who also built ST ANNE'S CHURCH, which is the only Georgian church to survive in the centre of Manchester. It was consecrated in 1712. The architect was probably John Barker, and it is a dignified piece of provincial Baroque executed in pink sandstone. The outside is decorated with two tiers of pilasters, the lower Corinthian and the upper without capitals. The tower originally had an elongated cupola, but this was later removed. The interior is dignified, with galleries and cut-down box pews. The impressive marquetry pulpit, with little Corinthian columns at the four corners, is sunk into a hole in the ground so as to bring it to a reasonable level without cutting it down. The apsidal chancel has sympathetic woodwork, designed by Waterhouse when he restored the church in 1887–9. The church has been more recently restored, by Donald Buttress, and in 1981 the interesting painted glass, dated 1769 by William Peckitt of York (originally at St Johns, Deansgate), was placed in the window nearest the choir vestry. In the Lady Chapel is the original eighteenth-century communion table given by Lady Bland, and an altar painting after Carracci, once in the now-demolished St Peter's Church.

Behind St Anne's, Deansgate (the longest street in central Manchester) leads to CHETHAM'S HOSPITAL and the cathedral. Manchester parish church was refounded as a collegiate establishment in 1421 under licence from Henry V. At the Reformation the college was suppressed but the buildings survived, becoming first a townhouse of the Earl of Derby; then in 1653 they were acquired by Humphrey Chetham, a rich and pious textile merchant. He founded there a boys' school and Manchester's first public library. Manchester Grammar School has moved

Manchester Cathedral.

to other premises and the Hospital buildings are now a music school. The buildings form an attractive fifteenth-century collegiate group of red sandstone with flagged roofs. It is a pity that the forecourt is tarmacked and used for car parking, and that utilitarian structures disfigure the Waterhouse wing. This group deserves better than that. Why not grass, cobbled paving and trees, as in Oxford and Cambridge? Inside the Hospital is the original fifteenth-century Great Hall, with timber screen and venerable open timber roof; it also has an attractive staircase and a small cloister quadrangle, which leads to the wonderfully atmospheric Library. This occupies the former dormitory and is L-shaped with an open timber roof, wide-boarded floor and mid-seventeenth-century bookcases of dark oak with gold press letters. These were heightened in the eighteenth century when the wooden security gates were added to the carrels. There is a nice smell of old books and an impressive number of seventeenth-century chairs and stools survive. The Reading Room is the former Warden's Chamber and has an unusual carved timber tympanum, with the Arms of Charles II and two obelisks over the fireplace – reminiscent of the proscenium over the Duke of Somerset's Pew in the chapel at Petworth.

The splendid Perpendicular collegiate church, now Manchester CATHEDRAL, was substantially restored and refaced in the nineteenth century, but still gives a good idea of the city's medieval prosperity. It was severely damaged by bombing in the Second World War and the atmosphere inside is now largely the result of Sir Hubert Worthington's post-war restoration and the taste of more recent clerics. The windows have clear glass (all the Victorian glass was destroyed by bombs), apart from two or three with rather garish modern stained glass, and the altar frontals and hangings belong to the tango-sackcloth school of ecclesiastical needlework. There are, of course, light oak low-backed chairs and a small central altar in the nave. A grand piano waiting in the wings to be wheeled on stage gives the unfortunate impression that this is a concert hall rather than a church. Of medieval work, the handsome timber roof, the pulpitum screen and the elaborate choir stalls with fretted canopies and carved misericords survive. These last are the best in the north-west. There are eighteenth-century brass chandeliers and excellent eighteenth-century wrought-iron altar rails and gates in the chancel – but these are thoroughly overshadowed by the 1960s' altar frontal. How this sub-Expressionist taste makes me, for one, long for the full-blooded historicist Stephen Dykes Bower approach!

Averting his gaze from the Arndale Centre, the sensitive visitor will quickly retrace his steps along DEANSGATE. This street owes its present appearance to widening in mid-Victorian times. Many of the buildings designed then by W. Dawes survive and more than hold their own against various modern interruptions. The BARTON ARCADE of 1871 by Corbett, Ruby and Sawyer has a frilly Victorian façade. The recently restored interior is the real point, however – a cast-iron *galleria* with glass-domed roof and three tiers of iron galleries reminiscent of the ironwork to be seen all over New Orleans. It is better than any of the much-vaunted shopping arcades in Leeds (*q.v.*). The finest building in

Rylands Library, Manchester.

Deansgate is of another order altogether. This is the RYLANDS LIBRARY, now part of Manchester University. It is the culmination of the Gothic Revival in Manchester and was designed in 1900 by Basil Champneys for Mrs Rylands as a memorial to her husband, a cotton manufacturer. It is Decorated Gothic at its most refined – a secular equivalent to Scott's Liverpool Cathedral (*q.v.*). The façade of red sandstone, with the main portal flanked by twin towers, is impressive enough, but the major impact of the building is its interior. Symmetrically duplicated staircases lead from the vaulted Entrance Hall to landings under the towers, open to their full height. This is an architectural effect of Fonthill-type extravagance. The Reading Room is perhaps the most beautiful room in Manchester and fully comparable with that of Yale University Library. It is like the nave of a church, stone-vaulted with aisles down each side. At either end are large windows with stained glass by Kempe and, beneath them, white marble statues by Cassidy of Mr and Mrs Rylands surveying each other across the full length of the room. All the original furniture, designed by Champneys, survives and not to be overlooked are the bronze *art nouveau* radiator grilles, electric lamps and light switches. The library itself (incorporating both the incomparable Crawford manuscripts and the rare

printed books from Althorp) is, like the architecture, on an American scale of munificence and one of the most magnificent historic collections in England.

Opening off Deansgate, south of the Rylands Library, is ST JOHN STREET. This is the best Georgian street to survive in central Manchester, with red brick three-storeyed houses. Note the collections of little brass name-plates on the panelled doors. Round the corner is BYROM STREET, a similar terrace distinguished by four Batty Langley Gothick doorcases. Retracing one's steps a little, Quay Street leads back to Deansgate and is continued in Peter Street, which returns you to St Peter's Square. In Quay Street is the OPERA HOUSE, a stucco neo-classical structure by Richardson and Gill, looking as if it belongs in St Petersburg. It has recently been restored to use. In Peter Street, the polished-looking faience of the MIDLAND HOTEL, the faience *art nouveau* of the YMCA, the 1845 stucco of the THEATRE ROYAL, and the spectacular Renaissance façade of the FREE TRADE HALL add up to a powerful architectural group. This last was gutted in the Second World War, but the interior has been rebuilt and the richly carved stone façade, designed by Edward Walters and built in 1853–6, survives. It celebrates and commemorates the triumph of Manchester's manufacturers over the landed interest in Peel's repeal of the

Corn Laws in 1848. It is famous as the venue for concerts given by the Hallé orchestra, which began here in 1857. Behind the Free Trade Hall is CENTRAL STATION. This has been closed and mouldering for decades but is now being refurbished as a conference and exhibition centre – a major project and a credit to the city. The train-shed has a vast semi-circular iron-and-glass roof designed by Sir John Fowler. With a span of 210 feet it is 10 feet wider than Lime Street Station in Liverpool (*q.v.*) and only a little narrower than St Pancras.

Bolton

35; 12 miles N of Manchester on A575

Situated beneath the moors, Bolton, with its great brick cotton mills, many of which have now been converted into small flatted industrial units, is the archetypal Lancashire industrial town. With Manchester, it had been the twin centre of the Lancashire textile industry since the Middle Ages, but it only really developed on a large scale from the late eighteenth century. The most active period was the years 1850–1900, which saw the population treble. Since the First World War the cotton industry has declined dramatically.

The centre of Bolton is well planned and has several impressive public buildings and statues. The *pièce de résistance* is the TOWN HALL – a remarkably monumental pile built between 1866 and 1873. It is the grandest of the classical Lancashire town halls and was designed by William Hill; he was an architect from Leeds, and his design was obviously influenced by Leeds Town Hall (*q.v.*). It is a splendid monument to Victorian prosperity, with a Corinthian portico approached from Victoria Square by an impressively wide flight of steps. The dominant feature is the tall clock tower topped by a domed cupola. The interior has recently been damaged in a disastrous fire but is to be rebuilt. Behind the Town Hall, the municipal buildings and Art Gallery (the latter by Bradshaw, Gass and Hope) complete a handsome piece of town planning. They are semi-circular in layout and make a grand display of inter-war classicism. Next to the Town Hall, facing Victoria Square, is the old EXCHANGE, a nice Greek Revival building built in 1825–9. VICTORIA SQUARE and NELSON SQUARE are both handsome formal spaces embellished with statues of local worthies – those in the latter including a fine bronze piece by Calder Marshal commemorating Samuel Crompton, the inventor of the revolutionary spinning mule, which opened the way for Bolton's eighteenth- and nineteenth-century expansion based on the textile industry and laid the foundations for Lancashire's prosperity – alas now dissipated. The Greek Revival Education Offices in Nelson Square were designed in 1825 by Benjamin Hick, a local man. Did he design the Exchange as well?

On the edge of Bolton two ancient houses survive and are well maintained as museums by the town council. HALL I' TH' WOOD is the old Lancashire manor house *par excellence*. It is situated 2 miles to the northeast of Bolton off the A58, and comprises two parts – one of black-and-white timber-framing, the other of dark local stone. The former is the oldest part, built in *c.*1500 by Lawrence Brownlow. Another Lawrence Brownlow added the Drawing Room in 1591, but not long after that the Brownlow family became impoverished and sold the house to Christopher Morris, a successful Bolton clothier. His son Alexander, a strong Puritan, was responsible for handling the confiscated estates of Royalist families in Lancashire after the Civil War – a profitable business. He built the stone south-west wing of the house in 1648. It is more monumental than the older parts, with a square porch, mullion-and-transom windows, and pointed finials on the parapet.

In the eighteenth century the house was converted into tenements, occupied by cotton spinners and farm workers; it was here that Samuel Crompton invented the spinning mule. Hall i' th' Wood was rescued in 1899 by Lord Leverhulme, who sensitively restored it to the design of Jonathan Simpson, and Grayson and Ould, with old panelling introduced from elsewhere. The elaborate plaster ceiling in the Drawing Room is copied from one at Chastleton House, Oxfordshire, and that in the Dining Room from an old inn in Bolton. Lord Leverhulme subsequently gave the house to his native town. Much of the good sixteenth-century oak furniture in the house was also given by Lord Leverhulme.

The Town Hall, Bolton.

SMITHILLS HALL, $1\frac{1}{2}$ miles to the north-east of Bolton off the A58, is a romantic house which, despite its proximity to the town, still has a rural setting, the moors rising to over 1000 feet behind it. Smithills came to a branch of the Radcliffe family in 1335, having previously belonged to the Knights of St John of Jerusalem, and Sir Ralph Radcliffe began the present house in the late fourteenth century. His Hall and adjoining buildings still survive, forming part of a three-sided quadrangle in the centre of the present house. The estate passed by marriage to the Barton family in the fifteenth century; they made a succession of additions and alterations, including the projecting wings at either end of the Radcliffe building and the stone-built Chapel. The house later belonged to the Shuttleworths of Gawthorpe (q.v.) but it remained largely unaltered until acquired in 1801 by Richard Ainsworth, who owned bleach works in Bolton. It remained in the Ainsworths' possession until 1930, when it was sold to Bolton Corporation for use as a museum.

Apart from the general picturesque effect of the house, with its varied elevations of black-and-white timber-framing and local sandstone, the principal antiquarian interest lies in the small late fourteenth-century Great Hall, which is the usual Lancashire/Cheshire type with speres framing the screens and quatrefoil bracing in the roof. The Parlour, or Drawing Room, in the east range is of Andrew Barton's time. It has moulded beams in the ceiling and elaborate early sixteenth-century Flemish-inspired linenfold panelling containing carved panels of heads. The Chapel next to the Parlour was damaged by fire in 1856 and later restored; the Tudor heraldic glass in the east window survived and includes the arms of Archbishop Cranmer.

Droylsden

36; 6 miles E of Manchester centre on A635

The FAIRFIELD MORAVIAN COMMUNITY is among the earliest Moravian communities in England and was established under the direction of Benjamin Latrobe in 1783. The Moravians were a German Christian sect, who had a great influence on Wesley. The community forms a well-laid-out group of buildings and was in the first place meant to be a self-contained unit. The centrepiece is the CHAPEL built in 1785 and approached by an avenue; it has a pediment and cupola. The other buildings are plain, of red brick, with sash windows and stone doorcases – like the standard Georgian townhouses of Lancashire. The men's accommodation was in the east wing and the women's in the west. The buildings behind the Chapel face cobbled streets with trees. The whole survives as an example of orderly planning in the midst of inchoate urban sprawl.

Heaton Hall

37; 6 miles N of Manchester centre off A665

Heaton Hall is the major surviving eighteenth-century house in Lancashire and a neo-classical design of international importance. It was built by twenty-three-year-old James Wyatt in 1772 for Sir Thomas Egerton, Tory MP for Lancashire and a man of taste keenly interested in art,

music, archery and travel. He had inherited Heaton at the age of seven and married Eleanor, co-heir of Sir Ralph Assheton of Middleton (q.v.), at the age of twenty-one; it was through his wife's relationship with Sir Nathaniel Curzon of Kedleston (q.v.) that he turned to the Wyatts.

Heaton was James Wyatt's first major country house commission, and is perhaps his best classical house design. It was not, however, a complete rebuilding. The centre block incorporates a small brick house of 1750 built by Thomas Egerton's father on an ancient site. Wyatt added the ashlar-faced south front with central domed bow, colonnaded links and octagonal end pavilions. Originally the colonnades did not have rooms behind but had blank rear walls with niches. The windows were inserted when the Music Room was designed in 1789 by Samuel Wyatt (brother of James), who had also designed the stables in 1777. Finally, Lewis Wyatt (nephew of James and Samuel) remodelled the north front, added the dramatic arcaded chimneystacks and designed the severely handsome lodges at the two main entrances into the park c.1806. Most of the interior is James Wyatt's work.

The principal rooms are, with one exception, on the ground floor and have characteristic delicate stucco work by Joseph Rose, exquisite marble chimneypieces by John Bacon and inset decorative paintings by Biagio Rebecca and Michael Novosielski. The rooms are arranged round the dramatic Staircase Hall, with its coved ceiling, yellow Siena scagliola columns and an imperial-plan stone staircase with an elegant lyre-patterned iron balustrade and lamp tripods based on a Roman design from Herculaneum. The exception is the circular Cupola Room behind the bow on the first floor of the south front, which is embellished with painted Etruscan decorations in pale green, yellow, pale blue, pink and *grisaille* by Biagio Rebecca.

Much of the original furniture was specially designed for the house by Wyatt, or was provided by Gillow, but all this was dispersed when the house was acquired by Manchester Corporation in 1906, though the fitted sideboard in the Dining Room apse fortunately remains. Samuel Wyatt's Music Room is plainer than his brother's work but has an interesting organ by Samuel Green dated 1790. Lewis Wyatt's octagonal Library in one of the end pavilions has fitted bookcases made by Gillow, now restored to their original position.

Manchester bought Heaton for its park and first used the house only as a tea room, but it later became a museum and in recent years an attempt has been made to redecorate and furnish the rooms in something like their original style. The park, laid out by William Emes and John Webb in 1770–1810, however, does not come under the aegis of the City Art Galleries, and has been partly disfigured by some ill-conceived municipal improvements.

Middleton

38; 10 miles N of Manchester centre on A6045

A former cotton town close to the moors, Middleton is now an indistinguishable part of the urban sprawl of Manchester. The parish CHURCH OF ST LEONARD stands conspicuously on a hill above the town, looking venerable and picturesque. It was rebuilt *c*.1412 by Thomas Langley, Bishop of Durham, who had been born at Middleton, and was rebuilt yet again – apart from the tower and south porch – in 1523–4 by Richard Assheton, the lord of the manor. It is long and low with battlements. The large west tower has a curious gabled and weatherboarded top storey, like a dovecote, added in the late seventeenth or early eighteenth century. The late Perpendicular interior creates a spacious, unified effect, as there is no division between the nave and chancel apart from the carved wooden rood-screen with Assheton heraldry in the lower panels and a 'restored' canopy and cresting. To the south of the chancel is the Assheton Chapel, where hang the crested helm, spurs and banner carried at the funeral of Sir Richard Assheton in 1765 – a late example of such medieval ceremonial. The south window of the chancel contains mutilated sixteenth-century stained glass. It is an early war memorial, as it commemorates the battle of Flodden in 1513 and has portraits, with their names attached, of those Lancastrians who took part and returned home safely after the crushing defeat inflicted on the Scots.

Apart from the church, the architectural interest of Middleton is confined to the turn-of-the-century work of Edgar Wood and James Henry Sellers – a talented and progressive pair of local architects who are the Lancashire equivalent of Charles Rennie Mackintosh in Glasgow. Wood designed at Middleton the METHODIST CHURCH in Long Street, two banks in the Market Place and some Voyseyish houses in the suburbs, including his own in Rochdale Road. They are all well worth looking at. The Methodist Church in particular is a beautiful piece of free Arts and Crafts Gothic with original and well-designed furnishings, especially the pulpit, screen and stalls. The exterior is stone and brick, forming an attractive courtyard group with various ancillary buildings. In 1901, Wood went into partnership with Sellers and together they designed two schools, one in ELM STREET and one in DURNFORD STREET, in 1908. Both are brick-built with stone trimmings and low towers; their cubic outlines and flat concrete roofs look decidedly 'modern', though much of the detail – such as the large mullion-and-transom and sash windows – is historicist. They are both remarkably interesting and impressive buildings.

Rusholme

39; 2 miles S of Manchester centre on B5117

PLATT HALL is a good Georgian house of medium size; it is now the property of the Manchester Corporation, which has used it as a museum since 1947. Platt was built in 1762–4 by John Lees (who married a Miss Carill Worsley and later changed his name to that of his wife's family) at a cost of £10,000. It was designed by Timothy Lightoler, whose drawings for the principal rooms are preserved at the house, though little of this internal work now remains. There are also unexecuted designs for Platt by R. Jupp and John Carr, the latter providing the basis for Lightoler's design.

The house is of red brick with a pedimented main block of seven bays, one-storeyed links and two-storeyed end wings with round-arched ground-floor windows. The best aspect of the interior is the staircase, approached from the Entrance Hall through a screen of two columns. It is of imperial plan, beginning in one flight and returning in two, and it has an elegant lyre-patterned iron balustrade. The Dining Room upstairs has stucco wall panels and a fine landscape by Richard Wilson still hangs in the position over the fireplace for which it was commissioned in 1764 (it was sold elsewhere but has now been bought back by the City Art Galleries). The house is a good example of English Rococo architecture just before the Adam neo-classical revolution.

The house and grounds remained in the hands of the Worsley family until the beginning of this century, when they were bought by Manchester, and the house has been put to good use by being made into part of the City Art Galleries.

Salford

40; 1 mile W of Manchester centre on A5081

ORDSALL HALL is an important fragment of the fifteenth-century house of the Radcliffe family; sadly, it is now engulfed in mean streets and industry. It comprises two ranges – the timber-framed south range of the fifteenth century, embellished in the sixteenth, and the brick west range of 1639. The other buildings that once completed the quadrangle have long since disappeared. The south range contains the Great Hall, measuring 43 feet by 25, and this, though partly refaced in harsh Victorian red brick, is internally surprisingly well preserved. The three doors to the service area and the dais end with mullion-and-transom bay window all survive. The walls are decorated with quatrefoils and the high-pitched roof also has quatrefoil patterns of wind-braces.

The Radcliffes of Ordsall were Royalists in the Civil War and never recouped their losses, being forced to sell in 1662. Ordsall subsequently changed hands several times and, with the development of Salford, degenerated into tenements. F.J. Shields, the artist and friend of the Pre-Raphaelites, converted part of the house into a studio in 1871. The Hall was bought by the Egertons of Tatton (*q.v.*) in 1883 and was drastically restored by them in 1896–8. (Up until then, the exterior timberwork had been covered with plaster.) The house was converted at that date into a training school for clergy. During the war it was used as a wireless station and was damaged by fire. Having been acquired by Salford Corporation in 1959, it was restored in 1972 with grants from the Historic Buildings Council and is now a museum.

Winstanley Hall

41; 4 miles W of Wigan off A571

Winstanley has the not entirely enviable distinction of being the only country house in industrial south-east Lancashire still to be inhabited as a private house by descendants of the original owner. The manor was bought in 1596 by James Bankes, a goldsmith and banker of Wigan and London, and is still in the possession of the Bankes family, who have been in the Wigan area since at least the reign of Henry VIII. The house built by James Bankes is of stone and its two projecting wings and recessed centre are similar to Bispham and Birchley – but unlike them the house has been extensively altered. The male line died out in 1784 and the house was inherited by a cousin, Thomas Holme, who took the name Bankes and celebrated his inheritance by reconstructing the interior of the house in 1785 in the fashionable Wyatt style to the design of Lawrence Robinson of Middleton, who had been clerk of works at Heaton Hall (*q.v.*) under James Wyatt. Many of the rooms – including the Library and Dining Room – retain elegant marble chimneypieces, mahogany doors and decorative stucco of that date. An even more drastic re-ordering took place in 1818–19, this time for Meyrick Bankes, to the design of Lewis Wyatt, who gave full reign to his enthusiasm for a personal and idiosyncratic version of the Jacobean style by removing the gables and replacing them with a monumental parapet; he also formed the large stable block, which has a fountain depicting Neptune in his chariot by William Spence, the Liverpool sculptor, in the centre of the quadrangle. The sloping park, with views over Wigan, was open-cast mined by the National Coal Board *c.*1950 but has since been roughly reconstituted.

Worsley

42; 6 miles NW of Manchester centre on M63

Francis, 3rd Duke of Bridgewater, built the Bridgewater Canal to the design of James Brindley in 1759–61 to carry coal from the Worsley mine to Manchester. This great enterprise was the basis of the huge fortune which was inherited in 1833 by his nephew Francis, second son of the 1st Duke of Sutherland, who took the name of Egerton and was created Earl of Ellesmere. Lord Ellesmere found Worsley 'a God-forsaken place, full of drunken, rude people with deplorable morals'. He did his best to civilise it and even now, with Worsley Hall demolished and the parish cut to pieces by motorways, Worsley is still an impressive Victorian achievement, combining

architecture and philanthropy. The Hall was built in 1840–6 to the design of Edward Blore in a full-blown Jacobethan style. The interior contained carved panelling from Hulme Hall (*q.v.*). The lodges remain, together with the memorial column erected in 1858 to the memory of Lord Ellesmere and designed by Driver and Webber, the model village of black-and-white houses, and the Gothic parish CHURCH OF ST MARK, proudly rebuilt to the design of Sir George Gilbert Scott in 1846. The eighteenth-century clock in the church tower strikes thirteen at 1 a.m., as it has done every day since 1789 when it was instigated at the command of the 'Canal Duke' in response to his workmen's complaint that they could not hear the bell and therefore did not know when it was their dinner time.

WORSLEY OLD HALL, a seventeenth-century black-and-white timber-framed house, was almost entirely reconstructed and restored for Lord Algernon Egerton in 1855 when a new west wing was built. The Billiards Room was added in 1905 and the small north-west wing in 1906.

Wythenshawe Hall

43; 7 miles S of Manchester centre on A560

This large, early sixteenth-century, partly timber-framed and formerly moated house is set in a spacious wooded park. It was for centuries a seat of the Tattons, but was given to Manchester Corporation in 1925 by Lord Simon of Wythenshawe, who had bought it from the Tatton family; it is now a museum. The house comprises a central Hall with a symmetrically placed porch and flanking wings. Above the Hall is the Drawing Room, which has a restored plaster ceiling, inlaid panelling and a chimneypiece dated 1650. It is approached by an eighteenth-century staircase with twisted balusters. The house was improved in 1813 when Gillow supplied the Library bookcases and was further extended and 'restored' *c.*1830 by Edward Blore, the work being completed by Salvin. The brick stables are eighteenth-century and the entrance lodge is dated 1878.

Bridgewater Canal, Worsley.

Leicestershire

Modern Leicestershire incorporates Rutland, once the smallest English county but reduced to the ignominious status of a district in 1974. The city of Leicester is situated bang in the centre of the county. To the west is a landscape dotted with nineteenth- and early twentieth-century industry, with rather dingy red brick villages and towns, and some coal-mining, but redeemed by the dramatic outcrop of Charnwood Forest – a piece of wild, rocky moorland. East of Leicester is more unspoilt country, part of 'the Shires' – famous hunting country and the home of the Quorn and Belvoir. There are grassy, humpy fields here, divided by properly maintained hedges punctuated by ash trees. (Only towards the Lincolnshire border have the hedges been removed on any scale.) For the most part this is still the landscape produced by eighteenth-century Parliamentary Enclosure, with red brick Georgian farmhouses and wide grass verges along the roads. The countryside is dotted with small fox coverts and copses, famous as the backgrounds to sporting prints. The villages contain brick and stone houses and cottages, and magnificent medieval parish churches with tall stone spires. The landscape of Rutland is similar, but even better; its villages used to be among the finest in England, their cottages built of gingery ironstone as well as creamy oolite. It is sad to have to report that since the early 1970s nearly every village has had added to it new houses of regrettably inappropriate design and materials, and more disappointing still to visit villages whose names are those of famous building stones, like Ketton or Clipsham, and to find them disfigured by new *bijou* residences of lavender brick or yellow concrete blocks. The hideous concrete street lighting in many villages is another wound for which we are indebted to the county council. There is no reason why these villages should not have been at least as carefully treated as those in the Cotswolds. The two reservoirs, however, at Stoke Dry and Rutland Water, although they have flooded areas of good farmland, are well landscaped and add a note of grandeur otherwise lacking in the mild Midlands landscape.

The chief architectural glories of Leicestershire are its Gothic parish churches. The area was prosperous in the Middle Ages thanks to farming and sheep, and the village and town churches are therefore surprisingly large, many of them with splendid tall spires, of which that at Market Harborough is the most beautiful. The thirteenth and fourteenth centuries were the heyday of Leicestershire architecture, but good buildings continue into later centuries. The church at Melton Mowbray, for instance, has a magnificent Perpendicular tower. Not to be missed are the delicious Gothick churches at Teigh and Stapleford, built at his own expense by an eighteenth-century Earl of Harborough who was in Holy Orders. The country houses of Leicestershire, for the most part, are comfortable Jacobean or Georgian squires' houses, often forming a picturesque group with the parish church, as at Nevill Holt, Prestwold, Noseley or Withcote. There are, however, some grander houses, including Belvoir, the culmination of early nineteenth-century Romanticism, and Burley-on-the-Hill (in Rutland), which is more like the palace of an eighteenth-century German prince than the seat of an average Midlands landowner. It has a huge colonnaded forecourt flanked by stable blocks, and was largely designed by its owner, the Earl of Nottingham himself. The villages and towns are also worthwhile. Uppingham and Oakham (both in Rutland) are pleasantly old-fashioned stone-built towns, which have hardly increased in size for 300 years. Ashby-de-la-Zouch in the north-west corner of the county, not far from the drab industrial area, is a fascinating and unspoilt place, whose architectural interest ranges from the massive ruins of a fifteenth-century castle to an abortive Regency spa. Leicester itself is largely a modern city built of red brick, but it contains an ancient nucleus of Roman ruins, Saxon and medieval churches, a Norman castle, a medieval Guildhall and a unique piece of Georgian town planning in the New Walk.

Although hardly to be described as 'unspoilt', Leicestershire offers much of architectural interest, set for the most part in attractive landscape. Late May is perhaps the best time to see it, when the leaves of the ash trees have at last come out, but while all is still fresh and green.

Appleby Magna

1; 6 miles SW of Ashby-de-la-Zouch off A453

The CHURCH OF ST MICHAEL, a large fourteenth-century church with west tower and thin spire, is unusual because it escaped Victorian 'restoration', and the appearance of the interior is largely the result of a Regency Gothick job of 1827. The roof has an elaborate plaster rib vault and there are Gothick pews and a west gallery. It is all a delightful surprise, as the outside gives no hint of what lies within. The east window has extremely odd, but original, Decorated tracery.

Ashby-de-la-Zouch

2; 6 miles NW of Coalville on A50

Although close to decaying industrial sprawl, this ancient and romantically named town is pleasantly unspoilt, thanks to the protection of the local landowners, descendants of the Hastings family, in the nineteenth century. Ashby is a very good place to study the revived feudalism of both the late Middle Ages and the Victorian era. It comprises a long, broad main street, Market Street, with the medieval nucleus of castle ruins and parish church at the north end and the unlikely remains of a Regency spa development at the south.

The CASTLE was slighted by the Parliamentarians in 1648, but it makes an impressive ruin and is neatly kept up, with immaculately mown lawns, by the Heritage Commission. It was founded in the twelfth century but in its present form is a grand late medieval country house rather than a fortification, having been largely rebuilt in the fourteenth century and then further remodelled and enlarged *c.*1473 by William, Lord Hastings, Chamberlain to Edward IV. The ruins surround two courtyards, with the Hall occupying the cross-range between the two. It dates from the fourteenth century, as does the solar adjoining it to the east. The huge kitchen is basically fourteenth-century but was refenestrated in the fifteenth; it was originally over 30 feet high and had a ribbed vault. Lord Hastings' main additions lie to the south and comprise a four-storeyed tower 90 feet tall, which was intended for his private apartments, rather like Ralph Cromwell's pretend-keep at Tattershall in Lincolnshire (*q.v.*). The source for this type of revived feudal display in fifteenth-century England is thought to be the châteaux of northern France and Flanders, which the English had come to know during the Hundred Years' War. The castle's private chapel also survives in ruins, its large Perpendicular windows now almost completely denuded of tracery.

Lord Hastings rebuilt the parish CHURCH OF ST HELEN in *c.*1474. It forms a group with the castle ruins and, like them, is proudly Perpendicular, with a west tower and broad-spreading nave. Some of the external stonework looks suspiciously new. This is because the two outer aisles were added by St Aubyn in 1878. Not normally a very sensitive architect, St Aubyn's additions here do little harm and transform the interior into a remarkably spacious affair, the nave being flanked by four wide aisles, two on each side. There is an air of well-being, derived not just from the church's spaciousness but from its general sense of being properly cared for. The wood-

work is lovingly polished; the pews have handsome needlework hassocks; there is heating in winter; and the Victorian clock at the back of the nave tells the right time and ticks contentedly. The nave is tall and channels the attention towards the altar in the chancel, but first look round and admire the brightly coloured and gilded Royal Arms on the west wall. The chancel has a carved Baroque reredos of attractively dark oak dated 1679 and reputed to be the work of Thomas Sabin, a local craftsman. The east window is a museum of sixteenth-century continental painted and heraldic glass roundels given to the church by the 3rd Lord Donington in 1924. More of it is displayed in the glazing of the Hastings Chapel adjoining. This is the climax of the church, full of monuments, hatchments and faded banners, and redolent of the sound of distant trumpets. It was carefully restored in 1924 by Lord Donington. The centrepiece is the magnificent alabaster tomb of Francis Hastings, 2nd Earl of Huntingdon, who died in 1561, and his wife Catherine de la Pole, niece of the Cardinal Archbishop of Canterbury. Hanging from the ceiling above are the cobwebby remains of Lord Huntingdon's Garter banner. All round the walls are further family monuments dating from the sixteenth to the twentieth centuries. The best is that to Theophilus, 9th Earl of Huntingdon, designed by William Kent. The sonorous epitaph was composed by Lord Bolingbroke and informs us of the Earl that 'HE ENOBLED NOBILITY BY VIRTUE. HE WAS OF THE FIRST RANK OF BOTH'. The beautiful bust of his widow Selina was carved by Rysbrack. Selina, Countess of Huntingdon, patroness of eighteenth-century Nonconformity and founder of the 'Countess of Huntingdon's Connexion', is herself buried under the chancel. (One wonders what she thinks of the mitre and episcopal vestments of the Bishop of Sarawak enshrined behind glass in the wall above her grave.) The churchyard is a perfect foil to the church, with lawns and attractive brick cottages along two sides and the former Ashby Grammar School, a seven-bay late Georgian house of 1807, next to the church gate.

There is much to be enjoyed in MARKET STREET as it descends gently to the south. The overall impression is of seemly Georgian brick but, as so often in English Midlands towns, there are one or two timber-framed survivors from an earlier age. The BULL'S HEAD pub claims to date from the fourteenth century – and why not? Opposite is the grandly Italianate TOWN HALL and market house – Victorian civic pride manifest in stone. Further down, two other timber-framed houses – one an antique shop and one a pub – face each other across the street. Bigger and better than the real thing is the jolly nineteenth-century Elizabethan of the MIDLAND BANK. There are several good old-fashioned shops and a merciful absence of boutiques, stripped pine and health-foodery. Owen's, the Chemist's, announces that it was 'established in the Reign of His Majesty King George IV' and Stones, Florists and Fruiterers, has an attractively painted and lettered late Georgian frontage. A detail that adds greatly to the townscape value of the street is the little island of houses in the middle where it is at its widest. The main defect is the heavy traffic pounding

Belvoir Castle.

through; it is scandalous that a by-pass has not yet been built – the benefit would be enormous.

Turning off Market Street into Bath Street there is a majestic view-stopper at the end of the latter in the form of a Gothic ELEANOR CROSS, taller than the surrounding houses, designed by Gilbert Scott in 1878 as a memorial to Edith, Countess of Loudon, Baroness Loudon, Tarrinzean, Mauchline, Botreaux, de Moleyns, Hungerford, and Hastings, Hereditary Bearer of one of the Golden Spurs. Note the heraldry. Just behind that, and equally arresting, is the Catholic CHURCH OF OUR LADY OF LOURDES, an ambitious structure with an arcaded apse and a tower with a little spire on top. It was built in 1908 to the design of F.A. Walters by the 15th Duke of Norfolk as a memorial to his first wife, Lady Flora Abney-Hastings, daughter of the Countess of Loudon, etc. (in her own right), and Lord Donington, the personification of late nineteenth-century new-Feudalism. Pevsner asks 'Why Norman?' The answer is that the founder of the Hastings family, Gilbert de Hastings, was a Norman (appointed Portreeve of Hastings by William the Conqueror). The interior of the church is movingly simple, with bare stone walls, majestic round arches, transepts and a painted and gilded *baldacchino* over the altar.

This leaves just one more area to be explored – that of the early nineteenth-century attempt at developing Ashby into a spa. It includes one rather moth-eaten terrace, the red brick ROYAL HOTEL with stone Doric porch, designed by Robert Chaplin in 1826, and, best of all, the former railway station – as Greek as possible, but now rather insensitively converted into a house. The Baths themselves have, unfortunately, been demolished.

Belvoir Castle
3; 16 miles SE of Nottingham off A52
Belvoir is the apotheosis of the early nineteenth-century castle and has remained remarkably untouched since its completion in the 1820s. The old Caroline house on the site was demolished in 1801 and replaced by the 5th Duke of Rutland and his wife (herself an amateur artist and a lady of pronounced aesthetic tastes) to the design of James Wyatt. In 1816 a terrible fire destroyed two sides of the castle. It was immediately rebuilt in an even grander version of Wyatt's Gothic to the design of the Duke's Chaplain, the Rev. Sir John Thoroton, though James Wyatt's three sons – Matthew Cotes, Benjamin Dean and Philip William Wyatt – were called upon to design the interiors in a variety of styles. These include Gothic, Norman, French, Italianate and Chinese, and form a fascinating cross-section of the whole spectrum of early nineteenth-century taste.

The Guardroom, staircases and Ballroom are all by Thoroton in a highly effective Gothic style and form a spatially dramatic sequence. The principal room in the castle, the Elizabeth Saloon, was designed in 1823 by Matthew Cotes Wyatt in the 'Louis XIV' style, of which it is the earliest example in England. The ceiling, depicting Jupiter, Juno and other gods, was painted by Wyatt, who also carved the white marble statue of the Duchess, after whom the room was named; it is dramatically placed in front of a looking-glass. The carpet was specially woven at Tournai for the room, while the black marble and Florentine mosaic cabinets against the walls are the acme of early nineteenth-century luxury. The white-and-gold Dining Room, by contrast, is Italianate,

The church of St Mary, Bottesford.

with a richly coffered ceiling. It contains examples from the famous Rutland collection of late seventeenth-century silver, and a jolly eccentricity is provided by the marble pedestal by M.C. Wyatt with a *trompe l'œil* tablecloth.

The Picture Gallery is a spectacular room influenced by the Baths of Diocletian in Rome. Apart from the paintings, it contains several exceptional treasures, including a splendid seventeenth-century state bed with its original cut-velvet upholstery, and a sixteenth-century silver-gilt and agate ewer and basin which are among the finest surviving pieces of English plate of that period outside the Kremlin. The most important paintings at Belvoir are the Poussin *Sacraments*, bought by the 4th Duke in Rome in 1786 on the advice of Sir Joshua Reynolds. There are also good Dutch paintings, swagger portraits by Reynolds, landscapes by Gainsborough, and Van Dyck's sketch of *The Procession of the Order of the Garter*, which was intended for a mural decoration at Whitehall Palace; there are also some good miniatures. The Regent's Gallery, 131 feet long, escaped the fire of 1816. It contains a series of rose-coloured Gobelins tapestries depicting the adventures of Don Quixote, bought by the 5th Duchess in Paris, and a notable series of portrait busts by Nollekens. The Gothic Chapel, which concludes the tour of the castle, has a soaring plaster vault and an altarpiece framing a painting by Murillo.

Bottesford

4; 15¼ miles E of Nottingham on A52

In June 1825 Elizabeth, 5th Duchess of Rutland, died suddenly of appendicitis at Belvoir (*q.v.*). Her funeral at Bottesford was a remarkable feudal pageant. The procession, accompanied by the tolling of many bells, took three hours to reach the CHURCH OF ST MARY from the castle. A long line of tenants and servants, all dressed in black, escorted the Duchess's empty carriage and her favourite white horse led by a groom. Finally came the hearse, flanked by four pages carrying silver-tipped staves. In front walked the house steward bearing her coronet on a cushion of purple velvet. She was not to remain at Bottesford for long, however, as her disconsolate husband built a Neo-Norman mausoleum in the grounds of Belvoir for her and all the later Dukes of Rutland are buried there; but from the sixteenth century to the eighteenth successive generations of the Manners family had been buried at Bottesford and their tombs fill the church; the array of sixteenth- and seventeenth-century memorials to consecutive Earls of Rutland is without parallel.

Architecturally, the church is rather upstaged by the funerary sculpture, but it is impressive enough in itself – mainly Perpendicular with a crocketed spire 113 feet high. The interior is well proportioned, with bare stone walls, tall arcades and clerestory. Over the chancel arch are displayed the Royal Arms of Queen Victoria, moulded in plaster; it looks rather like the proscenium arch in a theatre. It is almost impossible to see the altar for the serried ranks of tombs in the chancel. The first six Earls all have tombs of local alabaster. The 1st Earl, who died in 1543, is nearest the altar, with effigies of himself and his wife on a Renaissance tomb-chest. He is somewhat overshadowed by the 2nd Earl, whose tomb is also free-standing in the middle of the chancel, but further west; it is two storeys high with fat balusters at the corners, rather like the bulbous legs of an Elizabethan table or four-poster bed. The 3rd and 4th Earls face each other from the side-walls and have identical Jacobean monuments by Nicholas Johnson. The grandest of all is the 6th Earl, he and his two wives lying on shelves one above the other in a towering architectural framework the top of which almost scrapes the roof. The 7th and 8th Earls, by contrast, have seventeenth-century Baroque monuments of marble by Grinling Gibbons, no less, with figures in Roman costume and a theatrical flavour. The atmosphere of noble mortality is completed by an arrangement of hatchments and two sets of funeral armour hanging above.

Breedon on the Hill

5; 6 miles NE of Ashby-de-la-Zouch on A453

As you drive around the fascinating stretch of country between Derby and Ashby-de-la-Zouch in pursuit of architectural thrills, you are watched by the CHURCH OF ST MARY, dramatically placed on top of a rocky cliff like some robber baron's castle in central Italy. Visually the church is very impressive, but it is also of considerable archaeological interest, as it was a Saxon religious site and contains a museum-scale collection of Saxon sculptured fragments. It has a complicated history, and till the Dissolution was a monastic foundation – which explains various oddities in the architecture, a substantial portion of the building having disappeared at the Reformation. The tower, for instance, was originally a crossing-tower, while the present church (which dates from the thirteenth century) was merely the chancel of the monastic church. The nave has disappeared. The fact that the church is only a remnant of a grander composition explains various ambitious features, such as the stone vaulting of the aisles. The interior is memorable because it is crammed with seventeenth- and eighteenth-century furnishings, including box pews and a two-decker pulpit. The Shirley family pew, erected in 1627, is a theatrical fantasy, with heraldic cartouches and obelisks on the corners.

Burley-on-the-Hill

6; 3 miles NE of Oakham on B668

A proud and patrician pile which stands 500 feet up, overlooking the Vale of Catmose with the air of being monarch of all it surveys. It was built on an old site by Daniel Finch, 2nd Earl of Nottingham, between 1694 and 1705 under the supervision of Henry Dormer and John Lumley, local masons and surveyors. The layout is sweepingly Baroque, the central block being flanked by lesser office wings connected by short quadrant links. Beyond them are further colonnades and a pair of outer office ranges framing a palatial forecourt. It looks like a rural version of Bernini's Piazza in front of St Peter's in Rome. It seems likely that this grandiose design was Lord Nottingham's own idea. Before starting work he had obtained some advice from Wren and studied various recent houses in London for ideas. The interior of Burley was damaged by fire in 1912 but the staircase and Dining Room escaped. The former is like a magnified version of a staircase in a contemporary London house, with barley-sugar balusters and murals on the wall painted by

Lanscroon. The late eighteenth-century Dining Room is elegantly neo-classical, with attenuated Adamesque plasterwork, and was designed by James Lewis. The park was landscaped by Repton.

Tucked away behind one of the colonnades is the parish church, the CHURCH OF THE HOLY CROSS. It was largely reconstructed by Pearson *c*.1870 and is of comparatively little interest, though it contains a beautiful monument to Charlotte Finch, by Sir Francis Chantrey, in the form of a kneeling white marble figure inspired by Canova's Magdalene.

Clipsham

7; 7 miles NW of Stamford off A1

Famous as the name of one of the most splendid of English building stones, this village *was* a handsome demonstration of its merits, with medieval church and Georgian Hall side by side in parkland, and a loose layout of seventeenth-century cottages and farmhouses in pretty gardens to the south. Almost inconceivably, however, the planning authority has recently permitted to be built four little 'in-fill' houses of *orange* concrete blocks, totally wrong in colour and texture and irrevocably wrecking the visual harmony of the village. What can be done with them? They are too close to the road to be planted out, and they will never weather or mellow.

The CHURCH OF ST MARY is Victorianised. It has a complicated form of spire decorated round the base with little model castles. The interior is cream-washed and has one Norman arcade with round arches and scallop capitals. There is bad Victorian glass in the windows, which casts a pall. CLIPSHAM HALL is dignified eighteenth-century with a façade ten windows wide and a pediment. The approach from the east is along a unique nineteenth-century avenue of topiary figures, now maintained by the Forestry Commission and open to the public.

Burley-on-the-Hill.

Coleorton Hall

8; 2 miles E of Ashby-de-la-Zouch on A512

Coleorton was once the house of the distinguished Regency connoisseur and amateur artist, Sir George Beaumont. He was the patron of Constable and Landseer, and a prime mover in founding the National Gallery, to which he left his picture collection. He built this house in 1804–8, to the design of George Dance the Younger. Dance was one of the most original English architects of the day, equally happy working in a severe neo-classical style or playing around with exercises in Moorish-Gothic, as here. Beaumont described Dance as 'not only an able architect, but an old friend who I am persuaded will exert himself on this occasion'. The original conception has been somewhat altered by the addition in 1862 of a second storey by F.P. Cockerell. With its original landscape (now spoilt), Coleorton was a notable Picturesque composition. A dramatic stone-vaulted *porte-cochère* leads through a vestibule to a central polygonal Hall, where twelve thin-pointed arches surround an open well rising through the full height of the house. This Gothic tribune was obviously inspired by the work of Dance's old master, Sir John Soane. The spatial drama is strengthened by coloured stained glass in the windows of the lantern above. The austere, not to say stark, principal staircase rises to one side and is approached through one of the arches. The main rooms are plain and are not enhanced by the present use of the building as Coal Board offices.

Donington-le-Heath

9; 5 miles SE of Ashby-de-la-Zouch

The MANOR HOUSE is the oldest house in Leicestershire; it dates from *c.*1280. It is an irregular structure of stone and half-timber surrounding a small courtyard, with the Hall on the first floor and the great kitchen below. The house has been restored and refurnished by the county council.

The church of St Mary, Ketton.

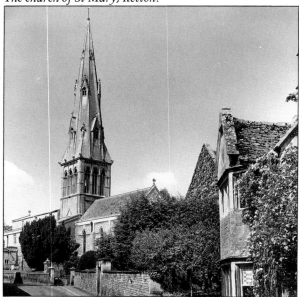

Empingham

10; 6 miles E of Oakham on A606

This is a large stone-built village with a central green. It is dominated by the thirteenth-century CHURCH OF ST PETER with its tall west tower and steeple. The nave is a century older, with unmatched arcades and lofty clerestory. The fifteenth-century roof of carved oak is enlivened with angels. In the chancel is a handsome sedilia combined with a piscina and embellished with sophisticated carved leaf decoration. The whole has an episcopal grandeur – not inappropriate, as the church was a Peculiar of the See of Lincoln in the Middle Ages.

Gaddesby

11; 6 miles SW of Melton Mowbray on B674

From a distance just the spire of the church is visible above the fields, as the village of Gaddesby lies in a hollow. It is made up of one or two brick cottages, a pub, far too much new housing of a suburban type, and the splendid central group of Hall and church.

The CHURCH OF ST LUKE is worth a long detour. The west front makes an attractive, balanced but not absolutely symmetrical composition. In the middle is the tower with a well-proportioned broach spire, and, to either side, the ends of the wide aisles have Decorated windows. The end of the south aisle is the more spectacular, with decorative carving and a triangular window with curvilinear tracery, and a doorway under, all forming part of the same elaborate composition. It is almost Iberian in its richness. The interior of the church has a gentle, poetic atmosphere, with old silvery-grey woodwork, limewashed walls, venerable oak benches and an uneven floor pavement of stone and tiles. Through the Victorian rood-screen, with polished brass gates, is the amazing spectacle of a life-size white marble horse in the sanctuary. This is the monument to Colonel Edward Cheney, who lost four mounts in succession on the field of Waterloo; this is one of them collapsing under him – a wonderfully realistic tableau by Joseph Gott. Note the Napoleonic colours on the plinth and the minutely carved wheat on the surface under the horse.

GADDESBY HALL stands well on a balustraded terrace next to the church and is surrounded by cedar trees. It is two storeyed and built of red brick, with canted bays at either end and white-painted sash windows.

Hallaton

12; 8 miles NE of Market Harborough off B664

Hallaton is an attractive village, full of prosperous houses and therefore less spoilt by badly designed recent development than many humbler, but once equally interesting, places have been. There are two greens, a large one on the edge of the village with a duck pond and white-painted rails round it, and a smaller one nearer the church with a war memorial cross and a less conventional VILLAGE CROSS in the form of a solid stone cone like an old-fashioned sugar loaf. The cottages and houses are partly brick and partly stone, some with stone-tiled roofs and some thatched.

The CHURCH OF ST MICHAEL makes a splendid picture from the sugar loaf, with its projecting chancel and

Kirby Muxloe Castle.

flanking recessed chapels of similar dimensions, all with large Decorated windows, and a tall broach spire rising above at the west end. The interior of the church contains Norman evidence but the general effect is Transitional/Early English. The roofs are, however, a Victorian rebuilding, and much of the stained glass, which casts an appropriately religious gloom over everything, is by Kempe. The outside is perhaps more impressive than the inside; and the churchyard is unusually attractive, with eighteenth-century stone and slate headstones and, against the chancel, a jolly late Rococo monument to the Rev. George Fennicke, who died in 1760.

Ketton

13; 4 miles SW of Stamford on A6121
A characteristic Rutland village with handsome seventeenth-century cottages built of local honey-coloured limestone. The parish CHURCH OF ST MARY, however, is of Barnack stone. It has one of the most distinguished spires in a county noted for fine spires. This dates from *c.*1300 and is of superlative proportions and design, shooting into the sky above the crossing; it took fifty years to build. The chancel, rebuilt in 1863 by T.G. Jackson, matches the spire in scale and is of a uniform grandeur; as a result, the best views of the church are from the east. The nave is older and more irregular. The west front is largely Norman. The interior has benefited from twentieth-century furnishings and decoration, which have contributed an aura of 'the beauty of Holiness' to the grandeur of the architecture. In the east window there is stained glass by Sir Ninian Comper, who also designed the high altar, and the chancel roof has colourful painted decoration by Sir Charles Nicholson. The graveyard is full of interesting gravestones dating from the seventeenth to the nineteenth century, all made of Ketton stone.

King's Norton

14; 6 miles E of Leicester off A47
The CHURCH OF ST JOHN THE BAPTIST is a *tour de force* of eighteenth-century Gothic Revival, designed by John Wing the Younger, of Leicester, in 1760–75. It is large and stately with a tall west tower, traceried windows under ogee arches, buttresses carrying pinnacles, and decorative pierced parapets round the top of the walls and tower. When it was first built there was also a spire on top of the tower, but this was struck by lightning and demolished in 1850. It would have added yet more to the seriousness of the design, which is a remarkably convincing exercise for its date. The interior is miraculously untouched, with the original box pews, pulpit, organ, communion rail and Gothic reredos.

King's Norton is one of the most impressive Georgian churches in England. It was built at the expense of William Fortrey, the local squire, whose handsome monument (he died in 1783) is situated in the graveyard near the east end of the church.

Kirby Muxloe Castle

15; 3 miles W of Leicester on B5380
The ruins are those of a great fifteenth-century country house rather than of a proper castle. It was built by Lord Hastings of Ashby-de-la-Zouch (*q.v.*) in the 1480s on the site of a fourteenth-century house, the foundations of which remain. Lord Hastings' castle-house is rectangular in plan, with four corner towers and a mighty Gatehouse, all surrounded by a moat 360 by 300 feet. It was built of red brick with diaper patterns of blue vitrified headers, brick being the height of aristocratic fashion in the fifteenth century. Only the west tower and the Gatehouse still stand to any height. The latter is broad and symmetrical with the central archway flanked by angular turrets. The west tower is three storeys high and battlemented, with a taller staircase turret.

Langham

16; 2 miles NW of Oakham on A606

The CHURCH OF ST PETER AND ST PAUL is a noble building of ashlar stone with battlements to the aisles and the top parapet. The south side, with its well-proportioned porch, is a beautiful composition. The west tower and richly ornamented spire are earlier than the nave — thirteenth- rather than fourteenth-century. The interior is spacious and full of light, as the windows are mainly clear-glazed.

The large village of Langham is partly red brick and partly stone, built on a complicated plan, which Hoskins attributed to the place having originated as a clearing in the forest.

Leicester

17; 16 miles S of Nottingham on A6

Leicester is reputed to have been the most prosperous town in England in the 1960s and a considerable amount of redevelopment occurred at that time, making the centre into something of a Midlands version of Croydon. Most of the new building, unfortunately, is not of any very high standard. James Stirling's ENGINEERING BUILDING at the University, however, is among the more important pieces of English post-war architecture, with its canted, geometrical composition, and its finishes of red engineering brick and patent glazing in romantic evocation of industrial buildings. It is something of an object of pilgrimage for architectural students from overseas.

Despite appearances, Leicester is an ancient town with Roman remains as well as several Norman and medieval buildings amidst the modern development. The centre of the old city is the CASTLE, founded in 1088. It houses the Assize Court, refronted in brick in 1690, but containing the castle's original Great Hall, which dates from between 1140 and 1160. It is a fine Norman room with stone walls and an open timber roof of braced beams. Adjoining the castle is THE NEWARKE (New Work), a walled enclosure of 400 acres containing Wyggeston's CHANTRY HOUSE of 1511, now a museum, and the Elizabethan SKEFFINGTON HOUSE. On the east side of the Newarke is a picturesque stone gateway with three arches.

In Castle Yard stands the CHURCH OF ST MARY DE CASTRO, a Saxon foundation but altered and enlarged at different dates in the Middle Ages. The pinnacled tower is thirteenth-century, its slender spire added a century later and then rebuilt in 1783. The exterior was thoroughly restored by George Gilbert Scott, which, as so often, makes the building seem more Victorian than it really is. The interior is an instructive patchwork of different architectural styles and dates, with important Norman bits. The chancel, rebuilt *c*.1160, is a sumptuous piece of late Norman architecture, with large round-arched windows and a richly carved sedilia with zigzag decoration on the arches. The whole of the south side of the church was rebuilt in the fourteenth century to form an aisle chapel as wide again as the nave. This has an enormous east window with geometrical tracery, which is splendid enough in itself but completely unbalances the original church to which it is attached.

ST NICHOLAS'S is even older than St Mary's, being built on a Roman site; the adjoining Jewry wall, in fact, is the most prominent survivor of Roman Leicester. St Nicholas's itself is an early Saxon church dating from the seventh century. The nave survives, with venerable rubble stone walls. The windows have arched heads re-using Roman bricks. The tower also re-uses Roman bricks, which are arranged in herringbone patterns as they are in the tower at St Alban's Cathedral, and has two tiers of blank round arches. It dates from the late eleventh century and was restored in 1904–5.

ST MARTIN'S was the parish church of Leicester, but was raised to cathedral status in 1927. It is medieval, but was substantially reconstructed in the nineteenth century by a series of architects, including Raphael Brandon, J.L. Pearson and G.F. Bodley, with the result that it looks more like a prosperous Victorian town church than anything else. The interior has been much enriched since becoming a cathedral; there are elaborate canopied stalls, and the Bishop's throne has a pinnacle of receding tiers of carved tracery 16 feet high, reaching nearly to the roof. These, together with the organ case, were designed by Sir Charles Nicholson in 1927.

Next to the cathedral is the medieval GUILDHALL, built originally for the Corpus Christi Guild, which had been founded in 1347. It became the Town Hall in the fifteenth century. It is L-shaped and timber-framed. The interior contains a seventeenth-century Library in the east wing and the old Mayor's Parlour with elaborate Jacobean woodwork.

Away from the nucleus of castle and churches, the other part of central Leicester worth a look is the NEW WALK. This was laid out as a promenade in 1785 and survives as a pedestrian walk, lined with trees and some late Georgian houses, though these are now, alas, mixed with unsympathetic later intruders. Some are stuccoed with incised pilasters, some are brick. The Crescent, which has a pedimented centre, is the most distinguished group, dating from 1810.

Lyddington

18; 22 miles E of Leicester off A6003

This is a pretty village of sixteenth- and seventeenth-century ironstone houses and cottages nestling comfortably in a hollow. There is a large green on which stands the stump of a medieval cross, and the main street is lined with neat grass verges. In the centre, set back behind a high wall with a watchtower resembling a gazebo on the corner, is THE BEDE HOUSE — a medieval summer palace of the Bishops of Lincoln. It dates from the fifteenth century and is an unusually well-preserved piece of late medieval domestic architecture, now maintained by the Heritage Commission. Next to it is the parish CHURCH OF ST ANDREW, surmounted by a dumpy broach spire dating from the fourteenth century. The main part of the church is fifteenth-century Perpendicular with an unusually light and elegant interior. There are tall moulded piers supporting the clerestory, the walls are limewashed, and the windows have clear glazing through which the light pours in. The fifteenth-century rood-screen has traces of original painting in the lower panels – some flowers can be made out but no figures. Unfortunately, the plaster was scraped from the chancel walls in 1890 leaving the rubble stone exposed as it was never meant to be; it ought to be plastered over again and limewashed like the nave. The most unusual feature of the church is the position of the altar, which sits in the middle of a raised enclosure – a rare survival of the Laudian arrangement. The rails date from 1635 but the oak communion table was made in 1662 and cost 19/6d.

Market Harborough
19; 12¼ miles SE of Leicester on A6

Founded by Henry II as a market town, the visual centre of the place is still the MARKET SQUARE. It is a spacious triangle focusing on the magnificent spire of the parish church – the most impressive and most beautiful spire in Leicestershire. The square is surrounded by pleasant late Georgian buildings, and the architectural sequence is continued along the High Street and Church Street, which run parallel to each other. In the High Street are some Georgian houses and the THREE SWANS INN, which displays an elaborate wrought-iron bracketed inn sign. The TOWN HALL dates from 1788 and contributes an air of stateliness with its arcaded ground floor and a Venetian window upstairs. North of the Town Hall the High Street widens and contains the best buildings, including the Victorian CORN EXCHANGE, the ANGEL HOTEL and various Georgian houses.

Retracing your steps to the Market Square, the parish CHURCH OF ST DIONYSIUS is the special glory of Market Harborough. The main part of the building is Perpendicular, with aisles and clerestory and battlemented parapets. But it is the fourteenth-century west tower that holds the eye, soaring upwards and perfect in its proportions and details. It has none of the eccentric chunkiness of some medieval spires; all is effortlessly graceful and dignified. The resources of the medieval builders were obviously lavished on the spire at the expense of the rest. The interior has a nice unrestored feel, with early nineteenth-century galleries in the aisles and the Royal Arms of Charles II in a plaster cartouche. The chancel has an impressive original timber roof, and stained glass by Hardman in the east window.

Melton Mowbray
20; 11 miles NE of Leicester on A607

Melton Mowbray was once the capital of hunting country, but now looks as if it has gone down in the world. The remaining Victorian hunting boxes round the edge of the town are engulfed in recent suburbs of 'Spec. Builders' allsorts', and the main streets are full of rather poor shops with cheap plastic shop-fronts. There is not much here to cater for the gentry now, but the fabric of the town survives and with very little effort could still be made to look attractive.

The principal building of Melton is the parish CHURCH OF ST MARY – the grandest church in the county. (Visitors should be warned that, like a village post office, it shuts for lunch and so you will not be able to get in round about midday.) The stately Perpendicular tower is 100 feet high, crowned with pinnacles and a little central lead cap. Much of the internal grandeur of the church derives from the addition of aisles flanking the transepts – a feature usually reserved for cathedrals, not mere parish churches; they add enormously to the drama of the diagonal vistas through the columns of the nave. Equally amazing is the clerestory – a continuous run of no fewer than forty-eight Perpendicular windows. Note the gargoyles, including a sheep and alligator, on the north choir aisle parapet.

The church stands in a pleasant backwater overlooked by pretty cottages on the south side. On the other side is the MAISON DIEU, a symmetrical Jacobean building dated 1640 and restored in 1891. Further out on the same side as the church is the HOUSE OF 'ANNE OF CLEVES', a medieval clergy house with some old traceried windows. It is now a restaurant. The Market Place is a good space, but not improved by some ugly paving and shop-fronts. The High Street and South Parade are largely three-storeyed Georgian brick with pubs and shops, but all a bit scruffy at the time of visiting. YE OLDE PORK PIE HOUSE sells the 'original' Melton Mowbray pies.

Mount St Bernard
21; 5 miles NE of Coalville off B512

The ABBEY here was founded in 1835 for Cistercian monks at the instigation of Ambrose Lisle March Phillipps de Lisle, a Leicestershire landowner and somewhat eccentric Catholic convert. The architect was A.W.N. Pugin. Building was slow, despite the generous backing of Lord Shrewsbury, and the monastic buildings were not finished until 1844. The church was begun in 1843. Pugin had a special talent for monastic buildings, clergy houses and subsidiary ecclesiastical buildings; he felt free to treat them more casually and simply than his churches, and their informal grouping and convenient plans make them among his most attractive works. The buildings at Mount St Bernard are built of rough rubble stone, which immediately gives them an air of authenticity. The ranges round the Cloisters have plain lancet windows and arched doorways, and broad strong buttresses and chimneystacks. Wistaria climbs the walls, and neatly maintained flower-beds enliven the lawns of the quadrangle. It is a remarkably convincing medieval picture. Pugin's original chapter house is now the Sacristy. It is rectangular with an arrangement of stepped lancets in the east wall. The present Chapter House dates from 1870 and is polygonal. Pugin's church was enlarged and altered in 1934–9. A large crossing-tower was added, together with a new nave. These additions are in a simple Gothic style that blends well with Pugin's work. The whole abbey makes an attractive group, set in the wild rocky landscape of Charnwood Forest, the most dramatic part of Leicestershire.

Nevill Holt
22; 8 miles NE of Market Harborough off B664

The road passes through heraldic gatepiers into parkland with a double avenue of limes and chestnuts, then turns a corner to reveal a knockout group: a long low medieval house, a Gothic church with spire and a late seventeenth-century stable block, all cheek by jowl in a drawn-out line along a ridge, surveying a grand view over the valley to Corby and Rockingham on the Northamptonshire hilltop opposite. The HALL is now a prep school – a good use for it because, unlike public schools, prep schools can use old houses without sprouting hideous shacks all around. It was heavily remodelled in the early nineteenth century, and much of the façade is stuccoed, but embedded in the middle are two spectacular fourteenth- or fifteenth-century bay windows and a mighty two-storeyed porch, all of richly carved stone with decorative battlements along the top. It makes a lordly ensemble.

The CHURCH OF ST MARY feels more like a private chapel than a parish church. It is quite small, but with a cruciform plan dating mainly from the thirteenth century. Unfortunately, the interior has been scraped and hideously pointed in grey cement. There is a dark Jacobean pulpit with all-over carving like embroidery. The south transept is a family chapel containing tombs to the Nevill family, who once lived here. A last delightful touch at Nevill Holt is the eighteenth-century *chinoiserie* clock cupola over the stable block.

Noseley

23; 8 miles N of Market Harborough off B6047

NOSELEY HALL and the CHURCH OF ST MARY sit side by side deep in a private park. If you wish to see the church it is best to ask at the estate office rather than braving the stone gatepiers crowned with eagles at the main entrance. The church is thirteenth-century and was originally a private chapel. It contains crisply carved fifteenth-century stalls arranged college-wise; they are embellished with wooden cockerels, the badge of the Staunton family. There is also a series of monuments to the Hazelriggs, who acquired Noseley by marriage in the fifteenth century and still live here.

Nevill Holt.

Oakham

24; 9¼ miles SE of Melton Mowbray on A606

The former county town of Rutland is hardly bigger than a village, but it is given dignity by several ambitious buildings and a well-proportioned L-shaped MARKET PLACE. Here stands a market cross in the form of a polygonal timber arcade with stone-tiled roof and a baby brother in the form of an old pump under a similar roof. The HIGH STREET, too, is lined with seemly stone buildings spanning the chronological range from medieval to Victorian. The town is dominated by ALL SAINTS, the parish church – a grand Perpendicular set-piece, except for the fourteenth-century tower and steeple flanked by four pepperpot turrets. The interior is spacious and well lit, with elegant arcades and tall clerestory windows. The capitals of the nave arcade are all carved with little biblical scenes demonstrating the Fall and Redemption of Man, including the Expulsion of Adam and Eve from the Garden and the Annunciation.

OAKHAM CASTLE is more a fortified house than a castle, and contains the best-preserved Norman Great Hall in England. This dates from *c.*1180–90 and is flanked by arcades of columns supporting the roof (as Westminster Hall originally was). The arches have dogtooth carving, and the capitals are of an elegant leaf design. Round the walls hangs a unique collection of ceremonial horseshoes: for centuries Oakham has exacted a horseshoe from any member of the Royal Family passing through.

OAKHAM SCHOOL, like so many English schools, comprises mainly Victorian buildings in Tudor style. But the original little block of 1584 still stands in the middle, embellished with learned inscriptions in Latin, Greek and Hebrew.

Prestwold Hall

25; 3 miles NE of Loughborough off A60

Prestwold is an eighteenth-century H-plan house remodelled and refaced in Ancaster stone by the architect William Burn in 1843 for Charles William Packe, and now chiefly of interest as a good example of early Victorian classical architecture. The Entrance Hall has excellent original decoration, with artificial marbling in green, brown and red, and rich polychrome ceiling paintings inspired by the Raphael *loggie* in Rome. The lunettes have simulated porphyry backgrounds. Similar decoration is continued in the adjoining vaulted passages. The other rooms are comparatively plain, but are nicely furnished and contain interesting family portraits. The Library was refitted by Gillow in 1875.

ST ANDREW'S, the parish church, is situated in the park close to the house and is largely a Victorian rebuilding with medieval bits. The chancel is crammed with family monuments and the atmosphere is one of continuing feudal patriarchy. (The present Packe squire has already had his coffin made from oak grown on the estate.) The procession of monuments through the centuries begins with a fifteenth-century alabaster tomb-chest and, for the moment, ends with a terracotta angel to Edward Henry Packe, who died in 1946. This is by Arnold Machin, best known for the profile bust of the Queen on English postage stamps. Of earlier monuments, Sir

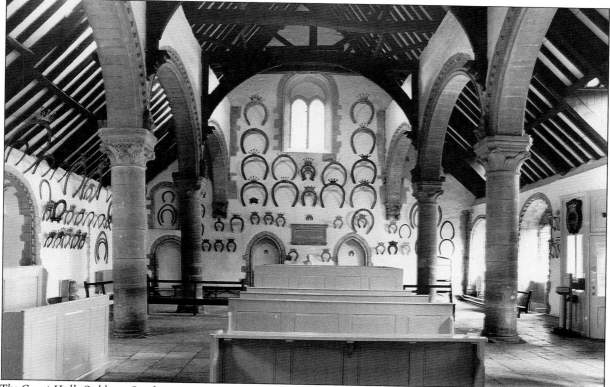

The Great Hall, Oakham Castle.

Christopher Packe's late seventeenth-century Baroque reredos tomb is typical of its date. Sadly poignant is that by Westmacott, Junior, for Charles Henry Packe, who died at school in 1842; he lies in his Eton clothes on a marble mattress.

Quenby Hall

26; 7 miles NE of Leicester off A47 [27]

Quenby is a handsome red brick Jacobean house built in *c.*1620 by George Ashby and carefully restored in 1906 under the direction of G.F. Bodley. It is well sited on a hillside with a wide prospect of good hunting country. The house was bought by Squire de Lisle in 1972 to replace his original family seat at Garendon, which was demolished in 1964. Quenby now contains the family heirlooms which once were housed at Garendon and it was extensively restored and redecorated in 1974–7.

The interior owes much to Bodley's rehabilitation of 1906. The Hall, for instance, was restored to its old proportions by him, though it retains the original panelled screen. The stone fireplace with the March Phillipps de Lisle arms was inserted by the present owner. The Ballroom was formed by Bodley and has an elaborate plaster ceiling copied from Knole and old panelling brought from elsewhere. The Library contains a Gothic chimneypiece from Garendon by E.W. Pugin. The Brown Parlour, Pomegranate Room (with intricate frieze), Library (with a fine ceiling) and Dining Room are the best of the original Jacobean rooms and have good panelling, stucco work and stone chimneypieces.

Queniborough

27; 6 miles NE of Leicester on A607

This village, near Leicester, comprises a wide street with brick, stone and timber-framed cottages focusing on the CHURCH OF ST MARY. This is of different dates, with a part-Norman chancel and Decorated nave aisles. The most impressive feature, as so often in Leicester and Rutland, is the magnificent west tower and spire. The spire is unusually thin and elegant, and richly crocketed with three tiers of lucarnes. The tower from which it rises is nicely polychrome, with pink stone walls and white stone dressings.

Stanford Hall

28; 4 miles SE of Lutterworth on B5414

Stanford Hall is a fine William and Mary house, designed and built by William and Francis Smith of Warwick, beginning in 1690, for Sir Roger Cave, the ancestor of the present owner, Lord Braye. He built it as a replacement for the old manor house, home of the family since 1430, which he pulled down. It is constructed of brick, but the main entrance front (on the south side) is faced in ashlar stone. The house stands in the centre of a system of eighteenth-century avenues in an attractive park through which the River Avon flows; it has been dammed to form a lake near the house. The stables adjoining the Hall are an admirable early eighteenth-century design of red brick by Francis Smith. They were restored in 1981 with the help of a grant from the Historic Buildings Council.

The church of the Holy Trinity, Staunton Harold.

The spine of the house is a marble-floored passage from which the main rooms open. The Library is lined with bookcases containing about 5000 volumes and some interesting historical documents, including an eye-witness account of the trial and execution of Charles I and a manuscript speech delivered by Sir Francis Bacon in the House of Commons. The Ballroom has a high coved ceiling with paintings by Joubert installed in 1880. The portraits belonged to Henry, Cardinal York, last of the royal Stuarts, and other Stuart and Catholic relics in the house attest to the Brayes' return to the faith of their ancestors. The Green Drawing Room has a seventeenth-century bolection-moulded chimneypiece and Rococo plaster ceiling, while the adjoining Grey Drawing Room, now the chief family sitting room, has a marble neo-classical chimneypiece.

Stapleford Park

29; 3 miles E of Melton Mowbray off B676
Situated in the middle of the Leicestershire hunting country, 5 miles from Melton Mowbray (*q.v.*) and surrounded by a large and finely wooded park, Stapleford is a composite house representing three main building periods. Its most striking feature is the earliest, the Gothic Old Wing, inscribed and dated 1500. This has an extraordinary display of carved decoration – both heraldry and standing figures of saints, kings and ancestors in canopied niches – which, like the top storey with its scrolly dormers, was added in 1633.

The main part of the house, forming a U, dates from the late seventeenth century and has sashed windows and a hipped roof. The open side was unfortunately filled in in the late nineteenth century with a new 'Jacobean' front and at the same time much of the interior was also remodelled in a variety of period styles. The work, however, was not completed and the Long Gallery has never received the elaborate plasterwork designed for it.

The Entrance Hall has a late eighteenth-century-style ceiling, while the Anteroom and Lady Gretton's Sitting Room have seventeenth-century panelling. The Library and Drawing Room are both Edwardian 'Georgian' of the type associated with the fashionable decorators Lenygon and Morant. The Dining Room has seventeenth-century woodwork from another room in the house but was entirely rearranged and embellished in the Edwardian period. At the time of visiting it seems likely that the house will be converted into a hotel.

Near the house in the park is the delightful Gothick CHURCH OF ST MARY MAGDALENE, built by the 4th Earl of Harborough in 1783 to the design of George Richardson. Inside there is a fine fifteenth-century brass and a tomb by Rysbrack.

Staunton Harold

30; 6 miles N of Ashby-de-la-Zouch on B587
Includes the church of the Holy Trinity (NT)
There is a poignant contrast between the dumpy dark stone CHURCH OF THE HOLY TRINITY (NT) and the gracious red brick STAUNTON HAROLD HALL with its palatial air and statue-inhabited roofline. A small lake, a few cedars, and a couple of bizarre Baroque gateways complete an ensemble that will always be haunted by the doomed Shirleys, who departed over twenty years ago – for ever? The house was saved by Group Captain Cheshire as one of his homes for old people and the church was given to the National Trust.

The church was built in the seventeenth century, in the middle of the Commonwealth, in pure Perpendicular style; it is a noble survival. Over the door is the proud inscription (which it is difficult to read without being moved to tears): 'When all things sacred were throughout ye nation Either demollisht or profaned Sir Richard Shirley Barronet founded this Church whose singular praise it is to have done ye best things in ye worst times And hoped them in the most callamitous. The righteous shall be had in everlasting remembrance.' And with these words ringing in our ears we pass into the interior, which is unequalled in England for the completeness and perfect preservation of its fittings. The piers are enclosed in oak panelling almost to the height of the capitals and there are oak box pews complete with their original brass candlesticks. At services, which are still held here every Sunday, the sexes are segregated – the men on the right and women on the left. In the west gallery is a seventeenth-century organ with an outsize semi-circular pediment like a large cocked hat; and at the other end of the nave are the original pulpit and lectern. The wooden-boarded ceiling is painted to look like the sky with grey clouds scudding across, and from it hangs an array of funerary banners and tabards; all around are hatchments of the arms of the Shirleys and their wives. The chancel is divided from the nave by a wrought-iron screen attributed to Robert Bakewell, the famous Derbyshire smith. The altar has its original frontal of purple velvet with silver trim and there are matching cushions for the clergyman to kneel on.

The best time to visit Staunton Harold is the late afternoon of an autumn day with a first tang of frost in the air and perhaps the smoke from a bonfire of damp leaves drifting across the grass; then you can contemplate in near solitude Lord Chief Justice Crewes' words in the reign of James I: 'And yet time hath his revolution; there must be a period and an end to all temporal things, *finis rerum*, an end of names and dignities and whatsoever is terrene'.

Stoke Dry

31; 2 miles S of Uppingham off A6003

The CHURCH OF ST ANDREW stands on a hill overlooking a reservoir near the old boundary between Leicester and Rutland. It has a little tower of ginger-biscuit-coloured stone and a blue slate clock. The interior is an idyll of an English country church. It has freshly whitewashed walls, an old stone floor, old oak benches, and an open timber roof faded to a beautiful silvery grey. Patches of old wall paintings of various dates enliven the general aspect. There are several rare and unspoilt furnishings. The Perpendicular rood-screen survives in unrestored condition. The little altar in the chancel is pushed off-centre by a large Tudor alabaster tomb in Renaissance style to Everard Digby. There are seventeenth-century communion rails and an extremely rare bier dated 1694. It is unusual to find a church with such an unrestored atmosphere. There is no electric light, only candles. Archaeologically, the columns on either side of the chancel arch, intricately carved with interlacing ornament and birds and beasts, are the most important feature.

Teigh

32; 6 miles N of Oakham off B668

The CHURCH OF THE HOLY TRINITY is a delightful effusion of Strawberry Hill Gothick built to the design of George Richardson in 1782 at the expense of the then rector, the Rev. the Earl of Harborough, who was also responsible for the Gothick church at his family seat at Stapleford (*q.v.*). Only the base of the tower survives from the medieval church, but the top with obelisk pinnacles is eighteenth-century. The body of the church is a serene performance in smooth grey ashlar with battlements and decorative frieze. The interior is a great treat, with a segmental plaster ceiling embellished with the Harborough arms, crest and the date 1782. The pews, arranged college-wise, are daintily carved in pine (recently cleaned of Victorian varnish) and similar fragile-looking woodwork frames the altarpiece – a seventeenth-century Flemish painting of the *Last Supper*. In a box-like enclosure in the middle of the north side are the fonts – the fragile original eighteenth-century one like a little mahogany vase, and a lumpy stone replacement carved by a Victorian vicar. The most startling feature of all,

however, is the pulpit. It is arranged in three parts over the west door, facing the altar, rather like little opera boxes. The wall behind is painted in naïve *trompe l'œil* to represent a window. Pevsner compares it to a weatherhouse and comments that you expect figures to pop out at any moment.

Tickencote

33; 5 miles NW of Stamford on A1 [29]

The CHURCH OF ST PETER is famous for its amazing Norman chancel arch. Photographs do not prepare you for the jazzy restlessness of the real thing: no fewer than five orders of colonnettes, with little cushion capitals, marshalled on either side and bands of every conceivable form of Norman decoration, from beak-head to zigzag, round the arch in textbook perfection. The church was reconstructed and restored by S.P. Cockerell in 1792, making it one of the earliest examples of Romanesque Revival anywhere in Europe. Cockerell rebuilt the nave, and was responsible for the megalomaniac west front – a serious but unscholarly exercise. He tidied up the chancel, giving its exterior a bogus smoothness; old engravings, however, show that the overall design is close to the original, with cylindrical stone buttresses like giant drainpipes against the walls, and round-arched windows with zigzag carving. The vaulting of the interior of the chancel is also original, the ribs again decorated remorselessly with zigzag. It is a church that gives you a headache if you look at it for too long.

Uppingham

34; 19 miles E of Leicester on A47

This little town built of ginger ironstone and cream oolite lies along a ridge overlooking green country. There is a good little MARKET PLACE, given an odd shape by one

The church of the Holy Trinity, Teigh.

small detached shop all on its own on the busiest corner, and the suave Regency post office next to the church. In the middle is a Gothic drinking fountain-cum-streetlight commemorating Queen Victoria's Jubilee in 1887.

On the south side of the Market Place is the parish CHURCH OF ST PETER AND ST PAUL. This has a medieval spire with lucarnes, but was largely rebuilt in 1860–1. What was lost can be seen in an early nineteenth-century watercolour at the back of the church; it shows the former condition of the interior, with old box pews, a flat plaster ceiling, and an iron stove in the middle. All these have gone, alas. But 'Look up and O how gloriously he has restored the roof', as Betjeman wrote; and, gazing aloft, one cannot but agree. The windows are full of dim stained glass. Of the furnishings, only the handsome carved and gilt early eighteenth-century organ case (brought from somewhere else) holds the attention.

The High Street runs east and west of the Market Place. In the west stretch are the SCHOOL buildings. Founded in 1584 and developed into a fully-fledged public school in the mid-nineteenth century, this is the dominating presence at Uppingham. The most important block is by Ernest Newton in a super-Elizabethan style inspired by Kirkby Hall over the hill in Northampton-shire. Oliver Hill was at school at Uppingham and nurtured his interest in architecture here with the encouragement of his housemaster, who let him off games in order to explore the surrounding villages and churches. Hill designed the WAR MEMORIAL LIBRARY, another of the school buildings, in 1949 – an unmistak-

able piece of architectural homage to Lutyens. In the east part of the High Street are the main shops, nice and old-fashioned looking, including such civilised establishments as bookshops, wine merchants and decent grocers. Several retain their Georgian shop-fronts.

Withcote

35; 12 miles E of Leicester off B6047

This is a most attractive English group of house and chapel side by side in green parkland. The CHAPEL was built as a private chapel at the beginning of the sixteenth century. It is rectangular and not very large, with a heraldic frieze and battlements all round. The interior is largely early eighteenth-century, the building having been restored in 1744. There is wonderful eighteenth-century joinery, including an impressive pedimented timber altarpiece with columns. It is flanked by two eighteenth-century marble monuments, and there are wrought-iron communion rails. The special glory of the chapel is the original Flemish-style early sixteenth-century stained glass that still survives in the windows. It shows large standing figures under transitional Gothic-Renaissance canopies and includes Tudor heraldry and symbols. It is thought to date from the 1530s and has been compared with the contemporary glass in King's College Chapel.

WITHCOTE HALL makes a delightful classical contrast to the Gothic chapel, with its pedimented stone façade and hipped roof. The porch is thought to be a later addition but blends in well enough.

Uppingham School.

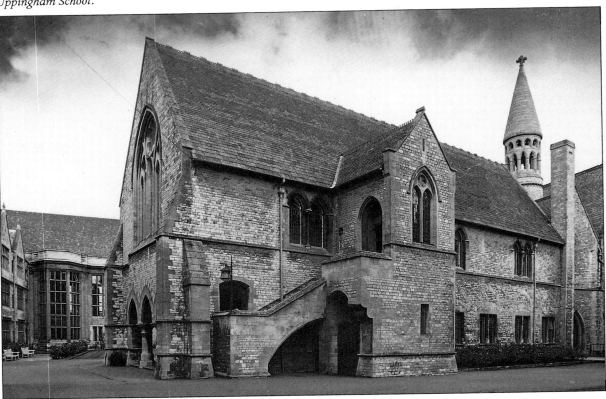

Lincolnshire

Lincolnshire is the second largest county in England and one of the least known. It forms a world of its own, between the Humber, the Wash, the Great North Road and the North Sea, to all intents and purposes cut off from the rest of the Kingdom. The south of the county is fen country and exceedingly flat, with vast empty fields of rich black soil; there are few trees and a large proportion of every view is made up of sky. The north of the county, by contrast, is divided into strips by two hilly ridges, the Cliff and the Wolds. The Cliff is a long narrow welt of limestone, about a mile wide, the beginning of the great oolite belt that sweeps across the English Midlands, by way of the Cotswolds, to Somerset. The Wolds are of chalk, like the Downs, and make marvellous rolling country with little hidden valleys and beech woods. To either side lie the flat coastal plain, and the equally flat Vale of Trent along the Nottinghamshire border. Everywhere the landscape is large-scale and the feeling of space has been intensified by recent agricultural changes. The land in Lincolnshire includes some of the richest arable in England, and as a result the county has been in the vanguard of agricultural progress for the last three decades. Everywhere old hedges have been removed, and in many areas an untidy new landscape has emerged. Sometimes the result just looks bare and scruffy, but where the removal of hedgerow timber has been balanced by new planting in belts and coverts, as on the Wolds, the result is visually satisfactory and makes the whole countryside look like eighteenth-century parkscape.

These prosperous, wide-open spaces are the setting for the county's architectural treasures. Chief among them are the medieval churches, the finest in England: Grantham, Louth, Boston, Heckington, Sleaford, Tattershall, Brant Broughton, Long Sutton, Claypole, just to mention a few of the most magnificent. Faced with this embarrassment of riches, it has been difficult to make a short list. Apart from the absolute tops like Heckington, Grantham and Boston, I have tried to concentrate on churches that have some special feature or atmosphere as well as purely architectural merit. Thus I have included the churches at Edenham and Heydour for their splendid eighteenth-century monuments; Laughton and Brant Broughton for their beautiful fittings by Bodley; Gosberton for its gargoyles; Irnham for its little-known

Easter Sepulchre; and Stragglethorpe for its humble, unrestored atmosphere. It is hard to generalise about so large and rich a group of buildings, but if one had to pick out any particular features of the Lincolnshire churches it would be their glorious spires and luscious Decorated window tracery. In the south of the county, dozens of spires seem to vie with each other. As A.K. Wickham has written: 'In these superb clusters in South Lincolnshire the Gothic church seems to have attained a perfect harmony of all its parts; the broach spire grows naturally from its base without any difficult transition, and the tracery of the windows expands like flowers from the soil.' Supreme, of course, is Lincoln Cathedral – the grandest, richest, and most beautiful of all England's Gothic cathedrals, and probably the greatest single work of architecture that these islands have produced.

If the medieval churches are the principal architectural thrill of Lincolnshire, they are not the only one. The county is a good place for unspoilt country towns. Horncastle, Sleaford, Spalding and Spilsby are all attractive, while Louth, Stamford and the 'High Town' at Lincoln merit a place in the first rank of English historic towns. Louth and Stamford are almost miraculously undisturbed, and in recent years Lincoln has been improved considerably thanks to a sensible conservation policy. It has to be pointed out, however, that Grantham, once an attractive brick market town, has been irrevocably ruined in the last twenty or thirty years, and Boston is well on the way to the same fate.

Lincolnshire is also a county of great estates and great houses. Grandest of all are Grimsthorpe Castle, with its spectacular Vanbrugh front; the extravagant early nineteenth-century Harlaxton Manor; and Belton, the acme of Caroline perfection. There is a whole series of agreeable middling houses like Doddington, Gunby, Casewick and Culverthorpe. The ideal Norman manor house at Boothby Pagnell and Lord Cromwell's fifteenth-century tower at Tattershall are of immense importance and would merit a place in any standard text on English medieval domestic architecture. The two most perfect pieces of eighteenth-century classical architecture in Lincolnshire, however, are not houses but garden ornaments: Sir William Chambers's excellent domed temple at Coleby, and James Wyatt's superb Corinthian mausoleum at Brocklesby.

Fountain, Belton House.

Aubourn Hall

1; 9 miles NE of Newark off A46

This house is Tudor in origin but was considerably remodelled, probably by Smythson, in the late sixteenth and early seventeenth centuries. It is of brick, with an L-shaped plan. The interior contains notable late sixteenth- and seventeenth-century woodwork. The study, for example, has an Elizabethan chimneypiece with tiered pilasters, while the Drawing Room has an interesting mid-seventeenth-century Mannerist-style chimneypiece. The best feature of all is the staircase with its strapwork-and-foliage balustrade of unusual design.

Belton House★

NT; 2; 2 miles N of Grantham on A607 [28]

Belton is the *beau idéal* of the late seventeenth-century house in the Anglo-Dutch taste. It was built between 1685 and 1689 by an unknown architect for Sir John Brownlow, whose grandfather had bought the estate with the proceeds from a successful legal career. The Cust family, created Lords Brownlow, inherited in the eighteenth century. The building was altered by James Wyatt for the 1st Lord Brownlow in 1776 and was brilliantly restored in *c.*1870, giving the whole place its special character as the most unaltered of Caroline houses.

The principal rooms have seventeenth-century-style panelling, richly embellished with naturalistic carvings by Grinling Gibbons, and moulded plaster ceilings. The Chapel is the best of the original interiors; it boasts a car-

ved and marbled altarpiece by Grinling Gibbons worthy of the grandest city church. The Chapel Drawing Room has its original green-and-gold marbled panelling and Soho *chinoiserie* tapestry. The Tyrconnel Room has a painted floor, one of only six to survive in England. The other 'Caroline' rooms, such as the staircase, Tapestry Room and the Entrance Hall, are largely effective late nineteenth-century recreations. The beautiful Library on the first floor is a magnificent piece of work by James Wyatt, with a delicately modelled barrel-vaulted ceiling. Much of the original furniture survives, including the seventeenth-century state bed with blue brocade hangings and chairs to match in the Blue Room, and the tall-backed chairs in the Saloon with their original velvet upholstery. There is also much eighteenth-century and Regency furniture of interest: the walnut bureau with mirror-panelled doors in the Blue Room is reputed to be the finest in existence.

Belton is regularly open to the public. The formal gardens were recreated in the nineteenth century and contain an Orangery designed by Sir Jeffrey Wyatville. Close by, the old parish CHURCH OF ST PETER AND ST PAUL is stuffed full of family tombs and monuments, including a neo-classical one by Canova. Harry Cust said of this church that 'it was built to the Memory of God and the Glory of the Cust Family'.

Bicker

3; 2 miles NE of Donington on A52

This brick-built village lies deep in the fens. ST SWITHUN'S CHURCH, cruciform with a central tower, is memorable for its powerful Norman work. The best thing is the Norman clerestory on the north side of the nave, which, unlike the rest of the church, escaped Victorian 'restoration'. The nave is so short that Pevsner assumed that it was a fragment only and that it had been intended to extend further west. The interior has fat round piers with scalloped capitals and round arches carved with zigzag and nailhead decoration. The crossing and central tower are Decorated, while the chancel is Early English with tall lancet windows. The whole building is a bit like a 3D illustrated glossary of medieval church architecture.

Boothby Pagnell

4; 4 miles SE of Grantham on B1176

The CHURCH OF ST ANDREW (key obtainable from Home Farm, up the lane opposite) has a low Norman west tower, with a crown of Perpendicular pinnacles, and Norman arcades to the nave; the chancel, however, is Decorated. The church was restored for Mrs Cecil Thorold in 1897 by Pearson and owes most of its present noble character to him. He fitted it out from end to end, giving it a unified elegance hitherto lacking. He designed the pews, the marble and tiled floor of the chancel, the pulpit, the organ case, the vestment chests in the vestry, the rood-screen with rich brass gates, the brass communion rails, and the carved and gilded tripartite reredos. Like all Pearson's work, the result is elegant, original and superior to anything of the date to be found anywhere in Europe.

BOOTHBY PAGNELL HALL is a relatively plain early nineteenth-century house, nice but not special. It therefore comes as a surprise to find on the lawn behind it a perfectly preserved Norman MANOR HOUSE. It dates from *c*.1200 and is two storeys high, with the Hall and solar raised over a rib-vaulted ground floor. A flight of stone steps leads to the round-arched door to the Hall. Some of the original windows survive, their two little round arches divided by a central colonnette. Inside the Hall, the fireplace has a projecting stone hood on corbels. The whole building is in remarkably good condition and is the best example in England of a small Norman house.

Boston

5; 15 miles NE of Spalding on A16 [**30**]

'The whole scene made an odd impression of bustle, decay, and a remnant of wholesome life, and I could not but contrast it with the mighty and populous activity of our own Boston, which was once the feeble infant of this old English town. . . .' So wrote the American Nathaniel Hawthorne when he visited the Lincolnshire Boston in 1855. Americans have long had a filial interest in this town because it was from here that the Pilgrim Fathers first attempted to sail, and whence many of the earliest settlers came to New England. By then the port had already declined because of the silting of the river with mud washed down from Yorkshire in the sixteenth century.

The heyday of Boston was from the twelfth to the fourteenth century, during which period it was second only to London as a port, and an important centre of the Hanseatic trade. This medieval prosperity is responsible for the spaciousness of the town layout and for one major surviving architectural monument, the CHURCH OF ST BOTOLPH. This is among the three or four largest medieval parish churches in England and is famous above all for its prodigious western tower, 272 feet high – the ironically named 'Boston Stump'. It is Perpendicular in five tiers, the lower ones with richly moulded stone panelling and the final one forming an octagonal lantern with open stone tracery and a fancy crenellated parapet on top like a tiara. It is reminiscent of the belfry at Bruges, but more elegant, and dominates the Lincolnshire fens for miles in every direction, visible even from the other side of the Wash. The body of the church is 'an almost pure example of the richest period of flowing Dec., built continuously through the whole reign of Edward III', to quote *Murray's Guide*. The huge chancel, with its phalanx of tall traceried windows and crocketed pinnacles, dominates the Market Place and offers a foretaste of the glorious interior. Immediately on entering, it is worth standing under the tower for a moment and looking up into the stone vault, soaring 137 feet above you – an unforgettable spatial experience. The vast, uniform nave has a carved wooden ceiling, brightly coloured; this was designed by Sir Charles Nicholson in 1928–33 as part of a general restoration that left the church in splendid order. It is sad to have to point out that the effect is now being spoilt by discordant new furnishings and trendy clutter. The chancel has an eighteenth-century

St Swithun's church, Bicker.

timber vault with thin ribs, gloriously coloured by Nicholson. The choir stalls have original misericords, but the canopies are Victorian restorations by Sir George Gilbert Scott, who was also responsible for the decorated tracery of the east window. This was copied from Carlisle Cathedral (*q.v.*) and contains vivid stained glass by O'Connor; Hawthorne described it as 'the richest and tenderest modern window that I have ever seen'. Many monuments around the walls commemorate prosperous medieval and eighteenth-century merchants.

The best place to begin a tour of the town is the MARKET PLACE, where there is a marble statue by Munro to Herbert Ingram who founded the *Illustrated London News* in 1842. The surrounding buildings are mainly Georgian and provide a good foil to the giant Gothic bulk of St Botolph's sailing high over all. On the riverside is EXCHANGE BUILDING, a brick-pedimented range of 1772, and next door are the ASSEMBLY ROOMS of 1826, a fine stuccoed block. The best secular building in the Market Place has, however, been demolished. This was the Peacock and Royal Hotel, described by Pevsner as 'the market place hostelry *par excellence*', and it is only one of a series of disgraceful demolitions in Boston during the last twenty years. While the general fabric of the town survives, and with a little intelligent effort and care could still be rescued, much of the architectural detail has been unnecessarily eroded and spoilt and many of the modern buildings leave much to be desired.

Some of the best of the remaining buildings of Boston are in South Street, off the Market Place. These include SHODFRIARS HALL, a romantic recreation of a medieval half-timbered house with a Hanseatic air, mainly by Oldrid Scott and of 1874, though the lower storeys contain genuine work; PILGRIM HOUSE is plain early nineteenth-century; the CUSTOMS HOUSE – trim and workmanlike – is dated 1725; and several good Georgian warehouses languish in various stages of neglect. The GUILDHALL is fifteenth-century but much altered; it contains a nice old-fashioned museum. Next to it is FYDELL HOUSE, the best Georgian building in the town. It dates from 1726 and has a handsome interior, with decorative plasterwork, chimneypieces and staircase and is now the headquarters of the Boston Preservation Trust. Beyond there are more warehouses in South Square; the ring-road, however, deters all further exploration in that direction.

Returning along the other side of the river up the HIGH STREET, there are more Georgian warehouses, a rare sixteenth-century survival of brick with crow-stepped gables and mullion windows; a gaunt, early eighteenth-century brick terrace with giant pilasters and a Vanbrughian air; and a ghastly new office block for the Transport and General Workers' Union. How on earth did that get planning permission? East of the Market Place is PUMP SQUARE, the centre of a labyrinth of little streets and a wonderfully intimate space, though shamefully treated. Bargate leads to WIDE BARGATE, an impressive funnel-shaped space, now partly the cattle market, full of rustic sounds and smells and surrounded by late Georgian and early Victorian houses. A last and unexpected treat is in Red Lion Street: the CENTENARY METHODIST CHAPEL, a megalomaniac piece of Edwardian

Baroque with grand corner towers and an Ionic portico designed by Gordon & Gunton. It is described in the *Shell Guide* as a building that 'might pass as a Christian Science Temple in San Francisco'!

Bourne
6; 10 miles W of Spalding on A151

This little town has some Georgian houses and a market place overlooked by an elegant neo-classical TOWN HALL, with a dramatic Doric centrepiece, designed by Bryan Browning in 1821. The principal sight in Bourne is the parish CHURCH OF ST PETER AND ST PAUL, the remnant of an Augustinian abbey founded in 1138. The domestic buildings all disappeared at the Reformation, but the church was kept as the parish church. It dates from the twelfth century and has a massive Norman nave with fat circular piers, scalloped capitals and semi-circular arches. The Early English west front is the beginning of an ambitious rebuilding programme which was never finished, hence the oddly truncated look of the outside of the church. It was meant to have a pair of towers flanking the entrance but only one of them was built. Many other vicissitudes have left the building with a rather knocked-about look. The transepts have been shortened and the medieval chancel demolished. The present chancel was built in 1807 but made more convincing in 1870 when a genuine Perpendicular window (taken from the west front, where it was replaced with a Victorian lancet) was inserted over the altar. The best of the furnishings is the magnificent brass chandelier, dated 1742, with three tiers of candles.

Brant Broughton★
7; 11 miles S of Lincoln on A17

Few English village churches are as glorious as the CHURCH OF ST HELEN. Much of the credit for its beauty goes to Canon Frederick Heathcote Sutton, squarson of Brant Broughton in the late nineteenth century, who employed G.F. Bodley between 1874 and 1876 to restore the building and to construct a new chancel. As a result the church is possessed of a remarkable unity and richness. It is in the Perpendicular style of the early fourteenth century, with a tall, elegant, much-crocketed spire 198 feet high – a landmark for miles around. The top 7 feet and the wrought-iron weathervane were added in 1897 to commemorate Queen Victoria's Diamond Jubilee. The exterior of the church is lavishly decorated with a variety of stone carvings, some described in *The Gentleman's Magazine* of February 1804 as 'too indelicate to be permitted to occupy one of your plates'. This carved decoration reaches its climax in the two splendid stone-vaulted porches to the north and south of the church.

Inside, the nave has tall arcades, a clerestory and the original timber angel roof, painted in its medieval colours of red, black and white (renewed by Bodley). The stained glass in the aisle and clerestory windows was designed by Canon Sutton and made in his own workshop at the Rectory. The latter illustrate the *Te Deum*. The wrought-iron light fittings and chancel gates, designed by Bodley, were made by F. Doldron & Son, the village blacksmiths at Brant Broughton, who subsequently executed work for Bodley elsewhere. The font cover, in the form of a carved spire and with a painted interior, was designed by Thomas Garner. A carved oak rood-screen in memory of Canon Sutton divides the nave from the chancel. The latter takes its cue from the nave but is even richer, encrusted with carving and with a timber lierne vault painted green and gold. The carved, painted and gilded reredos, installed in 1887, was designed by Bodley and Canon Sutton as a setting for the beautiful fifteenth-century panel of *The Ascension* by the Master of Leisborn (a Westphalian artist). This was given to the church by Canon Sutton and became a *cause célèbre* a few years ago when the rector and churchwardens, against the wishes of most of the parish, attempted to sell it but were prevented after an appeal to the Court of Arches.

After visiting Brant Broughton it is worth stopping off to see the little CHURCH OF ST MICHAEL at Stragglethorpe a couple of miles to the south but still in the parish. Here, in contrast to the High Church glory of St Helen's, is a simple, unrestored building, partly Saxon and partly Norman, reached through a farmyard. It has a bellcote at the west end and a humble red-tiled roof. The interior is delightful, with a flat plaster ceiling of *c*.1800, grey eighteenth-century box pews of scrubbed oak and deal, and a two-decker pulpit of the same date. Perched at odd angles on the pews are little wooden candlestands. On the whitewashed walls hang painted boards with the paternoster, Creed and Royal Arms; there is also one rather good eighteenth-century marble memorial to Sir Richard Earle by Thomas Green of Camberwell, Senior, the epitaph on which exhorts: 'STAY, READER AND OBSERVE DEATH'S PARTIAL DOOM. . . .' This delightful church has recently been saved from redundancy and has been repaired.

Brocklesby Park

8; 9 miles W of Grimsby on B1211
*Includes Brocklesby Mausoleum**

The Brocklesby estate, reclaimed from the wild in the eighteenth century, is, with Holkham in Norfolk and Alnwick in Northumberland (*q.v.*), one of the three greatest improved agricultural demesnes of eastern England. Today the great estate (over 30,000 acres) is still among the best-farmed and -forested in the country. In the words of Christopher Hussey, 'With the kennels to one side of the house, the old church on another, and a vast stable yard on a third, Brocklesby itself symbolises the traditional country life of England that, happily, persists so little changed around it.'

The nucleus of the estate was formed between 1565 and 1570 when Sir William Pelham started buying land in the area. His son built a fine Jacobean house on the present site in 1603. This was reconstructed and refaced in the early eighteenth century to form a three-storeyed brick block on the model of old Buckingham House in London. Additions were made in the nineteenth century, but in 1898 the interior was largely gutted by fire. It was subsequently reinstated and extended to the design of Sir Reginald Blomfield. Further work was done

after the Second World War, when most of the later additions, including Blomfield's, were swept away under the direction of Claud Phillimore, who restored the exterior to its eighteenth-century condition. Blomfield's formal garden round the house, however, with clipped hedges, topiary and formal pools, survives.

The exterior of the house is an elegant brick rectangle of nine bays by six. Decoration is restricted largely to carved stone window architraves and urns on the top parapet. Much of the interior was designed by Reginald Blomfield and has rich Edwardian plasterwork, and joinery in the style of Wren. The east Hall, on the other hand, was reinstated after the fire to its eighteenth-century form, with a coved plaster ceiling designed by Capability Brown, who also landscaped the Upper Park. There is excellent eighteenth-century and Regency furniture, and a good collection of paintings. In the ORANGERY to the north-west of the house is displayed a collection of antique sculpture, the remains of the Museum Worsleyanum from Appuldurcombe on the Isle of Wight, which was inherited by the 2nd Earl of Yarborough.

The parish CHURCH OF ALL SAINTS has a Perpendicular tower with a little lead spire. The interior contains many fine fittings, including a beautiful carved mahogany organ case from the house, which may have been designed by James Wyatt. There is also an array of Elizabethan and Jacobean tombs.

The church of St Helen, Brant Broughton.

The Brocklesby Mausoleum.

The greatest architectural thrill at Brocklesby, however, is the MAUSOLEUM* designed by James Wyatt and reached at the end of a long grassy ride through the park to the south of the house. It was completed in 1792 and is Wyatt's classical masterpiece. The 1st Lord Yarborough built it to commemorate his wife, Sophia Aufrère, who died young in 1787. The domed rotunda, a variation on the Temple of Vesta at Tivoli, stands on a mound and is surrounded by iron railings and stone piers in the form of classical sarcophagi carved with swags and rams' heads. The large entrance doors are approached by a flight of steps. Underneath them is a modest signature: 'JAMES WYATT ESQ ARCHT'. The interior is of great beauty, with crisply carved Corinthian columns of marble supporting a coffered dome. In the centre is a glazed oculus painted with clouds and cherubs by Francis Eginton; it was restored twenty years ago and throws light on the life-size marble statue of Sophia Aufrère by Joseph Nollekens. In three recesses round the walls are large sculptural groups, made in Italy, commemorating Pelham ancestors. It is a perfect expression of eighteenth-century monumental taste.

Casewick Hall
9; 3 miles E of Stamford off A16 [32]
An enchanting part Jacobean, part eighteenth-century Gothick house, Casewick was formerly the seat of the Trollop family but has recently been converted into flats. The house is quadrangular and was built by William Trollop in 1621 on an older site. The south range remains in its seventeenth-century state, with little gables and mullion windows. The east side has a jolly gateway, dated 1651, with three obelisks on top. The show front is that to the west, which was remodelled in 1785 to the design of William Legg of Stamford. It is fif-teen windows wide and two storeys high, and at either end are a pair of crow-stepped gables with large, jolly pinnacles on top. Most of the windows are plain square-headed sashes. An exception, however, is in the three-bay centrepiece, which sports the delightful solecism of a crenellated pediment and has a triple arrangement of two tiers of pointed arches divided by slimly elegant little columns. The middle window upstairs has an ogee dripstone over. The interior is plain apart from the Dining Room, which has pretty Rococo decoration.

Claypole
10; 9 miles NW of Grantham off A1
The CHURCH OF ST PETER is one of the grandest of the Decorated churches of Lincolnshire, with a cruciform plan, and a western tower and crocketed spire. The interior presents a proud, unified spectacle and is full of light from the large windows. The moulded piers of the nave have beautifully carved naturalistic foliage capitals, all of matching design. The chancel arch has two well-carved caryatid figures, which Pevsner thought might have once supported the rood-beam. The climax of the church is the noble chancel with its tall traceried windows, Decorated along the sides and Perpendicular at the east end. It is rather a pity that the latter has only clear glass in it. The handsome Perpendicular screen has ogee arches and tracery. The daintily carved pulpit and canopy is also Perpendicular, though partly made up; the pulpit desk, for instance, is supported on the brass stem of a medieval processional cross. The best feature of all is the sumptuous Decorated sedilia in the chancel, which has carved ogee arches and a crenellated top.

Coleby
11; 8 miles S of Lincoln on A607
The HALL itself is not very special, but at the end of the avenue in the grounds is a remarkably fine eighteenth-century garden building. This is the TEMPLE OF ROMULUS AND REMUS, designed in 1762 for Thomas Scrope, the then squire, by his friend Sir William Chambers. Although not large, it is a textbook example of Chambers' monumental classicism. It is circular with projecting apses on either side and two projecting pedimented porches, which have Tuscan columns of pronounced entasis. There is a well-detailed cornice and circular dome. Inside, the dome has splendid coffered plasterwork recently restored and painted blue and white. Scrope and Chambers had been in Rome at the same time and had inspected the antique ruins together; their temple does indeed recall the grandeur of the Ancient World. Coleby is situated on the old Roman road from the Humber and Lincoln, and Scrope saw himself as something of a latterday Roman. In a letter to Chambers in 1774 he referred to Coleby as 'the very seat of the Gothic Empire'.

Crowland
12; 14 miles E of Stamford on A1073
CROYLAND ABBEY is best visited late on a winter's afternoon. Then it is easy to imagine St Guthlac landing here, seeking refuge from the world on a little island in the

fens. The Benedictine abbey was founded in his memory by King Aethelbald in c.713 and was rebuilt after the Norman Conquest. From the Welland Bank Bridge the ruins still give an impression of the early monastic seclusion, and even as a part-ruin the church is a spectacular building. Only the north aisle of the nave is roofed, and this now serves as the parish church. It is entered through a two-storeyed Perpendicular porch in the base of the hefty west tower, with a stumpy spire, all added by Abbot Lyttington in the mid-fifteenth century. The rest of the west front dates from the mid-thirteenth century and is a perfect design in the manner of Westminster Abbey. The doorway is divided into two arches beneath a sculptured quatrefoil showing scenes from the life of St Guthlac. Above is a large window, now missing its tracery, flanked by a beautiful arrangement of blank geometrical tracery with statues in niches, similar to Lincoln Cathedral (q.v.). Through the openings can be seen the ruins of the Perpendicular nave and the solitary Norman arch at the crossing. The interior of the north aisle preserves its stone tierceron vault and has some nice furnishings, including Georgian communion rails and a Perpendicular screen with traces of original colouring. The outline of the Norman arch to the transept can be seen in the present east wall.

Crowland is a pleasant little town, with wide streets given extra dignity by late eighteenth-century tree planting. Its most famous feature is the TRIANGULAR BRIDGE, which Richard Gough, the eighteenth-century antiquarian and topographer, called 'the greatest curiosity in Britain, if not in Europe'. It was erected in the thirteenth or fourteenth century and comprises three arches that meet at their apex; these originally spanned three branches of the River Welland (now diverted from the town). Henry VI and Edward IV both landed here at different times during the Wars of the Roses. For over 200 years a weathered figure of Christ, enthroned and holding the world, has adorned the bridge. It is thought to have come from the missing apex of the gable of the west front of the abbey.

Culverthorpe Hall

13; 8 miles E of Grantham off A15
This stone-built house stands well on rising ground in a park, overlooking a lake. The three-storeyed central block is the original late seventeenth-century house; the flanking lower wings and much of the architectural detail, however, are eighteenth-century and are the result of a remodelling in the 1730s, possibly to the design of Robert Morris. With its steep-pitched roof, the house has something of the air of a French château – a feeling that is enhanced by the Edwardian formal garden with its symmetrical vistas and statues, and by the entrance forecourt flanked by older detached stable blocks. On the entrance (south) front, the lower wings have Venetian windows. The most distinctive feature of the north front is the central projecting square bay, almost like a tower, with an Ionic doorcase and prominent quoins. This bay was added in c.1700 to contain the main staircase, which, with its barley-sugar balusters and inlaid panels, is the best feature of the interior. Its walls

were originally painted with mythological murals by Louis Hauduroy, but these have been whitewashed over. The Entrance Hall fills the full width of the central block and has a pair of screens of fluted Corinthian columns. One Morris wing contains the Dining Room, the other the Drawing Room; both of these have good Georgian decoration of the 1730s or 1740s.

Doddington Hall

14; 5 miles W of Lincoln on B1190 [31]
This magnificent H-plan Elizabethan house of pink brick, with three bulgy domed cupolas on the roof, stands romantically amid courtyards, walled gardens and fields in a richly arable Lincolnshire landscape and is approached through a gabled Gatehouse. It was built between 1593 and 1600 by Thomas Taylor, Registrar to the Bishop of Lincoln, and is attributed to Robert Smythson, being associated with a group of advanced late Elizabethan Midlands houses, including Wollaton in Nottinghamshire and Hardwick in Derbyshire (qq.v.).

The exterior survives untouched: serene and symmetrical with a Tuscan porch and large mullion windows. The interior, however, was remodelled in 1760 by Sir John Hussey Delavel and is now entirely Georgian. Sir John employed as his designer Thomas Lumby, a Lincoln carpenter, and the splendid joinery of the main staircase is his *chef-d'œuvre*. The finest room is perhaps the Long Gallery on the second floor; it has Georgian decoration and a superb triple, full-length portrait by Sir Joshua Reynolds at one end.

Doddington has passed entirely by descent to the present owners and its rooms are full of good furniture and portraits accumulated over more than 380 years.

The Temple of Romulus and Remus, Coleby.

The church of St Michael, Edenham.

Edenham

15; 8 miles E of Colsterworth on A151

Edenham is the principal Grimsthorpe (*q.v.*) estate village. It is trimly maintained; the loosely spaced stone cottages have red pantiled roofs and cream-painted joinery. The CHURCH OF ST MICHAEL stands in a grassy graveyard with cedars and yew trees; its elegant tower crowned by tall pinnacles makes a lordly impression. The architecture is Perpendicular at its smoothest and most courtly. The interior is cream-washed, and the carved oak roof is adorned with angels. One is drawn immediately to the chancel and the magnificent array of memorials to the Willoughby de Eresby family, formerly Earls and Dukes of Ancaster. Chief among these are four vast Baroque tombs, arranged symmetrically, two to either side of the chancel. The variations on the theme of figurative sculpture against an architectural backdrop is worth a study in itself. The 1st Duke of Ancaster (d. 1723), by Scheemakers and Cheare, takes the form of a standing white marble figure in Roman armour against a black marble reredos with Corinthian columns. Robert, Lord Willoughby (d. 1738), is the most original design: a black marble sarcophagus supported on lions' paws carries a white marble urn, with seven marble busts, depicting the deceased, his wife and five children, arranged on brackets round it. The 2nd Duke of Ancaster (d. 1741) is by Roubiliac, the greatest sculptor to work in England in the eighteenth century, and shows the Duke life-size, leaning elegantly against an urn while a *putto* holds a

portrait of his wife, against a pyramidal background. The 3rd and 4th Dukes (d. 1778 and 1779) share the same monument, by Charles Harris, the two figures side by side; it is this sculptor's most important work and has great charm. Later marble monuments are arranged round the spacious Willoughby family pew to the left of the chancel. The blue carpet in this, by the way, was used for the Coronation of Queen Elizabeth II in Westminster Abbey and was a perquisite of the late Lord Ancaster as joint hereditary Lord Great Chamberlain.

Fiskerton

16; 5 miles E of Lincoln off B1190

The CHURCH OF ST CLEMENT has a tall, pinnacled Perpendicular tower with buttresses and gargoyles. The body of the building seems short in proportion to the tower, especially as the clerestory is so tall. The interior is dominated by dramatically different arcades: that to the north has short, thick Norman columns and round arches, while that to the south has graceful, clustered Decorated piers reminiscent of Lincoln Cathedral (*q.v.*). The surrounding landscape, with its views of Lincoln Cathedral, is well known from the watercolours of Peter de Wint.

Folkingham

17; 8 miles N of Bourne on A15

This is a former coaching village endowed with the dignified character of a town. The centre is a handsome wide street, or oblong square, climbing gently towards the GREYHOUND INN, which makes a splendid eye-catcher at the top. It is of red brick and three storeys, with sashed windows and a central archway. To the right is the former ASSEMBLY ROOM with its large Venetian window. The other houses lining the street are equally attractive – mainly late Georgian, of red brick and stone. The best building in Folkingham is the former HOUSE OF CORRECTION, the work of the interesting local architect Bryan Browning, who also designed the Town Hall at Bourne (*q.v.*). Although small, its severe stone facade exudes something of the drama of Vanbrugh or Ledoux. It is of three bays, the centre one with a dark recessed archway and a pediment over, the lower side-pieces with rusticated semi-circular windows. On the parapet is inscribed in deeply cut Roman letters 'HOUSE OF CORRECTION A.D. 1825'. It conveys the chill message – 'Abandon Hope All Ye Who Enter Here'.

Fulbeck

18; 10 miles E of Newark on A607

Fulbeck lies in a pretty valley under the Cliff. The village is distinguished, with stone cottages and houses arranged round a green off the main road. The MANOR HOUSE is seventeenth-century but much restored. It has a good setting with sloping lawns. FULBECK HALL, the seat of the Fanes since 1632, is approached through impressive iron gates and along a lime avenue. It has a distinguished Georgian front with Doric pilasters and Gibbs' surrounds to the windows.

ST NICHOLAS'S CHURCH is large and shows work of most dates, from Norman fragments to Perpendicular swathes. The west tower and clerestory are fifteenth-century – the former with big pinnacles – while the nave arcades are of *c*.1300 and the aisle windows Decorated. The church was over-restored in 1887 by Charles Kirk – the east window, for instance, is entirely his work. The walls inside are encrusted with marble tablets and memorials to the Fane family.

Gainsborough
19; 12 miles E of Bawtry on A631
GAINSBOROUGH OLD HALL, a complete fifteenth-century manor house, is rather an unlikely survival to find stranded on a piece of mown grass next to the war memorial in the centre of an unexceptional north Midlands red brick town. It was built in the 1470s by Sir Thomas Burgh, a Yorkist, after his old house had been burnt down by a Lancastrian army.

The house was altered in the sixteenth century by William Hickman, a London merchant. It later decayed, being used as a linen factory in the eighteenth century, but was restored in the nineteenth and twentieth. The buildings originally formed a quadrangle, but the south side has disappeared, leaving only three ranges. The chief survival from Burgh's time is the Great Hall, which has a splendid open timber roof and Perpendicular tracery in the windows. The west wing, which contained individual lodgings for different members of the household, is dominated by four projecting bays housing lavatories. The Ballroom in the east wing was formed in 1849 when the main reception rooms were altered.

Gosberton
20; 6 miles N of Spalding on A16
The CHURCH OF ST PETER AND ST PAUL is of model-type perfection – mainly Perpendicular, with a cruciform plan and central tower carrying a beautifully proportioned crocketed spire 160 feet high. The nave is taller and longer than the chancel and carefully related in scale to the spire. These well-managed proportions considerably enhance the beauty of the church. There are wonderful large windows with Perpendicular tracery, that in the south transept of an almost cathedral stature. Note also the well-carved gargoyles; one on the tower is an elephant with a long trunk. The interior is spacious with impressive vistas. The nave arcades have complex moulded piers with miniature-battlemented capitals and the crossing under the tower has an intricate stone lierne vault. The chancel was reconstructed in 1896, but the Decorated sedilia was re-incorporated. In the south transept is a good Decorated tomb with an ogee arch and carved angels.

Grantham
21; 21 miles E of Nottingham on A1
Includes Grantham House (NT)
Once an attractive Midlands market town comparable to Newark (*q.v.*), Grantham has been badly damaged during the last twenty years by unnecessary demolition and insensitive rebuilding; Watergate, formerly a fine street, the High Street and St Peter's Hill have all suffered from modern utilitarian 'development'. Grantham,

however, is still worth a stop for its magnificent medieval parish CHURCH OF ST WULFRAM – probably the finest in Lincolnshire and counted among the top dozen in England as a whole. Its spire is very tall – all of 272 feet – and, moreover, perfectly proportioned; Ruskin was spellbound by it. The body of the church is a large rectangle with the nave flanked by wide aisles and the chancel by side-chapels. The greater part of the church dates from the late thirteenth and early fourteenth centuries, mainly Transitional Early English to Decorated. The interior is remarkably spacious, but the restoration by Sir George Gilbert Scott in 1866–75 has left his somewhat heavy hand in the fabric and robbed the building of some of its life. There are bare rubble stone walls, and the three identical waggon roofs of dark oak are a bit too much of a good thing. The large windows have beautiful flowing and geometrical tracery of various patterns and competent Victorian stained glass. There are many eighteenth- and nineteenth-century marble monuments to local worthies hung around the walls like paintings in a gallery, while rich fittings of different dates include the rood-screen by Scott and the organ case and tall Gothic font cover, both by Sir Walter Tapper. The chancel has an enormous Perpendicular east window, and a large reredos by Sir Arthur Blomfield.

Facing the east end of the church is GRANTHAM HOUSE (NT), once the home of the Hall family. It is a picturesque gabled Elizabethan house, but with a medieval core. The sixteenth-century stables adjoining, restored by Dawber and Tapper in 1930, probably belonged originally to the house. CASTLEGATE and CHURCH STREET are the best remaining parts of the town, with stone, red brick and painted plaster houses. On the north side of the town, NORTH PARADE is a tree-lined street overlooked by one long brick terrace of little houses built originally for bachelors who leased them for the hunting season. In the mangled High Street the ANGEL AND ROYAL HOTEL survives – the most famous of Grantham's secular buildings and one of the best-preserved fifteenth-century inns in England, with stone bay windows. It was here that Richard III signed the death warrant of the Duke of Buckingham.

Grimsthorpe Castle★
22; 8 miles E of Colsterworth on A151
The sight of a very great house and estate fully kept up in traditional splendour is a rare and ennobling experience, and one which can still be savoured to the full at Grimsthorpe. The house and its contents are of the highest quality and all maintained with faultless taste. Everything is grand and unfussy, without a false note for miles in any direction.

With its inner quadrangle and mixture of medieval, Tudor and Baroque, Grimsthorpe is reminiscent of an Oxford college. The first impact is made by Vanbrugh's great north front – and what an impact! To stand in the forecourt facing the rusticated corner towers, the huge Doric columns, the phalanx of round-arched windows and the elaborately sculpted rapes on the balustraded roof is to feel that one has arrived at Giants' Castle. The same heroic theme is maintained within Vanbrugh's

Grimsthorpe Castle.

wing: in the austere stone-arcaded Hall with *grisaille* portraits of those English kings who had benefited the Willoughby de Eresby family; in the State Dining Room, with its tapestry, full-length swagger portraits, and thrones from the old House of Lords; and in the Chapel, one of the most beautiful rooms in England, its stone-coloured walls articulated by the Corinthian order, luscious plasterwork on the ceiling, and carved pulpit and pews. The state rooms along the east side of the house are smaller but also beautifully decorated. The King James Drawing Room has fluted Corinthian pilasters and a simple marble chimneypiece of Vanbrugh's time, but the plasterwork of the coved ceiling and Rococo *sopraporta* date from towards the middle of the eighteenth century. The State Drawing Room is entirely of this date – it is a breathtaking ensemble. The Rococo plasterwork of the walls is designed to fit round the full-length portraits in richly carved frames. This and the King James Drawing Room were redecorated in blue, white and gold by the late John Fowler. The third and last of the Drawing Rooms is hung with yellow-ground Soho tapestry from Normanton Park (now demolished) against a dark brown and gold ground. The Tudor inner courtyard is surrounded by galleries hung with family portraits, off which open the bedrooms, many of them Georgianised in 1911–14 by Detmar Blow. The private family rooms occupy the ground floor on the south and west sides of the house. The most interesting of these is the Chinese Drawing Room next to the Chapel. It has a wonderful black-and-gold Chinese fret dado and other joinery, blue-ground Chinese wallpaper, and huge pier glasses in gilt Rococo frames, one over the chimneypiece and the other facing the Gothick bay window.

Gunby Hall

NT; 23; 7 miles W of Skegness on A158

The Massingberd family have been in Lincolnshire since Saxon times and made their fortune in the fifteenth-century by a marriage to the Bernak heiress. They acquired most of the Gunby estate at the beginning of that century and the following fifty years saw them at their zenith, several members of the family holding important public appointments. The male line died out in the early eighteenth century and thereafter the property has passed many times through the female line, but each time the heir has added the name Massingberd to his own.

The present house was built in 1700 by Sir William Massingberd. It is of beautiful rose-red brick, nine bays wide and three storeys high. The architect is unknown, but it is a good example of the domestic architecture of its date. The north wing is a remarkably sensitive addition of 1873, copying the style of the old house.

The interior is relatively plain but unspoiled, with fielded panelling in the main rooms and a handsome staircase of oak with twisted balusters. The principal room is the Drawing Room on the first floor, over the Hall. All the rooms contain fine old furniture, pictures and china, most of which have been in the house for generations. Gunby is now the property of the National Trust and is beautifully kept up.

Harlaxton Manor

24; 2 miles SW of Grantham on A607 [33]

Here is a house that has to be seen to be believed. Glimpsed at the end of the long straight drive from the main road from Grantham, it spreads along its ridge like a gigantic fantasy of Ketton stone. It was the brainchild of George de Ligne Gregory, a bachelor landowner who scrimped and saved, then spent every penny and the greater portion of his life on the erection of this palace. As he told Charles Greville, Clerk to the Privy Council, in 1838, it was 'his amusement, as hunting or shooting or feasting may be the objects of other people; and as the pursuit leads him into all parts of the world, and to mix with every variety of nation and character, besides engendering tastes pregnant with instruction and curious research, it is not irrational, although he should never inhabit the house.' Two architects, Anthony Salvin and William Burn, were involved, but neither achieved the same pitch in any of their other works and there is little doubt that Gregory himself was the key figure in the evolution of the design. Building was started in 1832, but Gregory had already been studying and travelling for a decade in search of inspiration for the design. The place was largely finished by 1844. The layout of the house is, in Mark Girouard's words, 'a masterly combination of ingenious planning and picturesque composition'. It was literally dug into the hillside so that the main rooms, although on the first floor with the service rooms underneath as in an eighteenth-century *piano nobile* arrangement, still have direct access to the garden at the two sides of the house. The detailing inside and out provides a panoply of architectural vocabulary derived from Gregory's travels – not just English Elizabethan but also continental Baroque. The entrance front, for instance, is inspired by Burghley but

has even more swagger. The sensational fusion of Elizabethan and Baroque is demonstrated perhaps most clearly in the powerful gatepiers and pavilions flanking the entrance to the forecourt. This unique amalgam of styles is even more noticeable in the interior (the work of Burn, whereas the outside of the house is Salvin's). The Great Hall is a *tour de force* of carved woodwork and plaster, but it is the Staircase Hall that is the special glory of Harlaxton. 'Through struggling Caryatids, swarming cherubs and tasselled festoons it soars up to an illusionist Baroque heaven', wrote Girouard. On the ceiling a plaster figure of Father Time, holding a real scythe, unrolls a plan of the house against a background of painted clouds. The principal Drawing Rooms are decorated in a robust Louis Quatorze manner, with painted ceilings, huge looking-glasses and gilt plasterwork, all executed with the very best materials and brilliant craftsmanship.

Harlaxton is no longer a private house but now belongs to the University of Evansville, which maintains it well.

Harrington Hall

25; 8 miles E of Horncastle off A158

Harrington Hall was rebuilt in 1673, retaining parts of the Elizabethan house of the Copleydykes. The main front is of brick, with a hipped roof, a projecting porch with elongated Ionic pilasters, and sashed windows inserted in *c*.1700. The Hall has a seventeenth-century plaster ceiling and Doric panelling; other rooms also have painted panelling and are well furnished. The main staircase is early eighteenth-century with twisted and moulded balusters and carved tread ends.

The gardens were laid out with walls and raised terraces in the eighteenth century and are thought to have been the inspiration for Tennyson's *Maud*.

Harlaxton Manor.

Heckington

26; 6 miles E of Sleaford on A17

As one of the most magnificent village churches in Lincolnshire, ST ANDREW'S is therefore one of the finest in England. It is completely in the Decorated style, all of Ancaster stone, and owes its grandeur to Bardney Abbey, which appropriated the church in 1345 and lavished riches on it. The tower and spire, soaring to 180 feet, dominate the surrounding flat landscape – a landscape dotted with handsome church spires. Thanks to Victorian 'restoration', carried out by Kirk in 1866, the exterior is now a good deal more impressive than the interior, which, alas, is scraped, insensitively re-roofed, and darkened by poor quality stained glass. The outside, on the other hand, is richly carved, buttressed, pinnacled, and enlivened with beautiful flowing tracery. The south porch is an exquisite invention, its archway flanked by two large niches under pinnacled canopies and its gable adorned with a wavy carved parapet containing little sculptures of angels and of Christ, and decorated with heraldry. The transepts are lower than the nave but have especially splendid windows. The beginning of the chancel is punctuated by the staircase turret to the rood-loft, carrying a little crocketed spirelet. The east window of the chancel is among the most noble in England; it is of seven lights and its flowing tracery, showing the most fertile invention, is comparable to that of Selby Abbey or Carlisle Cathedral (*qq.v.*).

The interior, as I have mentioned, has lost much of its atmosphere; nevertheless, it is impressive for its enormous scale and for the magnificent Decorated fittings of the chancel. These comprise the sedilia, the piscina, the

The church of St Andrew, Irnham.

tomb of Richard de Potesgrave (chaplain to Edward III) and the famous Easter Sepulchre. All are of high quality, the tomb and sedilia with ogee arches, 'cauliflower' foliage, and beautifully carved little figures of saints and angels. The Easter Sepulchre is one of the three finest in England; only those at Lincoln Cathedral and Hawton in Nottinghamshire (*qq.v.*) bear comparison. It is in three tiers: at the bottom are the sleeping Roman soldiers; in the middle is a triangular-arched niche – the tomb itself – flanked by carvings of the three Marys and an angel; at the top is the figure of the risen Christ flanked by pinnacles and foliage carving. Although in my opinion not quite as beautiful as Hawton, it is nonetheless an exquisite creation.

Heydour

27; 7 miles NE of Grantham off A52

ST MICHAEL'S is a grand church with a lofty Perpendicular spire and Early English chancel. The east wall, over the altar, has the usual Early English arrangement of three stepped lancets – always a graceful effect. The windows of the north and south aisles contain fragments of fourteenth-century glass: knights, angels and saints. The special interest of the church lies in the Newton family Chapel, which houses a splendid array of monuments to the Newtons of Culverthorpe (*q.v.*). They include two by Rysbrack: one to Sir John Newton and one to the Countess of Coningsby. The little marble slab in the centre of the floor commemorates her baby son, whose untimely death caused the extinction of the Coningsby title; in 1733 he was dropped over the parapet of the house by the family's pet monkey.

Holbeach

28; 8 miles E of Spalding on A151

This little town in the heart of the bulb-growing district of the Fens boasts one dignified main street lined with Georgian buildings and Victorian ALMSHOUSES. William Stukeley, the antiquary, was born at Holbeach in 1687 and his house – so restored as to be almost a reconstruction – is now the local council offices. The CHURCH OF ALL SAINTS is situated on the south side of the High Street, its churchyard planted with unusual trees. It is late Decorated-going-on-Perpendicular and has a great plain spire 180 feet high. Inside, the nave arcades have tall arches and slender moulded columns. In the aisles are large Decorated windows with elaborate flowing tracery. The tomb of Sir Humphrey Littlebury, killed in the Wars of the Roses, is especially interesting: the tomb-chest has ogee-arched niches and coats of arms; the splendid effigy in armour rests his head not on a cushion but on his helmet, which bears his family crest – a Saracen's head in a net!

Horncastle

29; 18 miles E of Lincoln on A158

Situated at the south-west foot of the Wolds, where they meet the Fens, Horncastle is a small, neat market town of red brick and stucco, and slated or pantiled roofs. North Street has several good Georgian shop-fronts and, as a view-stopper at the end, the former COURTHOUSE – now a Job Centre – a decent Victorian municipal Italianate pile designed by C. Reeves in 1865. The HIGH STREET is the principal thoroughfare and is lined with nicely varied buildings, including the Tudor-style Midland Bank. The MARKET PLACE is an attractive, informal space of irregular outline. In the middle stands the Stanhope Memorial – a little Victorian spire, 31 feet high. Round the sides are several old-established shops: Hargrave's Gun Shop – note the wooden sign in the form of two crossed guns over the door; Perkin's the Stationer's with its Georgian shop-front; and the Horncastle Farmers' Club, which has some nice painted lettering. In West Street are more Georgian brick houses, several of which have good old shop-fronts.

Just off the Market Place is the parish CHURCH OF ST MARY with its low, squat west tower and its Perpendicular air. It was restored by Ewan Christian in 1860 (look for the date embossed on the rainwater heads). The nave and chancel are the same height, and round the whole church runs an embattled parapet, which is elaborately decorated at the east end. The interior has moulded piers and a clerestory, but the ugly chancel arch and general aura date from its Victorian restoration. The most extraordinary feature is the collection of thirteen scythe blades hanging on the walls of the south chapel. There is also a painted canvas hatchment or monument to Sir Ingram Hopton, killed at the battle of Winceby in 1643; the inscription refers to Oliver Cromwell as 'the arch-rebel'.

Irnham

30; 5 miles NE of Colsterworth off A151

Here is a pretty stone-built village. IRNHAM HALL, embosomed in trees, is a rambling early sixteenth-century house, long, low, and picturesque with its battlements, mullion windows and octagonal turrets. It forms a good group with the parish CHURCH OF ST ANDREW. This has a part-Norman tower but is largely Decorated. The great treat inside is the Easter Sepulchre – one of the finest in the country, though no longer in its original position. It is tripartite with gables, moulded ogee arches and little openwork vaults, and is encrusted all over with the most sumptuous foliage carving.

Kirkstead Abbey

31; 1 mile S of Woodhall Spa off B1192

Of the Cistercian abbey founded in 1139 by Hugo Brito, son of the Lord of Tattershall, hardly anything survives of the main buildings apart from a jagged fragment of the south transept, some bits of wall and a few mysterious bumps in the grass. To the south, however, the former chapel *ante portas* remains as the parish CHURCH OF ST CLEMENT. It was built in 1230–40 in rich Decorated style and was excellently restored according to SPAB (Society for the Preservation of Ancient Buildings) principles in 1913–14 by William Weir (who also did Tattershall Castle (*q.v.*) for Lord Curzon); as a result, it retains a lot of its early atmosphere. The west door has an arch carved with dogtooth, resting on foliage capitals; above is an arcade framing a central window. The cheerfully whitewashed interior has a low stone vault with dogtooth

The church of St Clement, Kirkstead Abbey.

carving on the ribs and large carved bosses, that at the east end depicting the *agnus dei*. The east wall is an excellent composition of three stepped lancets, also with foliage capitals and dogtooth arches. The oak screen separating the chancel from the nave is thought to be the second oldest in England. On the floor of the chancel is half the effigy of a thirteenth-century knight in chain-mail and a cylindrical helmet that resembles nothing so much as a tin of Heinz soup; it is among the earliest military effigies in England.

Laughton

32; 5 miles N of Gainsborough off A159 [22]

Set amidst a landscape of large-scale Forestry Commission plantations, ALL SAINTS is a sumptuous church in the Perpendicular mode. It owes much to Mrs Meynell-Ingram, builder of Hoar Cross church in Staffordshire (*q.v.*), who found the medieval church much dilapidated and in 1894–6 employed the great G.F. Bodley to reconstruct and restore it as a memorial to her husband. The west tower and nave arcades are original medieval work, but Bodley added the lofty clerestory, the impressive Perpendicular chancel and the south porch, so it is his contribution that dominates the church. He was also responsible for all the fittings, which give the interior its noble, unified character; among them are the organ case and stained glass. The chancel is divided from the nave by a carved rood-screen. Behind the altar is a tall wooden reredos by Bodley, and a triptych painted in 1903 by G. Jackson. The monument to Hugo Meynell – a white marble effigy by Thomas Woolner – is a replica of that at Hoar Cross.

Lincoln*
33; 16 miles NE of Newark on A15

THE CITY

As you approach Lincoln you are rewarded with a majestic, though intermittent, view of the cathedral on its hilltop. When you reach the outskirts, however, the first feeling is inevitably one of slight disappointment. Here you had not expected to meet dingy Victorian red brick streets, factories and ugly modern shops. Lincoln grew rapidly in the nineteenth century through the manufacture of agricultural machinery; the result is a classic case in England of Balzac's contrast between the *haute ville* and the *ville basse*. The former is Barchester-scape, with the cathedral, and houses for the clergy and gentry; the latter is peopled by the tradesmen and workers. Although the 'Above Hill' is the most picturesque part of the town, there is much to be seen down below, where interesting old bits remain amidst the more recent fabric: the churches of ST BENEDICT, ST PETER-AT-GOWTS and ST MARY-LE-WIGFORD all have Saxon or Norman towers; ST MARY'S CONDUIT, moved to its present site in 1540, is Perpendicular; JOHN OF GAUNT'S STABLES are the ruined medieval Hall of the Guild of St Mary; THE GREYFRIARS, now the city museum, dates from the thirteenth century.

BRAYFORD POOL, with its little boats and breathtaking view of the cathedral, is a Roman watercourse. For, even before its medieval grandeur, Lincoln was a Roman legionary fortress and showplace, with colonnaded streets and impressive stone buildings, fragments of which survive – an arch, for instance, in the cellar of Boots. Nor is Victorian Lincoln to be despised. Both railway stations are distinguished: ST MARK'S STATION is classical with an Ionic portico, while CENTRAL STATION is a white brick exercise in the Baronial Gothic style. The ARBORETUM along the foot of the hill is a delightful Victorian park with ornamental planting and a bandstand.

The old town proper starts to pull together in the High Street, beginning with the HIGH BRIDGE over the River Witham, where it runs east from the Brayford Pool. This dates from the twelfth century and, on one side, still has timber-framed buildings, including a sixteenth-century CUSTOMS HOUSE – just like old London Bridge. The High Street is a pedestrianised shopping street, Georgian buildings mixed with supermarkets. In the middle of the road, on the site of the Roman south gate, is THE STONEBOW, a late Gothic town gate completed in 1520, with, upstairs, the city Guildhall. Beyond, the street – and the architectural excitement – begins to mount. The STEEP HILL area is an evocative medieval scene: winding lanes and alleys lead off it, all cobbled and lined with old timber-framing, and there are two genuine Norman stone-built houses (still lived in), as well as Georgian brick. All this area as you climb the hill used to be very run down and its present condition owes much to a careful and successful conservation policy carried out since the mid-1970s. Old houses have been repaired and empty sites tactfully filled – a very creditable exercise.

The first stretch of street beyond the Stonebow is called THE STRAIT and here is the JEW'S HOUSE, which dates from the twelfth century and has a round-arched door. The walk uphill gives picturesque glimpses back over the roofs of the lower town and the green slopes of Canwick opposite. This stretch is especially picturesque, with some overhanging timbered houses and others seemingly sunk into the ground. Off to the right, on the side of the hill, is the USHER ART GALLERY, a dignified Frenchy classical design of 1927 by Sir Reginald Blomfield. The junction of Steep Hill with Michaelgate makes a particularly good townscape effect: iron railings, bollards and gas-lamps complement the intricate spaces and nice old buildings. Christ's Hospital Terrace branches off on the other side, and here is the former BLUECOAT SCHOOL of 1784. AARON THE JEW'S HOUSE is late twelfth-century, stone-built with a handsome round-arched doorway. At the top of the hill is a welcome open space called Castle Hill, with the EXCHEQUER GATE to the cathedral precincts on the right and the gate to the castle set back on the left. Straight ahead on the corner of Bailgate is a gabled, jettied timber-framed house which forms the *point de vue* as you come to the top of the hill. Good Georgian houses line the approach to the castle, among them the sleek neo-classical JUDGE'S LODGING of 1819, designed by William Hayward.

The CASTLE was first built by William the Conqueror in 1086 on the south-west quarter of the upper Roman enclosure. It covers an area of 13 acres (including the earthwork ditches). The Eastern Gateway has a Norman archway but dates mainly from the fourteenth century, and has corner turrets and battlements. It leads to the quadrangle – a grassy enclosure surrounded by Georgian red brick and fanciful nineteenth-century Gothic buildings. The former Gaol (now County Record Office) was built in 1787 by Carr of York and the Assize Courts, in Tudor Gothick, are of 1823–6 by Sir Robert Smirke. An impressive stone curtain wall with round towers encloses the site, and the two Norman mottes are planted with trees and daffodils, which help soften the harshness of the military architecture.

Retracing one's steps to Bailgate and continuing north, there are more good Georgian brick houses and the White Hart Hotel – a dignified hostelry of 1840. To the right, in EASTGATE are some early nineteenth-century houses. Deloraine Court has a Norman undercroft, while the Eastgate Hotel is 1960s' keeping-in-keeping. Returning to BAILGATE the scale is more cottagey and there are some decent shops. The ASSEMBLY ROOMS date from 1744 but were refronted in 1914. Inside is the best Georgian room in the town, with Ionic pilasters supporting a bold cornice. Beneath the west side of Bailgate are the foundations of a Roman colonnade marked out by setts in the pavement, and at the end is the major Roman monument of Lincoln: the NEWPORT ARCH, formed of a central arch spanning the carriageway and a smaller flanking arch to the east (there was once a similar small arch on the west side). The Roman road was 8 feet lower than the present surface, which explains the arch's squat proportions.

THE CATHEDRAL AND IMMEDIATE ENVIRONS

Returning to the Exchequer Gate – a large and impressive fourteenth-century Perpendicular triple gateway – we enter MINSTER YARD and the cathedral precincts. Opposite is the towering mass of the cathedral itself, surrounded by grass and trees. Minster Yard is paved with Yorkstone slabs. Facing the west front, and forming an excellent foil, is a gentle quadrant of Georgian red brick houses. The most important buildings lie to the south of the cathedral on the brow of the hill: the substantial medieval remains of the former BISHOP'S PALACE; the Victorian DEANERY and the fifteenth-century SUBDEANERY. VICARS' COURT was founded in the late thirteenth century for the Vicars Choral and comprises four ranges of stone Gothic buildings round a spacious turfed courtyard. From Minster Yard Greestone Place plunges dramatically downhill. Here is the handsome red brick Georgian ARCHDEACONRY, and a massive fifteenth-century TITHE BARN. East of the cathedral, in Pottergate, are several more picturesque stone houses and THE CHANCERY, which is partly fourteenth-century with Georgian additions.

Lincoln Cathedral is a truly marvellous building – without doubt the finest Gothic cathedral in England. The overall standard of the architecture and sculptural decoration is of staggering quality. The site, too, is most impressive – the mighty building perched on a limestone ridge above the surrounding flat plain, dominating the town and visible for many miles around. The central tower was the loftiest of the English Middle Ages, and one of the most beautiful; it is scaled perfectly to harmonise with the similar but more slender western towers. Part of the west front is Norman, but essentially Lincoln is a creation of the thirteenth century – the supreme English architectural expression of that century, which, all things considered, can perhaps claim to have seen the apogee of modern European civilisation.

The Norman cathedral at Lincoln was shattered, odd to relate, by an earthquake on 15 April 1185. Only the west front survived; the rest was reduced to such a parlous condition that it had to be taken down to the ground and, under the leadership of Bishop Hugh of Avalon and his 'constructor', Geoffrey de Noiers, the opportunity was seized to build afresh in the very latest style. Work began in 1192 and was completed in 1280; it was the work of a series of masters but, in general, followed the original plan, though the detail increased in richness at each stage. As a result, Lincoln has a majestic unity too often lacking in English medieval churches. First to be built were the choir and the eastern transepts, followed by the Chapter House and the lower part of the central tower; then came the nave and upper part of the west front; finally the Angel Choir at the east end and the upper parts of the three towers. In the Middle Ages these towers also carried three lead-covered spires, but the central one was blown down in the sixteenth century and the west ones removed in 1809; the central tower is, however, still 271 feet high.

The exterior of Lincoln is sublime. In distant views it looks perfectly balanced, its long nave and choir about the same length and balancing each other on either side of the central tower. Close up you are dazed by the ornate masses of masonry. There is carved decoration all over: statues, stiff-leaf foliage, clusters of quatrefoils, and exquisite refinements of detail such as the alternately high and low pinnacles on the transepts. The west front, though imposing, is the least satisfactory feature. There is a head-on collision of styles between the retained Norman work in the middle and the Gothic additions. The Norman core has austere masses of unadorned masonry, five darkly recessed Germanic archways and friezebands of figurative sculpture derived from the Old Testament. The Gothic work, on the other hand, takes the form of a wide, tall screen with tier upon tier of ornate little arches – an uncomfortable contrast to the serenity of the Norman work. Most unhappily, the two beautiful towers are not related organically to the screen but shoot up from behind in an unresolved way.

The interior is a vision of purity and splendour unmatched in England. The proportions are low and broad compared to French Gothic, but this is compensated for by the immensely long vista punctuated by the spiky Gothick organ case of 1826 on the pulpitum screen, and by the richness and variety of all the parts. The effect of spaciousness is enhanced by the absence of chairs, the expanses of clear stone paving recalling churches in Italy. The lierne vault is one of the earliest in Europe where the stone ribs are deployed for purely decorative effect. It is a pity that the vaults are painted starkly white rather than stone colour, but this solecism could easily be put right. The columns are lavishly embellished with Purbeck 'marble', brought by sea from Dorset. They alternate, some being all of Purbeck and the others of stone with applied Purbeck shafts. The capitals, bosses and the wall arcade are excellently carved. The rare Norman font of black Tournai marble is one of only ten in England. The highly competent Victorian stained glass is mainly by an amateur: Canon Sutton of Brant Broughton (q.v.). As you walk towards the tower, your eye is caught by the trellis-patterned stone carving in the spandrels over the crossing-arch, and by the glorious carving of the Decorated pulpitum screen – a *tour de force* comparable to that at Southwell in Nottinghamshire (q.v.) but much larger. Equally mind-blowing are the two Decorated arches to the north and south choir aisles with their incredibly deeply undercut foliage carving. (It is slightly vulgar to have lit these inside with electric bulbs, but the temptation must have been irresistible.) In the transepts are the two famous rose windows. That to the north is called the 'Dean's Eye' and contains the most complete piece of medieval stained glass in the cathedral. The 'Bishop's Eye' in the south transept is even more breathtaking with its extravagant Decorated leaf tracery and shimmering medieval glass. In fact, the latter was made up in the eighteenth century out of fragments, like a patchwork quilt of gorgeous colours, but it is nevertheless of great beauty. St Hugh's Choir was the first part of the church to be built, and here some of the effects that seem so effortlessly perfect in the nave have the air of being strained after. This is particularly true of the crazy lop-sided vault, where the arrangement of the ribs is obviously experimental. The carved wooden choir stalls, where you will find sixty-two misericords, date from 1360–80 and are surpassed in England, if at all, only by those at Chester (q.v.). The convincingly

Decorated-looking reredos of stone behind the high altar is eighteenth-century and was the work of James Essex, a pioneer of serious Gothic Revival. Genuinely Decorated is the Easter Sepulchre – crocketed gables, moulded shafts and pinnacles, and a carved frieze of sleeping soldiers at the bottom.

St Hugh's Choir is continued to the east by the supremely beautiful Angel Choir, begun in 1256 and completed in 1280. The whole of the east wall is filled by an astonishingly ambitious eight-light window with geometrical tracery, the earliest such window to survive anywhere in Europe. It is filled with decent thirteenth-century-style stained glass by Ward and Hughes made in the mid-nineteenth century. The east windows of the aisles, however, contain genuine medieval glass. The architecture is incomparably mature and sumptuous. In Pevsner's words: 'this abundance of rich and mellow decoration has the warmth and sweetness of August and September'. Purbeck marble piers support arches carved with large-scale dogtooth ornament; the triforium has Purbeck shafts, geometrical tracery and foliage carving. In the spandrels of the triforium are the twenty-eight eponymous angels – medieval sculpture of first-rate quality inspired by Westminster and Reims. Equally good are the bosses of the vault with their naturalistic leaf and figure carving. A final touch is the gloriously extravagant double tracery of the clerestory windows.

The Angel Choir was built to contain the shrine of St Hugh of Avalon, and the base of the shrine, decorated with nodding ogee canopies and carved foliage, survives in the retrochoir. Also here is a nineteenth-century cenotaph to Queen Eleanor, wife of Edward I, who attended the consecration of the Angel Choir in 1280; it is a copy of the gilt bronze effigy by Torel in Westminster Abbey. In the choir aisles, chapels and eastern transepts are many other rarities and furnishings of interest, including a wide range of tombs, murals by Duncan Grant, one of the four original copies of Magna Carta, and the finest thirteenth-century ironwork screens in the country.

But the glories of the cathedral are not exhausted yet. The CHAPTER HOUSE is the earliest of the English polygonal chapter houses. It is a decagon with a diameter of 59 feet and is therefore much more spacious than some of the later polygons elsewhere. The outside is supported by eight huge flying buttresses. The interior, dim with Victorian stained glass, is reached by a vaulted passage from the Cloisters. Round the walls is blank arcading and the central pier is enriched with ten shafts of Purbeck marble and carved capitals. It supports a stone star vault of twenty ribs fanning out from the centre, like the branches of a huge palm tree. The Cloisters have a wooden vault with carved bosses. The range on the north side was rebuilt by Wren as a colonnade of Tuscan columns supporting a library upstairs. Finally, walking round the outside of the cathedral, the Judgement Porch on the south side of the Angel Choir should not be missed. It is flanked by a pair of little Perpendicular chantry chapels and forms a deeply recessed archway with sculptural embellishment. The tym-

panum, which features a seated figure of Christ, was heavily restored in the nineteenth century, but surrounding it are three carved arches with filigree foliage embowering little statues of apostles, wise and foolish virgins, kings and queens, all in perfect condition. In flanking niches stand excellent life-size figures, including one said to be Margaret of Valois, the second wife of Edward I. It is suggested that these carvings may have been the work of royal sculptors brought from Westminster to Lincoln specially to undertake the task.

Long Sutton
34; 4 miles SE of Holbeach on A17

The tower of ST MARY'S CHURCH carries a lead-covered spire which, according to J.C. Cox, is the 'highest, oldest, and most perfect lead spire now extant'. Dating from the thirteenth century and rising to 162 feet, it was originally a detached *campanile* with open arches on the ground floor. The outside of the church gives off an aura of Victorian over-restoration, so the noble nave comes as a great surprise. It consists of seven Norman bays, with circular piers, triforium and clerestory sandwiched between the equally tall Decorated and Perpendicular aisles. The Perpendicular south aisle is particularly striking. There are interesting Georgian furnishings, including a poor-box dated 1712 and communion rails with turned balusters. Unfortunately, the reredos of the same date, with its fluted columns, has been moved to the south aisle. Could it not be put back in its proper setting?

Louth
35; 24 miles NE of Lincoln on A157

Louth lies on the eastern edge of the Wolds. As you drive over the top, the spire of the parish church can be seen in the distance, framed by rolling plantations. The town is the thriving capital of prosperous farming country and has an important cattle market and malt silo. Approaching from the west there are no modern suburbs: parkland gives way immediately to distinguished Georgian houses.

Louth is built largely of red brick, with red pantiled roofs which form an excellent contrast to the Ancaster stone of the church. WESTGATE contains the finest Georgian houses, several of which, including THE LIMES and LINDSEY HOUSE, are used by the girls' school and so are well maintained. WESTGATE HOUSE is particularly attractive, with bow windows supported on Tuscan columns, iron balconies, and a fragile fanlight over the door, which is reached by a curly horseshoe staircase. THORNTON HOUSE has a pediment and bow windows, and many of the smaller houses have handsome pedimented doorcases and tripartite sash windows. Westgate is altogether an exceptionally well-preserved and interesting Georgian street, and with its magnificent views of the church spire forms an excellent introduction to the town.

The centre of Louth has a complex plan and no obvious main axes or spaces. The Market Place and Cornmarket run parallel to each other and are more like two streets than an open square. They are surrounded by pleasant old buildings, many of them brightly painted. The MARKET HALL of 1866 is Venetian Gothic with a weird little clock tower. In Cornmarket is the CORN EXCHANGE, which has a delightfully incompetent classical façade of decayed stone. In Eastgate is the TOWN HALL, the magnificent façade of which was executed in 1854 by Pearson Bellamy, who copied it from the Palazzo Farnese in Rome. Throughout the town decent Georgian houses and old-established shops line the narrow winding streets. It is worrying, however, to hear that an inner ring-road is proposed – one would think it the very last thing that a town like Louth needs.

The CHURCH OF ST JAMES is one of the half-dozen most magnificent medieval parish churches in England, thanks to its majestic fifteenth-century west tower and spire, leaping upwards to almost 300 feet and perfectly proportioned. The arched windows of the tower increase in size as they go up, and the delicate corner buttresses support incredibly tall, slender pinnacles from which spring lacy openwork flying buttresses supporting the crocketed spire itself. Everything about it is perfect: proportions, detail, silhouette. It is a masterpiece, and one could happily contemplate it all day, watching the colour of the stone change in the different lights. The rectangular body of the church is long – 182 feet – and so is in balance when seen in conjunction with the spire. The whole of the exterior is faced in ashlar stone and has the noble, calm, courtly character of all top-quality Perpendicular architecture. There are large traceried windows, and *fleuron* friezes round the top beneath the battlements. The interior is disappointing after the glory of the exterior. It was, alas, 'restored' by the local architect James Fowler in the nineteenth century and as a result feels like a gutted shell. The nave is large and wide but the proportions are not entirely happy. The walls are cream-washed and there is an open timber roof, but there are few good fittings. The Victorian glass, the alabaster reredos and the encaustic tiles are all undistinguished, though one or two unusual old oil paintings hang in the nave.

St James's has an interesting history, for the sermon that incited 20,000 Lincolnshire men to join the Pilgrimage of Grace was preached from its pulpit. The vicar and sixty townsmen were hanged for their part in this ineffectual protest against the Dissolution of the Monasteries, and Henry VIII graciously described the inhabitants as 'rude commons of . . . one of the most brutal and beestlie [shires] of the whole realm'.

Marston Hall
36; 6 miles N of Grantham off A1
Marston is the ancient seat of the Thorold family, who are first recorded as living here in the fourteenth century. The house was severely damaged by the Roundheads during the Civil War, and then partly demolished in the eighteenth century. Thereafter Marston was used by the agent, or as a dower-house, till this century, which has seen it restored to its role as a family home.

In its heyday, Marston comprised an E-shaped Tudor house with a Gatehouse in front. What remains is the middle range, shorn of its wings. The old Great Hall was

St Mary's church, Long Sutton.

subdivided in the eighteenth century. The present Hall is only a quarter of the size of the original, but retains a sixteenth-century chimneypiece and a Tudor arch to the screens passage. The Library has an eighteenth-century marble chimneypiece after a design by Inigo Jones. Among the Dutch and Flemish paintings in the Drawing Room is a *Holy Family* thought to be a preliminary study for Rubens' altarpiece in Vienna. On the upper floor, the Burston Room has an elaborate plaster ceiling and panelling, dated 1699, brought to Marston in 1972. In the garden don't miss the Gothick gazebo with murals by Barbara Jones.

Scrivelsby
37; 2 miles S of Horncastle on B1183
SCRIVELSBY COURT, seat of the Dymokes – hereditary champions of England, who carry the Royal Standard in the Coronation procession – is buried deep in Lincolnshire, far from large centres of population, remote and romantic. The large park is beautifully kept, with a considerable amount of new tree planting as well as venerable old timber. Part of the ancient house was demolished in the 1950s and the present L-shaped building comprises the sixteenth-century gateway and fifteenth-century office wing, restored and converted to make an attractive smaller residence. It is built of narrow red brick and has steep gables and tall chimneys. Many of the windows are Georgian sashes, the old archway is now filled in and in the gable above it is a clock. The ENTRANCE LODGE by the roadside is charming; it has

retained its old stone archway, which is topped off with an over-sized heraldic lion. The little LODGE COTTAGE – possibly by Humphry Repton – is a double octagon, like an angular figure of eight, and has Gothick glazing bars in its pointed windows.

The CHURCH OF ST BENEDICT stands on its own in a stretch of parkland on the opposite side of the road. The graveyard is large and green, ablaze with daffodils each spring. There is no paved path to the church, which increases its feeling of rural peace. You will find it locked, but a polite notice on the door (signed by the squire-cum-churchwarden!) explains that the key can be obtained from Scrivelsby Court. The building was thoroughly restored in 1861 and the little tower and spire are entirely Victorian. The interior is crammed with Dymoke tombs, processing through the centuries (the Dymokes acquired the estate by marriage c.1350) down to the present time.

Sempringham
38; 10 miles N of Bourne off A15
Here St Gilbert founded the only English monastic order, the Gilbertines. The son of a rich Norman knight, he died at Sempringham in 1189 and was canonised in 1202. His monastery has disappeared, but the surviving parish church, ST ANDREW'S, was built by Gilbert's father. It stands alone amidst bumpy fields, marking the site of the vanished village. The transepts and chancel of St Andrew's were demolished in the eighteenth century, so the present structure combines the Norman nave and the Victorian apse. The building suffered somewhat from over-restoration by Browning in the 1860s and this has left it deprived of atmosphere, though still architecturally impressive. The central tower is Perpendicular, battlemented and pinnacled. The nave arcade alternates between circular piers and grouped piers, and several of the original round-arched Norman windows survive, as well as two lavish doorways. The south doorway is the showpiece of the church: stop and admire its carved tympanum, zigzag arches, the little grouped colonnettes on either side, and its beautiful thirteenth-century scrolling ironwork.

Sleaford
39; 11 miles NE of Grantham on A153 [34]
This is a stately little market town of stone-built houses. The Market Place, planted with pollarded trees, is dominated by the CHURCH OF ST DENYS, which has the nobility of a cathedral. The grand west front, 'pinnacled, niched, traceried and moulded', is surmounted by a sturdy tower supporting one of the earliest spires in the country; it dates from the late twelfth or early thirteenth century. The nave is Decorated, with lofty arches on slender piers, while the clerestory and chancel are Perpendicular. The windows are embellished with beautiful flowing tracery of a quality it would be hard to match in any other English parish church, and the rood-screen was considered by Pugin to be one of the most perfect in the land. The chancel is ennobled by beautiful fittings: seventeenth-century altar rails from Lincoln Cathedral and embellishments by Sir Ninian Comper, including the

rood and figures on top of the screen. St Hugh's Chapel contains Jacobean monuments – one by Maximilian Colt – to the Carre family, who were the great benefactors of Sleaford, founders of both the Grammar School and CARRE'S HOSPITAL. The latter, rebuilt by H.E. Kendall in 1830, stands to the south of the church and is planned round an open quadrangle. Kendall also designed the Gothic SESSIONS HOUSE facing the Market Place. The elaborate Perpendicular Revival CORN EXCHANGE was designed in 1857 by the local architects Kirk and Parry. Otherwise, the Market Place is lined with decent Georgian houses and in the middle is a Victorian Gothic fountain. Behind the church is the Elizabethan VICARAGE, dating from 1568.

The principal streets radiate from the Market Place. In EASTGATE is the seventeenth-century Old House, as well as the Victorian Italianate offices of Kesteven District Council, the Union Building by W.J. Donthorne and the Tudor-style Gatehouse to the old gasworks. In SOUTHGATE are the White Hart Hotel dating from 1691 and the Handley Monument, erected in memory of Henry Handley MP (who died in 1846) in the form of an Eleanor Cross. Westgate is generally attractive, though without any special buildings; several of the little Georgian houses and cottages are approached by individual bridges over the river. NORTHGATE contains the Grammar School, rebuilt in Tudor style by Charles Kirk in 1834. Among several interesting old houses in this street No. 2 is the best; it is late seventeenth-century with a pedimented door and carved keystones over the windows.

Somersby
40; 6 miles NE of Horncastle off A158 [21]
Somersby is nicely situated in a leafy hollow of the Wolds. SOMERSBY HOUSE was the birthplace of Alfred, Lord Tennyson, whose father was Rector here. It is a white-painted, rambling Georgian house, the Dining Room of which was added in 1819 to the design of the poet's father and built by the coachman. MANOR FARM, next door, is an embattled brick house with four square corner turrets. It was built in 1722 for Robert Burton and is attributed on stylistic grounds to Sir John Vanbrugh. The centre is pedimented and the arched door and window above form the centre of Venetian compositions on each floor with square-headed side-pieces. The upstairs windows in the turrets are circular portholes. The whole thing looks like a miniature barracks: you almost expect a line of lead soldiers to march out of the door at any moment.

The CHURCH OF ST MARGARET, although of no great architectural interest in itself, contains a bust of Tennyson and various other souvenirs of the poet, whose work is haunted by memories of Somersby and by the sound of the east wind as it comes whistling off the Wolds:

> *Come from the woods that belt the grey hill-side,*
> *The seven elms, the poplars four*
> *That stand beside my father's door....*

21 *Somersby Manor Farm, Lincolnshire.*

22 *All Saints' church, Laughton, Lincolnshire.*

23 *Leighton Hall, Lancashire.*

24 *Scarisbrick Hall, Lancashire.*

25 *St Mary and St John the Baptist, Pleasington, Lancashire.*

26 *Docks, Town Hall and Cathedral, Liverpool.*

27 *Quenby Hall, Leicestershire.*

28 *Belton House, Lincolnshire.*

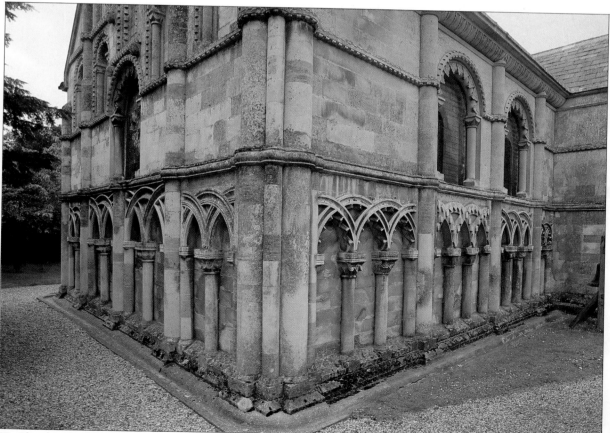

29 *The church of St Peter, Tickencote, Leicestershire.*

30 *St Botolph's – the 'Boston Stump' – Boston, Lincolnshire.*

31 *Doddington Hall, Lincolnshire.*

32 *Casewick Hall, Lincolnshire.*

33 *Harlaxton Manor, Lincolnshire.*

34 *The church of St Denys, Sleaford, Lincolnshire.*

35 *Tattershall Castle, Lincolnshire.*

36 *Alnwick Castle.*

37 *Callaly Castle, Northumberland.*

38 Cragside, Northumberland.

39 *Lindisfarne Castle, Northumberland.*

40 *Wallington Hall, Northumberland.*

41 *St Mary's church, Egmanton, Nottinghamshire.*

42 *Flintham Hall, Nottinghamshire.*

43 *Attingham Park, Shropshire.*

44 *Mawley Hall, Shropshire.*

South Stoke

41; 6 miles S of Grantham on A1

This estate still belongs to the Turnors (who live at Little Ponton) and is well kept, with an attractive group of 'Tudor' cottages designed by William Burn between 1840 and 1845 at the entrance to the park. STOKE ROCHFORD HALL, now used for educational purposes, is a large and grand Tudorbethan job, also by Burn, but its immediate setting has been somewhat spoilt by new buildings. The parish CHURCH OF ST MARY AND ST ANDREW is fascinating. The base of the tower and one of the nave arcades are Norman but the other nave arcade is French Transitional and recalls the choir of Canterbury Cathedral, while the east end is Perpendicular and Decorated. The special aura of the building can be attributed to Christopher Turnor, squire of Stoke Rochford in the early twentieth century and an amateur artist. He designed the three-tier Neo-Jacobean font cover with its gilded and painted decorations, and also the lectern and wrought-iron light fittings. The reredos, however, was the work of Mrs G.F. Watts. Lots of family memorials and hatchments can be seen inside the church. The north side is occupied by those of the Turnors of Stoke Rochford Hall and the south side by those of the Cholmeleys of Easton Hall. The largest, a Jacobean 'four-poster' to Henry Cholmeley, who died in 1641, has columns, obelisks and kneeling effigies. The Cholmeley monuments culminate in a tragic war memorial commemorating no fewer than seven of the family killed in the First World War. The Turnor monuments include an eighteenth-century one to Sir Edward Turnor with a large marble urn, and a curious Ruskinian Venetian Gothic reredos-type marble and mosaic monument designed by the artist-squire Christopher Turnor in memory of another Christopher Turnor and his wife.

Spalding

42; 24 miles E of Colsterworth on A151

Spalding brings a Dutch atmosphere to the centre of the most fertile district in England, renowned for sugar-beet, potatoes and bulb-growing. The River Welland flows through the middle of the town like a highway, its banks lined with trees and Georgian brick houses. It is crossed by seven bridges and, apart from some municipal 'improvements', it is an almost unalloyed pleasure to walk along it.

The best place to start a tour of Spalding is the MARKET PLACE, where the early eighteenth-century White Hart Hotel, the Victorian Corn Exchange and an interesting Barclays Bank are to be seen. Bridge Street leads down to London Road and the river, and WELLAND PLACE and WELLAND TERRACE form a procession of Georgian goodies, among them Welland Hall (the old High School), a dignified three-storeyed house standing in its own garden. On the other side of the river, in COWBIT ROAD, are several grander houses, including West-bourne Lodge, which has bow windows, and Langton House, with its Doric porch. Church Gate leads to AYSCOUGHFEE HALL, genuinely ancient but overlaid in the 1840s with *cottage orné* Tudor embellishments. It was the home of Maurice Johnson, lawyer and antiquary,

who founded the Spalding Gentlemen's Society (a society of antiquaries) in 1710. It is now a general museum and retains an eighteenth-century walled garden, albeit somewhat municipalised. The Council Offices next door were built in 1960–2 and, of course, replace an excellent eighteenth-century house which was specially demolished to make room for them. Beyond Town Bridge, dated 1838, is the HIGH STREET, where there are more decent eighteenth-century houses, including HOLLAND HOUSE built in 1768 and designed by William Sands, Junior; it is the best house in the town. Further Georgian and Regency houses can be found in Double Street on the other side of the river. In Broad Street the SPALDING GENTLEMEN'S SOCIETY MUSEUM, built in 1910, contains an amazingly heterogeneous collection of local antiquities and relics displayed in an attractively old-fashioned way. Of its sort, it is probably the most atmospheric and enjoyable museum in the country.

The parish CHURCH OF ST MARY AND ST NICHOLAS owes much to the restoration carried out by Sir George Gilbert Scott in the 1860s. It is basically a thirteenth-century cruciform plan but with later accretions, including secondary aisles and chapels. The elaborate north porch is Perpendicular and has a fan-vaulted interior. The south-west tower of the church carries a crocketed spire. The nave is spacious but lacks the unity of such great Lincolnshire churches as Boston, Grantham, Louth or Sleaford (*qq.v.*). Its wooden hammerbeam roof has carved angels, restored by Scott, while the chancel owes much to the recent redecoration by Stephen Dykes Bower, to whose credit is the beautiful painted ceiling. The dark Victorian stained glass in most of the windows is by Clayton and Bell.

Spilsby

43; 10 miles E of Horncastle on A16

Spilsby stands on the south edge of the Wolds – a small, neatly-kept town with a Georgian MARKET PLACE, which is given intriguing character by an island of houses down the middle. The west end has a huge Victorian bronze statue by Charles Bacon, dated 1861, of Sir John Franklin, the explorer of the North-west Passage, who is shown leaning on an enormous anchor. Facing this are some nice Georgian buildings, including the old TOWN HALL of 1764 and the WHITE HART INN. In the centre of the east part the old Market Cross stands on a stepped base.

The CHURCH OF ST JAMES lies to the west of the town. It has a squat Perpendicular tower with exaggeratedly crocketed pinnacles; otherwise, it all looks a rather dreary Victorian reconstruction. (It was indeed thoroughly restored and reconstructed by W. Bassett Smith in 1879.) But do not be put off, for the interior contains one of the best collections of church monuments in Lincolnshire. These are the Willoughby and Bertie monuments in the Willoughby Chapel – a fourteenth-century chantry chapel endowed by the will of the 1st Lord Willoughby in 1348. They make a wonderful array of medieval stone and alabaster knights and their ladies on tomb-chests. The whole of the west end of the Chapel, blocking the arch under the tower, is filled by the huge Elizabethan monument to Richard Bertie and his wife, formerly a Duchess of Suffolk. It is like a large stone reredos. The back is divided by three fluted Ionic columns and filled with inscribed stone panels from the Scriptures. The altar-like tomb beneath has three heraldic cartouches on the front.

Opposite the church is the best building in Spilsby: the former SESSIONS HOUSE – a severe Greek Revival building with a powerful Doric portico of 1824 by H.E. Kendall. It is now a theatre.

Stamford *

44; 21 miles S of Grantham on A1

Stamford is one of the best-preserved of the old country towns of England and has a remarkably dignified and homogenous character, thanks to the excellent local stone of which it is built. It stands on the rich oolitic limestone belt that runs across England like a Garter riband from the Humber to Somerset and has provided the building material for some of the best English architecture. Stamford is a place of great antiquity which grew up round the ford over the River Welland on the Great North Road. It has had three great periods of prosperity: the first in the twelfth and thirteenth centuries was ecclesiastical, producing churches and colleges (part of the University of Oxford migrated here for a time); the second, in the fifteenth and sixteenth centuries, was based on wool; the third came in the eighteenth century, when Stamford was an important coaching stage on the Great North Road. Each period has left a magnificent architectural deposit. Thanks to the Marquesses of Exeter, the dominant local landowners who resisted the railway in the nineteenth century (it went and ruined Peterborough instead), the town has survived in remarkably unscathed condition. There are no eyesores, no demolition sites, no new roads or large modern suburbs.

It is an extraordinary experience to walk or drive through Stamford from south to north: as the main street curves and winds through the town you keep coming across yet another large medieval parish church complete with tower or spire. These contribute greatly to the skyline in general views across the Welland Valley – as you can see, for example, in Turner's painting. The river, incidentally, forms the county boundary, with the result that ST MARTIN'S CHURCH, to the south of the town, is now really in Cambridgeshire – but it would be eccentric to ignore it here. It is late Perpendicular, with a soaring west tower. The Cecil family chapel contains the tombs of Lord Burghley, Elizabeth I's great minister, and his successors, the Earls and Marquesses of Exeter. That to the 5th Earl, made by Monnot in Rome in 1703, is an internationally important work of art. HIGH STREET ST MARTINS is an anteportas suburb of stone seventeenth-century and Georgian houses with stone-flagged roofs; it acts as a good overture to the town centre. Descend from here to the river, past the George Hotel of 1728, with its wooden sign over the street, and LORD BURGHLEY'S HOS-PITAL (a group of Elizabethan almshouses), and so cross the bridge. Pause now to admire the views of the water-meadows, which belong to the town, and the picturesque jumble of old roofs and warehouses climbing the slope from the opposite bank. The TOWN HALL, built in 1776, is on the right and in front of you is the majestic spectacle of ST MARY'S CHURCH. Its tower is Early English and its broach spire fourteenth-century, while most of the rest of the church is Perpendicular with a rich interior. The East Chapel has a ceiling studded with gold stars and a belated Pre-Raphaelite window of 1891 by Christopher Whall, described by Pevsner as 'the source of much that was and is evil in English twentieth-century stained glass'. The rood-screen and altar frontal are by J.D. Sedding, one of the most original of Arts and Crafts designers.

Facing St Mary's Hill are some specially fine Regency shop-fronts with Ionic columns, and from St Mary's Hill itself are good views back to St Martin's. St Mary's Place is of dog-leg shape, lying south and east of the church; it is described in *The Buildings of England* as a 'perfect expression of Georgian elegance', while Pevsner regards this whole sweep of the town as 'one of the best examples of Georgian townscape in England'. Turning left into St John's Street, the CHURCH OF ST JOHN THE BAPTIST is mostly Perpendicular, with a tower and an intimate interior, the outstanding feature of which is a carved timber roof embellished with angels. ALL SAINTS' CHURCH is the hub of Stamford. Facing down All Saints' Place and dominating Red Lion Square, it is a sumptuous Early English job with a Perpendicular steeple. All around here are excellent Georgian houses and the main streets fan out in different directions. BARN HILL is a complete and undisturbed sequence of Georgian houses with nicely varied doorcases, including some Gothick and some Greek.

In Broad Street is the finest medieval secular building of Stamford: BROWNE'S HOSPITAL, a foundation of almshouses endowed by William Browne, a rich merchant of the Staple at Calais who died in 1489. It is a thoroughly Trollopian set-up and provides for ten old men and one old lady, presided over by a warden in Holy Orders. Broad Street is a handsome wide thoroughfare with seventeenth- and eighteenth-century houses, as well as the CORN EXCHANGE of 1839 in mixed style. St Paul's Street leads to the HIGH STREET, where there are more Georgian houses (including a brick interpolation) and some good shop-fronts, one with Corinthian columns. Maiden Lane leads to St George's Square and ST GEORGE'S CHURCH, which dates from the thirteenth century, although the chancel was rebuilt c.1449 at the expense of William de Bruges, first Garter King of Arms. The north-east window contains old stained glass with about 200 mottoes of founder members of the Order of the Garter. The church's best feature is the marble monument by John Bacon to Sir Richard Cust, dated 1797. It shows a bust of the deceased on a column against which leans an allegorical female. The square is grouped round the church, forming a most attractive backwater, with good Georgian houses and the former ASSEMBLY ROOMS of 1725. In St Mary's Street is the surprisingly grand STAMFORD HOTEL – a large-scale classical façade with Corinthian columns designed by J.L. Bond in 1810 and adorned with sculpture by J.C.F. Rossi; it would not look out of place in St Petersburg (where, as it turns out, Bond

The church of St Mary, Stow.

had spent some of his career). From St Mary's Street several intriguing alleys lead down to the riverside, where it is worth taking a stroll to admire the fine views of the town from the meadows.

Stow
45; 6 miles SE of Gainsborough on B1241
In the centre of the flat plain north-west of Lincoln rises the castle-like Romanesque CHURCH OF ST MARY. The original Saxon church on the site was destroyed by the Vikings but rebuilt *c.*1040 by Eadnoth, Bishop of Dorchester, partly at the expense of Lady Godiva's husband, Leofric, Earl of Mercia. This work determined the size of the church when it came to be partly reconstructed once again after the Norman Conquest by Bishop Remigius. The Saxon work was notably monumental, as is demonstrated by the surviving crossing with arches 30 feet high. The nave, transepts and chancel are all Norman, the latter a spectacularly elaborate job owing much of its present splendour to the restoration carried out by J.L. Pearson in 1853–64. The chancel's original quadripartite stone-ribbed vault had been destroyed in a fire in the Middle Ages and the rents in the walls, formed when the vault collapsed, had been repaired with stones from the ribs. Pearson demolished the later east wall, which was 'in a shattered state', discovering in the process some carved stones from the Norman window arches. These enabled him to reinstate the original design of two tiers, each of two round-arched windows with carved mouldings. Likewise, the surviving bits of the ribs allowed him

to recreate accurately the whole of the original vault. This careful archaeological job is an architectural triumph and on the strength of his designs for the restoration Pearson was elected to the Society of Antiquaries in 1853.

Stragglethorpe
See Brant Broughton.

Swinstead
46; 5 miles NW of Bourne on B1176
Swinstead is an outwork of the Grimsthorpe (*q.v.*) estate. It has been suggested that Vanbrugh built a large house here for the 1st Duke of Ancaster, and certainly characteristic fragments survive, including a mighty rusticated doorway built into a cottage, and an extraordinary fireplace in the SCHOOL. On the hillside is a SUMMERHOUSE showing the unmistakable hand of the master. Flanked by two square towers, it has arched windows and on the first floor is a polygonal room with views over Grimsthorpe park.

Tattershall Castle
NT; 47; 7 miles S of Horncastle on A153 [35]
Tattershall was created by Ralph Cromwell, Lord Treasurer of England in the years 1433–43. As a young man he had fought in the Hundred Years' War and had been present at the battle of Agincourt. It is highly likely that the design of Tattershall was influenced by what he saw on the Continent – in particular the *wasserburgs* of

Tattershall Castle.

spire. The aisles and clerestory are battlemented, and there are prominent gargoyles at the corners of the roofline and at the ends of the aisles. The stone varies nicely in colour and the tower and porch are patched with medieval brickwork, all of which gives the exterior an attractively varied patina and a picturesque texture. The interior is spacious, with an open timber queenpost roof, octagonal piers to the nave arcades and a variety of interesting furnishings, including an array of carved screens. The main rood-screen is Perpendicular and part gilded, and in the south chapel is an ornate stone rood screen. But best of all are the two parclose screens – early sixteenth-century and English Renaissance with exciting wood-carving of dragons and human heads. The grandeur of the building is augmented by the monuments and memorial cartouches of local families, and it is attractively set in a graveyard bright with wild flowers.

Thornton Abbey
49; 6 miles NW of Market Rasen off B1205
The ruins of Thornton, covering nearly 100 acres, stand amidst flat fields half a mile outside the village of Thornton Curtis. The abbey was founded for Augustinian canons in 1139. Two walls of the polygonal Chapter House, decorated with beautiful tracery, are the only sizeable bits of the claustral buildings to survive; otherwise, the remains consist of low walls and foundations neatly marked out in the grass by the Heritage Commission. But at the entrance stands the largest of all English gatehouses – almost like a castle in its own right. It dates from the late fourteenth century and the elevations are a picturesque patchwork of soft red brick and weathered stone. Approached over a bridge between long fortified brick walls with niches and two round turrets, the Gatehouse is 68 feet high and divided into five sections by octagonal turrets. The entrance side is the most severe, with, in the centre, a tall archway beneath an array of statues of Our Lady, St John the Baptist and St Augustine; they stand in canopied niches with little arrow-slits on either side. The inner face, towards the precincts, is less forbidding, with an elegant oriel over the archway and one or two traceried windows. The oriel lights a large room, almost like a great hall, on the first floor, which has a beamed ceiling supported on carved stone heads and a pretty stone rib vault in the oriel – a good vantage point from which to survey the ruins.

Woolsthorpe Manor
NT; 50; 8 miles S of Grantham off A1
Famous as the birthplace of Sir Isaac Newton, Woolsthorpe is an unassuming T-shaped limestone manor house with mullion windows. The low homely rooms have moulded stone chimneypieces and are furnished with appropriate pieces of seventeenth-century furniture, acquired for the house by the National Trust. In the old kitchen are some *graffiti* said to be by Newton. It was while staying here to avoid the Plague in 1665 and 1666 that he made three rather important discoveries: the principles of differential calculus, the composition of white light and the law of gravitation.

northern France and Flanders – and the building accounts show that the bricks were made under the supervision of Balduin 'Dochman', a German. Over the centuries the castle fell slowly into ruin, but it was rescued by Lord Curzon in 1911 and carefully repaired under the direction of William Weir, a sensitive architect who specialised in the restoration of ancient buildings. The TOWER, which alone survives from the original building, is among the best examples of fifteenth-century domestic architecture in the country. One hundred feet high, it comprised Cromwell's private apartments and was a piece of neo-feudal display rather than a serious piece of fortification. The interior contains a series of Perpendicular carved stone chimneypieces decorated with Cromwell's arms and badges of office. These were saved by Lord Curzon after they had been removed for sale to America. He prevented their export and carried them back in triumph to their rightful home.

The adjoining CHURCH OF THE HOLY TRINITY was also founded by Lord Cromwell, built in 1438 as a collegiate establishment. It is large and cruciform with a west tower and enormous traceried Perpendicular windows, through which the light floods into the bare whitewashed interior. Only the east window now retains portions of medieval stained glass, most of which was removed in the eighteenth century. The overall effect is of being inside a vast Gothic greenhouse.

Theddlethorpe
48; 11 miles E of Louth on A1031
ALL SAINTS is sometimes called 'the cathedral of the marshes'. It is a large, rich church, chiefly Perpendicular, with a solid square tower sporting a thin little

Northumberland

Northumberland is frontier country, England's northern boundary. Beyond the Cheviot Hills and the River Tweed lies Scotland, for centuries a far from friendly neighbour. This fact dictates the character of both the landscape and architecture. For most of its history Northumberland was wild and unsettled; peaceful prosperity finally emerged only after the Act of Union, when the eighteenth and nineteenth centuries saw prodigious expansion, based on the exploitation of coal, in the south-east corner of the county round Newcastle, and the enclosure and reclamation of the wastes for high farming. Today the rural landscape of Northumberland is a classic combination of wild natural beauty, exemplified by the sweeping Pennine moors, and the improved farmland of the eighteenth- and nineteenth-century Agricultural Revolutions, characterised by model farms and cottages, large hedged fields and great expanses of recent tree planting. In many ways the county is closer in appearance to eastern Scotland than to more southerly parts of England. It is still exhilaratingly feudal with very large estates, of which the Duke of Northumberland's — nearly 100,000 acres — is the biggest. There are few towns, apart from Alnwick, Berwick-upon-Tweed and Morpeth, or large villages, and much of Northumberland is sparsely inhabited. The typical unit is the country house with a park, dependent farms and a cluster of planned model cottages at the gate. Much of the eighteenth- and nineteenth-century reclamation was carried out by old-established families, but more is the work of wave after wave of third-generation industrialists from Newcastle setting themselves up as landed families. Much of what you see in rural Northumberland was paid for by the coal, shipping and engineering of Tyneside.

Wide stretches of Northumberland consist of bare rolling hills, but the scenery is varied nonetheless: there is an attractive coastline with sandy beaches, sheltered bays and the odd dramatic outcrop like Dunstanburgh. In the north, the coastal plain is rich agricultural land; in the south it is heavily built up and industrialised, with coal-mines and new towns. The Tyne Valley west of Newcastle is the most gentle and wooded part of the county and such villages and small towns as do exist — including Corbridge and Hexham — are mainly concentrated there.

The chief architectural interest of Northumberland lies in its castles. There are few medieval churches here, and hardly any of national importance, apart from Hexham Priory with its Saxon crypt and St Nicholas's Cathedral, Newcastle, with the unique openwork stone crown on top of its west tower. But where military architecture is concerned, Northumberland is the best-endowed county in England, boasting excellent examples of many periods, from the Roman forts, like Chesters, on Hadrian's Wall to the mid-sixteenth-century Italian Renaissance fortifications at Berwick, the first of their sort in northern Europe. The history of English castles could be written drawing mainly on Northumbrian examples. There are splendid Norman fortifications — both circular shell keeps as at Alnwick, or square hall keeps as at Newcastle and Bamburgh. The more complex curtain walls of the later Middle Ages, with gateways and barbicans, can again be found at Alnwick and Bamburgh. At Dunstanburgh is an impressive example of the keep—gatehouse plan derived from Edward I's castle at Harlech. There are dozens of pele towers, of which Chipchase and Belsay are particularly impressive, and several compact later medieval castles with four corner towers and small internal courtyards, as at Ford or Chillingham. Finest of all is the fourteenth-century geometric keep at Warkworth — the culmination of English medieval castle design.

Increasing prosperity in the eighteenth and nineteenth centuries led to the remodelling of many old peles into comfortable country houses, like Callaly and Chipchase, or the building of a new country house nearby, as happened at Belsay. Many splendid houses were also built on fresh sites, notably Vanbrugh's Seaton Delaval. Northumberland was lucky in the late eighteenth and early nineteenth centuries in having a number of good local architects, especially the Greens of Newcastle and John Dobson. Their work is displayed in the grand early nineteenth-century commercial centre of Newcastle itself and also in country houses throughout the county. Dobson, in particular, created a series of beautifully planned and executed houses, of which Nunnykirk Hall is the best. He was also responsible for forming the central Hall on the site of a former courtyard at Wallington, which was decorated by Bell Scott under Ruskin's influence. A similar Pre-Raphaelite scheme of decoration was carried out in the village school at Ford by Louisa, Marchioness of Waterford. The best Victorian buildings in Northumberland, however, are the Italianate interior of Alnwick Castle and Norman Shaw's Cragside and Chesters. The story of successful design continues into the twentieth century with notable work by Lutyens at Lindisfarne and Whalton Manor, and with the 1960s' developments at Newcastle, where the Swedish-style Civic Centre and new Tyne bridges are something of which the citizens are rightly proud and which other cities might well envy.

In 1974 the south-east corner of the old county, including Newcastle, was lopped off to become the new metropolitan county of Tyne and Wear, but I have included it here, as the rural and industrial areas can only be properly understood in relation to each other.

Alnwick Castle★

1; 18 miles N of Morpeth on A1 [36]

There is a story of Proust repeating to himself again and again, as if to savour their feudal splendour, the syllables 'Duchess of Northumberland'. Although their great inheritance passed twice through the female line in the eighteenth century, the Percys can prove descent from Count Giselbert of Maasgau, who, in 864, married the great-grandmother of Charlemagne. There are few comparable examples in modern Europe of so old a family still in possession of such an extensive and historic hegemony – a dukedom, large estates, an Adam palace at Syon near London, a burial vault in Westminster Abbey, and this great castle with its incomparable art collection.

It is not clear exactly when after the Norman Conquest the castle was founded, but the first major stone buildings were erected in the mid-twelfth century in the form of a circular shell keep with a series of later towers surrounding a small inner court and two outer baileys encircled by curtain walls that are also punctuated with towers. This basic plan has survived all later changes and embellishments, though much of the fabric was rebuilt by Henry, 1st Lord Percy of Alnwick, who acquired the castle in 1309. The interior of the keep was completely remodelled by the 1st Duke of Northumberland in the 1760s to the design of Robert Adam – the park was landscaped by Capability Brown at the same time – and an even more sweeping 'restoration' was undertaken by the 4th Duke in the mid-nineteenth century. He assigned the external work to Salvin, who executed it in a solid medieval style appropriate to a castle. In the interior, however, the Duke – who was a great admirer of the Italian Renaissance and formed a remarkable collection of Italian pictures – turned classical and entrusted the decoration to a team of Italian artists under the Commendatore Luigi Canina, Director of Rome's Capitoline Museum, and to a number of indigenous craftsmen, of whom John Brown of Alnwick, a woodcarver, was the most accomplished. The result is probably the finest Victorian classical interior in England.

A modest Entrance Hall, hung with arms and armour, leads to the marble Grand Staircase and the Guard Chamber, the first of the principal apartments on the *piano nobile*. The Grand Chamber has a mosaic pavement made in Rome and frieze paintings by Francis Götzenburger; and the splendid Van Dyck of the 10th Earl of Northumberland, two Canalettos of Syon and Windsor, a landscape by Claude, gilt chairs and sofas by John Linnell and a magnificent Adam circular gaming table immediately introduce the visitor to the superb paintings and furniture of the Northumberland Collection. The Anteroom is hung with a group of Italian paintings that for quality has no equal in any English house: it comprises three by Titian, two by Tintoretto and two parts of an important fresco of *The Visitation* by Sebastiano del Piombo.

The Library, which contains 16,000 volumes – one of the best country house book collections – has a gilded coffered ceiling embellished with trophies representing History, Painting, Poetry and the Sciences; the oak and maple bookcases were designed by Giovanni Montivoli. The Music Room occupies the site of Adam's saloon; it has a richly coffered and gilded ceiling and a painted arabesque frieze by Mantovani. The walls are hung with yellow brocade and more fine paintings, including Canaletto views of Alnwick, Syon and Venice, and seventeenth-century portraits by Dobson, Van Dyck and Mignard. The palatial furniture in the French manner is partly nineteenth-century, but the chairs are Louis XV and were made by Lebas.

The Drawing Room is the most splendid of all. It has a gilded ceiling and a painted frieze by Mantovani, after Giulio Romano; its red and gold damask walls are hung with paintings by Palma Vecchio, Andrea del Sarto, Barocci and a copy by Poussin of Titian's *Bacchus and Ariadne*. The principal pieces of furniture are the two *pietra dura* cabinets made by Domenico Cucci for Louis XIV and acquired by the 3rd Duke in 1824 from Baldock, *the* London dealer in antique furniture. They are the grandest examples of their type in existence. The Dining Room is more sober, with a carved cedar-and-pinewood ceiling based on that of the Basilica of San Lorenzo in Rome. The walls are hung with full-length family portraits and displayed around the room are two important eighteenth-century Meissen services.

Bamburgh Castle.

Aydon Castle

2; 2 miles NE of Corbridge on B6321

This is really a fortified house rather than a true castle, since it has no keep but two walled baileys instead, with a stone-built range of living quarters facing the inner bailey. Licence to crenellate was granted in 1305, and it has been suggested that this was the date of completion, as the buildings look somewhat older than that. Few alterations have been made since, so Aydon survives as a remarkably intact country house of around 1300, like Markenfield Hall in Yorkshire (*q.v.*). Even better, it stands in beautiful wild landscape above the Cor Burn, surrounded by steeply wooded slopes.

The domestic range lies along the south side of the inner bailey. The Great Hall is on the first floor above a room with an original fireplace, the chimneystack for which still survives on the outside wall and is much illustrated in books on medieval secular architecture. It is a singularly beautiful design, having a conical top with a little lancet vent below for the smoke to escape from. The top of the walls of the domestic range is crenellated, the steep-pitched roof rising behind, and an army of plain stone gargoyles disposes of the rainwater. Several original windows survive, mainly comprising two lancets within a pointed arch, while some original doorways and chimneypieces are also preserved inside. The solar, to the east of the Hall, is the most beautiful room; its fireplace is enhanced by little columns and its windows by sparse but refined decorative sculpture. The ground floor, as is usually the case in medieval houses, is part vaulted. Aydon is now maintained by the Heritage Commission and is open to the public.

Bamburgh Castle

3; 18 miles SE of Berwick-upon-Tweed on B1340

This castle stands superbly on a precipitous coastal outcrop looking over the sand-dunes towards Holy Island. It is very large, covering about $4\frac{1}{2}$ acres, and comprises a twelfth-century keep and three baileys surrounded by restored medieval curtain walls, now all immaculately kept. The entrance is through a part-Norman gatehouse and a medieval barbican.

The ruins were patched up in the eighteenth century for charitable purposes by the trustees of Bishop Crewe of Durham; the castle was then bought and drastically restored between 1894 and 1905 by Lord Armstrong under the direction of C. Ferguson of Carlisle. Most of the building has been converted into flats, but Bamburgh is still owned and occupied by Lord Armstrong. The rather bleak state rooms are on the south side and are entirely by Ferguson, though the cellars beneath are medieval. These rooms, open to the public, house interesting collections and displays of furniture, porcelain, china, arms, armour and pictures.

Belsay

4; 19 miles NW of Newcastle upon Tyne on A696

In its present form, Belsay is the early nineteenth-century creation of Sir Charles Monck Middleton and is one of the most amazing of English Picturesque layouts. Travellers on the main road from Newcastle to Scotland via the Carter Bar are alerted to the proximity of interesting architecture by the sight of a range of model cottages with a stone-arcaded ground floor built by Sir Charles in the 1830s.

The Hall, Belsay Hall.

BELSAY HALL is the most perfect Greek Revival house in England, and was built to his own design by Sir Charles (with the practical help of John Dobson) between 1810 and 1817 to replace his old family seat. He was an enthusiastic Hellenist: he had spent his honeymoon in Athens studying ancient Greek architecture, and had called his eldest son Charles Atticus. In Athens he met the antiquary Sir William 'Rapid' Gell, who also helped with the designs for Belsay. These are uncompromisingly Grecian, more like a temple than a domestic building. The house is an exact square of 100 feet and stands on a low-stepped podium; it is of severest ashlar with a handsome Doric frieze and cornice, supported by plain pilasters. On the entrance front there is a porch of two giant fluted Doric columns, *in antis*, copied from the Theseion in Athens. That is the only decoration on the entire exterior of the house. The proportions and stonework are superb, the dimensions of each block of stone having been worked out to three decimal points. The stables, to one side, are in the same style as the house and are severely plain, except for a central octagonal clock turret inspired by the Tower of the Winds in Athens. The centre of the house is a two-storeyed Hall, like an atrium, surrounded by two tiers of columns, Ionic on the ground floor and Doric above (a reversal of the correct order), with a square, glazed lantern at the top from which light comes flooding down. The severity of the architecture is mitigated by a sumptuous scrolly balustrade of brass round the first-floor gallery. The Ionic capitals of the ground-floor columns were one of the items designed by Dobson. (He also drew the Doric capitals of the portico to

guide the masons.) The principal rooms, the former Dining Room, the Drawing Room and the Library, open off this peristyle Hall. They have simple Grecian detail, cornices of anthemion pattern copied from the Temple of Nemesis at Rhamnos and austere coffered ceilings. The Library is the most interesting, with fitted oak bookcases and a large Ionic chimneypiece of Siena scagliola.

Belsay has been empty since the Second World War and the original contents dispersed. It has now been taken into guardianship by the Heritage Commission, which preserves it as an empty monument. It would make a superb museum of English neo-classical sculpture (much of which is to be found in the cellars of national museums or on the back stairs of the Royal Academy, so presumably would be easily forthcoming as loans), rather like a Northumbrian version of the Thorwaldsen Museum in Copenhagen.

Surrounding the house are formal gardens with mown lawns and clipped yew hedges. These lead to one of the most dramatic artificial landscape experiences in England – a rocky, canyon-like cleft, sensationally planted with evergreens and rare shrubs. This was the quarry from which the stone was taken to build the new house. It leads to a great surprise: BELSAY CASTLE. When he built the new house, Sir Charles kept his old family home for picturesque and historical reasons. It comprises a massive fourteenth-century stone tower adjoined by the remains of a Jacobean wing. The tower has a vaulted ground floor, with the Hall on the first floor and solar at the top. The castle has recently been restored by the Heritage Commission and is to be used as an outstation of the Tower Armouries for their exhibition of arms.

Berwick-upon-Tweed★
5; 30 miles N of Alnwick on A1

Berwick is the most northerly town in England and makes a very picturesque, rather un-English spectacle when approached from the south, by road or train, across the River Tweed. It has a turbulent past and changed hands several times between England and Scotland in the Middle Ages, but was finally declared English by King Richard III in 1483. A special status lingered on into later centuries, and British declarations of war, down to the Crimean War in 1854, were made on behalf of England, Scotland and Berwick-upon-Tweed. The town occupies a little peninsula at the mouth of the Tweed and faces the river rather than the wild North Sea. It is compactly planned, encircled by walls, and contains the most concentrated proportion of 'listed buildings' of any town in England. The TOWN WALLS are part medieval, having been begun by Edward I, but were remodelled in the mid-sixteenth century by the Italian engineers Portinari and Jacopo a Contio, who added triangular stone-faced bastions. They are the earliest example of this type of Italian Renaissance fortification in northern Europe and the only one in England. There is a pleasant walk round the top of the walls, giving good views of the town, the river and the sea; the best view is from the bastion known as 'Meg's Mount'. The medieval castle of Berwick stood at the north-west corner of the town and its ruins were largely swept away by the Victorians to make room for the railway station – a characteristic act of vandalism, though Stephenson's mighty stone bridge is some compensation. The town is almost entirely of grey-brown stone with red-tiled roofs, and many of the streets that wind up and down at different levels are still cobbled.

HOLY TRINITY is an extremely rare mid-seventeenth-century parish church. It was built between 1648 and 1652 by Colonel George Fenwick, the Parliamentary Governor of Berwick. Unlike most early-mid-seventeenth-century country churches, it is not Gothic Survival but mainly classical and was the work of a London mason, John Young of Blackfriars. It is rectangular, with aisles down either side and no west tower, though the lack of a vertical accent has been partly made good by the two jolly octagonal stone cupolas with onion-shaped tops added to the west ends of the aisles in 1855; they add enormously to the idiosyncratic character of the façade. The nave has a plain parapet, without gables, all round, while the aisles have crenellated parapets. The most distinctive feature is the plethora of Venetian windows, which, despite their classical provenance, still have something of the feel of Jacobean mullion windows. The interior has well-proportioned arcades with Tuscan columns. Originally there were wooden galleries all round, including at the east end, but only that at the west end now survives. Both it and the pulpit are interesting pieces of Jacobean woodwork. The reredos behind the altar, which takes up the Tuscan theme of the arcades in a lighter key, is an early work by Sir Edwin Lutyens.

From the church, Church Street leads towards the TOWN HALL, which was built in 1750–5 and stares with grand assurance down Marygate, an exceptionally wide street. The Town Hall was designed by Samuel and John Worrall of London and executed by Joseph Dodds, a local builder. Not much is known about the Worralls except that they were involved in the development of Spitalfields in London, and an echo of Hawksmoor's great Baroque church of Christ Church, Spitalfields, as well as of Gibbs's St Martin-in-the-Fields, can be discerned in this building, with its mighty Tuscan portico and tall clock tower and spire. It is appropriate that the Town Hall should be so churchy, for it supplies the Berwick skyline with the spire which Holy Trinity lacks. The building was restored in 1969 – and won a Civic Trust Award – as part of a comprehensive programme of conservation in the town carried out over a period of twenty years with the help of grants from the Historic Buildings Council.

Marygate itself, sadly, was spoilt before the war when part of it was demolished to make a new street leading to the concrete road bridge of 1925–8. As soon as you turn off Marygate down WEST STREET, however, all expectations are fulfilled. Here are handsome Georgian houses and dramatic changes of level leading right down to the river and the OLD BRIDGE, which was built in 1610–34 and is over 1000 feet long with fifteen arches. A fascinating complex of streets can be explored from the bridge. Bridge Street leads to Southgate and Quay Walls, all with excellent late Georgian houses. Southgate leads under Quay Walls to Hide Hill, which then climbs up again to Church Street behind the Town Hall, while in Quay Walls is the CUSTOMS HOUSE, a five-bay Georgian house with arched windows on the ground floor and a Venetian doorway. Palace Street leads to PALACE GREEN, the *clou* of Berwick. It is a fine lawn planted with trees and surrounded by attractive buildings, such as the former Governor's house – an early eighteenth-century building with

The town walls, Berwick-upon-Tweed.

a five-bay, three-storeyed centre and lower flanking wings. Palace Street East leads to RAVENSDOWNE, where you will find the best Georgian houses in Berwick. At the end stand the BARRACKS, built in 1717–21 in response to local objections to billeting soldiers in public houses. They are in the 'house style' of the Royal Ordnance Department, which owes much to the influence of Vanbrugh. A large quadrangle is surrounded on three sides by massive stone ranges of accommodation and on the fourth there is a Gatehouse. The Barracks now contain the museum of the King's Own Scottish Borderers and are open to the public.

Blagdon Hall
6; 15 miles N of Newcastle upon Tyne off A1
Extensive new tree planting and trimly maintained farms and cottages with traditional maroon paintwork, spotted from the A1 as you head north from Newcastle, indicate the presence of a large estate. The ENTRANCE LODGE does not disappoint; it is by James Wyatt and is one of the best lodges he designed. It comprises a screen of Tuscan columns at either end of which are octagonal pavilions embellished with blank niches and dainty festoons. Each gatepier proudly carries the recumbent form of the Ridley bull.

The house is of *c*.1740 and has been attributed to James Paine but was substantially remodelled by James Wyatt in the 1780s. It was much extended in the nineteenth century, but after fire damage during the Second World War it was reduced to its original size and restored in 1949 under the supervision of Robert Lutyens, son of Sir Edwin and uncle of the present Viscount Ridley. Inside, the staircase survives from the mid-eighteenth century and has Rococo plasterwork. The best room by Wyatt is the former Dining Room; it has Tuscan columns and decorative plasterwork painted pale green and white. The Saloon in the middle of the south front was remodelled by Robert Lutyens and has a beautiful marble chimneypiece and a rich crimson flock paper as a background to family portraits.

The formal GARDENS round the house are by Sir Edwin Lutyens himself and were laid out in the 1930s. Since the war they have been simplified for ease of upkeep but they are still impressive. The main axis comprises a long rectangular canal pond flanked by clipped hedges, focused on the pedimented centre of the south front. At the end is a circular pond with a large marble statue in the middle.

Blanchland
7; 8 miles S of Hexham on B6306
Blanchland lies in the wooded glen of the Derwent with wild moorland all around. Approaching from the Hexham road, the village is announced by a medieval GATEHOUSE. Blanchland is a mid-eighteenth-century planned model village laid out by the Crewe trustees to provide accommodation for those employed by the nearby lead-mines (now extinct). Its layout was dictated by the fact that it occupies the site of the ruins of the Premonstratensian monastery founded here in 1165 by Walter de Bolbec. The stone-built cottages surround an

L-shaped square. They are two-storeyed and enlivened by the odd bit of medieval stonework that has been built in. The LORD CREWE HOTEL in the middle of the east side of the square is charmingly Gothick with ogee-headed windows. It occupies the site of the abbey guesthouse – a nice piece of historical continuity. Most of the abbey CHURCH has disappeared, but the thirteenth-century chancel was reconstructed in the eighteenth century by the Crewe trustees to serve as the village church. It was restored again at various dates in the nineteenth century: the transept was part rebuilt in 1854 and the east end in 1884. Much of the detail is now therefore Victorian, but some medieval lancets survive. In the transept floor are three stone coffin lids, two to abbots and one, carved with a hunting horn, to the abbey huntsman, Robert de Eglyston.

Brinkburn Priory
8; 6 miles SE of Rothbury off B6344
This is one of the most peaceful and beautiful parts of a beautiful county, with the River Coquet forming a rocky loop round the church – which is all that survives of the Augustinian priory founded here in 1135 by William de Bertram. The church was restored by Thomas Austin of Durham in 1858, so is partly Victorian; but it is archaeologically correct all the same. It is cruciform in plan with a short central tower, narrow chancel, aisled transepts, and a nave with an aisle on one side only. The style is Transitional 'Early English' of *c*.1300. The north door still has Norman zigzag ornament on its arches. The interior is spacious and lofty, with bare stone walls, vaulted aisles, and sturdy octagonal piers to the aisle arcade and crossing-arches. There are blank arcades round the lower part of the walls. The aisle arcade and the lancet windows at the east and west ends have painted arches but the triforium comprises semi-circular arches grouped in twos and the clerestory windows are also still semi-circular. The furnishings are all plain Victorian and of no particular interest. The church is now cared for by the Heritage Commission.

Callaly Castle
9; 10 miles W of Alnwick off A697 [37]
At Callaly a regular stone exterior covers a patchwork of buildings constructed over a period of nearly 500 years and incorporating an ancient pele tower. The tidying up was done in 1750, when the roofline was made even and much of the exterior faced in ashlar. The main front is U-shaped, with projecting wings and a centrepiece – dated 1676 on a sundial – thought to have been designed by Robert Trollope of Newcastle, which is a typical piece of artisan Mannerism with its amusing pediment.

The interior too was remodelled in the mid-eighteenth century and the Drawing Room is among the finest rooms of that date in the north of England. There are galleries with *chinoiserie* balustrades at either end, and the spirited Rococo plasterwork on the walls, ceiling and overmantel incorporates medallion portraits of poets and philosophers. The chandeliers are of *c*.1760 and the side-tables have *trompe l'œil* scagliola tops made in Florence by Laurentius Ucelli. An unexpected treat is

Chillingham Castle.

the group of four large Rococo paintings in the Smoking Room, which once formed part of the eighteenth-century decoration of the supper boxes at Vauxhall Gardens, London. The Smoking Room is altogether an entertaining piece of Victoriana, inhabited by a whole family of stuffed bears.

Chesters
10; 16 miles W of Newcastle upon Tyne off A69
The name is that of a Roman FORT on Hadrian's Wall, substantial remains of which survive (in the guardianship of the Heritage Commission). Still visible is the rectangular layout of the *Cilurnum*, surrounded by an earth mound and ditch, containing the stone foundations of the barracks and *principia* (headquarters). Nearby, on the river bank, is the Bath House, the stone walls of which survive to a reasonable height and give a clear impression of the plan of such an establishment, with its hot and cold rooms. A little museum (possibly designed by Norman Shaw) contains examples of Roman sculpture, altars and other objects from the Roman Wall. The collection was mostly formed by John Clayton, the Newcastle Town Clerk and owner of the estate for most of the nineteenth century, who bought many of the sites on the Wall to preserve them from destruction and then excavated them.

Clayton's house, also called CHESTERS, survives. It comprises a Georgian nucleus with grandiose Edwardian additions designed in 1891 by Norman Shaw, whose impressive classical architecture here was largely responsible for establishing the Neo-Georgian mode as *the* architectural style for the twentieth-century country

house. Sir Reginald Blomfield, in fact, thought Chesters was Shaw's finest country house. The ambitious classical style adopted was a response to the Roman site, since the house looked directly across at the camp. Shaw therefore applied himself to rivalling the antique past with breathtaking boldness, sandwiching the old house between projecting wings bristling with rugged rustication. These are particularly well managed on the entrance front, where his projections flank a deep-recessed forecourt; on the garden front the new wings lie at an angle, and on the west side he contrived a whole new façade of quite stunning drama: a segmental curve with an Ionic colonnade in the centre links the two diagonally set wings containing a new Drawing Room and Billiards Room. Shaw also remodelled the inside of the house. Nearly the whole main floor of the old block was gutted to create a huge Library 60 feet long, panelled in walnut and furnished with an organ, the case of which was painted by Robert Christie. Lutyens considered this room a masterpiece.

Chillingham Castle
11; 15 miles NW of Alnwick off B6348
Chillingham is famous for the herd of pre-historic white cattle, descendants of wild oxen, that has roamed the pastures and woods of the 600-acre park since it was enclosed in 1220. They are small, creamy-white creatures with black noses and black tips to their horns. Although they are shy, they can be fierce, and Thomas Bewick, the eighteenth-century engraver, found himself hastily climbing a tree in the middle of making a sketch for his famous study of the *Chillingham Bull*.

The castle, formerly the seat of the Earls of Tankerville, has not been lived in since the Second World War and is in poor condition, but it is good to report that it has recently been acquired and is to be restored by Sir Humphry Wakefield. Licence to crenellate was granted to Sir William Heton in 1344, which gives the approximate date of building. It is of the usual fourteenth-century plan, its four robust square corner towers connected by domestic ranges round an internal courtyard and the main rooms on the first floor above a vaulted ground floor. Alterations were made in the early seventeenth century, when the three-tier columned frontispiece was added to the entrance and large mullion-and-transom windows were inserted, and again in the early nineteenth, following the gutting of the east range in a fire in 1803. John Patterson of Edinburgh was employed to reinstate, and in 1828 Sir Jeffrey Wyatville was called in to do further work, including the landscaping of the approach with a new lodge, an avenue and an informal grass-banked forecourt.

The interior of the house, at the time of writing, is derelict, but some of the rooms have good Jacobean plasterwork, and in the former Great Hall are a pair of fine marble chimneypieces bought from Wanstead in the 1820s and installed here by Wyatville.

Chipchase Castle
12; 8 miles NW of Hexham off B6320
Chipchase is a terrific-looking castellated house in beautiful rolling, wooded country. It consists of a large fourteenth-century tower on one side and a Jacobean house on the other, the whole thing altered in 1784 to create a balanced façade, which would be symmetrical if it were not for the additional storey and machicolations of the tower. This west front is three storeys high, with sashed windows and a Doric doorcase in the middle. The back of the tower survives in its original condition, and features one or two traceried windows and projecting *garderobes* on corbels. The interior comprises a vaulted basement and three main rooms one above the other, two of which retain original medieval fireplaces. The Jacobean wing has an E-shaped façade facing south. It is symmetrical, with semi-circular bow windows at either end – Victorian restorations but none the worse for that – and also contains the main entrance. The square porch in the middle is carried up as a semi-octagonal bay, culminating in a fancy strapwork parapet. It is a beautiful design, with just enough in the way of bows and decoration to soften the northern austerity of the towering stonework.

Corbridge
13; 3 miles E of Hexham on A69
Now a pretty, sleepy little place of genteel stone houses, tea rooms and antique shops, Corbridge was among the most important towns of Northumberland in the Middle Ages; it had four churches, two pele towers, a mint and two members in the first English Parliament. It grew up around a Saxon monastery, of which the church survives as the parish CHURCH OF ST ANDREW. The lower part of the west tower dates from the early eighth century. The arch from this to the nave is perfectly preserved and seems to have been built of re-used Roman masonry. Two blocked Saxon windows can also still be seen, but the majority of the church is the result of a rebuilding in the thirteenth century in Early English style. The east end is the usual Early English arrangement of three graduated lancets. There are transepts, and the nave has aisles and arcades with octagonal columns.

On the south side of the graveyard lies the medieval VICARAGE, a fortified pele tower built of Roman stones in c.1318. At the east end of Main Street is another pele tower, this one incorporated in a Jacobean house called LOW HALL. MAIN STREET is remarkably wide and handsome with stone buildings – some genuine Jacobean, like the Angel Inn, and others successful Victorian imitations. Main Street is the continuation of Middle Street, one of three principal thoroughfares that radiate from the church and MARKET PLACE. In the latter is a nice cast-iron Gothick Market Cross of 1814 and the FOUNTAIN HOUSE, built of stone with a pyramidal roof supporting an iron signpost.

Cragside
NT; 14; 10 miles SW of Alnwick on B6341 [38]
Cragside is entirely the creation of the 1st Lord Armstrong, inventor, engineer and arms manufacturer, and it perfectly reflects his character. It began as a small weekend retreat but in 1869 Richard Norman Shaw was called upon to transform the existing lodge into a proper country house. Over the next fifteen years a series of additions changed it into the present picturesque building, which so admirably complements the romantic wooded setting created by Armstrong on the steep, rugged hillside. Equally interesting are the technological innovations found all over the house; Cragside was the first house in the world to be lit by electric light, which was installed here in 1878.

The interior is rambling, with many relatively modest rooms and a few very grand set-pieces. The Dining Room and Library remain as designed and decorated by Shaw in 1870–2 and are among the most unchanged Victorian interiors in the country. Both are in his 'Olde English' manner, with light oak joinery and the furniture specially made for the rooms by Forsyth and Gillow. The smaller rooms on both the ground and bedroom floors also retain most of their original furniture, fittings and paintings, and are charming examples of late Victorian decoration.

The most splendid room in the house is the Drawing Room on the first floor, which was Shaw's last addition to Cragside. It was completed in 1884, just in time for a visit from the Prince of Wales (later Edward VII). It has a coved and top-lit ceiling with lush plasterwork, and a staggering Renaissance-style double-storey inglenook chimneypiece of carved Italian marble provided by Farmer and Brindley. The furniture, specially made for the room, was probably designed by J. Aldam Heaton. Armstrong's collection of paintings was sold in 1910 but has been replaced by a collection by Evelyn De Morgan and Spencer Stanhope. Cragside now belongs to the National Trust and is regularly open to the public.

Dunstanburgh Castle

15; 7 miles NE of Alnwick off B1339

Here is an incomparably sublime spectacle of broken, jagged ruins on an invincible basalt promontory rearing up more than 100 feet out of the sea. One is not surprised to learn that Turner painted Dunstanburgh no fewer than three times. Nor is the drama purely visual, for the sound of the waves crashing on to the rocks below adds an appropriate booming background not unlike the rumble of distant gunfire, while the cries of sea-birds evoke a poetic melancholy. The whole creates a moving picture of transient human power and might dwarfed into utter insignificance by the force of nature.

The castle, covering 11 acres and so the largest in Northumberland, was built in the fourteenth century by Thomas, Earl of Lancaster, who was executed for treason in 1322. It then passed to the Crown, and John of Gaunt, as Lieutenant of the Northern Marches, added a new gatehouse and barbican on the west side in the 1380s. The site is so well defended by nature that strong fortifications were needed on the south side only, and there the main living quarters were also situated, incorporated in the original 1320s' Gatehouse. This has two mighty semi-circular towers flanking the central archway, with the Great Hall over, at second-floor level. These towers are the best surviving feature of the castle ruins, though stretches of the curtain wall and its towers stand to a reasonable height. The ruins are now in the guardianship of the Heritage Commission.

Ford

16; 10 miles SW of Berwick-upon-Tweed on B6354

'This old castle has much of its old romantic form left on one side, the rest being modernized after the taste of Strawberry Hill: but in the old towers of hoary stone overlooking the beautiful valley and field of Flodden, you can still imagine something of the time of Marmion. . . .' So wrote Louisa, Marchioness of Waterford, in September 1859 shortly after taking up residence at Ford, which her late husband had settled on her as her dower-house. She devoted the rest of her life to beautifying the estate: rebuilding the farms, making roads and bridges, planting trees and erecting a model village at the castle gates, with a fountain in memory of Lord Waterford. Augustus Hare continues the description: 'Above all, a beautiful schoolroom arose in the village, to be decorated with frescoes from "The Lives of Good Children", which will probably be the most lasting memorial of the pictorial genius of the lady of the castle.' It all survives as a testament of Victorian philanthropy, like Dorothea's dream in *Middlemarch* come true.

The village consists of one long street of yellow-grey cottages. The SMITHY is enlivened with a stone arch in the form of a large horseshoe. The memorial FOUNTAIN to the Marquess of Waterford is a polished granite column carrying a marble angel and was designed by Sir George Gilbert Scott. The SCHOOL is the *pièce de résistance*. The murals that line the schoolroom are not true frescoes but distemper and watercolour on paper mounted on canvas. They are colourful in a Raphaelesque way. The models were the actual children of Ford (they were

Cragside.

rewarded for their sittings with jam sandwiches) with their parents and grandparents. The school is thus a village portrait gallery, and for several years little Cain and Abel might have been sitting at their lessons beneath their own portraits. The subjects are *Cain and Abel, Abraham and Isaac, Jacob and Esau, Joseph and His Brethren, Moses in the Bulrushes, Samuel Lent unto the Lord, David and the Shepherds, Josiah Made King at Eight Years Old, The Three Children* and *Christ Blessing the Little Children*. On the end wall is *Christ Disputing with the Doctors*, in which the Jewish Rabbis are the village carpenter, schoolmaster, gardener and other local characters. Lady Waterford herself was a compulsive and talented artist. Once during an exceedingly dull sermon a friend was surprised by the rapt attention she was paying the preacher – she was sketching his portrait from beneath her pew! She also largely rebuilt the thirteenth-century CHURCH OF ST MICHAEL in 1853 to the design of John Dobson. Her own monument (she died in 1891) is in the churchyard and was designed by G.F. Watts.

Ford Castle.

FORD CASTLE itself is basically a fourteenth-century castle of typically rectangular plan, originally with four corner towers connected by curtain walls. The castle fell into decay in the early sixteenth century and one of the corner towers has disappeared. The north range was remodelled at the end of the sixteenth century to make an Elizabethan E-plan house. This was Gothicked in 1761–5 and further work was done in 1791–5, including the building of the pretty forecourt with its jolly rusticated archway, which, happily, still survives. Unfortunately, Lady Waterford's enthusiasm for architecture led her to call in David Bryce, the Scottish baronial architect, to remove much of the Gothick and reconstruct the main part of the castle in a dull and serious manner. The *tout ensemble*, however, remains romantic in the extreme.

Hexham
17; 18 miles W of Newcastle upon Tyne on A69

Hexham is a good old-fashioned market town in a pretty situation in the Tyne Valley. It is a popular centre for exploring Hadrian's Wall and its old-established shops provide an alternative, for the more discerning, to the chainstores of Newcastle. Its most important building – and the major medieval church of Northumberland – is the PRIORY CHURCH. The first church on the site was built by St Wilfred in 675–80. Of this the crypt alone survives. It is built of square dressed Roman stones, some of them with Latin inscriptions, and consists of a tunnel-vaulted relic chamber, the ceiling of which still retains its original iron-hard plaster. On either side are smaller vaulted vestibules and an original stone staircase leading up into the church. The Saxon church was damaged in the Viking raids and refounded after the Norman Conquest. The medieval part of the present building is largely thirteenth-century, in a no-nonsense north-country Early English style. Much of the total effect is owed to Victorian and Edwardian restoration. The east end was

rebuilt by John Dobson in 1858 and the nave built in 1907–9 to the design of Temple Moore. The plan is cruciform, with a low, embattled central crossing-tower. The two transepts are the most impressive parts, so it is best to start with them. The north transept has vaulted aisles, elegant moulded piers and arches, a triforium of paired arches with dogtooth carving, and a clerestory with little moulded columns dividing the window arches. The south transept is more austere but more sensational, the elevations taken up by two tiers of tall, narrow lancets. All round the bottom of the walls runs a beautiful blank arcade with trefoil arches and carved leaves in the spandrels. Also in the south transept is the famous Night Stair – a monumental stone staircase that allowed the monks to descend straight from the dormitory to the church for their night offices. Temple Moore's nave is beautifully proportioned and built, cleverly deploying a mild Decorated manner so as not to compete with the genuine Early English of the east end. Built into the walls are many Roman fragments. The chancel has vaulted aisles, the bosses of which are carved with stiff-leaf decoration. It is richly furnished, with a fifteenth-century rood-screen, choir stalls with medieval misericords, and, situated within the outline of the Saxon apse, St Wilfred's throne – a stone seventh- or eighth-century chair with a carved interlacing band along the arms and back. The painted wooden lectern is thought to have come from the priory refectory, and the painted medieval panels hanging above it were once part of the reredos. Not much survives of the monastic buildings apart from the fourteenth-century lavatorium (incorporated in the early nineteenth-century police station nearby), the chapter house and the twelfth-century priory gate.

To the north of the church is a pretty park crossed by the Cowgarth Burn. The east end of the church overlooks the MARKET PLACE, the old houses of which were removed in the nineteenth century to open up this vista.

Facing the church on the other side of the Market Place is the MOOT HALL, a severe machicolated pele tower of c.1400, now the public library. It was originally the Court House of the Archbishop of York, who held the Liberty of Hexham in the Middle Ages. In the centre of the Market Place is The Shambles, a square building with a Tuscan colonnade, erected by Sir Walter Blackett of Wallington (*q.v.*) in 1766, and the Temperley Memorial Fountain of 1906.

The main streets of Hexham have picturesque names – Priestpopple, Hencotes, Quatre Bras and St Mary's Chase. They are mainly lined with decent late Georgian buildings of stone, sometimes colour-washed, interrupted here and there by venerable antiquities. In St Mary's Chase is the ruin of ST MARY'S CHURCH, which was the medieval parish church but was superseded by the priory at the Dissolution. Behind the Moot Hall, and reached through the dramatic archway in the base of the tower, is HALL GATE, a quiet little backwater like an old Italian piazza, made resoundingly medieval not just by the back of the Moot Hall but also by the PRISON built in 1330 in the form of a massive rectangular tower with narrow little windows and a machicolated parapet – like something escaped from Gubbio or Perugia, or some other medieval hill town in Umbria. Behind the prison is the old GRAMMAR SCHOOL, a whitewashed Elizabethan-style building erected as late as 1684, though the school was founded in 1599. The main axis of Hexham, MARKET STREET and GILESGATE, runs east of the Market Place and contains nice simple Georgian buildings and one or two belated Elizabethan jobs actually dating from the seventeenth century. FORE STREET contains more Georgian houses and the wonderfully elaborate Victorian shop-front of Gibson's Chemist's Shop, the unusually well-preserved interior of which has migrated recently to the Science Museum in London, where a replica of the shop-front has been built.

Holy Island
See Lindisfarne Castle.

Howick Hall
18; 5 miles NE of Alnwick on B1339
This house stands in romantically landscaped grounds in a little valley a mile and a half from the sea. It was originally the seat of the Greys and now belongs to the Barings. The main block was built in 1782 to the design of William Newton of Newcastle and is flanked by a pair of five-bay pavilions, one originally the kitchen offices and the other the stables. The quadrants linking these to the main block are the work of George Wyatt, who altered the house in 1809 and added the Tuscan Entrance Hall on the north side. The main block was gutted by fire in 1928 and reconstructed to the design of Sir Herbert Baker. He reduced the size of the house by removing part of the centre of the garden front to make a recess behind a screen of columns carrying the old pediment – a picturesque, almost Piranesian idea, perhaps suggested by Aston Webb's similar treatment at Stourhead in Wiltshire after the fire there. The interior of the main block is entirely Herbert Baker's work, but is empty and disused

at the time of writing. The former kitchen pavilion was well restored and reconstructed to the design of Philip Jebb c.1970 to make a new house for the family.

Howick is perhaps best known for its beautifully planted GARDENS, with rare rhododendrons, flowering shrubs and trees, from where there is a romantic walk along the burn to Howick Haven, a little cove on the sea shore. The gardens are open to the public, but not the house.

Langley Castle
19; 6 miles W of Hexham on A686
One of the best examples in Northumberland of the fortified tower houses, rather than keeps, that emerged in the mid-fourteenth century, Langley is a large square, four storeys high with four projecting towers at the corners. It gives off an aura of good building, with its large, square dressed stones. It owes something of its spectacular and romantic appearance to the resoundingly named Cadwallader Bates, who restored it from a ruined shell to make a private house c.1900. He added the battlements, with stepped-up corner turrets and bartizans, which contribute so much to the castle's powerful silhouette; their reconstruction was based on archaeological evidence. Originally there was one large room on each floor and smaller rooms in the corner towers. The south-west tower was entirely devoted to latrines; they survive, and consist of rows of stone seats and chutes down inside the wall, discharging into the ditch at the bottom.

Hexham Priory.

Lindisfarne Castle

NT; 20; 12 miles SE of Berwick-upon-Tweed off A1 [39]
Glimpsed from the main railway line north to Edinburgh, Lindisfarne looks like a large grey battleship anchored off the Northumbrian coast. The origin of the castle is a Tudor block-house erected as a defence against the Scots in the 1540s, but it is now a romantic Edwardian country house and that is where its chief interest lies.

The ruins were discovered at the beginning of this century by Edward Hudson, the founder and proprietor of *Country Life*. In 1902 he bought the island from the Crown and commissioned Edwin Lutyens, an architect he much admired, to transform the remnants of the castle into a comfortable modern house: the result is the first and the best of Lutyens' 'castle-houses'.

He kept the walls of the old battery and the east and west guardhouses, but fitted a completely new L-shaped house inside. The silhouette was simplified and rounded at the edges so as to make the castle relate more naturally to the outcrop of rock on which it is perched. The interior is a successful example of Lutyens' ability to contrive 'romance without period'. The Entrance Hall has stout round columns with a 'Norman' feel. The Dining Room and Sitting Room – the Ship Room – were both contrived out of the Tudor magazines and have pointed stone-vaulted ceilings and subtly moulded arched fireplaces inserted by Lutyens. The rooms still contain Hudson's collection of oak furniture, carefully chosen to complement Lutyens' architecture. The castle is now the property of the National Trust and is open to the public.

The Town Hall, Morpeth.

Morpeth

21; 15 miles N of Newcastle upon Tyne on A1
Morpeth is an old market town situated in a U-shaped bend of the River Wansbeck. It grew up under the protection of its Norman castle, the remnants of which – including a motte and a restored fifteenth-century gatehouse – stand on a steep bank to the south of Ha Hill and afford good views over the rooftops of the town. The parish CHURCH OF ST MARY lies to the south of the town and dates mainly from the fourteenth century. There is a west tower carrying a little lead pagoda-like spirelet on top and, inside, the nave and aisles preserve their original timber roofs, while the east Jesse window contains the most important medieval glass in the county (it was restored by Wailes in the nineteenth century). In the churchyard is a little Gothic WATCH HOUSE of 1831, built there to guard against body-snatchers.

The New Bridge of 1829–31 is by Thomas Telford. Nearby are the remains of the former ALL SAINTS' CHANTRY CHAPEL, which dates from the thirteenth century. In the sixteenth it was incorporated into the Grammar School. Only the north wall and west porch survive in a building now used as a soft drinks factory – just like a plate in Pugin's *Contrasts*. Opposite is the somewhat whimsical PRESBYTERIAN CHURCH of 1860. It contains the memorial to Dr John Horsley, the pioneer archaeologist and author of BRITANNIA ROMANA, who died in 1732. Approaching the town centre from the south, you pass a large battlemented pele tower or gatehouse with hefty machicolated battlements. This is the COURT HOUSE AND POLICE STATION designed by John Dobson in 1822. In the Market Place is the handsome TOWN HALL designed by Vanbrugh for the Earl of Carlisle in 1714 and rebuilt, after a fire, in 1869–70. The general character of Vanbrugh's façade – band-rusticated with round-arched windows flanked by two pedimented towers – survives. From the Market Place it is worth walking along OLDGATE, where a fifteenth-century clock tower is firmly sited in the middle of the street – a very rare survival of an isolated medieval belfry, though the top is an eighteenth-century restoration. Its bells still ring a curfew every night. There are one or two good Georgian houses of brick or stone in Oldgate, including Collingwood House, once the home of Admiral Collingwood.

Newcastle upon Tyne★

22; 14 miles N of Durham on A1
Writing in his diary on 7 October 1862, W.E. Gladstone noted: 'At two we went to Newcastle and saw the principal objects, including especially the fine church and lantern, the gem of an old castle, and Grey Street – I think our best modern street.' Today's visitor could still make for the same objects and would not be disappointed. ★ Newcastle is an ancient town; it began as a Roman fortified camp on Hadrian's Wall and was prosperous in the Middle Ages. Its later greatness, however, was based on coal, iron, steel and engineering. In the eighteenth, nineteenth and early twentieth centuries it was the centre of one of the busiest areas of heavy industry in the world. Unlike many similar British commercial cities – which, like Topsy, 'just grow'd' – Newcastle in the late

Georgian and early Victorian periods was endowed with a magnificent planned centre of wide streets and handsome stone-built classical buildings. This was the achievement of three men: the Town Clerk John Clayton, the property developer Richard Grainger and the architect John Dobson. Their combined achievement survived into the mid-twentieth century and was largely intact when Newcastle was described by Pevsner in 1957. Then in the 1960s the centre was again replanned, with new roads and some large concrete or glass slabs of commercial building. T. Dan Smith and John Poulson were leading agents of this second great reconstruction. Not everything that was done then was regrettable, but it is sad that so much unnecessary damage was caused to the old city centre. John Dobson's Eldon Square and Richardson's Northern Academy of Art were both demolished to make way for a large new shopping centre; the Royal Arcade was also demolished, though a fibreglass replica of the interior has been reconstructed in a new block nearby; the settings of several old buildings have been spoilt by crude new roads or by ugly new blocks, of which the Norwich Union Tower, an illproportioned lump of stained concrete at the bottom of Westgate and Collingwood Street, is one of the worst offenders − it should never have received planning permission.

But Newcastle is proud of itself and its history, and happily there are also good things ro report from the last twenty years. Leazes Terrace and Grey Street have, on the whole, been well restored, as have many older buildings, including the Guildhall and remains of the city walls. There are two splendid new steel bridges over the Tyne, and the new CIVIC CENTRE at Barras Bridge is an impressive, if corny, modern municipal precinct. Though built in 1968, it was planned in 1951 and so is mercifully free from the worst 1960s' mannerisms. It has a jolly Festival of Britain air and is, in some ways, the final expression of the inter-war Scandinavian style that produced such buildings as the Norwich Town Hall. It was designed by the City Architect, George Kenyon, and is faced in Portland stone. The varied elements culminate in a tall tower and copper cupola adorned with what look like gilded sea-horses but are, in fact, the castles of the city arms. This tower houses a carillon of bells, which chime the hours and play well-known Newcastle airs four times a day. More worthwhile modern architecture can be found at Byker, a Newcastle suburb, where an influential new development of flats by Ralph Erskine helped to bring about a more humane approach to urban housing after the aberrations of 1960s' tower blocks.

It is best to arrive in the city by train. The first impression of Newcastle as you glide high over the Tyne is unforgettable: the river is steeply banked, almost a gorge, and the city is closely packed on the north side with mixed new blocks, old buildings, church towers, the castle keep, and the once busy quays down below. The river itself is crossed by five old iron or steel bridges and two new ones. The old HIGH LEVEL BRIDGE was designed by Robert Stephenson in 1849; the SWING BRIDGE, designed by Lord Armstrong, was built in 1876; the KING EDWARD BRIDGE − the main railway bridge − was opened

in 1906; and the old REDHEUGH BRIDGE and TYNE ROAD BRIDGE were built in the 1920s. This last is the most distinctive with its large single arch of steel from which the roadway is suspended. The new bridges, the METRO BRIDGE and the NEW ROAD BRIDGE at Redheugh, are worthy of their setting. The cumulative effect looks like an exhibition display of nineteenth- and twentieth-century British engineering: come here and choose your design before throwing a bridge across the Tagus, Amazon or Zambezi!

After this overture, the RAILWAY STATION comes as a magnificent climax. It was built in 1846−50 to Dobson's design and is among the most handsome railway stations in the country. The triple sheds are very long; the main platform is 1335 feet from end to end and is curved, like that at York, creating splendid oblique vistas when the sun shines through the glass roof, and increasing the elegant effect of the thin cast-iron Tuscan columns and shallow segmental arches. After Durham Cathedral, Newcastle Station, with its dramatic approach, is the most impressive architectural spectacle on the main east-coast line to Scotland. When you emerge, the station façade turns out to be fully worthy of the train-sheds. It is on a grand scale with a large *porte-cochère* of seven arches. This is enlivened by Tuscan pilasters, as are the two symmetrical pavilions at either end of the long façade, where the windows have rusticated surrounds and are set in shallow recesses.

The first building to be seen after leaving the station is the CASTLE, part of which was demolished to make way for the railway. A combined Victorian railway station and medieval castle is a not uncommon feature of English towns, and can be found also at Lancaster, Shrewsbury and Penrith (*qq.v.*). Two major bits of Newcastle survive: the keep and the Black Gate. The new castle was established on the old Roman site in 1080 and, of course, gave its name to the whole town. At first of timber, it was rebuilt in stone from 1172 onwards. The tall square keep is among the finest Norman keeps in the country and bears a marked resemblance to that at Dover. John Harvey considers that both were designed by the same military engineer, 'Mauricius Ingeniator'. The original elaborate forebuilding with gateway and stone staircase survives, but the battlements on top of the keep were restored by Dobson in 1809. It is worth climbing to the top for the impressive views of the city centre and river. The Black Gate with barbican dates from 1247 but was part reconstructed as a Jacobean house in 1618; the patchwork of medieval stone and later brickwork makes a highly picturesque composition. The interior of the castle now houses the museum of the Society of Antiquaries of Newcastle, which contains a display of Roman objects from excavations on Hadrian's Wall. As well as the castle, Newcastle preserves substantial traces of the medieval TOWN WALLS built as a defence against the Scots. They were begun in 1280 and originally extended for 2 miles round the town. A good stretch is visible in Bath Lane, where the wall has been restored and opened up with tree-planted lawns in front. The semicircular PLUMMER TOWER has also been restored and converted into a museum.

Fanning out into the town centre east of the station are two main walks – one through the old town clinging to the river banks, and the other through the nineteenth-century classical centre. Taking the old town first, turn right from the railway station down Westgate Street and Collingwood Street, until you reach ST NICHOLAS'S CHURCH, now the CATHEDRAL. It was made a cathedral in 1882 but dates largely from the fourteenth and fifteenth centuries. The principal feature of the exterior is the west tower, crowned with a dazzling openwork stone 'spire' of pinnacles and flying buttresses carrying a lantern. There is nothing else like this in England, though it recalls the stone crowns on such Scottish churches as St Giles' Cathedral in Edinburgh or St Michael's, Linlithgow. The interior of the church is fourteenth-century Decorated. Like many large town churches, it was expensively restored in the nineteenth century, the local architects Benjamin Green and John Dobson as well as Sir George Gilbert Scott all having a go. Much of the Decorated window tracery is nineteenth-century. The nave is strikingly plain: low-roofed, with simple unmoulded octagonal columns and stark arches, bare stone walls and no sculptural decoration. The choir is similar but more elaborately furnished: the large Perpendicular west window is filled with colourful Victorian glass; beneath it is an elaborate Victorian reredos with statues by Westmacott; and there are many monuments to local worthies. There is also an attractively carved late seventeenth-century organ case and a bronze eagle lectern of c.1500. In ST NICHOLAS'S SQUARE, beside the cathedral, the bronze *art nouveau* statue of Queen Victoria should not be missed; it is by Alfred Gilbert, the sculptor of Eros in Piccadilly.

Nearby, a network of steep streets or narrow flights of steps leads down to the riverside, which is one of the most exciting and undisturbed parts of Newcastle, overshadowed by the iron bridges and the castle hill above. In SANDHILL survives a picturesque group of old timber-framed merchants' houses, some dating from the sixteenth century. Surtees House is the most famous of these; it is seventeenth-century, five-storeyed with long continuous strips of window. The GUILDHALL has been well restored recently. It has a classical façade with attached columns and pediment added in 1796 to the design of David Stephenson and William Newton. The curved east side with its Tuscan colonnade was added by Dobson in 1827. The original building was medieval but was reconstructed by Robert Trollope in 1658 and much of Trollope's work survives inside, including the Great Hall with its double hammerbeam roof and other rooms containing fine late seventeenth-century panelling and carved chimneypieces. To the east is QUAYSIDE, where there are some Georgian brick houses. A lively market is held here on Sunday mornings, and an obelisk marks the spot where John Wesley first preached in 1742. In BROAD CHARE is Trinity House, which has a stuccoed Tudor façade of 1841 and a pretty courtyard overlooked by almshouses and a chapel. At the top of the sloping bank, in an entirely new setting of office blocks, is ALL SAINTS' CHURCH, designed by David Stephenson in 1786–96 on an elliptical plan; its tall elegant spire is even

now one of the principal accents on the Newcastle skyline. The interior has original box pews, and galleries carried on slender fluted Tuscan columns, all of finest mahogany. The church has been disused for years but is currently being repaired and converted into a concert hall. East of here is a desert of redevelopment and new roads, in the midst of which stands the now isolated HOLY JESUS HOSPITAL, restored as a museum after years of neglect – which makes it all the sadder that its setting has been ruined. The façade has an arcade of thirty arches on square piers, the end bays have shaped gables, and the centre has a semi-circular pediment.

Returning to the station and branching out in the other direction, the Grainger-Dobson centre is reached down Clayton Street. This part of Newcastle was developed between 1830 and 1844 on the site of Sir Walter Blackett's sixteenth-century house and grounds. In Clayton Street West is the Catholic CATHEDRAL OF ST MARY, designed by Pugin in 1844, with a spectacularly tall spire added in 1860–73 by Hansom. The exterior is an impressive piece of Victorian Gothic Revival. The interior, however, is spoilt by unsympathetic rearrangement and tasteless redecoration, though fortunately a bizarre scheme to re-orientate the whole church by ripping out the eastern altars, so destroying the focus of the architecture, has been scotched. In Clayton Street are THE MARKETS – a huge complex of glass-roofed halls with classical stone façades by Dobson. At the top of Clayton Street is the site of Eldon Square, now a run-of-the-mill modern shopping centre. A rapid detour to the north brings you to the LEAZES TERRACE, designed by Thomas Oliver and built by Grainger in 1829–34. This is the earliest surviving of the grand-scale Newcastle developments, and one of the most magnificent and massive blocks of terraced houses in England, with views over surrounding parkland – rather like an inside-out version of Regent's Park. The terraces have been restored to form a hall of residence for Newcastle University.

South of Clayton Street, Nun Street and Nelson Street lead to Grainger Street, all of them part of the original layout and containing stone classical buildings. The incomparable centrepiece, however, is GREY STREET, which forms an elegant sloping curve from the EARL GREY COLUMN at the east end of Grainger Street down towards Mosley Street and St Nicholas's. Professor Russell Hitchcock considered Grey Street one of the 'finest commercial streets ever built . . . the scale and the character of the detail provides consistency throughout', and Ian Nairn calls it 'one of the great planned streets of Britain'. Whatever one may think of some of the recent developments elsewhere in Newcastle, there can be nothing but praise for the way in which Grey Street has been preserved. The façades have been cleaned and garish fascia signs removed; any redevelopment has been carried out in stone as a replica of the original design, thus preserving the magnificent unity of the architecture. The whole length of the street is lined with large symmetrical classical ranges, all by different architects but all in the same Graeco-Roman style with impressive rolling sweeps of Corinthian columns. Particular accents are given by the domed 'Temple of Vesta' corners of the triangular central EXCHANGE near Earl Grey's column at the top of the west side, and by the grandly projecting Corinthian portico of Benjamin Green's THEATRE ROYAL almost half-way down on the east side. The curved portion of the east side of the street, from the Shakespeare Inn to Mosley Street, was designed by Dobson himself, but the other sections were by different local architects, including John Wardle, George Walker, and John and Benjamin Green. Part of the pleasure of Grey Street is watching the composition change from different angles and it is worth walking up and down on opposite sides to capture the full effect. It owes much to Nash's work in London, but is even better, as it is solidly built of stone rather than stucco and less slapdash in its detail.

Nunnykirk Hall
23; 8 miles NW of Morpeth off B6342

Nunnykirk is a good Greek Revival house designed by John Dobson in 1825; it is the best of his early houses, ingeniously incorporating an older house in the centre. The garden front has a recessed three-storeyed centre five windows wide, with an Ionic colonnade along the ground floor linking the two Dobson side-wings. These latter have tripartite windows on both floors and parapets embellished by large-scale anthemion motifs. On the entrance side there is a huge square Ionic *porte-cochère*. The house is built of a beautiful biscuit-coloured ashlar stone, and owes its chief distinction to the handling of this stonework. The whole of the centre block has channelled rustication, like a French classical building, while the side-pavilions are smooth with channelled corner pilasters like even quoins. The interior, like all Dobson's houses, is a model of lucid, rational planning, the main rooms opening off a full-height central Hall with a coffered plaster dome and handsome trellis-pattern metal railings round the first-floor landing galleries. The Drawing Room, in one of the flanking pavilions, is lit by a large bow window and retains its early nineteenth-century wallpaper and gilded pelmets.

Rothbury
24; 10 miles SW of Alnwick on B6341

A cheerful small town – or large village – on the banks of the River Coquet. With its decent small hotels, Rothbury makes a good base for exploring the surrounding county. The wide main street, lined with sycamores and grey stone houses, runs through to a sloping triangular green with houses and shops grouped around the grassy banks – an excellent townscape effect. Many of the buildings date from the eighteenth century and are pleasant though not outstandingly special. The parish CHURCH OF ALL SAINTS lies at the south end of the green. The chancel is thirteenth-century Early English with tall, thin lancets, but much of the rest of the church is a Victorian rebuilding of 1850 by Pickering. The chancel screen is a memorial to Lord Armstrong of Cragside (*q.v.*). Preserved in the church is the base of one of the most important Saxon crosses in England; it is thought to date from *c.*800, and its carvings represent the Ascension.

The Tyne bridges, Newcastle upon Tyne.

Seaton Delaval Hall.

Seaton Delaval Hall★
25; 9 miles NE of Newcastle upon Tyne on A190

Writers tend to indulge in purple prose when describing the setting of Seaton Delaval, but in fact I do not find the surroundings at all inspiring. Though the house is near the cliff edge, it does not face the North Sea. Between it and the coast there is a development of windswept, 1930s' villas, and the main axis is cut across by a busy road with hideous concrete lamp standards.

The house was designed by Sir John Vanbrugh in his most theatrical Baroque manner for Admiral George Delaval and built between 1718 and 1728. Pevsner has said that 'no other Vanbrugh house is so mature, so compact and so powerful'. It comprises a main block with ringed Doric columns, Mannerist turrets and a pedimented centre. The deep forecourt is flanked by arcaded stable and kitchen wings.

The centre of the house was gutted by fire in 1822 and, though re-roofed and refenestrated, the interior is now a bizarre ceilingless semi-ruin with calcined plaster statues gesticulating from blackened niches and proving themselves to be completely modelled beneath their peeling draperies and fig leaves. The west wing has been adapted as the occasional family residence and contains furniture and paintings originally in the Hall, with additional items brought from Melton Constable in Norfolk. The Drawing Room was originally the kitchen and has a bowed outer wall and simple groined ceiling. The stables in the opposite wing are equally monumental, with niches for the horses to eat hay out of.

It is the exterior of Seaton Delaval, however, which leaves the most lasting impression, its sombre cyclopic masses of stonework conveying a mood of Piranesian gloom that even the artist John Piper would find difficult to exaggerate.

Stamfordham
26; 10 miles NW of Newcastle upon Tyne on B6309

This is one of the best of the Northumberland villages built round a large rectangular green. The practical reason for such northern layouts is that cattle could be driven into the centre of the village, protected by the surrounding cottages, during the frequent Scottish Border raids. The houses are now all Georgian, with long stone or brick terraces facing the green. In the middle is the jolly village CROSS of 1735, its plinth of rusticated arches supporting a square pyramid. This seemly layout forms a handsome prelude to the CHURCH OF ST MARY — thirteenth-century but sadly over-restored by Benjamin Ferrey in 1848, who has left much of the detail not what it was before. There is a stalwart west tower, but the chief beauty of the church is the Early English chancel with a handsome stepped arrangement of three tall, thin lancets over the altar.

Wallington Hall
NT; 27; 11 miles W of Morpeth on B6342 [40]

Wallington, though built in 1688 by Sir William Blackett, is predominantly a Georgian house set in a fine landscape park. This is thanks to Walter Calverley Blackett, who owned the estate from 1728 to 1777 and employed the architect Daniel Garrett to design many alterations and improvements. On his death, childless, in 1777, Wallington passed to his nephew Sir John Trevelyan, and it belonged to the Trevelyans till 1941, when the Labour President of the Board of Education, Sir Charles Trevelyan, conveyed it to the National Trust. The Trevelyans were the acme of the intellectual, liberal Victorian family, equally active as politicians and scholars, and it is their earnest character that still pervades the house.

The outside of Wallington is solid and gentlemanly. The inside is more than that: all the rooms created by Garrett survive and have Rococo plasterwork. The Saloon is particularly fine, with a high coved ceiling and a marble chimneypiece by Sir Henry Cheere. The white-and-blue colour scheme devised by the late John Fowler is, rather perversely, a reversal of the original. The Dining Room has similar plasterwork and the attractive frames of the oval pier glasses between the windows are particularly noteworthy. Both these rooms contain good-quality mahogany furniture and portraits by Hudson and Reynolds. The Library is also of the eighteenth century, but now contains many of Lord Macaulay's books. Over the chimneypiece is a portrait of his brother-in-law, Sir Charles Edward Trevelyan, 'architect' of the modern Civil Service.

Upstairs, the most exciting room is the Needlework Room, hung with panels of embroidery worked by Julia, Lady Calverley, in c.1717–27. The most extraordinary room at Wallington, however, the central Hall, is not eighteenth-century but was created in 1855 by John Dobson out of the old open courtyard. It is a manifestation of the taste of Pauline, Lady Trevelyan, who was a close friend of Ruskin and the Pre-Raphaelites. It was decorated by William Bell Scott with large panels depicting Northumbrian history. The recent change of the surrounding colour from the original red to pink was a mistake that ought to be rectified as soon as the opportunity arises.

CAMBO, on the edge of the park, is an archetypal model estate village with neat eighteenth- and nineteenth-century stone cottages.

Warkworth★
28; 6 miles SE of Alnwick on A1068

Village and castle stand within a loop of the River Coquet. To approach from the north is to experience a townscape thrill comparable with coming to a great feudal stronghold somewhere in central France. A fourteenth-century bridge with three arches and sharp triangular cut-waters leads across the river, guarded on the village side by a fortified tower – a great rarity in England. From here a steep street lined with pleasant but plain stone terraces leads uphill to the castle keep.

WARKWORTH CASTLE came to the Percys in 1332 and belongs to them still, though the ruins are now maintained by the Heritage Commission. Three scenes in Shakespeare's *Richard II* take place at Warkworth. The castle comprises two baileys and was largely rebuilt in the late fourteenth century, on a Norman site, by the 1st Earl Percy. The outer bailey is entered from the south through a Gatehouse with a pair of polygonal towers flanking the portcullis arch. Inside the bailey is a quadrangle of domestic buildings resembling a university college, with Great Hall, Chapel and sets of apartments for the family and retainers. The Hall is large, arcaded down one side. Beyond the dais end is the solar, which retains its fireplace, and at the other the usual kitchen offices. At the south-east angle of the Hall is the Lion Tower, a proud piece of military display that serves as the Hall porch. It takes its name from the Percy crest, which is carved on the outside. The Chapel was planned on an ambitious scale and was intended to be a collegiate establishment; it seems never to have been completed, however, and only the foundations survive now. Next to

Wallington Hall.

it is the gateway to the inner bailey, which is small in comparison with the spaciousness of the outer one. Here stands the fourteenth-century keep on a conical Norman mound. It represents the apogee of English castle design. It is a compact square three storeys high, built round a narrow central light well. The corners are chamfered, and in the centre of each side is a projecting semi-polygonal bay (one of them the Chapel apse). High up on the twelve chamfered corners, carved angels hold stone shields of arms. In the middle rises a tall, slender staircase turret. On the village side, at second-floor level, there is a large carved panel of the Percy lion. The interior of the keep is ingeniously planned to provide all the accommodation of a comfortable late medieval country house. The Hall and Chapel (now roofless shells) are both two-storeyed with large traceried windows, and there are sets of living rooms at first- and second-floor levels. Some of the latter were repaired by Salvin in 1853–8 to make a romantic little fishing lodge.

The parish CHURCH OF ST LAWRENCE stands at the bottom of the hill. It is the only complete Norman church in Northumberland, albeit drastically restored in the nineteenth century by John Dobson and Ewan Christian. The interior is a dark stone affair; the chief thrill is the chancel, which has a twelfth-century rib vault with zigzag carving, rather like a baby replica of Durham Cathedral (*q.v.*). The chancel arch has a curiously squashed outline, as if an elephant has sat on top of it. It is supported on demi-columns with little cushion capitals. Most of the windows in the church are round-arched and flanked by little columns with cushion capitals, but many of these are the result of the Victorian restoration.

Whalton Manor

29; 5 miles SW of Morpeth on B6524

'Whalton Manor is not one of Sir Edwin's big works; but for its size there is a richness of invention and a quality in the detail which puts it high on the list.' So wrote A.S.G. Butler in his official biography of Lutyens. Whalton is one of its architect's most original and ingenious conversions, involving the welding together of practically a whole village street to make a large, comfortable Edwardian country house. Before Lutyens there were four houses or cottages on either side of a gap, all built in the local vernacular, with severe stone walls and slated roofs. In 1908–9 Lutyens knitted these together by building an arched link between the two blocks, so creating a house with six main rooms and twenty bedrooms. The house to the left of the new archway became the kitchen wing; to the right of the archway a dramatic arched vestibule, Hall and staircase gave access to a circular panelled Dining Room on the first floor over the archway (close to the kitchen) and to the existing Library and Drawing Room at the far end of the new Hall on the ground floor. Externally, Lutyens kept the long, low lines and the severity of the existing buildings in his new work, but by the introduction of tall sashes gave a hint of the elegance within. His new segmental archway from the street, with double oak-panelled doors, and his blank stone aprons under the flanking windows are reminiscent of Nicholas Hawksmoor. This subdued Mannerist quality is also apparent in the vestibule and Hall, which have ingenious blocky rustication round the arches and doorways, and characteristic flights of shallow steps. This progression of linked spaces is quintessential Lutyens. Splendid stuff!

Warkworth Castle

Nottinghamshire

Nottinghamshire is the Cinderella of English counties. Mention it to most people and they think of coal-mines and ugliness. How wrong they are. The raw red brick mining villages are there of course, but they are much less grim than those in Yorkshire or Durham. Many of the mines are relatively recent and so do less damage to the landscape than the more careless older developments elsewhere. They are scattered down the western boundary of the county on the Derbyshire border, from Worksop to Hucknall, divided from each other by farms and woods. Otherwise, industry is concentrated around Nottingham itself, the suburbs of which have expanded enormously in this century. The centre of the city, however, is still full of historic interest: a castle, three remarkably fine old parish churches, streets of Georgian houses and Victorian commercial buildings, and a huge market place dominated by the impressive inter-war classicism of the City Hall. The Park is a fascinating nineteenth-century suburb full of Regency and Victorian houses, while the modern suburbs of the towns are well planned and leafy, and contain several interesting factories in the modern style, of which Boots at Beeston is generally considered to be one of the most successful of pioneer English Modern buildings.

Otherwise, Nottinghamshire is largely rural. The centre of the county is Sherwood Forest and the Dukeries, still heavily wooded (by English standards) and dotted with the great estates carved out of the Royal Forest in the sixteenth century. Osberton, Worksop, Welbeck and Thoresby are still all privately owned; enormous in scale, they are models of enlightened land management with their trim model villages and farms and their excellent tree planting. Clumber now belongs to the National Trust and is similarly excellently maintained, while Newstead Abbey (Byron's old home) is the property of Nottingham Corporation. This juxtaposition of feudalism and coal-mining is reminiscent of parts of northern France or Belgium, and quite unlike anything else in England; indeed, the Dukeries has a strong continental feel and scale about it. Last but not least, the eastern and southern parts of the county are all gentle, rolling arable with attractive brick villages, large stone medieval churches, impressive farm buildings and the country houses of prosperous middling squires. Half the

Vale of Belvoir is situated in Nottinghamshire. It is a pleasure to explore both this part of the county and the unfrequented roads and unspoilt farmland of the area between the Dukeries and the Trent. It is particularly heartening to see a real effort being made here to preserve and enhance the character of the landscape — much new tree planting in the hedgerows, and in the villages new houses built of the right brick, with pan-tiled roofs to match the older cottages.

In the eastern part of the county are Nottinghamshire's two best towns: Southwell and Newark. The former is a miniature cathedral city with attractive Georgian houses and seemly streets grouped round the Minster. Newark is one of the least spoilt of English towns; its special glories are its huge medieval parish church, large dignified market place and impressive castle ruins guarding the Trent crossing. It is a pleasure just to wander round its streets, which are almost entirely free from hideous redevelopment; even the inevitable shopping centre and car park are tucked away out of sight behind the market place façades.

So much for the general setting. But Nottinghamshire also has much to offer the architectural enthusiast, and the pleasure to be derived is enhanced by being off the beaten track and by a feeling of personal discovery. It is a county to visit above all for its church architecture. There are no fewer than three important Norman naves: Blyth, Southwell and Worksop — a reminder of the fact that the Royal Forest of Sherwood was dotted with monastic houses after the Norman Conquest. In the Middle Ages, Nottinghamshire was prosperous and an artistic centre; it was close to Lincoln Cathedral, that powerhouse of art and learning, and the county was famous throughout Europe for its alabaster carving. The Early English choir at Southwell and the façade of New-stead Abbey are of exquisite beauty, but the supreme glories of Nottinghamshire are the Decorated Chapter House and pulpitum at Southwell and the chancel at Hawton with its wondrous Easter Sepulchre. St Mary's in Nottingham and St Mary Magdalene at Newark are two of the most ambitious Perpendicular parish churches in the whole of England. Nottinghamshire is also a county of less ambitious churches, which are nonetheless full of atmosphere, interesting fittings and old tombs. Teversal, with its monuments to the Molyneux family, and Ratcliffe-on-Soar, with the Sacheverell tombs, are both famous. There is interest to be found among the later churches, too – for instance the pretty eighteenth-century chapels at Papplewick and Ossington, one Gothick and one classical. The products of Victorian prosperity and piety, of which Bodley's noble fane at Clumber is the supreme example, are also evident. The visitor ought to be warned, however, that it is exceptional for parish churches to be left open and much time will be wasted tracking down keys. Whenever possible, I have tried to give some idea of where they may be found.

For country houses there is nothing in England to compare with the aristocratic conglomerate of the Dukeries. Here the great parks of Clumber, Thoresby, Welbeck and Worksop were landscaped in the eighteenth century by the Dukes of Kingston, Newcastle, Norfolk and Portland. The Dukes are now extinct or departed elsewhere and the main houses at Worksop and Clumber have been demolished, but the planting, garden buildings, lodges and avenues survive as impressive works of art. Thoresby Hall was rebuilt in the nineteenth century by Salvin as a Victorian Tudorbethan giant, while Welbeck is famous for its megalomaniac Victorian underground extensions – although less well known for its excellent Edwardian work above ground: Harry Wilson's beautiful Chapel and Library and Sir Ernest George's Neo-Georgian internal and external remodelling. Many of Nottinghamshire's middling squirearchical families are still *in situ* and cherish their houses – the Foljambes at Osberton, the Hildyards at Flintham, the Seymours at Thrumpton and, not least, the Stauntons of Staunton, who have been seated in the same place since before the Norman Conquest.

Beauvale
1; 3 miles W of Hucknall off B600

Although it lies in D.H. Lawrence land in the west of the county, characterised by collieries and red brick terraces of miners' cottages, Beauvale itself is a secret valley secluded in woodland and redolent of 'ancient peace'. Here are the remains of a CHARTERHOUSE – one of only nine in England – founded in 1343 by Nicholas de Cantilupe. The Carthusians differed from the older religious orders in that they were assemblages of hermits, rather than monks living a communal life. Each Carthusian lived alone and silent in a small house with his own little garden for manual work between stints of contemplation and prayer. He lived and ate there, his meals and the hot bricks he used for heating in winter being passed to him through hatches in the wall. He saw his confrères in church only, and never spoke. At Beauvale it is still possible to make out the lines of the cloisters and the little individual houses. A farm, built out of the stones of the Charterhouse, stands on part of the site; attached to it are the precarious ruins of the church and those of a tower house – the prior's lodging. The outbuildings of the farm incorporate the gatehouse range.

Beeston
2; 2 miles SW of Nottingham on A453

Beeston is a bleak suburb of Nottingham, all new roads and new housing, but dominated by the massive factory of the BOOTS COMPANY LIMITED. The firm moved to Beeston from the centre of Nottingham in 1928 and their new factory was built almost immediately. It is considered to be one of the major early Modern buildings in England and very impressive it is. Modern architecture is, of course, ideally suited to industrial premises and many of the most successful Modern buildings in England are factories or warehouses. The Boots factory, completed in 1932, was designed by Sir Owen Williams and is built of concrete, with mushroom-shaped columns supporting galleries round the full-height packing space in the centre. The whole of the exterior of the building is clad in glass, giving it a sleek look. The south front is 550 feet long, and cantilevered out over the loading space. One

reason why this factory is so impressive is that its appearance is a result of its structure. Reinforced concrete was used because it was the best way of achieving the space required, not because the designer wanted to be fashionable. One of the drawbacks of many Modern buildings in England is that the style was often chosen for aesthetic reasons alone and twisted to suit an antipathetic purpose.

This factory is exceptional in Sir Owen Williams's *œuvre*. Like the Victorian train-shed men, he was a civil engineer rather than an architect. Apart from the *Daily Express* buildings in London and Manchester, nothing else he did has the elegance and grandeur of this.

Bestwood
3; 3 miles N of Nottingham on A60

Set in the lush wooded landscape north of Nottingham are two arresting monuments to nineteenth-century prosperity. BESTWOOD PUMPING STATION, by the Nottingham–Mansfield road, is one of the proudest examples of Victorian engineering – a cathedral of steam technology. It was almost certainly designed in 1871–4 by Thomas Hawksley, the Nottingham water engineer. The north Italian style adopted shows the influence of Ruskin – round-arched windows and a projecting porch copied from some basilica or other on the Plain of Lombardy. The details are stone but the main part of the building is red brick and round the roof are elaborate curlicue cast-iron trimmings. The composition culminates in a tall chimney disguised as a *campanile* with a conical roof. The surroundings, carefully tended, are a museum-piece of Victorian gardening, the cooling pond embellished with an island and encircled by gravel paths, mown grass, clipped evergreens and cast-iron gas-lamps.

Equally grand and High Victorian is BESTWOOD LODGE 2 miles inland, a former seat of the Dukes of St Albans and built in 1862–5 by S.S. Teulon. It is eminently characteristic of Teulon's aggressively original polychromatic Gothic style, built of black and red brick and stone, effectively blending English and continental sources to create a wild, exciting skyline. The façade was decorated by Thomas Earp with finely executed stone carvings of scenes from local history, including, inevitably, Robin Hood and his Merrie Men. The ecclesiastical-looking appendage to the domestic offices on the left was originally the Servants' Hall. Perhaps not surprisingly, Bestwood ceased to be a private house many years ago: the 10th Duke's granddaughter described it bluntly as 'the most hideous house in England'. It is now a hotel.

Blyth
4; 7 miles NW of East Retford on A634
From the Great North Road the tall, Perpendicular, eight-pinnacled tower of the PRIORY CHURCH OF ST MARY AND ST MARTIN is a dominant landmark. It gives a false impression, however, for the real splendour of the building is the great, grim Norman nave, like that of a church in Normandy. The priory was founded in 1088 by Roger de Busli as an offspring of the Benedictine abbey of St Cuthbert at Rouen and it prospered as a centre of hospitality on the main road north. At the Dissolution in the sixteenth century the east end – including the apsidal chancel, choir and transepts – was demolished but the nave survived as the parish claimed it as theirs. It is thought to have been begun in the late eleventh century and is much more French in feeling than a lot of English Romanesque work. There is now simply a blank wall at the crossing and no altar. The wide south aisle was rebuilt in the late thirteenth century as the parish church, the function that it still serves; this explains why it is fully furnished with altar, organ, seventeenth-century pulpit and pews, as if it were a self-contained church on its own. This is one's first impression on entering through the south porch, and it comes as something of a shock to find the grand, austere Norman nave beyond: clustered columns with Frenchy capitals of elementary volute type, a plain round-arched triforium, small windows in the clerestory, and a remarkably early quadripartite ribbed vault.

There is much of interest in the church, in particular the tombs and hatchments of the Mellish family (formerly of Blyth Hall). The grandest is in the Lady Chapel, where a reclining effigy of the bewigged Edward Mellish is framed by Corinthian pilasters supporting a pediment. This is the work of John Hancock, as was discovered by the late Rupert Gunnis, who found the signature (top right) by climbing a ladder. There are also three medieval screens of carved wood in the south aisle, competent but not outstanding.

The village of Blyth is attractive and picturesque, with many good brick cottages and houses and two greens. It is a peaceful oasis now that it has been bypassed by the A1.

Bradmore
See Bunny.

Bunny
5; 6 miles S of Nottingham on A60
The 1930s' semis that line the main road, the ugly streetlights and a large petrol station do not inspire much hope

of architectural delights to come when one first arrives in Bunny. The village is, however, still just worth a visit, thanks to the 'Wrestling Baronet', Sir Thomas Parkyns (1662–1741). He was an amazing character indeed – an improving landlord, amateur architect, author of a Latin grammar and an enthusiastic wrestler. He designed several buildings in the village, including the old SCHOOL at the corner of the graveyard, dated 1700 and with a steep-pitched roof, chequered brick walls and Latin inscriptions. Sir Thomas also made a weird addition to his own house, BUNNY HALL, which can be seen peering over the wall behind the unsightly petrol station. It looks like a large folly with a castellated tower, an outsize segmental pediment containing a florid carving of Sir Thomas Parkyns' arms (his crest was a pineapple), and two mighty buttresses serving no clear purpose.

Sir Thomas is encountered again inside the large fourteenth-century CHURCH OF ST MARY. Almost the first thing one sees on entering is his monument on the opposite side, behind the font (it was originally in the chancel). It is a large reredos-type structure of marble, with Corinthian pilasters and two arched panels in front, on one of which is his life-size effigy in wrestling pose, and before the other his corpse stretched on a mat, kept company by a figure of Father Time. This extraordinary artefact was designed by Sir Thomas himself and 'wrought out of a fine piece of marble by his chaplain in a barn'. Pause to read the epitaphs in Latin, Greek and English; they too are by Sir Thomas. He also re-roofed the chancel in 1718. It is whitewashed and contains various monuments to deceased members of the Parkyns family, including another (later) Sir Thomas by John Bacon in 1805, and Dame Anne Parkyns (wife of the Wrestling Baronet) by E. Poynton. The sedilia and pretty double piscina are contemporary with the church.

Sir Thomas rebuilt much of the adjoining village of BRADMORE after a fire in 1716. The red brick houses and barns are signed 'SIR T.P.' in black brick and dated. His epitaph emphasises that he was responsible for 'contriving and drawing all his own plans' for buildings on the estate without the aid of an architect.

Clumber ★
NT; 6; 5 miles SE of Worksop on A614
Includes Clumber Chapel and Hardwick-in-Clumber (both NT)
Such is the scale, grandeur and variety of this great landscape PARK that no melancholy attaches to the loss of the ducal house at its heart. This is partly because Bodley's Gothic CLUMBER CHAPEL (NT), built for the 7th Duke of Newcastle in 1886–9, is more than worthy to be the sole focus of the avenues and vistas of so splendid a setting. It looks perfect among the cedars and lawns on the bank of the lake – a powerful monument to late Victorian aristocratic taste and piety. I first saw it during the annual Christmas carol service when the chancel was ablaze with dozens of candles and bright with the crisp white surplices of the choir. The well-known tunes rose up to the gilded bosses of the stone vault, making one feel very proud of England. Of course, this chapel – like

much else that is worthwhile – was paid for out of Victorian coal revenues, and the park is now merely a public playground. But that does not minimise by one jot its impact as a great work of art and as an expression of noble aspirations.

The exterior of the chapel is perfectly proportioned; the transepts, chancel and nave are well related to each other and form an appropriately scaled base to the excelsior of the central tower and spire – similar to that at Patrington in Yorkshire (*q.v.*). As if to save the church from the blandness of too harmonious a perfection, the outside stonework is strikingly contrasted – partly white and partly red Runcorn sandstone. The solemn interior is vaulted throughout, and the detail increases in richness as one proceeds eastwards to the altar. The chancel is lavishly decorated with carved and gilded woodwork by the Rev. Ernest Geldert. This rich display is entirely free from bright polychromy, relying on its effect on the natural colour of the stone and unpainted wood. But when the sun is shining the interior is nevertheless filled with reflected colour from the stained glass in the windows, all made by Kempe to Bodley's design. Throughout, there is a comprehensive and admirable attention to detail; Bodley even designed the needlework frontals for the altars.

Apart from the chapel, there is still much to be impressed by at Clumber. The park contains a wide range of landscape: rough heath, smooth lawns, woodland and arable. There are rare specimen trees and notable avenues, especially the famous lime avenue, stretching 4 miles from the Carburton to the Appley Head lodges. There is also a cedar avenue leading from the pleasure grounds to the kitchen garden, where the Vinery has recently been restored. The five principal entrances to the park are graced by stone Palladian gateways designed by Stephen Wright, the architect of the vanished mansion. He also designed two temples and an elegant balustraded bridge over the lake, which survive, as do the red brick Georgian stables and the red brick Victorian home farm and estate village at HARDWICK-IN-CLUMBER (NT). All this is now well maintained by the National Trust.

Egmanton
7; 2 miles S of Tuxford off A1 [41]
From the outside, ST MARY'S CHURCH looks like a run-of-the-mill medieval village church with a small Perpendicular west tower, a projecting late fourteenth-century transept, and a body of various dates from the twelfth century onwards. The interior (key obtainable from Manor Farm, next door), however, is a wonderful surprise thanks to the 7th Duke of Newcastle, who was patron of the living and enriched the church in 1896–8 with beautiful late medieval-style fittings designed by Sir Ninian Comper. Comper was introduced to the Duke by the historian St John Hope; it is one of Comper's earliest jobs and could easily be mistaken for the work of Bodley. The walls are painted white, and there are sturdy old oak pews, but the eye is immediately taken by the carved rood-screen, exquisitely painted in red, white, blue and gold, and bearing a finely proportioned

crucifix. Over the entrance door is a little painted balcony with the organ, a fine late German-inspired design with richly stencilled shutters and a gilded statue of Our Lady on top. The chancel is especially beautiful; the altar has gilded riddel-posts and rich hangings, and above it hangs a sacrament house, or pyx, protected by a little conical *baldacchino* like the symbolic umbrella carried over the Doge of Venice in processions. The statue of Our Lady of Egmanton on the north wall and the beautiful stained glass in the east window were also designed by Comper and complete a perfect ensemble. The south transept is the d'Avyll chantry, and a painted wooden effigy of the Knight himself (although no-one knows who – or even *if* – he was) reclines under an arch, his feet resting on a dog – more pet mongrel than heraldic talbot; he looks like a child's model in plasticine and is wholly delightful. The inscription reads 'GOOD CHRISTIAN FOLK WHO PASS THIS WAY FOR BARON ROBERT D'AVILLE PRAY'. It is a charming piece of late nineteenth-century self-conscious antiquarianism. In the window above are two attractive little panels of fourteenth-century stained glass showing St George and St Michael.

Flintham Hall
8; 10 miles NE of Nottingham on A46 [42]
Flintham is a magical house. On my first visit there I discovered a fox cub in the ice house – two bright eyes staring out of the dark pit below. It is best, perhaps, on a late summer or early autumn evening, when it is possible to sit in the Library and look through to the Conservatory in the dusk, with the exotic vegetation lit up and the sound of the little fountain splashing amidst the greenery. This Library is the *pièce de résistance* of the house. Originally added by Lewis Wyatt to an older house that once stood here, it was spectacularly reconstructed in 1851–4 by T.C. Hine of Nottingham for T.B.T. Hildyard. There are two tiers of bookcases all round and a massive carved chimneypiece in the *cinquecento* taste made by Holland & Sons to the design of T.R. Macquoid; this was shown at the Great Exhibition of 1851, where it won a prize. All the original furniture, upholstery, chandeliers and bric-à-brac survive to create a nostalgically unaltered Victorian interior.

The Conservatory of iron, stone and glass is as tall as the house and has a high, arched roof, like one of the transepts of the Crystal Palace transported to Nottinghamshire. Seen from the village street, looming over the red-tiled cottage roofs, it looks positively surreal. The rest of Hine's exterior is just as stimulatingly odd. Stone-faced, with a tower over the porch and most curious tracery in the windows, the style defies description. Mark Girouard calls it 'coarsely classical' but it looks more Jacobean to me. Hine's refacing, however, is only skin deep. The walls beneath are eighteenth-century, and the eighteenth-century house replaces a Jacobean and medieval house on the same site.

After the Library, the remainder of the interior is a more low-key affair, but also retains many Victorian features of interest. The Dining Room, for instance, has family portraits built into the panelling and a chandelier of cranberry-red glass, while the main staircase is suf-

Kelham Hall.

fused with multi-coloured light from heraldic stained glass in the large window. Flintham has been the seat of the Hildyards and their ancestors for centuries. All is lovingly cared for, making this one of the most enjoyable of all Victorian houses to visit.

Hawton
9; 2 miles S of Newark off A46
From the flat landscape surrounding ALL SAINTS' CHURCH the tall Perpendicular west tower built in 1482 by Sir Thomas Molyneux forms a notable landmark. However, the special glory of this church (if you can get in; the key is kept in the vicarage – a bungalow to the east – or at Pyke's Farm about half a mile away) is the chancel built in the early fourteenth century by Sir Robert de Compton in the richest Decorated style. There is a very large east window with elaborate flowing tracery and clear glass that fills the interior with bright light, to the great advantage of the magnificent carved fittings. On the south wall of the chancel is a double piscina, as well as a glorious tripartite sedilia with ogee arches and a canopy crisply carved with leaves and little figures. But even this is cast into the shade by the Easter Sepulchre filling the opposite wall. It rises the full height of the chancel and is a mass of richly executed, all-over decoration. Three cusped ogee arches are surmounted by pinnacles and a frieze of the apostles watching Christ ascend into heaven – his feet and the hem of his robe can just be seen flanked by angels in the topmost cornice. In the central niche is a relief of the Resurrection itself, and at the foot sit the sleeping Roman soldiers guarding the tomb. Nearly every inch of the stonework is covered with carved leaves, just like the inner face of the choir screen at Southwell (*q.v.*) and almost certainly by the same sculptors. There is a similar tripartite Easter Sepulchre at Heckington in Lincolnshire (*q.v.*), but this at Hawton is, in my opinion, the finer of the two.

Holme Pierrepont
10; 3 miles N of Newark off A1
HOLME PIERREPONT HALL comprises the remnant of a great early sixteenth-century courtyard house of brick, which for centuries belonged to the Pierreponts. It was partly demolished in the eighteenth century. The south range was originally the lodgings for retainers and still contains many sixteenth-century features; the other range was altered in the seventeenth and eighteenth centuries. The Drawing Room has a plasterwork ceiling of c.1660 brought from Wheelergate in Nottingham; the fine staircase with its foliated scroll balustrade is of about the same date and there is a Long Gallery, now used for the performance of concerts and operas. The attractive courtyard garden, with clipped box hedges and roses, was laid out in the 1870s.

Kelham Hall
11; 2 miles NW of Newark on A617
A first reaction on catching sight of the 'hard red brick' silhouette of Kelham rearing above the River Trent is to think: St Pancras! And it was indeed designed by Sir George Gilbert Scott. The owner was John Manners-Sutton, and the opportunity for rebuilding came when the former house on the site was burnt to the ground in 1857. In the words of Mark Girouard, 'any building so huge, so solid, so elaborately, learnedly and expensively Gothic, so redolently, earnestly and undilutedly Victorian is bound to exert a fascination that will increase'. As a private house, however, it was not a success; its character is more that of a public building, and so it is not inappropriate that it was used as a monastery for most of this century and now serves as the district council offices.

The plans for the house were worked out during 1858 and the foundation stone laid in April 1859. As a precaution against another fire in the future, the whole construction is fireproof, of brick, iron and concrete; the floors are all of marble, tiles or cement; only the roofs and staircase handrails are of timber. The façades are wildly asymmetrical, with innumerable different types of window (derived from Gothic cathedrals and Venetian palaces) and there is a handsome clock tower with a pointed top. The main entrance was placed not in the middle but at the north end, where there is a large covered court, so that visitors could alight from their carriages without getting wet, but this no longer serves its original function. The interior is very impressive, with spacious Gothic rooms opening off a vaulted spinal corridor. They were all elaborately carved, gilded and painted, though some of this original decoration has subsequently disappeared. The Drawing Room is the best preserved, with painted stencilling on the vaults and huge Gothic mirrors. Throughout the house the capitals of the columns, carved by Farmer and Brindley, are a great feature, embellished with a wide variety of flowers and leaves all done with the greatest botanical accuracy.

Milton
12; 5 miles S of East Retford off A1

In splendid isolation, away from the village and approached by an avenue of Lombardy poplars — and amazing the traveller — is a large stone Grecian church just like those to be found all over south London. This is the NEWCASTLE MAUSOLEUM, erected in 1832 by the 4th Duke of Newcastle as a memorial to his wife, who had died ten years earlier. It was designed by Sir Robert Smirke, the architect of the British Museum. It is cruciform in design, with a tall, octagonal domed cupola over the crossing, and was ingeniously planned in two parts to serve both as the parish church and as a private memorial chapel. The public half is to the west and stops that side of the crossing with a blank wall and Ionic reredos. The east end under the tower is the mausoleum proper. It is entered from the east through a solemn Doric portico with four fluted columns. Inside, the mausoleum is circular, with chapels in the transepts to north and south for tombs. The 4th Duke's is still *in situ*; rather incongruously it is Gothic, of carved wood. The tomb of the Duchess, the *raison d'être* of the whole edifice, has unfortunately been removed to the chapel at Clumber (*q.v.*); it ought to be returned here. It is by Westmacott, of purest Carrara marble, and shows the Duchess reclining with her twin children clinging to her as they watch an angel (on the back panel) beckoning their mother away. It is a fine example of English neo-classicism, chaste and poignant but not too overtly sentimental. After some years of neglect, the mausoleum has recently been restored and is now vested in the Redundant Churches Fund, which maintains it well, as it does all its churches.

Newark★
13; 20 miles S of East Retford on A1

Newark is a notably well-preserved and interesting old country town, though with a somewhat forlorn air. It is best approached from the north, where a long straight road, some of it built on a causeway, crosses the water meadows, railway and River Trent, arriving bang in the town centre beside the castle with no suburbs on this side to spoil the effect.

The riverside is lined with picturesque old brick warehouses, breweries and maltings, and is worth exploring. Just over the bridge, the eye is immediately taken by the russet grandeur of the OSSINGTON COFFEE HOUSE, given to Newark in 1882 by Lady Ossington (sister of the 5th Duke of Portland) and designed by Ernest George and Peto. It is a splendid display of Victorian architectural quality, but as an encouragement to temperance it was a failure. After a long period as offices, it was recently converted into a rather classy fish-and-chip shop but has now changed hands again.

On the other side of the road, the ruins of the CASTLE of the Bishops of Lincoln guard the crossing from the north into southern England. The castle was slighted in the Civil War but the twelfth-century Gatehouse and rectangular fourteenth-century curtain wall remain. The river frontage is very impressive, rising 170 feet above the water level. The ruins have belonged to the town since 1889 and have undergone various phases of restoration — hence the patchy effect of the stonework. There is a municipal garden, furnished with Victorian cast-iron benches, inside the walls.

KIRKGATE is an agreeable street, lined mainly with early to mid-eighteenth-century houses (or refrontings) of brick. One or two timber-framed buildings also survive in their original state. The King's Arms is enlivened with the Royal Arms in cast-iron, brightly painted. From the bridge, Kirkgate is aligned on the spire of ST MARY MAGDALENE'S CHURCH — 237 feet high and the major monument of Newark. The largest church in the county, it is a splendid monument to Newark's medieval prosperity. The overwhelming impact is of an ambitious Perpendicular structure with the nave and chancel dating from the fifteenth century, but the uniform plan actually goes back to the twelfth. The west tower is Early English in its lower parts, while the spire itself is fourteenth-century. The latter was a most welcome addition, its height matching the combined length of nave and chancel. The interior is equally striking — wide, high and airy. The columns are extremely slim and the arches so tall that the aisles, which are also unusually broad, feel part of the same space as the nave. The roof is continuous from end to end, and this also contributes to the impressive appearance of the church. The chancel has a huge Perpendicular window filling the whole of the east wall over the altar; it contains strongly coloured Victorian glass, by Hardman, which was given to the church as a memorial to Prince Albert. The magnificent gilded reredos in the style of the late fourteenth century was designed in 1937 by Sir Ninian Comper — a worthy twentieth-century contribution. Comper was also responsible for some of the woodwork in the south chapel. The choir stalls, on the other hand, date from *c.*1500 and have twenty-six genuine medieval misericords with amusing carvings. The rood-screen is of the same date and was made by Thomas Drawswerd of York. It is a *tour de force* of Perpendicular woodwork, its impact improved by cleaning in 1977.

To the south-west of the church lies Newark's famous MARKET PLACE; and remarkably monumental it is, comparable with the *places* of continental towns. It is roughly square, with cobbled paving and surrounded by regular Georgian buildings, many of which have Tuscan colonnades or 'piazzas' along the ground floor. The TOWN HALL on the north side forms a truly fine climax. It was designed in 1774 by Carr of York and is the acme of dignified civic architecture. Its stone façade has a Tuscan portico. The statue of Justice on top has been renewed recently. The ground floor contains the Butcher's Market, with stone colonnades, but upstairs there is a splendid Assembly Room, with apses at either end and Adamesque decoration. The other prominent buildings round the square were once nearly all coaching inns. The Clinton Arms and the Saracen's Head (now Barclays Bank, but still with a saracen's head in a niche) are prosperous Georgian brick – both carefully restored or reconstructed in the 1970s – while the Queen's Head and the WHITE HART are timber-framed. The White Hart is one of the most important pieces of fifteenth-century secular architecture in all England, its façade elaborately decorated with figures of saints in small tabernacled niches on the beams, all painted red and gold. The building has just been restored as offices for the Nottingham Building Society – it is a pity that the ground-floor frontage is glass, though.

The two other main streets of Newark run parallel to each other and to the river, north of the Market Place.

Middle Gate has the Victorian MARKET HALL of 1884 by Charles Bell, and one good big five-bay mid-Georgian house. Castle Gate, which runs alongside the castle, is spoilt by too much traffic but has stately Georgian houses, some with elaborate doorcases and some with pediments; also here is the splendid former CORN EXCHANGE of 1847, built in an Italian Baroque style worthy of an opera house; in fact it is now a bingo hall. How is that for *lèse-majesté*? These main streets and the Market Place are linked by a network of smaller streets lined with decent buildings, all in remarkably unspoilt condition. The inevitable modern shopping centre is relatively small and tucked away tactfully to the side of the Market Place; as a result it does little visual damage. Beyond, in Lombard Street, is the CASTLE BREWERY of 1882 by William Bradford, with an elaborately dressed façade, clock tower, polished brass name-plates and varnished woodwork – reeking of Victorian commercial confidence and still going strong. Poor Lady Ossington!

Newstead Abbey
14; 8 miles N of Nottingham off A60

The dissolved Augustinian priory was acquired by Sir John Byron in 1539 and belonged to his descendants until 1817, when the most famous of them, the poet Lord Byron, was forced to sell. It was bought and restored by his old schoolfriend Colonel Thomas Wildman. The Abbey was presented to Nottingham by Sir Julian Cahn in 1911.

Newstead Abbey.

The beautiful thirteenth-century façade of the priory church survives, but the remainder of the entrance front is as remodelled by Stedman, in Neo-Norman and mixed Gothic styles executed by the architect John Shaw in 1817–26. The fabric of the house, however, is largely medieval, and the main block still forms a quadrangle round the fifteenth-century cloisters. Entrance is gained through a thirteenth-century undercroft with a ribbed vault. The original chapter house was converted into a private chapel by the Byrons, and redecorated in polychrome in the 1860s.

The principal rooms are on the first floor. These include the rooms with marble chimneypieces at the north end, which were made habitable by Lord Byron and, in his time, formed an oasis in a scene of general decay. The poet's bedroom retains his pompous four-poster bed, ornamented with gilt coronets at the four corners. In the East and North Galleries is displayed a collection of Byron's manuscripts, letters and first editions. The state rooms, called after various monarchs, retain features of different dates: the Charles II Room has an early eighteenth-century painted ceiling and the Edward III Room has a sixteenth-century carved overmantel, one of three in the house. The Saloon occupies the site of the refectory and has an interesting wooden ceiling dated 1631 and 1633. The Great Hall was entirely refitted by Colonel Wildman with competent Gothic woodwork.

The south door, St Mary's, Nottingham.

Nottingham
15; 22 miles N of Leicester on A60

The centre of Nottingham will come as a surprise to most people, for, apart from Bristol, it is probably the only English industrial city that has been consistently prosperous since the Middle Ages and yet has managed to preserve much of historic interest from earlier periods. It is very different from the other cities of northern England, where the architectural interest is almost entirely Victorian and Edwardian, with only the occasional over-pickled antiquity to recall the more remote past. The comparison with Bristol is not an exaggeration, because Nottingham too has a spectacular medieval parish church, good Georgian houses, was damaged in the Reform Bill Riots in 1831, has a hilly Regency suburb, impressive early twentieth-century university buildings and an appalling 1960s' inner ring-road. The latter is called Maid Marian Way and has been dubbed the 'ugliest road in Europe'. It cuts through two of the best streets and does irrevocable damage to the townscape – but apart from that the old town centre is well preserved, rather like many historic continental towns where sprawling modern development surrounds the *belli arti* protected nucleus. The centre occupies a hilly ridge with a castle at one end and St Mary's church at the other. To the north is the huge Victoria Shopping Centre on the site of Victoria Station. To the north-west is THE PARK, an important Regency and Victorian residential development on the site of the castle park, promoted by the nineteenth-century Dukes of Newcastle. It is attractively landscaped, with villas in a variety of styles, from Grecian stucco to Jacobean red brick, and gas-lamps. The canal, railway, Broadmarsh shopping centre, industry and artisan housing (mainly replaced in the 1970s) fill the valley to the south and east.

The place to begin in Nottingham is the CASTLE, approached through a restored fourteenth-century gateway with two cylindrical towers. Most of the medieval buildings were destroyed in the Civil War and the present castle is a Genoese *palazzo* built between 1674 and 1679 by the Duke of Newcastle to his own design; it displays excessive rustication, Corinthian pilasters, elaborate architraves to the windows, and a rich modillion cornice. The interior was burnt in the Reform Bill Riots but was later reconstructed by T.C. Hine as an art gallery; it contains an interesting collection of paintings, part of which comes from the Duke of Newcastle's collection. In the cliff below the castle were troglodyte dwellings; one of them – the TRIP TO JERUSALEM, a famously 'olde' pub – still survives.

Houndsgate and Castlegate are both cut through by Maid Marian Way but nevertheless have some good Georgian houses: the SALUTATION INN is restored sixteenth-century; NEWDIGATE HOUSE is the same date as the castle, *c*.1675, and has rich iron gates in front; east of the ring-road, STANFORD HOUSE, of 1775, is a decent Adamesque building. ST NICHOLAS'S CHURCH, to the south, was built in 1671–82 to replace a medieval church destroyed by the Parliamentarians in the Civil War. It is of brick, with round-headed windows, battlements and a west tower. It has been well restored recently. The continuation of Castlegate is Low Pavement and High Pavement; both contain more Georgian houses. In the former is the POST OFFICE, once the Assembly Rooms, with a Regency façade, and WILLOUGHBY HOUSE, of *c*.1738, set back grandly behind a forecourt with iron railings. High Pavement has the JUDGES' LODGING, partly of *c*.1730 but with a dramatic Grecian extension of 1833. The neoclassical SHIRE HALL, which has an attached Ionic portico, is of 1769–70. It was designed by James Gandon, architect of the Dublin Customs House, and is signed by him on the pediment. The Italianate extensions on either side are by T.C. Hine.

At the end of High Pavement is ST MARY'S, the churchyard forming a square surrounded by Georgian houses and seemly Victorian warehouses. The church is a building of great splendour and size, Perpendicular and richly restored; it is something of which Nottingham is rightly proud. It nearly became a cathedral in the nineteenth century, but Southwell (*q.v.*) was chosen instead. It is cruciform in plan, with a tall central tower and very large Perpendicular windows; the north transept is a *tour de force* – more glass than wall. Entering through the south porch, the brilliantly imaginative bronze doors of 1904 by Henry Wilson form an admirable overture to the majestic interior. The general impression is of a remarkable unity: beautifully moulded piers and arches, the large windows full of Victorian glass by many of the leading nineteenth-century firms – Clayton & Bell, Hardman, Kempe, Heaton, Butler & Bayne. There are also regimental banners and impressive late Victorian fittings of the type described by Goodhart-Rendel as 'Public School Anglican', including the carved oak roodscreen, the high altar with riddel-posts, and a gilded reredos; all these are by Bodley. The whole church is beautifully kept, and is entirely free from the vulgar modern trivia that detracts from so many churches.

The area at the east end of the centre is known as the LACE MARKET, because in the nineteenth century, when their former inhabitants moved out to more fashionable suburbs, the houses were taken over by the lace industry. The lace manufacturers have gone in their turn, and the area is now being rehabilitated for other uses, rather as Covent Garden in London has been. The Lace Market is worth exploring, as it contains many interesting commercial buildings by the two idiosyncratic Victorian Nottingham architects T.C. Hine and Watson Fothergill – including the latter's own office, its façade decorated with busts of Pugin and Street. Victoria Street to the north contains a series of nineteenth-century Italianate stone *palazzi*, including the former Royal Insurance Company and several banks. It leads to the COUNCIL HOUSE and the MARKET PLACE, the *ne plus ultra* of municipal splendour. The Council House was rebuilt and the large Market Place, to one side of which it stands, remodelled in 1927–9 by T. Cecil Howitt in a super-classical style more usually encountered in the USA than in England; it perfectly expresses the inter-war prosperity of Nottingham – Players' cigarettes, Raleigh bicycles, and Boots the chemist's. The Council House has a huge dome on top and a cross-shaped arcade or *galleria* in the centre, with paintings showing

The church of the Holy Rood, Ossington.

progress and prosperity; there is more allegorical sculpture round the outside on the same theme. Nottingham's coat of arms is inlaid in mosaic into the pavement in front.

It is difficult to take one's eyes off this extravagant spectacle, but there are other buildings of interest round about, including the nineteenth-century Italianate NATIONAL WESTMINSTER BANK, originally Smith's Bank, and YE FLYING HORSE, established in 1483 – a rather over-restored old pub. To the south in St Peter's Gate is ST PETER'S CHURCH, medieval with a spire and an elaborate west door. It was excellently restored by Stephen Dykes Bower in 1951 and has many attractive fittings, including an organ by Schnetzler and two good altarpieces, one of carved wood and the other painted.

Osberton Hall
See Scofton.

Ossington
16; 6 miles S of Tuxford off A1
Buried deep in the park of a vanished house, with lake and cedar trees, and reached through romantic rusty iron gates and down an overgrown avenue, is a perfect neo-classical stone church. The CHURCH of THE HOLY ROOD was built in 1782–3 by Carr of York for the Denisons, whose descendants still own the estate and who now live in the old rectory. The rectangular body of the church is symmetrical with a pedimented Tuscan doorcase in the middle and two round-arched windows on either side. At the west end is a square tower of three slightly receding tiers, the top one of which has Tuscan columns and a low domed cupola above. The interior is one elegant room with a coved plaster ceiling and a

The Library, Papplewick Hall.

decent coffee-and-white colour scheme. The west wall is a symmetrical design and there is an interesting barrel organ in the middle, flanked by niches containing excellent marble statues by Nollekens of William and Robert Denison. William, who bought the estate in 1768, was a wool merchant, and there is a relief on the plinth of his statue showing bales of wool, sheep and a ship, all very delicately carved. His brother Robert conceived the church as William's memorial. At the east end the altarpiece is a good sixteenth-century Italian Mannerist painting, perhaps by Vasari. To the left is a tall Renaissance monument from the previous church on this site to William Cartwright, who died in 1602; his twelve children kneel below. The graveyard is attractively wild and contains two sundials; that to the south of the church is a baluster of 1812, but that to the east is a seventeenth-century piece of greater interest, in the form of a Tuscan column with a stone ball on top.

The site of the house, demolished in 1963, is next to the church and there is a good view from the former terrace over the lake and woods. If it were mine, I would build a new house there at once.

Papplewick

17; 6 miles N of Nottingham on B6011

Papplewick is an outpost of Horace Walpole's world. In the late eighteenth century it belonged to the Hon. Frederick Montagu, a friend of the poets Thomas Gray and William Mason; he built the house and church. The former is classical; the latter is Gothick and treated as an ornament in the park.

The CHURCH OF ST JAMES is extremely pretty, with a west tower and cardboard-looking battlements. The windows have Y-tracery and clear glass, except for the east window, which has eighteenth-century painted glass with courtly figures of Hope and Faith by Francis Eginton, after the Reynolds' glass at New College, Oxford. The interior is light and elegant, painted white, with a gallery running along one side supported on characteristic thin clustered columns of quatrefoil section. The squire's pew occupies the end of the gallery nearest the altar and has a fireplace so that he could listen to the sermon in comfort. Unfortunately, the box pews in the body of the church have been replaced with Victorian benches, but otherwise the Georgian atmosphere is undisturbed.

PAPPLEWICK HALL is almost square in plan. The external architecture is much as it has always been, with relatively plain façades, the main relief being different arrangements of Ionic pilasters on the park and garden fronts. The interior is elegantly appointed, with Adamesque plasterwork and doorcases. The Hall has a semi-circular staircase with wrought-iron balustrade, and the Morning Room contains an early Flaxman relief commissioned by Montagu. The Library is the best room; its chimneypiece is in an arched recess in the apsidal end wall, while the bookcases are set into blank arches. It is a suitable monument to Montagu's love of literature – though not the only one at Papplewick, for originally the grounds were embellished with urns commemorating Gray and Mason, of which the latter remains (Gray's has migrated to Eton).

Ratcliffe-on-Soar
18; 8 miles SW of Nottingham on A648
Set in the water meadows by the River Trent and liable to flooding, HOLY TRINITY CHURCH, with its venerable blackened stone spire, is famous for the Sacheverell family tombs. In *Tales My Father Told Me* Sir Osbert Sitwell, who was descended from the Sacheverell family, has described an abortive visit with his father to see them: 'When we reached what should have been the culmination of our pilgrimage, the church of Ratcliffe-on-Soar, we found the floor of the sacred edifice under water to the height of half a foot. It was impossible to examine the series of tombs closely without wading, but from the door they looked impressive and beautiful. Four or five great rectangular masses, fashioned of Nottinghamshire alabaster and Derbyshire marble, bearing on them the recumbent effigies of knights and their ladies, seemed to float on a flat mirror of water. . . .'

The spire and chancel are Early English but the main part of the church is an attractively patched hotchpotch, with bits of brickwork here and Georgian windows there. The interior is spacious. The tombs are in the chancel and their chronological sequence marks the change from Gothic to Renaissance. Ralph Sacheverell (d.1539) and his wife lie in a recess in the north wall under a Gothic canopy which still sports traces of the original gilding; Henry (d.1558) and his wife (on a tomb-chest with seventeen children holding shields), and another Henry (d.1586) and his wife (on a tomb with strapwork ornament) fill bays of the chancel arcade. And on the south wall is the large alabaster monument to the last Henry (d.1625); he lies on a tomb-chest with three babies carved on the side, and his three wives, kneeling in prayer, fill a sort of reredos structure hanging on the wall above him. It is thought that all these tombs were produced by the same Nottinghamshire workshop; they demonstrate how the once-famous local alabaster-carving industry continued after the Reformation by concentrating on tombs rather than altarpieces.

Scofton
19; 2 miles E of Worksop off A620
OSBERTON HALL is the seat of the Foljambes, one of the oldest families in Nottinghamshire. They had been prominent in the area since the Middle Ages and inherited Osberton in the eighteenth century through marriage to an heiress. The present house was built to the design of William Wilkins in 1806, but was substantially reconstructed in 1877 by J. MacVicar Anderson, who enlarged it, added bay windows, a large *porte-cochère* and a new roof. It is of red brick with stone trimmings and is an impressive classical design. Like the surrounding estate, it is beautifully kept up. The stables are a stone quadrangle designed by William Lindley of Doncaster. Although Osberton is not open to the public, a glimpse of the house can be obtained from the churchyard on the other side of the lake.

The CHURCH was rebuilt in 1833 by Ambrose Poynter for George Savile Foljambe; it is in the Norman style, with a west tower and round arches. It is beautifully furnished and contains Foljambe family monuments from the eighteenth to the twentieth centuries. For those who like a secret glimpse of a secluded, almost private world, this little church and the views over the surrounding well-managed estate, with its neat brick cottages and fine model farm buildings, is strongly recommended.

Serlby Hall
20; 3 miles N of Blyth off A614
A Georgian barracks of a house, built of rose-pink brick and three storeys high, Serlby stands well on a ridge overlooking steep grass terraces and eighteenth-century parkland. It was the seat of the Moncktons, Viscounts Galway; though the estate still belongs to the family, at the time of writing the house is being divided into flats. It was built piecemeal between 1754 and 1777 to the design of James Paine, but the austere form of the exterior is the result of alterations carried out by Lindley and Woodhead of Doncaster in 1812, when an extra storey was added and two flanking wings demolished. Paine's design was much more original and *mouvementé*, with a pedimented central block and flanking pedimented wings on the model of a Palladian villa.

The interior is very fine. The Saloon in the centre of the garden front is Paine's; it has an elaborately decorated ceiling containing inset paintings attributed to Zucchi. The Small Drawing Room is also by Paine, with a more sober Palladian character. Many of the other rooms retain their 1812 decoration — rather old-fashioned for its date, with Adamesque plasterwork and some of Paine's marble chimneypieces re-used; that in the main Drawing Room, with Bacchic carvings, however, was brought from a house in London. The Entrance Hall was remodelled in 1911.

The grounds of Serlby remain a good example of eighteenth-century design, with a lake, marble statues, grotto, Gothick eye-catcher and many splendid trees, especially cedars and magnolias. The whole *mise-en-scène* is of great beauty and is quintessentially English. Serlby has descended to Charlotte Monckton, who, through both her father and mother, is heiress to half a dozen estates, including Melbury in Dorset and Holland Park in London.

Shireoaks Hall
21; 2 miles NW of Worksop off A620
A blackened place of collieries in the north-west of the county — yet in the midst of this landscape of desolation stands the romantic fragment of a Jacobean house surrounded by formal gardens. Tall, gaunt, desolate, and looking like some abandoned villa or castle in the Campagna, Shireoaks Hall is three storeys high, with large mullion or sash windows, many of which are blocked up. Built *c*.1600 for Henry Hewett, almost certainly by Robert Smythson, it was cross-shaped, with a plan similar to the keep at Bolsover (*q.v.*). Originally the Great Hall was on the *piano nobile*, approached by an external flight of steps, with the state rooms on the top floor as at Chatsworth or Hardwick (*qq.v.*), but nearly all the original interior has gone. Much remodelling was done in the early eighteenth century; the two little stable blocks were built then and the grandiose formal gardens laid

out by Sir Thomas Hewett, Surveyor-General to King George I. Much of the house was demolished in 1810 when it became the residence of the agent to the Duke of Norfolk's Worksop estate (*q.v.*). For the last 150 years it has been a farmhouse and potato store, but now it has been acquired by an architect, Mr Leopold Godlewski, who is in the process of restoring it as his family home.

The special glory of Shireoaks is the eighteenth-century WATER GARDEN, the bones of which have survived a century and a half of decay, and which it is intended to restore to their original condition. There was a large radiating layout on the west front, similar to that at Hampton Court, with a central axial canal and flanking beech avenues. The canal, still filled with water, leads to a cascade of thirty-four steps with alternating stone basins fed from water in a large stone-lined pond half a mile away. On the north side of the house are two square ponds forming part of another formal layout. The grounds will have to be replanted as nearly all the trees have gone, including the clipped yews that lined the canal and all the intersecting avenues.

The Chapter House, Southwell Minster.

Southwell★
22; 6 miles W of Newark on A612

This conspicuously neat little town is like a miniature Barchester, complete with cathedral, sleepy close and Georgian main street all on a lilliputian scale.

The exterior of the MINSTER is lent a continental flavour by the pointed lead caps on top of the two west towers. The overall composition is very satisfying: every part is well proportioned and well related to the rest, the nave longer than the chancel, and the square central tower over the crossing more substantial than the thinner, more elegant west towers. Founded in about 956, the present building is largely Norman but with an Early English choir. The Norman detail of the nave and transepts is strong and simple, with large flat buttresses, round-arched windows lower down, circular windows in the clerestory and bands of blank arcading round the tops of the towers. The interior of the nave has fat round columns and three diminishing tiers of arches. It is massive and impressive, but also rather bare; there are few monuments or old fittings and the atmosphere is rather more Protestant than is usually the case in English cathedrals. The nice creaking old chairs have also been replaced with modern ones of obtrusively light oak with preposterously low backs – the sort of chairs that seem to be considered *de rigueur* in modern cathedrals but which do unnecessary visual damage. The chancel was rebuilt between 1234 and 1241 by Archbishop Walter de Grey of York (who also rebuilt the transepts at York Minster (*q.v.*)); it is excellently proportioned, noble and disciplined, with rib vaults, clustered lancet windows, and fine carving on the ceiling bosses and stiff-leaf capitals on the columns. The lower tier of eastern lancets over the altar contains sixteenth-century French Mannerist glass with rich colouring; it was rescued from the Temple Church in Paris when that was demolished during the Revolution and subsequently found its way to Southwell. The lectern in the middle of the choir, which at first you might think is the usual brass Victorian eagle, is in fact a genuine piece of late Gothic of *c.*1500. It has a romantic history: it comes from Newstead Abbey (*q.v.*), where it was dredged out of the lake in 1780 and given to Southwell. There is one similar, also of English manufacture, in the cathedral at Urbino in Italy. In looking eastwards, however, we are missing the best feature of all: the pulpitum screen – so turn round and swoon before one of the most elaborate pieces of Decorated architecture in England. It was erected in *c.*1330 and is of incomparable richness, with diaper and leaf carving, ogee arches, masses of small carved heads (albeit restored), and crocketed gables of a luxuriance otherwise encountered only in the Lady Chapel at Ely.

And so to the *pièce de résistance* – the famous CHAPTER HOUSE built on to the north side of the church in 1288. It is octagonal and approached by a short corridor. Although quite small, it feels more spacious than some of its larger peers because it has no central column to support the stone vault. The doorway into the Chapter House from the corridor is a most beautiful design, embellished with Purbeck columns, open geometrical tracery and exquisite naturalistic carving imitating buttercups, ivy, brambles and other easily identifiable plants. It is rightly considered one of the greatest works of art in England. The same stone foliage decoration embellishes the canopies of the arcaded seats round the walls of the Chapter House itself. It is best to sit here quietly and let the eye rove over the restrained richness of the design. You are unlikely to be disturbed, for Southwell is, fortunately, not a very touristy cathedral. It is easy to study the sculpture as the room is full of light; the windows are glazed with large areas of clear glass framing assembled fragments of English and continental medieval stained glass.

The setting of Southwell Minster is very attractive, with lawns on all sides and a scattering of prebendal houses and other ecclesiastical appendages. The BISHOP'S PALACE to the south was remodelled and covered with rough-cast by Caröe so that it looks almost entirely like an informal gabled Arts and Crafts job, but in fact it still contains much medieval work. VICARS' COURT to the north-east is an eighteenth-century U-shaped layout of brick, so chaste and well-proportioned that it looks more Neo-Georgian than the real thing. Along the north side of the precincts are several genteel Georgian houses, including CRANFIELD HOUSE, a perfect brick doll's house of c.1700. The west front of the Minster is open to Southwell's main street – Westgate – and its northern continuation, King Street. The late Georgian brick houses and shops are interrupted by the SARACEN'S HEAD, a picturesque sixteenth-century coaching inn with black-and-white timbering. A less welcome interruption is the unfortunate gap next to the Wheatsheaf Inn caused by redevelopment. It should be filled immediately with a well-designed new building. At the north end of King Street is Burgage Green, an attractive rectangular space with grass, and oak and lime trees, surrounded by varied Georgian houses and the cyclopic stone entrance archway to the former House of Correction.

Staunton in the Vale

23; 9 miles NW of Grantham off A1

Here is unspoilt and delectable Midlands country in the Vale of Belvoir, with hedged fields, old trees, winding lanes and impressive views of Belvoir Castle (*q.v.*) on the wooded hill to the south presiding in feudal splendour over all it surveys. The Stauntons have been seated at Staunton since 1041 and in the Middle Ages held the manor in return for the duty of castle guard at Belvoir. Their house and the parish church, full of their monuments, stand side by side in the centre of the park, forming a perfect manorial group.

The CHURCH OF ST MARY dates from the fourteenth century but was restored in 1853 by E.J. Willson of Lincoln. It is dominated externally by the tower, topped off with a pyramidal cap. The interior has octagonal columns dividing the nave from the north aisle, which is as wide as the nave. The whole church is full of light. Across the chancel arch is an early sixteenth-century wooden screen and there is a Norman font. The Staunton monuments are concentrated mainly in the north aisle, beginning in the thirteenth and fourteenth centuries with cross-legged knights in chain-mail, their ladies in

wimples, processing down the centuries to the conventional marble tablets of the eighteenth and early nineteenth centuries. The epitaph of Job Staunton Charlton tells us that his mother's ancestors had 'INHERITED THE ESTATE FROM THE TIME OF THE SAXONS'.

STAUNTON HALL, said to be the Willingham of Sir Walter Scott's *Heart of Midlothian*, is basically sixteenth-century; the porch is dated 1573 and another inscription gives 1554. Though some mullion windows, one gable and some tall chimneys survive, much of the pleasant character of the house comes from the Georgian remodelling carried out in 1794. The canted windows at either end of the entrance front and the garden elevation with a central bay window date from then. The family was not rich enough in the eighteenth and nineteenth centuries to rebuild the house entirely, so they just patched and mended what was there. The sixteenth-century Great Hall, for instance, is pleasantly Georgianised, with the main staircase occupying the site of the screens passage. The ancient front door is dotted with bullet holes commemorating the siege of 1645 when Mrs Staunton unsuccessfully defended the house for the King against the Parliamentarians, for of course the Stauntons were Royalists. Even today, whenever the Sovereign visits Belvoir Castle the Staunton of Staunton must be there to open the front door with a golden key.

Strelley

24; 3 miles W of Nottingham on B6004

The hilltop on which church and hall stand side by side in a pretty park is beleagured by the twentieth century: on one side is the M1 and on the other the sprawling suburbs of Nottingham (*q.v.*), but there is still a rural atmosphere – just.

The CHURCH OF ALL SAINTS is a splendid building, full of splendid things. It was largely rebuilt in the mid-fourteenth century by Sir Sampson Strelley. It is of pink sandstone and has an impressive west tower. The tall, spacious nave leads to the magnificent chancel, which was intended by Sir Sampson to be his family's mortuary chapel. It is separated from the nave by an exquisite rood-screen of carved wood with filigree ogee tracery and a projecting openwork cove. The cresting and cross on top were designed by C.G. Hare, who was also responsible for the beautiful furnishings of the sanctuary and south chapel. The chancel is one of the great medieval funerary chapels, and contains beautiful monuments to the once powerful Strelley family (they died out in the eighteenth century). Sir Sampson lies in the middle on an alabaster tomb-chest with angels holding shields round the sides. He wears armour and looks rather stern, but this is belied by a most touching gesture: he has removed his right gauntlet (which he holds in his left hand) in order to hold hands with his wife, who lies beside him in a richly decorated wimple and elegant dress. His feet lie against his crest (a lion) while hers rest against two little puppies. Inset into the floor are alabaster slabs and brasses to other members of the family. The most impressive tomb, however, is that to Sir John Strelley (d.1501) and his wife; it stands against the north wall in an elaborately crested recess carved with angels and heraldry. It is of high quality and would not be out of place in some old cathedral in Spain. Like Sir Sampson, Sir John is in armour, and his wife is in fashionable dress; his feet too rest on the Strelley lion, with two little figures of monks with rosary beads sitting on its back. No wonder it has a rather startled expression. Sir John's funerary helmet still hangs here, on the wall opposite his tomb. As well as these tombs, the chancel also has a complete set of medieval choir stalls with carved misericords. In the south chapel's east window is some excellent sixteenth-century Flemish glass. In Pevsner's words, the furnishings of Strelley church 'afford the most complete example in Notts of the riches of art which a generous and pious family would bestow on the church of its manor'.

Sutton on Trent
25; 8 miles N of Newark on B1164
I confess that I do not much care for the CHURCH OF ALL SAINTS, but feel that I ought to like it. For a start, the village has suffered from its position on the A1 and from too much new housing. Then the graveyard has been drastically tidied and the gravestones largely swept away to make room for neatly mown lawns and hybrid rose bushes. (I hate modern roses in graveyards.) The church itself is ambitious, mainly Perpendicular with a tall west tower, the nave with clerestory, and a large early sixteenth-century chapel on the south side. The church was restored and the west tower rebuilt in 1902 by William Weir – a good SPAB (Society for the Protection of Ancient Buildings) architect much employed by Lord Curzon – but even so the interior looks horribly scraped. This is because all the stonework of the walls is exposed and hideously pointed; one longs to plaster and whitewash it all. Perhaps this is a church which will appeal more to archaeologists than to aesthetes? There are a few nice things, however – old benches in the chancel with carved poppy heads; the 'Perpendicular' east window dated 1632 (an early example of Gothic Revival); and a dim oil painting of entertainingly poor quality in the nave. It depicts a not clearly identifiable New Testament subject and looks as if it might be by the daughter of an eighteenth-century vicar. The real disappointment is the Mering Chapel, south of the chancel. It looks promising from outside, with large Perpendicular windows and elaborate battlements. The effect inside, however, is entirely spoilt. Half is filled with an ungainly Victorian organ which blocks the vistas, while the other half is used as the vestry. There is not even an altar in it, though a well-preserved piscina can be discerned between the safe and a row of cassocks. The finely carved Perpendicular oak screen at the west end backs straight on to the organ, which detracts from its effect, though it is a fine piece of woodwork in itself.

Teversal
26; 2 miles NW of Sutton in Ashfield off B6014
Teversal is close to collieries, yet remains a rural backwater thanks to the protection of Hardwick Park, which has acted as a green belt holding ugly modern development at bay. The village is unspoilt, with stone cottages

– more Derbyshire than Nottinghamshire. The great thrill, though, is the CHURCH OF ST CATHERINE, which dates from the twelfth and thirteenth centuries. Its low arcades with circular piers carry round arches and support a later clerestory. It is the furnishings and unrestored atmosphere, however, that make it extra special. There are box pews throughout, the larger ones for more important members of the congregation. The squire's pew in the south aisle is like a four-poster bed, with barley-sugar columns at the corners supporting a canopy. This, like most of the furnishings, dates from the late seventeenth century, as do the Gothic roof and the panelled west gallery. The altar rails have turned balusters, the communion table has fat bulbous legs, the pulpit is combined with a reading desk, and the font sits in its own enclosure. All is remarkably complete and unaltered. The cushions in the squire's pew are embroidered with the Molyneux arms and the family's prayerbooks are still there, though the last descendant of the Molyneux family left Teversal in 1929. A wonderful array of seven Molyneux hatchments hangs around the nave between the top of the arches and the clerestory windows, and their monuments fill the chancel – a procession of eighteenth-century baronets culminating in Sir Francis, 'Gentleman Usher of the Black Rod during the long period of 47 years . . . the 7th and last baronet of this ancient family'. He died in 1812. None of these memorials are of the highest sculptural quality but they are dignified and quietly proud, with their marble portrait busts, heraldry, curly pediments, cartouches and well-composed epitaphs. It is a very English interior, old-fashioned and comfortable.

Thoresby Hall
27; 3 miles NW of Ollerton off A614
A Victorian house, and the third to occupy this site in the Dukeries, Thoresby was designed in 1864 by Anthony Salvin for the 3rd Earl Manvers. He demolished a beautiful house by Carr of York to make way for it and this, in turn, replaced a Baroque house designed by Talman for the Duke of Kingston which had been destroyed by fire in 1745.

The centre of the Salvin house is occupied by the Great Hall, three storeys high with a hammerbeam roof. At one end the Grand Staircase ascends through dramatic arcades; its wrought-iron banisters have a red velvet handrail such as you might find in an opera house. The bedrooms on the first floor contain suites of Victorian furniture specially made for the house, mainly of Amboyna wood. The principal rooms – Drawing Rooms, Library and Dining Room – form a richly decorated enfilade on the ground floor. The Blue Drawing Room is the best example in England of Second Empire French taste; it has blue brocade walls, walnut and maple joinery, and an enormous Sèvres vase presented by the Empress Eugénie to Lady Manvers. The Library is more English and more masculine, with dark oak bookcases and a carved chimneypiece showing Robin Hood beneath what seems a life-size oak tree. The other rooms are smaller but similar in style and all are finished in the most expensive nineteenth-century taste, albeit rather coarse.

The park of 3000 acres is superb and contains many old oak trees, venerable survivors of Sherwood Forest.

Thrumpton Hall
28; 6 miles SW of Nottingham off A648
Thrumpton Hall was built by Gervase Pigot in 1609–17 and is a fine example of brick Jacobean architecture with mullion windows. The unusual scalloped gables are an alteration of *c.*1662, when the house was modernised by Gervase Pigot's son. Further work was carried out in the eighteenth century, when Gothick glazing was added to some of the windows, but the best interior features all date from the late seventeenth century: the Caroline staircase with a pierced acanthus-foliage balustrade and carved pots of flowers on the newels is a remarkable example of its type; the Saloon also preserves its late seventeenth-century carved wainscot with pilasters, and a rich chimneypiece. There are good family portraits and inherited furniture of different dates. The house is set in well-maintained gardens and is very much the *beau idéal* of the middling English country house, while the adjoining eighteenth-century estate village of brick-built cottages with Gothic glazing bars is the best in the county.

Welbeck Abbey
29; 5 miles S of Worksop off A60
The PARK at Welbeck is vast, mysterious, magnificently kept, and guarded by more than thirty identical Tudor-style lodges. It makes almost every other English park look like a Japanese garden. The lake is 3 miles long. One drives for ever down informal lime avenues and eventually arrives at what looks like a Neo-Jacobean town – but this is merely the walled garden and estate office. The house itself, when finally reached, is not all that big, and is surprisingly nice and informal. It is U-shaped, of stone, and looks Georgian gone over in the late nineteenth century in a sensitive Arts and Crafts Baroque, with much excellent turn-of-the-century sculpture. All this is remarkably novel in an English country house, but various glazed skylights poking out of the surrounding lawns and shrubbery hint at something even more novel – half the house is underground! Welbeck was originally a Premonstratensian monastery. After the Dissolution it passed through several hands before coming to Sir Charles Cavendish, whose descendant Lady Anne Cavendish-Bentinck owns it today. Sir Charles began to rebuild Welbeck as a private house in the early seventeenth century; his son, the *haute école* Duke of Newcastle of Bolsover (*q.v.*) built the riding school and stables to the west to a design by Smythson. The east wing was remodelled in the eighteenth century by Lady Oxford and more work was done inside this in 1775–7 by John Carr for the 3rd Duke of Portland (later Prime Minister). The whole house was gone over again in 1900–2 by Sir Ernest George after a disastrous fire, and he is responsible for the rich Edwardian aura above ground.

The fame of Welbeck, however, rests on the 5th Duke of Portland's vast and crazy enterprises underground, which began in 1860 and for fifteen years employed hundreds of workmen, aided by traction engines and steam ploughs. Each workman was given a donkey and umbrella on arrival to make travel through the park easier. The Duke himself was a recluse, and his chaplain and anybody else who might encounter him had orders not to notice if they saw him. He burrowed for miles to the west of the house. One tunnel is $1\frac{1}{4}$ miles long; there is a suite of underground Libraries 236 feet long; a Ballroom 154 by 64 feet; several long conservatory-like corridors; and a riding school 385 feet long by 112 feet wide and 52 feet high, with an iron-and-glass roof. Originally all these rooms were lit by gas and there was hot-air heating. A subterranean railway was also built to convey food from the kitchens. The underground rooms and about half the house above ground are now let to the Army, while the family retains the other half in conjunction with a new Neo-Georgian house built in the grounds to the design of Walter Brierley in 1930.

Of the interiors of Welbeck, the two finest are the Library and Chapel made by the 6th Duke in 1891–6 to the design of Sedding and Henry Wilson. They are fitted into Smythson's riding school. The Chapel is Arts and Crafts Byzantine, with pink marble Ionic columns, its sumptuous bronze fittings designed by Wilson and made by Pomeroy. The Library is charmingly informal, with an alabaster inglenook fireplace also designed by Sedding and lavishly carved by Pomeroy. But the most impressive spectacle at Welbeck is the Plate Room – as large as a drawing room and surrounded by cupboards with glazed doors and baize-lined shelves groaning under the weight of the Cavendish-Bentinck silver and silver-gilt – perhaps the finest accumulation of its kind in England. The family wing is not accessible.

Winkburn
30; 8 miles NW of Newark off A617
House and church lie side by side, remote from the world in a beautiful corner of the county. Winkburn was the seat of the Burnell family from the reign of Edward VI, and the house has recently been bought back and is being restored by their descendants, the Craven-Smith-Milnes. The little estate hamlet otherwise consists of nothing except a couple of brick cottages and a farm.

The CHURCH OF ST JOHN OF JERUSALEM dates from the twelfth century and has a crumbly stone tower, rebuilt in the seventeenth century, while the body of the church has rubble walls covered in old stucco. The arch over the main door is decorated with fierce Norman beak-heads. The interior is unrestored and lovable. The walls are painted cream and there are Georgian box pews grained the colour of ginger biscuits, including the squire's pew. The double-decker pulpit is Jacobean, as is the simple triple-arched chancel screen with tympanum over. The Royal Arms are dated 1764. The Carolean altar rails are of a good design and the chancel is full of Burnell family tombs and hatchments. The two biggest monuments form an unmatched pair, balancing each other on either side of the altar; one is Jacobean and commemorates William Burnell, while the other is eighteenth-century with handsome marble figures of Death and Fame commemorating D'Arcy Burnell.

Overdoor carving, Winkburn Hall.

WINKBURN HALL is, thank goodness, unknown to architectural history, the date of its erection and the name of its architect remaining unidentified. It is an H-shaped block of red brick three storeys high. There are tall sash windows and a wooden modillion cornice below the attic storey; originally there was a circular cupola on the roof, of which the base remains. The nineteenth-century stone Tuscan porch leads into a circular vestibule and then to the Staircase Hall beyond. The overdoors here and in the central corridor are attractive pieces of Rococo work with carvings of rustic scenes. The Saloon in the centre of the park front has similar carved doorcases and a Palladian two-tier chimneypiece. The Drawing Room and Library also have doorcases with Rococo carving, the latter *chinoiserie*. In the Library and Dining Room there is also original painted bolection-moulded panelling. Winkburn is a fine house, and it is wonderful that it is once more lived in and loved.

Wollaton Hall

31; 2 miles W of Nottingham on A52

Though surrounded by the twentieth-century suburbs of Nottingham (*q.v.*), the park of Wollaton Hall is still attractively wild with bracken and deer. The house is among the most flamboyant of all Elizabethan prodigy houses and, for easily comprehensible reasons, was a great favourite of Victorian *nouveaux riches* families. It was erected between 1580 and 1588 for Sir Francis Willoughby, an enterprising landowner of ancient lineage who considerably developed his estates and became a pioneer sixteenth-century coal magnate.

The house was built by Robert Smythson, the leading Elizabethan 'architect' (really still part master mason), in a style derived from Longleat with regular grids of classical pilasters, and large mullion windows; Wollaton is much more showy, however, with dramatic recessions

and variations in height, corner towers with strapwork balustrades, columnar chimneys and a central keep-like prospect room over the Great Hall. The plan is supposed to be based on one in Du Cerceau's *Premier Livre* and is notable for its revolutionary symmetry. Unfortunately, very little of the original interior decoration survives. In the early nineteenth century, Lord Middleton feared that the dry old panelling would be a fire hazard should the house be attacked by a revolutionary mob from Nottingham, so he got Sir Jeffrey Wyatville to remove it and replace it with his own less combustible but, alas, infinitely more dreary brand of Tudorbethan.

The best surviving original feature is the hammer-beam roof of the Great Hall, a room that also retains its fine carved stone screen. The large painting on one wall is the *Toilet of Venus* by Thornhill. The Grand Staircase has a ceiling painting by Laguerre of an *Assembly of Gods*, altered by Thornhill to include *Prometheus Stealing the Fire*; the walls too were painted by Thornhill with other scenes from the story of Prometheus.

The house is now used as a museum and is full of stuffed birds and other creatures in glass cases. I particularly like the giraffe in the Great Hall.

Worksop

32; 17 miles SE of Sheffield on A57

Worksop is a ravaged little town that has lost most of its interesting old buildings and gained little in return; it is now known mainly as a centre of coal-mining. The PRIORY in its tidy graveyard, therefore, comes as a bit of a surprise, away from the present 'centre' and with a fourteenth-century Gatehouse to keep it company. It was founded in 1120 as an Augustinian house. The grand Norman nave built *c*.1170 survives, but the original east end disappeared at the Reformation – except for the Lady Chapel, which lay in ruins until this century. The most impressive feature of the outside is the west front – exceedingly plain and flat apart from the west door and large round-arched window above. The two flanking towers have simple square buttresses, and Perpendicular battlements and pinnacles on top. The interior of the nave has three tiers of arches and alternating circular and octagonal piers. All the carving of arches and capitals is very lavish, with a prominent use of nail-head decoration. The aisles are vaulted but the main roof is timber. After this the east end is a crashing disappointment. The transepts, rebuilt by Sir Harold Breakspear in the 1920s and 1930s, are fair enough, and the Lady Chapel, restored and re-roofed by Sir Harold at the same time, is a beautiful piece of Early English architecture, dating from the thirteenth century, with lancet windows and nice fittings. The crossing and chancel, however, are horrors designed in the 1960s by the late Laurence King, in my opinion one of the poorest of postwar church architects. The work here looks cheap – bare white plaster, aluminium-framed windows and plain flush doors like a modern office building. There is a new central altar under a sort of hanging corona of iron and glass. Behind it is the organ – an array of shining tin pipes – and, above that, the stepped-up square-headed east window is full of strident stained glass looking as if made of boiled sweets. All this, alas, replaces a rich Victorian high altar by Sir George Gilbert Scott. (The reredos is preserved in the south transept.) The Victorian stained glass in the side-windows has also been mutilated by removing the backgrounds and resetting the main panels in clear glass – pure vandalism. It is a pity, too, about the silly non-spire on top of the crossing; a simple slated cap like that at Westminster Abbey would have been preferable. Still, the Norman nave and the Lady Chapel make a visit well worth while. At the time of writing, though, there are deplorable plans to partition off the west end of the nave as a coffee room.

Two miles to the south-west of Worksop lies the estate of WORKSOP MANOR. This scene of past glories is one of the four great parks that make up the Dukeries, the others being Clumber, Thoresby and Welbeck (*qq.v.*). The park, of 3000 acres, was enclosed from Sherwood Forest in the sixteenth century by the Earls of Shrewsbury. The 6th Earl built a magnificent mansion here to the design of Robert Smythson, comparable in its splendour to Longleat, Hardwick or Wollaton (*qq.v.*). Indeed it was the tallest of all the Elizabethan prodigy houses, rising 90 feet from the ground to the top of the circular domed turrets on the roof. Along the upper floor of the house there was a vast Long Gallery. This palatial mansion burnt to the ground in 1761, by which time it had descended by marriage to the Dukes of Norfolk. The 9th Duke and his energetic wife Mary immediately set about rebuilding on a scale to emulate Blenheim. Their architect was James Paine, though the Duchess played a considerable role in the design and decorated the interior herself. The overall plan was intended to be a huge quadrangle, but only one range was actually built – twenty-three bays wide and three storeys high, with a rusticated ground floor and central carved pediment. This was senselessly demolished after the estate was sold

to the Duke of Newcastle in 1838 for what was then the world-record price for agricultural land. All that remains is part of the ground floor, the early eighteenth-century stables court – looking like a small Cambridge college – fronted with a stone Tuscan screen by Paine and, somewhat ironically, the carved stone pediment by Thomas Collins propped up in some nettles round the back; it shows the resurrection of Worksop after the fire in 1761. The park has reverted to agriculture, but traces of the vast formal gardens devised in the early eighteenth century by Lord Petre can still be seen, especially when the weather is dry. All this leaves a feeling of sadness for what once was and for what might have been.

But two good things survive at Worksop. One is CASTLE FARM, a delightful Gothick folly designed by the 9th Duchess of Norfolk herself and which, as well as serving as the home farm, contained her dairy and a little sitting room where she kept her books on gardening. It is now the home of the present owner of the estate. The other interesting survival is WORKSOP MANOR LODGE, a large Elizabethan lodge or 'stand'. It was almost certainly designed by Robert Smythson and recalls the lost glories of the sixteenth-century house. It has an ingenious cross-shaped plan, with the Hall and Great Chamber in the centre. Like the lost main house, it is prodigiously tall – soaring up through five storeys. The exterior is remarkably intact, except that the original entrance on the first floor has been converted to a window. Little of the Elizabethan interior decoration survives, however, though many of the rooms retain their original proportions and there are several sixteenth-century stone fireplaces in the lesser rooms.

Worksop Priory.

Shropshire

Shropshire is amazingly unspoilt. It seems to have the balance exactly right, exuding an air of old-fashioned prosperity without any of the hideousness that usually accompanies affluence. Nearly all recent development in the county is confined to the new town of Telford near the Staffordshire border and can therefore be avoided. The landscape itself is wholly wonderful: hilly and wooded, with magnificent long-distance views towards the Welsh mountains in the west. Everywhere there is rich and varied scenery: splendidly austere border country, and prosperous agricultural plains alternating with dramatic hills. In Shropshire the fields are still properly hedged and oak trees line the narrow lanes; there is none of the gappiness so often found in the English Midlands, where hedges and trees have been removed by 'agribiz' farmers. Here all is as it was.

The same is true of the towns. After a while you want to wipe your eyes and shake your head: can it be that there is still a part of England where little town after little town is full of attractive old buildings and decent, well-established shops, free from brash 1960s' redevelopment and roadworks on the one hand and 1970s' 'conservation' and tourist-boutique culture on the other? Even Shrewsbury, the county town of 45,000 people, though it does have some modern shops and two ugly multi-storey car parks, is still for the most part miraculously unchanged. Shropshire is an extraordinary phenomenon, and emphasises just how much has been lost in other counties. Towns like Bridgnorth and Ludlow are now hardly to be matched elsewhere in England for overall charm and unspoilt townscape. Shropshire has been lucky in that it escaped both nineteenth- and twentieth-century industrialisation; nor was it bombed in the war. But the same is true of Worcestershire and Herefordshire – and compare them with Shropshire. Compare Worcester with Shrewsbury, or Ross-on-Wye with Much Wenlock, and you will appreciate just how exceptional Shropshire is.

The county would be worth visiting for its unspoilt landscape alone, but it is also rich in buildings, though it lacks the supreme masterpieces of English architecture. It has no medieval church on a par with those of Yorkshire or Lincolnshire; it has no great cathedral; nor does it have the very finest English country houses, like those of Derbyshire. But, that said, it is enormously well endowed with a variety of good, middling-quality buildings: atmospheric Norman and Gothic churches; early castles, like Shrewsbury and Ludlow; untouched medieval country houses like Stokesay and the Abbot's House at Much Wenlock.

The two periods of greatest prosperity were the sixteenth and eighteenth centuries. The Elizabethan age witnessed the area flourishing because of its sheep; wool and cloth production throve and this resulted in a vast amount of black-and-white half-timbered architecture – houses, pubs, town halls, even bits of churches. All this survives, and in more genuine condition than in the adjoining counties. (Much of the similar architecture to be seen in Cheshire, for instance, is Victorian 'restoration'.)

The eighteenth century saw Shropshire in the vanguard of industrial development – at Coalbrookdale, for instance, the Darbys revolutionised the English iron trade and built the world's first iron bridge. Through the wealth such industry brought, the county is rich in Georgian churches – Pevsner lists over forty of them – and solid country houses of red brick or stone. Francis Smith of Warwick left a tremendous imprint with houses like Kinlet and Mawley, and he had many local followers. From later in the eighteenth century is Attingham Park, a major neo-classical house with a superbly decorated interior. One of the attractions of Shropshire is the considerable variety of building materials, thanks to its complex geology; churches and houses are found in grey, buff, or pink and red sandstone. Because of the natural drama of the landscape, the county is able to produce some of England's most sublime Picturesque gardens – notably Hawkstone on its rocky ridge, or Millichope with its highly romantic approach drive and lake.

The nineteenth century was a period of tranquillity and, unlike Staffordshire or Cheshire, Shropshire is not well endowed with Victorian buildings. There are few major Victorian churches built from scratch, though during the period much restoration was done to older churches, especially those built of the soft, friable local red sandstone. Victorian country houses are also thin on the ground in the county, compared to the multitude of Elizabethan or Georgian 'seats', though Adcote (now a school) is notable work by the distinguished architect Norman Shaw.

Shropshire, though not well-known in general, is a fashionable county and its many country houses survive in private hands, well maintained and rarely open to the public, for, despite the fine scenery, this is not really tourist territory. But if one had to advise discerning foreign visitors which part of England other than Oxford–Cambridge–Stratford would give them the best impression of all that was most admirable in our landscape, architecture and country life, it is this county that I would unhesitatingly recommend. It will not let them down.

Acton Burnell
1; 8 miles S of Shrewsbury off A49
The ruins of the CASTLE are tucked away behind an early nineteenth-century Greek Revival HALL with an Ionic portico and a roof bristling with dormer windows. These windows give away the building's institutional use: the Hall is now occupied by Concord College. The castle is a pink sandstone shell sitting on a smoothly mown lawn, like a large eighteenth-century garden folly, and guarded by a magnificent cedar tree. It was built in the 1280s by Robert Burnell, Lord Chancellor under Edward I and Bishop of Bath and Wells. It is not a fortified castle but a country house playing at being a castle for the sake of the lordly associations. The Great Hall and solar were on the first floor and, though nothing of the interior survives, the tall transomed and traceried windows mark their position. At the corners are four little towers. One contained an oratory and two of the others had dovecotes at the top.

The parish CHURCH OF ST MARY, its graveyard full of daffodils in spring, sits next to the castle and forms a group with it. Like the castle, it was built for Robert Burnell and is a fine, symmetrical, cruciform design with the courtly architectural detail to be expected of so important a client. It is very much *not* the work of a country bumpkin. The interior is impressive as a design but lacks atmosphere. A vigorous Victorian restoration has left it with an austere, colourless look. It is a pity that the beautiful tracery of the east window is filled with ugly plain glazing rather than stained glass. The church would also benefit enormously from a coat of limewash on its dirty plaster walls. The north transept is still paved with medieval tiles, and contains several memorials to the Lee and Smythe families. The best is that to Richard Lee, who died in 1591. It is good Elizabethan alabaster work with the effigy portrayed in rich armour reposing on a woven mat, his feet resting on a lion and a little pet dog lying in the empty gauntlet by his side – an unexpectedly playful detail.

Acton Round Hall
2; 5 miles NW of Bridgnorth off A458
This is a small brick house built in 1714 to the design of Smith of Warwick for Sir Whitmore Acton as a dowerhouse to Aldenham Park (*q.v.*). It is seven windows wide, with a pedimented centre and a hipped roof. The interior contains original panelled rooms and a staircase with twisted balusters.

Adcote
3; 7 miles NW of Shrewsbury off A5
In Mark Girouard's words, Adcote is 'the most controlled, coherent and masterly of the big country-houses designed by Norman Shaw'. Although the individual components of the architecture are all derived from English sixteenth-century examples, the calculated and brilliant asymmetry of the façades immediately marks out the building as a masterpiece of Victorian architecture, with its bay windows and buttresses, and carefully placed chimneystacks. It was designed in 1876 and completed in 1879. Though smaller than Cragside (*q.v.*), the 'scale of its parts is bolder and the total effect cooler and more dignified'.

The interior plan is arranged round a full-height Great Hall with a monumental stone-hooded chimneypiece and four sweeping stone arches supporting the roof. The staircase opens from the screens end: it is in the same monumental vein as the Hall and to climb it is a remarkable spatial experience, as the dramatic vista of the Hall roof comes into view at the top. The other rooms are less overpowering, but they are spacious and embellished with good craftsmanship: oak joinery, plaster friezes, carved inglenook fireplaces, Morris glass and De Morgan tiles. All the furniture has gone, however, for the house has been a school since 1927.

Aldenham Park
4; 4 miles NW of Bridgnorth off A458
Aldenham Park was for many centuries the seat of the Actons, ancestors of the Anglo-Neapolitan dynasty and of the historian Lord Acton, perhaps best remembered for his aphorism 'Power tends to corrupt and absolute power corrupts absolutely.' It is an early eighteenth-century Baroque house with an impressive stone façade eleven windows wide. It is rather a pity that the Georgian glazing bars have been removed from the windows, giving the somewhat plain, though well-proportioned, façades an air of additional austerity. At the back of the house is some earlier structure thought to date from the early seventeenth century, and also a part that was rebuilt by Sir Edward Acton in 1691. The main staircase, with barley-sugar-twist balusters, dates from then. Otherwise, the most impressive rooms are nineteenth-century, notably the central Hall, made in 1830 by roofing over a courtyard and decorated in the Grecian style with Ionic columns. Sadly, the large Library added by the historian Lord Acton has been demolished.

Attingham Park

NT; 5; 4 miles SE of Shrewsbury on A5 [43]

From the A5 bridge over the River Tern the view across the Repton landscape of the park towards the façade of Attingham Park is a perfectly contrived eighteenth-century set-piece, the creation of Noel Hill, 1st Lord Berwick. The architect of his new house was George Steuart, a Gaelic-speaking neo-classicist.

Attingham is a tall stone block with an elegantly etiolated portico and wings set far back. The interior is among the finest of its date and retains much authentic neo-classical decoration. The Entrance Hall has grey scagliola columns, marbling and very delicate stucco work. The main apartments to left and right are arranged in the French manner, with the Dining Room and Library forming the men's domain and the Drawing Room and Boudoir the ladies'. The Dining Room has bold stucco work painted a strong red and white, while the Drawing Room is an elegant ensemble of turquoise, white and gold. The circular Boudoir has exceptionally prettily painted Raphaelesque decoration.

The Picture Gallery in the centre of the house has porphyry Corinthian columns, dark red walls and a cast-iron coved ceiling; it was formed by Nash in 1807. At one end is an organ, and the walls are hung with the Old Masters collected in Italy by the 3rd Lord Berwick. Much of the furniture was also bought by him and is Neapolitan – rather a rarity in an English house.

Attingham Park.

Benthall Hall

NT; 6; 1 mile S of Ironbridge off B4375

Benthall, situated high above the River Severn close to Coalbrookdale, is a good example of late sixteenth-century domestic architecture. It was built of local sandstone, probably in *c*.1580, by the recusant Lawrence Benthall. In the entrance porch is a hiding place, evidence of the family's allegiance to the Old Faith. The property was sold to Lord Forester in 1844 and was part of the Willey estate till 1930, when it was bought back by a descendant of the original family, Miss Mary Benthall. It was she who gave it to the National Trust in 1958.

Despite fire damage at different dates, and the depredations of tenants, the interior still contains many original features, of which the staircase is the best. It was built in *c*.1618 and is a smaller-scale version of that at Aston Hall in Birmingham (*q.v.*), with carved newels and a strapwork balustrade. The Drawing Room has a carved wainscot, an elaborate overmantel and a strapwork plaster ceiling. The whole ensemble is painted white – a treatment frequently given in the eighteenth century to old oak panelling. The chimneypiece itself was inserted by T.F. Pritchard of Shrewsbury, the designer of the iron bridge at Coalbrookdale, in 1756. The Library, too, is a pleasing mixture of Jacobean and Georgian, with original panelling and mid-eighteenth-century fitted bookcases.

Bridgnorth

7; 8 miles SE of Much Wenlock on A458

Bridgnorth, situated on an outcrop of pink sandstone above the River Severn, is a hilltown – a rarity in England, where it was not as necessary to build towns in inaccessible defendable sites as it was in less settled countries. There are dramatic views of the town as you drive towards it, and equally good views outwards from the town over the surrounding wooded, hilly landscape.

The main street, the High Street, is exceptionally wide and is entered through a real town gate, the NORTHGATE. This was heavily restored in 1910 and looks splendidly medieval as a result. The street is so wide that the seventeenth-century gabled TOWN HALL stands comfortably in the middle and one lane of traffic passes underneath it, through the arcaded ground floor. The general townscape is unspoilt to a degree that is exceptional in England. It even retains its brick-paved footpaths and nineteenth-century cast-iron street name-plates. The buildings include old black-and-white half-timber, Georgian red brick, and painted stucco. The SWAN HOTEL is the most impressive black-and-white building, apart from the Town Hall; it has jettied upper floors, and a continuous row of sash windows at first-floor level. NORTHGATE HOUSE is the most stately of the Georgian brick buildings. Many of the shops have an old-established air and good shop-fronts. That of Beaman & Sons, Butchers, dates from 1890 and is an unspoilt piece of varnished oak joinery. George & Berties, Tailors, has a Georgian shop-front and a nice lettered sign.

Church Street leads east to ST LEONARD'S CHURCH, one of the two principal accents on the Bridgnorth skyline. Church Street is given presence by the ALMSHOUSES, erected in 1792 (and restored in 1952 after bomb damage). They are red brick, symmetrical, with a pediment and Gothick details. The church has an attractive grassy setting with interesting houses and cottages round it: PALMER'S HOSPITAL is a super-picturesque black-and-white reconstruction of 1889; No. 28 has a colourful little garden with a bird-table that is a model of Bishop Percy's House (see below); the old GRAMMAR SCHOOL, of brick, with gables and mullion windows, was built in 1629. St Leonard's itself is almost entirely a Victorian rebuilding of 1860–2 by Slater. With its tall red sandstone spire, its exterior is impressive.

Returning along the High Street, two decent narrow streets open to the west with mixed old buildings on a cottagey scale. To the east, alleys and flights of steps lead down the hill between interspersed houses and gardens. At the south end of the High Street the former NEW MARKET (now the Labour Exchange) is a welcome Victorian monstrosity of polychrome brick with an Italianate tower. Fixed to the flank wall is a painted board bearing a 'Chronological Table of Local Events', beginning in 912 with the founding of Bridgnorth Castle by Ethelfleda. Nothing is recorded between 1652, when the town was repaired after damage in the Civil War, and 1958, when it received a grant of arms.

Beyond, the street splits into West Castle Street and EAST CASTLE STREET. The latter is the most impressive street in the town. It curves, then straightens to make a formal axis focused on the portico of St Mary Magdalene, and is flanked by lime trees and seemly Georgian houses. Some are of red brick and some a chequer pattern of red and blue bricks; all have nice doorcases. The APLEY ESTATE OFFICE dates from *c*.1633 and is symmetrical, with a central gabled porch and mullion windows. ST MARY MAGDALENE was rebuilt in 1792 to the design of Thomas Telford. It is of yellow stone, with an Ionic portico and a tall cupola with a copper top. The interior is light and elegant, with arcades of Ionic columns, large round-topped windows with clear glazing, and a Victorian apse. From the churchyard there are good views outwards. The ruins of the CASTLE, next door, look precarious indeed. It was slighted by the Parliamentarians in 1646 and the twelfth-century keep undermined. Great masses of masonry lean at dizzy angles and look as if they will topple over at any moment. Below the castle and along the bottom of the cliff runs Underhill Road, with a good-looking mixture of old houses. Cartway used to be the only way up before the New Road was built in 1792. In it is BISHOP PERCY'S HOUSE, built in 1580 and one of the best surviving timber-framed Elizabethan buildings in Shropshire.

Broseley Hall

8; 2 miles S of Ironbridge on B4375
Broseley is a good example of a smallish early Georgian house built for a fairly well-to-do family, and it survives largely unaltered. It dates from 1727 and is five windows wide and three storeys high, with a pedimented door.

The interior was altered by Francis Turner Blythe in the 1760s to the design of the Shrewsbury architect T.F. Pritchard, and the carved chimneypieces and other

The Town Hall, Bridgnorth.

decorative features of the main rooms are Pritchard's work. Better known for his work at Ironbridge (*q.v.*), he also designed the little temple in the garden.

Buildwas Abbey

9; 2 miles W of Ironbridge on B4380
The setting of Buildwas is less idyllic than that of most abbey ruins. A large power station with pink concrete cooling-towers looms to the east, while by the abbey entrance is a bungalow with pretentious outworks in peasant-millionaire style. A little avenue of flowering cherries leads to the abbey and exacerbates the suburban aura. The ruins of the church are nevertheless impressive, many of the walls standing to full height.

The abbey was founded in 1135 as an offshoot of Furness Abbey in Cumbria (*q.v.*) and belonged briefly to the Savignac Order before being taken over by the Cistercians. Most of the buildings were erected in the twelfth century and remained unaltered until their abandonment at the Dissolution. The church survives almost complete, except for the roof, and typifies the austere style of the Cistercians in their early vigour. All the details are late Norman or Transitional, still with fat round columns and scalloped cushion capitals, but with pointed arches heralding fully fledged Gothic. The general effect is of a calm nobility. The nave originally had a flat timber ceiling, but the chancel was stone-vaulted. The flat east wall has three tall, narrow windows – almost lancets but still with round tops.

The walls of buildings round the cloisters are also well preserved. The Chapter House has a vaulted ceiling supported on slender octagonal and circular piers. To the east is a post-Dissolution country house, of different dates, which incorporates the monastic Infirmary. But unfortunately this cannot be seen close to, as the garden round it is private.

Claverley

10; 5 miles E of Bridgnorth off A454

You come through cuttings in the red sandstone to Claverley, which has the air of being a serious contender in the Best-Kept Village competition. Neat brick, stone or black-and-white cottages line the sloping village street, which also features a well-preserved cast-iron pump. ALL SAINTS' CHURCH, with its tall west tower, stands proudly in the middle of the main street. The entrance to the churchyard forms a picturesque group with the half-timbered old VICARAGE, a gabled LICH-GATE and the fourteenth-century CROSS (restored in 1903). From the outside the church looks all-of-a-piece Perpendicular, with red sandstone walls and red-tiled roof. It is a great surprise, on entering, to find oneself faced with a Norman arcade of strong round columns in the nave. This dates from the late twelfth century and is the oldest surviving part of the church; the rest was rebuilt at various later dates in the Middle Ages. The other arcade, with octagonal columns, is Decorated, and the clerestory is Perpendicular. The chief importance of All Saints lies in its remarkably well-preserved late twelfth-century wall paintings, which form a wide frieze beneath the north clerestory windows. They were discovered under whitewash in 1902 and restored. The colours are yellow, red and black, and the subject is a battle between the Christian Virtues and Pagan Vices, derived (according to Professor Tristram) from a fourth-century allegory by Prudentius. It takes the form of contemporary knights in armour with swords and shields and looks like the Bayeux Tapestry. On other walls there are traces of fifteenth-century paintings, including angels in the clerestory, a Doom over the chancel arch and the Royal Arms of Queen Elizabeth over the organ arch. To the north and south of the chancel are Perpendicular chapels. The North Chapel contains the eighteenth-century communion table – a charming piece of Gothick – and in the South Chapel is a monument to Sir Robert Broke, Chief Justice of Common Pleas in the mid-sixteenth century; it is a Renaissance design in alabaster, originally gilded.

Cleobury Mortimer

11; 10 miles E of Ludlow on A4117

Here is an attractive little town, its curving main street with pleached limes on one side and a nice variety of brick, stone, and black-and-white houses. The general atmosphere is cosily Georgian, with one or two bits of timber-framed antiquity to recall an older past. A granite Victorian horse trough makes a good piece of street furniture. The street curves round the graveyard, which is like a raised grassy terrace displaying the mainly fourteenth-century CHURCH OF ST MARY to great advan-

tage. It is of rubble stone with lancet windows and a homely red-tiled roof. The finely proportioned spire on the west tower is hung with wooden shingles. The interior is spacious, with a wide nave, arcades of circular columns, and an open timber roof. A thorough restoration in the 1870s by Sir George Gilbert Scott has left behind a markedly Victorian atmosphere; the walls are stripped to the rough stonework and there is a dado of cheerful red and white tiles round the altar, like the splashback of an old-fashioned washstand. The east window has good stained glass showing scenes from *Piers Plowman*; it was made in 1875 by Powell.

Coalbrookdale

See Ironbridge.

Condover Hall

12; 6 miles S of Shrewsbury off A49

The terrific E-plan late Elizabethan façade of Condover is framed in an archway when seen from the main road, and lies far back at the end of a long forecourt with mown grass, a cedar tree and clipped yews. It is of pink sandstone and the entrance front is symmetrical with mullion-and-transom windows; in the middle is a fancy two-storeyed porch culminating in a strapwork cartouche and obelisk, and there are clustered brick chimneystacks on the roof. It is very much the *beau idéal* of a grand Elizabethan or Jacobean country house. The park front is also symmetrical, with large mullion windows, and an arcaded *loggia* in the centre of the ground floor. The interior was remodelled by Robert Mylne in the eighteenth century, but his work was swept away earlier this century in a scheme of restoration that has left the rooms all Neo-Elizabethan. The house now belongs to the Royal National Institute for the Blind and the outside (the most exciting part) can be visited, by prior appointment, in August each year.

Cound Hall

13; 6 miles SE of Shrewsbury off A458

This oddly tall house stands in pretty country and enjoys views of the Wrekin. It was built in 1704 for Edward Cresset by John Prince of Shrewsbury in provincial Baroque style. It is of plum-red brick, with tall, narrow sash windows enhancing the exaggerated height of the building. The façade is given presence by giant Corinthian pilasters and by a broken pediment in the centre. Inside is an ingeniously arranged staircase, thought to be late eighteenth-century. It flies up in a narrow space, supported on slender columns, and has a thin iron balustrade. The house is now divided into flats.

Dudmaston

NT; 14; 4 miles SE of Bridgnorth on A442

For 850 years the Dudmaston estate has passed by descent or devise, never by sale. The present house, attributed to the architect Francis Smith of Warwick, was probably begun by Sir Thomas Wolryche in 1695 and was completed by the time of his death in 1705. The pediments and parapets were added to the roofline in the 1820s.

Hawkstone Park.

The Hall has changed little since Sir Thomas Wolryche's time and has bolection-moulded panelling with broad pilasters. The fine set of high-backed late seventeenth-century seat furniture with well-preserved upholstery was bought recently from Burley-on-the-Hill in Leicestershire (*q.v.*). The Library, which occupies the garden front behind the Hall, was remodelled in the 1820s; it is hung with part of the collection of flower pictures formed by Francis Darby of Coalbrookdale, a forebear of Lady Labouchère, who lives at Dudmaston today. The staircase, too, is an introduction of the 1820s, but the Oak Room retains its original panelling.

In the south wing, added in 1833, the rooms have been converted into galleries for the display of the twentieth-century British, French and Spanish paintings collected in the 1950s and 1960s by Sir George and Lady Labouchère. They generously gave Dudmaston as well as their collections to the National Trust in 1978.

Hawkstone Park
15; 5 miles E of Wem off A49

Contemporaries spoke of the 'Awful Precipices' and 'Elysian Fields' of Hawkstone, and this is indeed a sublime late Georgian PARK. Stone cliffs jut out of the plain and the park is planted with dark pines and gnarled oak trees. It is pure Salvator Rosa and makes Capability Brown seem placid and boring in comparison. A jagged stone archway, a huge Doric column, a (genuine) ruined castle and an octagonal Gothic tower enliven the skyline, while below are smooth swards of turf (now a golf course) and a long serpentine lake.

Climbing to the top of the rocky ridge, one finds long curving paths tunnelling through impenetrable thickets of overgrown rhododendrons. Just when you think you are totally lost you suddenly emerge into a clearing at the foot of the column, which rather perversely

is called THE OBELISK. It was erected in 1795 by Sir Richard Hill, who continued and embellished the layout begun by his predecessor, Sir Rowland Hill. It is 112 feet high and is dedicated to the memory of a sixteenth-century Sir Rowland Hill who was Lord Mayor of London and the founder of the family. It has a spiral staircase inside and commands spectacular views over the north Shropshire Plain. South-east of this, and facing in the other direction, is the SUMMERHOUSE, an octagonal tower of pink sandstone with pointed windows and battlements. Below, in the valley, is THE CITADEL, a polygonal Gothic castle built as a dower-house in 1824–5 to the design of Thomas Harrison of Chester. To the west, a long walk through the woods along the top of the ridge leads to a rocky bridge over the old main drive to the house. This narrow, natural-looking arch is the only link with the Grotto Hill, a vertical outcrop of stone with an eye-catching ruined arch on top. Crossing over to this, stone steps carved in the natural rock of the cliffs make it possible to climb to the top, where there is a worthwhile reward. Underneath the gaunt broken arch on the skyline is a huge eighteenth-century GROTTO. It was once lined with shells and coral but these have gone, leaving the bare stone walls and columns carved out of the rock like a natural form of Gothic church with nave and aisles. Dark tunnels lead off the sides. At the west end of the Grotto a little circular window bores through the wall, giving a spectacular view. In the foreground is another wooded outcrop, crowned with the scanty ruins of the thirteenth-century RED CASTLE. Far below is the mown grass of the golf course, with a large stone statue of a reclining river god, and the long lake curving out of sight to the north. As far as the eye can see into the west is a vast prospect of plain and mountain, stretching deep into Wales.

As so often in eighteenth-century landscape gardens, the layout forms an entity independent of the house – as at Studley Royal or Stourhead (*qq.v.*), for instance – and HAWKSTONE HALL itself lies in a stretch of more conventional parkland below the ridge. It too is of considerable interest, as it is of three main dates. The main block, tall and red brick with cream-painted dressings, was built in 1720 by Sir Richard Hill; flanking projecting wings were added *c*.1750 for Sir Rowland Hill; finally, the house was considerably remodelled between 1832 and 1834 by Lewis Wyatt for yet another Sir Rowland Hill. Wyatt heightened the quadrant links between the centre and the wings, built the Tuscan conservatory and remodelled much of the interior in a series of historicist styles: 'Louis Quatorze' in the Drawing Room and Pompeian neo-classical in the Library and Dining Room. The Saloon, however, survives from the early eighteenth century; it has a high coved ceiling, a two-tier chimneypiece, rich plaster wall panels and a pedimented doorcase.

The Hall is now a college of the Redemptionist Fathers. The park, on the other hand, is in various hands and regrettably much neglected. All the architectural features are in poor condition, and many have disappeared during this century. It is imperative that an effective scheme be put into operation to secure the survival of this highly important landscape – a garden that causes one to ransack *Roget's Thesaurus* for alternatives to 'dramatic' in an attempt to do it justice.

Ironbridge
16; 12 miles SE of Shrewsbury on A4169

In the eighteenth century this narrow wooded gorge of the River Severn below the Wrekin was the centre of English industry, with coal-mining, iron-smelting and china manufacture. The scene then, the satanic smoking furnaces contrasting with the picturesque landscape round about, appealed to Romantic tourists and artists alike, and was immortalised in the dramatic paintings of de Loutherbourg. As every schoolboy knows, Abraham Darby the First founded the Coalbrookdale Ironworks in 1709, and *c*.1713 made the great breakthrough of using coal instead of charcoal for smelting iron, which opened the way for a vast expansion of the iron industry. Other improvements in iron production followed later in the eighteenth century, making Ironbridge one of the true cradles of the early Industrial Revolution. The industry has now gone, but much of archaeological interest survives and in recent years has been brilliantly preserved and presented to make an outdoor museum of the Industrial Revolution, the best of its type in the country.

Abraham Darby's earliest furnace survives at Blists Hill, to the north of Ironbridge, and is open to the public, while the WHARF of the Coalbrookdale Ironworks stands near the bridge. It is mid-nineteenth-century, of red and yellow brick, and castellated. The town is rightly called after the IRON BRIDGE, the earliest in the world and perhaps Britain's best-known industrial monument. It was

The iron bridge, Ironbridge.

erected across the River Severn by Abraham Darby the Third; its opening in 1779 was watched by thousands of spectators, who came to admire the skill and daring of the great ironmaster. The bridge rises in the middle and is supported on a semi-circular arch. The cast-iron sections have a slightly Gothick pattern and the effect is exhilaratingly light and lacy. Along the arch is an inscription, picked out in white against the black paint of the ironwork: 'THIS BRIDGE WAS CAST AT COALBROOKDALE AND ERECTED IN THE YEAR MDCCLXXIX'.

At the bridgehead is a planned town square of substantial Georgian brick buildings, including the Tontine Hotel and the MARKET HOUSE, which has an arcade along the ground floor. The CHURCH OF ST LUKE, built in 1836 in mild Gothic style, lies higher up and is reached by a flight of 100 steps. On either hand the street is lined with a straggle of brick cottages and houses and the odd Nonconformist chapel. The cast-iron kerbstones lining the footpaths are, of course, a local product.

To the north and east of Ironbridge and Coalbrookdale is the new town of TELFORD. Although in itself it can offer only dual-track roads and clumps of new terrace housing, it is worth a trip there, for embedded in it is the old village of Madeley. Here is MADELEY COURT, the remains of an important mid-sixteenth-century house, the residence of Abraham Darby the First. After many years in a state of picturesque decay, it is now being restored. The best feature is the Gatehouse with octagonal turrets flanking the archway; its walls are decorated with little circular medallions around the mullion windows.

Kinlet

17; 6 miles NE of Cleobury Mortimer on B4363
The CHURCH OF ST JOHN THE BAPTIST stands in an island of mixed trees on a slope in the baldly agriculturalised park of Kinlet Hall. It is a largely medieval rebuilding of a Norman church, the most attractive feature of which is the fifteenth-century clerestory – timber-framed and painted black and white in the Shropshire vernacular manner. The interior has scraped stone walls and sturdy, round late Norman columns to the aisle arcades. The little transept is a family chapel and contains a large sixteenth-century alabaster 'six-poster' monument to Sir George Blount and his wife, who died in 1584. The front of the tomb-chest is an open arcade displaying a carved alabaster cadaver inside – rather a grisly conceit.

KINLET HALL stands well on a rise and is a dignified early eighteenth-century red brick house designed by Francis Smith of Warwick. The centre is of seven bays and three storeys, flanked by lower two-storeyed wings. There are prominent stone dressings, including quoins at the angles, architraves round the windows, and a little pediment and Tuscan columns to the front door. It is a thoroughly dignified job. Originally there were carved stone urns on the roof but these have been lost. Kinlet is currently let to a school.

Lilleshall

18; 6 miles SW of Newport off A518
An obelisk 70 feet high on a rocky crag heralds the return to civilisation on the north-east road out of Telford. The ABBEY stands on its own in a beautiful setting among fields to the south of the village, with mature woods as a backdrop. The ruins are surrounded by mown grass and old yew trees, and the pink sandstone walls and arches form a romantic picture. Even more might have survived if the place had not been converted into a stronghold during the Civil War.

The abbey was founded c.1148 and the buildings are late Norman. Through the round-arched west door is a fine vista down the length of the church to the east end, where the vast Decorated window has lost its geometrical tracery but nevertheless creates an impressive culmination to the view. The south door from the church to the cloisters is the finest remaining architectural feature, with an unusual and richly carved recessed moulded arch and flanking colonnettes. The south wall of the church has not yet been repaired and is therefore attractively overgrown with ivy and wallflowers – a reminder of how much more beautiful such ruins must have been before they received the ubiquitous antiseptic modern archaeological treatment.

Longnor Hall

19; 8 miles S of Shrewsbury off A49
South of Shrewsbury, in wonderful unspoilt country of narrow, hedged lanes, oak trees and spectacular views of the conical outline of Caer Caradoc – like the background of a landscape by Claude or Poussin – stands Longnor. The Hall was built by Sir Richard Corbett in 1670 and sits in the middle of a well-planted park. It is a Caroline dream-house of red brick, two storeys and a steeply pitched roof. The Flemish-style gables and dormers are Victorian alterations and add an enlivening dash to the mild perfection of the seventeenth-century architecture. On both the entrance and garden fronts are central doorways with half-round pediments carried on plump Ionic columns; they have a well-fed look. The Hall, Drawing Room and staircase are all splendid specimens of late seventeenth-century joinery, with enriched panelling and beautifully carved doorcases. The staircase has fat balusters carved with acanthus leaves, the treads having rich inlaid work and the tread-ends continuous carved laurel decoration. It is among the handsomest of its date. The Dining Room has panels of rare eighteenth-century Chinese wallpaper discovered under later wall coverings and restored to view.

Ludlow★

20; 24 miles S of Shrewsbury on A49
With its Norman castle, its medieval bridge over a roaring river, the grandest parish church in Shropshire, a prodigy of Elizabethan timber-framing as its principal hotel and, in Broad Street, what Pevsner has described as 'one of the most memorable streets in England', Ludlow is no ordinary town; and there are few in the Kingdom in which I feel happier to arrive of an evening. Unlike most towns, too, it looks equally good whether approached from the north or the south. From the road down from Shrewsbury it is the great tower of St Lawrence's that dominates the clustering houses; driving up from Leominster, one is tempted to leave the car by the pub at the

Ludlow Castle.

edge of the River Nene and walk out a little way on to the Ludford bridge, where you can stand in one of the projections over the cut-waters and – closing your eyes as far as possible to the peculiarly obnoxious garage in the right foreground – see the town climbing up the further bank. If you have time, follow the river round to your left to where it takes a sharp curve northwards; from there you will have a wondrous view of the CASTLE in all its glory.

Once upon a time this was the key stronghold defending the Welsh Marches, and it remains one of the biggest and bravest of English castles. Its heyday was in the fifteenth century when it was Mortimer property and thus, on the accession of Edward IV, came into the possession of the King; it was here that Edward's two little sons lived from 1472 until 1483, when they left for London to meet their death in the Tower. Subsequently it became the residence of the Lord President of the Council of Wales – an office long held by Sir Henry Sidney, father of Sir Philip – and was still palatially appointed when, in 1634, it saw the first performance of Milton's *Comus*. Later still, in the Civil War, it was the last mainland Royalist fortress to submit to the Parliamentarians. Now it stands a picturesque ruin, the centre of a summer festival with *Hamlet* performed nightly on the battlements; but the eleventh-century Norman Chapel – its circular nave now bereft of roof and chancel – is still beautiful, and the great coat of arms of the Sidneys still swaggers above the inner gateway.

The parish CHURCH OF ST LAWRENCE was probably begun only a century or so after the castle, but there is little surviving work earlier than about 1300. It raises high hopes, greeting you with a hexagonal south porch, one of only two in England. (The other is at St Mary Redcliffe, Bristol.) These hopes are not, however, entirely fulfilled. Although there is a fair amount of Decorated work – the porch, transepts, Lady Chapel and north aisle for a start – the nave is Perpendicular, and the prevailing atmosphere is of around 1400, or would have been if George Gilbert Scott and A.W. Blomfield had been a little more sensitive in their restorations. The best things for me are the tie-beam roof of the nave – prettily bossed, and with plenty of angels – and the square-vaulted roof under the crossing-tower, looking from below like a pattern in a kaleidoscope. And the stalls, though largely Victorian, have kept their medieval seats with simply splendid misericords.

From the churchyard there is a rather agreeable shortcut through the courtyard of the Bull to the FEATHERS HOTEL. Here is the apogee of all half-timbering – or, if you prefer it, the end of the line. Parts of it have been restored, but there is nothing remotely bogus about it as there is so often elsewhere – in Chester (*q.v.*) for example. With Little Moreton Hall in Cheshire (*q.v.*), this is one of the showpieces of the style, irresistible by reason of its sheer improbability. The principal room on the first floor, all oak panelled, with James I's coat of arms carved on the overmantel and a sensational plaster ceiling, deserves, I always feel, a more dignified appellation than 'Residents' Lounge'.

From the Feathers, a minute's walk will take you to the centre of the town, the BUTTER CROSS – an oddly medieval name for the pretty little classical Town Hall built by William Baker in the 1740s. Porticos and pediments are not really Ludlow's style, but here what might have been thought a rather misguided effort has worked surprisingly well. Would that the same could be said of the MARKET HALL a little further along to the west – an 1887 monster, which not even the most fanatical lover of Victorian architecture could possibly condone. Please, Ludlow, pull it down. You can if you want to. You *must*. And if you want to know what to replace it with, look in your civic museum in the Butter Cross, where there is an enchanting watercolour of its predecessor: unpretentious, arcaded, perfect in every respect.

These, in their different ways, are the most memorable buildings of the town. For the rest, one can do no better than wander – down BROAD STREET, for a start, under the arch of the medieval GATEHOUSE (with a delightful Georgian house perched on top of it) and on down to the river, returning via MILL STREET – parallel with Broad Street to the west, and very nearly as good. Fine town residences abound, in brick, stone and stucco. Some are safe, some quirkish; one has its entire fenestration composed of Venetian windows – a phenomenon I have seen nowhere else in the world. Finally, walk along to the castle, climb as high as you can, and look thankfully across to the Welsh hills. Wales, after all, is the reason for Ludlow's existence; we have every reason to be grateful.

Madeley
See Ironbridge.

Market Drayton
21; 18 miles NE of Shrewsbury on A53

The approach to the town from the west is spoilt by recent suburbs, messy street lighting and a cat's-cradle of electric wires; from the east, however, Market Drayton stands well on a little ridge, its tall church tower and the clustered roofs of old houses outlined against the sky. The two principal streets, High Street and Shropshire Street, lie at right-angles to each other. The High Street is wide, like a market place; here the CORBET ARMS is Georgian, of red brick clad in Virginia creeper. Shropshire Street is the best in the town, with good Georgian red brick and older black-and-white buildings. SANDBROOK'S VAULTS is dated 1653 but could be 100 years earlier, with its gables and jettied upper storeys. The ELEPHANT AND CASTLE is another picturesque half-timbered pub. On the opposite side is the best Georgian building, THE RED HOUSE, which has a pediment and Ionic doorcase.

St Mary's Street leads to the parish CHURCH OF ST MARY, the west front and tower of which are framed from this angle by neat brick cottages. The church has a grand fourteenth-century Perpendicular west tower, and dates generally from that period, though a Norman doorway survives. The building was heavily restored in the nineteenth century like so many old red sandstone struc-

tures, the surface of which proved to be too soft to withstand the passage of time. The interior is dignified and has good Perpendicular-style glass of late nineteenth- and early twentieth-century dates. The churchyard is attractive, with grass and trees, and contains one monument almost on the scale of a Georgian garden building. It commemorates William Beeston and takes the form of a classical marble urn under a pedimented canopy, which is supported on fluted columns with simplified Corinthian capitals copied from the Temple of the Winds in Athens. From here there is a view across the valley to the park of PELL WALL, a house designed by Sir John Soane, which is now derelict.

Mawley Hall★
22; 1 mile E of Cleobury Mortimer on A4117 [44]

At the time of writing Mawley Hall is open to visitors only by written appointment. Write then, and make one. It is not a particularly large house, but its interior decoration, a *tour de force* of Georgian craftsmanship in plaster and wood, is the most sumptuous in the county – and indeed for many miles beyond. It is marvellously situated on a spur of the Clee Hills just outside the village of Cleobury Mortimer (*q.v.*), with wonderful views over the surrounding country to the west; the fall of the land gives it four complete floors on one side and only three on the other. With a house so obviously important as this, it is faintly surprising that we should have no firm evidence of its architect, but indications point to Francis Smith of Warwick, with a strong contribution from the owner himself. It was built in about 1730 for Sir Edward Blount, of red brick with generous stone dressings (most of them recently renewed), including steep pediments – that over the entrance front flanked by statues – urns along the roofline and characteristic adornments above and below the rather tall, narrow windows. All very fine and distinguished, but giving little promise of the bounty that lies within.

Immediately inside the main Entrance Hall the house lays all its cards on the table. One's eye is first drawn to the overmantel, crowned by a tremendous trophy surmounting a plumed mask of vaguely Red Indian aspect. The ceiling and frieze, which are supported on attached composite columns with curious convex capitals, are also superlatively stuccoed, probably by Artari or Bagutti, or both. Three arches then lead you through to the back half of the Hall – it runs the whole depth of the house – and to a staircase unlike any other. Running round three sides of a splendidly stuccoed open well, it boasts a mahogany balustrade in the form of a snake, whose gentle undulations begin with its head on the bottom newel-post and continue without interruption to its tail, curled upward against the further wall of the first-floor landing. As if that were not enough, the prettily turned balusters rise from a broad string (i.e. the side of the stairs themselves, facing out into the well) carved with emblems of shooting, fishing and the arts.

At this point one begins to realise that exquisite woodwork is as much a feature of the house as the stucco – an impression confirmed by the two adjoining Drawing Rooms to the south. In the larger, there is some particularly fine oak carving in the Gibbons manner; in the smaller, the floor is of superb parquetry, with precious woods inlaid to form a radiating design within an embracing octagon. This same *tarsia* continues up the walls and along the cornice; extravagance could hardly go further.

But wander where you may in this wonderful house, the impact is the same: however precious the materials or luxurious the effects, there is no empty show. The taste is faultless, the craftsmanship breathtaking. Francis Smith was famous not only as an architect but as a supervisor of the work of others, and he had a national reputation for honest dealing and giving value for money. Sir Edward clearly took no thought for what he spent, but not a penny was wasted. The whole house was restored and redecorated in the 1960s and 1970s, having been saved by Mr Galliers-Pratt from threat of demolition.

Millichope Park
23; 8 miles NE of Ludlow off B4368
The house was designed by Edward Haycock of Shrewsbury for the Rev. Robert Norgrave Pemberton in 1835–40. It is a remarkable neo-classical design and has an exquisitely landscaped setting. The approach is along a romantic cutting through the rock, partly lined with dark yew trees. In front of the house, at a lower level, is a lake surrounded by rocks and pine trees; on the shore there is an Ionic rotunda, which forms a perfect foreground foil to the house in general views.

The house stands at the top of a steepish slope and is in the Greek Revival style, with a portico of fluted Ionic columns. The most original feature was the former entrance under the terrace; it had two massive stubby Doric columns and then a steep flight of steps straight up into the middle of the central Hall. This entrance has,

however, recently been closed as part of a series of alterations aimed at making the house easier to live in. It is nevertheless a great pity that such a splendid spatial contrivance should have been done away with. The central Hall is the principal interior, rising the full height of the house and lit through a glazed lantern decorated with plaster swans. Round the walls are two tiers of wooden Ionic columns supporting the first-floor landing Gallery and the lantern. The other rooms have fireproof ceilings, that in the Drawing Room forming a segmental tunnel vault decorated with papier mâché. As part of the recent alterations, the interior has been splendidly redecorated by David Mlinaric.

Morville
24; 3 miles W of Bridgnorth on A458
Includes Morville Hall (NT)
From the main road, the HALL (NT) and the CHURCH OF ST GREGORY form a splendid picture, almost like an architectural frieze. The main block of the house is flanked by spreading pavilions and the Norman church is to one side, with a large paddock in front. It is a quintessentially English view. The house is Elizabethan but was remodelled in two phases in the eighteenth century, with regular sash windows, giant pilasters with stone balls on top stuck on the front, and a pedimented front door. It is faced in grey stone. The polygonal Elizabethan staircase turrets remain in the angles; originally they carried little cupolas on top. The pavilions, designed by William Baker, are connected to the main block by curving walls with rusticated piers and stone balls, and they are crowned with pretty white cupolas with gilded weathervanes. The kitchen retains an elaborate Elizabethan plaster ceiling. Morville Hall belongs to the National Trust and is open by written appointment.

Wenlock Priory.

Much Wenlock

25; 12 miles SE of Shrewsbury on A458

This little town in a sheltered hollow consists of a T-plan of streets with the GUILDHALL of 1577 at the main junction. This is a wildly picturesque black-and-white timbered structure with gables and an open arcaded ground floor. In front of it, in the middle of the road, is a stone GRANDFATHER CLOCK commemorating Queen Victoria's Diamond Jubilee in 1897. Barrow Street, to one side, is lined with goodly brick and stone Georgian houses. The High Street, opposite, has a nice cottagey scale with several timber-framed buildings. REYNALD'S MANSION, dated 1682, has gables and jolly patterned timbers. The former CORN EXCHANGE is a dignified mid-nineteenth-century Italianate stone building, which introduces a more metropolitan note. At the top of the High Street, the GASKELL ARMS HOTEL is a seemly red brick Georgian hostelry with two bow windows. Retracing your steps to the other side of the Guildhall is Wilmore Street, where you will find some more Georgian houses and the parish CHURCH OF THE HOLY TRINITY, large and largely Norman. A little way along, behind the other side of the street, is a working farm with a real farmyard – a gentle *rus in urbe* touch. Bull Ring leads to the priory ruins, the great sight of Much Wenlock.

WENLOCK PRIORY was founded in 680 as a nunnery, but was destroyed by the Danes and subsequently refounded in 1050 by Leofric, Earl of Mercia, husband of Lady Godiva and a munificent patron of the Church throughout his earldom. After the Norman Conquest the priory was restocked with monks from Cluny in Burgundy by Roger de Montgomery and rebuilt in elaborate Cluniac Romanesque. The church was rebuilt again in Early English Gothic but some of the Norman monastic buildings survive.

The south side of the nave and the south transept still stand to full height and give a clear indication of the original appearance of the church, but only foundations of the choir and chancel remain. The cloisters are embellished with topiary, and in the centre of the garth is the base of the Norman lavatorium. On the east side is the shell of the Chapter House – a *tour de force* of elaborate Norman decoration. It is rectangular; with a triple entrance of zigzag decorated arches. The walls inside are a dazzling spectacle, tier upon tier of intersecting arches making patterns of almost Moorish elaboration.

From the cloisters, glimpses of the PRIOR'S LODGE may be obtained over the yew hedge. This is now a private house and not open to the public, but it is among the most perfect pieces of fifteenth-century domestic architecture in England. It is L-shaped, one side once containing a chapel and the other the main living rooms opening off two galleries or corridors (one above the other) that are lit by almost continuous rows of windows with traceried heads, divided into sections by thin elegant buttresses. The prominent steeply pitched roof, taller than the walls below, gives the house its cosy domestic feel, combining comfort and beauty to a rare degree. There can have been worse fates, one feels, than being Prior of Much Wenlock around 1500.

Newport

26; 8 miles NE of Telford on A518

Approaching from the north, the view of Newport is dominated by the church of St Nicholas with its low, fat west tower displayed to advantage. The town comprises one long winding main street, which divides into two in the middle round the islands of the church in its well-kept graveyard and a clump of Georgian and later buildings to the south. Pevsner, in praising the townscape beauties of this street, singles out for special mention the visual importance of the latter. He was writing in 1958, before the architectural holocaust of English towns. On the whole (and in comparison with its neighbouring counties), Shropshire emerged from the 1960s uniquely unscathed, but unfortunately the south part of the island in Newport was one of the few important sites to fall victim to redevelopment. It is now occupied by a flat-roofed square box, which ruins the view north up to the High Street. The only consolation is that it is built of such cheap materials that it cannot last very long and so the opportunity will soon arise to replace it with something more appropriate. How about something built of red brick with a pitched roof and possibly a little cupola with a gilt weathervane?

Otherwise, the town is intact. Starting from the north, the HIGH STREET rises gently towards the church, which from this side can be seen to its full extent, broadside on, because it lies at an oblique angle to the street. In this northern stretch are some of the most attractive buildings in the town, including a number of substantial red brick Georgian townhouses, such as Beaumaris House and the Royal Victoria Hotel, which has a Tuscan portico and a hanging sign in the form of a gilded bunch of grapes. The street splits into two round the church. The east part, ST MARY STREET, is still sett-paved, forming a most attractive backwater. The High Street proper continues to the west and has several nice old-established shops in the central stretch. Charles Plant, for instance, is a house of 1740 with an elaborate late Victorian mahogany shop-front. The same mixture of Georgian and Victorian, with some unobjectionable later façades and one or two ancient black-and-white buildings, such as the Jacobean GUILDHALL, continues to the south. The wide verges here are still part cobbled. Note the SHAKESPEARE INN with its gleaming gilt bust of the Bard in a roundel on the front.

The CHURCH OF ST NICHOLAS is a substantial Perpendicular town church of red sandstone, all thoroughly restored and refaced at different dates in the nineteenth century and again in 1904. The interior is dignified, with tall arcades of octagonal columns and a clerestory above. The fifteenth-century roof survives, low-pitched, with moulded beams and carved and gilt bosses. The chancel is largely Victorian and has carved and coloured angels in the roof, with a gold mosaic reredos. There is ugly modern stained glass in the aisle windows and modern light fittings looking like clusters of milk bottles, but the overall atmosphere is still prosperously Victorian. The south chancel window has good early stained glass by Morris & Co., and there is an elaborate Victorian lectern of brass and copper.

The Staircase Hall, Oakley Park.

Oakley Park

27; 5 miles N of Ludlow off B4365

The seat of the Earl of Plymouth, in its wild, oak-studded park on the banks of the River Teme near Ludlow, consists of an early eighteenth-century house altered first by William Baker in mid-century, then by John Haycock *c.*1784, and finally by the great C.R. Cockerell from 1819–36. The result is one of the most unusual and distinguished of late Georgian country houses, with a comfortable red brick exterior but also with many advanced and uncommon architectural details. Cockerell was responsible for the screen with the double Doric porticos (copied from the Delian order of the Olympiaeum at Syracuse) on the entrance front, which disguises the fact that the door is off-centre; he also added the attached portico with pilasters and superimposed balcony on the south front, and the Conservatory overlooking a little formal parterre of box-edged flower-beds. The glazed parts of the Conservatory were demolished earlier this century, but recently Lord Plymouth has reinstated to the original design Cockerell's square stone piers carrying well-proportioned urns.

The interior of Oakley is a magnificent spatial experience. A charming oval Entrance Hall with an unusual geometrical plaster ceiling of diagonal coffered pattern leads to a dramatic top-lit Staircase Hall in the centre of the house. The staircase, with a wrought-iron balustrade, curves slowly upwards to the landing, which is framed by Graeco-Egyptian fluted columns supporting a reproduction of part of the Bassae frieze (discovered and studied by Cockerell on his Grand Tour to Greece and Asia Minor in 1811). The main rooms are well proportioned, with plaster friezes, marble chimney-pieces and superb contents. The most attractive room is the Library, where there is a chimneypiece of the most dazzling green marble imaginable, rarer and brighter even than malachite. Upstairs there is an oval bedroom over the Entrance Hall. The rooms were partly redecorated by the late John Fowler and show all his usual sensitivity and flair.

Plowden Hall

28; 15 miles NW of Ludlow on A489

Like Devon or Cheshire, Shropshire is one of those few counties where some really long-established families have the proud distinction of being descended in the male line from a medieval ancestor who took his surname from lands that they still hold. (Most 'old' English landed families are really called Smith or Brown and changed their name on inheriting through the female line in the eighteenth or nineteenth centuries.) Of these genuinely ancient families, the Plowdens of Plowden in Shropshire are among the most venerable. Quietly recusant, they have lived at Plowden since time immemorial. Their house is romantically rambling and timber-framed with tall brick chimneys. It is largely Elizabethan, having been reconstructed by an eminent sixteenth-century lawyer, Edmund Plowden. Thereafter, being Catholic and long excluded from public offices, the family remained out of the limelight until after the Second World War and left their house in its sixteenth-century state. It is lovably irregular in outline, and the interior is largely panelled with carved Jacobean overmantels and little staircases going up and down in unexpected corners. There is a small and ancient private Catholic chapel.

Shipton Hall

29; 11 miles NE of Ludlow on B4368

Shipton Hall was built in *c.*1587 by Richard Lutwyche to the standard Elizabethan H-plan, though the grey limestone elevations are not strictly symmetrical. The gabled façades have tiers of mullion windows and over the entrance porch is a four-storeyed tower. The house was enlarged and the interior remodelled *c.*1762 by the Shrewsbury architect T.F. Pritchard. The Hall has nice Rococo plasterwork with a carved overmantel and open pediments over the doorways. The staircase is mildly Gothick with a fine plasterwork ceiling and leads to the Library, which has an especially handsome chimneypiece. Other rooms have Elizabethan and Jacobean panelling, while in the Dining Room the panelling is Victorian. It is all very mild and all very English.

The Market Place, Shrewsbury.

Shrewsbury★

30; 18 miles S of Whitchurch on A49
Includes Tower (NT)

The approach to Shrewsbury from the A5 is impressive: the town centre is heralded by Thomas Harrison's huge Doric column of 1814–16 commemorating Viscount Hill, and thereafter the road is lined with Georgian ribbon development down to the Abbey Foregate, with the mighty sandstone hulk of the abbey church, and then the elegant eighteenth-century English Bridge over the River Severn to the peninsula. The town centre occupies a rocky hillock almost entirely encircled by a loop of the Severn, except for a narrow neck of dry land guarded by the medieval castle and the Victorian railway station. Shrewsbury is a phenomenon almost without equal in England – an ancient county town that survives untouched, or almost untouched, by modern redevelopment, road improvements or even trendy 'conservation'. One has to say 'almost untouched' because some pretty dreadful things happened near the Welsh Bridge in the late 1950s and the 1960s, and that bit of town is now a mess of multi-storey car parks and so on. But otherwise the town is unscathed and is an almost unadulterated pleasure to visit. It has everything: castle, medieval churches, beautifully landscaped river banks, a good skyline of towers and spires, excellent hilly and curving streets with old buildings of all dates from the fifteenth century onwards, including an unequalled array of genuine (unlike Chester) Elizabethan black-and-white houses and a whole Georgian quarter.

It is best to park outside the loop of the river, preferably near Abbey Foregate, and then to walk. The first major building encountered is the ABBEY CHURCH OF HOLY CROSS, the major medieval church of Shrewsbury. The abbey was founded *c.*1080 as a Benedictine monastery. At the Dissolution the church survived, but the monastic buildings slowly disappeared, receiving their *coup de grâce* when the improvement of the Holyhead road (now the A5) in 1836 swept through their site. The church is cruciform, with nave, transepts and chancel. The nave and transepts are Early Norman and impressive in a rather brutal way, with squat, powerful round columns. The simplicity of the west front, however, is relieved by the magnificent Perpendicular window inserted later. The roof of the church and the whole of the present east end date from a restoration by J.L. Pearson in 1886–7. The space round the abbey could, with more attention and less traffic, be made very attractive. To the north are old brick houses and cottages, which form an effective foil. To the south, however, is an ignoble mess of shacks in the centre of which, surrounded by municipal shrubs so that it looks like a Gothic war memorial, stands the fourteenth-century refectory pulpit of richly carved stone.

The ENGLISH BRIDGE is an elegant late eighteenth-century design by Robert Mylne. It rises slightly in the centre and has sweeping stone balustrades and carved keystones to the arches. It affords a good view of the Shrewsbury riverside – mown lawns between the water and the old houses climbing the hill, and the back of the large early nineteenth-century former hospital building on the right.

WYLE COP, one of the most stunning streets in England, climbs the hill on a steep curve; here are jettied black-and-white-timbered houses, Georgian shop-fronts and the GOLD LION HOTEL, which has a gingery red brick façade and a large gilded lion over the porch. (Inside is an elegant Adam-style Assembly Room with plasterwork and marble chimneypieces.) The general scene fulfils all one's expectations of what an historic town should really look like – undisturbed old buildings free from self-conscious conservation. At the top of the hill is the High Street, where there are more half-timbered houses, including the GOLDEN CROSS INN and, at the corner of Mardol, IRELAND'S MANSION, the grandest in Shrewsbury, with three jettied storeys and canted bay windows. It was built *c*.1575 by a rich wool merchant, Robert Ireland. To one side of the High Street is THE SQUARE, an intimate open space in harmonious scale with the narrow streets and lanes round it. Here is the old stone MARKET HOUSE, built in 1596 with an open arcaded ground floor carried on Tuscan columns. In front is a bronze statue of Clive of India by Marochetti. On the other side of the High Street is a narrow network of steps and alleys, and a cluster of churches. ST JULIAN'S – now a craft centre – was rebuilt in 1745–50 by T.F. Pritchard, Shrewsbury's leading Georgian architect, who, however, kept the medieval tower with Perpendicular battlements. Almost next door is ST ALKMUND'S. This too has a medieval tower and Georgian body, the latter of 1793–5 by Carline and Tilley. The tower carries a beautiful slender spire 184 feet high. The interior, alas, is drearily Victorianised, with an ugly, flat timber ceiling, though it is still well worth visiting for the east window – a masterwork of the Georgian glass painter Francis Eginton. It is signed and dated 1795 and depicts Faith in beautiful shades of blue, yellow, brown and pink. Note the naturalistic thistles in the foreground. 'Be thou faithful unto death and I will give you a crown of life', reads the inscription. You might at first sight imagine that it shows the Assumption of Our Lady and wonder how so papistical a subject scraped into an eighteenth-century Protestant church. It is merely that Eginton cribbed his design from Guido Reni's famous painting of *The Assumption*.

All around St Alkmund's are the most enticing little backwaters: Fish Street, Butcher Row, St Alkmund's Lane, St Alkmund's Square. They are cobbled or stone-paved, free from traffic and lined with sixteenth–eighteenth-century buildings. Parallel to this sequence is DOGPOLE, another of Shrewsbury's curiously named main streets. It has a right-angle bend in the middle and the usual Shrewsbury mix of red brick Georgian and sixteenth-century black-and-white. On the bend stands the old GUILDHALL, a splendid brick townhouse of the 1690s with a richly carved pedimented doorcase protected by a Regency Doric porch. Dogpole changes imperceptibly into St Mary's Street, where you will find the early nineteenth-century Tudor Revival DRAPERS' ALMSHOUSES, and Shrewsbury's principal parish church, ST MARY'S. Almost incredibly, this large and important medieval church is currently threatened with redundancy. It has a Norman west tower and a doorway with a Perpendicular spire, on top of which is one of the three tallest medieval spires in England. (The top was rebuilt after a collapse in 1894.) Otherwise, the church is of various dates, but with a Perpendicular clerestory and a thorough Victorian going-over. The nave is well proportioned and has beautiful thirteenth-century arcades with clustered columns and carved capitals supporting the fifteenth-century clerestory and low-pitched timber roof. The transepts and east end retain substantial portions of Norman work. Much of the internal impact of the church, however, derives from the old, richly coloured stained glass. Much of this is foreign and was acquired for St Mary's by a nineteenth-century vicar; it makes the church a veritable museum of English and continental medieval glass. The chancel east window has a restored Jesse window from another Shrewsbury church. Elsewhere there are German, Flemish and French fifteenth- and early sixteenth-century panels. As you leave the church do not miss the heartless epitaph on the outside of the west tower:

> *Let this small monument record the name*
> *Of Cadman, and to future times proclaim*
> *How, by an attempt to fly from this high spire*
> *Across the Sabrine stream, he did acquire*
> *His fatal end. . . .*

Behind St Mary's is the former ROYAL SHROPSHIRE INFIRMARY. This was built in 1830 to the design of Robert Haycock in Greek Revival style with a Doric portico. The interior has been converted recently into a Neo-Regency shopping arcade. It is like the largest National Trust gift shop in the world, exuding a strong aroma of lavender bags.

At right-angles to St Mary Street is Castle Street, but before that PRIDE HILL descends sharply to one side. This is the chief shopping street and, fortunately, the only major street in the town to have been 'pedestrianised'. It is interesting to note how seriously the removal of the old footpaths and kerbstones and the substitution of wall-to-wall paving detracts from the proportions of an old street. When, as here, it is combined with continuous runs of modern shop-fronts along the lower storeys of old façades, it creates an unsettling visual effect whereby all the old architecture, above the 'snowline', seems completely cut off from the life below.

In Castle Street the NATIONAL WESTMINSTER BANK occupies a splendid Georgian house dated 1723, but it is a pity that the ground floor has been butchered. Surely a rich bank could afford to pay a decent architect to look after its buildings? Further along is the original SHREWSBURY SCHOOL building. The school was founded by Edward VI in 1552 and this building was erected from 1590 onwards. It is of stone in Elizabethan/Jacobean

Gothic, rather like several of the smaller colleges at Oxford. The school moved across the river in 1882 to its present Victorian Gothic buildings, and this old block is now the town museum and library. Almost opposite is SHREWSBURY CASTLE. It was founded in the 1070s, but the oldest masonry parts of the present building are twelfth-century. There is an impressive motte dating from the 1070s and now crowned by a delicious eighteenth-century Gothick folly built by Telford in 1790. This gives rather the wrong impression of the castle, perhaps, as there is much that is genuine, including the curtain wall, Norman gateway, several towers and the ancient Great Hall. Almost as grand as the castle is the Victorian-Tudor façade of the RAILWAY STATION jostling for attention next door.

Returning along Castle Street and down Pride Hill, MARDOL is reached. This descends the other side of the peninsula, towards the Welsh Bridge, and contains several more black-and-white timber-framed houses, notably THE RAVEN, where an upside-down green dragon supports the corner of the jettied upper storey, and the KING'S HEAD, a fifteenth-century pub, wonderfully drunken-looking.

The WELSH BRIDGE is a dignified classical design of 1791 by Carline and Tilley. On either hand hereabouts is the only post-war devastation in the town centre. ROWLEY'S HOUSE, the most famous sixteenth-century timber-framed house in Shrewsbury, and open to the public as a museum, is isolated in the middle of the bus station and car parks. Picking your way through there, Claremont Bank leads to the Georgian sector of the town, above Quarry Park and the riverside gardens. The *clou* here is

ST CHAD'S CHURCH, one of the best neo-classical parish churches in the country. It was designed by George Steuart, the architect of Attingham (*q.v.*), in 1790–2, after the old church on the site had collapsed. The plan is a characteristic neo-classical play on geometry, comprising three circles of graduated size; the porch under the tower, a connecting vestibule with stairs to the galleries, and the nave proper. The church has a Doric portico and an octagonal tower carrying a tall colonnaded cupola. The exterior is all faced in crispest ashlar stone from the Grinshill quarry. Inside, the body of the church is surrounded by a double arcade of Corinthian over Ionic columns, and a circular gallery; the pews too are curved to follow the circular lines of the church. The ceiling has elegant plasterwork similar to Steuart's work at Attingham. Round the walls are marble memorial tablets and hatchments arranged just like paintings in a gallery.

Walking round the town in a south-westerly direction, it is possible to enjoy a very fine sequence of Georgian houses and gardens in St John's Hill, St Chad's Terrace, Quarry Place and Swan Hill. Belmont has some positive mansions, including the JUDGE'S LODGINGS of 1701, while THE CRESCENT is indeed a short brick crescent of *c.*1800, with lacy fanlights over the doors. After this, the walk follows the line of the medieval town walls, the Georgian houses interrupted here and there by the odd bit of genuine thirteenth-century masonry, including a Gothic TOWER (NT), and the unmistakable little CATHOLIC CATHEDRAL, built by E.W. Pugin but based on his father's design. Beeches Lane, with BOWDLER'S SCHOOL of 1724, leads back to the English Bridge, where your explorations began.

St Chad's church, Shrewsbury.

Stokesay Castle

31; 8 miles NW of Ludlow on A49

Set in peaceful countryside surrounded by gently wooded hills, Stokesay is a fine example of a medieval fortified manor house and forms a perfect, uncontrived picturesque group with the jolly timber-framed GATEHOUSE and the adjoining parish CHURCH OF ST JOHN THE BAPTIST.

The core of the house is the Great Hall, which is flanked by two towers and was built c.1270–80 (licence to crenellate was granted in 1291). The builder, Laurence de Ludlow, was the son of a prosperous cloth merchant. The Hall is lit by tall traceried windows and has an open timber roof dating from the fifteenth century (patched in the sixteenth). The solar has Elizabethan panelling and a splendid fireplace decorated with strapwork and caryatids.

Upton Cressett Hall

32; 4 miles W of Bridgnorth off A458

This is a fourteenth- and fifteenth-century house encased in red brick with blue diaper patterns and given clustered chimneystacks of diamond and star-shaped sections during the sixteenth century. The gabled Gatehouse with an oak newel stairway, fine plaster ceilings and polygonal turrets was also added in the sixteenth century and the house itself was extended in 1580. The whole is set in beautiful countryside.

Inside, part of the fourteenth-century Great Hall roof with massive arched beams can be seen on the first floor; the Tudor oak newel staircase also survives, and the ground-floor rooms contain good Jacobean furniture. Both house and Gatehouse were restored in 1971.

Wem

33; 10 miles N of Shrewsbury on B5063

A wonderful forgotten and friendly little town in the middle of the north Shropshire Plain, Wem is known for its ales, which can be found in many pubs throughout the county. It is dominated by the CHURCH OF ST PETER AND ST PAUL, which looks as if it is Victorian with a Perpendicular west tower. In fact, its building history is more complicated than that. While the chancel is Victorian, the nave was built in 1809–13 in Regency Gothick, as is demonstrated by the frieze of little stone fans round the top of the walls. It was gone over in the 1840s when the more serious-looking traceried windows were inserted. The interior retains early nineteenth-century galleries supported on thin iron columns and has a good-looking eighteenth-century brass chandelier. The churchyard has impressive eighteenth-century gateways with rusticated piers carrying florid stone urns.

The backbone of the town is the long curving High Street, mainly of Georgian red brick. The former MARKET HOUSE is an unassuming late Georgian building with a Tuscan colonnade along the ground floor, now enclosed. The TOWN HALL is Edwardian municipal and jolly to look at. Over the door of the public LIBRARY are carved reliefs of children, looking just like Edwardian book illustrations. Kynastone's, the ironmonger's, has a splendid

hanging sign in the form of a giant iron padlock, while the CASTLE HOTEL has a model castle, like a sandcastle, perched over the front door.

Wenlock Priory

See Much Wenlock.

Whitchurch

34; 18 miles N of Shrewsbury on A49

An old-fashioned place, dominated by the great west tower of the parish church, which has stone urns on its parapet and a newly painted and gilded clock face, Whitchurch is situated right in the middle of the wide plain that stretches between the hills of the Peak District and the mountains of Wales. There was a Roman settlement on the site halfway between Worcester and Chester, and recent excavations have revealed the remains of several buildings and of the encircling rampart and ditch.

The main street still follows the line of the axial Roman road. It is called the HIGH STREET and rises gently towards the church. At the top, beyond the churchyard, are HIGGINSON'S ALMSHOUSES, an attractive Georgian building with a central pediment. Nearby are some good eighteenth–twentieth-century school buildings. On the south corner of the churchyard is a picturesque half-timbered pub. The body of the High Street comprises red brick Georgian houses with half-timbered highlights, some genuine and some, like the National Westminster Bank, later variations on a theme. BARCLAYS BANK was originally the Market Hall with an open arcaded ground floor on Tuscan columns, which is now closed in. There are one or two flat-roofed, set-back 1960s' interruptions, such as the Civic Centre, but on the whole Whitchurch has escaped lightly from unsympathetic modern redevelopment. At the bottom of the High Street, Green End contains some larger Georgian houses and also the WHITCHURCH INSTITUTE, a mid-nineteenth century stucco building. At this end of the town, reached via Watergate Street, is the suburb of DODINGTON, which contains timber-framed buildings and the MANSION HOUSE, an ambitious eighteenth-century house with a central pedimented doorway and a decorative window above.

The principal building of Whitchurch is its parish church, ST ALKMUND'S, the largest Georgian church in the county outside Shrewsbury itself. The old church that stood on this spot collapsed on 31 July 1711, and the present building was erected then by William Smith and John Barker, the former a mason, the latter a carpenter. It is not clear which of them was mainly responsible for the design – perhaps they both were. Anyway, it is a remarkably handsome job, with its tall west tower, eastern apse, and semi-circular south porch. This last was accurately reconstructed in 1925, but the capitals have never been carved. A tablet in the porch explains that buried beneath is the heart of John Talbot, 1st Earl of Shrewsbury, killed fighting for Henry VI in France. Shakespeare immortalised him with the words

Is this the scourge of France?
Is this the Talbot, so much fear'd abroad
That with his name the mothers still their babes?

The interior of the church is impressively monumental, with giant Tuscan columns of pink sandstone supporting arches and a coved ceiling. There were originally side-galleries in the aisles, but these were removed in 1972 because of dry rot. The pews are the original box pews, although they were cut down in the nineteenth century. There are two original brass chandeliers, one with the Egerton crest and a coronet, and there is also a splendid carved organ case of *c*.1715. The apsidal chancel was enriched in the Victorian age, when the stained glass by Warrington was installed in the east windows. The altar and reredos were erected in 1911 as a memorial to Lieutenant C.F. Dugdale. The carved oak pulpit is only part of the original three decker: it has been cut down and altered at various dates in the nineteenth and twentieth centuries. In the Lady Chapel is a large painting of *The Last Supper*; it is an old copy of a painting by Veronese and comes from the redundant chapel-of-ease in Dodington. Here also is the tomb of the 1st Earl of Shrewsbury. Its Gothic canopy dates from 1874 and the bones were re-interred at that date. When the Earl was moved there was found in the great man's skull a mummified mouse. She was reburied too, with this inscription:

The skull which once upreared great Talbot's crest,
Gashed by a foeman, gave this mouse a nest.

Wilderhope Manor

NT; 35; 6 miles E of Church Stretton on B4371

Wilderhope stands in Corve Dale, between Wenlock Edge and Aymestrey Ridge, among some of the most remote and least-spoiled landscape in Shropshire. It was built for Francis Smallman in the 1580s and is a good example of a smaller Elizabethan house. It is of local limestone, except for the tall chimneys, which are of beautifully executed brickwork. The main feature of interest inside is the contemporary plasterwork decoration of many of the ceilings; it is rich with geometrical ribbed patterns, various emblems and the initials of the builder and his wife. The house is now a youth hostel.

Willey Park★

36; 3 miles S of Ironbridge off B4375

Willey stands in a large park, hilly and wooded, traversed by a long winding drive. The house itself is a noble neo-classical design, with a rich Corinthian portico on the entrance front and a domed bow ringed with Corinthian columns round the corner in the centre of the front facing the park. It is the masterpiece of Lewis Wyatt, nephew of James Wyatt, and was begun in 1812 for Lord Forester, who was probably introduced to the Wyatt architectural clan by his brother-in-law the Duke of Rutland, who had employed no fewer than four of the family at Belvoir Castle (*q.v.*). The designs were prepared in 1812–13 and Willey took ten years to complete. The exterior is much influenced by James Wyatt's late classical style. The portico, which served as a *porte-cochère* so that visitors could alight from their carriages under cover, was inspired by James Wyatt's at Dodington in Gloucestershire.

The Central Hall, Willey Park.

The interior is notable for the sequence of processional spaces through the centre of the house: Entrance Hall, Great Hall, Staircase Hall. The main rooms are arranged on either side, with the Library and Drawing Rooms on the right and the Dining Room on the left. The great Central Hall is treated as an *atrium*; it is a magnificent neo-classical ensemble with a glazed lantern above the central open coffers of the wide-spanned segmental ceiling. Corinthian columns of yellow scagliola support a Gallery, the brass railing of which is punctuated by bronze candelabra of a Roman pattern derived from Piranesi. Halfway down either side of the Hall are simple chimneypieces of black marble, while the floor is paved in yellow and white marble. It is all very splendid, and retains original furnishings, statuary and marble urns. The Staircase Hall, divided from the Central Hall by a double screen of Corinthian columns, is oval with two symmetrical flights of stairs sweeping up on either side in the most elegant curve imaginable and meeting at the central landing. The other rooms are less exciting spatially, but they are richly decorated. The Library, which has the bow window on the park front and a matching curve to its inner wall, has built-in mahogany bookcases and a segmental ceiling with a sparse pattern of large-scale honeysuckle motifs. The Dining Room is simpler and was hung with full-length family portraits to create a masculine background to after-dinner port drinking. The Drawing Room, by contrast, is so richly decorated as to seem Victorian before its time.

Staffordshire

Of all the counties of England, Staffordshire is, I suspect, the most consistently underestimated. To most people the name conjures up visions of the Potteries, the Black Country, grim, grimy towns like Wednesbury, Wolverhampton or Walsall, and the bleak, unromantic industrial Midlands. Of rural Staffordshire (if, they might murmur in parenthesis, such a thing exists) they have no very clear vision; as for architecture, surely that must be mostly a matter of factory chimneys, cooling-towers and kilns.

How wrong they are. Parts of Staffordshire, principally the north-west and south-west corners, are admittedly given over to heavy industry and all its attendant apparatus – though they can always throw up the sudden, unexpected jewel, like a diamond in a piece of coal. They can also, even when at their most depressing, exude a stolid Victorian grandeur which, with all its overtones of *Hard Times* and the engravings of Doré, has its own smoky appeal. But they are only one aspect of a county whose greatest single industry remains agriculture. The whole centre of Staffordshire, from the border of Shropshire to that of Derbyshire, is still predominantly rural – rich and rolling farmland, flecked with quiet villages but possessing few towns of any real or significant size. Even Stafford itself numbers only 55,000 souls, and yet manages to be more than twice as big as Lichfield, the cathedral city. Then, as you move up towards the north-east beyond Uttoxeter, the countryside suddenly takes on a new character, wild and dramatic; this is the remote and somehow mysterious region of the Churnet valley, the Pugin-land of Alton and Cheadle. Beyond this are the Weaver Hills, dropping to the valley of the little River Manifold, where Izaak Walton loved to fish, and which runs into Dovedale, the Derbyshire border. By now we are approaching the country of the Peak and, though we are still in Staffordshire, those desolate industrial wastes seem light-years away.

Fortunately for us, it is the rural parts of the county that seem to contain most of the best architecture; indeed, there is one point – that from which one first catches the distant prospect of Wootton Lodge – at which natural and architectural beauty combine to create an effect that has few parallels anywhere in the Kingdom. Of all the buildings of Staffordshire, Wootton – at least its entrance front – must surely be the loveliest. Noblest, for me, will always be the great Gatehouse of Tixall, a monument both to Elizabethan glory and to the work of the Landmark Trust which alone has saved it from ruin. Most magnificent is Weston Hall, where Lord Bradford's superb collection of furniture and pictures are given a setting worthy of them. Most fantastic, beyond a doubt, is Pugin's Alton Castle. For elegance, I should hand the palm to Chillington; for charm to Blithfield; for interior decoration and parkland to Shugborough; and for sheer mad freakishness, to Alton Towers every time. Then there are Pillaton and Moseley, Caverswall and Ingestre and Swynnerton – the list is almost infinite, but the length of this book is not.

As for churches, Lichfield Cathedral must inevitably take pride of place. A flawed masterpiece it may be today, thanks to the violence done to it in the Civil War and the not always sensitive attentions of Victorian restorers; but if it cannot rank among the first league of English cathedrals, at least it holds a high and honourable place in the second. Of the parish churches, there is fine Norman work to be seen at Gnosall, Stafford (St Chad's) and above all at Tutbury; relatively little Early English, at least where whole buildings are concerned (the tiny church of Coppenhall looks lovely from the outside, but having failed to get in I thought it better not to list it); one masterpiece of Decorated in St Andrew's, Clifton Campville; and, for Perpendicular, Dr John Taylor's one-man, all-of-a-piece creation at Barton-under-Needwood. It may seem odd that this last style, which saw its most brilliant flowering during the Wars of the Roses, should best be represented by a church built in the latter half of the reign of Henry VIII; but good Perpendicular is unexpectedly rare in Staffordshire, and better late than never. The seventeenth century witnessed the creation of Ingestre, of which Sir Christopher Wren himself might have been proud, and probably was; and the eighteenth saw churches suddenly begin to spring up all over the place – Pevsner effortlessly lists thirty-five still standing – none of them, however, of outstanding quality.

And so we come to the Victorians; and the Victorian churches of Staffordshire merit a book of their own. In this single county – and a fairly obscure one as counties go – three of the greatest architects of the Victorian age produced their best work, together bridging the whole of that interminable reign. Inevitably we start with Pugin, whose grand Gothic manifesto, *Contrasts*, appeared the year before the Queen's coronation. His churches at Brewood and Dudley and his little chapel in the convent garden at Stone may be undistinguished; setting, as he did, so much store by inessential decoration, he could never work satisfactorily to a tight budget. But his achievements for the Earl of Shrewsbury at Alton and above all at Cheadle show, as conclusively as the Palace of Westminster itself, just what he was capable of

when he was given free rein. Twenty years or so later, George Edmund Street was to achieve his ecclesiastical masterpiece at Denstone – and another, very different but almost as remarkable, at Hollington, for which there is unfortunately no space for anything more than an Honourable Mention. Finally, in the 1870s, there was the Hoar Cross of G.F. Bodley, who was to survive well into the twentieth century.

Do not, then, avoid Staffordshire. Stay a day or two in some little market town in the west, centre or north-east – best of all, if you are unusually far-sighted or prodigiously lucky, in the Tixall Gatehouse – and see for yourself what variety and beauty and quite extraordinary architectural interest this most heterogeneous of counties has to offer. You will not be disappointed.

Abbots Bromley

1; 10 miles W of Burton upon Trent on B5234

Abbots Bromley is famous for its Horn Dance, a festival of pre-Norman origin held every September. Six local men in medieval costume carry reindeer horns and (accompanied by a hobby horse, a boy with a crossbow, a jester and a musician) perform the dance. It is all to do with the rights of the townsfolk in Needwood Forest. For the rest of the year the reindeer horns hang in the parish CHURCH OF ST NICHOLAS. This is of medieval origin but was largely rebuilt by G.E. Street in the 1850s. The handsome classical west tower, however, with its balustraded parapet and corner urns, dates from 1688 when the medieval tower collapsed and had to be replaced.

This little market town is very attractive; it is really now hardly more than a village, progress having passed it by in the nineteenth century. The centre is the MARKET PLACE, where there is an unusual seventeenth-century hexagonal timber market cross and several timber-framed and red brick Georgian houses. The GOAT'S HEAD HOTEL is sixteenth-century and in Bagot Street is an especially good timber-framed building, CHURCH HOUSE, with decorative timbers, as well as the red brick BAGOT ALMSHOUSES, dating from 1705 and ornamented with a curly pediment in the centre. The largest buildings in Abbots Bromley belong to the SCHOOL OF SS MARY AND ANNE, a Woodard Girls' School founded by Provost Lowe in 1874. The chapel rises above the main street – Gothic, red brick, with an apse. The interior has a polished marble reredos and painted vaulting above. Behind the chapel, and not visible from the street, is a series of attractive garden quadrangles surrounded by ranges of brick buildings, some Gothic but mainly Neo-Georgian.

Alton★

2; 4 miles E of Cheadle on B5032

Staffordshire has not anything to show more flabbergasting than ALTON TOWERS and its associated architecture. Here the early nineteenth-century English passion for the Picturesque is dragged to its ultimate extreme – the greatest and most monumental folly in the country, surrounded by countless smaller follies in a setting of secret valleys and romantic crags that does it full justice:

a Midlands Transylvania touched with occasional breaths from Athens, Tuscany and Canton.

This gigantic pile stands – or rather slowly crumbles; it has not been lived in for over half a century – as a monument to the megalomania, and indeed the wealth, of two successive Earls of Shrewsbury. It was the 15th of that line who began to enlarge his agent's unassuming little lodge around 1810, starting work on the gardens in 1814; his nephew who, succeeding in 1827, embarked on a career of compulsive fantasy building, on a scale equalled only by Ludwig II of Bavaria, which continued until his death twenty-five years later. At least eight architects were involved in Alton Towers. James Wyatt was one of the first, but as he died in 1813 he cannot be held responsible for much. One of the last, appearing at Alton in 1837, was Augustus Welby Pugin; but Pugin's work in the house – as opposed to the castle, which we shall come to in a moment – was largely confined to decoration. His, however, is the Banqueting Hall, with its tremendous oriel window looking out towards the lake. The Chapel, for which he is usually given credit, predates his arrival, though he may have remodelled it to some extent and certainly supervised the interior painting. It now houses – *sic transit!* – a model railway.

Then there is the PARK; and it is the park, even more than the model railway, that brings people to Alton in their thousands on summer afternoons. The 15th Earl simply crammed it with buildings or follies of one kind or another. For his own monument he chose a copy of the Choragic Monument to Lysicrates at Athens – doubtless aped from 'Athenian' Stuart's at Shugborough (*q.v.*); but by that time his architects, Thomas Fradgley and Robert Abraham, had produced a vaguely oriental Conservatory, an Orangery, a Rotunda, a 'Harper's Cottage', a mini-Stonehenge, the intriguingly named Screw Fountain, a Gothick Prospect Tower, a *Loggia*, an Iron Bridge, and a Chinese Pagoda in a lake – a piece of eighteenth-century *chinoiserie* fifty years behind its time. On the way out there is a pretty pink Italianate Lodge, and a larger Tudor one, probably by Pugin; we then return to Italy for the delightful little Railway Station, now alas abandoned by British Rail but, thankfully, maintained and cherished – and rented to visitors – by the Landmark Trust.

The Conservatory, Alton Towers.

All this is admirable fooling; but now raise your eyes heavenward, and there on a beetling crag above you is ALTON CASTLE, straight out of the Brothers Grimm, the fantasy creation of Shrewsbury and Pugin built between 1847 and 1852. The fragments of a real Norman castle stand in front of it; to one side, across the deep ravine that serves the office of a moat, is Pugin's HOSPITAL OF ST JOHN, built at Shrewsbury's expense as a hospice for retired Catholic priests and now a convent, associated with the prep school that now occupies the castle. This is not open to the public; but a polite request at the door will normally gain you admittance to the Pugin CHAPEL, which is all you really need to see. From the outside it appears as a strangely truncated projection to the right, roofed with green and white tiles in the Burgundian style; the interior too is distinctly French in feeling: only some 15 feet across but unusually tall in proportion, with a high polygonal apse and rib-vaulted in stone. The walls are hung with tapestry woven by the monks of Prinknash Abbey in Gloucestershire and in the bottom – as it were the predella panels – of the slender traceried windows are charming representations of Shrewsbury and Pugin, surveying the works with justifiable pride.

Barton under Needwood
3; 5 miles SW of Burton upon Trent on B5016
The founder of ST JAMES'S CHURCH, Dr John Taylor, was the eldest of triplets, a fortunate accident which induced the normally close-fisted Henry VII, in his astonishment, to pay for their education. Later, under Henry VIII –

whom he attended at the Field of the Cloth of Gold – he served as Archdeacon of Derby and Buckingham and Master of the Rolls.

His church is a splendid all-of-a-piece example of late Perpendicular, broad-shouldered and foursquare, with a nice stalwart pinnacled tower (insensitively beclocked) and embattled wherever there is room for battlements to be. Taylor's coat of arms (three babies' heads) proudly crowns the nave arcade, which still keeps its original wooden roof; this in turn leads to a long chancel, with a broad polygonal apse and three transomed windows of three lights each in which there remains some good sixteenth-century glass.

Biddulph Grange
4; 5 miles N of Tunstall on A527 [45]
The house is now an orthopaedic hospital but it is still well worth visiting for the extraordinary GARDENS made here in the mid-nineteenth century by James Bateman, whose father had made a fortune out of manufacturing steam engines in Manchester. From his earliest youth Bateman was interested in plants and gardens. (His best-known work is the layout of the University Parks at Oxford.) The gardens at Biddulph, laid out between 1842 and 1869, are among the most imaginative in England. The centrepiece is the Chinese garden encircled by a tall hedge, 'the Great Wall of China', and approached by two mysteriously dark tunnels. There is a lake surrounded by large rocks and planted round with bamboos and Chinese maples. Brightly painted bridges cross the

streams feeding the lake and once there was also a fret-work Chinese pavilion with pagoda roof; alas this has recently been destroyed by vandals – it is to be hoped that it will be rebuilt. In addition to the Chinese garden, there is an Egyptian court. Here is a temple of clipped yews, treated as pyramids and guarded by stone sphinxes. A feature of the Egyptian garden is the Obelisk Walk, a *trompe l'œil* fantasy where the perspective and the gradient are so arranged as to make the path ahead look like an obelisk. Other features include a long Wellingtonia avenue, magnificent specimen trees and old plantings of rhododendrons, many of them the earliest introductions of the species to this country. All this has been well maintained by the hospital for over fifty years.

Blithfield

5; 3 miles W of Abbots Bromley off B5013

BLITHFIELD HALL (pronounced 'Bliffield') is that rare combination: a large house and yet a lovably intimate one. Its core is medieval; the Bagot family have lived here uninterruptedly – save for a few months just after the Second World War – since the early fourteenth century, and building seems to have continued spasmodically from about 1500 until the 1820s. Then, thank goodness, it stopped in the nick of time; and the house as we see it today falls, roughly speaking, into three main periods – Tudor, mid-Georgian and Regency, this last (and most obvious, since it includes nearly all the entrance front) being almost certainly the work of John Buckler – a man better known for his beautiful architectural drawings than for actual buildings themselves. What makes the house intimate is first of all the fact that it is built round a little enclosed quadrangle, like a minor Oxford or Cambridge college, and, second, that it has no really big or imposing rooms. Even the Great Hall is only one storey high and without any serious pretensions to grandeur; on the contrary, its enchanting plasterwork of about 1820 (by Francis Bernasconi) gives it the same light-hearted, almost frivolous, effect as Sanderson Miller's rather similar *jeu d'esprit* at Lacock in Wiltshire. Here, once again, are all the trappings of Gay Gothick, beautifully conceived and carried out – the elaborate lierne-vaulted ceiling with pendants and bosses, the pinnacled doors and chimneypiece and, best of all, the long niches crowned by canopies positively exploding with crockets and cusps.

Above and behind this ceiling, the old oak rafters remain from the original Hall; for this, not surprisingly, is the earliest part of the house. It forms most of the northern side of the quadrangle, facing southwards on to the enclosed space; in this range too is a glorious late seventeenth-century staircase, with carved openwork panels in the style of those at Ham or Sudbury, leading to the green-and-gold Elizabethan panelling of the Dining Room and through that to a more soberly panelled Study (fluted pilasters and triglyph frieze – very noble) dating from the 1740s, when a new series of rooms was added to the north front.

These, together with the jolly little Gothick 'cloister' that runs along the south side of the quadrangle, are the most memorable features of Blithfield; but, as I have said, it is a large house and the present Lady Bagot – who, with her late husband, repurchased it from the Water Board in 1946 and has since been almost solely responsible for its survival – tells me that she is now planning to convert it into four separate houses. Given its shape and character, this should present no major problems; the essential architecture will not be affected, and the project means that the long-term future of Blithfield should thus be assured.

Do not leave without visiting the lovely little CHURCH OF ST LEONARD, 100 yards away to the north. It is thirteenth–fourteenth-century – the restoring hand of Pugin is barely perceptible – with splendid Bagot tombs, including a particularly enjoyable one to Sir Lewis, who died in 1534. He is portrayed surrounded by his nineteen children, a number of dogs, and three wives – the youngest of whom, who must have died when little more than a child herself, is being elbowed out by the others and barely gets a look-in over her husband's shoulder.

Brewood

6; 7 miles W of Cannock off A5

This is an attractive little town near to the Shropshire border in country redolent of Charles II's adventures after the battle of Worcester. The Boscobel oak tree where he hid from the Cromwellian soldiers is close by, though over the Shropshire border. The narrow streets of the town are lined with agreeable houses, and over all presides the tall Perpendicular spire of the parish CHURCH OF ST MARY AND ST CHAD.

The body of the building is of various dates, the nave being fourteenth-century, the chancel Early English with lancets; much was restored and reconstructed by Street in 1878–80. The interior is notable for the tombs of the Giffards of Chillington (*q.v.*), especially a group of sixteenth- and seventeenth-century alabasters in the chancel. There is also a modern memorial to Colonel Carless, who is buried here: 'HE NOT ONLY ASSISTED CHARLES I OF EVER BLESSED MEMORY, BUT WAS ALSO THE CHIEF PRESERVER OF HIS SON KING CHARLES II IN THE ROYAL OAK AT BOSCOBEL.'

Thanks to the Giffards, there is a strong recusant presence at Brewood and the Catholic CHURCH OF ST MARY was designed by A.W. Pugin in 1843–4. It is a little cruciform building with a broach spire, rather like a Gothic model. The stained glass in the east window was given by Pugin himself. Forming a group with the church are the PRIEST'S HOUSE and SCHOOL, gabled brick buildings also by Pugin.

Near to the parish church are several good Georgian houses, including THE CHANTRY, WEST GATE and DEAN STREET HOUSE. The best building in Brewood, however, is SPEEDWELL CASTLE in the Market Place – a delightful Rococo Gothick job of 1750, with two canted bay windows and ogee-arched windows. Originally there were octagonal-patterned glazing bars; let's hope that one day somebody will restore them. The house was paid for by a successful bet on a horse called Speedwell belonging to the Duke of Bolton – hence its name.

Broughton

7; 7 miles E of Market Drayton on B5026

Here is a spectacular manorial group of church and Hall standing side by side in beautiful empty country in the west of the county. It is the stem seat of the Broughton baronets who later inherited Doddington in Cheshire (*q.v.*) in the eighteenth century, but who continued to be buried here. The CHURCH is seventeenth-century Gothic (it was built in 1630–4), Tudor in feeling, with round-topped mullion windows. The interior is a great thrill and well worth the effort of getting in. (The key is obtainable from the vicarage at Wetwood, half a mile towards Eccleshall.) The nave is full of tall box pews, the walls are painted white and the light fittings are Victorian oil-lamps. The east window of the chancel has fifteenth-century stained glass, with little portraits of the members of the Broughton family, and there is good seventeenth-century heraldic glass in the side-windows. Lots of Broughton memorials and tablets line the walls; nothing individually spectacular, but they are historically impressive as a group. In the chancel are brasses to Thomas Broughton, who built the church, and his wife and daughter. Many handsome seventeenth- and eighteenth-century marble tablets and cartouches can be seen in nave and chancel; I particularly like that to Sir Thomas Delves Broughton, the builder of Doddington Hall, who was, we are informed, 'endowed by Nature with Superior abilities'.

BROUGHTON HALL is a glorious half-timbered mirage, the beams forming dazzling black-and-white patterns. Three storeys high, with gables and jettied upper storeys, it was built in 1637 though it owes some of its impact, it has to be admitted, to the improvements and additions of W. & S. Owen in 1926–39. They doubled the original size of the house but maintained its original character. There are several interior features of interest, including a grand seventeenth-century staircase and the Long Gallery on the top floor with its elaborate Jacobean plasterwork. The Hall now belongs to the Franciscans.

Burton upon Trent

8; 11 miles SW of Derby on A38

The first thing that strikes the visitor is the smell of hops – for, of course, Burton means beer. Brewing was started here in the Middle Ages by the Benedictine monks of Burton Abbey (founded in 1004). The excellence of the ale is due to the local water, which contains gypsum. After the Dissolution of the abbey in the sixteenth century, the local inns continued to brew their own beer and, with the vast improvement of water-communications in the eighteenth century, Burton beer came to be widely exported – not just to London but to the world, from Russia to India, thus gaining an international reputation. The heyday of Burton beer came in the late nineteenth century, when there were no fewer than forty independent breweries at work in the town. These have been reduced in recent years by amalgamations, and the town has been somewhat spoilt by 'planning' and insensitive redevelopment: avert your eyes if you can from the two ugly shopping centres and the lumpish telephone exchange, which ruins the views down Lichfield Street.

Broughton Hall.

There are two areas of Burton that are still worth exploring: the old town around the Market Place and parish church, and the nineteenth-century suburbs, including the Victorian Town Hall and churches, which owe much to the beneficence of the Bass brewing family (raised to the beerage as Lords Burton). In the old town, the stretch along the river is pleasantly green and leafy. Bridge Street and Horningshow Street have prosperous eighteenth-century houses. The High Street is the heart of the brewing industry, with the BASS BREWERY OFFICES, founded in 1777, and WORTHINGTON HOUSE, where William Worthington started brewing in 1744. The Market Place has a Victorian MARKET HALL (alas, replacing one by the Wyatts) and ST MODWEN'S, the old parish church, a good Georgian building rebuilt in 1719 by William and Francis Smith of Warwick. The interior of the church was much remodelled and redecorated in the nineteenth century, but is none the worse for that. Its most notable feature is the princely neo-classical organ case designed by James Wyatt in 1771 and enlarged in 1902; it is the best of its date in the country.

It is worth trawling the Burton suburbs to see the other breweries and the splendid churches and public buildings paid for by rich nineteenth-century brewers. The TOWN HALL, standing isolated from the old town to the west of the railway, was erected in 1878 by Michael Bass to the design of Reginald Church, and completed at the expense of the 1st Lord Burton. It is Tudor Gothic, of brick and stone with a tall clock tower, and a glass and iron *porte-cochère*. In the square in front is a bronze statue by Pomeroy of Michael Arthur Bass, 1st Lord Burton. The group is completed by the ambitious CHURCH OF ST PAUL, paid for by Michael Bass and designed in 1874 by J.M. Teal and Lord Grimthorpe. It has a large central tower, and the interior is distinguished for its fittings by Bodley, such as the enormous and elaborate organ case. The best building in Burton, however, is ST CHAD'S CHURCH to the north. This was paid for by Lord Burton and designed by Bodley; it was begun in 1903 and completed in 1910 by Cecil Hare, and is generally considered to be one of his late masterpieces. The exterior is dominated by the tall bell-tower at the north-west corner; it is almost free-standing, connected to the body of the church only by a vaulted passage. The lower part of the tower is plain but the upper part is fitted with large traceried bell-openings, executed with all the refinement of which Bodley was capable. On top is a small lead cap or spirelet. The interior is serene and splendid, with a long, well-proportioned nave. The chancel has distinguished fittings of an ascending order of grandeur, culminating in the high altar and the towering reredos of the Lady Chapel on the north side.

Caverswall Castle
9; 1½ miles E of Longton off A50

A castle was first built at Caverswall in 1275 – oblong, with polygonal angle-towers at the corners. Into this frame, in 1614 or so, one Matthew Cradock inserted a fine Jacobean mansion with projecting bays and big, broad, mullioned bay windows – a building, in fact, as unlike a castle as could possibly be imagined. (The

The church of St Giles, Cheadle.

present battlements are only a nineteenth-century substitute for the original balustraded parapet.) The architect was probably Robert Smythson's son John, but the real interest lies in the contrast between the world of medieval fortification and that of the new, self-made, Renaissance man of the early seventeenth century.

Cheadle★
10; 5 miles E of Longton on A521

If one lived in Cheadle one would have to be a Roman Catholic. It is one of the few English towns in which, architecturally speaking, the Church of Rome beats that of England into a cocked hat – and no wonder, because it was here, in the Catholic CHURCH OF ST GILES, between 1841 and 1846, that Augustus Welby Pugin created his masterpiece. His patron, as at nearby Alton (*q.v.*) with which he was simultaneously involved, was the 16th Earl of Shrewsbury, which meant that his funds were almost unlimited – a fact of which he took the fullest possible advantage. For miles in every direction that spectacular 200-foot spire proclaims the ancient faith of England with triumphant assurance, just as its designer intended that it should; within, he has created what he once described as 'a perfect revival of an English parish church of the time of Edward I.'

In fact, I should be very surprised if any English parish church of King Edward's time – or anyone else's for that matter – looked remotely like St Giles's; but that is not altogether Pugin's fault. What actually happened, as he admitted in 1851 (the year before his death), was that St Giles's had been 'originally designed for a plain parochial country church, and it was quite an afterthought of its noble founder to cover it with coloured enrichment.' In other words, the Earl changed his mind; but we can be glad that he did, because one of the things that makes the church so visually stunning today is its polychrome brilliance. Pugin was as inspired a colourist as he was a designer, and here we see him at his most inventive and exuberant. The chancel alone (lightswitch just inside the screen to the left) is painted all the colours of a merry-go-round, with saints in huge rosettes all over the north and south walls; and virtually the whole interior (except Wailes's glass) is of his own personal design. His are the font, font cover and reredos, the screen and the huge rood surmounting it, which seems to have burgeoned forth in so many flowery protuberances as to have become practically a vegetable. Yet there is much subtlety too. Note the difference of colouration on the piers of the arcade; all have the same basic design, but the reds and greens follow, from one pier to the next, an intricate pattern of their own. The church is not large but, like the House of Lords – its secular equivalent in the Pugin canon – its wealth of detail makes it perennially fascinating. '*Perfect Cheadle*,' wrote Pugin, 'Cheadle my consolation in all my afflictions.' One can only hope that its fortunate parishioners feel the same way.

A mile away on the B5417 is an enchanting small house of 1712 called HALES HALL. It has a hipped roof with three dormers, the middle one especially ornate with volutes framing a little pinnacle; and this same central emphasis continues down the garlanded first-floor mid-window to a similarly voluted pediment above the front door. It belongs to the council; I wish it belonged to me.

Checkley
11; 6 miles NW of Uttoxeter on A50

ST MARY'S is a fine church, though not by any means a pure one. The tower alone begins Norman and finishes up Perpendicular, with a burst of Decorated in between. Once inside the south doorway (1300 or so) your eye is immediately caught by the soaring chancel arch, and you note to your surprise that the arcade arches, which look to be of around 1200, go very nearly as high. (Pevsner suggests they may have been heightened later.) The climax is the chancel itself, raised up three quite steep steps, Decorated through and through, and obviously a replacement by some late thirteenth-century benefactor; it boasts a really beautiful five-light east window with intersecting tracery, and three-light windows to north and south. Good fourteenth-century glass too, including a nice Martyrdom of Thomas à Becket. (The strategic light-switch will be found halfway along the north wall, just past the end of the stalls.) The south chapel has an excellent parclose screen by Sir Ninian Comper.

Chillington Hall
12; 8 miles NW of Wolverhampton off A41

It was in 1178 that the Giffards – the 'G' is soft, as in George – first came to Chillington, and they are still there. The house, however, though built round a Tudor core of which only a few traces remain, is to all intents and purposes an eighteenth-century building, the work of two separate and strongly contrasting architects with an interval of some sixty years between them. The first of these architects was almost certainly – documentary evidence is lacking, but the attribution can hardly be doubted – Francis Smith of Warwick. His is the three-storey south front and all that lies immediately behind it, including the glorious Staircase Hall – reminiscent of his masterpiece at Mawley in Shropshire (*q.v.*) (though rather more restrained) and decorated, like Mawley, with much fine plasterwork, probably by Artari or Vassali or both.

North of the staircase the mood changes dramatically – though not surprisingly, since we are now entering the world of the young John Soane. He was only thirty-two when he arrived, and Chillington was his most ambitious work to date; yet his style was already formed to a remarkable degree. Those familiar hallmarks turn up again and again – the tall, round-headed arches, the unexpected vistas, the top lighting, the almost studied avoidance of the classical orders and entablatures, at least where interior decoration is concerned. His east front is more conservative, with its giant portico of four unfluted Ionic columns in streaky Tunstall stone; the problem that obviously faced Soane here was how to make the junction at the southern end with Smith's earlier work.

At this point Soane's habitual assurance seems to have left him. His new front was to be of only two storeys, and to accommodate the consequent change in window levels he decided to convert the eastern end of Smith's work into a sort of flanking tower, repeating the pattern in the north-east corner for symmetry's sake. It ought to have worked, but it didn't: the join is clumsy, the differing fenestrations struggle disagreeably with each other, and there is no doubt that Smith comes off the better from the encounter.

Where Soane is seen at his best is in his Saloon, once the Tudor Great Hall – an intricate and adventurous design which we can now see as a sort of prototype for what, a few years later, he was to achieve at the Bank of England. Its central feature is a huge elliptical dome, coving upwards to a lantern of the same shape and supported on heavily emphasised pendentives – to which the elliptical plan lends an agreeably rakish shape – bearing stylised reproductions of that memorable but apocryphal moment around 1500 when Sir John Giffard shot a tame panther that had escaped from its cage and was about to savage a mother and child. (This device appears on the Giffard coat of arms and on the curious Saloon fireplace, the scene of the incident itself being marked by a rough wooden cross at the end of the Oak Avenue in the park.)

The park, which was laid out by Capability Brown in about 1770, contains several small buildings which make nice objectives for walks. They include an Ionic temple, possibly by Robert Adam, a Doric and a Gothic temple, and a pretty bridge by James Paine where the ornamental lake meets the canal.

Clifton Campville★

13; 7 miles NE of Tamworth off A453

Staffordshire is lucky indeed to possess Clifton Campville. One tiny wiggle of the county boundaries – and they have wiggled enough, God knows, in the past few years – would have put the village in Warwickshire, Leicestershire or Derbyshire, and Staffs would have lost its loveliest church. Its spire is as distinctive a landmark as that of St Giles's, Cheadle (*q.v.*) – though built nearly 500 years earlier, recessed, and supported by four flying buttresses from the corner pinnacles of the tower. As you approach across the churchyard from the north, the first surprise is to see right *through* the tower at ground level; there are twin three-light windows with intersecting tracery facing each other on the north and south sides, both of them with plain glass (and, incidentally, another of similar size on the west). The effect is of wonderful airiness and makes the whole structure seem more ethereal than ever.

Inside, the impression of lightness persists. At first the church appears double-naved Decorated; but this is only because the south transept of the original Early English cruciform church was extended westwards, thus becoming a broad south aisle, when the church was rebuilt and almost doubled in size by Sir Richard Stafford in 1361–76. (The two-storey vaulted north transept was not similarly enlarged; it remains as the Chantry Chapel, and very beautiful it is.) An eastward extension of the south transept made at the same time produced the Lady Chapel, another broad and sunny space notable for a fine alabaster tomb, dated 1545, to Sir John and Lady Vernon and even more for the parclose screens enclosing it. Two of these are original – late fourteenth-century – which makes them rarities indeed; a third is dated 1634, contemporary with the doors of the rood-screen.

We are left with the chancel, separated from the Lady Chapel by a three-bay arcade, adorned with a fine wooden roof with a cusped zigzag design running between the purlins, but dominated by a superb five-light east window with reticulated tracery. A fitting climax to a wonderful church.

Croxden Abbey

14; 4 miles W of Rocester off B5031

The ruins of the Cistercian abbey founded by Bertram de Verdun in 1176 lie in a remote valley near the Derbyshire border and must be one of the least-known monastic sites in the country. The setting is delightfully rural. A deep tree-lined lane leads to the little village of Croxden, with a few cottages and farms forming a foil to the majestic remains of the abbey's west front and south transept. These are the two best features still standing – Early English at its most austerely splendid, with tall, thrilling lancet windows. Little remains of the rest. The lane cuts across the site of the church and in the middle of the former nave is a splendid large walnut tree; otherwise, just foundations laid out in the grass or sparse fragments of wall remain. The east end of the church was unusual for England, being apsidal with five radiating chapels rather than the usual square end, and is copied directly from French practice.

Denstone

15; 1½ miles N of Rocester on B5031

ALL SAINTS' CHURCH, Denstone, will not be everyone's cup of tea; but Staffordshire is quite extraordinarily rich in Victorian churches and this is one of the very best. On the other hand, it has none of the obvious, immediate appeal of a Cheadle or a Hoar Cross (*qq.v.*). G.E. Street was not that sort of architect, and anyway, he had no fantastically rich patron to back him. His object was simply to build a working church, tough and sensible, not puritanically plain by any means but without any fussy art-historical or continental fripperies. He was only thirty-six when he designed it in 1860, and it was finished two years later.

As you enter the lich-gate – also Street's – one of the first things you notice is that the chancel is higher than the nave; and before you go into the church, walk round the apse to the north side, past those curious low buttresses that stop at the sill level of the windows. Look, too, at the plate tracery: not really tracery at all – simply blocks of stone with holes punched through them – but the only kind known to the architects of the first half of the thirteenth century and with just that sort of no-nonsense masculine chunkiness that Street preferred. Only in the round tower, with its outside staircase and conical top, has he perhaps allowed his imagination, very slightly, to run away with him.

The inside is broad and spacious, both in nave and chancel, with little or no sense of narrowing as it goes east. Nor is there much mystery – the last thing Street would have wanted. The feeling of robust strength persists, but not of austerity: there are bands of colour on the rough stone walls and both screen and pulpit are heavily decorated – the latter just the place for a good, stiff, muscular Victorian sermon.

Enville

16; 5 miles W of Stourbridge on A458

A spruce estate village, wooded park and large old house approached by a lime avenue make up the seat of the Greys, who have been here since the fifteenth century. The present house dates from the sixteenth century, but the façade was done up in Gothick style with pinnacles and battlements in the mid-eighteenth. The interior was burnt and rebuilt in 1904, when the entrance porch was added. The special glory of Enville, however, is its landscaped GARDEN, which is among the most glorious in Staffordshire, a county very generously endowed with eighteenth- and nineteenth-century gardens. To the west of the house is a wide lawn adorned with a large pond containing a fountain in the form of a triton and four horses; beyond rises the park, hilly, wooded and dotted with follies. To the south is a lake. William Shenstone, the poet and landscape gardener who had created a reputation for himself with his own garden at the Leasowes (over the Worcestershire border) was responsible for the original mid-eighteenth-century layout, but further embellishments and improvements were carried out in the late eighteenth and nineteenth centuries. Shenstone died at Enville, and the Chapel is dedicated to his memory. It has a round tower with a conical roof and is surrounded by romantic dark planting. Nearby are the cascade and the Gothic gateway with three arches and castellated walls. This gateway, recently restored, once led to walks through the woods and the little valley with a classical temple. Originally there was also a hermit's cottage with a thatched roof, and a pagoda, but these have almost completely disappeared. The finest of the surviving garden buildings is the MUSEUM near to the house. This is a delightful piece of eighteenth-century Gothick, faced in stone, with ogee gables, clustered columns and fanciful window tracery. It was designed by Sanderson Miller in 1750. At the time of writing it is in poor condition, but plans are in hand for its re-roofing and repair.

Gnosall
17; 8 miles W of Stafford on A518

If Clifton Campville (*q.v.*) wins the prize for the best medieval church in Staffordshire, Gnosall (pronounced 'Nozzle') is not very far behind. But where the beauty of the former lies in the Decorated style, the grandeur of Gnosall is Norman. This is a rare thing on this scale in Staffordshire. The building gives little enough away on the outside: Early English west window of three stepped

The church of the Holy Angels, Hoar Cross.

lancets; Decorated five-light east window; Perpendicular clerestory and top stage of crossing-tower; a south porch of 1893 that defies categorisation. But the moment you get inside, the whole picture changes: standing in the nave, you see to your astonishment that that lovely east window is framed by two Norman arches of tremendous power; indeed the whole crossing and much of the south transept is simply splendid work of the late twelfth century. Just look at the west wall of that transept: there you see the old Norman triforium still in position, and below it first a carved string-course and then the blank arcading that probably extended all the way round. Alas that so much has been destroyed; but the church was much enlarged in the thirteenth century, and medieval architects were poor respecters of their predecessors' achievements.

Hales Hall
See Cheadle.

Hoar Cross★
18; 4 miles E of Abbots Bromley off B5234

The CHURCH OF THE HOLY ANGELS at Hoar Cross is, like that of St Giles's, Cheadle (*q.v.*), its architect's masterpiece; in this instance, however, the architect concerned was G.F. Bodley, and he was working thirty years later. There is another difference too, not so much liturgical – for the gulf that lies between the Roman Catholicism of the one and the High Anglo-Catholicism of the other is narrow indeed – as in the purposes for which the two buildings were intended. Lord Shrewsbury and Pugin saw their church as a beacon, a proclamation of the true faith to the lost and benighted sheep of the industrial Midlands; Mrs Emily Meynell Ingram and Bodley saw theirs as a candle at a shrine. St Giles's is extrovert, ablaze with colour; the Holy Angels is secret, mysterious and contemplative. St Giles's is rich; the Holy Angels is even richer.

Though technically (and quite unnecessarily) a parish church, this astounding creation is in essence a memorial chapel, erected between 1872 and 1876 by Mrs Meynell Ingram in memory of her husband. Its exterior is noble but austere; the tall embattled crossing-tower has none of the fireworks of Pugin's spire. But to enter is like walking into a jewel. A dark jewel, admittedly; the glass, by Burlison and Grylls, allows little light to penetrate. But, in the chancel especially, from the black-and-white marble floor to the high tierceron-vaulted roof, there is wealth and sumptuousness everywhere, and superb craftsmanship to boot. How easy it would have been, with so much money available for every element – statuary, stations of the Cross, altarpieces, reredoses, glass, plate, stalls, screens, candelabra and the rest – to lose control; yet Bodley's handling is faultless; nothing is overdone or overstated. Here is the High Victorian Gothic Revival at its most solemn, and its most glorious.

In the Chantry Chapel just south of the chancel lie the tomb effigies of the foundress and her husband, his under a canopy of carved stone, hers under one of painted and gilded oak. His spirit must feel deeply honoured; hers, I hope, infinitely proud.

Ingestre

19; 5 miles E of Stafford off A51
Includes St Mary's Church★

INGESTRE HALL will not detain you long. The south front, apart from its faintly ridiculous central cupola, is a pleasantly distinguished Jacobean composition; the other two principal façades, however, having been ill-advisedly brought up to date in the eighteenth century, were re-Jacobeanised by – of all people – John Nash in 1808–10. To make matters worse, in 1882 much of the house was gutted by a fire, which also destroyed all, or nearly all, of Nash's work; and John Birch, to whom the restoration was entrusted, was not the most sensitive of architects. Console yourself, then, if the representatives of the local authority to whom the Hall is now entrusted show themselves something less than welcoming to visitors. You are missing nothing.

If, on the other hand, you return home without visiting ST MARY'S CHURCH★ opposite, you will be missing a very great deal. (The key can be obtained by asking in the big Victorian stables – Birch again – just behind.) It is almost certainly by Sir Christopher Wren, and if it isn't it ought to be. The quality alone makes it difficult to attribute it to a lesser hand. There is nothing grandiloquent here – unless it be the tremendous Royal Arms over the exquisitely carved screen – only cool, confident perfection. The stucco ceiling is a joy to behold – flat over the nave, barrel-vaulted over the chancel – and there is an admirable pulpit with spreading tester. The only incongruous feature is a window on the north side by Morris & Co. Not bad in itself, but what can it be doing here?

Leek

20; 13 miles S of Macclesfield on A523

Leek is an unspoilt little old industrial town high among the moors of the Peak District. The overall atmosphere is dictated by the terraced houses of brick or darkened stone lining the steep streets, some of them still cobbled, and several large silk mills. Leek's days of prosperity were the eighteenth and nineteenth centuries, and were based on the manufacture and dyeing of silk hosiery.

All the main roads into the town meet in the MARKET PLACE – a cobbled space surrounded by decent eighteenth-century buildings, including the Red Lion Inn, Foxlowe and other Georgian houses, as well as good Victorian banks. West of the Market Place is the large and impressive parish CHURCH OF ST EDWARD THE CONFESSOR, with a many-pinnacled west tower. The nave has octagonal columns, a panelled sixteenth-century timber ceiling and a large eighteenth-century west gallery, like the dress circle in a theatre. The chancel was rebuilt by Street in 1865–7 and is a Victorian period piece with all its fittings by Street. There is also good stained glass by Morris & Co., especially that in the Lady Chapel. The needlework frontals on the various altars are the work of the Leek School of Embroidery founded by Lady Wardle in the 1870s. The VICARAGE, dated 1714, at the east end of the churchyard is reputed to have been occupied by Bonnie Prince Charlie on his way to Derby in 1745.

St Mary's church, Ingestre.

The finest street in Leek is St Edward Street to the south of the church. It contains several good eighteenth-century houses, and at its end (actually in Broad Street) are the ALMSHOUSES founded by Elizabeth Ash in 1676. East of the Market Place is Stockwell Street, which contains two or three good things. GREYSTONES is a fine late seventeenth-century stone house with a symmetrical front. Behind it is the NICHOLSON INSTITUTE, established in 1884 by Joshua Nicholson (owner of a local silk firm) as an art school, gallery and library. It was designed by William Sugden, the local architect who more or less monopolised the profession in late nineteenth-century Leek, being responsible for the banks, police station and even the silk mills. The Institute is a friendly red brick building in Caroline style with a tower. At the end of Stockwell Street is the WAR MEMORIAL in the form of a clock tower, designed by Thomas Worthington and also given to the town by the Nicholsons.

Lichfield
21; 13 miles SW of Burton upon Trent on A38

THE CATHEDRAL AND IMMEDIATE ENVIRONS

Of all the cathedrals of England, Lichfield is the easiest to recognise. No other has three spires. It comes as something of a surprise to learn that the central one over the crossing is largely the work of James Wyatt, whose controversial career as a cathedral restorer began here between 1788 and 1795. As for the other two, fourteenth-century though they unquestionably are, they sit uncomfortably on the west façade rather than being continued to the ground as towers. The west front of *c*.1280 is now very largely a Victorian restoration by Sir George Gilbert Scott, and as a result has a rather hard and mechanical feel.

Still, the cathedral is nicely situated in its intimate little close, and its orange-pink sandstone silhouette reveals itself beautifully as you walk along the narrow lane leading up from Beacon Street. And once inside, things improve immediately. Here again Gilbert Scott and his son John Oldrid Scott were at work from 1846 onwards – despite the efforts of Wyatt and others, the building had never really recovered from the appalling devastation it suffered during the Civil War 200 years

Lichfield Cathedral.

before – but they remained faithful to the spirit, and often indeed to the letter, of the original late thirteenth-century designs and the Lichfield nave of *c*.1260 offers a vista both impressive and exciting. Unusual too – take, for example, that extraordinary motif in the clerestory of three circles enclosing cusped trefoils and themselves enclosed in a single triangle with slightly bulging sides. It can be seen in the tribune at Westminster Abbey, but in no other English church that I know of is it used as a regular motif for the clerestory. This theme is continued, with variations, down the elevation of each bay towards the ground. At triforium level, amid much dogtooth, we find the more frequent figure of an inscribed quatrefoil; just below that, and once again peculiar to Lichfield, are the huge flowing moulded cinquefoils, framed in circles and bisected by the triple shafts that go rocketing up from floor to vault. At Lichfield, the love of linear pattern so characteristic of English Gothic was taken further than ever before. The capitals of the main arcade, and vault too, show a new naturalism with recognisable leaves of oak. Here is all the imagination and invention of the early Decorated style at its resplendent best.

Now walk up the nave to Scott's beautiful iron screen at the entrance to the choir. Standing under the crossing, you can look along the transepts, north to the Early English window of five equal lancets, south to the huge if somehow characterless Perpendicular one of nine lights, above which – though from your present position you would never guess it – is an elaborate rose window in the crowning gable.

The choir is a remarkable Victorian set-piece with a rich marble floor, reredos and fittings, all by Scott. Much interest lies to each side of it. Halfway along the south choir aisle you will find a little flight of steps leading up to the Chapel of St Chad's Head. How Lichfield's patron saint became decapitated we do not know; he was a gentle seventh-century bishop who died peacefully in his bed. But while the rest of his body lay in a shrine just behind the high altar, his head was kept here and occasionally raised aloft to be venerated by the pilgrims as they passed in procession below. As the triple-lancet windows show, this is pure Early English – probably about 1225 – though the stone gallery in front is obviously a later, fourteenth-century, addition. Also in the south choir aisle is Chantrey's affecting monument to the Robinson children, showing two white marble babies asleep. Many other genteel marble monuments and tablets, especially in the transepts, recall Lichfield's Georgian heyday, when it was the elegant centre of the county's social life.

Opposite, on the north side, is one of the best things in the whole cathedral: the Chapter House of *c*.1240. It is connected to the north aisle by a vestibule – used, apparently, for the washing of pilgrims' feet. There is lovely carving on the capitals of the colonnettes; but the virtuosity is greater still in the Chapter House itself. In shape it is a decagon, or ten-sided building, though with the two middle sides in a straight line, vaulted from a central cluster of shafts which, even if it cannot boast the soaring grace of Wells, is nonetheless a considerable work of art. (The capital of the central pillar was given to four men to carve and each adopted his own pattern without reference to the others.)

And so to the eastern end, behind the high altar. This is the Lady Chapel, completed about 1330. The nodding ogee arches of the wall arcading, the statues under their canopies (Victorian, but *tant pis*), the polygonal apse, the tall, three-light untransomed Decorated windows (still almost lancets in shape but bursting out into a spray of trefoiled tracery as their lines begin to converge), and above all the tall, slender proportions and lack of aisle are unusual in this country at that period and give one the impression of being in northern Europe rather than in England – an impression increased by the early sixteenth-century Flemish glass brought from Herckenrode by Sir Brooke Boothby of Ashbourne in 1802. The altarpiece was carved at Oberammergau in 1895 and looks it.

The close contains, among several nice houses, two buildings of outstanding merit. The first is the BISHOP'S PALACE. There is nothing palatial about it as there is, for example, at Wells; it is simply a fine two-storey house designed and built by Edward Pierce (one of Wren's masons, whose most important architectural commission this was) in 1687–8 – ashlar-faced, with a hipped roof and dormers and a nice episcopal crest within its pediment. Alas, it is no longer used for the purpose for which it was intended – a fact which, if I were Bishop of Lichfield, would occasion me much sorrow. The two side-pavilions date, almost unbelievably, from 1868. Who said the Victorians couldn't build sensitively if they tried? Next to the Palace is the DEANERY, twenty years later and, very properly, on a slightly smaller scale – but none the worse for that.

THE CITY

The city of Lichfield itself benefits enormously from the two great pools that separate the cathedral precinct from the rest. It has a fair amount of good architecture, but nothing outstanding. ST JOHN'S HOSPITAL, whose eight formidable chimney-breasts present such a frowning face to the visitor as he enters the city from the south by St John Street, proves to be an attractive little quadrangle, mostly of 1495 but completed (west side) by Louis de Soissons in 1966. As to churches, ST CHAD'S is a bit of a hotchpotch, ranging from an Early English south arcade to a Gothic Revival clerestory; ST MICHAEL'S CHURCH is too Victorianised to give any real pleasure but does command just about the best available view of city and cathedral.

Finally, we must on no account forget Lichfield's most celebrated son, Samuel Johnson. It would in any case be hard to do so, owing to the distinctly alarming mosaic portrait of him, about fifty times life size, on the side-wall of the GEORGE HOTEL; but his real memorial is his BIRTHPLACE, a pleasant house with a steep hipped roof, unremarkable except for a recessed ground floor with Tuscan colonnade, which must have been newly built when the Johnsons settled there in 1707, two years before Samuel was born. It is now a museum, and there is a first-rate statue of the great man, hunched in his chair, just outside. (Boswell is a few yards further down.)

Moseley Old Hall

NT; 22; 4 miles N of Wolverhampton off A460

There are two sad things about Moseley: the flat industrial sprawl in which it stands and for which we must blame the Cannock Chase coalfield, and the grim Victorian brick in which the old house was encased in 1870, when the original timber-framing was found to have deteriorated to the point where the whole structure was endangered. There is nothing much to be done about the first, but I still hope that one day some enlightened benefactor will enable the National Trust to remove the brick, restore the half-timbering and leave Moseley Old Hall looking once again as it did when King Charles II took refuge here for two days and a night after his defeat at Worcester in September 1651.

This would be well worth doing, since the inside of the house has changed remarkably little since King Charles's day. You can still see the 'orchard door' through which he entered, disguised as a woodman, in the early hours of 8 September, the room which he occupied and the four-poster bed in which he slept, its original linsey-wolsey hangings still intact. In the corner of the room is a concealed closet within which is a trap-door, only exposed when the two opposing closet doors are shut, leading to the small recess where Charles hid on the following day to escape his pursuers. None of this, it should be emphasised, is in any way tradition or legend; it was all scrupulously recorded at the time by the master of the house, Thomas Whitgreave, and later by the King himself, dictating to Samuel Pepys. Thus, for some forty hours of its long history, this unassuming manor house was the most critical point in all England.

The garden and surrounding orchard have been imaginatively laid out by the National Trust in the style of the time, using only such plants as might have been grown there in the seventeenth century.

Okeover Hall

23; 2 miles NW of Ashbourne off A523

Okeover is situated on the Staffordshire–Derbyshire border at the entrance to Dovedale, and has the distinction of having passed down in the same family for 800 years. On the death of Mr Haughton Ealdred Okeover in 1955 it was inherited by his nephew Sir Ian Walker, Bt, grandson of the donor of the Walker Art Gallery in Liverpool (*q.v.*), who at that time lived in a large Victorian house, Osmaston Manor, near Derby. He had no hesitation in making up his mind about which house to keep. He added Okeover to his name, demolished Osmaston and moved here in order to perpetuate the exceptional continuity of the family and estate. The existing house at Okeover was a hotchpotch of Victorian buildings stuck on to the back of a mutilated wing built c.1750 by Joseph Sanderson for Leake Okeover. This peculiar plan was the result of a drastic reduction of the house in the early nineteenth century, followed by piecemeal enlargement later. The architect Marshall Sisson evolved a plan whereby the eighteenth-century block could be retained as one wing of a new U-shaped house with the entrance centred on a pedimented temple in the garden to the north. This plan was adopted and the reconstruction was begun in 1957, being completed in 1960. The result is one of the finest country houses built in England since the Second World War.

The new main block was given a principal façade facing south over the park, made symmetrical by re-using half the stone dressings from the east pavilion to form a matching pavilion on the west, while the central three bays were given prominence by making them a semi-circular bow. The new entrance facing north was treated in a simpler, more Vanbrughian, manner with square staircase towers in either corner and a central projecting porch the full height of the house; it has a pediment and on top there are giant lead statues brought from the garden at Osmaston. A subtle unifying feature of this façade is the broken string-course which is carried right across in the form of simple 'capitals' to the pilasters of the porch and towers, and the entablatures of the upper windows. One of the reasons for the success of Okeover is the lucid economy of the design, which relies on simple clean details in the new work or cleverly re-used features salvaged from the demolished parts. There is also a sense of inevitability about the way the house fills the site between a steep hillside and existing old buildings, such as the medieval parish church.

The interior is equally successful. The entrance porch gives on to a transverse corridor, or gallery, the length of the centre block; its generous width is dictated by the eighteenth-century staircase at one end, which has a splendid wrought-iron balustrade by Robert Bakewell, who was also responsible for several gates and sets of railings in the grounds. The main rooms open off to the south, facing the park and ancient oak trees, the predecessors of which gave the place its name. The Drawing Room and Boudoir at the east end survive from the eighteenth century and have exceptionally fine Rococo plasterwork and joinery, but the Garden Hall in the centre, behind the bow, is entirely Marshall Sisson's. It has a late rather than mid-eighteenth-century character, thanks to the Ionic columns and excellent mahogany doors salvaged from James Wyatt's Henham Hall in Suffolk, which was demolished in the early 1950s.

Penkridge
24; 5 miles S of Stafford on A449
ST MICHAEL'S, a grand church of red sandstone, formidably embattled, was once one of the six collegiate churches of Staffordshire, with its own Dean and four canons. Looking at it from Station Road in the east there is only the huge Decorated east window to suggest that the building was even thought of before about 1400, or even later. It comes, therefore, as quite a shock to go inside and find yourself in an interior which, apart from that east window again and those in the clerestory, is purest Early English – a good 150 years earlier, mutton dressed as lamb. The lower windows of chancel and aisles are agreeably ambiguous; actually Perpendicular, but with shapes that fall so smoothly into the thirteenth-century idiom that Pevsner has suggested that they might even be earlier material, re-used. There are splendid sixteenth- and seventeenth-century monuments to the Littletons of nearby Pillaton Hall.

PILLATON HALL lies a mile or so away to the south. It was built in the fifteenth century as four ranges around a quadrangle, but there remains only the northern one, with a Henry VIII Gatehouse and, to the east of it, a tiny Chapel of 1480, which is very beautiful. In the eighteenth century the Littletons moved to Teddesley Hall, a couple of miles away, but this was demolished after the Second World War and Pillaton has recently been restored as the family house after a long period of neglect.

Pillaton hall
See Penkridge.

Sandon
25; 4 miles NE of Stafford on A51
The CHURCH OF ALL SAINTS is a lovely, broad country church, alone in the middle of the park. Its story begins with the south aisle, which was the nave of the original thirteenth-century church and then in about 1300 was enlarged northwards, being simultaneously relegated to its present status. Soon after that, a north aisle was added, as the Decorated tracery shows. But the real beauty of the church lies less in its architecture than in its furnishings: benches, chancel screen with gallery on top forming the Harrowby family pew (an unusual arrangement), pulpit with tester – all are of the mid-seventeenth century. The chancel, which was discreetly refitted by Samuel Wyatt in 1782, is a further fascination. Very long, with a wonderful arch-braced roof, it contains some tremendous tombs, the best of which is to Samson Erdeswick, the antiquary and first historian of Staffordshire, who died in 1603. There he lies against the north wall, half as large again as he was in life, with two full-size beruffed and bonneted wives kneeling in niches above him. His, too, is the *trompe l'œil* window and painted family tree nearby. Much of the impact of the church is from a sensitive restoration in the 1920s by Caröe.

The Sandon estate is a feudal oasis midway between Stoke and Stafford. The large and abruptly undulating PARK is well planted; the eighteenth-century landscaping is by William Eames and John Webb, and there are many Victorian trees of botanical interest. In a surprise valley to the east of the house is an excellent quadrangular model farm of pink sandstone designed by Samuel Wyatt in 1778; and on a hilltop nearby is an Italianate pavilion, which in fact is the top of Barry's tower from Trentham, brought here in 1910. The HALL itself is by Burn and is a typical early Victorian house – just asymmetrical and just Jacobean. The interior is pleasant, with large, airy rooms containing magnificent eighteenth-century marble chimneypieces and excellent paintings and furniture – the family heirlooms of the Earls of Harrowby who live here. The Victorian gardens contain a conservatory, an Orangery, a temple (made out of the eighteenth-century front door of the previous house), and an excellent Coade stone sundial dated 1808. The gates at the entrance to the park and the adjoining group of cottages, pub and club were all designed by Guy Dawber in 1902 and make an impressive Arts and Crafts overture to the splendours within the park wall.

Shugborough

NT; 26; 4 miles E of Stafford on A513

Shugborough as it stands today is essentially a monument to two brothers, Thomas and George Anson.
Thomas, who inherited the estate in 1720, was an enlightened and cultivated patron of the arts, a founder
member of the Society of Dilettanti for the encouragement of 'Greek Taste and Roman Spirit'; his younger
brother George was the greatest admiral of his day, who
transformed the Navy as dramatically and successfully
as Thomas was to transform their family home here in
Staffordshire.

In 1740 the two brothers set sail in different directions. Thomas headed for the Levant, in search of classical antiquities – for which, however, he possessed
nowhere near enough money to indulge his taste as he
would have liked. George sailed west in his flagship
Centurion, to return four years later after an epic circum-
navigation of the world during which, among many
nightmarish disasters, he had had the good luck to capture the annual Spanish 'Manila Galleon' with its cargo
worth £400,000.

From that moment on the Admiral was able, through
his prize money, to finance his brother's building work
at Shugborough, and when he died childless in 1762
Thomas was his sole heir. By then the seven-bay,
three-storey house of 1693 had been substantially enlarged by
the addition of flanking pavilions, attached to the centre
by single-storey links – the work, almost certainly, of
Thomas Wright; but Anson, suddenly at sixty-six finding himself a rich man, was now able to call on his old
friend James Stuart – another Dilettanti member – to
design further improvements to the house and, above
all, the PARK.

'Athenian' Stuart had travelled widely in Greece and
Turkey in 1751–5, accompanied by his fellow-architect
Nicholas Revett, with whom in 1762 he had published
his *Antiquities of Athens*, thereby effectively launching
the neo-classical style. Few traces now exist of his work
in the house, unless the addition of a second storey to the
two link buildings can be ascribed to him; but the copies
of Athenian monuments with which he adorned the park
are, after the Doric Temple at Hagley in Worcestershire
(*q.v.*), the earliest manifestations of neo-classicism in the
country. They include the TOWER OF THE WINDS, THE
CHORAGIC MONUMENT OF LYSICRATES (more usually, if
inaccurately, known as the Lanthorn of Demosthenes),
and the ARCH OF HADRIAN – this last transformed into a
memorial to the Admiral, with commemorative carvings
by Peter Scheemakers. Among the slightly earlier garden
monuments (as opposed to those in the park), the DORIC
TEMPLE may also be by Stuart – there are obvious
similarities to the one at Hagley – but documentary
evidence is lacking and we cannot be sure.

The park still looks much as Thomas Anson and Stuart
left it; the house, on the other hand, was due for further
important changes at the hands of Anson's great-
nephew, the first Viscount. His architect was Samuel
Wyatt (James's elder brother), whose most obvious alterations were the building of the octostyle Ionic portico
along the central block of the east front and the simul-

The Library, Shugborough.

taneous transfer of the balustrade from this block to the
two wings. These wings he enlarged to the west,
developing the Dining Room bow upwards into a
projecting centre that runs the whole height of the
house. Finally, yet another bow was constructed to the
south – bows were very much his speciality.

Inside the house, the best things are Wyatt's elliptical
Entrance Hall, the magnificent Dining Room (formerly
the Drawing Room and the creation of Thomas Wright)
and – surely everybody's favourite – the Library, its two
parts linked by a transverse depressed arch so thick (5
feet) that it is almost a tunnel, since it in fact penetrates
the outer wall of the original house. It is supported on
small Ionic columns, on each side of which are cunningly
placed mirrors that continue the lines of bookshelves
and as a result make the room look considerably longer
than it is.

Shugborough's great tragedy occurred in 1842, when
the 1st Earl of Lichfield, having reduced himself to
penury by disastrous speculations on the Turf and
elsewhere, had virtually the entire contents of the house
put up for sale, including the pictures and statuary
amassed by Thomas Anson and a good deal of the
Admiral's *memorabilia*. Fortunately, his son proved a
discriminating collector of French furniture, and several
of the most important items sold have gradually returned to their own home, so there is plenty left to see.
But if all the original belongings were still here, what a
treasure-house it might have been!

Stafford

27; 16 miles S of Stoke-on-Trent on A34

The SHIRE HALL in the Market Place at Stafford is the only complete work by Samuel Wyatt's assistant John Harvey. It is remarkably good – so good that one finds oneself wondering whether he was indeed solely responsible; might his master not have had a hand in it himself? Apart from that, I find Stafford a rather disappointing town; though half a century ago there would probably have been much to admire, post-war planning and modern traffic have taken a hideous toll. The best thing is ST CHAD'S CHURCH. The outside, with its Perpendicular crossing-tower and its west front by the ubiquitous G.G. Scott, is scarcely promising; but the great sturdy Norman nave and clerestory and the splendid chancel arch make up for a lot.

Stone

28; 8 miles S of Stoke-on-Trent on A34

Though close to the industrial sprawl of the Potteries, Stone still has some of the atmosphere of an old country town. The High Street has several seemly red brick Georgian buildings, of which the CROWN HOTEL, designed by Henry Holland in 1778, is the best. It has two suave semicircular bow windows flanking an Ionic porch detailed with all Holland's usual refinement and elegance, but the interior is a crashing disappointment, for it has been done up in 'Brewers' Olde Worlde' style; how on earth was this allowed? The most prominent building in Stone is JOULES' OLD BREWERY, established here in the early eighteenth century. It is no longer a working brewery, just a distribution depot for Bass Charrington, but the original Georgian Brewers' House survives as offices.

The parish CHURCH is an interesting example of eighteenth-century Gothick. It was designed by William Robinson of the Board of Works and executed under the supervision of William Baker, a gentleman-architect from Cheshire. It is a rectangular box with a square tower at the west end, the whole building ornate with battlements and two tiers of windows with Y-tracery. The body of the church survives, with galleries on either side and box pews miraculously intact. As so often, however, the chancel was remodelled in the nineteenth century and, though not bad of its kind, it spoils the appearance of the church. The Georgian altar painting – a large canvas of the church's patron saint, Michael the Archangel – has been relegated to the north gallery. Admiral St Vincent, whose family came from Stone, is buried here, and his monument is embellished with a long epitaph and a lifelike marble bust by Chantrey. In the graveyard, the Jervis MAUSOLEUM was also designed by Robinson.

The CATHOLIC CHURCH at the other end of the town forms part of a convent, and in the garden is a little chapel by A.W. Pugin, although it is not among his best works.

Swinfen Hall

29; 2 miles S of Lichfield on A38

Stranded like a zoo curiosity behind the barbed-wire of an open prison is the earliest surviving work of the Wyatt family of architects. They originated in Staffordshire, at nearby Weeford. Benjamin Wyatt, a farmer turned builder, designed and built Swinfen in 1755; he was assisted by his sons William and Samuel, but not by James, who was to become the most famous of them all. It is an old-fashioned house for its date, red brick and three-storeyed, with giant Ionic pilasters at the corners and a pedimented Tuscan doorcase in the middle.

In the centre of the house is a two-storeyed Hall with good plasterwork of the date of the house. Other rooms are decorated in a similar rich mid-eighteenth-century style. They should be viewed with a certain amount of caution, however, for in 1913 considerable alterations and additions were carried out in a sympathetic adaptation of the original style; the large wing to one side is of that date.

The house is not really used by the prison and has been empty for years, though it is well maintained. It is a great shame that such a fine building does not have a proper occupant; presumably prospective new owners would be deterred by the Nissen-hut-type structures occupied by the prisoners and the wire fences around the place?

Swynnerton

30; 8 miles S of Stoke-on-Trent off A51

The village of Swynnerton is unusually arranged: two imposing CHURCHES, one Protestant, one Roman Catholic, within a few yards of each other; and, looming up between them, in the village but not entirely of it, the haughty aristocratic back of SWYNNERTON HALL facing outwards, Petworth-like, across the glorious parkland behind. The Catholic Church is Victorian, of 1868, opulent enough for anybody but of no real interest. The Protestant one is originally Norman – see in particular the west door *inside* the tower – but with later accretions of various periods. Its most precious treasure is the 7-foot seated statue of Christ, which could not be later than about 1280. Its origins are a mystery. The Hall, which is not open to the public, can be properly seen only from the park. It is attributed, almost certainly rightly, to Francis Smith of Warwick – though the interior was much altered early in the last century by James Trubshaw, one of that remarkable Staffordshire family who produced five competent architects in five successive generations.

Tamworth

31; 7½ miles SE of Lichfield on A51

In the eighth century Tamworth was the principal capital of Offa, King of Mercia and builder of the celebrated Dyke. Alas, the post-war planners have shown it no mercy, even to the extent of erecting six huge tower blocks of flats, which are not only visually disastrous but, in a country town of some 40,000 souls, totally unnecessary. Why, then, include it here? Because it possesses two buildings that cannot possibly be omitted. One is the castle; the other is the parish church.

The CASTLE has a splendid seat on a high mound overlooking the River Tame, with access up a steep and narrow path. The earliest surviving fabric is the late eleventh-century herringbone masonry just below the entrance; the roughly circular shell keep probably dates from about 1150. But what really gives the place its interest is not the Norman work, but the fact that a large and quite opulent house has been rather uncomfortably and incongruously squashed inside it. The Great Hall of this house, in which you find yourself immediately upon entering the castle, was probably built by Sir Thomas Ferrers around 1430, though the huge mullioned-and-transomed window is obviously a Jacobean addition. It was in the seventeenth century, too, that the house acquired its present proportions; the other principal rooms – the State Drawing Room, the Oak Room (with a tremendous overmantel) and the State Dining Room on the first floor and the Long Gallery on the second – all date from between, say, 1620 and 1660. A particular pleasure is the little open walkway running inside the castle wall at second-floor level; from it you can look down on to the house and see what an extraordinary construction it is. The whole castle, incidentally, is now the borough museum, and is blessed with a particularly helpful and well-informed staff.

The CHURCH OF ST EDITHA is a good deal more interesting than it looks at first glance, since the exterior suffered from *three* separate Victorian restorations, by Benjamin Ferrey, G.G. Scott and William Butterfield respectively. The interior, without escaping as it were Scott-free, still retains much to wonder at, beginning with the tremendously Baroque monument which is the first thing you see when you enter under the tower. It is to Sir John Ferrers, and was designed – though probably not actually carved – by Grinling Gibbons. The tower originally stood over the crossing, where the grand Norman arches still exist to north and south. The western arch and the chancel arch, however, have gone and were not replaced; the result is a long and uninterrupted vista right up to the high altar and – more unexpected still – westwards from the chancel through the empty-traceried inner west window (i.e. inside the tower) to the outer one beyond. At the south-west corner of the tower is a fascinating staircase in a double spiral – two staircases winding up a single newel, starting from opposite sides and never meeting. (If the door to this is locked, ask for it to be opened; the authorities seem to be unaccountably reluctant to show it.)

One other building, I think, deserves special mention. It is the TOWN HALL, a delightful little job of 1701, brick, with pretty round-headed windows at the front – the narrow end – three rows of Tuscan arches supporting it underneath, and a white ogive-capped lantern with weathervane on top. It was a present to the town from Thomas Guy, the founder of Guy's Hospital and MP for Tamworth, who made a killing with the South Sea Bubble. In front of it stands the statue of one of Guy's even more distinguished parliamentary successors, Sir Robert Peel. His son thought it looked exactly like him.

Tean
32; 6 miles W of Uttoxeter on A50
A classic example of a patriarchal industrial village, Tean is set in wild moorland country south of Cheadle (*q.v.*) and complete with mill, Nonconformist chapels and terraces of weavers' cottages; the early nineteenth-century parish church and big house were both built for the mill owner John Burton Philips to the design of Thomas Johnson of Lichfield. The Philips family established the tape industry here in the mid-eighteenth century; tradition says that they brought over a Dutchman in 1747 to instruct the locals in how to build looms.

The large MILL is of various dates. The original eighteenth-century section is of eleven bays with a pediment and cupola; the bell in the latter is dated 1833. In 1823 a four-storeyed extension of twenty-three bays was added and further additions were made in 1885. This huge building dominates the village like a medieval castle, the cottages arranged loosely in terraces round it. The MANAGER'S HOUSE is a splendid affair, incorporating a half-timbered building of 1613 to which was added an eighteenth-century brick wing with sash windows and stone corner pilasters. The home of the Philips family, HEATH HOUSE, stands on high ground to the east in a beautiful wooded setting. It was built in 1836 in the Jacobethan style and is an excellent example of the genre, built of rough ashlar stone with shaped gables, a tower and a *porte-cochère*. The interior retains much original decoration and has an impressive Staircase Hall. The grounds are embellished with a classical temple, an Orangery and three sets of lodges.

Tixall
33; 3 miles E of Stafford off A513
The Elizabethan mansion, built for Sir Walter Aston around 1575, in which Mary Queen of Scots was held prisoner eleven years later, was burnt down in the eighteenth century and its successor demolished in 1926. Mercifully – almost miraculously – the GATEHOUSE survives, the largest and most majestic of its date in the country. Three storeys high – four in the polygonal angle turrets – it has four-light windows, mullioned and transomed, framed by pairs of columns of all three orders – Doric below, Ionic above, Corinthian on top; and in the spandrels of the central archway are reclining figures, crumbling a bit but still recognisable – angels on one side, soldiers on the other. A few years ago this glorious building was a hollow, roofless shell; then, thank heaven, it was acquired by the Landmark Trust, faultlessly restored and made comfortable for those well-advised families who rent it by the week or month for their holidays. Four gilded weathervanes, one on each turret, mark the completion of this splendid work. '1', they say, '9', '7', '6' – 1976, and Tixall lives again.

Trentham
34; 3 miles S of Stoke-on-Trent on A34
Just where the suburban sprawl of Stoke-on-Trent begins are the impressive gates to Trentham Hall, a vanished ducal palace, and on the opposite side of the road the squat, sombre form of a neo-classical mausoleum. Trentham was originally a priory of Augustinian monks but was acquired by the Levesons in 1540. Subsequent generations married heiress after heiress, becoming Leveson-Gower, Barons, Earls and Marquesses of Stafford, and finally Dukes of Sutherland, and

the greatest and richest landowners of nineteenth-century Britain, 'leviathans of wealth'. Although they owned many seats, Trentham remained the chief one and underwent many transformations. The seventeenth-century manor house was replaced in the early eighteenth century by a classical brick house by Smith of Warwick; this in turn was enlarged and remodelled in the late eighteenth century by Capability Brown and Henry Holland. Finally, in the middle of the nineteenth century Sir Charles Barry doubled the size of the house and transformed it into a grand Italianate *palazzo* with tower, *porte-cochère* and vast formal gardens designed by Nesfield. Most of this was demolished in 1910 because of the pollution of the river with effluent from Stoke-on-Trent. The top of the tower was bought by Lord Harrowby and has migrated to Sandon (*q.v.*). The gardens survive in a modified form and are open to the public in the summer. The remaining fragments recall the glory that once was here. Formal flower-beds still overlook the vast lake, with Capability's hanging woods framing the opposite shore where, on a distant hilltop, a giant bronze statue on a squat column commemorates the first Duke. But when you turn around, there is a great emptiness where the house was. The *porte-cochère*, the dull south side of Barry's church and an ugly utilitarian exhibition hall form a poor substitute for the architectural grandeur of the house.

The CHURCH OF ST MARY AND ALL SAINTS contains an impressive array of Leveson monuments, beginning in the sixteenth century and culminating in the marble tombs of the 1st Duke and Duchess, which have statues by Chantrey and Noble. The best surviving building at Trentham is the MAUSOLEUM designed by C.H. Tatham in 1807 and situated on the roadside because 'the Ancients usually built their tombs near the highways, which reminded them of their ancestors', as a commentator pointed out on its completion in 1808. It is a ruthless cyclopean design of ashlar stone with sloping sides and a small central tower topped by a gold cross. It is a pity that new housing development has been allowed to creep so close; this is a building that needs to be seen in splendid isolation.

Tutbury
35; 6 miles N of Burton upon Trent on A50
TUTBURY CASTLE, crowning its hill and commanding splendid views over the River Dove to Derbyshire, was once the residence of John of Gaunt, time-honoured Lancaster, to whose Duchy it still belongs today. He would still recognise the remains of the twelfth-century Chapel, and also the north-east gateway, completed only a few years before his arrival in 1361; the rest is a magnificent jumble of styles and periods. To the south, near the entrance, stand the former King's Lodgings of the 1630s, when the castle served Charles I as a hunting lodge; east of them is the South Tower – really two towers – of the fifteenth century, as is the North Tower opposite. West of the King's Lodgings, to the north, is the agreeably dotty early nineteenth-century Folly Keep.

But all these buildings seem insignificant compared with the terrific west front of ST MARY'S CHURCH, a little

below the castle to the east. The doorway is set inside no less than seven orders, richly and fancifully carved with dogtooth, beak-heads, animals, the lot. One of these orders is of alabaster, alleged to be its earliest use in England. I confess to having been unable to decide which it was; and since Pevsner claims it is the outermost, while the local guide leaflet identifies it as the second one outwards from the door, others seem to have had the same trouble. No matter; the effect is just as overwhelming whatever the material. Above the door is another great three-layer arch, enclosing a Decorated window that looks wildly incongruous in so robust a setting; interlaced blind arches, lavishly zigzagged, run off to each side, with three similarly adorned roundels above them. There is another noble Norman door on the south side; its lintel depicts a boar hunt, but the carving is too worn to be of any real pleasure.

Pleasure is renewed, however, by walking inside. Of the old Norman monastic church there remains only the nave, but a very magnificent one it is – the eastern piers circular, the western ones with two half-columns attached to them at opposite sides, giving them a curious cross-section like an elongated quatrefoil. Above the two eastern bays is what at first appears to be a Norman clerestory but is in fact the remains of a gallery. Look at the way the vaulting shafts are suddenly cut off at the top; once they soared up to a real clerestory, but that has gone and the roof has been lowered accordingly.

The original apsed chancel was destroyed at the time of the Dissolution of the Monasteries in 1538. (The nave owed its preservation to the fortunate fact only that, as in so many abbeys, it was used as the parish church.) The present chancel is a replacement of 1867 by Street: a great broad apse – he followed the line of the old foundations – lit by three two-light windows, widely spaced. In Street's day the floor was 2–3 feet higher to allow for heating pipes underneath; in 1937 it was restored to its original level, with the result that the apse looks rather more lofty than it was meant to and the sedilia are unusable. Nonetheless, the whole thing seems to me a beautiful and sensitive reconstruction which does its designer much credit.

Uttoxeter
36; 12½ miles SE of Longton on A50
Well known for its racecourse, Uttoxeter is an ancient market town on the border between Staffordshire and Derbyshire, set in lovely country where the Midlands meet the north. It is best approached from Derbyshire over the River Dove, via the medieval bridge and down narrow streets to the MARKET PLACE. This comprises two irregular spaces surrounded by an unspoilt assemblage of old timbered buildings, red brick Georgian houses, and jolly Victorian interpolations. In the centre of one of the squares is the domed and pedimented WEIGHING HOUSE designed in 1854 by Thomas Fradgley, the local architect. He was responsible also for the classical TOWN HALL in the High Street, built in 1853. In the other square is a Gothic MARKET CROSS erected as a war memorial in 1922. All the adjoining streets have worthwhile houses; Church Street is the best with a pretty Gothick house

(now County Court Offices), the pedimented Manor House, and Jervis House with its canted bay windows. ST MARY'S CHURCH has a fourteenth-century tower and a spire that forms the principal accent of the town, but it is not otherwise architecturally special, having been reconstructed and gone over at different dates in the nineteenth century; nevertheless, it has a nice atmosphere. ALLEYNE'S GRAMMAR SCHOOL nearby is a large assemblage of Victorian buildings.

The Market Place at Uttoxeter was the scene of Dr Johnson's penance. He had once refused to help his father with his bookstall there; in later life he bitterly regretted this, and at the age of seventy went back to the spot, bare-headed in the rain: 'In contrition I stood, and I hope the penance was expiated.' A tablet commemorates the event.

West Bromwich

37; 5 miles NW of Birmingham on M5

In 1953 something very exciting happened at West Bromwich. Half a mile or so west of the parish church, in Hall Green Road, a group of derelict, apparently nineteenth-century tenements awaiting demolition were found to conceal, beneath layers of brick and crumbling stucco, the fourteenth-century MANOR HOUSE of Bromwich, complete with a Great Hall almost intact, a solar wing, south wing, chapel, kitchen block and even a timber-framed Elizabethan gatehouse. The Hall is the oldest part – about 1300, perhaps even very slightly earlier. It has a tremendous central truss, a dais and a screens passage – to which two ogee-headed doorways give access – with a stairway at the end leading up to the solar.

Hats off to the local council, who decided to restore this splendid building and stuck to their decision, in spite of the considerable expense and a barrage of criticism, in the years following. The Manor House is now a pub and restaurant, most of whose patrons appear sublimely unaware of their venerable surroundings. No matter; a rare treasure has been saved. Protected and profitable – an all too infrequent combination – its future is assured, and we are the beneficiaries.

There is one other quietly spectacular building in West Bromwich; that is OAK HOUSE in Oak Road, now the borough museum. Timber-framed and grandly gabled, it seems mostly of the early sixteenth century, though the prospect tower is presumably rather later and the brick part behind must be Jacobean. But if your time in the town is short (and there is no reason to linger) it is to the Manor House you must go.

Weston-under-Lizard

38; 17 miles SW of Stafford on A5

WESTON PARK is more a village than a house; the tightly packed complex of brick and stone emphasises that this is the capital of a large estate. Like most great houses, Weston occupies a medieval site, as the proximity of the parish church bears witness. Although it has passed by inheritance, it has seen more changes of family than most, owing to successive failures of male lines. From the de Westons it passed to the Myttons, the last of whom –

The Temple of Diana, Weston Park.

Elizabeth – married Sir Thomas Wilbraham in the mid-seventeenth century. They had no son and so Weston passed again by marriage, this time to the Newports, Earls of Bradford of the first creation. But after one generation they too failed, and once again the house passed through a daughter, to the Bridgemans of Castle Bromwich, who were descended from Charles II's Keeper of the Privy Seal. Sir Henry Bridgeman, who inherited in 1762, was created Lord Bradford, and in 1815 his son Orlando was created Earl of Bradford of the second creation.

Weston Park is a remarkably early example of the classical style. It was designed in 1671 by Lady Wilbraham herself; a copy of Palladio annotated by her is still treasured in the Library, but the house owes as much to French example as to Italian – particularly in the two semi-circular pediments on the park front. Despite its size, it has a domestic feel. The warm brick, which contributes so much, was stuccoed in the nineteenth century and only revealed again in the 1930s.

Inside the house nothing survives from the seventeenth century and the light cheerful rooms that the visitor passes through are the result of three later remodellings. In the mid-eighteenth century the screens of columns in the Library and Drawing Room, and the splendid marble chimneypieces, were introduced. From the 1860s to the 1890s the house was reoriented and the large Dining Room and marble staircase installed. Finally, in the 1960s the Victorian rooms were remodelled and several other rooms were cleverly redecorated by the Dowager Countess of Bradford. One is glad, however, that the Tapestry Room and Library have not been altered and still retain an elusive mellow quality. The Library, with grained woodwork, has great charm; the Tapestry Room is hung with one of the six sets of Boucher-Neilson tapestries woven for English clients at the Gobelins factory in France in the late eighteenth century. (Five of the sets still remain in English country houses.)

The palatial Dining Room is the most dramatic of the redecorated rooms, with its lofty ceiling embellished with new stucco by Jacksons and rose-coloured wallpaper specially made in Italy. It was finished in time for the coming of age of the present Earl of Bradford in 1968. The former Billiards Room and Smoking Room in the centre of the house have been rearranged as picture galleries; they are redolent of English eighteenth- and early nineteenth-century taste, with Dutch cabinet pictures and landscapes by Vernet and Salvator Rosa. One of the purposes of the rearrangement of Weston has been to display the pictures to their best advantage. The most interesting smaller portraits, including Holbein's *Sir George Carew*, now hang in the Breakfast Room, while the Dining Room is ablaze with newly cleaned Van Dycks of the highest quality.

The PARK at Weston was landscaped by Capability Brown. It contains subsidiary buildings designed in the 1760s for Sir Henry Bridgeman, who was among the great 'improvers' of his generation; the Home Farm has been called 'one of the noblest architectural products of the agricultural revolution'. There are two lakes, a Roman bridge, Swiss cottage, obelisk, Grecian mausoleum, Gothic tower, boathouses, seats and well-sited urns. The finest piece of architecture is the TEMPLE OF DIANA by James Paine, which contains an Orangery, tea room, music room and china room within its small compass and commands arcadian vistas.

In addition to the house, Lady Wilbraham also designed the stables and parish CHURCH OF ST ANDREW. The latter contains a typical series of family monuments, the finest of which is that by Peter Hollins to the 1st Countess of Bradford; it is dated 1842.

Wightwick Manor★

NT; 39; 3 miles W of Wolverhampton on A454
Standing only 3 miles from the centre of Wolverhampton, Wightwick (pronounced 'Wittick') just manages to remain a country house. Despite its considerable size, however, it is not in any sense a stately home. It was built in black-and-white timber-framed style by Edward Ould, of the famous Liverpool firm of Grayson and Ould, between 1887 and 1893, and was designed for comfort and good solid Victorian domesticity; there is no attempt to impress. Yet impress it does, less because of its architecture than because it has been preserved as a shrine to William Morris and the Pre-Raphaelite Brotherhood. Nothing is allowed to spoil the atmosphere of late nineteenth-century aestheticism. Thus the Great Parlour – the principal room of the house, which rises through both floors to a panelled open-timber roof and a gallery at one end – contains a plaster frieze by C.E. Kempe (who also provided the stained glass for many of the windows) telling the story of Orpheus and Eurydice, tapestry by Morris, tiles by William De Morgan and pictures by Burne-Jones (*Love Among the Ruins*), Watts, Millais and Holman Hunt. In the Drawing Room, over the piano – made for the Crystal Palace Exhibition of

1851 and winner of a gold medal in Paris in 1878 – is a portrait of Mrs Morris begun by Ford Madox Brown and finished by Rossetti, who added the unmistakable red hair of his own wife, Elizabeth Siddal, for good measure, and another of Effie Ruskin (later Millais) by Watts. The Drawing Room walls are covered with Morris's silk-and-wool tapestry; the chimneypiece has a surround of De Morgan tiles. Upstairs in the Oak Room you will find a gesso *cassone* by Burne-Jones, a settle designed by Bodley and decorated by Kempe, and Swinburne's folding bed and cupboard from The Pines (Swinburne's home in Putney), bought at Sotheby's for a guinea in 1939. The list can be prolonged *ad infinitum* – yet Wightwick is never a museum; it remains a house that is lived in and loved. With Standen in Sussex and 18 Stafford Terrace, London, it is one of the country's three great monuments to enlightened greenery-yallery Victorian taste – thanks to Lady Mander, and her late husband Sir Geoffrey, who gave the house to the National Trust and greatly enriched the collection.

Wootton Lodge★

40; 5 miles N of Rocester off B5032
The distant prospect of Wootton Lodge is, for my money, the most serenely beautiful architectural vision to be had in all Staffordshire. It stands in that wild, remote, romantic country that people tend to associate with Derbyshire; the road rounds a hill and suddenly there is the house before you – and a little below you too, so that you are looking at it from roughly the height of its first-floor windows. It was almost certainly built in the first decade of the seventeenth century, and very probably by that greatest of Elizabethan architects, Robert Smythson – perhaps the very last house that he ever designed and perhaps the loveliest. The setting, first of all, is perfect; the house rises from a little spur, which distances it from its background of woodland and rolling hills and, on a day of changing light, can allow it to stand out in dramatic relief in a way that few houses in England are able to do. Then there are the proportions; it is tall for its breadth – three storeys over a high basement and only five bays across – but there is an unusually long distance between the outer bays and the angles; and this space, together with the two semi-circular bays that project to each side from points just round the corners, gives the building, as it were, elbow room. It also allows the architect to emphasise the height, just as at Hardwick (*q.v.*), by increasing the verticality of the windows as they ascend – the basement untransomed, the first floor with one transom, the two upper floors with two each. There is a balustrade around the top, above which the chimneys rise in neat, orderly groups, looking rather like castles on a chessboard.

None of the original Jacobean interior survives at Wootton. The house was largely gutted during the Civil War and contains nothing predating the eighteenth century. But the interior is not, and never has been, the point. It is the outside that counts, and above all that staggering show front. With it the late Elizabethan style of building reaches its ultimate perfection – and stops, in a gentle glow of glory. An epoch is at an end.

Warwickshire

Warwickshire is rolling, wooded, uneventful Midlands country, quintessentially English with its pretty villages, unspoilt market towns and prosperous country houses. The post-1974 county is almost entirely rural, because the heavily industrialised north-west corner, containing Birmingham and Coventry, was hived off into an independent unit called the 'West Midlands'. But historically these two industrial cities are part of Warwickshire and it is from them that much of the county's recent wealth derives. If the roads seem crammed to the gills with cars, if the cottages are lavishly done up to make tasteful *bijou* residences, if Leamington is a smart commuter town, if the country houses have the comfortable air of knowing that there is a sound ballbearings-manufacturing fortune underpinning them – all this is due to the proximity of swarthy Birmingham. The county is as haunted by nearby industry as it is by the ghost of Shakespeare. It is because of the Bard that Warwickshire is prime tourist country, walked over by millions of visitors' feet every year. The tourists come primarily to see Shakespeare's birthplace at Stratford-upon-Avon rather than any special beauties of landscape or interesting historic architecture, but they will not be disappointed by the latter. The south-east of the county, bordering Worcestershire, Gloucestershire, Oxfordshire and Northamptonshire, is the most agreeable part, rather like the Cotswolds but less austere and with a richer mixture of natural building materials, thanks to a more complex geology. But even close to Coventry and Birmingham there is surprisingly unspoilt country; its dairy farms are neatly hedged and the plentiful woodland recalls that this was once the Forest of Arden. As for architecture, Warwickshire contains one of the most interesting conglomerations of good buildings of all periods to be found anywhere in England.

There are impressive medieval churches, including some especially lavish Perpendicular work in the parish church at Stratford, the chancel and Beauchamp Chapel at Warwick, and the two large medieval parish churches of Coventry. The secular architecture of the Middle Ages is even more richly represented: Kenilworth, Maxstoke and Warwick Castles, Baddesley Clinton, Coughton Court and Compton Wynyates are all first-rate examples of their type, as are such timber-framed public buildings as Leycester's Hospital in Warwick, the three hospitals in Coventry, or the Grammar School and Almshouses at Stratford. The latter, like many other villages and towns, has good sixteenth-century timber-framed houses, albeit much restored. The best pieces of Elizabethan architecture in the county, however, are the delightful Gatehouse at Charlecote and the ruins of Leicester's Building at Kenilworth Castle – one of the most dramatic demonstrations of Elizabeth I's policy of not spending money on her own palaces but instead getting her courtiers to build suitable houses in which to entertain her during her summer progresses. Aston Hall, now stranded in the middle of Birmingham, is among the most spectacular of Jacobean houses, even in its present dingy setting. The late seventeenth century is particularly well represented in the richly decorated state rooms at Warwick Castle, the chapel and stables at Arbury, the austerely grand exterior of Ragley Hall, and not least Honington Hall – one of the most desirable of all Caroline country houses, which, together with its neighbouring parish church, forms a perfect manorial group.

The eighteenth century in Warwickshire is especially interesting because of the activities of several talented native-born architects. Thomas Archer was born at Umberslade and his unique (for England) Borromini-esque Baroque style is demonstrated in Birmingham Cathedral. William and Francis Smith of Warwick, who were active in the country house field all over the Midland counties, left their masterpiece in the mighty west wing of Stoneleigh Abbey. Later, William and Francis Hiorn also operated from Warwick. William Hiorn was involved in the origination of the plan for Arbury Hall, that most perfect of eighteenth-century Gothick houses. Hardly less attractive than Arbury is Alscot Park, near Stratford. Indeed, Warwickshire has a notable place in the history of the English Gothic Revival. The nave and tower of St Mary's, Warwick, are among the earliest major eighteenth-century Gothick church work. Sanderson Miller, of Radway Grange, was a pioneer of Gothick and, as well as embellishing his own house and erecting the Tower on Edgehill, was much consulted by his neighbours. Gothic Revival can be seen to perfection, at the moment it gets serious, in Rickman's splendid church at Hampton Lucy – still with plaster vaults and cast-iron tracery, but solidly executed and archaeologically correct.

In England, Gothick was a manifestation of Rococo, and more conventional Rococo decoration is not lacking in Warwickshire either. The Hall at Ragley, designed by James Gibbs, has the most sumptuous plasterwork and equally good, though smaller-scale, interior decoration of the same date is to be found in the octagonal Saloon at Honington and in the rooms at Farnborough, where there is also a beautiful mid-eighteenth-century landscaped garden with terrace walk, obelisk and temples laid out with the advice of Sanderson Miller. Capability Brown was responsible for several masterpieces, including the grounds at Warwick Castle and the park of Packington. The latter is a notable eighteenth-century house containing a unique large-scale scheme of Pompeian decoration in the gallery. The adjoining parish church, designed by the owner Lord Aylesford himself and his architect Bonomi, is a powerful work of the neo-classical imagination, comparable with Boullée or Ledoux.

Architectural riches continue into the nineteenth century with such characteristic Victorian country houses as Merevale and Ettington, the remarkably well-preserved interiors of Charlecote, the Roman temple of a town hall in Birmingham, and, of course, Leamington – that complete Regency and early Victorian spa town, its stucco terraces and its villas all beautifully kept. The architectural interest of Warwickshire continues up to the present. While the 1960s' centre of Birmingham is a crashing disappointment compared with city centres in America, or even Germany, Coventry is, for better or for worse, a pioneer example of post-war planning, and particularly worth a visit for Sir Basil Spence's Arts and Crafts cathedral. The current proposals for rebuilding the burnt Victorian part of the Royal Shakespeare Theatre at Stratford look promising, while the town's new National Farmers' Union headquarters gives grounds for confidence that the county's tradition of good and original architecture will be continued.

Alcester

1; 7½ miles W of Stratford-upon-Avon on the A422

This small, ancient town stands astride a Roman road at the confluence of the Rivers Arrow and Alne. It was a Roman market centre and recent excavations have turned up some evidence of the layout of the Roman buildings, although nothing remains above ground. The general impression is of a well-kept Midlands town, free from eye-sores and modern redevelopment. The main axis is the High Street, with one or two half-timbered houses, the Italianate former CORN EXCHANGE of 1857 and a couple of decent Victorian banks. BUTTER STREET, opening off the High Street, is a particularly attractive thoroughfare, very narrow and curving below its picturesque jumble of ancient roofs. At the top is CHURCHILL HOUSE, dated 1688 – small but stately, with a well-proportioned brick façade and modillion cornice. The TOWN HALL was given by Sir Fulke Greville in 1618; it has a timber-framed upper storey carried on stone arcades with Tuscan columns, now enclosed. From here Henley Street runs north. It has one good old timber-framed house, with a jettied upper storey carried on carved braces. CHURCH STREET, to the east and south of the church, has a remarkably unspoilt group of middling Georgian houses, some with bay windows, iron balconies, or restrained classical decoration. Off Church Street is Malt Hill Lane, with the oldest house in Alcester: the OLD MALT HOUSE, a timber-framed job with gables dating from c.1500.

The CHURCH OF ST NICHOLAS at first sight looks medieval but is not. The tower does indeed date from the thirteenth and fifteenth centuries, but the chancel and the nave windows are all Victorian Gothic and not very distinguished at that. The body of the church was in fact built in 1729–30 by Edward and Thomas Woodward of Chipping Campden 'under the advise, direccion and Government' of Francis Smith of Warwick, and the interior is a pleasant surprise. It is plain Georgian classical, the nave separated from the aisles by a simple coved ceiling and Tuscan columns. The east end was unfortunately messed up in 1871. The chief feature is the grand mid-sixteenth-century tomb of Sir Fulke Greville (who died in 1559), with alabaster effigies of himself and his wife on top of a tomb-chest ornamented with barley-sugar-twist colonnettes and stiff little statues of their children along the sides. The church also contains a scatter of white funerary marble to the Seymours of nearby Ragley Hall (*q.v.*); the Marquesses of Hertford are still lords of the manor of Alcester, and patrons of the church living.

Alscot Park

2; 4 miles S of Stratford-upon-Avon on the A34

Alscot Park may be little known, but it is nonetheless among the finest surviving eighteenth-century Gothick houses in England – even Horace Walpole would approve. Part of an old house survives at the back, remodelled but with the old mullion windows still showing through. A new wing, larger in scale, was added in the mid-eighteenth century by James West, Joint Secretary of the Treasury, and it is this that contains the main rooms and the entrance front. The latter has battlements, sash windows with ogee arches, and a pair of octagonal turrets topped by onion cupolas. The work was carried out by Edward Woodward to the design of Messrs Shakespear & Philips, Surveyors of London. The porch in the same style was added in the early nineteenth century to the design of Thomas Hopper, best known as the architect of the gigantic Neo-Norman Penrhyn Castle in Wales.

The interior is a feast of Gothickry, with much elaborate plaster decoration. The Hall has plaster panels with ogee arches and a pair of chimneypieces carrying busts of Shakespeare and Prior, the Drawing Room a sumptuous papier mâché fan vault, while the secondary staircase has a wrought-iron handrail and Gothick plasterwork. The main staircase is Victorian, as is the Dining Room, which contains a superb Victorian sideboard carved by William Cookes of Warwick with trophies of the chase, including a life-size dying stag.

The Saloon, Arbury Hall.

The house is beautifully maintained and in recent years has been sympathetically redecorated. The park, too – along the banks of the River Stour – is very attractive, with a Gothick greenhouse and lodges. An obelisk designed by Edward Woodward in 1757 has since disappeared.

Arbury Hall★

3; 2 miles SW of Nuneaton off B4102 [47]

Arbury is generally regarded as one of the finest unaltered examples of Gothic Revival architecture in England. Although only about 6 miles from Coventry and 9 from Meriden, it stands in a particularly attractive landscaped garden and park, rich in lakes and woods, and surrounded by an extensive area of farmland. The novelist George Eliot, who was born in one of the farms on the estate, described it in *Scenes of Clerical Life* as Cheverel Manor.

Originally an Elizabethan mansion built out of the ruins of an Augustinian monastery, Arbury was remodelled in the Gothic style by Sir Roger Newdegate, the 4th Baronet, during the last half of the eighteenth century. While on the Grand Tour he had been greatly impressed by Roman architecture, making a number of sketches of examples that particularly appealed to him. On his return he sought the advice of the architect Sanderson Miller of Radway and engaged William Hiorn of Warwick, followed by Henry Keene, the surveyor of Westminster Abbey, to carry out the work of conversion. The style adopted throughout is a fluid Perpendicular Gothic, resulting in most attractive interior

decoration; note, in particular, the fan- and barrel-vaulted ceilings in plasterwork – they are both unique and spectacular. The influence of Keene can be seen in the Saloon ceiling, which was strongly influenced by Henry VII's Chapel in Westminster Abbey. Surviving from the pre-Gothick period is the Chapel, with a sumptuous Baroque ceiling executed by Edward Martin in 1678, and also the stables, which were built at about the same time; their entrance was designed by Sir Christopher Wren.

The Long Gallery, which contains a magnificent Elizabethan fireplace, Chippendale Gothic furniture and a desk and chair once the property of the Duke of Suffolk (father of Lady Jane Grey), is used for the display of a large quantity of correspondence from the Newdegate family archives. Some items from this collection date back to the eighteenth century and are of considerable interest.

Aston Hall

See Birmingham.

Baddesley Clinton

NT; 4; 3 miles E of Hockley Heath off B4439 [64]

An ancient moated manor house, Baddesley Clinton retains its historic character to an unusual degree, thanks partly to the impoverishment of some of its owners as a result of their adherence to Catholicism. It is not large and the entrance front of grey stone looks austere; the side elevations, patched with brick, are more lovable.

The moated site of the house was probably established in the thirteenth century, though the earliest substantial remains in the present structure date from the fifteenth. Much of the house's character is given by the alterations carried out by Henry Ferrers, the antiquary, in the late sixteenth and early seventeenth centuries. He introduced most of the panelling and carved chimneypieces, and established in the house a tradition of armorial glass. His major work was the construction of the timber-framed Great Hall on the south side of the quadrangle.

The romantic atmosphere of Baddesley Clinton was carefully preserved and enhanced in the nineteenth century by Marmion and Rebecca Ferrers, the latter's aunt, Lady Chatterton, and her second husband, Heneage Dering. This eccentric quartet added the service wing, laid out the courtyard garden, recreated the Chapel in 1875 and added some portraits, Spanish leather hangings and old oak furniture to the indigenous contents of the house. These include the Ferrers family portraits and armorial glass; Flemish and Aubusson tapestries; Civil War armour; and a half-tester bed of wood from a wrecked ship of the Spanish Armada. Baddesley Clinton now belongs to the National Trust and is open to the public.

Birmingham

5; 12 miles W of Coventry on M6

The generally held view of Birmingham is that the place is an architectural rubbish dump – and it is not hard to see how that view is reached. It is not worth pausing over the tangled web of new roads or the heaps of 1960s' 'development' – like the Bull Ring – that make up the city centre and were described as 'ultra-modern' when built. Let us pass straight on, instead, to two or three buildings in the midst of all this that merit a place in this book.

ST PHILIP'S CHURCH, now BIRMINGHAM CATHEDRAL, is by Thomas Archer, a Warwickshire man, the younger son of Thomas Archer of Umberslade, country gentleman and MP. He was an amateur architect in that he did not have to rely on the profession to earn his livelihood. After Oxford he had travelled abroad and been influenced by continental Baroque, especially Bernini and Borromini, from whom he gained his fondness for convex and concave planes. That direct experience is strongly expressed in this beautiful church, which was built of stone from the family quarries at Umberslade (refaced in the nineteenth and twentieth centuries). Archer produced his design in 1709 and work was largely completed in 1715, though the tower took longer. The latter is the cathedral's most impressive feature – octagonal, with concave sides and scrolling brackets recalling Roman Baroque. Many of the details show similar Roman influence, such as the doorways with bulbous triglyphs carrying pediments, and the circular windows, which have elaborately carved frames with weird lion's-head keystones. The interior is equally impressive, but owes much of its impact to a Victorian remodelling. The chancel was added in 1883 in a remarkably accurate evoca-

Aston Hall, Birmingham.

tion of the original style. The nave is divided from the aisles by square fluted columns carrying round arches. The great thrill is the magnificent stained glass in the windows, made by William Morris and designed by Sir Edward Burne-Jones, who was born in Birmingham and baptised in this church. The unscreened kitchen, complete with sink, under the tower comes as rather a shock!

Birmingham's TOWN HALL is a full-blown Roman temple on the model of the Temple of Castor and Pollux in the Forum, standing aloof on a high, rusticated plinth and looking as if it has been left behind from a Cecil B. de Mille setting for a Hollywood epic about the Roman Empire. It comprises eight columns at the front and fifteen along the sides, with crisply carved capitals. The architect was J.A. Hansom, better known as a designer of Catholic Gothic churches and as the inventor of the Hansom cab. As a young man in 1830 he won a competition held to find an architect for the Town Hall and building began in 1832. There were financial troubles, however, and the builder went bankrupt, so the Town Hall was not actually finished until 1861. It is of brick but faced in Mona marble from Anglesey. The interior consists of one large room, redecorated by Sir Charles Allom in the 1920s in a convincing classical manner.

Until recent years, the Town Hall formed part of a group of distinguished Victorian public buildings, but some of them, including the Reference Library, have been demolished and replaced with new buildings, so unfortunately the Town Hall no longer enjoys a homogenous setting.

Situated half a mile to the north-east of the city centre, beside Aston Villa football ground, ASTON HALL lies like the skeleton of an extinct animal amidst industrial buildings and motorways. This, the finest Jacobean house in the Midlands, was begun in 1618 by Sir Thomas Holte, who moved there in 1631, though the final touches were not added until 1635. The house comprises a main block and projecting wings of diapered red brick. The east front is entirely symmetrical with a central stone Doric doorway. The strongest feature of the exterior is the romantic skyline with shaped gables and ogival-capped square turrets.

The interior is as grand as the exterior. The Hall has interesting original woodwork, though the convincing-looking plaster ceiling is probably an early nineteenth-century introduction. The main staircase is an especially splendid piece of joinery, with Ionic newels and intricate carved embellishments, including rippling sea monsters on the strings. The Great Drawing Room on the first floor has an ornate plaster ceiling, a high-relief frieze and an elaborate stone chimneypiece; there are good friezes and chimneypieces of carved stone and alabaster in some of the other rooms too. The Long Gallery is remarkably well preserved; it is 136 feet long, with oak panelling and a moulded plaster ceiling.

Aston was occupied in the early nineteenth century by James Watt, Junior, son of the pioneer manufacturer of steam engines, but it has not been used as a house for over 130 years. It is now run as a museum by Birmingham City Council.

Birmingham Cathedral.

Charlecote Park

NT; 6; 4 miles E of Stratford-upon-Avon on B4086 [48]

Set in an ancient-looking park with oak trees, avenues and deer, Charlecote has been the home of the Lucy family since the twelfth century. The house was rebuilt in the sixteenth century and substantially reconstructed in 1828–44 by George Hammond Lucy and his heiress wife Mary Elizabeth Williams; it is of special interest now as an outstanding example of early nineteenth-century Elizabethan Revival taste. Only the Gatehouse survives as a genuine piece of Elizabethan architecture — and a very charming piece it is, with little ogee-domed corner turrets and an oriel window.

The early nineteenth-century work was planned by the owner himself with the advice of Charles Smith and Charles Willement, the former a pupil of Wyatville, the latter best known as a designer of stained glass. Willement was chiefly responsible for the decoration of the three main rooms at Charlecote, designing wallpapers, carpets, textiles and furniture. The Hammond Lucys also assembled a great collection of works of art, purchasing many objects from the sale of William Beckford's collection at Fonthill; apart from the more valuable Old Masters, their collection survives intact.

The Great Hall was formed in the 1830s and makes a good introduction to the interior. Weapons, portraits and trophies of the chase are arranged on the walls, which are painted to resemble stone, and in the centre of the room is the large table with a magnificent *piètre*

Charlecote Park.

commesse top from the Borghese palace on a Gothic base designed by Beckford for Fonthill. The windows contain heraldic glass, partly sixteenth-century and partly by Willement. The Dining Room has crimson-and-blue flock paper by Willement, a panelled dado, and furniture by J.M. Willcox; the latter includes the colossal Charlecote Buffet, a virtuoso piece carved with the help of his assistant, Kendall of Warwick. Queen Victoria, to whom it was offered, described it as a 'masterpiece of genius and skill', but politely turned it down. The Library was also decorated by Willement, with bookcases carved by Willcox; the first-rate collection of books was formed partly by Sir Thomas Lucy in the sixteenth century and augmented by George Hammond Lucy in the nineteenth. The Ebony Bedroom contains the seventeenth-century Portuguese bed from the Lancaster State Bedroom at Fonthill. The Drawing Room was formed in the 1850s and contains its original furnishings, including *pière dure* cabinets from Fonthill and other continental works of art. The sense of richness is completed by amber silk wall hangings, which have recently been rewoven to the original design.

Shakespeare is said to have been accused by Sir Thomas Lucy of poaching deer at Charlecote and to have taken his revenge by caricaturing Sir Thomas as Justice Shallow in *The Merry Wives of Windsor*.

Compton Wynyates★
7; 8 miles W of Banbury off B4035

Ideally, Compton Wynyates should take you by surprise. You should be out for a drive one summer afternoon, bowling aimlessly along the leafy lanes of south Warwickshire, and then suddenly glimpse it through the trees – a mellow flash of russet-gold brickwork that at the next clearing resolves itself into a house, revealed at a distance below you in a gentle hollow. It is a house that makes no concessions to style or symmetry, a house at once rambling and foursquare; topped sometimes with crenellations, sometimes with half-timbered gables, crowned with a wild forest of chimneys, glancing with unequal windows, bow, bay and oriel; breathing all the strength and confidence of Tudor England.

And early Tudor at that. But then, by Compton standards, the Tudors were upstarts. One Philip de Compton was already lord of the manor here in 1204 – nearly three centuries before his descendant, Edmund, pulled down the old medieval house and, on the same moated site, began the marvellous building we know today. Its walls, 4 feet thick and enclosing a central quadrangle, were firmly in position by the time of Bosworth Field and Henry VII's accession in 1485; and when Edmund died a few years later, his eleven-year-old son William was appointed page to Prince Henry, then aged two.

which, had it survived, would have brought him even closer. Alas, 'King Harry's Gilt Bed' was sold, with the rest of the furniture, in 1774; it fetched £10, and has since disappeared without trace. By this time the family fortunes were at a low ebb, the Comptons were living at their other, more recently acquired seat of Castle Ashby in Northamptonshire, while the older house had remained largely untenanted for half a century; indeed, had the local agent obeyed his instruction, the house would have been demolished altogether – a loss that one cannot to this day contemplate without a shudder.

But poverty and neglect can preserve as well as destroy; and perhaps it was these two factors as much as anything else that kept the sixteenth-century spirit of the house so miraculously intact. Virtually nothing of later stylistic date (except the mildly regrettable Victorian staircase) has been added; most of the other accretions, surprisingly, are from an earlier building – the little fifteenth-century castle of Fulbroke, another gift of the King to William Compton, which provided the timber ceiling and bay window in the Big Hall, and probably some of the smaller stone-mullioned windows elsewhere. In atmosphere as well as in fabric, the house is still essentially as William knew it; and though the moat was drained, by order of Parliament, in the 1650s (revealing his tomb effigy and four others, flung into it by furious Roundheads, but now returned to the church nearby) there are still moments at Compton Wynyates when one seems to hear the echo of battles long ago – nowhere more than in the Priest's Room, with its three separate escape staircases for panic-stricken Catholics in hiding or on the run.

Such sounds, however, are rare. They normally yield to others: the rustle of summer leaves, the inconsequential bleating of sheep on the hillside. After its long and turbulent past, Compton Wynyates is now once again a place of peace – a peace that permeates it through and through until the very bricks begin to glow and time itself is held suspended.

Coughton Court

NT; 8; 3 miles N of Alcester on A435 [49]
The Throckmortons, one of the small group of English recusant families, have lived at Coughton for five and a half centuries, and the house reflects their turbulent history. As it now stands, it is the work of Sir George Throckmorton, who inherited at the beginning of the sixteenth century, and the magnificent stone Gatehouse, one of the best of its type, dates from his time. The house was a regular quadrangle surrounded by timber-framed ranges, but the east wing containing the chapel was destroyed by a Protestant mob at the time of the Glorious Revolution in 1688 and was never replaced. The front range, apart from the central Gatehouse, was refaced in the eighteenth century with Gothick windows and Roman cement rendering.

The interior has features of different dates. The front Hall, which occupies the ground floor of the Gatehouse, has its original stone fan vault. The Drawing Rooms are predominantly Georgian in character and have good eighteenth-century furniture and family portraits, in-

The boys grew up together; Henry became King Henry VIII, William his First Gentleman of the Bedchamber, with the privilege of keeping his hat on in the royal presence. The house is full of reminders of their friendship, which never wavered. The screen in the Big Hall (*Big*, not *Great* – a nice Tudorish touch) carried a panel depicting the battle of Tournai in 1512, in which William fought beside his King, to be knighted immediately afterwards on the steps of the cathedral; the room in which Henry and his first Queen Catharine slept displays his monogram (and those of three of his successors) on the ceiling and, in the window, the royal crest beside the insignia of Castile and Aragon; in the Dining Room, an illuminated parchment confers on the Comptons the right to include the Lion of England in their own armorial bearings. Most splendid of all, however, is the main entrance. Above the arch – deeply grooved by the chains of the old drawbridge – are emblazoned the Royal Arms, supported by the Dragon and Greyhound (emblems used only by Henry VII and Henry VIII) and surmounted by a crown, around which runs the proud inscription 'DOM REX HENRICUS OCTAV'. Some of the Comptons' neighbours may well have asked themselves whether William was not pushing his loyalty a little too far.

Henry VIII never seems very far away at Compton Wynyates; there is, however, one tremendous object

cluding a splendid canvas of Sir Robert Throckmorton, 4th Baronet, by Nicolas de Largillière in a contemporary French Rococo frame. The Dining Room, however, retains its carved Tudor panelling and chimneypiece, showing Renaissance influence. The eighteenth-century chapel, now a Saloon, is used to display family treasures.

Coventry
9; 12 miles E of Birmingham on M6

This is a town that has been consistently prosperous since the Middle Ages but, thanks partly to heavy aerial bombardment in the Second World War, it has rather less to show than most historic towns. In fact, the destruction of the old centre was begun by the city council before the war; the *Luftwaffe* merely lent a helping hand. Much of the flattened area was rebuilt on a cross-plan in the 1950s as a pedestrian shopping precinct. Though it now looks much like anywhere else, it is of some historical interest as the earliest example in England of what has become a planning cliché. As architecture, it is no worse than the centre of Rotterdam or most rebuilt German towns. A small fragment of the old town survives around the cathedral and the medieval CHURCH OF HOLY TRINITY (over-restored Perpendicular, but with a truly splendid spire). Here are one or two cobbled streets of black-and-white half-timbered or red brick Georgian houses and ST MARY'S HALL, a picturesque fourteenth-century guildhall. How it makes one regret the rest! On the other side of the new shopping centre an attempt has been made to create another historic precinct in SPON STREET, where several old timber-framed buildings have been reconstructed. Purists may feel unhappy about this, but timber-framed houses were often moved in the past, and it is better to reconstruct them on another site than to demolish them entirely. There are also three picturesque old groups of alms-houses: BONDS HOSPITAL, FORDS HOSPITAL and the HOSPITAL OF ST JOHN.

Most people, however, visit Coventry solely for its CATHEDRAL: this fascinating church is one of the few post-war English buildings that is genuinely popular. The reason for this is that, while in the Modern style, it is really a late work of the Arts and Crafts movement, its impact coming more from high-quality traditional materials, fine craftsmanship and a wide range of specially commissioned works of art than from its spatial qualities or beauties of proportion. It has a deliberate Gothic air, with a nave arcade, vaulted roof and rich stained glass. It is perhaps the best and most distinctive example of the 1950s' indigenous response to the Modern movement, before English architects succumbed to copying badly buildings that had been erected in the USA twenty or thirty years earlier.

Its predecessor was a large Perpendicular parish church raised to cathedral status in 1918. This was gutted by German incendiary bombs in November 1940, leaving just the outer walls and the noble tower and spire – one of the finest in England. The interior could have been reinstated – photographs existed of the destroyed timber roof, and traditional craftsmanship in wood and stone has never been a problem in England. Many medieval churches in northern Europe contain less genuine fabric than a restored Coventry would have done! After some controversy, it was decided instead to leave the old church as a shell and to build a new cathedral alongside, the architect to be chosen by competition. This was a perfectly valid alternative, but was hailed at the time as if it were a moral victory. The competition was thrown open in 1951 (the year of the Festival of Britain) and won by Sir Basil Spence. His building, with all the fittings by a range of different artists, arose in a mere six years, between 1956 and 1962. The new cathedral is set at right-angles to the old, the surviving shell of which serves as a forecourt; this brilliantly picturesque stroke was suggested to the architect by Siena Cathedral, where the unfinished shell of the over-ambitious fourteenth-century nave acts as a piazza in front of the earlier cathedral. A wide flight of steps ascends to the entrance porch, which can also be approached from east and west. On the wall outside the east entrance is Epstein's large bronze group of St Michael, the patron saint of the church. The outer face of the walls is beautiful pink sandstone from Hollington in Staffordshire – an admirable material, endowing the building with an air of distinction that concrete could never aspire to.

The cathedral is entered from the porch through a large glass screen engraved with Expressionist angels and saints by John Hutton. This looks best from outside, with the engravings silhouetted against the darker interior; looking back from the nave they lose much of their impact against the dazzle of daylight and could be smears of soap on the glass. Immediately upon entering, one's attention is caught by the *coup d'œil* of the Baptistery window – a large, swelling bow filled with orange, green, blue and crimson glass by John Piper and Patrick Reyntiens. The font, which at first sight you might take for a middle-period work of Henry Moore, is a natural boulder from the Holy Land. The overall plan is that of a hall church, with nave and aisles of the same height, like Bristol Cathedral. The slender, tapering concrete columns support an elegant rib vault of concrete and timber. Looking towards the altar, the windows cannot be seen because the sides of the nave form zigzags, like the flats on a stage. From the entrance they look like continuous walls of grey roughcast carrying stone tablets inscribed with arty-crafty lettering by Ralph Beyer; it is only when you reach the chancel and look back that the full blaze of the vividly coloured abstract stained glass by Lawrence Lee, Geoffrey Clarke and Keith New is revealed. The chancel is arranged traditionally, with timber choir stalls, the thorn-pattern canopies looking like assemblages of coat-hangers. All is dominated by the huge tapestry filling the end wall. It was designed by Graham Sutherland and made at Felletin in France. Both in design and colouring, it is fully worthy of its role. Around the church and in the side-chapels there are many other works of art contributed by Sir Basil Spence's team. Opinions vary as to their relative artistic merits, but the cumulative effect is impressive and they provide a fascinating cross-section of English art at the beginning of its post-war Renaissance.

Ettington Park

10; 6 miles SE of Stratford-upon-Avon on A422
Described by Mark Girouard as a 'triumph of Ruskinian polychromy and sculptural adornment', this impressive Victorian Gothic pile is built of no less than five different varieties and colours of stone arranged in stripes. The style is an exciting amalgam of English, French and Italian Gothic; the exact thirteenth-century sources could provide an art historian with many happy hours of research. Not the least amazing aspect of Ettington is that it is not a complete Victorian rebuilding but merely the remodelling of an earlier house. The mind boggles . . .

The main front is easily seen from the Stratford road. The recessed centre has projecting wings with bay windows of subtly different design and tall turrets or towers in the angles, one circular and the other square but both with conical roofs. The centre is symmetrical, the ground floor with a projecting cloister-type arcade and porch. As well as being brightly striped all over, the façade is further embellished with excellent stone carving of scenes from Shirley family history by Thomas Earp, the leading Victorian purveyor of architectural sculpture. Ettington may not be everybody's dream of the ideal country house, but it certainly gives the traveller a visual jolt when he rounds a bend on the road to Stratford and finds it before him. The house has for some time been a hotel and has recently been well restored, but less Victorian work remains inside.

Farnborough Hall

NT; 11; 16 miles SE of Leamington Spa off A41
Little evidence remains of the old manor house of Farnborough. The west end was refaced in the early eighteenth century by the first William Holbech, and the rest of the house was reconstructed in the mid-eighteenth century by the second William Holbech with the advice of his friend and neighbour, the amateur architect Sanderson Miller. The exterior is a dignified Palladian affair of golden ironstone, while the interior has charming Rococo decoration with plasterwork by William Perritt and contains the second William Holbech's Grand Tour purchases.

The Entrance Hall has a marble floor and chimneypiece, and a compartmented ceiling. In ovals round the walls are displayed a collection of restored antique busts and reliefs from Italy. The Dining Room, the best room in the house, has pretty plaster decorations and framed copies of paintings by Pannini and Canaletto (the originals bought by the second William Holbech were sold in 1929 and have gone abroad). The furniture includes a set of mid-eighteenth-century mahogany chairs and a pair of neo-classical side-tables with marble tops. The staircase was installed in *c.*1700 by the first William Holbech, and the attractive dome, part glazed and part decorated with stucco by Perritt, was added by the second William Holbech in *c.*1750.

The great glory of Farnborough is the long terrace walk, planned with the advice of Sanderson Miller and embellished with an obelisk, a pavilion and an Ionic temple, from which can be enjoyed magnificent views across the Warwickshire Plain towards the Malvern Hills.

Great Packington★

12; 8 miles W of Coventry off A45
That there is still any attractive green country between Birmingham and Coventry is thanks to a chain of historic estates that were successful in holding back the tide of urban and industrial development before post-war town and country planning successfully imposed the concept of green belts between large towns. The chief of these estates is PACKINGTON HALL, the seat of the Earls of Aylesford, whose wooded park designed by Capability Brown in 1751 is an oasis of eighteenth-century taste, enclosing an imposing house, monumental stable block and revolutionary neo-classical Chapel. A seventeenth-century house was enlarged and encased in 1766—72 for the 3rd Earl by Mathew Brettingham (whose father had supervised the construction of Holkham in Norfolk). The result is grandly classical, of three storeys, with a pedimented centre to both fronts and excellent ashlar stonework.

The interior was badly damaged by fire in 1979, but has since been carefully restored. The little Library, Drawing Room, Entrance Hall and main staircase are all agreeable examples of late eighteenth-century taste, but the exceptional feature of Packington is the Pompeian Room or Gallery, which fills the whole of the park front and which was designed by Joseph Bonomi in 1782 but not completed until twenty years later. In scale and quality of decoration it could easily be the inside of one of the palaces of the Bourbon monarchies — Caserta, say, or Aranjuez. (This is not fanciful, for Bonomi applied and failed to become architect to the King of Naples.) The Gallery is divided into three sections by screens of scagliola Corinthian columns made by Domenico Bartoli, and the walls and ceiling are entirely covered with Roman-style paintings executed by J.F. Rigaud in strong classical colours with much black, red and terracotta. The set of Greek *klismos*-style chairs were specially designed for the room by Bonomi; they have needlework cushions with decoration matching the wall paintings and are said to have been worked by Lady Aylesford. This wonderful room was Lord Aylesford's own idea and was inspired by the illustrations in Ponce's *Description des Bains de Titus*, published in 1786; it is a remarkably thoroughgoing example of this type of 'Pompeian' taste.

Hardly less impressive than the house is the Palladian stable block — a spacious quadrangle, attributed to William Hiorn of Warwick and inspired by Colen Campbell's quadrangle at Althorp, with pyramidal-roofed corner pavilions and a Tuscan portico.

Architecturally ST JAMES'S CHURCH is more important than the house, and is, in fact, among the most exciting neo-classical buildings anywhere in the country. It was built in 1789—90 to the design of Joseph Bonomi and Lord Aylesford himself, who was a noted amateur of the arts. There has been a certain amount of controversy about whose was the inspiration behind the uncompromising Greek features of the design, but it seems likely to have arisen from Lord Aylesford's studies of antique originals. The church is square and sombre, with four little domed corner towers, large lunette windows and austere expanses of brick. It recalls some of the neo-classical churches in and around St Petersburg, which in turn were inspired by the work of the French neo-classicists. St James's has all the drama and 'progressive' qualities of a radical student's *Prix de Rom* design or a *Barrière* by Ledoux. The interior is a staggering experience. The walls, completely unadorned, are painted to resemble ashlar stonework (in itself a rare survival of this once common form of interior decoration), while the groin-vaulted ceiling (also painted to resemble stone) is supported on four corner columns of primitive Doric order without bases and with the pronounced entasis of over-stuffed sausages. The altarpiece has a marble pediment carried on Corinthian columns, which frame a painting by Rigaud of angels inscribing the name of Jesus, 'IHS', bordered by clouds. This is an oddly Catholic – indeed positively Jesuitical – subject to find in an eighteenth-century Anglican church, but it does not seem incongruous amidst the continental grandeur of the architecture.

Hampton Lucy
13; 5 miles E of Stratford-upon-Avon off B4086
On the edge of Charlecote Park (*q.v.*), and paid for by the Lucys, stands ST PETER'S CHURCH. The Rev. John Lucy (brother of the Squire) was left £900 by his mother in 1778; by the 1820s this had increased to £9000 and he used the money to rebuild the church. It was designed by Thomas Rickman, who invented the typological

St Peter's Church, Hampton Lucy.

sequence of 'Norman', 'Early English', 'Decorated' and 'Perpendicular' to describe English medieval architecture. He taught himself architecture after going bankrupt in the corn trade and after the death of his first wife; to recover, he started to take long country walks, studying in detail the old churches he came across. As a result, he was able to secure several jobs from the Church Building Commissions after the Napoleonic Wars and to put his knowledge into practice, opening an architect's office in Birmingham in 1820. The church at Hampton Lucy is his most important work, as here he was not hampered by the stringent economies of the Commissioners. It is faced in fine ashlar stone and has a high west tower with prominent pinnacles. The style is Decorated! The window tracery is cast-iron – a material of which Rickman made lavish use in his churches, much to the disgust of a later generation; to Ruskin, for instance, such 'shams' were anathema. All is very richly finished, with frilly battlements and lots of carving.

The interior is most impressive – clustered piers, a tall clerestory and a noble ribbed vault (of plaster, to look like stone). It is a convincing job, and could easily be mistaken (if it were not for the use of plaster and cast-iron) for the work of fifty years later. This convincing Victorian feel is reinforced by the apse, which was, in fact, rebuilt in 1856 by George Gilbert Scott with slightly thicker and richer detailing, but reincorporating the original stained-glass east window. This is by Willement, who was responsible for much of the interior decoration at Charlecote itself. An anonymous contemporary described it as 'the most magnificent window in stained glass that has been produced in modern time, in imitation of the ancient style'.

Serious Regency Gothic is not a style that is fashionable at the moment, but in examples like Hampton Lucy it is well worthy of respect.

Honington
14; 2 miles N of Shipston on Stour off A34 [50]
Amidst mild, unassuming English landscape, a bridge over the River Stour, embellished with stone ball finials, heralds something architecturally exciting. The small village of Honington has a triangular green surrounded by prosperously done-up cottages and, facing them, a magnificent gate, the rusticated brick piers of which are decorated with carved swags and masks. This is the entrance to HONINGTON HALL, one of the most perfect Caroline houses in England. It was built in 1682 for Sir Henry Parker, an MP who had bought the estate in 1679 and died in 1713. The entrance front of seven bays has a recessed centre and a hipped roof; it is built of dark red brick, with stone dressings the colour of ginger biscuits, and beneath the first-floor windows are busts of Roman emperors in little arched niches – a delightful feature. On either side of the house are rusticated archways with pediments; originally these were connected to curving screen walls but only that on the right survives.

From the Parkers, Honington passed to the Townsends, and Joseph Townsend considerably remodelled the interior of the house in the mid-eighteenth century to the design of William Jones, surveyor to the East India

Kenilworth Castle.

Company and architect of Ranelagh in Chelsea. He added the large canted bay in the middle of the park front. This contains an octagonal Saloon — the outstanding feature of the house and a gem of second-generation English Palladian architecture, its classical details softened by Rococo warmth. It has a coffered, domed ceiling, a Corinthian doorcase inspired by that in the Double Cube Room at Wilton, and a two-tier chimneypiece with broken pediment. Dripping down the angles of the room are magnificent Rococo garlands in stucco. This beautiful room has recently been restored and repainted in its original colours of blue, white and gold. The Entrance Hall has decoration of the same date and quality. Its chimneypiece is surmounted by an elaborate stucco relief, and on the opposite wall is a companion piece of stucco mythology. The ceiling is likewise embellished with Rococo plasterwork. In the rear wall are 'windows' open to the staircase, which rises through the middle of the house and has a good scrolly ironwork balustrade. The Staircase Hall and passages display further excellent Rococo stonework, and the Dining Room ceiling has a delightful relief of Flora. The Oak Room, however, retains seventeenth-century panelling of the same date as the house. The best surviving original room is the Chinese Room upstairs, which has leather wall panels painted to resemble oriental lacquer — a rare survival.

The CHURCH OF ALL SAINTS sits on the lawn beside the house, completing a perfect manorial picture. The short west tower is medieval, but all the rest of the church was rebuilt in the 1680s in the same style as the house, though faced in stone not brick. There are large arched windows with many small panes of clear glass, which glitter in the afternoon sunlight. On the parapet are flaming stone urns. The inside is festive and perfect — just the place for weddings. The aisles are divided from the nave by arcades of Tuscan columns, and there is a shallow segmental plaster vault reflecting the gentle apsidal arrangement of the east end. The plasterwork is painted blue and white — a good foil to the dark oak joinery, many marble memorials to the Parkers and Townsends, and the cheerful heraldic colours of the funerary hatchments hanging on the walls. The best monument stands in the middle of the west wall, rather grander than the altar that it faces. It commemorates Sir Henry Parker and his son Hugh, who predeceased him; their near-life-size statues, standing in front of a marble reredos, show them dressed in loose cloaks, curly wigs and buckled shoes and looking as if they are in the middle of an animated conversation. Joseph Townsend is commemorated by an exquisitely macabre tablet in the south aisle, with a pile of marble books, bones and oak leaves supporting a cherub (described by Arthur Mee as 'perhaps the most unpleasant cherub in all England, a nightmare of sculpture'). Above the chancel arch are the original Royal Arms supported by a Lion and Unicorn. Many of the seventeenth-century fittings survive, including the communion rails, carved oak choir stalls and pulpit. The pews, though mainly cut down, are formed out of the old box pews. The pulpit is a good piece, the steps with barley-sugar-twist balusters, and perched on the newel is a startlingly lifelike dove holding a single olive leaf in her beak.

Kenilworth Castle★
15; 4 miles SW of Coventry off A452
The splendid ruins of Kenilworth, among the grandest in England, are approached via the old village HIGH STREET and CASTLE GREEN, whose pretty houses and old cottages make a good foil to the towering, cliff-like masses of the castle's red sandstone walls. The castle was royal from the twelfth century down to 1563, when Elizabeth I gave it to her favourite, Robert Dudley, Earl of Leicester. The mighty keep was built by Henry II in c.1170–80; the curtain wall with square and polygonal towers that sur-

Leamington Spa.

rounds the whole site was erected under King John and Henry III in the thirteenth century. Much of the castle was remodelled by John of Gaunt in the 1390s. He built the kitchen, the Great Hall, and the range of medieval private apartments to the south. Finally, between 1563 and 1570 Robert Dudley, Earl of Leicester, converted the castle into a great Elizabethan country house, remodelling the keep, inserting large mullion-and-transom windows and erecting 'Leicester's Buildings'. Here the Queen was entertained by him in July 1575 with pageants, fireworks and banquets – a description of the event forms the high spot of Sir Walter Scott's eponymous novel, *Kenilworth*. It is difficult not to view the castle ruins through Scott's eyes: to see Elizabeth and her party entering the base-court through Mortimer's Tower, its archway flanked by semi-circular turrets, and 'moving on through pageants of heathen gods and heroes of antiquity, who offered gifts and compliments on bended knee'; to imagine the now roofless state apartments overlooking the inner court 'gorgeously hung for her reception with the richest silken tapestry, misty with perfumes, and sounding to the strains of soft and delicious music'; and to see the vast shell of John of Gaunt's Great Hall, with its huge traceried windows and polygonal bow at the high table end, still with a 'highly carved oaken roof', hung from which was a 'superb chandelier of gilt bronze, formed like a spread eagle, whose outstretched wings supported three male and female figures, grasping a pair of torches in each hand'. Leicester built the vast new range of state apartments to the east of the medieval ones (which he also remodelled) especially to house the Queen and her retinue; it has a nearly symmetrical façade with canted bay windows.

Kenilworth's end came with the Civil War in the 1640s, when the castle was dismantled on Cromwell's instructions and the mere that protected it on the west side was drained. Today all is roofless; even the vaulted undercrofts on the ground floor are open to the sky. The main rooms, which were all on the first floor and approached from outside by a flight of steps, have vanished. The vast masses of the walls, in places 15–20 feet thick, still convey a powerful impact, however, and the empty windows with stone mullions and broken tracery make a romantic impression, silhouetted against the light. The ruins are now carefully maintained by the Heritage Commission, the lawns round the walls neatly mown.

Leamington Spa
16; 8 miles S of Coventry on A445

A former spa, Leamington is now a prosperous residential town for the industrial area to the north. The curative qualities of the waters were discovered by William Camden, the antiquary, in 1586, but it was not until 1786 that William Abbots built the first bath. The heyday of the spa, however, came in the nineteenth rather than the eighteenth century and Leamington owed its success to Dr Henry Jephson, a well-known physician who received Queen Victoria here in 1838 and played a dominant role in the planning of the town and in attracting the famous to take its waters – not just the Queen, but the Duke of Wellington, Sarah Bernhardt, Longfellow and Nathaniel Hawthorne too. Napoleon III lived for a short time in Clarendon Square, after the defeat and collapse of the Second Empire in 1870.

The general character of Leamington is late Regency, with stuccoed classical terraces or detached and semi-detached villas, some of them Tudorish. The buildings are well kept and the stucco smartly painted in cream. The main axis runs north from the river and Pump Room via the Parade to Beauchamp Square. On either side are wide, tree-lined residential streets. Along the river banks are the attractively landscaped JEPHSON GARDENS, laid out as a memorial to Dr Jephson. At this end of the town are the parish CHURCH OF ALL SAINTS and the PUMP ROOM, connected by the elegantly balustraded Victoria Bridge. The Pump Room was originally built in 1813–14 to the design of the local architect C.S. Smith, but was largely rebuilt in 1926, only the Tuscan colonnade surviving from the original. All Saints is an amazing apparition in French cathedral style; it was begun in 1843 by the vicar, Dr John Craig, acting as his own designer but with the assistance of a little-known local architect, J.C. Jackson. The nave and tower were completed to the design of Arthur Blomfield in 1888–92. The interior is impressive because of its scale: the roof is 80 feet high. The chancel is apsidal with rich, glowing stained glass made in 1851 by Chance of Birmingham.

The main street is called THE PARADE and was developed between 1815 and 1834. It contains Leamington's most important shops, which have carefully controlled signs and shop-fronts. The architecture increases in grandeur as one walks north, culminating in the symmetrical terraces with giant pilasters, iron balconies and Doric porches that lead into BEAUCHAMP SQUARE. This was laid out in 1825. Originally it had a Neo-Norman church in the middle, designed by P.F. Robinson; this has been demolished, but is no loss to the amenities of the square. The surrounding residential streets are worth exploring, as they contain many attractive stucco houses with iron balconies and Doric porches. CLARENDON SQUARE is the best preserved; it, too, dates from 1825 and shows the transition from grand Grecian terraces to Tudorish villas. These villas continue in HAMILTON TERRACE, REGENT GROVE and HOLLY WALK, where there are some entertaining Gothic and Jacobean as well as classical designs. This combination of rather light-hearted Regency and early Victorian stucco architecture, further enhanced by beautiful planting of mature trees and shrubbery, is the hallmark of Leamington.

Maxstoke Castle
17; 9 miles NW of Coventry off B4102
Situated in an unspoilt landscape of dairy farms in the remarkably well-preserved rural belt between Birmingham and Coventry, the castle presents a perfectly symmetrical outer face to the world and is surrounded by a moat, which is surprisingly deep in parts. With its red sandstone walls it could be a small crusader-fortress in the Holy Land. In form it is a rectangle with four polygonal corner towers and a grand gatehouse on the north side. Licence to crenellate was obtained in 1346 by William de Clinton, Earl of Huntingdon, and the castle, like Warwick but unlike Kenilworth (*qq.v.*), has been continuously inhabited ever since. It was partly remodelled in the fifteenth century by the 1st Duke of Buckingham. In 1589 it came to Sir Thomas Dilke, who reconstructed the residential ranges within the medieval curtain wall to form a comfortable Elizabethan country house. A fine avenue of trees leads to the bridge across the moat and through the fifteenth-century wooden doors of the vaulted gateway to the spacious inner courtyard with its lawn and gravel sweep. Originally there were ranges of living quarters on all four sides, but the house as it is today is essentially an L-shaped building on the south and west sides, partly of stone and partly timber-framed. The rooms contain fine panelling and paintings, and furniture dating mainly from the sixteenth and seventeenth centuries. In a first-floor room of the north-west tower is an original medieval tiled floor – a rare survival. Maxstoke remains the seat of the Dilke, now Fetherston-Dilke, family.

Merevale Hall
18; 2 miles W of Atherstone on A5
From the main-line railway north to Glasgow the observant traveller, just after Atherstone, is rewarded with a glimpse of what looks like a Rhineland *Schloß* with turrets and two towers on a dramatically wooded hilltop. This is Merevale Hall; in fact the house is smooth Victorian Tudor when seen close up, and it is more the site than the architecture that is responsible for the drama of the distant views. The architect was Edward Blore, a purveyor of dull but respectable Tudorish mansions to the Victorian Tory squirearchy. Merevale is of special interest, however, for the completeness and undisturbed nature of its Victorian furnishings and atmosphere. It was built for William Stratford Dugdale, MP, a descendant of Sir William Dugdale, the seventeenth-century herald and antiquary. Work began in 1838 and was finished in 1844. The exterior is faced in very smooth ashlar and embellished with carved strapwork and other 'Elizabethan' frills round the doors and windows. Like several Victorian houses, the main entrance is at one end rather than being in the middle. This was a change of plan while work was in progress and is supposed to have resulted from Mrs Dugdale's complaint that if callers had to pass her windows to get to the front door it would make it embarrassing for her to say she was 'not at home' when she did not wish to be disturbed.

The Entrance Hall is lined with glass cases of stuffed birds, and a wide corridor or Gallery leads from it to the staircase in the centre of the house. The latter has an arcaded landing at first-floor level, and heraldic stained glass in the windows. The main rooms, which are light and spacious, are arranged round it. Their most striking features are their great height and their original Victorian furniture. The Dining Room is 19 feet high and retains all the solid, comfortable furnishings provided for the room in 1844 by W. & E. Snell of Albemarle Street, London – including a Turkey carpet, twenty-four chairs upholstered in red Morocco leather, and the matching sideboard and side-tables in Jacobean style. The Library is L-shaped, with built-in Jacobean-style shelves and comfortable, over-stuffed armchairs. Even upstairs the bedrooms and dressing rooms are full of Victorian fittings and bric-à-brac, as well as mementos of Balliol, where both W.S. Dugdale's sons were undergraduates. Dr Jowett, the famous Master of Balliol, was a friend of the family, and there is a nice contemporary description of him reading Homer to the eight-year-old son of his host in the nursery at Merevale.

Packington Hall

See Great Packington.

Packwood House

NT; 19; 2 miles SE of Hockley Heath off A4023
Packwood House lies in pleasant, though slightly sub-urbanised, country in the Forest of Arden, about 11 miles south of Birmingham, and is chiefly famous for its TOPIARY GARDEN. The house, too, is of interest – not least for the restoration carried out by Graham Baron Ash in the 1920s and 1930s, and for the collection that he assembled at the same time.

The main block is a timber-framed building dating from the mid-sixteenth century, with additions of *c.*1670. It is plastered with steep gables and tall brick chimneys. The twentieth-century alterations are chiefly evident on the inside. The Hall was substantially remodelled in 1931–2, when the Gallery and timber ceiling were inserted; the walls are hung with Flemish tapestry. The Long Gallery was built to lead to the Great Hall, which was formed out of a barn and byre. The fireplace and overmantel in the latter were brought from Stratford, and in the centre of the room is a magnificent long oak table from Baddesley Clinton (*q.v.*); the eighteenth-century Soho tapestries depicting Four Continents also came from there, as did the Antwerp tapestries in the Long Gallery. The staircase, made by Wood, Kendrick and Reynolds, was also inserted in 1931–2 and leads to a series of bedrooms, all with tapestries and interesting seventeenth- and eighteenth-century furniture. The Drawing Room faces south over the topiary garden and contains some especially fine Queen Anne walnut marquetry pieces. The Dining Room has altered Jacobean panelling and Flemish glass in the windows, brought from Culham Court in Oxfordshire.

The Tower, Radway Grange.

Preston on Stour

20; 4 miles S of Stratford-upon-Avon off A34
This is the Alscot (*q.v.*) estate village, and a model of intelligent upkeep when so many Warwickshire villages have been dolled up to the nines by people with more money than taste. The village street has several sixteenth-century timber-framed houses and one good early eighteenth-century brick house opposite the church, still with wooden cross-mullions, as well as several typical Victorian estate cottages – red brick Tudor with lattice windows. ST MARY'S CHURCH was reconstructed in the Gothick style in 1753–7 by Captain James West of Alscot Park under the direction of Edward Woodward, a mason of Chipping Campden. The tower is genuine Perpendicular, but the nave has eighteenth-century windows with archaeologically convincing tracery, and the chancel was rebuilt. It has good Georgian fittings, and in the east window is a collection of seventeenth-century glass given to the church by James West at the time of the rebuilding. There is also fine eighteenth-century glass.

Radway Grange

21; 7 miles NW of Banbury off A422
This is a place of pilgrimage for architectural historians as the birthplace and family home of Sanderson Miller (1716–80), the gentleman-architect and purveyor of Gothick follies and grottoes to his aristocratic friends and neighbours. He was the son of a prosperous merchant of Banbury and was educated at Oxford. As well as architecture, he had tastes for literature and landscape gardening. Between 1744 and 1746 he rebuilt the south and east fronts of Radway in enthusiastic Gothic style, with crocketed pinnacles and pointed arches. It is pioneer work of its kind, more effectively picturesque than any previous eighteenth-century Gothick building. Radway shows many of the hallmarks that Miller was later to reproduce elsewhere for an ever-widening circle of uncritical antiquarian-minded landowners who asked him to embellish their parks and houses. The hallmarks include the pair of two-storeyed bay windows, the cusped stone panelling, on the south front, which he was later to repeat at Arbury (*q.v.*), Adlestrop in Gloucestershire and Rockingham in Northamptonshire.

As well as improving the house, Sanderson Miller also embellished the grounds by adding a couple of Picturesque buildings on Edgehill to complete the view. THE COTTAGE, built in 1743–4, has pointed windows and when first built had a thatched roof. It is important as the earliest English Picturesque building of that type to survive. Even more impressive is THE TOWER, an irregularly composed castellated folly with a prominent octagonal tower, built in 1746–7. This again had a great effect and led to Miller's being commissioned to design half-ruined towers or castles for the parks at Ingestre and Hagley (*qq.v.*), and Wimpole in Cambridgeshire; it was to the latter that Horace Walpole was referring when he mentioned 'the true rust of the Barons' Wars'. The Edgehill Tower was intended to contain a statue of Caratacus in chains but, when carved, it was found to be too large to fit in its niche and so was placed on the lawn

Ragley Hall.

of Radway Grange instead. The tower windows originally contained stained glass embellished with heraldry, but this has disappeared. Somewhat improbably, the Edgehill Tower is now a pub, though, alas, with a disappointing interior. One hoped that it might be furnished with Gothick fittings and serve beer in large Gothick tankards!

Ragley Hall
22; 3 miles S of Alcester on A435
Externally, Ragley Hall is a large, plain, late seventeenth-century house designed by Robert Hooke, one of the founder members of the Royal Society and a friend of Wren. The original formal plan survives, with four state apartments flanking the central Hall–Saloon axis, and duplicated staircases, but the interior decoration was all redone in two phases in the eighteenth century – first by Gibbs, and then (in the hope of a visit from George III, which did not materialise) by James Wyatt in his most etiolated neo-classical manner. After having fallen into a somewhat neglected state, the whole house has been restored and redecorated by the present Marquess of Hertford over the past twenty-five years.

The first interior seen by the visitor is also the best – the Gibbs' Great Hall, with its sumptuous Rococo plasterwork. The Rococo hall chairs were made for the room in 1756. The whole ensemble is one of the finest in England. The Study and Billiards Room are also by Gibbs, with similar but more restrained stucco ceilings.

Wyatt's work is mainly confined to the garden front and can be seen in the sequence of Drawing Rooms and the central Saloon; all have elegant Adamesque ceilings and carved marble chimneypieces. The two staircases are in their original positions but were replaced in the nineteenth century. One of the Staircase Halls has been decorated recently with huge murals by Graham Rust in clear bright colours – an appropriate modern addition to the house.

Stoneleigh Abbey
23; 2 miles S of Coventry on A444
The mighty Baroque west front, built in 1714–26 to the design of Francis Smith of Warwick, conceals the older pink stone courtyard behind; this was developed out of the cloister of the small Cistercian abbey that once occupied the site. The vanished church was on the north side, where the main entrance now is. That façade of the house incorporates part of the south arcade of the nave, and in the lower parts of the surrounding ranges many medieval features survive, including ribbed vaults, Gothic piers and arched doorways. The fourteenth-century Gatehouse also still stands, facing the north side of the house across the lawn. The upper parts of the rear ranges were remodelled c.1600 and contain panelling and staircases of that date. These smaller rooms now form the private residence of Lord Leigh, while the large Georgian rooms in the west wing are open to the public. The west range was badly damaged by fire in 1960: the upper parts were gutted, and the main rooms on the ground floor spoilt by water and smoke. After lying empty for twenty years, this range has now been reconstructed under the supervision of Neville Hawkes of Warwick. The upper part has been converted into offices for commercial letting, to help with funding the maintenance of the building, while the main rooms have been carefully restored, redecorated and the principal surviving contents displayed in them; Claud Phillimore has advised on the rearrangement of the furniture and pictures.

A long enfilade, with excellent panelling and plasterwork, extends the length of the west range. In the centre is the Saloon, with yellow scagliola Corinthian columns and rich stucco work – especially the panels over the chimneypieces depicting the Labours of Hercules and the ceiling, which fortunately survived the fire. The large carpet, incidentally, was woven c.1970 for the Great Room at Boodles Club in London and when replaced recently was snapped up for Stoneleigh at a bargain price! To the north, the rooms are furnished as the Drawing Room and as the State Bedroom; the furniture in the latter is that prepared for an upstairs room in which Queen Victoria slept when she visited Stoneleigh in c.1858 and includes white-painted Chippendale chairs. To the south are the State Dining Room and Library. A feature of Stoneleigh is the sequence of magnificent gilt gesso furniture acquired for the Georgian rooms in the 1720s. Most of the south side of the house is taken up by a mildly Gothick Long Gallery, formed by C.S. Smith in the 1820s, which serves as the main entrance hall. In the Anteroom between this and the west wing is heraldic sixteenth-century glass brought from Brereton Hall in Cheshire (q.v.). The main staircase behind the Saloon is an impressive piece of early eighteenth-century joinery, and there is Rococo stucco work on the walls and ceiling. The Chapel also has a mid-eighteenth-century stucco ceiling, and pews, pulpit and communion rail of the same date. There is a Family Gallery at the north end at the level of the main rooms, with red-baize hassocks and an eighteenth-century feel of worshipping God in comfort; this has been excellently restored as part of the recent programme. Altogether, Stoneleigh is one of the most ambitious restorations and adaptations of a large country house to have been undertaken in the 1980s.

Stratford-upon-Avon

24; 16 miles SE of Birmingham on A34
Includes Stratford-upon-Avon Canal (NT)

Stratford is England's prime tourist attraction outside London. The cult of Shakespeare was begun here in the eighteenth century by David Garrick and has flourished ever since, the place now being visited by millions of tourists every year. For that reason it is best seen out of season, in autumn or early spring. The results of the enthusiasm for Shakespeare could have been terrible, but on the whole Stratford has withstood the pressure remarkably well and maintains its character as an unspoilt Midlands market town. The various showplaces are well managed and well presented by the Shakespeare Birthplace Trust, and the general appearance of the town displays a level of intelligent and understated care well beyond the English norm. The various new developments of the 1960s and early 1970s are already of some historical interest for their attempt to be 'of our time, yet in keeping'.

Most people enter the town from the east across the River Avon by the CLOPTON BRIDGE of fourteen arches, built by Sir Hugh Clopton in c.1480–90. The little folly-like tower was built in 1814 as a toll house. To the east is the ALVESTON MANOR HOTEL, a blaze of over-restored timber-framing, which promises Olde Englishe Hospitalitye. Along the river and round the CANAL (NT) wharf are attractively landscaped gardens. This stretch of the Birmingham Canal, which was opened in 1816, is smartly maintained by the National Trust, and very festive it looks with its neat white trim and pleasure boats. Surveying the scene with a look of approval is a bronze statue of Shakespeare made in 1888 by Lord Ronald Gower. The east–west axis is continued by Bridge Street,

at the top of which the white-painted MARKET HOUSE forms an appropriate *point de vue*. It is best, however, to walk along the river to the ROYAL SHAKESPEARE THEATRE and then to the parish CHURCH OF HOLY TRINITY. The theatre was built in 1874–9 in Victorian Gothic. It was partly burnt in 1929 but is now to be rebuilt, in a style that captures the drama of the original Victorian building, as an annexe to the new theatre erected in 1928–32 to the design of Elizabeth Scott and looking for all the world like an Odeon cinema. Holy Trinity lies to the south of the town, now somewhat away from the centre. With its central spire (rebuilt by William Hiorn of Warwick in the eighteenth century) rising out of the trees of the churchyard, it forms a *Country Life* front-cover picture when seen from the river. It is large and largely Perpendicular, and was restored in the 1890s by Bodley and Garner. They designed the organ case, for instance; the tall rood-screen is mostly a recreation. The interior is dominated by the large east window, flanked by tall niches for statues (note the flying insects carved in their corbels), and the chancel is richly furnished. In the Clopton Chapel, at the east end of the north aisle, are several interesting tombs – especially the elaborate monument to George, Lord Clopton, who died in 1629, with a richly carved military trophy on the front. But what everybody comes to see is Shakespeare's tomb in the chancel. He was baptised at Holy Trinity, and was buried here in 1616. The tomb is a slab inscribed:

> Good friend for Jesus sake
> forbeare
> To digg the dust enclosed
> heare!
> Bleste be the man that spares
> the stones
> And curst be he that moves
> My bones.

On the wall above is the alabaster memorial with a bust of the Bard by Gerard Johnson and an epitaph informing us that he 'LEAVES LIVING ART, BUT PAGE, TO SERVE HIS WITT'.

From the church it is possible to reach HALL'S CROFT, a picturesque half-timbered and gabled house (where Shakespeare's daughter Susannah and son-in-law John Hall lived), and then to walk along the main axis of the town – CHURCH STREET, CHAPEL STREET, SHEEP STREET and the HIGH STREET. (Foreign visitors are always amazed in English towns to find that what looks like one rambling street can very often change its name four or five times within a comparatively short distance.) Church Street is the most attractive in Stratford, with several nice Georgian houses and, at the junction with Chapel Street, a classic stretch of English townscape made up of the ALMSHOUSES, GRAMMAR SCHOOL and the tower of the GILD CHAPEL. The Almshouses have a timber-framed frontage, 150 feet long, with a jettied upper storey: they were erected in c.1427. The Grammar School was originally the Guildhall of the Gild of the Holy Cross, and was built in 1417: it too has a timber-framed front with an overhanging upper storey. The square tower of the Gild Chapel makes a fine eye-catcher in the general street scene. The Gild was founded in the thirteenth century, but the chapel was largely rebuilt in the fifteenth by Sir Hugh Clopton; it has a light and spacious Perpendicular interior with interesting wall paintings, including a lively Doom painting over the chancel arch.

North of the tower, in Chapel Street, is a good stretch of Georgian houses interspersed with restored timber-framed frontages, including the SHAKESPEARE and FALCON HOTELS. The MIDLAND BANK of 1883 is decorated with amusing red terracotta reliefs of scenes from Shakespeare's plays. Continuing into Sheep Street, more half-timbered houses make a foil to the well-bred Palladian façade of the TOWN HALL, designed in 1767 by Robert Newman. The lead statue of Shakespeare by John Cheere in the middle of the front was given by David Garrick. The continuation of Sheep Street is the High Street, with more late sixteenth-century houses, of which HARVARD HOUSE (dated 1596), with its ornate carved woodwork, is the best. On the corner of Sheep Street and the High Street is a new development of black-painted concrete 'beams' with red brick panels carried out by Sir Frederick Gibberd in 1963–4 – very Civic Trust Award.

To the west is the Market Place, called Rolher Street – more workaday, with the AMERICAN FOUNTAIN in the middle: this is a strong Victorian Gothic design by Jethro Cossins and was erected in 1887. To the north, in Henley Street, is SHAKESPEARE'S BIRTHPLACE, romantically timber-framed; it was restored in 1858. To the east, Bridge Street leads back to the riverside gardens and Clopton Bridge. The extraordinary Post-Modern building north of the car park is the new HEADQUARTERS OF THE NATIONAL FARMERS' UNION.

Upton House

NT; 25; 6 miles NW of Banbury on A422

Upton House is not itself of much architectural interest, being largely a plain Neo-Georgian remodelling of 1927–8, carried out by Percy Morley Horder for the 1st Viscount Bearsted. It is nevertheless notable for its fine collection of paintings – one of the best brought together in the inter-war years. The English pictures – most of them portraits by Reynolds, Raeburn and Devis, and sporting works by Stubbs, Sartorius and Ben Marshall – are displayed in the principal rooms: the Dining Room, Staircase Hall, Billiards Room and Boudoir. The Long Drawing Room – a gallery that occupies nearly the whole of the garden front – contains a beautiful group of seventeenth-century Dutch works by Ruisdael, Steen and their contemporaries, as well as a remarkable collection of English porcelain, among which late Chelsea pieces predominate.

The cream of the picture collection is displayed in a special gallery – originally a squash court, but converted for this purpose by Trenwith Wills. Particularly notable are the Bosch triptych, *The Adoration of the Magi*, a pair of small portraits of unknown men by Memlinc and Rogier van der Weyden, and a small version by El Greco of his famous *El Espolio* in the sacristy of Toledo Cathedral.

An unexpected treat at Upton is the eighteenth-century walled and terraced garden, concealed in a little valley in front of the house.

Warwick

26; 6 miles SW of Coventry on A46

The county town of Warwickshire was founded by Ethelfleda, a daughter of Alfred the Great, in 914. It flourished in the Middle Ages under the protection of the Beauchamp Earls of Warwick, who at times were more powerful than the King himself. In 1694 much of the town was destroyed by fire, but it was solidly rebuilt in a unified classical style. During the nineteenth and early twentieth centuries it was protected from unsuitable industrial development by the Greville Earls of Warwick. As a result, it is a remarkably well-preserved old town. If one has a criticism, it is that everything is too done-up and over-restored – but at least that is better than being pulled down.

Warwick stands on a low hill above the River Avon and comprises a cross of streets – known as Jury – High Street running from east to west, cut in the middle by Northgate, Church Street and Castle Street. Parts of the medieval TOWN WALLS survive, as well as the two main gates at either end of the High Street axis. The EASTGATE has a plain fourteenth-century tunnel-vaulted arch, and above it is a fantastical Gothick chapel with a pretty pinnacled clock turret on top, like a pagoda; it was designed in 1788 by Francis Hiorn. The WESTGATE also carries a chapel, approached by a steep flight of steps, but this one is genuinely medieval with a tower. This chapel now serves LEYCESTER'S HOSPITAL, which forms an ultra-picturesque group adjoining. The Hospital was founded by the Earl of Leicester in 1571; for the purpose he took over the premises of the Guild of the Holy Trinity and St George, which dated from the fifteenth century. The front to the street is a riot of half-timber with a jettied upper storey. A stone gateway gives access to the courtyard, which, if possible, is even more picturesque than the outside; a balustraded open gallery runs round at first-floor level, there are two Great Halls, and also the Master's House, this last rebuilt in the mid-nineteenth century, the Victorians going rather over the top in the way of decorative heraldry and other ornament. In West Street, outside the gate, a number of lesser timber-framed houses still stand, as the seventeenth-century fire did not spread this far. The High Street itself, and its continuation in Jury Street, is largely late seventeenth- and early eighteenth-century, following the fire. On the corner of Castle Street is a particularly fine townhouse of 1696, with a hipped roof, central window with curly broken pediment, and Tuscan corner pilasters. The best building on this axis, however, is the COURT HOUSE, which faces Church Street. It was designed by Francis Smith *c*.1725–8 and is entirely faced in stone with channelled rustication, giving it a French air. The *piano nobile* is distinguished by very tall sash windows, Doric pilasters, a triglyph frieze and elegant balustraded parapet concealing the roof. In the centre is a statue of Justice by Thomas Stayner, with carved coats of arms, brightly painted in gold and colours, above and below. South from here in Castle Street is OKEN HOUSE, a sixteenth-century timber-framed structure, now a doll museum. Further east along Jury Street are more late seventeenth- and early eighteenth-century houses.

Leycester's Hospital, Warwick.

At Eastgate it is worth making a detour outside the town walls to see ST NICHOLAS'S CHURCH – eighteenth-century Gothick with a pretty tower and spire. At the foot of the hill, Castle Bridge offers the classic view of Warwick Castle rising in glory, sheer from the river, the ruined arches of the medieval bridge and the little Gothick MILL at its feet. Mill Street, leading towards the latter, escaped the 1694 fire and as a result is full of gabled, timber-framed houses, though all a bit *bijou* now.

Returning to the Court House, Church Street forms the other major axis of Warwick. It focuses on the mighty west tower of St Mary's Church and is lined with eighteenth-century houses, several of them now antique shops.

In most views of Warwick, ST MARY'S, the parish church, is more prominent than the castle, because it is set at the highest point of the ridge on which the town lies, and the large square west tower is no less than 176 feet high. The main body of the church was destroyed in the fire that engulfed Warwick in 1694, but the fourteenth-century chancel and the fifteenth-century Beauchamp Chapel survived. The latter is the most famous feature of the church and is one of the grandest of all medieval chantry chapels. It was begun in 1443 and completed in 1465 under the will of Richard Beauchamp, Earl of Warwick, who had died at Rouen in 1439. It cost £2481.4s.7½d; the accounts survive and throw a great

deal of light on large-scale building work in the late Middle Ages. The windows, for instance, were among the first to be glazed with glass made in England (before then all glass was imported). The east window survives, albeit much restored. The interior of the Chapel is a set-piece of Perpendicular at its most lavish, with a rich lierne vault and its walls almost filled with large six-light windows. Round the bottom runs an arrangement of stone panels like blank tracery, and the original oak choir stalls. The east window is framed in a continuous sequence of excellently carved stone angels, which somehow escaped the attentions of sixteenth- and seventeenth-century iconoclasts. The reredos, equally beautiful, is eighteenth-century, with a lovely relief by William Collins of the Annunciation. The centrepiece of the Chapel is, of course, the Earl's own tomb – a free-standing chest of Purbeck marble topped by an effigy of gilt copper rivalling the royal ones in Westminster Abbey. Round the sides are enamel coats of arms and little gilt figures of mourners in rich canopied niches. The effigy itself is protected by a contemporary hoop-shaped grille – a most unusual feature. The Earl is in armour, his head resting on his helmet and his feet on his family crests – a bear and a griffin. He holds his hands apart, looking more as if he were clapping than praying. The effigy was cast by William Austen of London and the gilding was executed by Bartholomew Lambespring.

The chancel is earlier Perpendicular, begun in the 1360s and completed in 1392; but again it has blank panelled tracery on the east wall and a six-light window (containing good Victorian glass by Kempe). The most striking feature is the tierceron vault, looking more as if made of moulded metal than carved stone. In the middle of the floor is the large monument to Thomas Beauchamp, Earl of Warwick (who died in 1369), and his wife. It is an alabaster tomb-chest, with a pair of effigies holding hands. In niches round the chest stand pretty little carvings of mourners (many of them restored). This Earl began the chancel and intended it as his burial place, but most of it was built after his death by his son, another Thomas. Beneath it is the Norman crypt with fat circular piers – hinting at the scale of the vanished Norman church founded on this site in 1123.

The main part of the church, including the transepts, nave and west tower, was rebuilt between 1698 and 1704, and is a noble example of Baroque-Gothic, similar to some of the hybrid monastery churches built in Bohemia at the same time. Gothic was obviously chosen to match the chancel and Beauchamp Chapel, and thus to preserve the historical continuity of the building. After the fire of 1694, the Warwick Commissioners approached both Sir Christopher Wren and his 'man' (whom Kerry Downes has identified as Nicholas Hawksmoor) for plans for rebuilding. The architect finally chosen, however, was Sir William Wilson, a mason-sculptor of Sutton Coldfield, and the contractors were Francis and William Smith of Warwick. The interior is a remarkable piece of construction for its date with a wide, light nave, a plaster vault and side-aisles of the same height as the centre. It appears superficially medieval, but in fact neither the mouldings, nor the piers, nor the carved capitals are anything like real Gothic work. The window tracery and the exterior are a jolly scramble of medieval and Renaissance such as is found in Transitional French churches of the sixteenth century.

The tower is the most impressive part of the rebuilt church. Wilson's tower was intended to rise over the first bay of the nave, but the foundations could not take it; after only a small part had been erected it was taken down again and the present grander tower, projecting from the west front, was built instead. It is carried on open arches and has square corner pieces and a crown of mighty pinnacles on top. The whole surface of the walls is covered with patterns of little arches and other Gothic decoration. It has been suggested that the basic design for this tower was Wren's, but that the surfaces were modified in execution. Whoever the designer, it is a noble piece of work, fully worthy of its dominant role on the Warwick skyline.

Beyond the church tower is Northgate Street, dominated by the SHIRE HALL and former COUNTY GAOL – an unusually good group of Georgian public buildings. The Shire Hall was built between 1753 and 1758 by David and William Hiorn and Job Collins, to the design of the Warwickshire gentleman-architect Sanderson Miller. The centre has a pediment, and inside is a large Hall, 93 feet long, with rich early nineteenth-century ormolu chandeliers. Flanking the entrance are little clipped box trees, like Easter eggs. The County Gaol was added in 1777–83 by Thomas Johnson and is a powerful neo-classical design with archaic Greek Doric columns and triglyph frieze. Across the end of Northgate Street, forming a perfect view-stopper, is NORTHGATE HOUSE (actually a semi-detached pair), built of brick with a central pediment and dated 1698.

Behind the Shire Hall are modern COUNTY OFFICES. The main block, designed by G.R. Barnsley in the late 1950s, forms the north side of the Market Place and is a good example of the tactful, unassertive Modern architecture of that decade. It is joined to a splendid stone-faced house of 1714, with fluted Corinthian pilasters. The MARKET PLACE is L-shaped and has recently been re-paved in a decent manner; in the centre is the former Town Hall of 1670, originally with an open arcade on the ground floor. It is now the COUNTY MUSEUM and was well restored in the 1960s.

WARWICK CASTLE

Warwick Castle has long been a leading tourist attraction, famed for its architecture, setting and legendary associations, as well as for its contents. In the eighteenth century Lord Torrington described it as 'the most perfect piece of castellated antiquity in the kingdom', and later visitors have endorsed that view. Among others, Prince Pückler-Muskau, the Polish count whose published journal gives a vivid picture of Regency England, thought it exceeded even Ashridge and Woburn in interest and magnificence.

The original motte-and-bailey castle was built by William the Conqueror in 1068, rebuilt in stone in the twelfth and thirteenth centuries, and enlarged in the

The Beauchamp Chapel, St Mary's, Warwick.

Warwick Castle.

fourteenth by the Beauchamp Earls of Warwick. Thomas the Elder, who held the castle from 1329–69, built Caesar's Tower and the Gatehouse. His son, Thomas the Younger, extended the curtain wall and built Guy's Tower in 1394. Further work was done in the fifteenth century by Richard Neville, Earl of Warwick, 'the King Maker', whose political intrigues during the reign of Henry VI were immortalised by Shakespeare. The 'King Maker's' daughter married the Duke of Clarence, Richard III's brother, bringing the castle to the Crown. It remained in royal hands until 1547, when it was granted to John Dudley, Earl of Warwick, but it reverted to the Crown in 1590. It was subsequently granted in 1604 to Sir Fulke Greville, later created Baron Brooke. The Earldom of Warwick was revived for the Grevilles in 1759.

In the Civil War the Grevilles supported the Parliamentary side, which saved the castle from the ruinous fate of nearby Kenilworth (*q.v.*). After the Restoration, Lord Brooke remodelled the lodgings on the south side of the courtyard to form a handsome sequence of state rooms within the thirteenth-century walls. The fabric was further altered and embellished by his successor, the 1st Earl of Warwick, who also commissioned the four Canaletto views of the castle that remained at Warwick from 1748 until 1977. The 2nd and 3rd Earls collected many of the treasures that have enriched the interior for nearly two centuries. The 4th Earl, in the mid-nineteenth century, employed Salvin on the castle and also restored it after the fire of 1871.

The visitor entering through the fourteenth-century Gatehouse in the middle of the east side will be impressed by Caesar's Tower on the left and Guy's Tower on the right. The austere grandeur of the medieval military architecture is softened in the courtyard by the eighteenth-century landscaping – a brilliant early scheme of Capability Brown's. A side-door leads to the Chapel, which was remodelled in 1753, when it was given a pretty plaster ceiling; an assortment of Flemish medieval stained glass was installed in the east window

in 1759. The white-and-gold Dining Room is another piece of eighteenth-century Neo-Elizabethanism, designed by Timothy Lightoler. The portraits of Frederick, Prince of Wales, and his wife Augusta sport the most lavish Rococo frames in England – a good match for the gilt English tables beneath. Ironically, in view of the early Grevilles' Parliamentary sympathies, the room is dominated by a version of Van Dyck's vast equestrian portrait of Charles I.

After this, the Great Hall, as remodelled in 1872, is something of a surprise. It has a red-and-white marble floor and a terrific carved oak sideboard created by Cooke Brothers of Warwick for the Great Exhibition of 1851. It was in this room in 1312 that Piers Gaveston, Edward II's favourite, was sentenced to death – an act which, more than anything, led to the bloody deterioration of English political life in the fourteenth century. Other historic events associated with this room are two visits of Queen Elizabeth I in 1566 and 1572.

From the Hall, the state rooms open in a continuous enfilade. The Red Drawing Room has panelling lacquered a strong red – an effective contrast to the dark cedar wainscot in the Cedar Drawing Room beyond, where English gilt-wood Rococo sconces flank full-length portraits by Van Dyck and his school, and a lavish stucco ceiling completes a princely ensemble. In the Green Drawing Room, the seventeenth-century panelling is complemented by a late seventeenth-century stucco ceiling. Queen Anne's Bedroom takes its name from her bed and chairs (originally at Windsor Castle) which came to Warwick in the late eighteenth century. The apartments end with the Blue Boudoir, which has the most magnificent of the seventeenth-century stucco ceilings.

The castle remained the property of the Greville family until 1978, when it was sold to the present owners. The private apartments were reopened in April 1982 and contain a waxworks recreation by Madame Tussaud's of a house party of the 1890s.

45 *Biddulph Grange, Staffordshire.*

46 *Nostell Priory, South and West Yorkshire.*

47 *Arbury Hall, Warwickshire.*

48 *Charlecote Park, Warwickshire.*

49 *Coughton Court, Warwickshire.*

50 *Honington Hall, Warwickshire.*

51 *Burton Constable Hall, East Yorkshire.*

52 *Bolton Abbey, North Yorkshire.*

53 *Broughton Hall, North Yorkshire.*

54 *Castle Howard, North Yorkshire.*

55 *Castle Howard.*

56 *Newby Hall, North Yorkshire.*

57 *Ribston Hall, North Yorkshire.*

58 *Ripon Cathedral, North Yorkshire.*

59 *Whitby, North Yorkshire.*

60 *The Temple of Piety, Studley Royal, North Yorkshire.*

61 *Wentworth Woodhouse, South and West Yorkshire.*

62 *Sutton Park, Sutton-on-the-Forest, North Yorkshire.*

63 *Harewood, South and West Yorkshire.*

64 *Baddesley Clinton, Warwickshire.*

65 *Carlton Towers, North Yorkshire.*

Yorkshire

Yorkshire is the heart of the north and the largest English county. It is also the most richly endowed architecturally, as it contains the biggest and best of everything. York Minster and Wentworth Woodhouse are, respectively, the largest of English medieval churches and Georgian country houses, while Beverley Minster and Castle Howard can claim to be the most beautiful of their respective genres. Yorkshire contains about a third of the medieval parish churches of England, many of them much grander even than those of East Anglia; more monastic ruins than any other county; over twenty Norman castles; innumerable small country towns with handsome main streets and unspoilt market places; and the magnificent historic city of York itself, as well as the Victorian industrial towns of the old West Riding. But the dominant architectural character of Yorkshire is Georgian. It remains the most Georgian part of England, with great estates, model farms, country houses, racecourses and landscape gardens all on a scale and of a perfection met with nowhere else.

Until 1974 Yorkshire was divided into three 'Ridings', or thirds – East, North and West; but in that grey year the Heath–Walker rearrangement of local government came into force and swept away these ancient territorial divisions as well as shifting all the boundaries around. No other part of England was as badly affected by these indefensible changes; and, of a population of four and a quarter million souls, hardly a voice was raised in opposition. So much for that famous Yorkshire independence and outspokenness! Under the new dispensation North Yorkshire has lost a small strip along the River Tees to Cleveland but gained all the rural part of the West Riding as well as the northern section of the East Riding. The remains of the latter were combined with a chunk of north Lincolnshire to form something called 'Humberside' (though East Yorkshire is still allowed as a postal address). The old textile towns of the West Riding between Halifax and Leeds remain as the nucleus of a much-shrunken West Yorkshire. The coalfield between

Sheffield and Doncaster was also taken out of the West Riding and renamed South Yorkshire. At the time of writing, proposals to abolish the metropolitan counties would allow the Ridings (if not their original boundaries) to be restored by re-amalgamating South and West Yorkshire to form the West Riding, and renaming North Yorkshire and Humberside.

In the following pages I have arranged my material into three sections, putting South and West Yorkshire together, and sticking to East Yorkshire for Humberside. This does not make complete topographical or historical sense, but it is the best that can be done with the present dog's dinner. It leaves North Yorkshire out of balance, as the section on that area takes in all the county's most beautiful landscape – including the West Riding Dales and North York Moors – as well as all the best architecture – abbeys, towns and country houses, and, of course, York itself. This is, by any standards, the finest part of England. The country here contains all that is most marvellous in our landscape, including two hilly National Parks in addition to the unspoilt agricultural vales and plains. East Yorkshire is less spectacular, though it has the Wolds, sweeping and empty, and many large and well-managed estates. West Yorkshire contains the most dramatic combination of old industry and landscape, with wild empty moors dividing the sprawling stone-built textile towns in the valleys below. This is perhaps not everyone's idea of tourist country but there are wonderful things to see, and if the textile industry continues to decay at its present rate its towns will soon be one with the wool villages of Suffolk and the Cotswolds. South Yorkshire is the least exciting part. This is the area of nineteenth-century heavy industry and coal-mines. The plain around Doncaster, with ugly brick colliery villages and sprawling new housing developments, is dreary indeed. But even here there are splendid oases – country houses that hold out against the odds, churches that have not yet fallen down coal-mines, and impressive relics of medieval greatness. They are all worth seeking out.

East Yorkshire

Beverley★

1; 8 miles N of Hull on A1079

Thomas Gent, a painter and historian of York, described Beverley in the mid-eighteenth century as 'in every way delightful, the houses handsome and well-built, the streets neat and clean, the gardens many and beautiful'. This still applies. There are two good approaches to Beverley. The railway from Hull streaks across the flat intervening fields, straight as a die, on axis with the Minster. The main road from York crosses the beautifully landscaped Georgian racecourse and enters the town near the North Bar, with no intervening suburbs, thus giving a very good picture of the town as it was in the eighteenth century when it was a centre of fashion full of the houses of the East Riding gentry. But Beverley was an important market town and port as long ago as the Middle Ages, and its major monuments – St Mary's Church and the Minster – date from then.

The MINSTER rises cathedral-like (though it is not in fact a cathedral) on its own at the south end of the town. It was founded *c.*690 by St John of Beverley, Bishop of York, whose shrine stood behind the high altar until the Reformation and, as an object of pilgrimage, was the reason for the ambitious scale of the church. The present building was begun in the thirteenth century. The chancel and transepts are Early English while the nave, west

Beverley Minster.

front and towers are Decorated with Perpendicular touches, but sensitively deferring to the earlier work. It has a unified perfection, within and without, which makes it one of the most beautiful of all English churches. The west front, with a pair of graceful flanking towers, is especially successful.

The interior makes an immediate and overwhelming impact because of the exquisite golden stone, contrasted here and there with thin shafts of black Purbeck, and the subtle manipulations of proportion and light in the vistas. Note, for example, the consummate way in which the bosses of the choir vault diminish in size from west to east – a visual trick that exaggerates the apparent length of the building. The rich perfection of the detail owes much to an early eighteenth-century restoration under the direction of Nicholas Hawksmoor and the ingenious carpenter-architect William Thornton, who, among other triumphs, jacked the end of the north transept back into an upright position. The magnificent Baroque-Gothic west doors carved with the Four Evangelists are also Thornton's work. At first the interior strikes you as remarkably even and uniform, but in fact there is considerable variation in the detail. Note, for instance, the differences in the blank arcading round the bottom part of the nave walls. The Minster was restored again by Sir George Gilbert Scott in the 1860s and it is a stiff test to decide what is the work of the medieval masons, what was done by the eighteenth-century restorers and what is Scott's. He replaced some of the more outrageous eighteenth-century Gothickries, including Hawksmoor's choir screen. The masonry from this now adorns various gardens in Lincolnshire, but a pair of lead statues of King Athelstan and St John of Beverley that adorned it still stand in the south aisle. These are masterpieces of intricate lead casting, painted with sandy paint to resemble stone. Nearby is the gruff Norman font on which sits a splendid scrolly eighteenth-century font cover. It is a pity about the trendy low-backed pale oak chairs in the nave, and the new central circular altar under the crossing looks like the dining table from an Edwardian tycoon's yacht. Could anything be more absurdly incongruous? Raise your eyes, however, and admire the splendid twirling carved eighteenth-century boss in the oculus of the crossing-vault. The deceptive medieval-looking stained glass in the south transept windows was made by Powell in the 1930s – a most impressive achievement.

The choir is the earliest part of the building – Early English maturity with masses of Purbeck, dogtooth-encrusted mouldings and lush stiff-leaved capitals. The choir stalls are basically late Gothic (they date from 1520) but again owe a great deal to eighteenth- and nineteenth-century restorers. Look for George II, in his crown, on the canopy. The *trompe* geometrical pavement of coloured marbles is also due to the eighteenth-century restorers and would be disconcerting for inebriated brides to process down! The Clayton and Bell stencilled decoration in the vaults (recently restored) reaches a climax of elaboration over the altar. The Percy screen or reredos is an exquisite piece of Decorated work. On the altar side it is embellished with Victorian mosaics but the back, towards the Lady Chapel, is in its original state and is a masterpiece of medieval stone carving; hours could be spent studying the details. The Percy screen is an extension of the Percy tomb between the chancel and north choir aisle. This is the richest Decorated monument in England, its nodding ogee canopy so encrusted with carving that it looks like a pile of cauliflowers. Facing it is a Baroque monument of white marble to Sir Charles Hotham with haunting empty suits of armour flanking a severely truncated obelisk (the top 30 feet were lopped off by Gilbert Scott). There is another fine eighteenth-century monument in the Lady Chapel. It is by Scheemakers, to a design by Gibbs, and commemorates Sir Thomas Warton, who raised the money for the eighteenth-century restoration of the church – so perhaps it is not *too* shocking that he has usurped the site of the Lady altar. The huge Perpendicular window filling the upper part of the east wall contains all the surviving medieval stained glass in the church, placed here in the eighteenth-century and restored by Shrigley and Hunt in 1927. It makes a fine climax to the long vista through the church.

The WEDNESDAY MARKET was originally a large triangular open space along the whole of the north side of the Minster, but it was encroached on by squatters in the fifteenth century and is therefore a much-reduced shadow of its former self. The bulk of the Minster now rises from streets of small-scale old houses of different dates. Some splendid cast-iron lamp-posts made at the Thorncliffe Iron Works in 1824 have recently been repaired and can be found around the Minster and in several of the main streets.

The central axis through the town comprises BUTCHER ROW, TOLL GAVEL and WALKERGATE, displaying some pleasant seventeenth- and eighteenth-century brick houses with projecting brick cornices and red pantiled roofs. They lead to the TUESDAY MARKET, the major open space of Beverley, which is endowed with considerable style by the Market Cross – an elegant Baroque confection erected to the design of Samuel Shelton of Wakefield in 1714. The MARKET PLACE has a nice informal shape and is surrounded by good buildings with interesting shopfronts: Akrill, the gunmaker, with a gold-lettered sign; Seller, the chemist, with a new carved and gilt mortar and pestle; and Michael Philips', with a green-painted Regency shop-front rescued from elsewhere. East of the Market Place, the grain of the old town has been disturbed by a new road and too much 'vernacular'-style housing – well-intentioned enough but threatening to swamp the real old buildings of the town.

North of the Market Place is ST MARY'S, the parish church – one of the most beautiful in England, with a massive central tower and a west front flanked by fretted octagonal turrets. The interior is spacious and an impression of unity is given by its late Perpendicular reconstruction after the old tower collapsed in 1520. The eye is immediately caught by the unique roof paintings, with panels of forty English kings in colours on a gold

ground. These were first painted in 1445 and restored in 1863 and 1939. Another lovable feature of the church is the series of little carvings, such as the famous Minstrels' Pier, to be seen all over the interior. Most stunning of all, however, is the chancel aisle, with its superb tierceron star vault and large Decorated east window.

The principal sequence of Georgian houses in Beverley stretches to the north of the Market Place. First comes NORTH BAR WITHIN, where there are several stately houses. On the right, behind trees, is St Mary's Manor, built in 1815 with a columned porch and circular Dining Room. On the left is the Beverley Arms Hotel, originally known as the Blue Bell and built in 1794 by the local joiner-architect William Middleton. It features in Trollope's novel *Ralph the Heir* as the Percy Standard. The NORTH BAR itself is the sole survivor of Beverley's five medieval gateways. It was built of locally made brick in 1409–10 and cost £96.9s.11½d. It is Gothic and has a Hanseatic air. Beyond, the street continues as NORTH BAR WITHOUT; it is wider, its cobbled verges and chestnut trees giving it the feel of a boulevard. It contains several more good Georgian houses. No. 62 was the town house of the Sykes family of Sledmere (*q.v.*) and dates from 1725. No. 56 has a beautiful doorcase of 1740 carved with a shell and palm branches. The continuation of North Bar Without is called NEW WALK – a piece of planned Georgian development dating from 1782 and dominated by the Ionic portico of the Greek Revival SESSIONS HOUSE on the west side; the carved and coloured figure of Justice is by Watson of York.

Retracing one's steps to the south, a detour can be made down Lairgate and into NEWBEGIN, which can show one or two good houses, notably Newbegin House of *c.*1690 and, set back in a garden to its east, a house the front porch of which is made out of the Tuscan columns that supported Hawksmoor's galleries in the Minster until they were thrown out in a later restoration. In Lairgate stands LAIRGATE HALL, the former town house of the Pennymans of Ormesby (*q.v.*) and now council offices. It is early eighteenth-century but has a beautiful Drawing Room added by Carr of York with a rare green ground Chinese wallpaper. Champney Road leads to Cross Street off which is the GUILDHALL – basically fifteenth-century but remodelled in the eighteenth and disguised externally by a severe Greek Doric portico. The Court Room is by William Middleton and has a rich stucco ceiling embellished in three phases by Giuseppe Cortese. Behind the dais is a frilly Rococo carving of the Royal Arms.

Bridlington
2; 9 miles SE of Filey on A165
Bridlington comprises two parts: the old market town, which is half a mile inland, and the staithe, or harbour, on the coast. The undistinguished modern resort has grown up between them but the old parts retain their character. The old town comprises one long HIGH STREET running up to the Gatehouse of the priory. The street curves a little and is lined with a varied assortment of good Georgian houses, many still retaining late eighteenth-century shop-fronts. It survives in remarkably unspoilt condition, thanks partly to the efforts of

The Great Hall, Burton Agnes Hall.

Francis Johnson, who has his architectural office here at Craven House (No. 16) – a seemly red brick house with an elegant late eighteenth-century doorcase.

The PRIORY was founded *c*.1120 as an Augustinian establishment. At the Reformation the east end of the church and the monastic buildings were demolished, but the nave was preserved as the parish church. Even in its truncated state, the church is impressive, if somewhat gaunt. Two huge buttresses at the east end mark where the old crossing and choir once abutted. The west front is curiously asymmetrical, with one ugly stumpy tower and another somewhat more aspiring with hefty Perpendicular pinnacles. The body of the church dates from the thirteenth century but was partly remodelled in the Perpendicular period. The tall nave has beautiful clustered columns supporting a tall clerestory. The north side has a triforium, but the south side has the more unusual feature of double tracery in front of the lower part of the clerestory windows, which creates a remarkably intricate architectural effect. The church was substantially restored by George Gilbert Scott in the 1870s and the reredos behind the present altar is his.

SEWERBY HALL is a white-painted Georgian house of two different dates – the central pedimented section of 1714 and the wings, bow windows and semi-circular Tuscan porch added in 1808. The interiors are mostly of *c*.1714, with enriched panelling in some rooms and a good staircase with twisted balusters. The house is now used as an art gallery by the local authority and the ground floor rooms are filled with glass cases displaying archaeological bits and pieces, while the rooms upstairs contain paintings by local artists.

Burton Agnes Hall
3; 6 miles SW of Bridlington on A166

Burton Agnes Hall is one of the most attractive of late Elizabethan mansions; the south front with gables and bowed windows and the Gatehouse with ogival-capped turrets form a perfect composition.

The house was built between 1601 and 1610 by Sir Henry Griffiths, a member of a Welsh family long established in the Midlands, and it has been little altered since. The warm brick symmetrical elevation is the overture to one of the most notable surviving Jacobean interiors in the country. The Great Hall has panelling with blank arches; a carved screen decorated with sibyls, the Twelve Tribes of Israel and much else; and an equally elaborate early alabaster chimneypiece depicting the Wise and Foolish Virgins, which was brought from Barmston, some 6 miles away.

The Drawing Room has similar arched panelling and a carved chimneypiece decorated with the Dance of Death. King James's Bedroom and the Queen's Bedroom on the first floor both have superb Jacobean stucco ceilings. On the top floor is the Long Gallery, which was subdivided into bedrooms in the eighteenth century; it has been restored in recent years, however, and its plaster tunnel vault reconstructed to the original design from surviving fragments.

Burton Constable Hall
4; 8 miles NE of Hull off B1238 [51]

This seemingly Jacobean house was in fact extensively altered in the 1750s by William Constable, an unusually discerning patron, who kept to the original style. Constable consulted a number of different architects, including James Wyatt, Thomas Lightoler and Thomas Atkinson of York, and landscaped the grounds to the design of Capability Brown. The house was much neglected for a number of years after 1932 and the present owner is carrying out a substantial programme of restoration, which is still not complete.

The contents of the house are remarkably well documented, and the names of the makers and original prices are known for nearly everything, even the customs duty paid on marble table-tops imported from Italy. The most unusual interior is the Long Gallery on the first floor, formed out of a series of bedrooms between 1740 and 1770 and embellished with convincing Jacobean-style plasterwork copied from old examples. The family portraits displayed here include an outstanding Marcus Gheeraerts of Lady Constable, dated 1599, and a pastel by Liotard of William Constable, *c*.1770, showing him dressed in Rousseau's clothes.

Of the other main rooms, two – the Hall and the Dining Room – are excellent examples of Rococo work by Lightoler, while the rest are neo-classical. The Catholic Chapel and Blue Drawing Room are by Atkinson with plasterwork by Giuseppe Cortese. The Great Drawing Room was designed by James Wyatt in 1775 and contains the original furniture made for it by Chippendale (whose bills are preserved). The large plain Staircase Hall contains historical paintings by Andrea Casali from Fonthill.

Everingham Hall

5; 5 miles S of Pocklington off A1079

Until its sale by Lady Herries in 1983, the Everingham estate had passed down entirely by descent from the twelfth century when it was acquired from the Archbishop of York by the de Everinghams. In the early sixteenth century it came by marriage to the Constables of Flamborough. 'Little Sir Marmaduke' Constable commanded the English left wing at Flodden. His younger son, also Marmaduke, was knighted after the battle and was the first of the family to live at Everingham.

The Constables remained Catholic – Sir Robert, the eldest son of Little Sir Marmaduke, was executed for his part in the Pilgrimage of Grace – and in the seventeenth century were royalists, created baronets by Charles I in return for their support. On the death in 1746 of Sir Marmaduke, 4th and last Baronet, the estate was bequeathed to his great-nephew William Haggerston, who changed his name to Constable. William married Winefride Maxwell, great-granddaughter of the Jacobite 5th Earl of Nithsdale and 9th Lord Herries of Terregles, who was attainted and condemned to death for his part in the 1715 Rising but, with the help of his wife, escaped from the Tower disguised in a cloak.

At the time of his marriage, William decided to demolish the old house and replace it with a new one. He chose as his architect John Carr of York, whose designs, and some of the building accounts, survive among the family papers in Hull University Library. The new Everingham is a compact Anglo-Palladian villa seven bays wide and three storeys high, built of local red brick with stone dressings; it is comparable to Carr's slightly grander design for the Catholic Clifton family at Lytham in Lancashire (*q.v.*).

The exterior is restrained, but the interior was embellished with excellent work by York craftsmen such as the carver David Shillito, who was responsible for the Doric set-piece on the landing, and the joiner Richard Bainton, who made the handsome mahogany doors. The placing of the principal rooms on the ground floor, rather than on the *piano nobile* in the Italian manner, was a striking innovation on Carr's part. The Drawing Room has good plasterwork on the walls and a contemporary marble chimneypiece.

Everingham was inherited in 1819 by William Constable (whose father Marmaduke had added the name of Maxwell to his own) and he eventually succeeded as 10th Lord Herries of Terregles in 1858 following the formal reversal of the attainder against his ancestor. William Constable-Maxwell made large additions, partly to accommodate his expanding family, and in 1836–9 erected the adjoining Catholic CHAPEL (dedicated to Our Lady and St Everilda) – a great architectural treasure. This, at first sight, rather improbable Roman basilica is a striking demonstration of the Constable-Maxwell family's adherence to Catholicism. The designs were made by the Italian architect Agostino Giorgioli, while construction was supervised on the spot by John Harper, a pupil of Benjamin Dean Wyatt. The exterior is stuccoed, with the main entrance inset in a dramatic arch and a noble Latin inscription on the cornice. The interior

is magnificent, with grey marbled walls, Siena scagliola Corinthian columns and a white-and-gold coffered tunnel vault. Many of the fittings were specially made in Italy, including the plaster statues of the Apostles by Leopold Bozzoni of Carrara, the altar of granite and porphyry by Giuseppe Leonardi of Rome, and possibly the font. The contemporary organ in the west gallery is of considerable historical importance as it has never been altered or modernised. It was made by William Allen of Bristol in 1839.

Lord Herries' additions to the house, which detracted from the symmetry of the original design, were demolished in 1960. At that time, Carr's house was restored by the 16th Duke of Norfolk, who had inherited the property from his mother in 1945. The architect for the restoration was Francis Johnson, who carefully replaced missing features, such as the front porch and the main staircase. The date of the restoration is inscribed on the lead rainwater hoppers: 'AFH 1962'. It is largely as a result of this exemplary restoration that today Everingham is the perfect smaller Georgian country house – which, by chance, happens to have a Roman basilica on the lawn beside it.

The Chapel, Everingham Hall.

Garrowby Hall

6; 13 miles E of York on A166

Garrowby, formerly a small shooting box on the edge of the Yorkshire Wolds, is now the principal seat of one of England's more interesting twentieth-century aristocratic families: Charles Lindley Wood, 2nd Viscount Halifax (who died in 1934) was the learned champion of Anglo-Catholicism, while his son, the 1st Earl, was Viceroy of India and Foreign Secretary. The present Lord Halifax has the distinction of numbering two Prime Ministers among his great-grandfathers: the Liberal Lord Rosebery and the Conservative Lord Derby.

The Woods were a Whig family from the West Riding (their main seat was at Hickleton (*q.v.*)) who rose to prominence in the early nineteenth century. Garrowby, a small hunting lodge surrounded by farmland, had been bought by the 2nd Baronet in 1827 and in the late nineteenth century was used mainly for holidays. The 2nd Baronet's grandson, the 2nd Viscount, enlarged the house in romantic semblance of an old manor round two courtyards (one the stables) and made the park by removing the hedges and planting avenues and clumps of trees.

After the Second World War, the Halifaxes moved permanently to Garrowby and when the present Lord Halifax inherited he decided to rebuild it as a proper country house. He appointed Francis Johnson and Malcolm McKie to design it in a Georgian style reminiscent of Carr of York. Work began in 1980 and the last touches were added in 1984.

The new Garrowby forms three sides of a quadrangle. The rear (north) wing is the original 1803 house and contains Francis Johnson's Library of 1973, with guest bedrooms above. The 2nd Viscount's little castellated tower at the west end has been converted into a Chapel by removing the first floor and opening the interior to the full height. This has created space for the large Victorian Gothic altarpiece ornamented with woodcarvings, which was made in Oberammergau to Tower's design, and the Jacobean-style gallery and pews from the previous chapel. The new Chapel also contains many of the family's religious relics and mementoes and reflects their strong High Church tradition.

The long east wing is also old, but has been remodelled inside to contain the family's own accommodation; this opens off a long corridor, part of which has plaster vaulting. The main block, facing south over the freshly re-landscaped park, is entirely new and contains the Drawing Room, summer Sitting Room, Dining Room, front Hall, main staircase and principal bedrooms. The house is cleverly planned so that it can be expanded or contracted as required. This makes it economical and easy to manage.

The interior is beautifully finished throughout and is a tribute to the great care taken by the architects and by Lord Halifax himself. The Library has architectural bookcases designed round inset paintings and at one end is a screen of Ionic columns with capitals copied from the temple at Bassae. The main rooms have decorative plasterwork designed by Francis Johnson and handsome chimneypieces; that in the Sitting Room was designed by Johnson and made by R. Reid of York, but the others are eighteenth-century ones re-used. The mahogany panelled doors downstairs are all new, but the painted ones upstairs are from the old house. The Dining Room has an apsidal serving recess with built-in electric hotplates flanking an equestrian bronze of Louis XIV – a nice combination of modern convenience and eighteenth-century grandeur. The Entrance Hall is divided from the staircase by Doric columns painted to resemble Siena marble, and the elaborate wrought-iron balustrade was made by Hammond of Kirkbymoorside from Francis Johnson's full-scale drawings.

Hedon

7; 6 miles E of Hull on A1033

It is a considerable surprise to find the vast, proud CHURCH OF ST AUGUSTINE in this little town. But once upon a time Hedon was a port to rival Hull, and in the Middle Ages was three times its present size. The church, larger than the largest of the East Anglian wool churches, is a monument to this long-vanished prosperity. It is 165 feet long and the central tower is 128 feet high. The church is mainly thirteenth-century, in the Early English style, but the tower, crowned with no fewer than sixteen pinnacles, was added in the fifteenth in a blaze of Perpendicular splendour. The ends of the transepts make magnificent architectural compositions, with three tiers of lancet windows, steep gables and mighty corner buttresses and pinnacles. If they seem to have a super-Gothic perfection about them, this is thanks to a restoration by G.E. Street in 1868–76. He removed the Perpendicular windows and reinstated the original thirteenth-century design – an admirable decision from an aesthetic point of view, whatever William Morris might have thought. The nave is the most impressive part of the interior, the tall clustered columns and richly moulded arches contrasting with the large expanses of bare stone and the smaller windows of the clerestory above – a highly satisfying design. The transepts and chancel have been slightly spoilt by the demolition of the eastern aisles and the blocking of the arches that once led to them. Hedon does not have the uniform beauty of Patrington or Beverley (*qq.v.*), but it has a strong masculine dignity and grandeur that impress even in its slightly truncated state.

Hornsea

8; 11 miles NE of Beverley on B1244

ST NICHOLAS's is a large Perpendicular church built mainly in the fourteenth and fifteenth centuries. The walls are of rough cobbles – a nice humble touch reminiscent of East Anglia. The west tower once had a spire, but this fell down in 1733. The interior is strangely impressive. The nave of five bays has continuously moulded piers and arches with no capitals – always an effect of noble simplicity – supporting large clerestory windows. The impression of more window than wall reaches a climax at the east end around the altar, where solid masonry gives way entirely to three large Perpendicular windows making the chancel a glazed lantern structure.

St Peter's church, Howden.

Houghton Hall

9; 4 miles S of Market Weighton off A1034

Francis Johnson, the Bridlington-based architect, has since the Second World War been responsible for the design of several fine new houses in the Georgian style in his native county. He has also supervised several imaginative and enterprising restorations and reconstructions of eighteenth-century buildings. Houghton Hall, carried out between 1957 and 1960, is one of the most ambitious of these jobs. The original house, built by Philip Langdale in 1760, had been faced with dreary stucco in the 1820s and altered again so detrimentally that the Historic Buildings Council did not deem it worthy of grant aid when the reconstruction was begun in 1957. Francis Johnson's work consisted of stripping away these accretions and replanning the interior. It took three years, being completed in 1960, and produced a house with a Palladian plan of main block and symmetrical wings. Externally the stucco was removed to reveal the brick; glazing bars were restored to the windows; the billiards room, the chapel and the Victorian porch were demolished. On the garden front dressings of Ancaster stone were added, and so were architraves and cornices to the ground-floor windows and a pediment to the central door. On the entrance front a prominent new porch was built. Thus the original symmetry and dignity were restored.

Inside, the rooms were replanned, keeping the best existing features, including the Drawing Room with its attractive Edwardian plasterwork and the two-storeyed Hall with eighteenth-century staircase. The Library, opening off the Hall through Edwardian arches, was enlarged by throwing in a redundant corridor and embellished with an eighteenth-century-style chimney-piece. The old dining room was converted into a Smoking Room, and a new Dining Room was made nearer to the kitchen out of space formerly occupied by the lowest flight of the back stairs and a ground-floor bedroom. The retention of the upper flights of the back stairs posed a problem, as the underside of the steps jutted into the room, but the architect got round this by giving the room a Soanic ceiling with a segmental arch over half the space. The poor lighting was overcome by inserting a large Venetian window in the west wall. Both wings were also replanned: the west to contain domestic offices, the east to contain bedrooms.

Houghton is a good example of the way in which old country houses were rehabilitated and adapted for continued family life after the Second World War, following a period of decay when it looked as if they might follow the monasteries and leave just ruins behind them.

Howden

10; 8 miles SE of Selby on A63

Written descriptions do not prepare you for the amazing sight of ST PETER'S, the parish church, framed in its own ruins as you approach from the Market Place, its huge, gaping east window acting as a decorative surround to the view of the rest of the building, like a Gothick border round an eighteenth-century architectural illustration. The manor here belonged to the Bishops of Durham in the Middle Ages and they were responsible for erecting and embellishing the huge collegiate church. After the Reformation it proved too much for the parish and by the early seventeenth century only the western half was being used, as now. The lead was taken from the chancel roof to repair the nave, then in 1696 the upper part of the chancel collapsed in a thunderstorm. The roof of the Chapter House followed suit in 1750.

Even in its present half-ruined state, however, Howden is a magnificent church. It is 255 feet long and the crossing-tower is 135 feet high. The latter was begun by Bishop Skirlaw *c*.1400. It has only two tiers of windows, the lowest being prodigiously tall – a gloriously exaggerated effect – and the top is finished off with plain battlements and no pinnacles. The main part of the church was built remarkably quickly during the last decades of the thirteenth century and it illustrates well the transition from Early English to Decorated. The west front has a tall, narrow Decorated window in the centre, set off by four octagonal turrets pierced and pinnacled with crocketed spirelets – a bold staccato effect. The interior is impressively unified, with tall arcades of clustered piers enhanced by carved foliage capitals and beautiful moulded arches supporting a clerestory. The timber roof is a mid-nineteenth-century reconstruction to the original design. The east end is formed of the blocked chancel arch, but the beautiful Perpendicular rood-screen survives as a reredos to the present altar with its four fretted tabernacle niches, two on either side of a central ogee arch. They contain the four original fifteenth-century statues – a rare survival in England.

Hull

11; 8 miles S of Beverley on A1079
Includes Maister House (NT)
In the late Middle Ages Hull was the leading port on the east coast of England; it continued to flourish, especially in the eighteenth century and the early twentieth, on trade with northern Europe. The port, however, has recently closed and, sad to say, the historic centre of the town has been ruthlessly maltreated since the Second World War. The Georgian area to the north-west of the old centre has been decimated, while the ancient nucleus, filling the peninsula between the River Hull and the eighteenth-century docks, presents a sad and moth-eaten spectacle. It all makes a shaming contrast to the old cities of Holland and northern Germany. Hull was, it is true, bombed in the war, but the worst damage has been perpetrated since: swathes of fine buildings, including the whole of the old Market Place, have been pointlessly destroyed. Nevertheless, the city does contain a lot of architectural interest that is well worth seeking out.

The visitor by train finds himself in the modern centre of the town, its wide streets exuding a clean, well-planned air. Here are the principal shops. This part of the town dates almost entirely from the 1950s and, with its mixture of timid Modern and Neo-Georgian, already

seems a period piece. It will be noticed that all the telephone kiosks are painted cream rather than red; this is because Hull has its own independent telephone company. QUEEN VICTORIA SQUARE makes a good introduction to the old town. It is a triangular space containing, in the middle, a bronze statue of Queen Victoria by C. Fehr dated 1903, erected on top of a subterranean public lavatory. The square's character is determined by three impressive public buildings: on the west side is the CITY HALL of 1903 by J.H. Hirst (the City Architect), with a copper dome and carved frieze; on the south side is the FERENS ART GALLERY – a chaste 1920s' *Beaux Arts* classical affair containing a decent collection of Old Masters; to the east is the Old Dock Office, now the TOWN DOCKS MUSEUM – a florid triangular building with three little domes and richly carved detail with a nautical flavour – note the intertwined rope pattern of the friezes and the tridents and anchors on the railings. It was designed in 1867 by Christopher Wray. The best of Hull's civic buildings lies to the east of Queen Victoria Square. This is Edwin Cooper's GUILDHALL of 1906–14, the acme of Edwardian Baroque splendour. The carved Roman armour over the doorways is thrilling in the extreme. This is Real Architecture! Behind it and to the east of the Docks Museum stretches QUEEN'S GARDENS on the site of Queen's Dock, which was sadly filled in between the wars and is now a poorly landscaped garden focused on the re-sited WILBERFORCE MONUMENT – a Doric column 90 feet high. It stands in front of the truly dreadful 1960s' Hull College building – a large, boring symmetrical block, which, to my mind, wholly negates the punctuation value of the column. To the south of Queen's Square stretches PRINCES DOCK, still containing water and therefore a visual asset to the town. Almost incredibly it is proposed to fill this and cover it with commercial development. Princes Dock Street, which runs along the east side of the dock, has several good brick and stucco Georgian buildings (actually the back of Trinity House). ROLAND HOUSE, its pediment decorated with an anchor, is an early nineteenth-century office block (note the extrawide windows on the ground floor). Next door, the VICTORIA ALMSHOUSES of 1842 sport a handsome Ionic gateway.

WHITEFRIARGATE to the east recalls the medieval friary that once stood here. Its site is now occupied by Trinity House, which fills the entire south side of the street and forms an unbroken sequence of Georgian frontages, some of high quality but all disfigured by modern shopfronts. The most interesting buildings are the former BANK OF ENGLAND – which has an Ionic centrepiece and pediment with the Smith arms and, in the pediment, a jolly figure of Neptune by John Earle, the father of a local dynasty of sculptors – and the former NEPTUNE INN. Opposite the Inn, and focused on it, is Parliament Street, a planned late eighteenth-century layout with more or less uniform Georgian houses sporting pedimented doorcases. Whitefriargate is continued in Silver Street, which has several Victorian Italianate banks and the MARKET HALL. In an alley just off is the OLDE WHITE HARTE, an Artisan Mannerist house of the 1670s. And in The Land of Green Ginger (a street that gave its name to

Quiller Couch) are several old buildings. Note the GEORGE HOTEL, which has a tiny glass window three blocks up on the left of the double doors. It was a lookout for the Press Gang, so that customers could be warned and escape through the back door.

To the south is Trinity House Lane, with TRINITY HOUSE, the great five-star attraction of Hull. It fills a whole block of the old town between Princes Dock, Whitefriargate and Posterngate. The façade in Trinity House Lane was rebuilt in 1753 and is now faced in cream-painted stucco. The doorcase, incidentally, is one of the few examples of a true Tuscan order in England. The pediment contains a jolly coloured and gilded relief of the Royal Arms. Trinity House was founded in the fourteenth century and at one time controlled all the shipping and navigation of the port; it still supports many maritime charities and maintains pilots on the north seas. Behind the street range is a paved courtyard. The Georgian brickwork here hides the medieval structure. A large part of the building was once occupied by almshouses. The Entrance Hall and main staircase have walls painted to resemble Siena marble; they also have gleaming oak graining and beautifully polished floors of encaustic tiles. In the Canoe Room the most arresting object is the kayak hanging from the ceiling with an eskimo in it; it was brought back from an expedition to Greenland in 1613. Admiring the stuffed crocodile at its foot, we mount the staircase to the Court Room, an eighteenth-century interior with a high coved ceiling and stucco work by Joseph Page. Like many of the rooms, it has well-preserved (or carefully renewed) 1840s' decoration, including gold *trompe* Rococo *grisaille* work. Around the room are portraits, models of ships and a pair of fine globes. The portrait of William III has an especially good gilt Baroque frame. The Council Room has 1840s' stencilled decoration on the walls, amber glass panels in the window and rushes strewn on the floor. The Library wing was added in the 1840s to the design of William Foale, the then Surveyor to Trinity House. These rooms have idiosyncratic plaster ceilings, such as the dome in the round Reading Room. The Anteroom to the Library is a museum full of fascinating curiosities, including narwhal tusks, polar-bear paws, Captain Cook's log-book, an eider duck's nest from the Davis Straits, the tattooed head of a New Zealand chieftain and the pickled hand of an orang-utan. Architecturally, the most distinguished interior is the Chapel, with its complex vaulted ceiling.

Nearby is the major monument of medieval Hull, the CHURCH OF HOLY TRINITY. It is the largest medieval parish church in England, still surrounded on three sides by decent old buildings, including the old GRAMMAR SCHOOL of *c*.1580 with brick mullions. At the east end of the church, however, is a large incongruous block of bronze-tinted glass which replaces part of the old Market Place. The remainder of the Market Place has disappeared under new road works – an unforgivable piece of civic vandalism. The gilded statue of William III by Peter Scheemakers, which was once the proud centrepiece of a beautiful stretch of townscape, now surveys a scene of indescribable devastation.

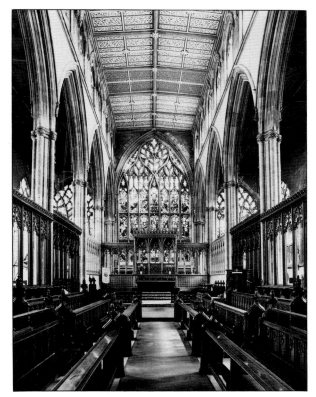

The church of the Holy Trinity, Hull.

Turning back with relief to the church itself, it will be noted that, apart from the stone west front and crossing-tower, much of it is built of brick, making it one of the earliest English uses of this material for a monumental building. (The present surface brickwork is, however, largely Georgian restoration.) The interior is vast and uniform, with an impressively long east–west vista – nearly 300 feet. The ground on which the church was built is marshy and the resulting need to reduce the weight of the structure is the practical reason for the vast size of the windows and the excessively slender section of the stone piers. The low-pitched timber ceiling has new painted decoration by George Pace in his toffee-wrappings style. There are many good furnishings, mainly Georgian and Victorian. The eighteenth-century altarpiece and communion table – excellent pieces of Rococo wood-carving by Paty – are tucked away at the back of the present high altar. The large painting by James Parmentier, which used to hang above, is now in the north choir aisle; it looks as if the Last Supper is taking place on a large sofa. There are rich Victorian fittings too, including the swagger Flamboyant Gothic pulpit and lectern by Lockwood of 1847. The present rood-screen has an attractive lacy outline when seen from the west end of the nave. Parts of the earlier Perpendicular rood-screen are incorporated in the side-screens of the crossing. There are many monuments, ranging from the medieval tombs of the De la Poles (wholesale fish merchants and Hull's most prosperous fourteenth-century family, ancestors of the ultra-aristocratic Dukes of Suffolk, who were later to be more or less exterminated by Henry VIII because of their Plantagenet blood!) to several nineteenth-century works by the Earles, a local family of sculptors. Many of the windows have clear glass, but in the nave are a pair of Arts and Crafts windows by Walter Crane – strikingly audacious in both design and colour.

Hull's other major parish church is ST MARY LOWGATE, begun in the fifteenth century and over-restored by George Gilbert Scott in the mid-nineteenth. The best external feature is the projecting western tower. It was built in the seventeenth century but refaced by Scott in 1862 in stone Perpendicular dress. Cutting through from here along Scots Lane, with one lonely sixteenth-century timber-framed house (now being repaired after years of neglect), the HIGH STREET is reached. This runs along the west bank of the River Hull and is narrow and winding. Here the Hull merchants had their houses and warehouses facing the river. It is a most interesting street, but sadly gap-toothed. CROWLE HOUSE (NO. 41) is reached down a narrow alley and has recently been restored. It is dated 1664 and is an example of Artisan Mannerist brick architecture. WALKER'S WAREHOUSE is late Georgian brick (1829), and the CORN EXCHANGE, now a museum, has a florid Corinthian façade. Opposite it is MAISTER HOUSE (NT). It was built in 1743 and has a five-bay, three-storeyed brick front with an Ionic doorcase. The new iron railings in front were designed by Francis Johnson. The finest feature within is the staircase, which

St Patrick's church, Patrington.

has lyre-patterned ironwork by Robert Bakewell, Rococo plasterwork by Joseph Page, and an octagonal lantern overhead. WILBERFORCE HOUSE, with another Artisan Mannerist brick façade, is the best surviving late seventeenth-century merchant's house in Hull. It now faces a municipal 'open space' occupying the site of a row of Georgian houses demolished in the 1960s to the severe detriment of the street's appearance. (The two Georgian houses next door were saved from a similar fate by the exertions of the late Colonel Rupert Alec-Smith to whom is due much of the credit for the surviving bits of Hull.) The interior of Wilberforce House was remodelled in the 1760s and has a nice staircase with Rococo plasterwork. It is open to the public. The PEASE WAREHOUSE of 1745 was restored as offices and flats by Benjamin Hudson in 1981 after it had been left to rot by the town council. To the north of the main road is BLAYDES HOUSE, with another good Georgian interior saved by the skin of its teeth from road 'improvements'; it is now architects' offices.

Little survives in the Georgian area north of Queens' Gardens; there is a fragmentary terrace in Albion Street and part of Kingston Square survives. The most exciting building in this part of Hull is the Catholic CHURCH OF ST CHARLES BORROMEO, built in 1829, the year of the Emancipation Act, but much remodelled later. The interior is an amazing spectacle, with Baroque plasterwork, coloured marbling and a dramatically lit cupola over the altar recalling the *Transparante* at Toledo.

Hull's best Victorian suburb, now called THE AVENUES, has survived completely intact. It was laid out in the 1870s by a local businessman, John Spivey Cooper, with wide tree-lined avenues, florid dolphin-encrusted fountains at the main intersections and a number of interesting Queen Anne-style villas – notably a group by George Gilbert Scott, Junior. It deserves to be better known; it is the Bedford Park of Yorkshire.

Patrington★
12; 15 miles SE of Hull on A1033

ST PATRICK'S CHURCH is rightly famous for its beautiful Perpendicular spire, which is among the most perfect in England. It is 189 feet high and can be seen for miles across the empty flat landscape of Holderness, beckoning the traveller onwards. The village itself is not very special and it is a matter for regret that the church authorities have treated the setting of this magnificent building with such cavalier disregard. The site of the rectory immediately opposite the church has been sold off and covered with a development of little houses, while between the church and road is an unkempt visitors' car park that looks like a bombsite. The church, however, rises above all this in serene perfection. The spire is beautifully proportioned and derives its unique character from an open Perpendicular arcade or lantern round the lowest stage – a source of inspiration for several later architects, including Nash at All Souls, Langham Place in London, and Bodley at Clumber in Nottinghamshire (*q.v.*). The early fourteenth-century interior shares the same perfection as the exterior. All is uniform and well proportioned. There are enticing vistas through the arches and across the transepts with their double aisles. The aisles are stone-vaulted, and it is thought that the original intention was to vault the nave and chancel as well, but this never materialised because the Black Death interrupted construction. A feature of the church is the lavish stone carving of the capitals, the font, the sedilia and the East Sepulchre (in the chancel). The latter is comparable with those at Heckington in Lincolnshire and Hawton in Nottinghamshire (*qq.v.*). It rises in three tiers with remarkably lifelike figures of the sleeping soldiers and of Christ rising from the tomb, the latter looking as if He is rolling out of bed. The top tier would originally have shown the Ascension but is now blank. The elaborate carved and gilded altarpiece was designed by J. Harold Gibbons in 1936. The Lady Chapel in the south transept has a canted apse containing a beautifully carved stone reredos by the same hand as the Easter Sepulchre. Note the extraordinary arrangement of access steps and gallery above the south crossing-arch. It makes you dizzy just to look at it. Much of the glass in the windows is clear, which enhances the spacious effect of the interior.

Pocklington

13; 13 miles E of York on B1246

ALL SAINTS is one of the lesser churches of the East Riding, though it would make a splash in any less well-endowed area. The main part dates from the thirteenth century but the clerestory, chancel and west tower are all Perpendicular, and they give the church its dominant character. The tower is very fine, with large traceried windows and battlements round the top. The nave has Early English circular columns with prettily carved capitals. The Perpendicular clerestory has flat-topped windows. The best feature, however, is the impressively tall west arch to the tower, the inside of which was intended to be vaulted. The large Perpendicular east window has colourful Victorian stained glass by Gibbs and there is an important early sixteenth-century carved Flemish altarpiece that would have sent Pugin into raptures.

Sewerby Hall

See Bridlington.

Skipwith

14; 10 miles SE of York off A163

ST HELEN'S is a very interesting church with parts of several different dates, like a chronological textbook of medieval architecture, beginning with a Saxon west tower. This now has a Perpendicular bell-storey on top, but inside the church, towards the nave, there is a well-preserved Saxon archway. The nave has one Norman arcade and one Transitional. The chancel is the best part, remarkably unified by contrast with the palimpsest of the western parts. It is fourteenth-century, with square-headed windows full of rich interlacing cusped tracery. The church was well restored by Pearson in 1877 and he was responsible for its most impressive feature – the magnificent south door with its all-over geometrical wrought-iron decoration, possibly incorporating fragments of the original.

The south door, St Helen's, Skipwith.

Skirlaugh

15; 8 miles E of Beverley on A165

ST AUGUSTINE'S is not large, but it is perfect – like a model for a Perpendicular church. It was the gift to his native village of Bishop Skirlaw of Durham and was built very quickly, beginning in 1401. It is of six bays divided by buttresses carrying pinnacles and has large traceried windows of identical design. The west tower is rather short in relation to the body of the church but in itself is a good design, with openwork tracery round the top. The inside is more like a college chapel than a parish church, with no division between nave and chancel, and no aisles. It is lofty and light but spatially dull and lacks rich fittings. One rather wishes that Bodley or Comper had passed this way.

Sledmere House

16; 7 miles NW of Great Driffield on B1252

Sledmere House was designed by its owner, Sir Christopher Sykes, and built between 1776 and 1783. It is in the neo-classical style and shows the influence of Samuel Wyatt and John Carr of York, both of whom were consulted by Sir Christopher. He also landscaped the park under the direction of Capability Brown and executed an enormous programme of agricultural reclamation of the surrounding Wolds. The interior of the house was embellished with superb plasterwork by Joseph Rose.

Sledmere was gutted by fire in 1911, but was immediately restored under the direction of Walter Brierley. He accurately reinstated the main rooms, using the original moulds for the plasterwork, but made a number of clever improvements and redesigned the main staircase to create a more dramatic effect. The principal ground-floor rooms – Music Room, Drawing Room and Dining Room – are all richly decorated in the late eighteenth-century style and contain all their original contents (salvaged in 1911), including chairs made for the house in 1792 by John Robbins, an organ in a huge mahogany case and portraits by Lawrence and Romney. The latter's painting of Sir Christopher Sykes is one of the artist's best works.

The most important room at Sledmere – the great Library – is on the first floor and, 100 feet in length, occupies the whole of the front of the house. It has a coved plaster ceiling, inspired by the Baths of Diocletian in Rome, and marbled Ionic pilasters framing the bookcases. The original collection of precious and antiquarian books was sold in 1824 and replaced with a more workaday country house assemblage of sermons and novels.

Sledmere House.

South Dalton
17; 6 miles NW of Beverley off B1248
ST MARY'S CHURCH is one of the most amazing of what, in his novel *Lothair*, Disraeli called those 'celestial fanes raised to the revealed Author of life and death' by pious Victorian landowners. The 200-foot western steeple, 'planted like an enormous arrow in the breast of the wolds', beckons the visitor through long miles of beautiful empty landscape improved by the enterprise of eighteenth-century agrarian reformers. It is a major work of perhaps the greatest of all Victorian Gothic Revival architects, J.L. Pearson, and his noble client here was the 3rd Lord Hotham. Local gossip had it that Lord Hotham spent his entire fortune in building this 'cathedral of the wolds' (as Anthony Quiney called it in his biography of Pearson), partly in order that there should be little for his nephew and heir to inherit. The start of work coincided with the Great Eclipse of 15 March 1858 and the church was finished in 1861, though the vestries were added later. The sources of the architecture are thirteenth-century English, not continental, and the spire shows the influence of Salisbury and Grantham but is not the less High Victorian for that.

The most amazing aspect of the church is the superabundance of ornate decoration inside and out; there is stone carving everywhere: 'lizards bask on its stone and birds in its crannies' and grotesque animals are liberally dispersed over its surfaces. This intense richness was responsible for the high cost of the church – £25,000. What makes the building an architectural masterpiece of the highest order, however, is Pearson's attention to the overall proportions – for instance, the way in which the transepts are carefully scaled to the rest of the church. The effect is of a perfect unity; all the furnishings and fittings were designed by Pearson himself: 'My wish is to make the church look as complete as possible and that the several things in it should bear a proportion to it and to one another and appear to be designed for the positions they are severally placed in.' The magnificent stained glass in the east window was made to Pearson's design by Clayton and Bell, as were the iron screens to the south chapel by Skidmore. In the latter is a seventeenth-century monument to Sir John Hotham which was brought from the old church on the site; it is a splendid Baroque conceit with the deceased's effigy in white marble on a black marble slab supported at the corners by four icy white figures of kneeling Virtues. Underneath on a straw mat is a highly convincing marble skeleton.

Welton
18; 10 miles W of Hull on A63
This is one of the few non-estate villages in East Yorkshire that retains any sense of visual coherence. So many others have been ruined by unsympathetic new housing, unnecessary demolitions of old buildings, or ill-considered 'improvements'. For some reason it seems more difficult to preserve the character of brick villages than stone ones – at least in Yorkshire. Welton has a large green with an early nineteenth-century Perpendicular PUMP, like a lost turret from a church. The stream, which

runs through, has been dammed to form an ornamental pond and there are several genteel eighteenth-century houses, enviable country retreats, including WELTON MANOR, WELTON HALL and WELTON GRANGE. The latter is the finest and is faced in stone rather than brick. The one-bay centre has a front door with Gibbs' surround, Venetian window over and pediment on top. It has good interiors, with Rococo plasterwork and chimneypieces. The parish CHURCH OF ST HELEN was largely reconstructed by Sir George Gilbert Scott in the 1860s, which rather stripped it of its atmosphere, but it is redeemed by six windows with stained glass by William Morris.

Winestead

19; 14 miles SE of Hull on A1033
ST GERMAIN'S is an attractive little church standing on its own in a well-kept graveyard. It has something of the feel of a proprietary church – an effect increased by the absence of a tower and the care with which it is maintained. The dedication to St Germain is rare – he was a fifth-century Bishop of Auxerre in France. The patronage of the church living passed by inheritance to the Hildyards in 1417 and remains with them still.

The nave dates from the twelfth century and the chancel from the late fourteenth. The south aisle was rebuilt, using old bricks, by Temple Moore in 1897 as part of a sympathetic restoration of the building, which left it with atmosphere and patina. The interior is most attractive, with whitewashed walls and eighteenth-century brass chandeliers with candles; there is no electric light. The lower parts of the walls are panelled with wood from the eighteenth-century box pews and the present Jacobean-style benches were designed by Temple Moore. The chancel is divided from the nave by a Perpendicular wooden screen restored in 1890 in memory of T.B. Thoroton Hildyard. The lectern is by George Gilbert Scott, but the pulpit with canopy is late seventeenth-century. Between them is the large tomb-chest of Sir Christopher Hildyard, who died in 1610. If you climb the pulpit steps, you can look down on the fine effigy, which, in full armour, rests its feet on the Hildyard crest – a cockerel.

The Hildyard Chapel in the south-east corner behind the pulpit was added in the early seventeenth century by Sir Christopher Hildyard. It is now used as the vestry. The wooden screen round it is made of sixteenth-century panelling from the former Hildyard pew. In here are more family memorials and the displaced seventeenth-century communion table – the present altar in the chancel is by Temple Moore.

North Yorkshire

Aske Hall

1; 3 miles N of Richmond off B6274
The seat of the Marquess of Zetland near Richmond is situated in a beautifully planted park. The house itself was substantially remodelled to the design of Claud Phillimore between 1961 and 1963. It had developed round a fifteenth-century pele tower into a large pile of eighteenth- and nineteenth-century buildings with an incoherent plan. Phillimore demolished the Victorian ballroom, dining room and a large area of redundant service quarters at the back of the house, reduced the projecting wings on the entrance front and entirely refaced the front of the house in stone. A new roof was built with a steel structure. The interior was rationalised, the former Great Hall subdivided to form a new Entrance Hall and Library. The old library became the Dining Room. Chimneypieces and other fittings were introduced from elsewhere, including the splendid marble one in the new Hall, brought from Clumber in Nottinghamshire (*q.v.*). The Victorian Chapel adjoining the house, however, was retained in its existing form. This was once the stable block, built *c.*1763 to the design of John Carr of York, and the handsome arcaded façade is as Carr left it. The interior, with an apse and plaster barrel vault, dates from 1887 and was formed by Thomas Oliver of Newcastle. At the same time new stables and a home farm were built to Oliver's design at a cost of £10,345; they make a splendid Victorian pile.

The finest thing at Aske is the TEMPLE – a Gothic folly on a hill in the park overlooking the main house, and one of the most ambitious of its type in England. It was built in the 1740s for Sir Conyers D'Arcy and was almost certainly designed by Daniel Garrett. It stands on an arcaded terrace and has a central tower and flanking turrets. It was probably influenced by William Kent's illustrations for Spenser's *Faerie Queene*, which show fantastic Gothick structures of this type in their backgrounds.

Bedale

2; 7½ miles SW of Northallerton on A684
To approach Bedale from the north is a great visual surprise. The open country becomes parkland with old limes and other trees. Across the park can be seen the dignified façade and outbuildings of a Georgian country house with a large medieval parish church sitting next to it. The usual manorial group, you think to yourself; but the road dives in between the church and the Hall and, hey presto, you find yourself bang in the main street of a busy country town. From the back the Hall reads as part of the general street scene. It is the most extraordinary transformation. The street itself forms an almost perfect piece of townscape. It is wider in the centre than at the ends and is slightly curving – in other words banana-shaped. The middle is called Market Place and the extremities North End and South End respectively. The houses on the west side are taller than those on the east, but otherwise it is lined with remarkably uniform buildings – three-storeyed red brick Georgian houses with sash windows upstairs and unspoilt nineteenth-century painted-timber shop-fronts at ground level. There are pubs and old-established shops and one or two banks. The broad verges are still cobbled, just the central roadway being covered with tarmac. The only accent is the

The staircase, Beningbrough Hall.

ancient stone Market Cross on the west side – a tall, thin stone shaft with a simple gilded iron cross on top.

BEDALE HALL is now the local council offices. It is built mainly of brick, though the main front facing the park is stone. It has a pediment and doorcase with Doric columns but is otherwise plain. The interior contains fine stucco decoration of the 1730s. The main room fills all five bays of the centre and has a coved and decorated ceiling, wall panels and a two-tier chimneypiece. The staircase has equally lavish stucco decoration on the walls and ceiling.

The CHURCH OF ST GREGORY is an ambitious thirteenth-century church with a tall square west tower forming an excellent view-stopper at the north end of the main street. Close up much of the detail is Victorian restoration, which is rather a pity. The interior has a wide and spacious nave with curiously variegated columns like a non-matching 'Harlequin' set of Chippendale chairs. The chancel is raised over a vaulted crypt, in which are preserved some fragments of ninth-century sculpture. The altar end has interesting made-up 'Wardour Street' panelling, including sixteenth- and seventeenth-century Flemish and English wood-carvings. Lying on the floor are several medieval effigies, among them a fourteenth-century alabaster pair to Sir Brian Fitzalan and his wife. They are well carved and look the very models of the medieval knight and his lady. She wears a long, simple flowing dress; he has his legs crossed and wears chain-mail, a surcoat and sword, and carries a shield showing his arms.

Beningbrough Hall

NT; 3; 7 miles NW of York off A19

Here is a remarkable Baroque house of red brick set in the flat Vale of York and built in 1716 by John Bourchier. The architect was the York carpenter-architect William Thornton, who was much influenced by contemporary engravings of seventeenth-century Roman buildings. The house has recently been extensively restored and redecorated by the National Trust to house some early eighteenth-century paintings from the National Portrait Gallery, which look well here; the Gallery deserves credit for the imaginative policy of lending its reserve collection to appropriate historic buildings.

The plan and much of the decoration of the house, including some exceptionally fine joinery, remain largely untouched, though the new colour schemes are not an unqualified success. The front door opens straight into the Hall, which rises through two storeys and is one of the most impressive English Baroque interiors. It has fluted composite pilasters and an unusual coved ceiling. The stone floor has recently been restored and the room sparsely furnished in the authentic manner. The main apartments occupy the garden front of the house on the ground and first floors. They are notable for their fine wainscotting with richly carved cornices and overdoors. The State Bedchamber on the ground floor contains the late seventeenth-century state bed from Holme Lacy in Herefordshire (*q.v.*) – possibly the work of Francis Lapière, the leading Huguenot upholsterer. A rare survival are the two pelmet boards above the windows *en suite* with the bed. The adjoining Dining Room contains the portraits of members of the Kit Kat Club; these are on loan from the National Portrait Gallery and formerly hung at Bayfordbury in Hertfordshire. It is to be regretted that Lady Chesterfield's walnut-grained decoration in this room has been replaced with white paint. The Saloon upstairs is the most impressive room in the house, its wainscot embellished with finely carved fluted pilasters. Again, it seems rather a pity to have changed the colouring from a dramatic blue-green to white. The staircase to the first floor is a supreme masterpiece of the joiner's art. The steps and landings are of finest marquetry and the balustrade is so intricately carved that it could be mistaken for wrought-iron.

Bolton Abbey

4; 5 miles E of Skipton on B6160 [52]

Despite its name, Bolton was not an abbey but a priory (which was one grade down) of Augustinian canons. At the Dissolution the nave became the parish church and the choir became a ruined shell. The church stands in gentle wooded parkland beside the River Wharf, the untamed moors stretching to the horizon all around. It was a scene loved by romantic painters and immortalised by, above all, Turner and Landseer – though, as the 6th Duke of Devonshire said of the latter's *Bolton Abbey in Olden Time*, 'it could be any other abbey'. The impact of Bolton derives from the contrast between the 'power and border sternness' of the wild encircling moorlands and the 'sweet peace and tender decay' of the ruins, as Ruskin pointed out in *Modern Painters*.

The priory was founded by Alicia de Romilly in 1151 and the church was begun soon after, parts of the chancel being Norman. The nave, however, dates from the mid-thirteenth century and is a fine piece of Early English design. The interior is somewhat bleak, perhaps because of the restoration by G.E. Street in 1875–80, and the crossing-arch is entirely filled by a blank stone wall. At the Dissolution the priory reverted to the Cliffords, who owned the surrounding land, and descended from them via Lord Burlington to the Dukes of Devonshire, who own it today. The marks of their enlightened estate management can be seen for miles around.

The gatehouse of the monastery was converted into a little SHOOTING LODGE for Lord Burlington by William Kent, and its drawing room was decorated by him. The castellated wings on either side were added for the 6th Duke by Joseph Paxton.

Bolton Castle

See Castle Bolton.

Broughton Hall

5; 3 miles W of Skipton on A59 [53]
The beautiful classical façade of smooth golden ashlar, seen to such advantage across the Broughton beck from the main Clitheroe–Skipton road, conceals a house built in 1597, only the walls of which survive. The staunchly recusant Tempests have had a house here since at least the fourteenth century. The main block was refronted in *c.*1750 and the pedimented wings to either side were added in 1810 to the design of William Atkinson. But it is the additions of the 1840s – the Chapel tower and the *porte-cochère* – designed by George Webster that make

the house such an interesting composition, perfectly adapted to the lovely landscape around.

The interior has a sequence of remarkably well-preserved early nineteenth-century rooms – the Red and White Drawing Rooms, Library and Dining Room – all full of furniture supplied by Gillow of Lancaster, and an interesting collection of Italian paintings, formed by Mr and Mrs Stephen Tempest in Italy in *c.*1818. Much has already left the house, sold to meet death duties. The Gothick Chapel has a plaster rib vault and richly stencilled redecoration executed in 1901 and recently restored. The Italianate terraced gardens were designed by W.A. Nesfield in 1855. The large Conservatory at the back of the house dates from 1853, thus predating Nesfield's work, though it is usually attributed to him.

Byland Abbey

6; 11 miles SE of Thirsk off A19
The Cistercians settled here in 1177 after various false starts elsewhere. They drained the marshes in the broad valley bottom, built their church and monastic quarters, and lived an uneventful life till the Dissolution. Byland makes a hauntingly beautiful ruin, standing by a bend on the road to Coxwold with nothing else around except a little inn opposite.

The west front of the church is dramatic, with a large broken circular rose window and a single turret. The whole of the north side of the church survives, but only the foundations and lower parts of the walls of the rest of the church remain. A fine geometrical pavement of glazed green and yellow tiles has also survived. Great cliffs of masonry from the monastic buildings still stand, making a highly picturesque composition.

Byland Abbey.

Carlton Towers

7; 6 miles S of Selby on A1041 [65]

Carlton Towers has been passed down entirely by inheritance since the Norman Conquest, through the Bruces, Bellews and Stapletons, coming to the present Duke of Norfolk through his mother, the last of the Stapletons and 11th Baroness Beaumont in her own right. It is perhaps the largest, most spectacular and most complete of inhabited Victorian Gothic country houses to be found anywhere in England. The Victorian decoration of the rooms open to the public was refurbished in 1982 and the bedroom wallpapers replaced to the original design and colours.

The overwhelming Victorian appearance is, however, only skin deep, and beneath the stunning array of battlements, turrets, towers, coats of arms and gargoyles remains the fabric of the original 1614 house, and the stables and chapel added by Thomas Stapleton in 1777. The house was first Gothicised in the 1840s by the 8th Lord Beaumont to celebrate the successful resurrection in his favour of the dormant barony of Beaumont. He was heir through the marriage of his ancestor Sir Bryan Stapleton to Joan Lovel, niece of the 7th Baron Beaumont who had died without direct issue in 1507. The Beaumonts were descended from the princely house of Brienne and claimed kinship with the last Christian King of Jerusalem as well as with the Royal House of France. This illustrious but complicated genealogy furnished material for the heraldic decoration, which was worked out by General John de Havilland, York Herald of Arms, and is remarkably extensive, even by Victorian antiquarian standards.

The exterior of the house was again remodelled, by E.W. Pugin, for Henry, 9th Lord Beaumont, between 1873 and 1876. Both patron and architect were slightly unbalanced and both of them died bankrupt in their forties. They quarrelled while work was in progress and Lord Beaumont chose a different, younger architect to decorate the interior – John Francis Bentley, the most accomplished Catholic architect of his time and designer of Westminster Cathedral. His work at Carlton is his only major country house commission and it remains largely as he left it. Bentley also designed much of the furnishing, down to such details as pokers, curtains and towel-rails.

The great Victorian state rooms – Armoury, Venetian Drawing Room, Card Room and Picture Gallery – open up to form an enfilade nearly 200 feet long, which would have been twice as long again if Lord Beaumont's money had not run out. These rooms, with their original dark, rich colour schemes, contain interesting furniture as well as a collection of paintings by obscure Italian masters typical of English Catholic houses. Carlton also retains a number of smaller eighteenth-century rooms, such as the Bow Drawing Room and the Dining Room, and it is these, with their chintzes, Turkey carpets, silver-framed photographs and Edwardian family portraits, that give the house much of its charm and its happy, lived-in atmosphere – an agreeable contrast to the Gothic megalomania of the exterior. Carlton is regularly open to the public in summer.

Castle Bolton

8; 6 miles W of Leyburn off A684

The beautiful, timeless landscape of Wensleydale is best in winter when there is no one about except for the occasional shepherd. High on the northern slopes, guarding the valley, lies BOLTON CASTLE the mighty fortress of the Scropes, with a little fourteenth-century church and a few stone cottages arranged around a rectangular green under the castle's shadow.

Sir Francis Knollys, writing in 1568, described Bolton Castle as 'very strong, very fair, and very stately after the old manner of building. ... It is the highest walled house that I have seen' – words that are still appropriate. It is a fortified country house rather than a castle proper, and was built in c.1378–99 by Richard de Scrope. It forms a large rectangle with an inner courtyard and four stalwart corner towers of four storeys. The connecting ranges are of three storeys and have square projecting bays in the centre of the long sides. Though largely gutted, the walls stand to full height (except for the north-east tower, which has collapsed) and so it looks as impressive from the other side of the valley as it did on the day it was built. Nor is one disappointed close-up, for it is maintained in perfect ruinous condition – neither a tidied-up monument nor falling into decay. There is ivy, and evidence of farming up to the walls. The west range is still roofed and lived in and is now, of all things, a restaurant. It is an extraordinary experience to arrive here on a cold, misty day in winter, to drive up to the forbidding walls and then to go inside to find a snug bar where one can order Theakston's beer, Scarborough fish pie and blue Wensleydale cheese (which, it is encouraging to know, is now made in the valley again, rather than in Leicestershire).

The castle remains entirely as first built, apart from a few sixteenth-century mullion windows and one or two Georgian sashes fitted into fourteenth-century window openings. The ground floor is tunnel-vaulted throughout (as are the first-floor rooms in the towers) and was originally used as stables or stores. The principal rooms were on the first floor, approached from the courtyard by archways, each with a portcullis and flights of stone stairs. The Great Hall occupies the north range. Though now open to the sky it is still impressive, with tall arched windows and a stone fireplace. The private apartments were to the west and the domestic offices to the east. The Great Chamber in the centre of the west range is now the restaurant and has a recent ceiling and the original stone fireplace with a hood carried on simple projecting corbels. The kitchen was in the north-east tower, and the Chapel filled the top two storeys of the south range. At the west end of the Chapel is a Gallery, which was probably the Lord's pew, as it connects with the Great Chamber. The chaplain's rooms and vestry were in the south turret. Other accommodation included at least twelve independent lodgings for retainers, each comprising one or two rooms like the 'sets' in Oxford or Cambridge colleges. On a fine day it is worth climbing the spiral staircase to the top of the south-west tower to admire the terrific view over Wensleydale.

Castle Howard.

Castle Howard★

9; 6 miles W of Malton off A64 [54,55]

From whichever direction he approaches, the visitor is made aware of the proximity of this great seat of the Howards by long avenues of beech and lime and impressive architectural outworks. The house itself was the first work of Sir John Vanbrugh, dramatist turned architect, for the 3rd Earl of Carlisle, and is perhaps the most insouciant and attractive of the English Baroque palaces. As Horace Walpole remarked, it is not merely gigantic but sublime. The richly embellished main façades face north and south and were inspired by Wren's unexecuted plans for royal palaces at Hampton Court and Whitehall. But the feature that makes the exterior of Castle Howard so glorious is the tall central dome with a gilded lantern over the Entrance Hall.

Unfortunately, Lord Carlisle's attention was directed to his park and outbuildings before the house itself was finished, and the west wing was eventually completed only in 1750 to a different design (by Lord Carlisle's son-in-law Sir Thomas Robinson) spoiling the overall symmetry of Vanbrugh's layout, though the differences between Vanbrugh's and Robinson's work provide a graphic demonstration of the English reaction from Baroque to Palladian architecture.

Castle Howard is now owned by the Hon. Simon Howard, great-grandson of the 9th Earl, and his wife. Like several of the great Whig houses, it has always been open to the public. The visitor arrives through the eighteenth-century tourists' entrance in the west wing and climbs an imposing Victorian staircase to the *piano nobile*. On the China Landing is displayed a series of Meissen, Derby and Chelsea services. Beyond stretches a dramatic stone-vaulted corridor lined with antique

sculpture and marble-topped side-tables. But first there is a detour through a group of attractive Regency bedrooms, all of which retain their original decorations and furniture. The climax of the house is the Hall, which rises the full height of the central block and is open to the dome, 70 feet above the marble floor. The effect is like the crossing of a large Italian church but even more dramatic, as open arches reveal the staircases at either side and the vaulted vistas along the passages that traverse the length of the house.

The beautiful painted decorations of the Hall are by Pellegrini. Unfortunately, his work in the dome was destroyed by fire during the Second World War (when, incidentally, the house was occupied by a girls' school). Many of the state rooms along the south front were also burnt. But the slow work of restoration is well in hand. The dome was recreated with the aid of photogrammetry, as was the fresco, which was painted by Scott Medd. The Garden Hall has been recreated too, with romantic landscape paintings by Felix Kelly, and to the east is a new Library in the Vanbrugh manner, designed by Julian Bicknell. The rooms to the west escaped the fire – the Music Room, Tapestry Room and Orléans Room. They have superb carved woodwork by Nadauld, a Huguenot refugee, and by Samuel Carpenter from Yorkshire, and later marble chimneypieces. In these rooms are concentrated the finest furniture and paintings in the house.

The interior of the west wing was fitted up to the design of C.H. Tatham for the 5th Earl of Carlisle, and the Museum Room and Long Gallery are his work. The Chapel was redecorated in the 1870s and is a Pre-Raphaelite gem with stained glass designed by Burne-Jones and frescoes by pupils of Kempe.

The architectural excitement of Castle Howard extends into the grounds, which contain some of the finest of all English garden buildings – notably Vanbrugh's TEMPLE OF THE WINDS, its interior richly embellished with scagliola and plasterwork by Vassali, and Hawksmoor's sublime Doric MAUSOLEUM, which Horace Walpole thought 'would tempt one to be buried alive'.

Constable Burton Hall
10; 12 miles W of Bedale on A684

Not to be confused with Burton Constable Hall in East Yorkshire (*q.v.*), Constable Burton is a very good mid-Georgian villa designed by John Carr of York in the 1760s for Sir Marmaduke Asty Wyvill; he was away on his Grand Tour at the time and it is said that the old house was demolished and replaced by mistake instead of being repaired.

The house is a neat cube of fine ashlar stone with an Ionic portico *in antis* on the main front and a canted bow window on the other front. The principal rooms are on the *piano nobile*, arranged round a central Staircase Hall. The Saloon is placed behind the bow window, on axis with the Staircase and Entrance Halls. The main rooms have nice stucco cornices and carved marble chimneypieces.

Coxwold
11; 10 miles E of Thirsk off A19

One of the most attractive of the North Riding villages, Coxwold has a wide main street lined with mown grass strips and golden stone cottages, with the church situated at the top. All is maintained properly thanks to the protection of the Newburgh Priory estate (*q.v.*), which has been able to resist the vulgarisation that has overtaken some other 'show villages'. The setting in the gentle rolling Howardian Hills could not be better.

Temple, Duncombe Park.

The FAUCONBERG ARMS is a nice Georgian pub with a display of family heraldry at the front. The proprietor has the right to graze four cows on the village's common pasture. SHANDY HALL to the north of the village was the home of Laurence Sterne, vicar of Coxwold and author of *Tristram Shandy*. It has recently been restored as a literary museum. Other interesting buildings in the village are OLD HALL, early seventeenth-century and formerly the Grammar School, and FAUCONBERG HOSPITAL, a nice range of late seventeenth-century almshouses.

ST MICHAEL'S CHURCH has an unusual octagonal west tower with buttresses running up the angles like seams and an openwork parapet round the top. The fifteenth-century nave is attractive, with a low-pitched timber roof. The chancel was rebuilt in the eighteenth century to the design of Thomas Atkinson and is full of monuments to the Bellasis family (also of Newburgh Priory) – a wonderful clutter of marble columns and coronets, urns and effigies. The eighteenth-century communion rail, box pews and pulpit all survive.

Duncombe Park★
12; 2 miles W of Helmsley off A170

The grounds of Duncombe Park are, according to Sacheverell Sitwell, the 'supreme masterpiece of the art of the landscape gardener'. They stretch on a vast scale to the east of the house; there a wide, curving grassy terrace overlooks the Rye Valley and gives dramatic, contrived views over the surrounding beautifully planted country. The estate was laid out in the 1730s by Thomas Duncombe, whose uncle, a London banker, bought it in 1689. At either end are classical temples – that at the north in the form of an open Ionic rotunda with a lead dome (attributed to Vanbrugh) and that at the other a domed temple attributed to Sir Thomas Robinson. In the woods to the north-west is yet another temple, this one with a large arched window flanked by niches. At the point where the lawn in front of the house debouches on to the terrace stands a big carved sundial with a statue of Father Time attributed to Van Nost.

The house is a handsome masculine Baroque pile with a mighty Doric portico and a fanfare of urns on the roof. Once attributed to Vanbrugh, it is now known to be by William Wakefield, a Yorkshire gentleman-architect. The interior was gutted by fire in 1879 and cleverly reconstructed (largely to the original design) by William Young, architect of the War Office in Whitehall. It is a splendid Edwardian reinterpretation of eighteenth-century Baroque architecture, with giant columns and elaborate plasterwork.

Duncombe graphically illustrates the revival of the English country house and landed estate in the late twentieth century. Having been let to a girls' school for many years, it is currently being restored by the present Lord Feversham so that he can move back into his family seat instead of living in the smaller house used by his predecessor. If only the city fathers of England's historic towns had shown half the enterprise, courage and taste manifested by historic house-owners over the last thirty years, an architectural tour of Britain might be even more enjoyable than it is.

Ebberston Hall

13; 9 miles E of Pickering on A170

Ebberston Hall was built in 1718 by William Thompson, MP for Scarborough, to the design of Colen Campbell, architect of such houses as Stourhead in Wiltshire and Houghton in Norfolk. It is a little casino, or villa, set in a contemporary formal garden, of which the outlines and cascades of the original water-garden still remain.

The rooms are small but well appointed, with carved wooden friezes and enriched architraves by William Thornton, who was responsible for work at Castle Howard and Beningbrough (*qq.v.*). The Drawing Room, with fluted Corinthian pilasters and bolection-moulded panels, is particularly fine. On the garden front is a delightful *loggia* (now enclosed) decorated with carved stonework and stucco. The house, which contains eighteenth-century furniture – mainly English, but including a set of French chairs with tapestry covers – and family portraits, is open to the public in a wonderfully unselfconscious way.

Fountains Abbey*

NT; 14; 4 miles W of Ripon off B6265
Includes Fountains Hall (NT)

'I wept when I remembered the days when the Abbey lived, and was the glory of the country; when the poor were fed and warmed in the wintry cold, when "hospitality" was kept, and all men rejoiced in the Catholic Faith.' Not Pugin, but John Hungerford-Pollen, Private Secretary to the Marquess of Ripon, and written at the time of the historical pageant given at Fountains in 1896. The most perfect monastic ruins in England, or indeed anywhere in Europe, have evoked similar sentiments from a stream of antiquarian-minded visitors for the past 200 years. The situation in a secret wooded valley could not be bettered, and the beauties of nature have received the helping hand of an eighteenth-century landscape gardener (in connection with the creation of the adjoining Studley Royal Estate (*q.v.*)). The visitor is immediately struck by the vast scale of the buildings. Here, for once, the reality turns out to be larger than photographs had led one to believe. A great portion of the fabric, including the church, is preserved almost *in toto*, apart from the loss of the roofs. It is easier, therefore, to imagine Fountains still occupied and used than is possible in the case of more fragmentary ruins. The haunting sadness of the place is, however, partly mitigated by the fact that the Dissolution in 1539 spared the building from later alterations and 'restoration'. Here, unlike any of the Gothic cathedrals of Europe, is a great medieval church where the stonework is almost entirely genuine and medieval.

The west front is flat, plain and precise, with no frills. Entering through the west door one could be in Burgundy. This is early Cistercian Gothic at its simple best, with a long procession of unmoulded circular columns, pointed arches and austere lancets stretching far into the distance. The transepts and crossing, like the nave, date from the twelfth century, but the east end was rebuilt in the early thirteenth to form a transeptal chapel of nine altars on the pattern to be repeated shortly afterwards at

Fountains Abbey.

Durham Cathedral (*q.v.*). This is in the Early English manner and originally the columns had attached shafts of Nidderdale marble, but these have disappeared, leaving the stone cores of the columns soaring upwards, improbably tall and thin, as if part of a romantic dream.

Finally, in the early sixteenth century, Abbot Huby built the huge square tower attached to the north transept. It is 170 feet high and of a beautiful Perpendicular design, with four tiers of windows and exquisite diagonal buttresses clustered at the corners of the final stage. This tower provides a wonderful asymmetrical yet balanced feature that enhances the overall composition of the abbey ruins and is one of the chief reasons for their picturesque beauty from almost every angle.

The monastic buildings around the cloisters to the south of the church are also remarkably well-preserved and provide a textbook illustration of medieval monastic planning, with the Chapter House, Refectory and Warming Room in the enclosing ranges. The western side is the most impressive, with its vast vaulted undercroft and, above it, the remains of the dormitory of the lay brothers who were responsible for farming the extensive monastic estates. To the south are the ruins of the reredorter and infirmary and the Abbot's lodging, all less well preserved than the principal monastic buildings, as it was these parts that Stephen Proctor, Collector of Fines on Penal Statutes and a characteristic *nouveau riche* of his day, plundered for stone c.1611 to build FOUNTAINS HALL (NT). Centuries of weathering and mild decay, however, have softened the brashness of his domineering new house and it now shares some of the same poetic architectural melancholy as the abbey ruins. It is dazzlingly improbable, with vast mullion windows and low circular clipped yews beneath the garden wall – appropriately like Yorkshire puddings. It is very tall at the front – five storeys – but much less so at the back because of the steep rise in the ground; it has flanking castellated towers, fancy gabled wings and a recessed centre with a columned porch approached by a long flight of steps, with a semi-circular oriel window above. The whole thing has the dramatic, theatrical quality of a stage-set for a Shakespeare play. You expect Hamlet to emerge from the central doorway and start proclaiming his lines.

Harrogate

15; 2 miles W of Knaresborough on A59

The best approaches to Harrogate are by train, as the lines from York and Leeds are both dramatic. From York, after crossing the flat plain, the train suddenly enters hilly country and glides on a dramatic castellated bridge high over the River Knidd at Knaresborough. From Leeds, the line sweeps through Wharfedale, with incomparable views on all sides, and enters Harrogate on the long, low Crimple Viaduct of thirty-one stone arches over a shallow valley. Once in the town, the splendid landscape setting is always apparent because of the hilly topography and the way large areas of grass planted with trees, collectively known as 'the Stray', penetrate right into the centre. It is this relationship of landscape and buildings that gives Harrogate its character. The architecture itself is dignified Victorian with dark stone terraces of houses, large hotels and good classical public buildings. Harrogate is no longer a spa, but a conference and shopping centre and a dormitory for the industrial towns of the West Riding. The atmosphere is strongly northern middle class: comfortable, solid, value-for-money and pleasantly old-fashioned. There are lots of tea rooms, ladies in hats and Regent Street-type shops. As you walk around, it is fun to imagine Bateman-cartoon situations: 'The man who asked the way to the red-light district in Harrogate'!

The mineral springs that were the *raison d'être* for the town were discovered in 1571 by Sir William Slingsby. He had travelled abroad and was therefore able to recognise the curious taste of the water in the TEWIT WELL on his estate. In 1598 Thomas Bright called Harrogate 'the English Spa', and thereby converted a place-name in Flanders into an English noun. The little domed pavilion on the site of the well was built in the eighteenth century and encircled with Tuscan columns in 1842. Large-scale urban development did not really begin until the late eighteenth century and the early nineteenth, the 1840s being the most important decade. The first public bath, the ROYAL PUMP ROOM was built in 1842 to the design of B. Shutt, an architect of the most glorious obscurity. It is debased Grecian with a dome. The much larger ROYAL BATHS, forming a grand classical composition with towers and a dome, were built in 1897 by F.T. Baggalay

& F. Bristowe, a London firm. They were extended as late as 1937, but in 1949 were nationalised and rapidly declined under the dead hand of state control; they were eventually closed in 1969 but have now re-opened. As well as the baths, a number of hospitals and convalescent homes were connected with the spa, and these survive.

The most distinguished buildings in Harrogate are perhaps the hotels, of which there is a whole series dating from the 1820s onwards. GRANBY HOTEL is perhaps the oldest, built in c.1800 though with many later enlargements. It is a long, low building, painted white and with a four-columned porch. The former WHITE HART HOTEL, right in the town centre, was built in 1846 with an Ionic porch and handsome ashlar-faced façade. The CROWN HOTEL dates from 1847 and is impressively Italianate with wings, tower and large centre. The CLARENDON HOTEL is smaller and plainer, but it too has a Grecian porch. And there are lots of others, culminating in the towering rubicund pile of the HOTEL MAJESTIC, designed by G.D. Martin in 1900 with a symmetrical red brick front and a large dome.

Helmsley

16; 14 miles E of Thirsk on A170

This attractive little town lies in the valley of the River Rye, below the Yorkshire Moors. You descend into it gently, so that your first impression is of the red-tiled roofs of the houses, the pinnacled church tower and the stark silhouette of the castle ruins. The centre of the town is the square, a large open space surrounded by stone Georgian houses and one picturesque sixteenth-century timber-framed house with its beams arranged in herringbone patterns; this is the former VICARAGE. ALL SAINTS' CHURCH lies to one side and is a not particularly interesting rebuilding of 1866–9 by Banks and Barry, though it has some nice fittings by Temple Moore. He also designed the Jacobean-style TOWN HALL in the Market Place. From the Market Place, the HIGH STREET runs to the north-west. Its stone-built houses have long narrow gardens at the back (a medieval plan) and down the middle of the road runs a tree-lined stream, creating a most dramatic effect.

The CASTLE lies in the other direction, to the south-east of the church. It was begun in the early twelfth century by Walter l'Espec, but most of the present buildings date from later. The earthworks, with a double ditch surrounding the curtain wall, are very impressive. The keep, built on an unusual semi-circular plan, was remodelled in the fourteenth century and makes a handsome picturesque object. The castle was knocked about in the Civil War and replaced as the major house on the estate by Duncombe Park (*q.v.*) in the early eighteenth century, so subsequently fell into ruins. Its remains are now in the guardianship of the Heritage Commission and are neatly maintained.

Hemingbrough

17; 6 miles E of Selby on A63

ST MARY'S is a large cruciform church of white Tadcaster stone. The central spire is an exaggeratedly tall needle 126 feet high set on a squat 60-foot tower. It lures the

Hovingham Hall.

visitor across the Plain of York like an enormous obelisk. It is worth looking at the tower with binoculars in order to see the worn washing tuns, or tubs, carved on the top moulding in punning reference to Prior Washington, who built the tower in the early fifteenth century. The church is part Early English and part Perpendicular, the whole of the clerestory being of the latter period. The interior is distinguished by its well-preserved medieval woodwork. There are Perpendicular parclose screens and stalls with poppy heads in the choir, and a wonderful array of (restored) Perpendicular benches in the nave. The bench ends have amusing carvings: one has a jester in a belled cap and a dragon, another the bust of a young man and a grotesque mask.

Hovingham
18; 8 miles NW of Malton on B1257
This is a well-kept estate village with a grassy green and stone cottages. The HALL is just off the green and is approached by a short avenue. It is an extraordinary eighteenth-century house with the main rooms on the first floor above a vaulted riding school and stables. It was designed by its owner, Sir Thomas Worsley, *c*.1750. He was Surveyor-General to King George III, and horses and architecture were the great interests of his life – as his house makes clear! With Whiggish prejudice, Horace Walpole called him 'a creature of Lord Bute, and a kind of riding master to the king'. His interest in architecture dated from his boyhood; there is still preserved here a drawing of a Doric column that he made at Eton. Hovingham is his main architectural work and, as well as its unique plan, has very competent façades in the Palladian style. It was intended to have two flanking projecting wings but only one of these was executed. The main

rooms have high coved ceilings and screens of columns. The Saloon, in the centre, has painted decorations by Sebastiano Ricci and Cipriani. Over the staircase is a copy by Andrea Casali of Guido Reni's famous *Aurora*, one of the paintings in Rome most admired by eighteenth-century *milordi inglesi*.

Jervaulx Abbey
19; 12 miles NW of Ripon off A6108
The ruins of the Cistercian abbey are still privately owned and therefore not too tidied up. Although not extensive, the old walls make a beautiful picture: bushes, wildflowers and trees are suffered to remain among the ancient stones in eighteenth-century Picturesque fashion. What a relief after the antiseptic mown-grass neatness and curators' huts of routine Ministry-maintained ruins. The ground-plan of the abbey buildings can still be followed clearly, and the wall of the monks' dormitory, pierced by a row of noble lancet windows, stands to an impressive height.

The abbey was founded here in 1156 (after a false start near Aysgarth). The last abbot was hanged in 1537 for taking part in the Pilgrimage of Grace.

Kirkham Priory
20; 10 miles W of Malton off A64
Here is a perfect ruin, situated in a secluded pastoral valley on the bank of the River Derwent. Lawns stretch gently down to the river and the opposite bank is thickly wooded. The priory was a house of Augustinian canons founded *c*.1125 by Walter l'Espec, who also founded Rievaulx (*q.v.*). According to legend it was built in memory of his only son, who was killed in a riding accident near the present entrance to the monastery.

Of the Norman church an arched doorway survives, embellished with unusual carved mouldings and cushion capitals. The east end of the church was rebuilt in Early English style and one romantic fragment of this, with a tall lancet window, still stands. The general outline of the monastic buildings is also preserved, including the Norman doorway to the Refectory. The two most impressive features are the LAVATORIUM and GATEHOUSE. The Lavatorium adjoins the Refectory and is where the monks washed their hands before meals in lead-lined stone sinks beneath a beautiful late thirteenth-century geometrical arcade. The Gatehouse has a sumptuous decorated façade, embellished with ten shields of arms, and two traceried windows over the low archway. The carving is well preserved and all the heraldry is easily identifiable. It looks like a Strawberry Hill Rococo Gothick bookplate – especially as the archway frames a beautiful landscape view.

Kirkleatham

21; 4 miles S of Redcar on A1042
Kirkleatham is situated close to modern suburban development, but still retains its own character. It owes its special interest to the philanthropy of the Turners, who were the squires here in the eighteenth century; their house, Kirkleatham Hall, was demolished in the 1950s. The centrepiece of the village is TURNER'S HOSPITAL, founded by Sir William Turner, a rich London draper, in 1676 and partly rebuilt in 1742 on a most generous scale, with three ranges surrounding a courtyard and several statues, including one of Justice. One of the wings was designed for ten old men and the other for ten old women. The back range contains the Chapel, which is comparable with Wren's London churches; the name of the great architect is often linked with it, though there is no proof that it is his and James Gibbs is a stronger contender. Four wooden fluted Ionic columns support a plaster-groined vault. There are original box pews, and galleries on three sides. The arrangement over the west door is spectacular, with the gallery stepped up in the middle and embellished with a flowing wrought-iron railing by Tijou, who was also responsible for the altar rails. The Venetian window over the altar contains stained glass of the Adoration of the Magi designed by Sebastiano Ricci. Sir William Turner's death-mask is preserved in a glass case at the back of the Chapel. The almshouses are now administered by the Charity Commissioners, who since 1951 have carried out an excellent programme of restoration and modernisation.

Sir William also built the school, now called the OLD HALL, in 1708–9. It is of brick and stone, three storeys high, with a stone centrepiece of Doric pilasters carrying a semi-circular pediment flanked by pairs of *œils-de-bœuf* windows. It is a building of altogether surprising grandeur for an eighteenth-century village school.

The third major building in the village is ST CUTHBERT'S CHURCH. The main part was rebuilt in 1763, with beautiful smooth stonework and round-arched windows. The interior has arcades of Tuscan columns, and a Venetian window over the altar. Attached to one side,

and in striking contrast to the demure classicism of the church, is Marwood William Turner's MAUSOLEUM, designed by James Gibbs in 1740. It is octagonal with a pyramidal roof 63 feet high culminating in a large flaming urn. The lower parts of the walls have crinkly rustication, and incised on the string-course is a finely lettered inscription: 'THIS MAUSOLEUM WAS ERECTED 1740 TO THE MEMORY OF MARWOOD WILLIAM TURNER, ESQUIRE THE BEST OF SONS'. Inside, in the middle, is the plain sarcophagus tomb of Sir William, and in a niche against the wall is the beautiful monument to Marwood William Turner himself; he died on his Grand Tour. It was designed by Gibbs and made by Peter Scheemakers. Various other interesting marble monuments to different members of the Turner family are scattered around the church, giving it a well-furnished look.

Knaresborough

22; 2 miles NE of Harrogate on A59
Knaresborough is a picturesque place, almost continental in feeling, built along a sandstone cliff overlooking the River Nidd. The views from the medieval road bridge or nineteenth-century railway bridge over the river are especially memorable, with the ruins of the castle and the church tower rising above the houses and the river running far below. A curious, possibly unique, feature of the town is the number of buildings painted in chequers of black and white, like great chess boards.

The CASTLE was originally royal and was largely rebuilt between 1310 and 1340. The most substantial fragment is the keep, a rectangle of 64 by 52 feet rising three storeys over a vaulted basement. This basement is now a museum and its exhibits include armour picked up on the battlefield of Marston Moor. In the former outer bailey is the Court House of the Royal Forest of Knaresborough, which has a medieval ground floor and a seventeenth-century upper floor. Nearby is the Market Place with the nice little TOWN HALL of 1862 and the oldest chemist's shop in England.

The CHURCH OF ST JOHN is on the other side of the railway that the Victorians pushed straight through the middle of the town – a deplorable piece of vandalism. It stands in a large and grassy churchyard surrounded by attractive houses. It is a Perpendicular rebuilding but retains a late twelfth-century tower in the middle. The interior is notable for the Slingsby family monuments, including two dating from the reign of Charles I. Sir William Slingsby (who discovered the mineral springs at Harrogate (*q.v.*)) stands in a niche and is dressed as a cavalier in hat and boots – remarkably lifelike. He leans against his sword, his head resting on his hand, and you expect him to move at any moment. Also not to be missed is the poor-box of about 1600 shaped like a clock.

From the church a very steep cobbled street leads down to Waterside, just off which is the CHAPEL OF OUR LADY OF THE CRAG, a tiny shrine cut into the cliff in 1409. It has a pointed doorway and one traceried window, and on the front is carved St Robert of Knaresborough, a hermit who lived in a cave nearby. He is more than life-size and is a startling apparition. The whole ensemble is delightfully dotty.

The spine of Knaresborough is the remarkably unspoilt HIGH STREET, which winds right through the town parallel to the river and is lined with good eighteenth-century houses of brick and stone, several old coaching inns and many well-preserved Georgian shop-fronts. The grandest houses are at the north end, where the name changes to York Place. Also in the High Street is KNARESBOROUGH HOUSE, a detached stone-fronted late eighteenth-century house, which is now council offices. It is set back from the street and has flanking wings lower than its main block.

It is a pity there is so much traffic in Knaresborough – a by-pass would be a great improvement.

Langton
23; 4 miles S of Malton off B1248

This is a typical early nineteenth-century Picturesque estate village of stone cottages with some mildly Gothic pointed-arched windows and doors. They are arranged in semi-detached groups or short terraces with wide grass verges in front, and focus on the heraldic stone gatepiers of the Big House, LANGTON HALL. The village was developed from the 1820s to the 1850s by two generations of the Norcliffe family, but it sticks to the same late Georgian style throughout, which suggests a local builder under squirearchical direction rather than the hand of a professional architect. There is clear evidence that it is not all Georgian: the date-stones on the fronts of the cottages give the game away, beginning 'A.N. JAN 24 1824' and ending 'N.N. 1857'; and the charming single-storeyed former SCHOOL has a more explicit inscription: 'THIS SCHOOL HOUSE WAS BUILT BY LT. COLONEL N. NORCLIFFE 1841'.

There is a small green planted with trees and surrounded by a protective wooden rail. Don't miss the two early nineteenth-century fluted cast-iron water pumps that stand here. The centrepiece of the village is the parish CHURCH OF ST ANDREW, rebuilt in 1822 out of old materials. The interior is very pleasant, with a flat plaster ceiling, whitewashed walls and old panelled pews. It has a nicely unrestored atmosphere and, like everything at Langton, benefits from being immaculately maintained.

Markenfield Hall
24; 5 miles SE of Ripon off A61

Built by John de Markenfield by licence dated 1310, then added to and adapted in the fifteenth century, this wonderfully little-altered building is the most complete surviving example of a medium-sized fourteenth-century country house in England. Having later become a farmhouse, it escaped fashionable remodelling in the seventeenth and eighteenth centuries and has merely been kept in repair. Surrounded by a moat (with ducks on it) and approached through extensive farm buildings, it remains much as it was when the last of the Markenfields fled abroad in 1569 after taking part in the abortive rising of the north against Elizabeth I.

A stone bridge leads across the moat and through the Gatehouse to the courtyard. The main part of the house is L-shaped with battlements, an octagonal stair turret and its original chimneys. The ground floor is part vaulted, and the Chapel and Great Hall are on the first floor; they are distinguished by their tall traceried windows. Because it has been used continuously as a farmhouse since about 1600, little of the original decoration survives, but the main lines of the place remain relatively unchanged.

Masham
25; 8 miles NW of Ripon on A6108

A little stone-built town with a feudal atmosphere, Masham lies on the edge of the Dales and is surrounded by large estates and old families. It has a cattle market, Theakston's (real ale) brewery and several nice old-established shops selling country houses or tweeds, and repairing clocks.

The *clou* of the town is the large, regular MARKET SQUARE, part cobbled, with an old stone cross in the middle flanked by four lime trees and green-painted cast-iron benches of snake pattern. Along one side is the King's Hotel – built of stone, with a pediment, and looking quite stately. At one end is the eighteenth-century Café Royal (fish and chips) and a domestic-looking Barclays Bank.

At the other end of the square is the CHURCH OF ST MARY, with its square Norman tower and fifteenth-century octagonal top with a broach spire and blue-and-gold clock – a very elegant arrangement. The graveyard is undisturbed, with good old trees and eighteenth- and nineteenth-century headstones; it is open to the country to the south. Opposite the entrance porch is the base of an important ninth-century cylindrical cross with elaborate carving depicting figures and animals; it has been the subject of many learned articles in antiquarian journals. Inside, the dominant impression of the nave is Perpendicular, with a well-proportioned clerestory over the arcade. The wide aisles are full of family monuments: those in the south aisle commemorate the Danbys, the Harcourts, and the Listers of Swinton Park (*q.v.*). At the end, like a Lady altar, is a Baroque reredos of marble erected to the memory of the splendidly named Sir Abstrupus Danby and decorated with his crest: a golden crab. This wonderfully incongruous piece of heraldry can also be seen in the five hatchments hung aloft in the nave. In the north aisle is a Jacobean alabaster tomb of four-poster type commemorating Sir Marmaduke Wyvill and his wife; their children kneel below, while the cherubs in the spandrels above look as if they are blowing bubbles. Over the chancel arch is a large oil painting in a gilded Gothick frame. It is the upper part of the *Nativity* cartoon by Reynolds intended for the central light of the west window at New College, Oxford. How did it find its way here? (The lower half was at Belvoir Castle (*q.v.*) but was burnt in 1812.) The high altar dates from the Victorian restoration and has a carved reredos of alabaster and Italian marble given by Lady Lavinia Bertie in 1882. It is now disused and the chancel is somewhat cut off by a clumsy new central altar. One wonders why advantage was not taken of the handsome eighteenth-century mahogany communion table for this purpose, rather than using it as a postcard stall at the back of the church.

Drawing Room, Newburgh Priory.

Newburgh Priory
26; 8 miles SE of Thirsk off A19

The Augustinian priory, founded in 1145, was dissolved in 1538 by Anthony Bellasis, Chaplain to Henry VIII. He then bought the estate for £1062 and left it to his nephew, Sir William Bellasis, who converted the priory into a private house in 1546. The estate has since passed by descent to the Wombwells. The great mystery of Newburgh is whether or not Oliver Cromwell is buried here. His third daughter, Mary, married Thomas Bellasis, 2nd Viscount Fauconberg and 1st Earl of Fauconberg, and she is reputed to have rescued her father's body after it had been exhumed from Westminster Abbey at the time of the Restoration.

Newburgh has recently been excellently restored and re-roofed; the largely sixteenth-century exterior conceals a series of well-maintained eighteenth-century rooms. The Dining Room has a sumptuous alabaster Jacobean chimneypiece and interesting family portraits. The two best rooms are the small and large Drawing Rooms, which have Rococo plasterwork by Giuseppe Cortese and good eighteenth-century furniture, as well as some fine family portraits by Mary Beale, Romney and Andrea Soldi. The needlework of *c.*1760 on the Drawing Room chairs was restored by the actor Ernest Thesiger.

The recent restoration programme did not include the derelict Long Gallery, which has been reduced to a shell and converted into a garden. It contains the tombstone of Sir George Wombwell's favourite horse, The Turk, who survived the Crimean War and lived to the age of twenty-three. Three of his hooves are kept in the house as inkpots.

Newby Hall
27; 3 miles SE of Ripon off B6265 [56]

Newby is set in attractive though unspectacular country between Ripon and Boroughbridge on the north bank of the River Ure. The eighteenth-century parkland has been augmented in this century by elaborate formal gardens, which include spectacular double herbaceous borders stretching down from the house to the river.

The house comprises a seventeenth-century three-storeyed red brick main block with a pair of lower eighteenth-century wings, attributed to Carr of York. Its chief interest, however, is the sequence of rooms created by Robert Adam for William Weddell, an eighteenth-century connoisseur and collector. The Entrance Hall, with a built-in organ, and stucco work – including excellent Piranesian trophies of arms – by Joseph Rose, is a perfect example of Adam's middle period. The floor of marble and stone has a geometrical pattern related to the design of the ceiling. The Tapestry Room contains one of the series of Boucher-Neilson tapestries from Gobelins (here with a grey ground) – for which Adam also designed settings at Osterley, Moor Park (now at Aske) and Croome Court (now in the Metropolitan Museum, New York) – with matching chairs and the original carpet designed by Adam. The Library, with apsidal ends screened by Corinthian columns, was designed by Adam as the Eating Room and converted into a library in the early nineteenth century. The original decoration, including arabesque stucco work and inset paintings, is still in place. Opening out at the south end is the famous Sculpture Gallery containing Weddell's collection of much-restored Roman sculpture, the finest neo-classical ensemble of its type to survive in England. The Gallery is formed of a series of domed spaces, the stucco work painted in different shades of pink and intended to evoke a Roman catacomb.

Northallerton
28; 7½ miles NE of Bedale on A684

The county town of the North Riding has an air of dignity and consequence. It comprises one long main street, the HIGH STREET, running from north to south and gently curving. It is very wide, with three-storeyed Georgian houses of brick and stone and several decent old shop-fronts. The houses would benefit from the wholesale restoration of glazing bars in their window sashes, and the tall streetlights should be removed, but otherwise the High Street presents a handsome spectacle – still with a strong coaching atmosphere about it. The widest part of the street serves as the market place. It narrows at the north end as you approach the CHURCH OF ALL SAINTS, which overlooks a triangular green planted with trees and is surrounded by decent houses. The great feature of

All Saints is the tall Perpendicular crossing-tower which dominates the town. The main part of the church was heavily gone over in the 1880s and, at the same time, its pretty eighteenth-century chancel was replaced to the design of C. Hodgson Fowler. An old guide-book says of the eighteenth-century work: 'These errors were happily rectified at the great restoration of 1882–5'. Alas!

Norton Conyers
29; 4 miles N of Ripon off A1
Norton Conyers has been the seat of the Grahams since 1623. An early Tudor manor house, it was substantially remodelled in the seventeenth century, when the shaped gables and mullion-and-transom windows were added. The Great Hall is in the original position, and the early sixteenth-century timber roof still exists above the coved plaster ceiling. Many of the other rooms were remodelled in *c*.1773, when some of the windows were sashed and good marble chimneypieces were installed. The interior looks especially attractive at Christmas, when, every year, peacocks are made out of yew by the gardener as decorations.

The house contains the accumulated possessions of a squire's family over three and a half centuries, including good Georgian furniture and a long run of family portraits. The James II Bedroom upstairs is reached by a fine seventeenth-century oak staircase and has a richly carved Jacobean bed. It is here that James II, then Duke of York, and his wife Mary of-Modena slept while travelling to Scotland in 1679.

Nunnington Hall
NT; 30; 7 miles SE of Helmsley off B1257
Nunnington stands by the River Rye in a valley below the Yorkshire Moors. It dates from the sixteenth and early seventeenth centuries but was refronted in the 1680s in a harmonious classical style by Richard Graham, 1st Viscount Preston, a Catholic supporter of James II and one of the five peers to whom James entrusted the government of the country when he fled in 1688. Nunnington remained in the Graham family till 1839. It was modernised in 1921 by Mrs Ronald Fife under the supervision of Walter Brierley, the York architect, and, on her death in 1952, passed to the National Trust.

The interior owes much to Brierley's restoration and, at the time of writing, some of the colour schemes – such as the strong blue-green in the Dining Room – date from his time. The Entrance Hall was formed out of Lord Preston's kitchen and the Mannerist chimneypiece with a cartouche of arms was designed by Brierley. A remarkable feature of the house is the ceiling of Lord Preston's Room, which has late seventeenth-century heraldic paintings on canvas. The Great Hall has oak panelling and doorcases inserted by Preston, and a carved stone chimneypiece. The furniture here, as elsewhere in the house, comprises good pieces from the late sixteenth century to the early eighteenth, and among the paintings are allegories of Wealth and Poverty, after Breughel. The Drawing Room, on the first floor, contains Regency satinwood furniture and some interesting pictures.

Ormesby Hall
31; 4 miles SE of Middlesbrough on A174
The seat of the Pennymans is a middling-sized Georgian country house. The present house, with its plain exterior, was built in the 1750s by Dorothy, widow of Sir James Pennyman. The architect is not known, but the original interior decoration suggests the work of the York school of craftsmen. The interior was further embellished and the handsome stable block built by Sir James Pennyman, 6th Baronet, in the 1770s to a design of John Carr of York. Both the Dining Room and Drawing Room are his, and these rooms are the best in the house. They have pretty plaster ceilings and chimneypieces in the Adam manner. Ormesby contains appropriate eighteenth-century furniture, family portraits (including one of Sir James Pennyman by Reynolds) and a handsome silver race cup by Smith and Sharp, hallmarked 1772, presented by Sir James to be raced for at Northallerton Races and recently bought back at auction for the house.

Pickering
32; 8 miles N of Malton on A169
A picturesque old market town of brick and stone with red-tiled roofs, nestling at the foot of the North York Moors. Distant views of the town are attractive because of the way in which the higgledy-piggledy roofs pile up towards the church spire.

The most interesting part of the town is away from the main road. The Market Place is a wide street, running uphill, with narrow alleys and flights of steps leading off it. The parish CHURCH OF ST PETER AND ST PAUL at the top is reached by flights of steps as if it were in an Italian hill town. It is basically Norman, though it was much altered and enlarged later in the Middle Ages. The tower at the west end dates from the early thirteenth century, but the spire was added 100 years later. The great feature of the church is the cycle of fifteenth-century wall paintings in the nave – not of very high artistic quality, and heavily restored, but nevertheless giving a good impression of the way in which the interior of a medieval church was decorated. They were first discovered under whitewash in 1851, but the then vicar thought them 'purely ridiculous' and feared that they would 'distract the attention of the congregation', so he had them covered over again. They were not fully revealed and restored until 1880. The dominant colours are black and red, and they show scenes from the lives of the saints, vividly depicted like comic strips. The mouth of Hell is a particularly enjoyable image.

The other main sight of Pickering is the great CASTLE of the Duchy of Lancaster. The ruins, surrounded by trees, stand on a hill overlooking the stream that runs through the town. The castle was founded by William the Conqueror – or at least that is the tradition, though none of the present fabric dates from before the late twelfth century and most of the castle was built in the thirteenth and fourteenth. The curtain wall was built between 1323 and 1326, and has square projecting towers, each with a romantic name – Rosamund's Tower, the Mill Tower, Diate Hill Tower. There are two baileys, one within the other. The keep, a circular shell keep of c.1220, stands on a large artificial motte and is the castle's most impressive feature. Many of the medieval domestic buildings within the walls were timber-framed and have disappeared. The castle was besieged and ruined in the Civil War.

The bridge over the river is part medieval. Beside it, set back behind trees, is BECK ISLE, once the home of William Marshall, the late eighteenth-century agricultural reformer and theorist. He was responsible for the Gothick alterations to the front of the house, including the two tall pointed windows to one side of the door.

Ribston Hall
33; 4 miles N of Wetherby off A1 [57]
Ribston gives its name to the most delicious of all English eating apples. The house is long and low, of red brick, with fifteen bays on either front. It was built by Sir Henry Goodricke in 1674. The entrance front is the plainer of the two and has a simple late Georgian front door. The park front retains more of its original character, with a broken segmental pediment over the front door. The glory of the house is the late Georgian Saloon. It was remodelled by Carr of York c.1775 in his Adam-esque style, and has a high coved ceiling enriched with filigree plasterwork. Round the walls in plaster frames are eighteenth-century copies of famous Italian paintings by Guido Reni, Guercino and others. The striking colour scheme – sage green, dark blue, and red – is that of Charles Moxon, who redecorated the room in 1846; it gives body to the thin elegance of the plasterwork and one is very glad of it.

Attached to one end of the house is the thirteenth-century CHAPEL OF THE KNIGHTS TEMPLAR. It has a vaulted crypt, and many fine furnishings were provided as part of a scheme of improvement in 1700. The carved panelling round the altar also dates from then. In the east window is Regency stained glass copied from Reynolds' at New College, Oxford.

Riccall
34; 9 miles S of York on A19
ST MARY'S is a Norman church altered later and heavily restored by Pearson in 1864–5. He rebuilt the tower, clerestory, nave roof and south aisle, and added the south porch. (The church had been closed two years earlier because it was in a dangerous condition.) The work was done with considerable care, all the old stones being numbered and put back in their original positions. Pearson deliberately left the columns of the nave arcades leaning drunkenly (they were solid enough) as a reminder of the condition of the building before he set to work on it. To those interested in Victorian church restoration, Pearson's sensitive treatment of the nave makes an instructive contrast with Ewan Christian's unsympathetic revamping of the chancel for the Church Commissioners before Pearson was called in by the rector. The most important feature of the church is the Norman south doorway, which Pearson protected by his new porch; it dates from c.1160 and sports much elaborate

carving. The arch is carried on little columns, the capitals of which are carved with St Peter and St Paul. The thrice-recessed mouldings round the arch are also elaborately carved with beak-heads, roses and miscellaneous naturalistic motifs.

Richmond ★
35; 8 miles N of Leyburn on A6108
This is one of the least spoilt and most picturesque of all English country towns. Its hilly setting at the entrance to Swaledale could not be better, and the drama of the landscape is matched by the silhouette of the town and the powerful ruins of the castle. The streets rise steeply from the bridge over the river to the Market Place, and the houses are built almost entirely of grey stone.

Richmond was important in the Middle Ages but later declined – though, as so often, there was a rallying in the eighteenth century. Henry VII was Earl of Richmond before he seized the crown at Bosworth in 1485. He perpetuated his old title in the name of his new palace on the Thames near London – Richmond in Surrey. Thereafter the title was raised to a dukedom and reserved for royal bastards.

The roofs of the town cluster round the ruined CASTLE, with its exceptionally tall and well-proportioned stone keep, standing on a sheer rock. The castle was begun by Alan Rufus, 'the Red', in 1071; it was an important fortification in what was still disputed border country, though it was never the scene of a great siege and it was already being allowed to decay in the sixteenth century. The keep was begun in 1150 and completed in about 1180. It is unusual in being sited next to the gate rather than in the most inaccessible part of the castle. It is square (like Castle Hedingham in Essex), with flat buttresses and four corner towers, and is over 100 feet high. A large part of the curtain wall, punctuated by lesser towers, also survives – as do the ruins of the domestic buildings, including the Great Hall, which was begun in 1080 and is the oldest in England. It is worth climbing to the top of the keep both for a bird's eye view of the town and for the beautiful views over Swaledale and the surrounding moors.

The MARKET PLACE is large, sloping and still cobbled. It is surrounded by stone-built Georgian and Victorian buildings. The TOWN HALL on the south side was built in 1756 and is said to have been designed by Thomas Atkinson. The adjoining MARKET HALL dates from 1854. What gives the Market Place its special picturesque aura, however, is the romantic island of buildings in the middle, including HOLY TRINITY CHURCH. This is a basically medieval structure, but has been encroached on by secular uses and so is now a wonderfully dotty jumble of cottages, shops, offices and a medieval church tower. Vying with the latter is the MARKET CROSS – a fat obelisk erected in 1771 and looking a bit like a stone cucumber on a classical plinth.

It is well worth exploring the streets opening off the Market Place. Friars' Wynd leads to the THEATRE ROYAL, a perfectly preserved small Georgian theatre. It was built in 1788 by the actor-manager Samuel Butler, and was closed in 1848. After a long period as an auction room and furniture warehouse it was rescued and re-opened in 1962. The outside is plain, but the interior is complete in every detail, with a little stage, pit, boxes, and a gallery carried on Tuscan columns; all is original. It is a miraculous survival and its small, cosy interior must make it a marvellous experience to come to a play here. The stage scenery, dating from 1836, is the oldest and largest set to survive in this country.

Back to the Market Place. Finkle Street leads to NEW-BIGGIN STREET, the stateliest Georgian street in Richmond. It is wide and lined with trees and has remarkably good houses with stone doorcases and sashed windows. NO. 47 is a charming essay in Gothick, with two bay windows – a harbinger of things to come, for at the junction of Newbiggin Street and Craven Gate is the entrance to TEMPLE LODGE, a property of 35 acres. The house was built in 1769 and is symmetrical and castellated with ogee-arched windows. Even more delectable is the CULLODEN TOWER in the grounds. Erected in 1746 to commemorate the defeat of the Jacobites, it is a spectacular octagonal tower with beautiful interiors. The first-floor room has a plaster ribbed vault and a lively Gothick chimneypiece with scrolly decoration and two pinnacles flanking an ogee pediment.

Richmond is altogether a good place for towers. The most beautiful of all is the GREYFRIARS' TOWER in Queens Road – a fifteenth-century ruin looking extremely impressive on its own, as the rest of the church of which it was once a part has disappeared, leaving this square bell-tower soaring upwards with sheer expanses of stone culminating in the Perpendicular tracery of the windows in the lantern storey and an openwork parapet with twelve short pinnacles. ST MARY'S, the parish church, is away from the centre of the town, having been built outside the town walls. Its tower is much less impressive than the Greyfriars', and the church was excessively restored in the nineteenth century. The chancel, for instance, is almost entirely by Sir George Gilbert Scott, but it contains a set of early sixteenth-century choir stalls brought from Easby Abbey after the Dissolution. They have amusing carvings on the misericords.

Rievaulx Abbey★

36; 4 miles W of Helmsley off B1257
Includes Rievaulx Terrace and Temples (NT)
This is the most poignant of all English monastic ruins – partly because of its hauntingly beautiful site; partly because so much is known about life here at the height of the abbey's prosperity under the congenial Abbot Aelred in the mid-twelfth century and can be recalled across the centuries as you survey the broken walls and shattered arches. This part of the Rye Valley is narrow and sheltered from the moors that rise all around it; the river banks are luxuriously wooded now and probably always were. It is also possible to look down on to the buildings snuggling into the valley below, just as the youthful Aelred did when he decided to turn back from his journey and join the new abbey, in time becoming its abbot and the head of a community of 140 monks and at least 500 lay brothers.

The abbey, the first Cistercian house in England, was founded by Walter l'Espec, who in 1131 granted this site

Rievaulx Abbey.

Ripon Cathedral.

in the wilderness to a group of twelve Cistercian monks from Clairvaux. (William, the first abbot, had been St Bernard's secretary there.) There are substantial remains of both the church and the monastic buildings, and it is possible to trace the whole plan – regular, civilised and vast. The east end and transepts of the church stand to their full height. They are Early English and of great nobility, with clustered columns, richly moulded arches, a triforium of paired arches, and lancets in the clerestory. The east end, formed of two tiers of three perfectly proportioned lancet windows, is, after the north transept of York Minster (*q.v.*), perhaps the most satisfying of all English lancet designs. The nave, by contrast, has largely disappeared. The walls of the monastic buildings stand to a good height, part Norman and part Early English. The romantic counterpoint between these towering masses of masonry and the dream-like perfection of the east end of the church is what gives Rievaulx its drama.

Along the top of the hill overlooking the ruins, a spectacular grass TERRACE (NT) was laid out in the eighteenth century as part of the landscaping of Duncombe Park (*q.v.*). The date is about 1758, and it was the work of third-generation Thomas Duncombe in emulation of his father's older grass terrace at the house. It has a similar formula, with TEMPLES (NT) at either end and contrived vistas down into the valley below. The only difference here is that the views are not merely of country but of the abbey ruins. There is no more superlative landscape experience in England than walking along this terrace. It was painted by Turner, sent Dorothy Wordsworth into raptures and made Cowper wish to stay forever. It now belongs to the National Trust and visitors are allowed to

picnic, just as visitors did in the eighteenth century. The temples are open to the public. One is rectangular with an Ionic portico, and inside is a painted ceiling by Giovanni Borgnis, the central panel copied from Guido Reni's *Aurora* in Rome; there is also original furniture in the style of William Kent. The temple at the other end is a domed rotunda with Doric columns, and the circular room inside has a coffered ceiling.

Ripley Castle
37; 4 miles N of Harrogate on A61

The CASTLE, PARK and Gothick MODEL VILLAGE form a fine late eighteenth-century landscape composition, though it incorporates older fabric and has some Victorian highlights and eccentricities. The house was largely rebuilt in *c*.1780, almost certainly to the design of John Carr of York, with a castellated exterior and chaste neo-classical interiors. The fifteenth-century Gatehouse survives from the old castle, as does the Tower, dated 1555, which contains three Jacobean rooms, including the Tower Room. This has a decorative plaster ceiling and oak panelling. The Dining Room, Hall and Drawing Room in the eighteenth-century block all have good marble chimneypieces, family portraits and Georgian furniture.

The serpentine lake in the valley below the house was made in 1844 by Sir Thomas Ingleby. He called the house 'the *Schloß*' and was responsible for the notice in the Gatehouse, which reads: '*Parlez au Suisse*' – 'Speak to the Swiss [porter].' He also built the elaborate French Gothic house in the village called the HOTEL DE VILLE; legend has it that he wanted to make Ripley look like somewhere in Alsace.

Ripon

38; 10 miles N of Harrogate on A61 **[58]**

The little town of Ripon has a slightly dusty, continental atmosphere, with humble red-roofed houses crouching below the cathedral, and a large Market Place. This latter derives a certain stateliness from the 90-foot obelisk in its centre and the faultlessly well-bred classicism of James Wyatt's TOWN HALL façade, with pious red-and-gold inscriptions on its frieze.

The CATHEDRAL is small (by English as opposed to Italian or Spanish standards) but architecturally interesting. It occupies the site of a Saxon abbey built by St Wilfred in the seventh century, the crypt of which survives under the crossing of the present church. This is one of the earliest Christian structures in England; it is small, dark and tunnel-vaulted, with niches in the walls for relics. The best part of the cathedral is the west front. It is among the earliest and most perfect pieces of Early English Gothic, with flanking towers and tiers of carefully arranged lancets increasing in size as they go up, so that the tallest are at the top of the towers. There were also, until the seventeenth century, two little spires on top and, until the nineteenth, tracery in the lancets – but one is glad that these fripperies have all gone, their absence enhancing the square-cut perfection of the design with nothing finicky to detract from the scale and proportions. The interior of the church is late Norman–Transitional Gothic, but partly remodelled in Perpendicular taste. Unfortunately, this latter scheme was never finished, leaving the church neither one thing nor the other. This is particularly noticeable at the crossing, where the Norman columns and arches have been partly encased in Gothic stonework, leaving the church looking horribly lop-sided and unfinished. In the nave, the Perpendicular transformation was more successfully carried through and it is only by dint of serious looking that it is possible to discover traces of Norman work at either end. The transepts and chancel retain more of the twelfth-century work – Transitional in the former and maturely Early English in the latter, making it one of the earliest examples of fully-fledged Gothic. The wooden vault throughout the church is a Victorian restoration, but incorporates many old carved bosses.

The hotch-potch character of the architecture at Ripon is partly redeemed by the way in which the cathedral is lovingly maintained, and by the beauty of its furnishings. The choir has splendid late fifteenth-century stalls with two tiers of elaborately pinnacled canopies. The sedilia is rich Decorated work, comparable to Lincoln or Southwell (*qq.v.*). The high altar and reredos, glowing with gold and colour, are by the late and underrated Sir Ninian Comper. Similar good things can be found throughout the church. Not to be missed are the pulpit in the nave by Harry Wilson, with scrumptious Arts and Crafts relief decoration in silver and bronze, and the Grecian monument in the south transept to William Weddell of Newby (*q.v.*), which consists of a sensitive marble bust by Nollekens set inside a copy of the Choragic Monument of Lysicrates at Athens designed by drunken 'Athenian' Stuart.

Robin Hood's Bay

39; 7 miles SE of Whitby off A171

This village, to paraphrase Dr Johnson, is worth seeing, but not worth travelling to see. It is a small, eminently picturesque fishing village on the side of a steep cove, with little red-roofed houses crowded along small paved alleys and up flights of steps above the steep curving road down to the shore. Most of the houses were built in the eighteenth century when the old village on the site fell into the sea in a storm. The present parish CHURCH OF ST STEPHEN, by G.E. Street, is stern and Victorian with a saddleback-roofed tower.

What makes the place worth a special visit, however, is the OLD CHURCH (also dedicated to St Stephen) about a mile inland, situated in a wonderfully overgrown graveyard with headstones to the seafaring dead. No fewer than 260 of those commemorated are buried abroad or at sea. The building is simplest Gothick. and was built in 1821 to replace a ruined Norman church. Having been itself replaced in 1870, the interior has been left completely alone and is a perfect example of a small Georgian layout, with box pews and a three-decker pulpit all painted a milky cocoa colour. There are galleries on Tuscan columns, a Gothic mahogany shelf for hymn books, the Royal Arms of George IV over the chancel arch, a barrel organ in the west gallery, a little gourd-shaped font, boards painted with psalms behind the altar, an old-fashioned iron stove and, in a glass case, a large model of SS *Pretoria* built in Sunderland in 1900 for the International Line Steamship Co. Ltd of Whitby. The church is altogether one of the most undisturbed and unspoilt specimens of its kind. Unfortunately, at the time of visiting, after having been quietly kept ticking over for 100 years, and used for Evensong on summer evenings, it is now being declared redundant. It is essential that it be taken on by the Redundant Churches Fund and preserved as it is.

Rudding Park

40; 3 miles SE of Harrogate off A661

The present Rudding Park is almost entirely a late Georgian creation, the house and landscape forming one integrated composition. The overall architectural unity is such that it might be assumed that everything was designed at one time for the same client. In fact, the work was carried out in three stages for three different owners. The landscaping of the park was executed for the Earl of Rosslyn *c.*1790 by Humphry Repton. Following Rosslyn's death in 1805, the Rudding estate was sold to the Hon. William Gordon (a cadet of the Aberdeen family), who began the new house in 1807 to the design of an unidentifiable architect. In 1824 Gordon sold the house, as an unfinished shell, to Sir Joseph Radcliffe, 2nd Baronet of Milnebridge in the West Riding, who wished to move because of the effect of industrial development on his former property. He employed R.D. Chantrell to fit out the interior, creating the rooms we admire today – especially the Library with its fitted mahogany bookcases – and to add a large service wing at the back. (Chantrell was a pupil of Sir John Soane and, though born in London, spent most of his working life in

Yorkshire. He was pre-eminently a church architect, being responsible for over twenty-five new churches in the Leeds area. Rudding is his only country house interior.) Various alterations were made later in the nineteenth century, including the erection of the splendidly incongruous Victorian Gothic CHAPEL to the north of the house.

Rudding is currently being converted into a conference centre, which will detract from its character somewhat. Nevertheless, the exterior, with severe ashlar stonework and no fewer than five segmental bow windows, is an admirable example of simple Regency architecture.

Scampston Hall
41; 5 miles NE of Malton off A64

Scampston is set in a well-wooded park on the south side of the broad, flat Vale of Pickering, beneath the Wolds. The main road from York to Scarborough crosses the estate, offering a glimpse of the house half a mile away at the end of Capability Brown's long lake. This forms part of an extensive scheme of improvement carried out in the 1770s by Sir William St Quintin, 4th Baronet. An early nineteenth-century topographer commented 'a sterile plain destitute of every natural advantage has at considerable expense been rendered beautiful by art'. The present appearance of the house is due to Sir William's nephew and successor, William Thomas St Quintin, who called upon Thomas Leverton in 1803 to remodel it. The core of the house, which is built of brick, probably dates from the seventeenth century. Leverton was an interesting but slightly obscure neo-classicist, responsible for Bedford Square in London and Woodhall Park in Hertfordshire. At Scampston he encased the house in fashionable stucco and added central bows to the entrance and garden fronts. The former is encircled by giant Tuscan columns and contains the front door, while the latter has pilasters and is topped off with a shallow dome (once carrying a tall cupola, but this has disappeared). Leverton also remodelled the interior to form a symmetrical enfilade of state rooms along the south front: Drawing Room, Library and Dining Room, all in a simple Regency style, with marble chimneypieces, moulded cornices, and a discreet use of the Tuscan order as pilasters framing the bookcases in the Library and as columns flanking the sideboard recess in the Dining Room. The most original feature of these rooms is the series of fine mahogany double doors with circular central panels. The interior of Scampston is splendidly undisturbed and contains excellent Georgian furniture and an impressively long series of family portraits.

As a final treat, Capability Brown's park is embellished with both an Ionic Palladian bridge *and* a Gothick tea house.

Scarborough
42; 7 miles NW of Filey on A165

Scarborough is the best of all English seaside resorts. For a start the site is marvellous, on a bay with a sandy beach framed by dramatic rugged headlands; the cliffs on which the town is built are carefully landscaped with bushes and trees. There are two distinct parts – the old town with the parish church, castle and harbour to the north, and the nineteenth-century planned development with hotels and classical terraces at the south end. In the middle, acting as a giant visual pivot between the two parts, is the GRAND HOTEL, a Victorian Second Empire whopper by Cuthbert Broderick of Hull. (It is now a Butlin's Holiday Camp and the interior is a nightmare, but the exterior looks as splendid as ever.)

From the railway station it is best to walk straight through the shopping centre (an unspectacular pedestrianised street with Munich-style globe lights, decent cast-iron litter bins, and the usual chainstores) to the old town, which climbs up to the medieval parish church of St Mary and the castle. At this end of the town there are little shops selling fishing tackle, woolly Balaclavas and excellent fish and chips. There are also several steep, narrow cobbled streets with unpretentious brick Georgian houses and a certain amount of quiet 1950s' suburban rebuilding, although this is all disguised from the waterfront by a façade of vibrant vulgarity – day-trippers' Scarborough, described by a snooty neighbour as 'all pies, peas and piss'.

The old HARBOUR, full of fishing boats, is enclosed by eighteenth-century stone piers and at the end is a good-looking white-painted lighthouse of 1800 designed by Matthew Short. It was rebuilt after being bombarded by the Germany navy in 1914. From here there are splendid views of the CASTLE on top of the cliff. It is best admired from afar, as there is not all that much to see close up. But from below, the immensely long curtain wall enclosing an area of 19 acres makes it seem like a crusaders' castle in the Middle East – a seaside Krak des Chevaliers. At the top of the old town is the parish church, mainly of *c*.1300, with a crossing-tower rebuilt in 1669 after the old one collapsed. The church was heavily restored in the nineteenth century and most of the window tracery is Victorian, as is much of the scraped-looking stonework. Anne Brontë, who died in Scarborough at a house on the site of the Grand Hotel, is buried in the graveyard.

From the old town it is best to walk back along the beach to catch the most splendid view of the Grand Hotel. Unfortunately, this has been somewhat compromised by the Olympia Leisure building next door. Incidentally, the Neo-Jacobean building poking out of the trees above and looking rather like a chunk of Hatfield gone astray, is the TOWN HALL. Beyond the Grand Hotel is the Valley, and the beginning of elegant Scarborough. The iron footbridge on tall stone columns is dated 1827 and is thrilling to walk over. But first explore the ROTUNDA MUSEUM, built in 1828–9 for the Scarborough Philosophical Society to the design of R.H. Sharp. Its circular interior is lined with the original showcases and is lit from above through the glazed centre of the coffered dome. On the wooded banks beyond this are a group of handsome Loudonesque villas of yellow stone in their own grounds. One of these, WOOD END, was the winter home of the Sitwells. The villa entrances face THE CRESCENT, a handsome stone classical terrace with black iron balconies, reminiscent of Edinburgh.

Scarborough.

Now, crossing the Spa Bridge, THE ESPLANADE is reached, though the first object to greet one is the SPA CHALET, a nineteenth-century fretwork Swiss cottage painted in improbable shades of blue. The Esplanade is a grand classical terrace of cream stucco with Corinthian columns rolling away into the distance. The Crown Hotel in the centre has a large brightly painted plaster crown in the pediment. The crescents and villas carry on for a long way beyond this. The ultimate object of an exploration in this direction, however, is ST MARTIN'S CHURCH, designed by G.F. Bodley in 1861–2. This is the major architectural thrill of Scarborough and one of the great Victorian churches of England. It is of dark stone with a powerful saddleback-roofed tower and a rose window punched in the west gable. The interior is immensely tall, with chamfered arches supporting a clerestory and expanses of plain wall in the aisles. The chancel, by contrast, is richly decorated, like a Pre-Raphaelite dream. The east wall was designed by Bodley and painted by Burne-Jones and William Morris; it shows the Adoration of the Magi and angels against a gold ground with leaf patterns. The chancel ceiling is by Morris and Philip Webb. The square oriel-like pulpit has ten painted panels on gold grounds by Rossetti, Morris and Ford Madox Brown. The reredos, rood-screen and organ case were all designed by Bodley, the latter with paintings by Spencer Stanhope. Much of the stained glass is by Morris, designed by himself, Rossetti, Burne-Jones and Ford Maddox Brown – a glow of red, green and blue. *Sursum corda!*

Selby Abbey
43; 14 miles S of York on A19

The abbey was founded in 1069 by Benedict of Auxerre, who was directed in a vision to go to Selby in England. Forbidden by his superiors, he went nevertheless, taking St Germain's finger (a valuable relic) with him. Sailing up the River Ouse, three swans landed in the water beside him and he took this to be a sign that he had reached Selby. He landed, built a hut and planted a wooden cross. By a remarkable coincidence, the place where he squatted turned out to be royal property and William the Conqueror assented to Benedict being given the land and becoming the first abbot. That, at least, is the legend – but I feel there must have been more to it than that! The present church was begun by Abbot Hugh de Lacey *c.*1100 and is largely Norman, but with a Decorated chancel. None of the monastic buildings remain but the whole of the church does (in excellent condition, thanks to a series of nineteenth- and twentieth-century restorations), having become the parish church at the Dissolution. It now seems entirely urban, its west front facing the market place and main street of an uneventful but pleasant little town. In England it is usually either the church or the monastic buildings that survive, depending on what use overtook an abbey after the Dissolution. If the church became a parish church, the monastic buildings have nearly always gone, but if the latter became a private house it is usually the church that has disappeared. It is only where a monastic establishment was left to fall into ruin that the whole lot still remains in layout, as at Fountains or Rievaulx (*qq.v.*).

The church at Selby is large and cruciform with transepts, a central crossing-tower and two west towers – more like a cathedral than a parish church. Although of different dates, the architecture is remarkably harmonious and organic, thanks to the carefully proportioned relationship between the different. parts. The central tower is partly Norman but has a restored Gothic top with a continuous arcade of lancets and four excellent corner pinnacles. The west towers are a storey lower and, in their present form, are largely restorations by Oldrid Scott, but they give just what is needed in the way of height to the west front without competing with the dominant role of the central tower in general views. The most beautiful part of the exterior is the east end: a symmetrical Decorated set-piece with the large, elaborately traceried east window flanked by clustered buttresses and fat pinnacles.

The Folly, Settle.

Entering through the Norman west door you are immediately struck by the great length of the building and the nobility of the Norman arcades of the nave, with clustered and cylindrical columns (like Durham (*q.v.*)) carrying a triforium gallery and clerestory. The flat timber roof is a restoration from after the fire of 1906, but it incorporates some old bosses salvaged from the flames. As your eye adjusts you will note that the upper parts of the south side are Early English Gothic and do not match the north side, but such is the strength of the Norman arcade below that the eye only slowly takes in the many differences of detail. The shadows under the crossing, and Oldrid Scott's florid oak rood-screen, disguise the transition to the choir, which is entirely Decorated with multi-shafted columns, cauliflower capitals, statues in tabernacle niches above, and a stone vault. The whole of the east end is filled with the magnificent flowing geometrical tracery of the large window, which miraculously retains some of its medieval stained glass depicting the tree of Jesse – a final excelsior effect in a splendid church.

Settle

44; 11 miles SE of Ingleton on A65
This little market in the Ribble Valley is a well-known centre for walkers and pot-holers in the Pennines. The chief focus is the cobbled Market Square with a jolly Elizabethan-style TOWN HALL on one side designed in 1832 by George Webster of Kendal. Next to it is

THE SHAMBLES, a continental-looking building – seventeenth-century below with later living quarters above opening on to the balcony over the ground-floor arcade. This was originally an open market, but is now enclosed. Leading off the Market Square are several narrow streets and alleys with good Georgian houses built of stone, some sandstone and some limestone, for Settle is built on a geological divide. The most famous building in Settle, however, is THE FOLLY in the High Street – an amazing example of Yorkshire vernacular architecture, dated 1679. It is called the Folly because its owner is supposed to have run out of money before he could finish the building, but the name could apply equally to the crazy design. It is a three-storeyed townhouse with recessed centre and asymmetrical flanking wings. The doorway is a hybrid of Gothic and classical with cucumber-shaped columns flanking the entrance; the lintel has two pointed arches and on top are three weird pinnacles looking like *petit fours*.

Settrington

45; 3 miles E of Malton off A64
This is a neat estate village of pairs of plain semi-detached late Georgian cottages set back behind wide grass verges. And in the centre, side by side, are the Hall and parish church.

The cobbled forecourt of SETTRINGTON HALL opens straight on to the village street. It owes much to a reconstruction by Francis Johnson following a fire in 1963.

Formerly a rather dull three-storeyed late Georgian house, it is now an unusual Burlingtonian Anglo-Palladian villa with a pedimented centre and flanking wings with Venetian windows. The interior is perhaps Johnson's best work; it includes a dramatic plaster-vaulted top-lit passage down the centre of the house and richly decorated principal rooms.

The adjoining ALL SAINTS' CHURCH is early thirteenth-century and has a Perpendicular tower but, like the Hall, it owes much to a stylish later reconstruction – in this case by Pearson, who rebuilt the chancel *c.*1867. He was responsible too for the geometrical tracery of the windows, the stained glass by Clayton and Bell, the decoration on the east wall by J.W. Knowles, the herringbone boarding of the roof, and all the chancel fittings.

Sheriff Hutton

46; 10 miles N of York off A64

The broken ruins of the CASTLE form a zany jagged silhouette that can be seen for some distance across the flat landscape of the Plain of York. The castle was often occupied by the Lieutenant of the North, responsible for marshalling armies against the Scots, up to the sixteenth century (when the Council of the North was established in St Mary's Abbey, York (*q.v.*), by Henry VIII). It is similar in plan to Bolton Castle (*q.v.*), with four large corner towers connected by ranges of buildings round an inner courtyard about 100 feet square. It fell into ruin in the sixteenth century and is now situated in a farmyard – a pleasant shock for those who are used to the antiseptic neatness of Ministry-maintained ruins.

The adjoining CHURCH OF ST HELEN AND THE HOLY CROSS has a stolid little Norman tower and an atmospheric interior with old box pews and some important medieval monuments, including one said to represent Edward Plantagenet, the son of Richard III whose premature death in 1484 dashed Richard's long-term hopes of keeping hold of the throne and opened the way for the usurpation of the Tudors – the sound of distant trumpets.

Skelton

47; 5 miles SE of Ripon off B6265

CHRIST-THE-CONSOLER is one of the two Yorkshire churches designed by William Burges and paid for with the ransom money of Henry Frederick Grantham Vyner, who was murdered by Greek brigands in 1870 during an expedition to Marathon. The church was begun in 1871 and consecrated in 1876 as 'a memorial church in a pastoral setting, hung around with drooping willows'. The silhouette is dramatic from every angle, forming a jagged pyramidal composition culminating in the spire. The exterior is decorated with sculpture by Nicholls – the Good Shepherd on the porch (flanked by sheep looking up to be fed), Christ-the-Consoler in a nimbus on the east gable and the Four Ages of Man around the rose window on the west gable.

The interior is a *tour de force* of Victorian Gothic – rich, passionate, magnificent. The nave seems much taller than the outside would lead you to expect. The intricately carved stone piers and mouldings of the arcades and clerestory are enlivened by shafts of Irish black marble. Over the chancel arch is a complicated sculpture by Nicholls of the Ascension. The congregation, in the words of Dr J.M. Crook, is 'bombarded with sculptural images. The corbels are alive with carving'. The painted Gothic organ case projects forward and is supported on carved angels. The font of Tennessee marble was given by the Marquess of Ripon in memory of his only daughter and has a crocketed cover with figures of Christ and John the Baptist. The windows are full of stained glass made by Saunders under Burges's direction and they irradiate the interior with coloured light. The richness increases towards the east and reaches a climax in the chancel. Lower than the nave, from which it is divided by a low Italianate screen of white marble inlaid with panels of porphyry, gold mosaic and alabaster, it has a rib vault carried on shafts of coloured marble. Behind the altar is a carved reredos of white alabaster. The entire chancel floor has colourful encaustic tiles, but the most magnificent effect of all is created by the double geometrical tracery of the windows. Goodhart-Rendel thought Skelton 'one of the most remarkable churches of the nineteenth century, and to my thinking one of the most beautiful. . . . The chancel is a dream of richness and beauty.'

The church of Christ-the-Consoler, Skelton.

Stillingfleet

48; 8 miles S of York on B1222

The CHURCH OF ST HELEN is well known for its two Norman doorways, the south one with five orders of columns, carved capitals and arches, and the north one with zigzag and dogtooth ornament. Both retain original doors with bits of Norman iron decoration – an extremely rare survival. The south door, like its surround, is the more elaborate and, as well as the surviving portions of metalwork, much of the original pattern can be traced in marks on the planks. It had an overall lattice pattern of criss-crossing strips of iron and elaborate scrolling hinges showing dragons' heads, little figures and a ship with a large oar and a dragon prow. The rest of the church is not in the same league; it is a palimpsest of all dates of medieval architecture – Early English, Decorated and Perpendicular. Attractive enough, but it is the Norman doorways that reward the effort of a special visit.

Stockeld Park

49; 3 miles W of Wetherby on A661

Stockeld Park is among the most impressive smaller Georgian houses in Yorkshire. It was designed and built by James Paine between 1758 and 1763 and is a tightly knit composition with its pedimented three-storeyed centre and lower pedimented wings. The windows have rusticated surrounds and on the garden front there are canted bay windows with dramatic, deep semi-circular recesses above. The interior is arranged round a beautiful Staircase Hall in the centre with a glazed oval dome and restrained plasterwork.

The house was extensively altered by Detmar Blow in 1890, when a portico was added, so reversing the aspect of the house; a complete new wing was also added. At the same time the Chapel was moved from within the house and relocated in a converted Orangery.

Stokesley

50; 8 miles S of Middlesbrough on A172

An enchanting little market town at the foot of the Cleveland Hills, Stokesley is composed of Georgian brick houses arranged in a special townscape sequence of irregular squares. The River Leven, crossed by several footbridges, including a pretty iron one, runs along one side and is reached by a series of cobbled alleys between the houses. Forming an island in the middle of the long, wide Market Place and High Street with cobbled verges is the severe ashlar-faced TOWN HALL of 1854. Facing it across the Market Place is the former MANOR HOUSE, approached by splendid eighteenth-century gatepiers and with a pedimented doorcase. It is now used as council offices. Nearby is the parish CHURCH OF ST PETER AND ST PAUL – plain Georgian with round-headed windows but retaining a Perpendicular west tower and chancel from an earlier building on the site, which prop up the Georgian nave at either side like a pair of bookends. At either end of the Market Place and High Street are the East and West Greens. The latter has an endearingly irregular shape with grass and trees. Its north side comprises a terrace of houses with bow windows, in the middle of which is HANDYSIDE HOUSE, the grandest in town, with a pedimented doorway and flanking wings. It is the residence of the suffragan Bishop of Whitby.

It is worth walking through the churchyard and along the leafy riverside. The trees were planted in the nineteenth century to commemorate Jane Page, a native of Stokesley, who was the first white woman to settle in Melbourne, Australia. In September each year the whole centre of Stokesley is filled with a fair.

Studley Royal

NT; 51; 3 miles W of Ripon on B6265 [60]

Studley is among the best preserved of English eighteenth-century landscape gardens. Here, and perhaps only here, the landscape is still almost entirely as its creator intended, relying for its effect on trees, still and moving water, mown grass and an artful scatter of temples. The garden, created between 1716 and 1781 by John Aislabie and his son William, is situated in the flat bottom of a narrow winding valley at one end of which, as the spectacular climax, are the ruins of Fountains Abbey (*q.v.*) and, at the other, a lake, deer park and an amazing Victorian church. It is the perfect fusion of natural beauties and the polished planning of the eighteenth century.

John Aislabie inherited in 1699 and when he began his garden he was an important political figure. The South Sea Bubble, however, ruined his career; he resigned as Chancellor of the Exchequer and was expelled from the House in 1721. He returned to Yorkshire, where he spent his premature retirement in improving his garden – largely to his own design, though the Palladian Colen Campbell may have provided features for some of the structures. By the time of his death in 1742 the general aspect of the garden was much as it is now. The spine of the layout is the River Skell; this was canalised by Aislabie into long straight stretches with geometric ponds on either side. Cascades mark the changes of level and at the park boundary a waterfall flanked by little square fishing pavilions announces the beginning of the lake. The slopes on either side of the valley are densely planted with yew, beech and pine trees, and dotted with temples and other decorative buildings. These include the BANQUETING HOUSE high up on the north bank, originally intended as an orangery. The façade, with three arches divided by rusticated Tuscan pilasters, is attributed on stylistic grounds to Colen Campbell. The interior has fine wood-carving by Richard Fisher of York. From the lawn in front of the Banqueting House there is a good view across the valley to the OCTAGON TOWER on the other side. This was first built as a serene classical building but it was Gothicised in 1738 when the parapet, pinnacles and porch were added. The centrepiece of the garden is the TEMPLE OF PIETY, in front of which are the geometrical layout of the Moon Pond and three fine lead statues of Bacchus, Neptune and Endymion, attributed to Andrew Carpenter (a Huguenot craftsman). The Temple of Piety, built in 1740, was originally dedicated to Hercules, but John Aislabie's son William rededicated it after his father's death as a symbol of filial piety. The exterior has a Greek Doric portico

– a remarkably early example – while the interior has Rococo plasterwork by Giuseppe Cortese, the York plasterer whose work is frequently encountered in the neighbouring country houses.

After John Aislabie's death, William continued the garden along the same lines but made several improvements of his own. For instance, he moved the rotunda from near the Banqueting House to the other bank, gave it a shallow dome and renamed it the TEMPLE OF FAME. His great *coup*, however, was the acquisition of the neighbouring Fountains estate with its spectacular ruin. In 1768 this was incorporated with incomparable panache into the garden. To walk now along the south path from the Moon Pond to the Half Moon is one of the supreme experiences of eighteenth-century landscape art; suddenly, as one rounds the bend, the ruins come into view – first some low walls, then the chapter house, then the east end of the church, and finally the tall Perpendicular tower. The whole Gothic vision is framed exactly between plantings of yew and beech at the end of the water. It is difficult to think of a more gasp-making prospect than this 'surprise view'.

Nor is the other end of the layout at Studley Royal an anticlimax for, climbing the little hill to the north of the lake, one finds oneself in a dramatic eighteenth-century AVENUE of limes and chestnuts planted by John Aislabie, and there, 3 miles away, framed by the trees, is the west front of Ripon Cathedral (*q.v.*)! And at the near end is the extraordinary triangular silhouette of ST MARY'S CHURCH, the ecclesiastical masterpiece of William Burges and, though not enormous in scale, a building of cathedral grandeur. As Dr Cook has remarked, this is 'a church which in its purpose, setting and design serves almost as an epitome of the High Victorian Dream.' Like the church at Skelton (*q.v.*), also designed by Burges, it was built in expiation of the murder in 1870 of Henry Frederick Grantham Vyner by Greek brigands. His family decided to devote the ransom money they had raised but had no chance to pay, and which amounted to one million drachmas, to these two estate churches. St Mary's was begun in 1871 and finished in 1878. The exterior, dark and powerful, is characteristically Burges with its idiosyncratic mix of French, English and Italian sources. But nothing prepares one for the glories within. The nave is of plain stone, with Purbeck columns and an oak roof. At the west end is an elaborate Jesse window. This comparative austerity is in marked contrast to the gorgeous chancel, which is surrounded by continuous windows with double tracery and excellent stained glass that suffuses the interior with tinted light. The lower parts of the walls are lined with Egyptian alabaster. The floor is covered with mosaic depicting shrines of the Holy City. Above, all is ablaze with gold and rich painting; it is the nearest thing in English architecture to a Gothic dome. Everywhere there is evidence of Burges's personal genius: not least the Winged Lion of Judah, which supports the south arcade and gazes across the choir 'with red-eyed basilisk stare'. The brass door to the vestry, made in 1876 by T. Nicholls, was a gift to the church from the architect. Hardly less wonderful is the font of brown Tennessee marble with four inset brass panels, also by Nicholls, depicting the Four Ages of Man. Finally, not to be missed, the Edwardian chantry of the noble founders, the Marquess and Marchioness of Ripon. Their effigies rest on a sarcophagus of *verde antico* and Cippolino marble. The Marchioness looks as if she has just stepped out of a portrait by Sargent, and nothing could be more of its period than the marble collie dog at her feet.

Sutton-on-the-Forest
52; 12 miles N of York on B1363 [**62**]
SUTTON PARK is an enviable brick mid-Georgian house designed by Thomas Atkinson and built by Philip Harland. It comprises a central block and flanking pavilions, surrounded by attractive gardens, in one of the least-spoilt parts of England. The Sheffields moved here from Normanby Hall, Scunthorpe, in 1963 and brought with them the finest contents of that house, including much eighteenth-century English mahogany, as well as Dutch and French furniture. The extensive family collection of porcelain is displayed in a special Porcelain Room designed by Francis Johnson, who is also responsible for various other recent improvements.

The main rooms have good Rococo plasterwork, attributed to Giuseppe Cortese. The Drawing Room has rare Chinese wallpaper and the Dining Room has splendid eighteenth-century panelling brought from elsewhere. The tea room is painted in *trompe l'œil* to represent tortoiseshell – an unusual form of decoration based on eighteenth-century examples.

Swinton Park
53; 2 miles SW of Masham off A6108
'. . . there are no towers in the land more time-honoured than my gloomy, grey, hereditary halls.' Edgar Allan Poe's sentence comes automatically to mind as one peers through impressive iron gates and a dusky evening forecourt at the bogus castellated silhouette of Swinton. The present appearance of the house is entirely due to the romantic Gothic dress thrown over an older building in 1821–4 to the design of Robert Luger; he rearranged the interior, added a storey, battlements and turrets, and built the large circular tower with the entrance *porte-cochère* in front of it. This tower was heightened in 1889, improving the composition further. The core of the house, however, dates from the early eighteenth century. Inside, the White Room, with panelling and a secondary staircase, survives from that date. This relatively small house was greatly enlarged for William Danby by John Foss of Richmond, who added the north wing in 1791–6 and the south range in 1813–14. The Drawing Room was decorated by James Wyatt in 1793–4 but the other splendid state rooms in the south range were richly redecorated in c.1890. The grand staircase under an octagonal lantern was also reconstructed in 1890. The grounds were romantically landscaped in the Reptonian style by William Danby in the 1830s. He was also responsible for the DRUIDS' TEMPLE 3 miles to the west of the house; it is a full-scale copy of Stonehenge.

Swinton is now a Conservative Party conference centre, but it still belongs to the Earl of Swinton.

Thirsk
54; 10 miles NE of Ripon on A168

Thirsk was once an important coaching station but is now by-passed. Several Georgian inns recall its past: the THREE TUNS is the oldest and has a seemingly eighteenth-century front and good staircase inside; the CROWN INN claims to date from 1682; the FLEECE was the main coaching inn and has a nice unspoilt interior with horse paintings and Gothick glazing bars in the windows. The market place at Thirsk is called THE SQUARE and is still cobbled. From the north-west corner, Kirkgate, lined with seemly Georgian houses, leads to THIRSK HALL and ST MARY'S, the parish church, which sit side by side as if they were in the country. The Hall is an ambiguous cross between townhouse and country house, and comprises a five-bay centre with later wings and a top storey added by Carr of York in 1771-3. One of the wings contains a grand Dining Room with elegant Adamesque decoration. St Mary's is a spectacular all-of-a-piece Perpendicular job with a tall west tower braced by stepped buttresses. The interior has a notable wooden barrel roof with carved bosses. The monuments include one to Aurelia Frederica Storre, daughter of the Swedish Minister to the Court of George II. How on earth did she end up in Thirsk, one wonders?

Whitby★
55; 12 miles SW of Loftus on A171 [59]

As every schoolboy knows, Dracula landed at Whitby after sailing to England from Transylvania, leaping from the ship on to the stone quay in the form of a black dog. As you might expect, Whitby is an extraordinary place. It comprises two parts, east and west, on either bank of the mouth of the River Esk, with little red-roofed houses and narrow curving streets climbing the steep cliffs. The oldest part is the east side, where the abbey ruins and the parish church stand in lonely wind-swept splendour at the top of the hill.

The ABBEY is sublimely picturesque, with jagged broken arches and empty windows silhouetted against the sky. It was founded in 657 by St Hilda and was the scene of the Synod of Whitby where the Roman date of Easter was accepted by the Celtic church. At the Dissolution the abbey was acquired by the Cholmley family, who built a large quadrangular house to the south-east of the ruins. This has sixteenth-century, eighteenth-century and Victorian bits, but its somewhat startling character is a result of the sombre eleven-bay Baroque front added in the 1670s. This is now an empty shell, with all the windows blocked; the Cholmleys abandoned the house in the mid-eighteenth century after storm damage. In its present state it looks just like one of John Piper's more gloomily dramatic paintings.

The CHURCH OF ST MARY is approached from the town below by a long, curving flight of 199 stone steps, and sits in a splendid graveyard full of hefty gravestones. Seen at night with the waves crashing at the foot of the cliff, clouds scudding across the sky and the abbey walls looming dark in the moonlight, it makes a more than perfect setting for Dracula. The church is basically Norman, but was delightfully Gothicked and enlarged in

1819-29. It is ever memorable for its amazing interior crammed with box pews, grained and lined with red or green baize, and any number of lovable fittings and assorted eccentricities. In the centre is a cast-iron stove with a chimney shooting up into the roof, and polished poker and tongs by the grate. All round the sides are galleries built by ships' carpenters and supported on Tuscan columns with naïvely painted orange marbling. Hanging at the west end is an eighteenth-century vamp horn, and in the centre is a splendid Baroque brass chandelier with an anchor on top. On the walls are wooden pegs for hats, eighteenth-century marble memorial tablets and painted boards with texts from scripture. Across the Norman chancel arch, like a rood-loft, is the Cholmley pew – a white-painted gallery with carved cherubs' hands on the front, and supported on barley-sugar-twist columns. (This is approached from outside by a timber staircase of Chinese Chippendale design.) On the pew front hangs an eighteenth-century brass Rococo clock of high quality, recalling the design of contemporary nautical instruments. In the midst of the sea of woodwork the eye is held by the triple-decker pulpit of 1778: it is Gothick with mulberry plush hangings and, supported by scrolls on top of the sounding board, is . . . a carved wooden pineapple. At the back of the pulpit hang a pair of Georgian ear trumpets once used by the deaf wife of an early nineteenth-century rector to listen to her husband's sermons. Despite all this priceless clutter, the interior seems light and cheerful, thanks to the large windows with their clear glass and Gothick glazing bars, and the flat dormers in the roof reminiscent of ships' cabins. The chancel survives in its Norman state and was well restored by Caröe in 1905, when it was brought back to use. In the vestibule at the west end of the church is a free-standing marble memorial in the form of a little domed temple; it commemorates a lifeboat disaster of 1861. The church notices are worth reading – 'Funerals precisely at one o'clock'.

At the foot of the steps of St Mary's the spine of the east side of Whitby is CHURCH STREET – a long street lined mainly with Georgian brick houses, and also some not bad 1950s' in-fill. Opening off to the west is the little MARKET PLACE with one or two timbered buildings and, in the centre, the small classical TOWN HALL with armorial pediment, Venetian window and clock cupola, all raised up over an open ground floor on Tuscan columns. It was given to the town by Daniel Cholmley in 1788 and was designed by Jonathan Pickernell. The shops in Church Street mainly sell jet, junk and kippers. One antique shop has its façade plastered with old enamel advertisements for cocoa, tea and soap. On a wall nearby is an elaborate barometer given to 'the Fishermen of Whitby' by Lord Grimthorpe. At the south end of Church Street, overlooking the river, is a dramatic Neo-Jacobean range of ALMSHOUSES for seamen designed by Sir George Gilbert Scott in 1842. Perched on the central gable are three large model ships. In Grape Lane, leading to the bridge over the Esk, is CAPTAIN COOK'S HOUSE. It was from Whitby that he set sail on his exploratory voyage to the South Seas. The town bridge is cast-iron with a little circular office at the west end. On a board

Whitby.

outside are chalked up the times of high water. Facing the bridge is the CUSTOMS HOUSE, a domestic-looking brick building on a curved corner site, with the Royal Arms and a nice painted sign. This, together with the fishing boats in the harbour, ensures that Whitby still has a convincing nautical flavour.

The west side of the town is more extensive and less self-consciously picturesque than the east. Here are the banks and shops, and the handsome stone railway station with its arcaded portico in front. Baxtergate leads up the hill, lined with eighteenth- and nineteenth-century buildings. Here is ST NINIAN'S CHAPEL, eighteenth-century brick and Gothick; the interior has galleries on dark green Tuscan columns, and later Anglo-Catholic fittings. Lesser streets of Georgian brick houses wind off to left and right, and at the end of Baxtergate is ST HILDA'S TERRACE – a very good group of ambitious eighteenth-century brick and stone houses forming a long curving terrace overlooking a neatly kept park. In this is the PANNETT MUSEUM, 1930s' Neo-Georgian, and full of fossils, water colours, stuffed birds and much else, all effectively displayed in old mahogany cases. It is one of the most attractive and least-spoilt museums in England. A notice reads 'All these geological specimens have been collected within ten miles of Whitby.' Here are the Whitby crocodile, a fossil millions of years old, and a set of Eskimo's false teeth carved from walrus ivory.

On top of the cliff, reached by a steep road carved out of the rock and known as 'the Khyber Pass', is WEST CLIFF, a planned Victorian development undertaken by George Hudson, the railway king. The earliest bit is East Terrace, which overlooks the town and offers magnificent views over the harbour to the wind-blasted abbey ruins on the opposite cliff-top. It was designed by John Dobson of Newcastle in 1850. Behind, there is a rapid drop in voltage, the houses becoming coarser and plainer and the whole thing fading out halfway through the

Royal Crescent. In the centre, however, is ST HILDA'S by R.J. Johnson of Newcastle (1884–6), a good Victorian Gothic church with a well-proportioned central tower. Last, but not least, is the HARBOUR itself at the mouth of the river, enclosed by massive semi-circular stone quays with columnar LIGHTHOUSES on the ends, one low and Tuscan, the other taller and fluted Doric. They were designed by Francis Pickernell, engineer to the harbour, in 1831.

Yarm

56; 8 miles E of Darlington on A67
Yarm stands on the south side of the River Tees and is approached by a bridge built by Bishop Skirlaw of Durham in 1400. The HIGH STREET is one of the most impressive in the north of England – long and wide with cobbled verges and one side greatly curved. Only the excessively tall lamp-posts spoil the scene. The street is lined almost entirely with red brick three-storeyed Georgian houses with pantiled roofs and no fewer than eight pubs (there were sixteen in 1848!). One of these, the KETTON OX, is late seventeenth-century and has four tiers of little Tuscan pilasters and blank ovals in the attic storey. It is called after a short-horn reared nearby that weighed 220 stone when it was slaughtered in 1801. The GEORGE AND DRAGON INN is of some historical importance, for it was here that the first meeting of the promoters of the Stockton and Darlington Railway was held in 1820. In the centre of the High Street, forming a little island, is the TOWN HALL of 1710. It is of brick with a white-painted cupola on the roof. The parish church of ST MARY MAGDALENE stands away from the main street, alongside the River Tees. It is largely of 1730, but retains a Norman west front with a little tower perched on the centre of the gable and an oval window over the door. Unfortunately, the interior was gone over in a most depressing way in 1878, ruining its Georgian character.

The Minster and Treasurer's House, York.

York★

57; 18 miles E of Harrogate on A59
Includes the Treasurer's House (NT)

York is the most intact of England's larger historic towns and among the most interesting and best-preserved of the medieval cities of northern Europe. As well as the Minster, it retains a circuit of fourteenth-century walls nearly 3 miles round, a complete set of thirteenth-century town gates, nineteen medieval parish churches and an intricate network of narrow streets lined with old houses of different dates but predominantly medieval and Georgian.

York began as a Roman legionary fortress found in AD 71 on the north-east bank of the River Ouse. Here Constantine was proclaimed Roman Emperor in 306. Parts of the Roman walls survive, including the multangular tower in the garden of the Yorkshire Museum, and the line of several of the streets follows that of their Roman predecessors; Stonegate, for instance, was the *via praetoria* and Petergate the *via principalis*. The Minster is built on the site of the *praetorium* (the legionary headquarters), foundations of which were revealed in recent excavations and can be seen in the new Minster undercroft. The eighth century, when York was the centre of the 'Northumbrian Renaissance', was the most distinguished in the cultural history of the city, but nothing remains of that date thanks to the burning of the town by William the Conqueror in 1069. Recovery was swift, however, and in the Middle Ages York was the second

city of England, with a thriving commercial and religious life. In the sixteenth century there was a decline, largely caused by the policies of that grizzly monster Henry VIII, and it was not until the eighteenth century that York recovered as a prosperous county town, which it remains today. During the last fifteen years the city has benefited from one of the most successful urban conservation policies in the country.

THE MINSTER AND IMMEDIATE ENVIRONS

York Minster is the largest English medieval cathedral and, apart from the Norman crypt, is entirely Gothic, built in slow stages beginning in the early thirteenth century and ending in the fifteenth. All the phases of English Gothic are represented in textbook perfection, from Early English in the transepts to Decorated in the Chapter House, nave and west front, and Perpendicular in the east end and the three towers. The overall effect is grand and noble, all the work being of highest quality. York Minster also has the distinction of possessing no less than half the medieval stained glass in England, and the strong heraldic colours fill the interior with a rich glow and sparkle. The west front is among the most majestic in England. It was completed, except for the towers, in 1345. Bold projecting buttresses give it strength and assurance and the sumptuous west window, 75 feet high, is a remarkable *tour de force* of flowing tracery, incorporating a Sacred Heart in its design. The pair of elegant symmetrical towers were the last part of the Minster to be built; they date from c.1450 and 1470, and, though Perpendicular, their elaborate all-over decoration sits well on the rich Decorated façade below.

The vast interior seems remarkably unified and coherent; only Salisbury is more uniform among English medieval cathedrals. The nave was begun in 1291 but took fifty years to complete; at one stage a long strike paralysed the work. The immediate impact is extremely imposing, though the proportions leave something to be desired, the great width detracting from the overall feeling of height. The over-sensational restoration of the building in the 1960s has, alas, left the interior with some rather incongruous trivia, and this is felt most strongly in the nave. One enters through horrid glass and metal draught-porches; the vaults, which should be stone colour, are painted white and gold; the floor of the nave is awash with the detritus of modern churchmanship – bits of beige carpet and light oak benches arranged diagonally so that it is difficult to see William Kent's and Lord Burlington's fine geometrical pavement.

It is best to pass rapidly to the transepts. There some of the proud nationalism that was once the hallmark of the Established Church can still be savoured. There are no fewer than three regimental chapels with military memorials, regimental colours with battle honours, and beautiful iron screens, altars and appropriate fittings by G.F. Bodley, Sir Walter Tapper and Bainbridge Reynolds. The large astronomical clock is a memorial to the RAF of the Commonwealth in the Second World War and was designed by Sir Albert Richardson. The architecture of the transepts is the best in the church. The south transept was begun c.1230 by Archbishop Walter de Gray and its unprecedented width set the scale for the whole of the existing building. The timber vault was burnt in 1984 and at the time of writing is being repaired. The Archbishop's own monument of Purbeck marble with a tomb-chest and pinnacled canopy escaped fire damage and still stands proudly in the midst of his own creation. (A painted coffin cover with his portrait was discovered during the restoration in 1968 and is now displayed in the new undercroft.) The north transept, also built by Archbishop de Gray, is slightly later, c.1253, and is the noblest of all lancet designs. The whole of the north wall is taken up by the famous Five Sisters – pointed lancets each 55 feet high, with only a beautiful blind arcade below and smaller graduated lancets in the gable above. It is a design of the utmost serenity, and the chaste, austere architecture is matched by the original *grisaille* glass in which there is just the odd flash of red and blue where bits of alien glass have been fitted in by later repairers.

Accessible from the north transept is the octagonal Chapter House. It was begun shortly after Southwell (*q.v.*) but, unlike many of the other English polygonal chapter houses, it has no central pier to obstruct the effect of spaciousness. The lofty lierne vault is ingeniously constructed of wood imitating stone and has good Victorian painted decoration by Willement. The large windows have beautiful geometrical tracery and excellent fourteenth-century glass, while the stone seats below have rippling Decorated canopies richly embellished with carving.

The choir and eastern parts of the Minster were begun in 1360 and closely follow the design of the nave, but have better proportions, the central vault being 102 feet high. The choir aisles are full of interesting monuments: recumbent Victorian archbishops, painted sixteenth-century four-posters with stiff figures, eighteenth-century marble worthies in togas amidst weeping *putti* and decorous urns. There is also a pretty fourteenth-century alabaster effigy of Prince William (a son of Edward III who died young), which has recently been restored to its original canopied niche in the north choir aisle. As well as monuments, various bits of ecclesiastical bric-à-brac contribute to the atmosphere, including a group of eighteenth- and nineteenth-century needlework banners and a pair of superb thirteenth-century cope chests with decorative ironwork. In the choir itself the carved wooden stalls and the Perpendicular stone screen behind the altar are decent early nineteenth-century copies made by Sir Robert Smirke to replace the originals, which were burnt in a fire started by the artist Mad Martin's equally mad brother. But everything else is dwarfed by the enormous Perpendicular east window; it has 117 panels arranged in thirteen rows, and 144 compartments in the tracery full of stained glass provided in 1405 by John Thornton of Coventry. This, as Pevsner says, forms 'the most extensive Apocalypse series in medieval art and is unique in glass painting.'

In order to avoid an anti-climax after all this glory, it is best to leave the crossing till last. The west face of the pulpitum was carved in the late fifteenth century with a remarkable array of statues of English kings, from William the Conqueror to Henry VI – an interesting demonstration of medieval historical sense. Look up into the dizzy vault in the tower – a sublime architectural experience of the type that James Wyatt tried to recreate at Fonthill and Ashridge.

Leaving the Minster by the south door, the exterior should be circumnavigated and the precincts explored before plunging into the town proper. The south transept has a somewhat fussy façade, with steep little gables over the doorway and a rose window set too high in the gable; the east end, however, has a unique cliff-like grandeur and the elevation of the north transept is a noble design identical to the interior. The huge bulk of the building rises out of neat mown grass and cobbled paving surrounded by medieval half-timber and Georgian brick – the characteristic York architectural mix.

To the east is the TREASURER'S HOUSE (NT), a large stone building of the seventeenth and eighteenth centuries, well restored by Temple Moore c.1900 and with the air of a country house. It has a good interior and is regularly open to the public. The beautifully furnished rooms contain many features and fittings rescued from demolished buildings elsewhere, including several fine chimneypieces. The Great Hall is largely by Temple Moore. The Dining Room has a good early eighteenth-century plaster ceiling and the main staircase is of similar date. Behind is GRAY'S COURT, also restored by Temple Moore – an attractive garden offering a good view of the city walls. Next door to the Treasurer's House, MINSTER

COURT makes a villagey contrast with informal brick houses nicely grouped. The Neo-Georgian brick DEANERY in the north-east corner enjoys a breathtaking view of the Minster, broadside on with the Chapter House, Five Sisters window, huge central tower, and the west towers in enfilade. The row of weathered arches to the west is a remnant of the vanished Archbishop's Palace, and the two-storeyed LIBRARY behind, now standing in splendid isolation, was originally his private chapel. In odd corners hereabouts are neat ecclesiastical gardens with rows of onions and cabbages and herbaceous borders. The whole informal, yet perfect, ensemble is a masterpiece of English townscape. PRECENTOR'S COURT, opposite the west front of the Minster, should not be missed. It is a narrow Georgian cul-de-sac. Walk to the end, then turn round. The view back is an Axel Haig vision of the Middle Ages with the majestic west front and towers of the Minster framed by low brick houses and one projecting iron gas-lamp bracket.

THE CITY

The visitor to York is well advised to arrive by train, or if by car to park near the station, and then to walk, because many of the old streets are closed to traffic. The station itself has a most impressive Victorian TRAIN-SHED, dating from 1877 and designed by Thomas Prosser. The triple-aisled interior is 800 feet long and forms an elegant curve which looks marvellous when shafts of sunlight stream down through the iron-and-glass roof. Leaving the station and the towering yellow brick hulk of the former Station Hotel (also by Prosser, and dated 1877–8), the walled city is reached immediately. Straight ahead the west front of the Minster can be seen looming across Lendal Bridge at the end of Duncombe Place. From this angle there is some Neo-French Gothic competition from the tower of the Roman Catholic ST WILFRED'S CHURCH, built with ultramontane insensitivity in Duncombe Place in 1862–4 to the design of George Goldie. At the corner of St Leonard's Place, an elegant Regency stucco crescent, is THE RED HOUSE, a Georgian townhouse of 1714, its plaster front painted a robust shade of maroon and the glazing bars recently restored to the windows. Further towards the Minster, we pass on the right the fiery red brick Gothic of the former DEAN'S COURT HOTEL and Bodley's more elegant BOER WAR MEMORIAL CROSS of 1905.

Turn left here, pass out through Bootham Bar and then smart left again to see the Assembly Rooms, the King's Manor, the Art Gallery and the ruins of St Mary's Abbey. The ASSEMBLY ROOMS were designed by Lord Burlington in 1730 and refaced with an Ionic portico by Pritchett in 1823. The Hall inside is a noble Palladian room 112 feet long, 40 feet high and 40 feet wide. It is lined with Corinthian columns painted to resemble Siena marble, and above is a tall clerestory and rich plaster frieze derived from Inigo Jones. The original glass chandeliers add a festive note. Sarah, Duchess of Marlborough, who visited the Assembly Rooms soon after their completion, mocked the 'correct' Palladian proportions, for the narrow spacing of the columns made it impossible for ladies in fashionable hooped skirts to pass between them. The KING'S MANOR was the Abbot's House of St Mary's Abbey. After the Dissolution of the Monasteries it became the headquarters of the Council of the North. It now houses the Institute of Advanced Architectural Studies of the University of York. The general impression is of a mellow Tudor building of brick and stone with some of the feel of a Cambridge college. The second court was completed in 1963 by a new west block designed by Feilden and Mawson in brick and concrete and 'frankly Modern'. The site of ST MARY'S ABBEY itself is a beautifully landscaped early nineteenth-century park. The thirteenth-century architecture of the ruins forms a Pugin contrast to the severe Greek Doric architecture of the YORKSHIRE MUSEUM, designed in 1823 by William Wilkins. The museum contains a large and interesting assemblage of architectural and sculptural fragments of many dates.

The ART GALLERY, in an appropriate Victorian Italian style, was the work of E. Taylor in 1879 and contains an unusually good collection of pictures, including the Lycett-Green bequest of Old Masters, a room full of Etty's work, and a cross-section of eighteenth- and nineteenth-century English paintings. There is a classic view from the portico – the Minster, a skyline of old gables and chimneypots, and BOOTHAM BAR. Bootham itself and GILLYGATE form a handsome but slightly shabby old suburb with brick Georgian houses saved (just) from demolition by archaeological enthusiasts (to reveal the walls behind) and traffic engineers (to make a ring-road).

Returning through the walls into the city, the best medieval streets lie to the south of the Minster. They include HIGH and LOW PETERGATE, STONEGATE, GOODRAMGATE, COLLIERGATE and THE SHAMBLES. They are now largely free from traffic and contain a most enjoyable mixture of Georgian brick and old jettied timber houses enlivened with odd eccentricities, as well as many excellent shop-fronts, some old and some sensitively restored. The best street of all is Stonegate, long and narrow, running from the Minster to the Mansion House. It has been restored excellently, with painted shop-fronts, hanging signs and Yorkstone paving, and represents a triumph of conservation with hardly a false note throughout its length. On the corner of High Petergate is a delightful painted statue of Minerva, goddess of Wisdom and Drama, dated 1801, and, halfway down, the painted signboard of the Star Inn goes right across the street. Of the many excellent shop-fronts, that of Messrs Greenwood, antique dealers, is the best, with its green and gold heraldic cartouche and framed photographs of Queen Mary. At the bottom, in St Helen's Square, is the dignified MANSION HOUSE of 1725 by John Etty, with a pediment and Ionic pilasters. The Saloon upstairs is one of the most imposing rooms in York, with its coved and gilded ceiling, Corinthian doorcase and full-length portraits of monarchs and mayors. Behind the Mansion House, facing the river, is the fifteenth-century GUILDHALL, damaged in the war but now restored; the interior has an open timber roof supported on octagonal timber columns. With the adjoining MUNICIPAL OFFICES in Victorian Gothic style, it presents an almost Venetian pros-

Riverside and Guildhall, York.

pect to the river. North of the Mansion House is LENDAL; the former judge's lodging (now a restaurant) is another good Georgian house of 1718–25, with giant brick pilasters and an elegant horseshoe staircase leading to the Venetian doorway. South of the Mansion House stretches CONEY STREET, rather workaday with ordinary chainstores (in contrast to the specialist luxury shops of Stonegate), but redeemed by the large and jolly clock projecting on a scrolly wrought-iron bracket from ST MARTIN-LE-GRAND. This church was bombed in the war and is now partly a ruin, although one aisle was ingeniously restored by George Pace in 1961 and is full of his characteristic spiky fittings. Also to be admired in Coney Street is the *art nouveau* shop-front of Dewhurst, the butcher's. A few steps beyond St Martin's is ST MICHAEL SPURRIERGATE, the refaced Perpendicular exterior of which conceals an unexpectedly spacious interior, with whitewashed walls and elegant Transitional Gothic colonnades, the columns part-sunk into the floor like grandfather clocks in a cottage. There is an early eighteenth-century reredos of carved wood and a matching draught-porch; and there is medieval glass in the windows, and an elegant marble memorial tablet by Fisher of York to William Martin. Extra attractions are the old embossed leather altar frontal in a glass case, and the loudly ticking clockworks in one corner.

Out once more into the busy street and down Low Ousegate to OUSE BRIDGE. (The two plaster cats nonchalantly climbing the façade of Wigfall's shop should not be missed.) From here is to be enjoyed the best riverside view. To the north are converted warehouses and the Gothic frontage of the Guildhall. To the south is KING'S STAITHE, an attractive cobbled quay with two old pubs and the early eighteenth-century Cumberland House, its front door above flood-level in the side street. Over the bridge (classical by Atkinson in 1810) and on

towards MICKLEGATE – the 'great street', the grandest in York. Immediately on the right is ST JOHN'S CHURCH, with bits of Norman work and a picturesque brick belfry. It is now an arts centre and the inside is a welter of 1960s' Civic Trust-style conversion – bright pine woodwork, spiral staircases and the smell of coffee.

The start of Micklegate is anything but inspiring. On the left is an empty gap, the site of the demolished Queen's Hotel, and on the right is a 1960s' Co-op. From here a detour should be made to ALL SAINTS, North Street, one of the best of York's medieval parish churches. It has a fifteenth-century hammerbeam roof and medieval stained glass, but it is made especially memorable by the clutter of High Church fittings, furnishings and general oddments brought together earlier this century by the Rev. Patrick Shaw. Is this what a medieval church was really like? Do not miss the concrete HERMITAGE built against the south-west corner by Fr Shaw to house a twentieth-century anchorite. Back in Micklegate, things rapidly improve as the street curves gently uphill, with sett paving and several very grand Georgian townhouses on the right and two picturesque medieval churches in grassy graveyards on the left. At the end MICKLEGATE BAR (thirteenth-century, repaired in 1727) leads out to Blossom Street, the Mount, Knavesmire Racecourse and the main approach to the city from the south-west (the Great North Road, or A1, leading to London and the industrial towns of the West Riding). On the corner of Nunnery Lane and Blossom Street is the BAR CONVENT, one of the oldest recusant convents, founded by Mary Ward in the seventeenth century. It has a pretty eighteenth-century neo-classical chapel with a domed chancel by Thomas Atkinson. Blossom Street also contains the BAY HORSE, with its atmospheric Victorian pub interior. Further out, the Mount is a broad tree-lined street where stands the famous QUAKER GIRLS' SCHOOL.

Clifford's Tower, York.

Retracing one's steps, it is a good idea to make forays into the side-streets off Micklegate. Here, in somewhat forlorn surroundings, several treasures are to be found, from old enamel advertisements for Rowntree – 'Cocoa and Chocolate Maker to H.M. the King' – and Roman, medieval and Georgian fragments, to ST MARY BISHOPHILL JUNIOR, which has a Norman doorway, the oldest tower in York and an Anglo-Catholic interior smelling of incense and adorned with a carved and painted reredos by Temple Moore. In Skeldergate is a good group of eighteenth- and nineteenth-century warehouses and Lady Anne Middleton's ALMSHOUSES, now a hotel.

Now cross SKELDERGATE BRIDGE (Victorian cast-iron of 1881 with Gothic lanterns identical to those on Westminster Bridge in London); an inscription records that the bridge was formally declared free from tolls on 1 April 1914. A joke? Noting the pink granite obelisk on the traffic roundabout and the row of charming Regency cottages with bow windows in Tower Place, we make straight for the CASTLE, where William the Conqueror's steep earth motte is crowned by an impressive stone keep, CLIFFORD'S TOWER, facing a formal layout of eighteenth-century prisons and law courts (parts of which now form a museum). Clifford's Tower was built in 1250–75 and has a unique (for England) quatrefoil plan. It was saved from destruction in 1596 when the city corporation petitioned for its preservation as 'an especial ornament for the beautifying of this city'. This makes it, with the Colosseum in Rome, one of the earliest examples in Europe of a building consciously preserved as an ancient monument. It has been the scene of many horrible incidents, notably the massacre of the York Jews in 1139, and the execution on Henry VIII's orders of Robert Aske, leader of the Pilgrimage of Grace in 1537; he was hanged alive in chains from the battlements and took a week to die.

The monumental stone building opposite was originally the DEBTORS' PRISON and dates from 1705; it has been attributed to the gentleman-architect William Wakefield. Flanking it are a pair of elegant neo-classical blocks of 1773–7 by John Carr, York's most distinguished native-born architect. They were originally the FEMALE PRISON and ASSIZE COURT. The latter has an extremely handsome interior, the two courtrooms with Pantheon domes and scagliola columns.

From Clifford's Tower, Castlegate leads back to the city centre. It contains two especially fine Georgian townhouses. CASTLEGATE HOUSE by John Carr dates from 1759–63 and has a remarkable interior, with chimneypieces and plaster ceilings beginning to show Adam's influence. FAIRFAX HOUSE opposite is also by Carr, but of 1750–5 and still Rococo, with magnificent plasterwork, carved doorcases and a wrought-iron staircase balustrade. The interior has been splendidly restored under the supervision of Francis Johnson and was opened to the public in 1984 to show the Terry collection of Georgian furniture. ST MARY'S CHURCH has a prominent Perpendicular tower and spire, which is a considerable landmark. The close-up impact of this large regular building has been marred by its recent conversion to a 'heritage centre'. An incongruous glass and stainless-steel porch has been plonked on to the outside, and the interior (never as impressive as the exterior) is now full of spotlights and trendy hangings. The new churchyard paving impiously incorporates former headstones; one, to the memory of Elizabeth Wilson, reads 'WEEP NOT FOR ME'.

At the end of Castlegate there is a choice between Victorian and Georgian. Clifford Street to the left is the only consistent Victorian street in York, with harsh brick elevations and a busy skyline culminating in the flamboyant piled-up silhouette of turrets on domes of the LAW COURTS. Copper Gate is largely demure Georgian, but with some timber-framed houses. It leads to ALL SAINTS, Pavement, the grandest of York's parish churches, with an elegant octagonal lantern on top of the tower and a uniformly Perpendicular appearance – though the east end is, in fact, of 1887. (The original chancel was demolished in the eighteenth century for road widening.) The best feature of the interior is the west window, which has rich fourteenth-century glass brought from elsewhere and the north door has a rare thirteenth-century lion's head door-knocker. To the south of the church is SIR THOMAS HERBERT'S HOUSE – one of the best known of York's fifteenth/sixteenth-century timber-framed houses. LADY PECKITT'S YARD at the back is extremely picturesque. Continuing eastwards, FOSS-GATE is reached; it is one of the main streets radiating from the city centre to a medieval gate, and has several nice buildings with good shop-fronts. On the west side is the MERCHANT ADVENTURERS' HALL, reached through a seventeenth-century brick gatehouse and across a little courtyard; it is two-storeyed and timber-framed. The Hall, raised up above a brick-vaulted undercroft, has an open timber roof and some interesting fittings, including the Georgian sheriff's seats with pediment and fluted pilasters. The Chapel has an attractive seventeenth-century interior with pews, stalls and panelling. Over the FOSS BRIDGE, built by Atkinson in 1811 with elegant balustraded parapets and two iron lamps, the street changes its name to Walmgate. Just by the bridge is DOROTHY WILSON'S HOSPITAL – a tall late Georgian brick house with a nice inscription – and a little further on is ST DENYS'S CHURCH, with its Norman doorway and decent graveyard, full of snowdrops in spring. Beyond this, the street becomes somewhat threadbare, but WALMGATE at the end is the only one of the town gates to retain its medieval barbican.

Back towards the centre and, averting one's eyes from the monstrous concrete office block in Stonebow, it is best next to explore ST SAVIOURGATE and ST SAVIOUR'S PLACE. These contain some of the best Georgian terraced houses in York, as well as the seventeenth-century UNITARIAN CHAPEL. The dreary 1960s' block for HM Inspector of Taxes is rather a blow, but otherwise this is a good area in which to admire the excellent restoration work carried out in York since the early 1970s.

PEASEHOLME HOUSE, in particular, is an arresting mid-eighteenth-century house rescued from the depths of degradation in 1975 by the York Civic Trust, which demolished a garage built in front of it. Further restoration work and careful in-fill development can be found in ALDWARK, where the proposals set out in Lord Esher's Report of 1968 to reintroduce residential accommodation into the walled city have recently been implemented. The important building hereabouts is the MERCHANT TAYLORS' HALL, the only remaining hall of a craft guild in York. The seventeenth-century brick hall, set back behind a large open lawn, conceals a fourteenth-century Hall with original open timber roof and heraldic glass in the windows. All this east part of York has an attractive cottagey scale, with restored old houses and new neo-vernacular brick housing; there are also wonderful glimpses of the east end of the Minster riding high above.

At Monk Bar it is worth going outside the city walls for a quick look at the LORD MAYOR'S WALK, a leafy eighteenth-century parade laid out beneath the walls. Then go back along Goodramgate, another of York's medieval streets. OUR LADY'S ROW, dating from 1316, is the oldest surviving group of houses in the city. It is long and low with a pantiled roof and jettied upper storey plastered over. Behind is HOLY TRINITY, Goodramgate, reached through an eighteenth-century brick arch; it is now vested in the Redundant Churches Fund. It has an atmospheric 'unrestored' interior with an uneven stone floor and, with its seventeenth- and eighteenth-century fittings, is a splendid example of how a church was furnished after the Reformation: old brown box pews, communion table and double-decker pulpit. Continuing along Goodramgate, COLLIERGATE branches off to the south. It is the continuation of Low Petergate and is largely Georgian, with the odd eruption of half-timber. Then go back through The Shambles, the best-known of York's medieval streets and so narrow that the jettied upper storeys of the houses almost touch one another across the roadway. The restoration carried out since the mid-1960s varies in quality, but errors of detail are partly atoned for by the openings to the NEW MARKET on the west side with its bustling crowds of shoppers and smells of cauliflowers and kippers. The medieval street-plan is so complicated at this point that it is possible to get lost and suffer the nagging feeling that some parallel alley contains something marvellous that one is missing. Patrick Pool has a fifteenth-century timber-framed house, which forms a picturesque group with ST SAMP-SON'S CHURCH, now an old people's day centre. In Sampson Square the MAIL COACH INN contains the remains of a Roman bath in its cellar, including part of the *frigidarium* and *calidarium*. Finally, back to the Minster along Low Petergate. Among many splendid buildings and shops, the star is SCOTT THE PORK BUTCHER – a model of how to maintain a medieval building. Its jettied and gabled upper storeys are still plastered and painted cream; it has sliding casements, the woodwork painted smart red; lead downpipes, dated 1763; and a wonderful *trompe* 3-D lettered sign 'York. Ham. Bacon. Lard'. If only The Shambles were still like this.

South and West Yorkshire

Ackworth

1; 1 mile N of Ackworth Moor Top on A628

The FRIENDS' SCHOOL at Ackworth is a remarkably ambitious Georgian school. In fact, the buildings were erected as a Foundling Hospital, or orphanage, in 1758 as a country outpost of the London Foundling Hospital, and only became a Quaker school after they were bought by Dr John Fothergill in 1778. The layout is on a grand scale, with an ample quadrangle surrounded on three sides by two-storeyed ranges of thirteen bays, each with a central pediment but otherwise plain. They are connected to each other by semi-circular colonnaded links, and the side-wings have little cupolas – the only touches of light relief in the severely elegant architecture. The Chapel is attached to the north wing and dates from 1847. Behind the east wing is a smaller courtyard surrounded by Tuscan colonnades.

Ackworth is a co-educational boarding school, still run by the Society of Friends. The buildings are open to the public during the school holidays.

Birstall

2; 6 miles SW of Leeds on A643

OAKWELL HALL, a house of smoke-blackened stone, features as Fieldhead in Charlotte Brontë's novel *Shirley*. It dates from the sixteenth century but was reconstructed in the seventeenth in the Yorkshire Jacobean vernacular, with mullion windows of different sizes, including one enormous affair of thirty lights giving on to the Great Hall. Many of the rooms have seventeenth-century panelling and are furnished with oak pieces of the same date.

The Staircase Hall, Brodsworth Hall.

Bolling Hall

See Bradford.

Bradford

3; 9 miles W of Leeds on A650

BOLLING HALL is a mid-seventeenth-century house built on to a fifteenth-century tower. It is a good example of Yorkshire vernacular, with its canted bays and variegated mullion windows. The house was altered internally in the eighteenth century to the design of Carr of York.

The Hall has a Rococo plaster ceiling. One room on the upper floor, however, retains a Jacobean plaster ceiling decorated with strapwork, birds and fruit, and other rooms have old oak panelling. The house has been somewhat over-restored and is now used as a museum, with some of the rooms allocated to exhibitions of paintings and local life.

Bramham Park

4; 9 miles NE of Leeds on A1

Bramham is famous chiefly for its exceptionally well-preserved early eighteenth-century formal GARDENS with related woodlands, which have recovered remarkably well from the effects of a seemingly catastrophic gale in 1962. The house itself is a fine example of English Baroque architecture, built between 1700 and 1710 by Robert Benson, 1st Lord Bingley, Treasurer of the Household to Queen Anne. His architect is not known.

The house, apart from a few rooms south of the Hall, was largely gutted by fire in 1828. The Hall, constructed in limestone, with fine Corinthian pilasters and carvings and rising to the full height of the house, survived the fire, though, sadly, the ceiling was destroyed and is yet to be restored. Restoration of the rest of the house commenced in 1906 when the architects Detmar Blow and his French partner Billery were called in by George Lane-Fox, later Lord Bingley of the third creation, to carry out the work and to copy closely the stucco work and wood-carving that remained in the undamaged rooms at the south end of the house. The Gallery, converted from three rooms and occupying most of the width of the garden front, is very fine; it contains some good pieces of French furniture, including a rare Louis XV back-to-back bureau bought from Rudding Park (*q.v.*) in 1973. The Sitting Room, with good carved joinery, also survived the fire and is hung with a number of continental paintings by lesser masters, including works by Vogelsang, Campidoglio, Pourbus and Jordaens.

Brodsworth Hall

5; 6 miles NW of Doncaster on B6422

The landscape round Doncaster is rather dispiriting. It is flat, dotted with coal-mines and, far worse, every village is swamped with Barratt-type housing. In the midst of this, the Brodsworth estate comes as a welcome surprise, its park surrounded by great belts of trees and the Italianate house reigning secretly in the middle, stand-

Conisborough Castle.

ing proudly among sweeping lawns and banks of rhododendron.

Brodsworth was designed by an obscure Italian architect, Casentini, and executed by Philip Wilkinson for Charles Sabine Thellusson, one of the heirs of the notorious Thellusson will, in which a huge sum of money was left three generations ahead to accumulate at compound interest. The exterior is symmetrical and, to quote Mark Girouard, 'endowed with considerable bravura' by the urns crowning the parapet and the grand *porte-cochère* with rusticated Tuscan columns on the entrance front. It conceals the great feature of Brodsworth: its sequence of remarkably well-preserved rooms. It is perhaps the best Victorian house interior in the classical style now remaining in England, with long marbled vistas, myriad neo-classical statues reflected glistening white in looking-glasses, crimson *portières*, ormolu chandeliers and dark gilded plasterwork. A splendid procession of ceremonial spaces runs down the centre of the house: Entrance Hall, Staircase Hall, marble corridor and pillared Garden Hall. The walls of these halls and corridors are marbled in different shades of red, green, grey and yellow, and the floors are paved with bright Minton tiles. The Drawing Rooms to the south are most splendid, their walls hung with crimson damask and their ceilings painted with arabesques of pink and green. The furniture and carpets were all provided by Lapworths' of Bond Street; stuffed and buttoned Victorian chairs, ottomans and sofas still fill the rooms. On the other side of the central corridor, the top-lit Billiards Room is a wonderful Victorian period piece, with padded leather benches round the walls on raised

platforms for watching the game and excellent horse paintings hanging above. The little Library at the end of the corridor is divided from it by a glowing stained-glass window and is hung with a stunning Victorian wall-paper of dark blue, pink and gold.

Cannon Hall
6; 5 miles W of Barnsley off A635
A good solid plain stone house of 1700 enlarged in 1764 to the design of John Carr of York and set in a nice park landscaped by Richard Woods. It was acquired in 1951 by Barnsley and is now run as a museum.

Various collections have been built up since 1951, including eighteenth-century and *art nouveau* furniture and a comprehensive collection of glass, but the chief attraction of the house is the National Loan Collection — a fine collection of Old Masters, mostly by Dutch and Flemish painters, formed in the mid-nineteenth century by William Harvey of Barnsley and well exhibited. The atmosphere is that of a well-arranged art gallery rather than of a house, and as such it is one of the pleasantest galleries of its size in the country.

Conisborough Castle★
7; 4 miles SW of Doncaster on A630
The South Yorkshire coalfield may seem an unlikely place for picturesque sights, but Conisborough is exceedingly so: the little town in a hollow between hilltops supporting the Norman church and the castle, and the River Don flowing past in a narrow limestone gorge.

Conisborough Castle is one of the most impressive in England and has a thrilling circular keep with projecting

The Mansion House, Doncaster.

buttresses on a mighty battered base, surrounded by a curtain wall with semi-circular towers. It was built c.1180 by Hameline Plantagenet, the bastard half-brother of Henry II. He had already built an identical keep on his estate at Moretemer in Normandy. The Conisborough keep is 90 feet high and 52 feet in diameter; the walls are 15 feet thick and the buttresses 9 feet wide. The exterior is faced in beautiful white ashlar stone of a quality rare for a Norman building, and this enhances the severe geometry of the form. Originally there was a conical roof, but this has disappeared. The basement retains its domed vault. The Great Hall was on the second floor and this room still has an interesting fireplace with a stone hood supported on short columns with leaf capitals; it looks like an illustration by Violet le Duc or some similarly romantic nineteenth-century medievalist. On the third floor is the solar, over the Hall, and built into one of the buttresses is a tiny polygonal Chapel with an ingenious rib vault.

The castle features as Coningsborough in Walter Scott's *Ivanhoe* and, as you gaze from the top of the keep over a landscape blackened by collieries and industry, it is worth recalling the opening words of the novel: 'The sun was setting upon one of the rich grassy glades of the wide tract of forest that covered the hills and valleys between Sheffield and Doncaster. . . .'

Doncaster

8; 14 miles E of Barnsley on A1

Doncaster is the heart of the South Yorkshire coalfield and a centre of declining heavy industry, but it is famous chiefly for its eighteenth-century racecourse, where the St Leger was first run in 1776 (four years before the Derby, making it the oldest of England's five 'classic races'). Doncaster is worth visiting for two major buildings, though the centre is now the usual planners' mess of new roads in the wrong places, boring shopping precincts and mediocre multi-storey office blocks for nationalised industries.

ST GEORGE'S CHURCH replaces the medieval parish church burnt in 1853, only the vaulted crypt of which remains. It was rebuilt by Sir George Gilbert Scott in 1854–8, taking its cue from the old church but bigger and better. It is 170 feet long, and the massive central tower is 170 feet high. The latter is Perpendicular but the inspiration for the remainder is Decorated. The tracery is of the most elaborate geometrical patterns. Everywhere there is rich carving and ornament. Indeed, the exterior positively bristles with pinnacles.

The interior is impressive for its lofty proportions – the nave is 75 feet high. The *tout ensemble* is resoundingly High Victorian, with all the fittings designed by Scott and made by the best firms – stone carving by Birnie Philip and stained glass by Hardman, or Clayton and Bell. It has to be added, however, that the whole place now feels depressingly gloomy and forlorn: the church is cut off from the rest of the town centre by a badly sited road; buckets in the aisles catch the drips from leaking roofs. Built at the height of Victorian confidence and prosperity, one feels that the size of its present congregation would not fulfil its founder's expectations – indeed any racing man would hesitate before betting heavily on the future of the Church of England after paying even a brief visit to Doncaster parish church!

The MANSION HOUSE in the High Street recalls the eighteenth-century elegance of Doncaster before it sunk under the impact of coal and the railways. It was built in 1745–8 and was designed by James Paine, the most talented of second-generation Anglo-Palladian architects. It was intended as the official residence of the Mayor, with state rooms for him to entertain in. It is like a Venetian palace: the tall front has a rusticated ground floor supporting a *piano nobile* with Corinthian columns and a Venetian window; the attic storey is an addition of 1801 by William Lindley. Ideally one should be able to arrive by gondola. A low, columned Entrance Hall leads to the imperial-plan main staircase, which begins in one flight and breaks into two at the half-landing. It is among the earliest examples of this type of staircase in England, and it provided the inspiration for Carr of York at Lytham Hall and Wentworth Woodhouse (*qq.v.*). The whole front of the building is occupied by Paine's Ballroom, its walls and ceiling magnificently decorated with Rococo stucco by Joseph Rose. The Mansion House is still used for civic functions, but Doncaster's Mayor has not actually lived on the premises since the nineteenth century.

East Riddlesden Hall

NT; 9; 8 miles NW of Bradford on A650

There is a charming and rather dotty tradition that the name 'Riddlesden' means 'The Red Lion's Den'. The house itself has some of the same eccentric appeal, with its dark gritstone Jacobean façades enlivened by the odd dash of Gothic Survival, such as the rose window over the front door.

The main part of the house was built by James Murgatroyd in 1642 and the 'VIVE LE ROY' carved on the battlements demonstrates that he was not afraid to show where his allegiance lay at the opening of the Civil War. A new wing was added to the west in 1692 but of this only the façade still stands. East Riddlesden was let in the nineteenth century and so escaped Victorian 'improvement'. The principal rooms all have their original oak panelling and moulded plaster ceilings. The contents include a portrait of the Airedale heifer bred at East Riddlesden by Mr Slingsby in 1830 – a notable example of 'improved' livestock, she weighed 41 stones 12 lb per quarter!

Halifax

10; 6 miles SW of Bradford on A58

Halifax is not large as nineteenth-century industrial towns go – it is no bigger than Cambridge and now possesses rather less in the way of manufacturing industry – but its setting amidst the crags and bleak moors of the Pennines endows it with tremendous grandeur, and the fact that it is all built of gritstone gives it a solid, monolithic quality. Modern planning has, of course, done its best to ruin the place with unnecessary road 'improvements' and new developments, but again this is no worse than in most historic cathedral cities.

For once it is better to arrive by road than by train, as Halifax's spectacular setting, with dramatic changes of level, is best appreciated from a car. The station, on the other hand, is best avoided; as the Save Britain's Heritage pamphlet on Halifax puts it mildly: 'The station is at present a dispiriting place and one of the worst possible introductions to the town.' It possesses a handsome symmetrical façade of 1855 by T. Butterworth and it is typical of the helplessness of the old industrial towns that this splendid asset is now wasted.

Of the historic core of the town, almost all that remains are some over-restored fragments in THE WOOLSHOPS – a street of eighteenth-century houses with weaving garrets at the top, now stranded in the middle of a new Arndale shopping centre and car park. The sole survivor of the medieval town is the parish CHURCH OF ST JOHN. This is the grandest medieval church in the area, a large fifteenth-century building in Perpendicular style with a big west tower, nave, aisles and chancel, all in blackened stone. A striking feature of the exterior is the array of far-projecting gargoyles supported by the buttresses. Entering through the south porch (note the dark oak doors dated 1650), the first thing you see inside will put you in a good mood for the rest of the day. This is the poor-box, leaning against a stone column in the form of a carved and painted wooden figure holding a note: 'Remember the Poor'. He is called Tristram and dates from the seven-

teenth century. The interior of the church is spacious, the aisles nearly as wide as the nave, and, thanks to the Victorian stained glass, all is pleasantly dark and gloomy. Stand under the tower at the west end and behind the monument to Charles Musgrave (a marble effigy on a tomb-chest); from here the vista down the church is terrific, not least because the floor slopes gently downhill towards the altar. The only other church I know that does this is Cartmel Fell in Cumbria (*q.v.*), but here in St John's the scale is much grander. The nave is full of carved Jacobean pews and the font has a fifteenth-century cover in the form of a spire. The ceilings — low-pitched, of dark oak, with moulded beams — are also Jacobean, dated 1636. The nave is divided from the chancel by a rood-screen and has nice furnishings, especially the late seventeenth-century communion rails with carved barley-sugar balusters.

To the south-west of the church, and slightly uphill, is the PIECE HALL. This is the major monument to the eighteenth-century wool trade in Halifax, and has recently been excellently restored. It was built in 1775 by Thomas Bradley and forms a large regular square of stone. From the outside it has plain walls with central

The church of St John, Halifax.

Harewood.

doorways – that on the north side with Tuscan columns; that to the west an arch with a pediment over and topped by a cupola with a gilded weathervane in the form of the golden fleece. The building contains rooms for 315 cloth merchants opening off colonnades round the quadrangle. Because of the slope of the ground there are three storeys on the east and only two on the west, though the roofline is even. The arrangement comprises an arcade at the bottom, square rusticated piers in the middle and Tuscan columns above. The roof has stone flags and the quadrangle is paved with setts and Yorkstone slabs. A market is held here on Saturdays.

In Market Street is the BOROUGH MARKET, a large stone block of 1895 by Leeming and Leeming with a jolly skyline and busy stone façades decorated with little colonnettes and carved panels, just like an Elizabethan four-poster bed or a carved wooden overmantel magnified a thousand times. In Princess Street and Crossley Street are distinguished Italianate buildings of stone enriched with carving and a discreet use of granite for highlights. These form the setting for the TOWN HALL, designed by Sir Charles Barry in 1859 and given to the town by Sir Frank Crossley. Its most prominent feature is its clock tower, which looks like a classical pagoda. Unfortunately the setting of the north side of the Town Hall is spoilt by a new road and new buildings.

Further to the north, in the valley, are DEAN CLOUGH MILLS; once the largest carpet factory in the world but now empty, it is among the noblest factory buildings in the country. This was the source of the Crossley fortune, which contributed so much to Victorian Halifax. On the hill above is AKROYDEN, the model development made for his workers by Colonel Akroyd, the Crossleys' chief rival. This is dominated by ALL SOULS, Haley Hill, Sir George Gilbert Scott's best church, with a terrific spire and richly appointed interior. Having been abandoned by the Church of England, it is now being restored by a private trust.

Returning to the south through the Victorian centre, note LLOYDS BANK on Crown Street – a rich confection of stone and pink granite. In George Street is SOMERSET HOUSE by Carr of York, the best Georgian house in town but spoilt by the insertion of shop-fronts. At the end of Crown Street is the dominating new headquarters of the HALIFAX BUILDING SOCIETY, the largest in the world, built in 1974 and the only good piece of modern architecture in the town. Behind is a pleasant area of stone Georgian houses around the CHURCH OF HOLY TRINITY, which was designed by Thomas Johnson in 1795. This elegant neoclassical church has been closed and its fittings removed to a restaurant. It has been empty and neglected for seven years.

Harewood

11; 7 miles N of Leeds on A61 [63]

Harewood is the most distinguished of the houses and estates created in eighteenth-century England out of a West Indian fortune. The property was bought in 1738 by Henry Lascelles, who had made a great deal of money from his sugar plantations. His son Edwin, 1st Lord Harewood, built the house to the design of John Carr and Robert Adam, landscaped the beautiful park with the help of Capability Brown and other gardeners, and laid out the estate with model farms and two villages. Much of his achievement survives, though the house itself was remodelled externally in 1843 by Charles Barry for the 3rd Earl of Harewood to make it look more like an Italian *palazzo*.

Successive generations enriched the collections, buying Old Master paintings and drawings, silver and Sèvres porcelain. Since the Second World War this policy has been reversed and there have been no fewer than twenty-three sales of works of art from the house. But though half the Sèvres, all the Regency silver gilt and some important paintings, drawings and pieces of furniture have gone, a lot remains, including the family portraits, a significant proportion of the Old Master paintings and most of the furniture made specially for the house by Chippendale.

Adam's designs for the interior of Harewood are dated 1765. The Entrance Hall is a noble room, with attached Roman Doric columns round the walls and fine plaster panels. A tour of the house starts here, on the *piano nobile* – where all the rooms are open to visitors – and continues with the Old Library, which has Adam plasterwork by Joseph Rose and paintings by Biagio Rebecca. Then comes the China Room, originally a dressing room but restored in 1958 to display china; some of the Harewood collection of Sèvres is now on show here, including a *Bleu du Roi* tea service made for Marie Antoinette in 1779. A series of rooms at the east end of the house was occupied by the late Princess Royal; her Dressing Room was designed in 1929 in the Adam manner by Sir Herbert Baker and her Sitting Room, originally the State Bedroom, still has the original alcove for the bed, exceptional Chippendale marquetry furniture made for the house, and watercolours of Harewood and Wharfedale by Turner, Varley, Girtin and other leading landscape artists. Barry converted the original central saloon into a Library, and his severe mahogany bookcases make a strong counterpoint to Adam's delicate stucco ceiling and chimneypieces. The four landscapes by Dall and two by Turner were specially commissioned for the room. The Rose and Green Drawing Rooms contain most of the remaining Old Masters, including important works by El Greco, Bellini, Catena, Titian, Tintoretto, Veronese, Sodoma and Cima da Conegliano.

The Gallery is one of Adam's finest interiors, though it was slightly altered by Barry. The furniture provided by the Chippendales, father and son, includes the *trompe l'œil* painted wooden 'curtains' over the windows, carved and gilt looking-glasses and an extensive group of chairs, sofas and window seats. The Chinese celadon porcelain, with eighteenth-century French ormolu mounts, was collected, like the Sèvres, by Viscount Lascelles, eldest son of the 1st Earl of Harewood. Most of the family portraits are hung in the Gallery and include several notable works by Reynolds, Gainsborough, Hoppner and Lawrence. The Dining Room was remodelled by Barry but is redeemed by the Chippendale marquetry side-tables, wine-cooler and urns, which are among the finest English furniture ever made. The most complete of the Adam rooms at Harewood is the Music Room, the acme of late eighteenth-century perfection, with an original carpet (reflecting the ceiling pattern), original gilt Chippendale chairs and marquetry side-tables, and large wall paintings by Zucchi.

Heptonstall

12; 6 miles W of Halifax off A646

Heptonstall is grimly grand, with gritstone houses jumbled up on a hillside around two parish CHURCHES. The medieval parish church of St Thomas, with its stubbly west tower, was dismantled in the mid-nineteenth century and replaced by a lavish new one in the Perpendicular manner – to the advantage of the picturesque appearance of the village. Most unfortunately, the amazing old churchyard was cleared, in the interests of suburban tidiness, in the 1960s. Where did this despicable taste for clearing old graveyards originate?

Heathcote

See Ilkley.

Hickleton

13; 5 miles W of Doncaster on A635

At the time of writing, the CHURCH OF ST WILFRED is falling down a coal-mine. It is to be hoped, however, that one day it will be restored and re-opened, as it is one of the most interesting parish churches in England, thanks to the 2nd Viscount Halifax, who presided over the Anglo-Catholic wing of the Established Church throughout the last third of the nineteenth century and the first third of the twentieth.

The church, close to the gates of Hickleton Hall, is a large Perpendicular edifice with a west tower. It owes its glory to the restoration carried out for Lord Halifax by G.F. Bodley, and it is appropriate that the church should contain a monument to Bodley himself in the form of an alabaster bust. He was responsible for the seemingly medieval perfection of the interior. The effect was much enhanced by the rich furnishings provided by Lord Halifax, many of continental origin. They include Italian *quattrocento* paintings, German or Flemish medieval wood-carvings, and much Baroquery of various dates and provenance. It is to be hoped that not too much of this rich collection will be sold off to pay for the restoration. Indeed, one wonders why the National Coal Board cannot pay for all the work out of the billions that taxpayers provide in subsidies?

Huddersfield

14; 15 miles SW of Leeds on A62

Huddersfield is a spectacularly sited nineteenth-century mill town. Descending into it from the M62 is like going down into the centre of an extinct volcano, as the town lies in a deep hollow surrounded on all sides by bleak moors. The place was built largely of smoke-darkened gritstone, which used to give it a massive dignity. The best building is the RAILWAY STATION erected in 1847–8 to the design of J.P. Pritchett. It is a palatial job, with a large six-columned Corinthian portico in the centre carrying a pediment with a clock, and long, spreading colonnaded wings on either side. It has been cleaned to reveal the whitish-yellow colour of the stone. Personally, I preferred it when it was sooty black. Then it had a Piranesian grandeur that was infinitely preferable to the Civic Trust blandness of its new state.

Ilkley
15; 18 miles NW of Leeds on A65
HEATHCOTE is a manufacturer's villa designed by Sir Edwin Lutyens, and probably the most magnificent of his early classical designs. Just as at Castle Drogo in Devon he turned his client's request for an 'Olde English' house into a powerful variation on a castle theme, so here what could have been tamely Neo-Georgian is the richest imaginable Anglo-Palladian pile, with elaborately carved stonework, arched and rusticated chimneys and a steeply pitched red pantiled roof. All Lutyens' mannerisms are apparent. On the garden front a tiny little door under the terrace is almost crushed by the massive cushion rustication around it; and in the terrace parapet there are little gaps, flanked by miniature cushion rustication, for pots of flowers. The fenestration is extraordinarily varied; it sounds rather house-agent blurby to say that no two windows are the same, but it is almost true. And oddest of all is the double set of quoins flanking the recessed centre of the garden front. None of these idiosyncrasies shouts at you because of the power of the overall composition, with the tall three-bay centre block flanked by lower wings. It is often claimed that a particular building is a masterpiece: here is one – and indeed it is one of the most original buildings designed by a twentieth-century English architect.

Ledsham
16; 7 miles E of Leeds off A1
ALL SAINTS is a Saxon church of great importance and rarity, albeit restored here and there in Norman times. It dates from the eighth century and comprises a nave with a two-storeyed porch, now the base of the tower, and a portico, now the south porch. The original stonework is rough rubble, while the Norman masonry is ashlar. (The little spire on top of the tower is Perpendicular.) The great feature of the church is the tower doorway, much restored in 1871 but dating from the early eleventh century and retaining its original form. It is an archway surrounded by a band of scrolly carving, unlike any other door of its date in the country. Inside, the church is quite light, as several Perpendicular windows have been inserted into the thick Saxon walls. There is a grand army of seventeenth- and eighteenth-century Baroque marble tombs of the owners of Ledston Hall (*q.v.*) – black and white marble, effigies and obelisks, allegories and sarcophagi.

Ledston Hall
17; 9 miles E of Leeds on A1
Here is a large and spectacular mid-seventeenth-century mansion that ought to be better known. It is three storeys high and the main front, built by Sir John Lewis, has a centre eleven bays wide, flanked by projecting wings with square end turrets carrying ogee caps, like Hatfield. The most distinctive feature is the array of fancy Dutch gables along the skyline. The pedimented front door and the sash windows were inserted in the early eighteenth century and add to the uniformity of the façade.

The building itself is much older than it seems. It originated as a grange of Pontefract Priory and various medieval bits survive inside, including a thirteenth-century undercroft. The interior is part sixteenth-century with panelled rooms embellished with elaborate plaster ceilings, and part early eighteenth-century, as in the dignified Georgian Dining Room, Entrance Hall and several other rooms.

Leeds
18; 8 miles N of Wakefield on M1
This sprawling city, the largest in Yorkshire, has a German feel to it. The wide, regular streets of the centre, lined with slightly coarse brick Victorian buildings, brash 1960s' blocks and garish, over-lit shops could be in Westphalia. Even the guttural northern speech of the inhabitants sounds slightly German until you attune your ears to it. Leeds does not have the transatlantic grandeur of Manchester or Liverpool (*qq.v.*) but it does have a strong sense of civic pride and a range of interesting buildings. It is a commercial city, the prosperity of which was based originally on wool before it diversified into other trades.

The centrepiece of the city is the TOWN HALL, a splendid Victorian monument built between 1853 and 1858 to the design of Cuthbert Broderick. It is a large square pile, grandly classical, with a rusticated plinth supporting the main façades of giant Corinthian columns and pilasters. Round the top is a balustraded parapet with urns and in the centre a square colonnaded tower carrying a clock turret and dome. It makes a sumptuous display. Inside, the main room is a large Concert Hall with a plaster tunnel vault supported on paired columns; it has benefited from a recent restoration of the Victorian colour scheme. The Town Hall is one of a group of civic buildings. Next door are the MUNICIPAL OFFICES, a rich Italianate block, and next to that is the CITY ART GALLERY. The new part stuck on to the front makes the whole building look curiously like a ruin or an unfinished façade. Behind, in Calverly Street, is the CIVIC HALL by Vincent Harris. This is among the most impressive inter-war civic buildings in England, with a Corinthian portico of Portland stone and two Wren-Baroque towers with gilt owls on top. South of the Town Hall is an interesting area containing the best-preserved Georgian houses in Leeds and some jolly Victorian warehouses. PARK SQUARE is a more or less intact Georgian square, the centre grassed and planted with trees, and, along the sides, terraces of red brick houses with stone Tuscan doorcases and sash windows,

The Town Hall, Leeds.

the Neo-Georgian Water Board offices, and the less tactful but very welcome Moorish ST PAUL'S HOUSE. This warehouse was built in 1878 by Ambler and is an extravaganza of brick and terracotta, culminating in four corner minarets. It backs on to St Paul's Street, which contains several other warehouses, and Park Place which has Georgian houses almost identical to Park Square.

To the east of the Town Hall is THE HEADROW, a *via triumphalis* laid out in a wide, straight line through the centre of Leeds by the corporation in 1924. Only the north side was completed to a unified design in brick and stone, with 'features' incorporating Tuscan columns. This was the work of Sir Reginald Blomfield and is dignified enough, though in my opinion the changes in level between the sections are curiously ill managed. To the south, between the Headrow and the railway, are the principal commercial and shopping streets, with Gothic and classical Victorian banks and offices, and also some more recent and less agreeable Modern interpolations. Park Row leads down to City Square, where are to be found the Italianate POST OFFICE of 1896 by Sir Henry Tanner, modern office buildings and an entertaining group of bronze sculpture in the middle, including an equestrian statue of the Black Prince by Brock and various bronze nymphs, holding electric lamps, by Alfred Drury.

Boar Lane leads north. Here is HOLY TRINITY CHURCH, designed by William Halfpenny in 1721–7; it is the only one of Leeds's three Georgian churches to survive. It is in the Gibbs manner, with heavy rusticated window surrounds. The elegant tower with diminishing stages

was added by Chantrell in 1839. The interior has giant Corinthian columns supporting a shallow tunnel vault, an unusually monumental effect for a provincial Georgian church. Boar Lane leads to Duncan Street where, framed at the end, is the CORN EXCHANGE of 1861–3 by Broderick. It is circular with a dome, heavy-faceted rustication and a rich carved frieze showing swags and bulls' heads. It is one of the most original and impressive buildings in Leeds. The interior is equally good; it has an oval dome decorated with a curious pattern of elliptical ribs, rather like a Baroque church in Turin.

Briggate is the main shopping street. The most characteristic of its Victorian buildings are the glazed ARCADES, such as Barton's Arcade and County Arcade. At the top, in New Briggate, is ST JOHN'S CHURCH, the oldest surviving building in central Leeds. It was erected in 1632–4 in late Perpendicular style and is a considerable rarity, as few large parish churches were built in England at that time. It has a west tower, nave and chancel, all with battlements; straight-headed windows with cusped lights; and the whole exterior is in blackened stone. The interior is exciting both spatially and for its furnishings. It comprises two low naves of similar character; the arches between them could be reflecting mirrors rather than openings. Above, there is an open timber roof with carved beams and moulded plaster panels, but no clerestory. And across both naves are carved Jacobean screens with elaborate strapwork cartouches on top. The pulpit, with its frilly crested top, is *en suite*, and all the original carved pews also survive. It is a remarkably well-preserved ensemble. What a miracle that some energetic Victorian vicar did not sweep it all away.

Nostell Priory.

To the south-east of the city centre is TEMPLE NEWSAM, now administered as an art gallery by the City of Leeds. It is the most impressive Tudor-Jacobean house in West Yorkshire. The earliest part dates from the time of Lord Darcy, who was beheaded for taking part in the Pilgrimage of Grace. He determined the plan of the large square building round a courtyard, but it was substantially reconstructed after its acquisition by Sir Arthur Ingram in 1622. Ingram was a henchman of the Earl of Suffolk and, like his master, made enough money out of unscrupulous governmental financial deals to build for himself on a grand scale. He constructed the many bay windows, the columned porch and the biblical inscription round the balustrade (originally stone but replaced in cast-iron in 1788).

The exterior survives much as it was left by Sir Arthur but the interior was largely remodelled in the eighteenth century by his descendants, the Viscounts Irwin, to the designs of a succession of architects, including Daniel Garrett, Carr of York and an obscure Mr Johnson. Further interior work was done by Mrs C.E. Meynell Ingram and the splendid carved oak staircase by C.E. Kempe (copied from the Slaugham Place staircase in Sussex) is hers.

The state rooms are the creation of the 7th Viscount Irwin and comprise rooms with Rococo plaster ceilings by Thomas Perritt and William Rose of York. The most spectacular is the Long Gallery, with chimneypieces designed by William Kent (their overmantels enclosing paintings by Antonio Jolli) and a Rococo ceiling. The adjoining Library, designed by Garrett with Corinthian columns framing the bookcases, was restored in 1974

when nineteenth-century alterations were removed. The Chinese Drawing Room has a hand-painted oriental wallpaper hung in 1828 and enriched with birds cut out of Audubon's *Birds of America*.

Temple Newsam was sold to the City of Leeds in 1922 by the Earl of Halifax, together with some of its original contents. These have been augmented over the years by furniture, paintings and much else of very high quality, including the great marquetry library table by Chippendale from Harewood (*q.v.*) and the gilt furniture in the Gallery by Vile and Cobb from Croome Court in Hereford and Worcester (*q.v.*). The park, however, has suffered from open-cast coal-mining, although an imaginative scheme to recreate the formal gardens around the mansion has recently been started.

Lotherton Hall
19; 7 miles NE of Leeds on A1
Now an outstation of Leeds City Art Gallery, Lotherton is a somewhat amorphous Edwardian house developed in 1897–1908 round an eighteenth-century core with additions of 1828. It is surrounded by a large Edwardian garden and parkland. The estate was bought by the Gascoignes of Parlington in 1825 and succeeded the latter as their family house in the 1890s. It still contains the family collection, including splendid portraits — among them a swagger Pompeo Batoni of Sir Thomas Gascoigne, 8th Baronet — and the late eighteenth- and early nineteenth-century racing cups won by his horses. Since being acquired by Leeds City Council and opened to the public in 1969, the original contents have been greatly augmented.

Nostell Priory
NT; 20; 5 miles SE of Wakefield on A638 [46]

The exterior of Nostell is not as satisfactory as one could wish, as neither the original Palladian design of a centre block with four quadrant wings nor Robert Adam's amended scheme was completed. The present house, therefore, comprises a large, lumpish main block and an exquisitely modelled smaller block side by side, looking for all the world like a demonstration of how and how not to design a house using the Ionic order. The park, though large and full of venerable timber, with a lake and various eighteenth-century outbuildings, is, alas, much tarnished by the close proximity of coal-mining.

The interior, however, is of the first rank. It was designed partly by James Paine in c.1750 and partly by Robert Adam in c.1760–70. The principal rooms are on the *piano nobile* and are notable for the Chippendale furniture made specially for the house. The large Hall was designed by Adam in 1771 and has characteristic plasterwork. The Library was the first room here to be decorated by him and his drawings for it are dated 1766. Rose's plasterwork, Zucchi's paintings and the pedimented bookcases form a striking unity, though the room was repainted in c.1819. The large carved mahogany library table is the finest piece by Chippendale at Nostell. The Tapestry Room has an Adam ceiling and Brussels tapestries woven after designs by Teniers. The exquisite marble group of Flora and a Zephyr is one of R.J. Wyatt's best early works. The Saloon, on axis with the Hall, is as designed by Adam, with a complete set of Chippendale furniture – pelmets, chairs, sofas, pier glasses and side-tables – all conceived as an integral part of the original decoration.

After the chaste neo-classical refinement of the Adam rooms in the centre and north part of the house, Paine's heavier Rococo rooms at the south end seem remarkably old fashioned. The best is the Dining Room (redecorated by the late John Fowler), which has a good ceiling and chimneypiece, while the State Bedroom and Dressing Room are notable for the Chinese wallpaper supplied by Chippendale and a complete set of green japanned *chinoiserie* furniture provided by Chippendale in 1771.

Oakwell Hall
See Birstall.

Saltaire
21; 5 miles N of Bradford on A6038

Saltaire is best approached by train, from which you get the feel of the valleys cutting through the Pennines, enclosing the railway, roads and Leeds–Liverpool canal, with the eighteenth- and nineteenth-century industrial villages and towns threaded along them. Saltaire is by far the most handsome of the West Riding industrial towns and, unlike many of the others, is spankingly kept up. It was built as a model settlement by Sir Titus Salt, who moved his alpaca mills out of Bradford in the 1850s. The MILL dominates the valley – a spectacular affair, 550 feet long and six storeys high. It is Italianate with a prominent cornice, two towers and a tall chimney. What is more, it is still in operation. It forms the centrepiece of

the town, together with the RAILWAY STATION and the CONGREGATIONAL CHURCH. The former has recently been restored and is embellished with new cast-iron lamps. The latter was built in 1858–9 and was designed, like everything else at Saltaire, by the local firm of Lockwood and Mawson. It has a semi-circular portico with Corinthian capitals carrying a domed circular cupola. It is of excellent ashlar stone and is richly ornamented. On the north side is the domed Salt family mausoleum.

Beyond the station is a fine MODEL VILLAGE. The park is beautifully laid out in the Victorian municipal-landscape manner and affords fine views over the surrounding valley and hills. Across the railway tracks the workers' houses are laid out in even terraces to a grid-plan and were designed by Lockwood and Mawson. They share the Saltaire Italianate house-style and are solidly built in local stone. There are no pubs – always a possible drawback in model villages.

The Congregational Church, Saltaire.

Sandbeck Park

22; 6 miles E of Rotherham off A631

This estate of 5000 acres forms an eighteenth-century enclave close to Doncaster, Rotherham and other industrial towns. The park was landscaped by Capability Brown and the house designed by James Paine. It is a dramatic composition, with none of the blandness of much mid-Georgian architecture. The ground floor is heavily rusticated and on the garden front there is an exceptionally deep Corinthian portico. The Piranesian effect is enhanced by the weird weathering of the stonework, caused by the polluted industrial atmosphere of the West Riding. The interior is magnificent and is being splendidly restored and redecorated by Lord Scarbrough, who lives here in preference to his other seat, Lumley Castle in Durham (*q.v.*). A low Entrance Hall and an Edwardianised Dining Room occupy the central axis of the ground floor. On either side are comfortably proportioned family living rooms with good marble chimneypieces and other features. The house has post-war work by both Claud Phillimore and Francis Johnson. In the well of the main staircase is the Elizabethan alabaster fountain with a pelican, brought from the Great Hall at Lumley. The whole centre of the first floor is occupied by the great Saloon, recently refurnished as a drawing room. It is among the most beautifully decorated rooms in the north of England, with its high coved ceiling, in Paine's later Adamesque manner, and its sumptuous neo-classical plasterwork.

Sheffield

23; 12 miles N of Chesterfield on A61

Sheffield enjoys the best site of any large English city, with hills and moors all around, like the background of a classical landscape by Claude or Poussin. Unfortunately, the architecture of the town does not rise to the same level; nor do the amenities. It is fashionable to claim that the place has been greatly improved since the Second World War; it is rather more difficult to agree. Nonetheless, there is much to be excited about in Sheffield. The general atmosphere is like nowhere else in England: part feudal, part socialist republic. The lord of the manor and largest landowner is the Duke of Norfolk, but the town council has been Labour consistently since the war and runs to such utopian extravagances as a free bus service.

The growth of Sheffield, and its past prosperity, was based on the steel industry. This was developed in the sixteenth century by Gilbert, 7th Earl of Shrewsbury and warder of Mary Queen of Scots. Stuck all the year round on his northern estates near to his charge, and being of a scientific turn of mind, he devoted himself to the exploitation of the minerals on his land and to the expansion of the local knife-making craft, introducing Flemish artisans to train the locals. This fledgling industrial empire was carried by his granddaughter Aletheia to the Howards, Dukes of Norfolk in the seventeenth century.

The proud centrepiece of the city is the TOWN HALL, erected to the design of E.W. Mountford in 1890–7 while the 15th Duke of Norfolk was the first Lord Mayor. It is one of Mountford's best works – Baroque-Jacobean –

The Town Hall, Sheffield.

with a tall cupola carrying a gilt statue of Vulcan on top. The interior is staggeringly well preserved, down to details like the original *art nouveau* light fittings. The state rooms on the first floor retain their original decorations and furniture, looking just as they do in Bedford Lemère's photographs, which were taken soon after the building was opened. The Entrance Hall and staircase, which form the processional approach, are lined with alabaster and marble, and at the foot of the staircase is a striking marble statue by Onslow Ford of the 15th Duke with his mayoral chain-of-office tucked into his Garter riband. Nearly as impressive is Sheffield's other great public building, the CITY HALL, designed by E. Vincent Harris in 1920 and completed in 1934. It contains two concert halls and is a twentieth-century version of St George's Hall in Liverpool (*q.v.*) and hardly less successful than its nineteenth-century precursor. This is undoubtedly Harris's best building and is a belated tribute to nineteenth-century municipal architecture. The main façade has a monumental portico of eight Corinthian columns, without a pediment. The most original feature is the apse at the back with free-standing square piers at the top – a feature copied from the Harris Art Gallery in Preston (*q.v.*).

Sheffield's CATHEDRAL is something of a disappointment. It is the old parish church, raised to cathedral status in 1914 and enlarged and enriched by a sequence

of architects, including Sir Charles Nicholson, George Pace, and Ansell and Bailey. As a result, the general effect is of a nice old building that has been spoilt by having far too much money spent on it. The trouble is that there has been no consistent plan, and the orientation has changed three times in the course of work, leaving the building with no sense of direction and all sorts of bits left over as appendages from previous plans. The best part is the Shrewsbury Chapel, with its two grand alabaster Elizabethan monuments to the 4th and 6th Earls of Shrewsbury (restored by Hadfield for the 15th Duke of Norfolk). ST MARIE'S, the Catholic cathedral, is an ambitious Puginian Gothic church of 1846–50, with a tall spire by Hadfield, on the site of the eighteenth-century house of the Duke of Norfolk's agent (and Sheffield's recusant Catholic chapel). The interior, which has good fittings by a series of designers including Pugin, Goldie and Bentley, has been spoilt by insensitive reordering and tasteless decorations. The great shrine of Sheffield, however, is not a church but the CUTLERS' HALL, a dignified Grecian building reminiscent of the City Livery Companies in London. It was designed by Samuel Worth and B.B. Taylor in 1832 and has a splendid interior with an imperial-plan staircase and a grandiose Banqueting Hall. Here the annual Cutlers' Feast is held. The Cutlers of Sheffield possess a magnificent collection of silver dating from the eighteenth century to the present day.

Of the street architecture of central Sheffield, the best is the area round PARADISE SQUARE on land belonging to the Shrewsbury Hospital. This is a complete square of early Georgian red brick houses (now offices), which has been carefully restored in recent years. Further off, a number of buildings are worth seeking out. The MAPPIN ART GALLERY in Weston Park is a pure Grecian building of 1886 with an Ionic portico, such as you might expect to find in Glasgow or the USA. On the other side of the town is MANOR LODGE, with its sixteenth-century 'stand' or summerhouse – all that survives of the seat of the Earls of Shrewsbury. It was restored in the late nineteenth century by the 15th Duke of Norfolk and is let on a long lease to the corporation. The SHREWSBURY HOSPITAL is a large set of early nineteenth-century almshouses in Jacobean style by Woodhead and Hurst. They were moved here from the town centre by the 12th Duke of Norfolk. Later ranges of almshouses commemorate comings-of-age and similar events in the Norfolk family. Opposite, in a small park, is the CHOLERA MONUMENT of 1832 by Hadfield – a Gothic spire described by Pevsner as 'the Gothicist's equivalent for an obelisk'.

Shibden Hall
24; 1 mile E of Halifax off A58
Shibden Hall is a house of many dates – fifteenth, sixteenth and seventeenth centuries – which owes a lot of its picturesque appeal to a drastic restoration carried out

in the 1830s for Anne Lister by the architect John Harper, who also added a stone tower. The exterior is part timber-framed and part stone-faced. The interior contains oak panelling of different dates (much of it brought here in the nineteenth century), and in the Dining Room is some original Elizabethan painted decoration lying behind the hinged panelling, which can be opened on request. Now a museum, the rooms are appropriately furnished.

Temple Newsam
See Leeds.

Tickhill
25; 10 miles E of Rotherham on A1
ST MARY'S is a large, proud Perpendicular church, a monument to the medieval greatness of Tickhill, which, though now no more than a village, was once a flourishing market town under the protection of its castle – one of the most powerful in the north. The west tower of the church is 124 feet high, embattled and richly decorated with heraldry and religious imagery. The nave is very tall, while the chancel is lower, which helps to give the

exterior a good silhouette. The interior is full of light from the large aisle windows and also from a window over the chancel arch. The church has good fittings and monuments and has recently benefited from being looked after by George Pace, who has added various things of his own, one of the most interesting of which is the Comperish font cover.

Wentworth★
26; 4 miles NW of Rotherham on B6090 [**60**]
WENTWORTH WOODHOUSE is a vast and palatial house, exuding a strong sense of *sic transit gloria mundi*. Beyond the boundaries of the estate, industrial ruin stretches in all directions as a squalid memorial to nineteenth-century prosperity and late twentieth-century economic decline, and in the damp inner courtyards the shade of doomed Strafford lingers . . .

Wentworth Woodhouse is really two huge houses back to back, both of them built for the same client, the 1st Marquess of Rockingham, but radically different in style. One is Baroque, of brick, with lively carved detail and a deeply recessed centre. The other is Palladian, of stone, dignified, immensely long and perfect. Embedded

Wentworth Woodhouse.

in the middle between them are the remains of Lord Strafford's house. His front door can still be seen, opening now on to one of the inner courtyards, and there is a fine seventeenth-century Mannerist gateway copied from the engravings of Dietterlin. The Baroque garden front was added in the 1720s. Until recently this building was retained as a private house by the family and it has several good interiors, including the West Hall, with its elaborate Baroque plasterwork reminiscent of central Europe, especially Prague. The Dining Room has a well-preserved eighteenth-century French wallpaper with an apple-green ground, and there are sets of bedrooms, such as Clifford's Lodgings and the Yellow Rooms, with panelling and good plasterwork. The Long Gallery stretches 130 feet to the east range and in its purer Palladian decoration is an overture to the architecture of that side of the house.

The main front of Wentworth Woodhouse is 600 feet long – the longest of any English country house – and was designed by Harry Flitcroft, with a huge Corinthian portico on the model of Colen Campbell's Wanstead. The flanking wings were heightened and their Tuscan centrepieces added by Carr of York in the 1780s. As a lighter counterpoint, the end pavilions are treated as little towers, with jolly glazed cupolas on top almost like lighthouses. What photographs and written descriptions can never convey is how perfectly proportioned this whole vast composition is.

The state rooms fill the *piano nobile* of the Flitcroft range and are among the finest in the country. It is little short of a tragedy that Wentworth Woodhouse did not become a stately home open to the public after the war, but instead the main part was let to the local authority for educational purposes. The furniture, fittings and paintings, all of the highest quality and specially commissioned for the state rooms, have been removed and are currently at Bourne Park in Kent. One day they ought to be returned and the rooms restored to their original glory and opened to the public.

The *piano nobile* is approached via the low Pillared Hall – note the marble statues and Italian plaster casts after the antique in niches – and the semi-circular Grand Staircase by John Carr. The Saloon in the centre of the east front is inspired by Inigo Jones's Hall at the Queen's House, Greenwich. It has marbled wall decoration in brown, siena and white. In niches round the walls are marble copies of classical statues by various Italian sculptors. Above them are plaster neo-classical reliefs by 'Athenian' Stuart. The chimneypieces have marble relief sculptures by John Gibson. North of the Saloon are the Statue Room, the State Dining Room with its grand stucco decoration, and the Libraries, originally the state bedroom and dressing room. To the south are the Anteroom, Van Dyck Room and Whistlejacket Room, all of a mounting degree of splendour, reaching a climax in the gilt plasterwork of the last. This room takes its name from Whistlejacket, the famous racehorse whose life-size portrait by Stubbs was once framed into the wall. It is reputed to have been Whistlejacket's winnings on the racecourse that paid for the gigantic stables, designed by Carr of York on a scale to match that of the house.

The park at Wentworth Woodhouse was landscaped by Repton but badly damaged after the Second World War when Emanuel Shinwell, as Minister of Fuel, had it open-cast mined to produce a small quantity of low-grade coal. The damage has now been largely restored by the Fitzwilliam estates. In the park and grounds there are many subsidiary buildings of interest, including the ROCKINGHAM MAUSOLEUM, designed by Carr of York, and the heroic TERRACE with an Ionic Rotunda to the south of the house. (This collapsed during the mining but has been rebuilt.) Outside the park proper there are various Whig eye-catchers, such as the HOOBER STAND, commemorating the defeat of the '45 Rebellion, and KEPPEL'S COLUMN, marking the acquittal at court martial of Admiral Keppel.

The village of Wentworth is a remarkably intact eighteenth-century estate village, unusual in being utilitarian rather than picturesque. The eighteenth-century estate improvements, combining agriculture, mining and industry, at Wentworth Woodhouse were the cynosure of those who advocated planned economic development in the age of Enlightenment. A forlorn relic is the dairy farm at ELSECAR designed by Carr of York to provide milk and butter for the colliers employed in the new mine there. Last but not least at Wentworth is HOLY TRINITY, the parish church built for Lord Fitzwilliam in 1872–7 by J.L. Pearson. It is a noble design with a central spire and is stone-vaulted throughout. A straight walk half a mile long extends from the centre of the west front of the house to the church – just the thing for funeral processions.

Wentworth Castle
27; 3 miles SW of Barnsley off M1

This huge house was built as a direct rival to Wentworth Woodhouse (*q.v.*) by a cousin who considered himself to be the main-line descendant of the Wentworths. The Wentworth Woodhouse family won in the end by making their house the largest in England – but only just! Wentworth Castle is a T-shaped pile on the side of a hill, with fine views across the valley to the east. The short stroke of the T is the north range, dating from *c.*1670 and now very much the back of the house. At right-angles to this is the east range of 1708, a Baroque palace frontage based on an elevational drawing by General Jean de Bodt, architect of the Arsenal unter den Linden at Potsdam. The Earl of Strafford had met de Bodt while British Ambassador in Berlin. Indeed, the building works at Wentworth Castle were directed through letters written by the Earl from Berlin. Finally, round the corner there is a long, rather dull, Palladian frontage, added in 1759 to the design of an obscure London architect, Charles Ross.

The de Bodt façade is the glory of Wentworth Castle and is a unique example of Franco-German architecture in Georgian England. It is faced in stone and is three storeys high, the end pavilions and the centrepiece being decorated with crisply carved Corinthian pilasters and swags of flowers. It is a pity that a car park has been made off-centre in the foreground, spoiling the setting. The environs have been further disfigured by 1960s' con-

Wentworth Castle.

crete buildings to the north erected by the training college that occupied the house after the war. The nearby stables and outbuildings, which could easily have been converted to provide less obtrusive subsidiary accommodation, have been allowed to fall into ruin. The climax of the house is the great Gallery designed by James Gibbs. It occupies the whole of the first floor of the east range and is approached by a staircase, also by Gibbs, with ornate Baroque plasterwork by Italian *stuccatores*. The Gallery has a coved ceiling, marble chimneypieces (once with carved eagles holding festoons) and two screens of marble Corinthian columns. It should look like the Colonna Gallery in Rome, but, unfortunately, at the time of writing it is disfigured by modern partitions.

The grounds at Wentworth Castle are of great interest and are embellished with a considerable number of ornamental buildings, two obelisks, various temples and follies, which, hopefully, will one day be restored.

Womersley
28; 3 miles SE of Pontefract off A1

ST MARTIN'S stands in the grounds of the HALL, a subsidiary seat of the Earl of Rosse. The church is cruciform with a well-proportioned spire and bits of different dates, but mainly Decorated. It is made special by the late nineteenth-century restoration carried out by Bodley and by many brought-in continental fittings, including altar furnishings and sculpture. The church is also beautifully kept. Bodley was responsible for its roof and also designed the rood-screen in Perpendicular manner. The stained glass in the aisle windows was made by Kempe as part of the Bodley restoration. The new monument to the late Earl of Rosse is appropriately classical for the co-founder of the Georgian Group.

Bibliography

As well as the books listed below, the *Shell Guides* – in those counties for which they exist – form excellent introductions to the architecture of specific areas of England.

Allen, Thomas. *History of the County of York*, 6 vols, 1828.
Barley, M.W. *The English Farmhouse and Cottage*, London, 1961.
    Nottingham Now, London, 1975.
Brock, Clutton. *York Minster*, 1899.
Cannadine, David. *Lords and Landlords: The Aristocracy and the Towns, 1774–1967*, Leicester, 1980.
Chapman, S.D. *History of Working-class Housing*, Newton Abbot, 1971.
Charleton, R.J. *History of Newcastle upon Tyne*, 1950.
Clifton-Taylor, Alec. *The Cathedrals of England*, London, 1967.
    The Pattern of English Building, revised edn, London, 1972.
Cobb, Gerald. *English Cathedrals*, London, 1980.
Colvin, Howard. *A Biographical Dictionary of British Architects 1600–1840*, London, 1978.
    Calke Abbey, London, 1985.
Cox, J.C. *Notes on the Churches of Derbyshire*, 4 vols, 1875–9.
Darley, Gillian. *Villages of Vision*, London, 1975.
Devonshire, 6th Duke of. *Handbook of Chatsworth and Hardwick*, 1845.
Devonshire, Duchess of. *The House*, London, 1982.
Dugdale, Sir William. *Antiquities of Warwickshire*, 2nd edn, 1730.
Duncomb, John. *Collections Towards the History and Antiquities of Hereford*, 6 vols, 1804–1913.
Dyos, H.J., and Wolff, Michael. *The Victorian City: Images and Realities*, 2 vols, London, 1973.
Eller, I. *History of Belvoir Castle*, 1841.
Fallow, T.M. *Memorials of Old Yorkshire*, London, 1904.
Fleetwood-Hesketh, Peter. *Murray's Lancashire Architectural Guide*, London, 1955.
Frost, Charles. *Early Notices . . . [of] Hull*, 1827.
Girouard, Mark. *Robert Smythson and the Architecture of the Elizabethan Era*, London, 1966.
    The Victorian Country House, London, 1979.
Gunnis, Rupert. *Dictionary of British Sculptors 1660–1851*, London, 1951.
Hall, Ivan and Elizabeth. *Historic Beverley*, York, 1973.
    Georgian Hull, York, 1979.
Hamilton Thompson, A. *Military Architecture in England*, London, 1912.
Harvey, John. *English Medieval Architects*, London, 1954.
Hickman, D. *Birmingham*, London, 1970.
Hill, Sir Francis. *Georgian Lincoln*, Cambridge, 1965.
Hitchcock, Henry Russell. *Early Victorian Architecture in Britain*, 2 vols, London, 1954.
Hoskins, W.G. *The Heritage of Leicester*, Leicester, 1950.
Hughes, Quentin. *Seaport*, London, 1969.
Hussey, Christopher. *The Picturesque*, London, 1927.
    English Country Houses: Early Georgian, London, 1955.
    English Country Houses: Mid Georgian, London, 1955.
    English Country Houses: Late Georgian, London, 1958.
Linstrum, Derek. *Architecture of the West Riding of Yorkshire*, London, 1980.
Lloyd, David. *The Making of English Towns*, London, 1984.
Lobel, M.D. (Ed.) *Historic Towns*, London, 1969.

Macauley, James. *Gothic Revival*, Edinburgh, 1975.
Mee, G. *Aristocratic Enterprise*, Edinburgh, 1975.
Morris, J.E. *Little Guide to the East Riding of Yorkshire*, London, 1932.
Mowl, Tim, and Earnshaw, Brian. *Trumpet at a Distant Gate*, London, 1985.
Ormerod, R. *History of Cheshire*, 2nd edn, 3 vols, 1872.
Peters, J.E.C. *Development of Farm Buildings in Western Lowland Staffordshire*, Manchester, 1969.
Pevsner, Nikolaus. *The Buildings of England*, London, various dates and in constant revision.
Picton, J.A. *Architectural History of Liverpool*, 1858.
Pitt, W. *Topographical History of Staffordshire*, 2 vols, 1817.
Quiney, Anthony. *John Loughborough Pearson*, London, 1979.
Reid, Peter. *Burke's Guide to Country Houses II*, London, 1980.
Rennie, Sir John. *British and Foreign Harbours*, 2 vols, 1854.
Richardson, G. *New Vitruvius Britannicus*, 2 vols, 1802 and 1808.
Ritchie-Noakes, Nancy. *Liverpool's Historic Waterfront*, London, 1984.
Robinson, Rev. C.J. *Mansions and Manors of Herefordshire*, 1872.
Robinson, John Martin. *The Wyatts: An Architectural Dynasty*, Oxford, 1979.
    Georgian Model Farms, Oxford, 1984.
    The Latest Country Houses, London, 1984.
Royal Commission on Historical Monuments: Westmorland, London, 1936.
    Herefordshire, London, 3 vols, 1931–4.
    City of York, London, 5 vols, 1962–81.
    Stamford, London, 1977.
Shaw, S. *History of Staffordshire*, 1801.
Smiles, S. *Lives of the Engineers*, 2 vols, 1861–2.
Smith, D.M. *Industrial Archaeology of the East Midlands*, Newton Abbot, 1965.
Simmons, J. *The City of Leicester*, London, 1957.
Stanton, Phoebe. *Pugin*, London, 1971.
Stranks, C.J. *This Sumptuous Church*, Canterbury, 1973.
Summerson, John. *Architecture in Britain, 1530–1830*, London, 1953.
Taylor, Henry. *Old Halls in Lancashire and Cheshire*, 1884.
Taylor, H.M. and J. *Anglo Saxon Churches*, London, 1965.
Taylor, M.W. *Old Manorial Halls of Westmorland and Cumberland*, 1892.
Thoroton, Robert (Ed. John Throsby). *Antiquities of Nottinghamshire*, 1790–6.
Twycross, Edward. *Mansions of England and Wales: Lancaster*, 3 vols, 1847.
    Chester, 2 vols, 1850.
Underhill, C. *History of Burton-on-Trent*, London, 1961.
Whittaker, Neville, and Clark, Ursula. *Historic Architecture of County Durham*, Newcastle upon Tyne, 1971.
Wilkes, Lyall, and Dodds, Gordon. *Tyneside Classical*, London, 1964.
Wilson, D.M. *Archaeology of Anglo-Saxon England*, London, 1976.
Winter, J. *Industrial Architecture: A Survey of Factory Buildings*, London, 1970.

CUMBRIA

1 Appleby
2 Barrow-in-Furness
3 Brampton
4 Broughton in Furness
5 Carlisle
6 Cartmel
7 Cockermouth
8 Corby Castle
9 Crosthwaite
10 Dalemain
11 Dallam Tower
12 Dalton Hall
13 Dent
14 Grange-over-Sands
15 Greystoke
16 Holker Hall
17 Hutton-in-the-Forest
18 Isel Hall
19 Kendal
20 Kirkby Stephen
21 Kirkoswald
22 Lanercost Priory
23 Levens Hall
24 Lowther
25 Morland
26 Muncaster Castle
27 Naworth Castle
28 Penrith
29 Plumpton Wall
30 Rose Castle
31 St Bees
32 Scaleby Castle
33 Sizergh Castle
34 Temple Sowerby
35 Ulverston
36 Warwick Bridge
37 Wetheral
38 Wharton Hall
39 Whitehaven
40 Wigton
41 Windermere
42 Witherslack
43 Workington
44 Wreay
45 Yanwath Hall

DURHAM

1 Barnard Castle
2 Chester-le-Street
3 Durham
4 Egglestone Abbey
5 Escomb
6 Gibside
7 Jarrow
8 Lumley Castle
9 Penshaw Monument
10 Raby Castle
11 Rokeby Hall
12 Roker
13 Sunderland
14 Ushaw
15 Wynyard Park

NORTHUMBERLAND

1 Alnwick Castle
2 Aydon Castle
3 Bamburgh Castle
4 Belsay
5 Berwick-upon-Tweed
6 Blagdon Hall
7 Blanchland
8 Brinkburn Priory
9 Callaly Castle
10 Chesters
11 Chillingham Castle
12 Chipchase Castle
13 Corbridge
14 Cragside
15 Dunstanburgh Castle
16 Ford
17 Hexham
18 Howick Hall
19 Langley Castle
20 Lindisfarne Castle
21 Morpeth
22 Newcastle upon Tyne
23 Nunnykirk Hall
24 Rothbury
25 Seaton Delaval Hall
26 Stamfordham
27 Wallington Hall
28 Warkworth
29 Whalton Manor

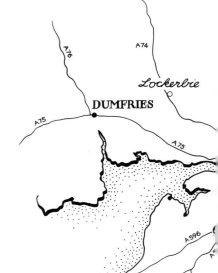

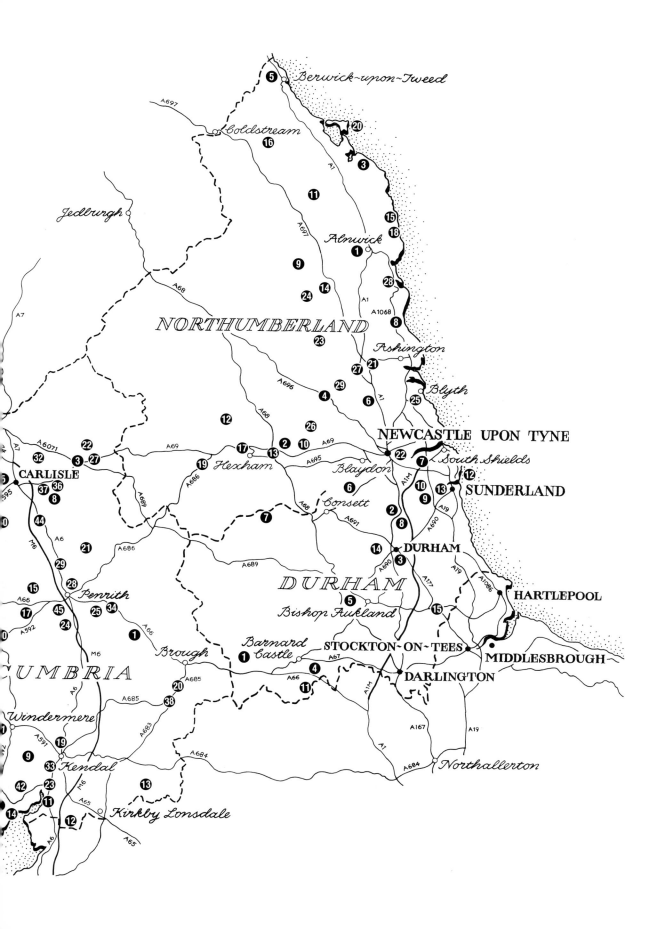

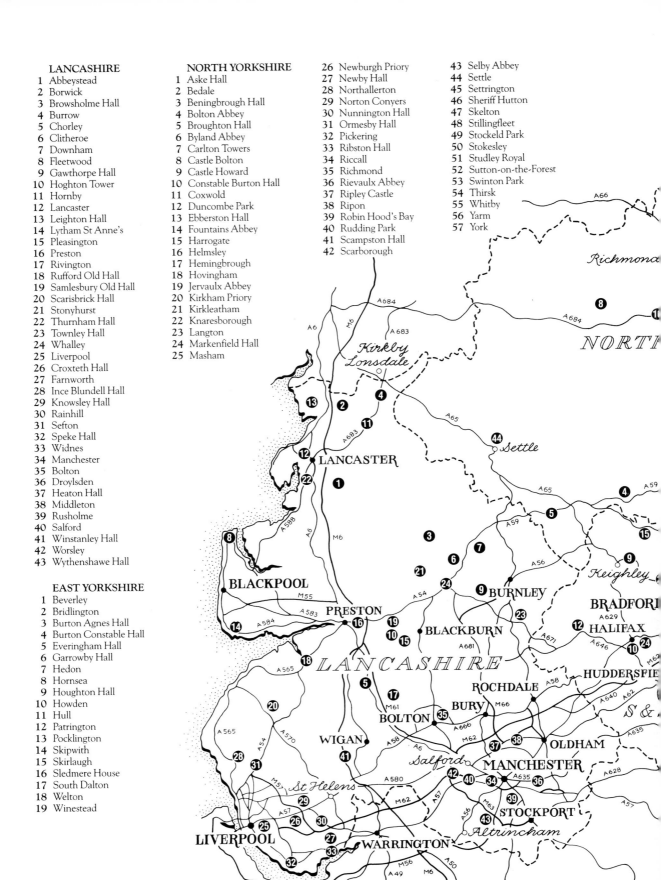

LANCASHIRE

1 Abbeystead
2 Borwick
3 Browsholme Hall
4 Burrow
5 Chorley
6 Clitheroe
7 Downham
8 Fleetwood
9 Gawthorpe Hall
10 Hoghton Tower
11 Hornby
12 Lancaster
13 Leighton Hall
14 Lytham St Anne's
15 Pleasington
16 Preston
17 Rivington
18 Rufford Old Hall
19 Samlesbury Old Hall
20 Scarisbrick Hall
21 Stonyhurst
22 Thurnham Hall
23 Townley Hall
24 Whalley
25 Liverpool
26 Croxteth Hall
27 Farnworth
28 Ince Blundell Hall
29 Knowsley Hall
30 Rainhill
31 Sefton
32 Speke Hall
33 Widnes
34 Manchester
35 Bolton
36 Droylsden
37 Heaton Hall
38 Middleton
39 Rusholme
40 Salford
41 Winstanley Hall
42 Worsley
43 Wythenshawe Hall

EAST YORKSHIRE

1 Beverley
2 Bridlington
3 Burton Agnes Hall
4 Burton Constable Hall
5 Everingham Hall
6 Garrowby Hall
7 Hedon
8 Hornsea
9 Houghton Hall
10 Howden
11 Hull
12 Patrington
13 Pocklington
14 Skipwith
15 Skirlaugh
16 Sledmere House
17 South Dalton
18 Welton
19 Winestead

NORTH YORKSHIRE

1 Aske Hall
2 Bedale
3 Beningbrough Hall
4 Bolton Abbey
5 Broughton Hall
6 Byland Abbey
7 Carlton Towers
8 Castle Bolton
9 Castle Howard
10 Constable Burton Hall
11 Coxwold
12 Duncombe Park
13 Ebberston Hall
14 Fountains Abbey
15 Harrogate
16 Helmsley
17 Hemingbrough
18 Hovingham
19 Jervaulx Abbey
20 Kirkham Priory
21 Kirkleatham
22 Knaresborough
23 Langton
24 Markenfield Hall
25 Masham
26 Newburgh Priory
27 Newby Hall
28 Northallerton
29 Norton Conyers
30 Nunnington Hall
31 Ormesby Hall
32 Pickering
33 Ribston Hall
34 Riccall
35 Richmond
36 Rievaulx Abbey
37 Ripley Castle
38 Ripon
39 Robin Hood's Bay
40 Rudding Park
41 Scampston Hall
42 Scarborough
43 Selby Abbey
44 Settle
45 Settrington
46 Sheriff Hutton
47 Skelton
48 Stillingfleet
49 Stockeld Park
50 Stokesley
51 Studley Royal
52 Sutton-on-the-Forest
53 Swinton Park
54 Thirsk
55 Whitby
56 Yarm
57 York

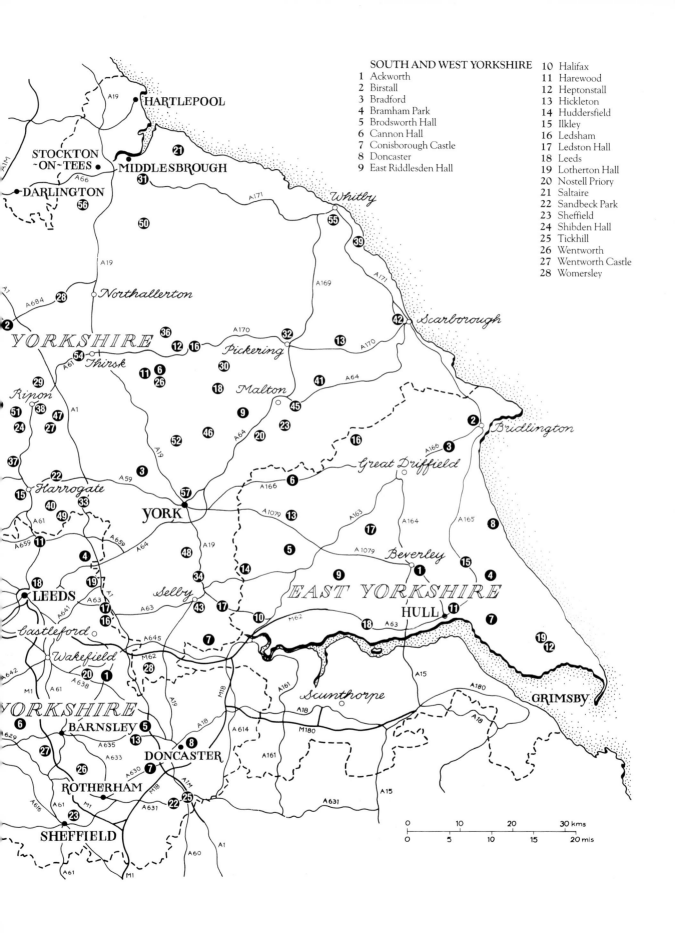

SOUTH AND WEST YORKSHIRE
1 Ackworth
2 Birstall
3 Bradford
4 Bramham Park
5 Brodsworth Hall
6 Cannon Hall
7 Conisborough Castle
8 Doncaster
9 East Riddlesden Hall
10 Halifax
11 Harewood
12 Heptonstall
13 Hickleton
14 Huddersfield
15 Ilkley
16 Ledsham
17 Ledston Hall
18 Leeds
19 Lotherton Hall
20 Nostell Priory
21 Saltaire
22 Sandbeck Park
23 Sheffield
24 Shibden Hall
25 Tickhill
26 Wentworth
27 Wentworth Castle
28 Womersley

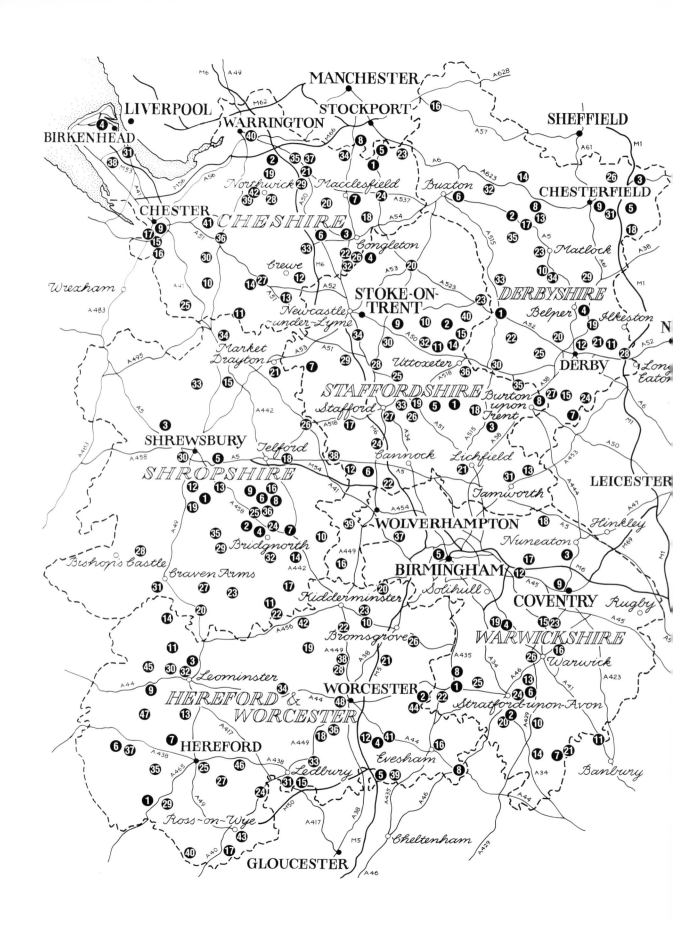

INGHAM

CHESHIRE

1 Adlington Hall
2 Arley Hall
3 Astbury
4 Birkenhead
5 Bramall Hall
6 Brereton Hall
7 Capesthorne
8 Cheadle
9 Chester
10 Cholmondeley Castle
11 Combermere Abbey
12 Crewe Hall
13 Doddington Hall
14 Dorfold Hall
15 Dunham Massey
16 Eaton Hall
17 Eccleston
18 Gawsworth
19 Great Budworth
20 Jodrell Bank
21 Knutsford
22 Little Moreton Hall
23 Lyme Park
24 Macclesfield
25 Malpas
26 Mow Cop
27 Nantwich
28 Northwich
29 Over Peover
30 Peckforton Castle
31 Port Sunlight
32 Rode Hall
33 Sandbach
34 Styal
35 Tabley House
36 Tarporley
37 Tatton Park
38 Thornton Hough
39 Vale Royal
40 Warrington
41 Willington
42 Winnington Hall

DERBYSHIRE

1 Ashbourne
2 Bakewell
3 Barlborough Hall
4 Belper
5 Bolsover
6 Buxton
7 Calke Abbey
8 Chatsworth
9 Chesterfield
10 Cromford
11 Dale Abbey
12 Derby
13 Edensor
14 Eyam
15 Foremark Hall
16 Glossop
17 Haddon Hall
18 Hardwick Hall
19 Horsley
20 Kedleston Hall
21 Locko Park
22 Longford
23 Matlock
24 Melbourne
25 Radburne Hall
26 Renishaw Hall
27 Repton
28 Sandiacre
29 South Wingfield
30 Sudbury Hall
31 Sutton Scarsdale
32 Tideswell
33 Tissington
34 Wirksworth
35 Youlgreave

HEREFORD AND WORCESTER

1 Abbey Dore
2 Abbots Morton
3 Berrington Hall
4 Besford
5 Bredon
6 Bredwardine
7 Brinsop
8 Broadway
9 Burton Court
10 Chaddesley Corbett
11 Croft Castle
12 Croome Court
13 Dinmore Manor
14 Downton Castle
15 Eastnor Castle
16 Evesham
17 Goodrich Castle
18 Great Malvern
19 Great Witley
20 Hagley Hall
21 Hanbury Hall
22 Hartlebury Castle
23 Harvington Hall
24 Hellen's
25 Hereford
26 Hewell Grange
27 Holme Lacy
28 Holt
29 Kilpeck
30 Kingsland
31 Ledbury
32 Leominster
33 Little Malvern Court
34 Lower Brockhampton
35 Madley
36 Madresfield Court
37 Moccas Court
38 Ombersley
39 Overbury
40 Pembridge
41 Pershore
42 Rock
43 Ross-on-Wye
44 Rous Lench
45 Shobdon
46 Stoke Edith
47 Weobley
48 Worcester

SHROPSHIRE

1 Acton Burnell
2 Acton Round Hall
3 Adcote
4 Aldenham Park
5 Attingham Park
6 Benthall Hall
7 Bridgnorth
8 Broseley Hall
9 Buildwas Abbey
10 Claverley
11 Cleobury Mortimer
12 Condover Hall
13 Cound Hall
14 Dudmaston
15 Hawkstone Park
16 Ironbridge
17 Kinlet
18 Lilleshall
19 Longnor Hall
20 Ludlow
21 Market Drayton
22 Mawley Hall
23 Millichope Park
24 Morville
25 Much Wenlock
26 Newport
27 Oakley Park
28 Plowden Hall
29 Shipton Hall
30 Shrewsbury
31 Stokesay Castle
32 Upton Cressett Hall
33 Wem
34 Whitchurch
35 Wilderhope Manor
36 Willey Park

STAFFORDSHIRE

1 Abbots Bromley
2 Alton
3 Barton under Needwood
4 Biddulph Grange
5 Blithfield
6 Brewood
7 Broughton
8 Burton upon Trent
9 Caverswall Castle
10 Cheadle
11 Checkley
12 Chillington Hall
13 Clifton Campville
14 Croxden Abbey
15 Denstone
16 Enville
17 Gnosall
18 Hoar Cross
19 Ingestre
20 Leek
21 Lichfield
22 Moseley Old Hall
23 Okeover Hall
24 Penkridge
25 Sandon
26 Shugborough
27 Stafford
28 Stone
29 Swinfen Hall
30 Swynnerton
31 Tamworth
32 Tean
33 Tixall
34 Trentham
35 Tutbury
36 Uttoxeter
37 West Bromwich
38 Weston-under-Lizard
39 Wightwick Manor
40 Wootton Lodge

WARWICKSHIRE

1 Alcester
2 Alscot Park
3 Arbury Hall
4 Baddesley Clinton
5 Birmingham
6 Charlecote Park
7 Compton Wynyates
8 Coughton Court
9 Coventry
10 Ettington Park
11 Farnborough Hall
12 Great Packington
13 Hampton Lucy
14 Honington
15 Kenilworth Castle
16 Leamington Spa
17 Maxstoke Castle
18 Merevale Hall
19 Packwood House
20 Preston on Stour
21 Radway Grange
22 Ragley Hall
23 Stoneleigh Abbey
24 Stratford-upon-Avon
25 Upton House
26 Warwick

0
10
20
30
40 kms
0
5
10
15
20
25 mls

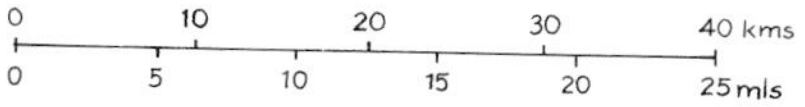

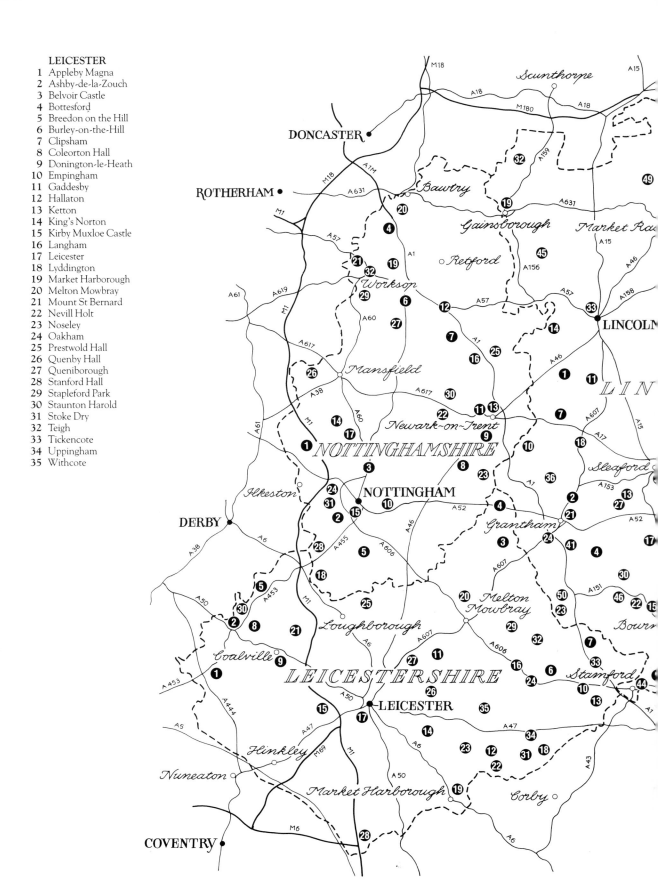

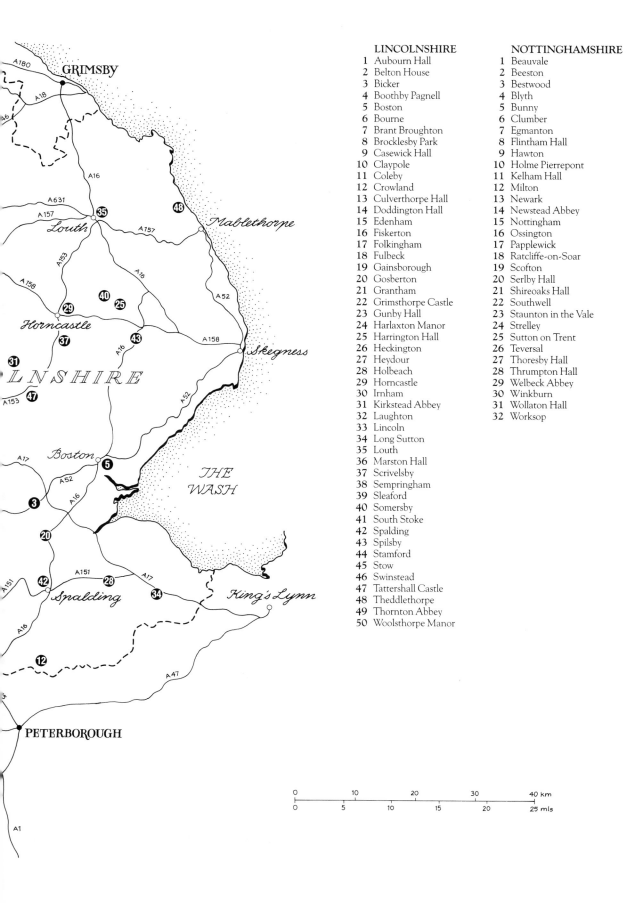

LINCOLNSHIRE

1 Aubourn Hall
2 Belton House
3 Bicker
4 Boothby Pagnell
5 Boston
6 Bourne
7 Brant Broughton
8 Brocklesby Park
9 Casewick Hall
10 Claypole
11 Coleby
12 Crowland
13 Culverthorpe Hall
14 Doddington Hall
15 Edenham
16 Fiskerton
17 Folkingham
18 Fulbeck
19 Gainsborough
20 Gosberton
21 Grantham
22 Grimsthorpe Castle
23 Gunby Hall
24 Harlaxton Manor
25 Harrington Hall
26 Heckington
27 Heydour
28 Holbeach
29 Horncastle
30 Irnham
31 Kirkstead Abbey
32 Laughton
33 Lincoln
34 Long Sutton
35 Louth
36 Marston Hall
37 Scrivelsby
38 Sempringham
39 Sleaford
40 Somersby
41 South Stoke
42 Spalding
43 Spilsby
44 Stamford
45 Stow
46 Swinstead
47 Tattershall Castle
48 Theddlethorpe
49 Thornton Abbey
50 Woolsthorpe Manor

NOTTINGHAMSHIRE

1 Beauvale
2 Beeston
3 Bestwood
4 Blyth
5 Bunny
6 Clumber
7 Egmanton
8 Flintham Hall
9 Hawton
10 Holme Pierrepont
11 Kelham Hall
12 Milton
13 Newark
14 Newstead Abbey
15 Nottingham
16 Ossington
17 Papplewick
18 Ratcliffe-on-Soar
19 Scofton
20 Serlby Hall
21 Shireoaks Hall
22 Southwell
23 Staunton in the Vale
24 Strelley
25 Sutton on Trent
26 Teversal
27 Thoresby Hall
28 Thrumpton Hall
29 Welbeck Abbey
30 Winkburn
31 Wollaton Hall
32 Worksop

Glossary

abacus flat slab on top of a *capital*

achievements (heraldic) a complete display of armorial bearings

acroterion a foliage-carved block on the end or top of a classical *pediment*

aedicule the framing of a window or door by columns and a *pediment*

ambulatory a semi-circular or polygonal aisle enclosing an *apse*

amorino a cherub; a popular motif in Renaissance art

angel roof a timber roof decorated with carved wooden figures of angels

apse a vaulted semi-circular or polygonal end of a *chancel* or chapel

arcade a range of arches supported on *piers* or columns, free-standing or blind, i.e. attached to a wall

architrave the lowest of the three main parts of an *entablature*; also, more loosely, the moulded frame surrounding a door or window

Artisan Mannerism a term coined by Sir John Summerson to define a style of the best London craftsmen – particularly bricklayers – which flourished in England between 1615 and 1675.

aumbry a cupboard or recess in which to keep sacred vessels

baldacchino a canopy supported on columns

ball-flower a globular three-petalled flower enclosing a small ball, a decoration used in the first quarter of the fourteenth century

barrel vault see **tunnel vault**

basket arch an arch whose curve resembles that of the handle of a basket, formed by a segment of a large circle continued right and left by two segments of much smaller circles

bas-relief a shallow carving or sculpture on background, raised less than half its full depth

beak-head a Norman decorative motif consisting of a row of birds' or beasts' heads, with beaks usually biting into a roll moulding

belvedere a raised turret from which to view the surrounding scenery

blank arcading a range of arches supported on *piers* or columns attached to a wall

blank arch an arch attached to a wall; also known as a blind arch

blind arcading see **blank arcading**

blind arch see **blank arch**

bolection moulding a projecting moulding used to cover the joint between two members with different surface levels

boss an ornamental knob or projection covering the intersection of ribs in a *vault* or ceiling; often carved with foliage or other decoration

braces diagonal subsidiary timbers strengthening the frame of a roof and connecting either a *tie-beam* with the wall below or a *collar-beam* with the rafters above; they may be straight or arched

bressummer a beam in a timber-framed building which supports the (usually) projecting superstructure; a massive beam spanning any wide opening, especially a chimneypiece

broach spire a spire, usually octagonal in plan, placed on a square tower with each of the angles of the tower not covered by the base of the spire filled with an inclined mass of masonry or broach, built into the oblique sides of the spire to effect the transition from the square to the octagon

bucrania a favourite motif in antique architecture, consisting of a row of ox skulls, usually garlanded

campanile a bell-tower, usually separate from the main building

cap-à-pie from head to foot

capital the top part of a column

cartouche a tablet with an ornate frame, usually enclosing an inscription

caryatid a sculpted female figure used as a supporting column

celure a panelled and adorned part of a *wagon roof* above the *rood* or altar

chancel the part of the east end of the church in which the altar is placed; usually applied to the whole continuation of the *nave* east of the crossing (though not to the eastward extensions of cathedrals, etc.)

chevet the French term for the east end of a church, consisting of *apse* and *ambulatory* with or without radiating chapels

cinquefoil see foil

clerestory the upper storey of the nave walls of a church, pierced by windows above the roofs of the aisles

clunch a hard chalk used as building stone

Coade stone artificial (cast) stone invented by Mrs Eleanor Coade in the 1770s and widely used in the late eighteenth and early nineteenth centuries for all types of ornamentation

coffering recessed square or polygonal panels forming a decoration on a ceiling or *vault*

Composite a classical *order* whose *capital* combines the foliate bell of the *Corinthian* with the *volutes* of the *Ionic*

console an ornamental bracket with a compound curved outline

corbel a projecting block, usually of stone, supporting a beam or other horizontal member

Corinthian a classical *order* featuring an intricately moulded *capital* with acanthus leaves

cornice in classical architecture, the top projecting section of an *entablature*; also any projecting ornamental moulding along the top of a building, wall, arch, etc. finishing or crowning it

cottage orné a deliberately rustic or romantic building, usually of asymmetrical plan and often thatched; a product of the late eighteenth- and early nineteenth-century cult of the Picturesque

cove/coving a large concave moulding, particularly where wall and ceiling meet

crocket/crocketing a decorative feature carved in various leaf shapes and projecting at regular intervals from the angles of spires, pinnacles, canopies, gables etc. in *Gothic* architecture

crownpost a vertical timber standing centrally on a *tie-beam* and supporting a collar *purlin*

cruck a big curved wooden beam supporting both walls and roof of a building

cupola a small polygonal or circular domed turret crowning a roof

cusp a projecting point formed at the intersections of circles or arches (*foils*) in *Gothic* architecture

dado a decorative covering of the lower part of a wall

Decorated a historical division of English *Gothic* architecture covering the period from *c*.1290 to *c*.1350

dentil a small, square block used series as a decoration for a classical *cornice*

diaper a surface decoration, usually of brickwork, made up of repeated small squares, rectangles or lozenges

Diocletian window a semi-circular window divided vertically by two mullions; much used in Palladian architecture and named after the Baths of Diocletian in Rome. Also known as a thermal window

Doom painting a painting of the Last Judgement, usually facing west over the *chancel* arch of a church

Doric a classical *order*, primarily distinguished by the *triglyphs and metopes* in its *frieze*

Early English a historical division of English Gothic architecture covering the period from *c*.1180 to *c*.1280

encaustic tiles glazed and decorated tiles of earthen-ware, much used in the Middle Ages and in Victorian churches for flooring

enceinte in military architecture, the main enclosure of a fortress surrounded by a curtain wall

enfilade a system of aligning internal doors in sequence so that a vista can be obtained through a series of rooms

entablature in classical architecture, the horizontal elements of an *order* supported by the columns, comprising the *architrave*, the *frieze* and the *cornice*

entasis a slight convex deviation from a straight line; used on Greek columns and sometimes on spires to prevent an optical illusion of concavity

fan vault a late medieval *vault* composed of inverted concave cones overlaid with numerous ribs of the same curve and length, radiating at equal angles from one *springer*, thus giving a fan-like pattern

fenestration the arrangement of the windows in a building

finial a formal ornament at the top of a gable, pinnacle or canopy

flèche a slender wooden spire rising from the centre of a roof; also called a spirelet

flushwork the decorative use of knapped flint in conjunction with dressed stone so as to form patterns of tracery, initials etc.

fluted having shallow concave vertical channels in the shaft of a column

flying buttress an arch or half arch transmitting the thrust of a *vault* or roof from the upper part of a wall to an outer support or buttress

foil a lobe- or leaf-shaped curve formed by the *cusping* of a circle or an arch; the number of foils involved is shown by the prefix, i.e. trefoil, quatrefoil, cinquefoil

frieze in classical architure, the central part of the *entablature*; otherwise, the decorated band along the upper part of an initial wall, immediately below the *cornice*

galilee a chapel or vestibule usually at the west end of a church; sometimes called a *narthex*

gargoyle a waterspout projecting from a roof, or the parapet of a wall or tower, carved into a grotesque human or animal shape

garth an enclosed open space, as in a cloister

Gothic/Gothick Gothic is the architecture of the pointed arch, the *rib vault*, the *flying buttress*, the walls reduced to a minimum and spacious *clerestory* windows; the style started about 1130 in England and continued until the end of the sixteenth century. Gothick is used to decribe the early part of the Gothic Revival, in the mid-eighteenth century, started by Horace Walpole at Strawberry Hill and characterised by a light-hearted, almost *Rococo* decoration; it continued into the first quarter of the nineteeth century

green man a wild man of the woodland; also called a jack-in-the green

grisaille a way of painting in grey monochrome

ha-ha a sunken ditch to keep livestock out of gardens and eliminating the need for a fence or wall

hammerbeam a horizontal roof bracket projecting at

the level of the base of the rafters to carry arched *braces* and struts

hood mould a moulding, projecting from round an arch, doorway or window, or from a wall, to keep the rain off

impost a bracket in a wall, usually formed of mouldings, on which the end of an arch appears to rest

in antis a term used to describe a *portico* when it recedes into a building and the columns range with the side walls

Ionic a classical *order* characterised by the *volutes* of its *capital* and the *dentils* in its *cornice*; the shaft is generally *fluted*

jack-in-the-green see **green man**

Jesse window a window in which the tracery represents the branches of the tree of Jesse, a genealogical tree showing the ancestors of Christ ascending from the root of Jesse

jetty the projection of an upper storey in a timber-framed building beyond the storey below, made by the beams and joists of the lower storey oversailing the external wall

keystone the central stone of an arch or *rib vault*, sometimes carved

kingpost a vertical timber standing centrally on a *tie-beam* or *collar-beam* and rising to the apex of the roof to support the ridge

label stop a decorative *boss* at either end of a *hood mould*

lancet a slender pointed-arched window, characterising the *Early English* style

lantern a small circular or polygonal turret, with windows all round, crowning a roof or dome

lesene a **pilaster** without base and capital, also called a pilaster strip; usually found on exteriors of later Anglo-Saxon and early Romanesque churches

lierne vault a tertiary rib, i.e. one which springs neither from one of the main *springers* nor from a central *boss*

linenfold Tudor panelling ornamented with a conventional representation of a piece of linen laid in vertical folds

long-and-short work Saxon *quoins* consisting of long stones on end between flat ones, all bonded into the wall

louvre an opening, often with a *lantern* over, in the roof of a hall to let out the smoke from a central hearth

lucarne a small opening in an attic or spire, originally to let in light but often purely decorative

lunette a *tympanum* or semi-circular opening; the term can also be applied to any flat, semi-circular surface

machicoulis/machicolation a projecting gallery on brackets built on the outside of castle towers or wall, with openings in the floor through which to drop missiles

mandorla an upright almond shape, found chiefly in medieval art, to enclose a figure of Christ enthroned; also known as a *vesica*

mathematical tiles small yellowish-white facing tiles, the size of brick headers, popularised by Henry

Holland and very much used, especially in the South of England, between *c*.1780 and *c*.1840

merlon the raised portion of the battlement of a castle or house

metope and triglyph the *frieze* of a *Doric* order; triglyphs are the blocks separating the metopes or square space between. They have two vertical grooves, or glyphs, in the centre and half grooves at the edges

meurtrière in military architecture, a small loophole, large enough for the barrel of a gun or musket

misericord a bracket, often elaborately carved, placed on the underside of a hinged choir-stall seat, which, when turned up, gave support to the occupant when standing during long services

modillion a small bracket of which a series (modillion *frieze*) is often placed below a *cornice*

motte and bailey the usual post-Roman and Norman defence system, consisting of an earthen mound (the motte) topped with a wooden tower eccentrically placed, with a bailey (open space) surrounded by an enclosure ditch and palisade

mouchette a curved dagger-like motif in curvi-linear *tracery*, popular in the early fourteenth century

mullion a vertical post or other upright dividing a window into 'lights'

narthex see **galilee**

nave the part of a church west of the crossing, often flanked by aisles

newel-post the central post in a circular or winding staircase; also the principal post where a flight of stairs meets a landing

nogging the name given to brickwork used to fill the spaces between the timbers in a timber-framed building

oculus window a circular opening in a wall or at the apex of a dome

oeil-de-boeuf a small round or oval window

ogee/ogival a double-curved line made up of a convex and a concave part; an ogee arch is pointed and uses this compound curve. It was introduced *c*.1300 and is also called a keel arch

opus Alexandrinum a form of wall or pavement mosaic composed of small pieces of coloured marble and gilded tesserae

oriel a bay window on an upper storey or storeys of a building

ormolu a gold-coloured alloy of copper, zinc and tin; gilded bronze or lacquered brass. Widely used in French cabinet-making for furniture ornaments in the seventeenth and eighteenth centuries

order in classical architecture an order comprises a column, with or without a base, a shaft, *capital* and *entablature*, decorated and proportioned in one of the accepted modes: *Doric, Tuscan, Ionic, Corinthian* or *Composite*

pantile a roofing tile of curved S-shaped section

parclose screen a screen, usually of wood or iron, separating a chapel or tomb from the body of a church

pargetting exterior plastering of timber-framed buildings, usually modelled with ornamental patterns or figures, popular in the sixteenth and seventeenth centuries, especially in East Anglia

pediment a low-pitched gable above a **portico** or above doors, windows etc.; it may be straight-sided or curved segmentally. A broken pediment has a gap in the upper moulding

pele tower a term used in northern England and Scotland, signifying a small tower or house suitable for sudden defence

pendentive a concave *spandrel* leading from the base of a dome to the angle of two supporting walls

Perpendicular the style of English Gothic architecture succeeding the Decorated. First appearing *c*.1330 and continuing throughout the fifteenth century, it is characterised by the strong vertical lines of its *tracery*

piano nobile the principal storey of a house, usually above ground level, containing the main reception rooms

pier a solid masonry support

Pietà a devotional type of the suffering Virgin bearing the dead Christ on her knees

pilaster a shallow *pier* or rectangular column projecting only slightly from a wall

piscina a shallow basin with a drain, in which Communion or Mass vessels are washed; generally placed in a niche in the south wall of the chancel

poppy-head the ornamental *finial* of a church pew, often carved with ornamental patterns or figures; the name is derived from *poupée*, doll, and has nothing to do with the flower

porphyry a kind of rock with crystals embedded in a red or other ground mass

porte-cochère a porch large enough to admit wheeled vehicles

portico a roofed space, open or partly enclosed, forming the entrance and centrepiece of a house or church; often with classical detached or attached columns and a *pediment*

prodigy house extravagant country house built *c*.1570–*c*.1620, many of them designed primarily to entertain Queen Elizabeth and her court; examples are Longleat, Wollaton, Hardwick, Burghley, Audley End and Hatfield

pulpitum a screen, usually of stone, in a major church, erected to shut off the choir from the *nave*

putto a little boy, often winged, developed from the god Eros, and a frequent motif of decorative art in the classical, post-classical and Renaissance periods

purlin a longitudinal timber of a roof laid parallel with the wall plate and apex, usually at one-third or two-thirds interval up the slope of the roof

pyx a vessel in which the Host is reserved during Mass

quadripartite vault a rib *vault* in which two diagonal ribs divide each bay into four compartments

quatrefoil see foil

queenpost pairs of vertical or near-vertical timbers placed symmetrically on a *tie-beam* and supporting side *purlins*

quoins the dressed stones at the corners of buildings, usually laid so that their exposed faces are alternately large and small

Red Book a book specially produced by Humphry Repton for each of his more important clients, containing watercolours of their existing house and grounds with ingenious lift-up flaps showing his suggested improvements

repoussé decoration of metalwork by relief designs, formed by beating the metal from the back

rere-arch the inner arch or a window or door opening, when it differs in size or form from the original (outer) arch

reredorter a privy, situated at the back of the dormitory in a convent or monastery

reredos a wall or screen, usually of wood or stone and often decorated, rising behind an altar

respond a half pier bonded into a wall and carrying one end of an arch

reticulated a form of tracery typical of the early fourteenth century, consisting entirely of circles drawn at top and bottom into *ogee* shapes, giving a net-like appearance

retrochoir the space behind the high altar in a major church

rib vault a system of cross-vaulting in which the groins are replaced by arched ribs constructed across the sides and diagonals of the vaulted bay to act as a framework or support for the infilling

rocaille originally the stone or shell decoration for artificial grottoes; later used to describe *Rococo* decoration of any work

Rococo a form of decoration developed from the late Baroque but lighter and more elegant; fashionable in England in the mid-eighteenth century

Roman cement Parker's Roman Cement, patented in 1796, was made from burnt septaria; it surpassed all previous stuccos for durability and imperviousness to damp, and is said to have made Nash's architecture possible

rood a cross, usually wooden or painted on the *chancel* arch, at the east end of the *nave*

rood-screen a screen at the west end of the chancel, separating *nave* and choir and below the rood-loft

rose window a circular window with patterns of concentric or radiating *tracery*

rotunda a building circular in plan and often domed

roundel a circular panel, disc or medallion; also a similarly shaped panel in a stained-glass window

rustication masonry cut in massive blocks separated from each other by deeply recessed joints and often with a roughened surface; see also *vermiculated*

sarcophagus a stone coffin

scagliola imitation marble, composed of cement or plaster and marble chips or colouring matter, often used for columns and in interior decoration in eighteenth-century classical architecture

scissor-braces a pair of *braces* which cross diagonally between pairs of rafters or principals

screens passage the entrance passage of a medieval house separating the hall screen from the kitchen, buttery and pantry

sedilia a series of seats (usually three) on the south side of the *chancel* for the use of the clergy. Often recessed into the wall at three different levels and linked decoratively with the *piscina*

sexpartite vault a form of vaulting in which each bay is divided into six parts by two diagonal ribs and one transverse rib

shell keep a circular or oval wall surrounding the inner portion of a castle

solar a parlour or private room in medieval and Tudor manor houses, usually at first-floor level, approached by a stair from the dais end of the hall

spandrel the triangular surface between one side of an arch, the horizontal line taken from its apex and the vertical drawn from its springing (see *springer*); also the surface between two adjacent arches and the horizontal moulding above them; also the surface of a *vault* between two adjacent ribs

spirelet see **flèche**

springer the point at which an arch rises from its support

squinch a small arch or series of concentric arches built across the angle of a square or polygon to support a superstructure, i.e. a dome or spire

stiff-leaf a late twelfth-century and early thirteenth-century type of sculptured foliage, found chiefly on *capitals* and *bosses*

strainer arch an arch inserted across a *nave* or aisle to prevent the walls from leaning inwards, or to support a superstructure

strapwork decoration originating in the Netherlands *c*.1540 and popular in Elizabethan and Jacobean England, consisting of interlaced bands similar to fretwork or cut leather; generally executed in plaster or stone on ceilings, screens or parapets

sub-arch one of a small group of arches (usually a pair) enclosed within a single embracing arch

tester the horizontal board or canopy over a pulpit; also called a sounding-board

tie-beam a beam spanning the space from wall plate to wall plate of a timber roof, preventing the wall from spreading

tierceron a secondary rib of a *vault* which springs from one of the main *springers* and leads to a place on the ridge-rib

tracery ornamental intersecting work in the upper part of a window, screen or panel, or used decoratively in *blank arches* and *vaults*

transepts the transverse arms of a cruciform church

Transitional a term usually referring to the transition from the Norman to the Early English style of architecture in the late twelfth century

transom a horizontal bar of stone or wood across the opening of a window

trefoil see **foil**

tribune gallery the upper storey above an aisle in a church, with arches to the *nave*

triforium the arcaded wall passage, or *blank arcading*, facing the *nave* at the height of the aisle roof and below the *clerestory* windows

trompe-l'oeil a style of painting which, through precise draughtsmanship and a careful placing of shadows, attempts to deceive the eye by producing a three-dimensional effect

trumeau a vertical stone mullion supporting the *tympanum* of a wide doorway

tunnel vault an uninterrupted *vault* of semi-circular or pointed section, the simplest form of vault; also called barrel vault or wagon vault

tympanum the space between the lintel of a doorway and the arch above it, or the space between the enclosing mouldings of a *pediment*

undercroft a vaulted chamber, sometimes wholly or partly underground, below a church, chapel or hall

vault an arched ceiling or roof of stone or brick, sometimes imitated in wood or plaster

Venetian window a tripartite window, with an arched central opening higher and wider than the side openings, which have flat heads

vermiculated a form of masonry decoration in which the stone is scored with irregular shallow channels like worm tracks

vesica see **mandorla**

volute a spiral scroll, the distinctive feature of the *Ionic* capital, used in modified form in *Corinthian* and *Composite* capitals and in *consoles* and brackets

voussoir one of a series of wedge-shaped stones or bricks used to form an arch

wagon roof a roof formed by closely set rafters with arched braces and often panelled or plastered; so called because it looks like the stretched canvas roof of a wagon

wagon vault see **tunnel vault**

water-leaf a leaf shape used in later twelfth-century *capitals*, with a broad, unribbed, tapering leaf curving up towards the angle of the *abacus* and turned in at the top

wild man see **green man**

wind-brace a diagonal timber *brace*, usually curved, crossing the rafters to stiffen the roof longitudinally; sometimes decorated with *cusping*

Definitions of other architectural terms, and illustrations of some of those given above, can be found in *The Penguin Dictionary of Architecture* by John Fleming, Hugh Honour and Nikolaus Pevsner.

Index